THE SERBS AND
RUSSIAN PAN-SLAVISM
1875–1878

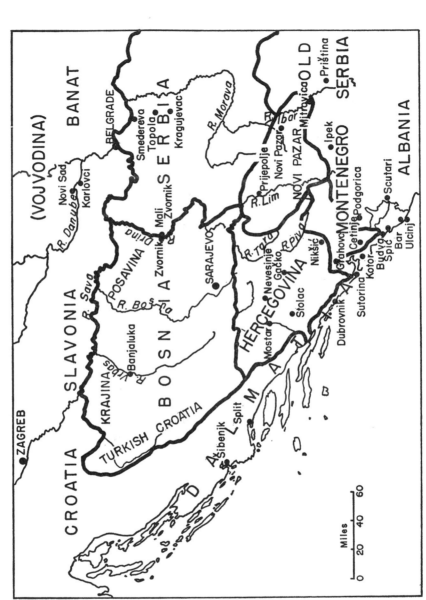

The Serbian lands (heavy lines indicate boundaries in 1875).

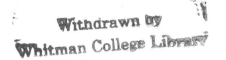

THE SERBS AND RUSSIAN PAN-SLAVISM 1875–1878

By David MacKenzie

Wells College

CORNELL UNIVERSITY PRESS

Ithaca, New York

CORNELL UNIVERSITY PRESS

First published 1967

Library of Congress Catalog Card Number: 67–12306

PRINTED IN THE UNITED STATES OF AMERICA
BY KINGSPORT PRESS, INC.

TO PAT

PREFACE

SERBIA and Montenegro in the nineteenth century, like Yugoslavia since 1948, exerted influence in European power politics incommensurate with their size. They lay between Russia, to which they were attracted by linguistic, ethnic, and religious ties, and western Europe, which exerted increasingly powerful cultural and economic pressure upon them. In an age of rising nationalism, the Serbian people, divided between the Ottoman and Austro-Hungarian empires, dreamed of independence and unity. In the 1870's Serbian and Montenegrin statesmen sought to follow the path which had led the Italians to liberation and unity in the 1860's. Because of its strength, historical traditions, and relative size, Serbia, although still a vassal of Turkey, hoped to lead the Serbian people to create a greater Serbia or Yugoslavia, just as Piedmont had led the Italians; and Serbian nationalists in other lands recognized this leadership.

When revolts against Turkish rule broke out in Bosnia and Hercegovina in 1875, these nationalists looked to Russia to deliver them from foreign oppression. In Russia, sympathy for the Serbian Christians existed in Court circles, among nationalist diplomats, and in the lower classes, and was actively expressed through the Slav committees. These sympathies, however, did not necessarily induce Russians to favor creation of a large, independent Serbian state. Furthermore, the Russian government's desire for peace to consummate domestic reforms, and for harmonious relations with Austria-Hungary, suggested maintenance of the *status quo* in the Balkans. Russian policy under Alexander II and A. M. Gorchakov therefore fluctuated indecisively, and rivalry among the Serbian states as well as the fortunes of war added greatly to the difficulties faced by Serbian statesmen. Cleverly assessed and manipulated by Austrian diplomats under Count Julius Andrassy, such difficulties helped dash hopes for Serbian unity at the Congress of Berlin.

In a doctoral dissertation for Columbia University, "Serbian-Russian Relations, 1875–1878," I confined myself to a description and analysis of diplomatic and unofficial relations between Russia and Serbia during the Eastern Crisis. It appeared desirable subsequently to include the entire Serbian people—in Bosnia, Hercegovina, Montenegro, and the Vojvodina as well as Serbia proper—and their relations with Russia. Since unofficial nationalist organizations and the press played significant roles in the events of the 1870's, it seemed essential to devote considerable attention to public opinion. But it was difficult to ascertain public views in Russia and the Serbian lands, which were predominantly illiterate, although occasionally attitudes of the uneducated masses were expressed in the Serbian Assembly or in tsarist police reports. The views of what the Russians call *obshchestvo* (society) could be more readily determined. *Obshchestvo* refers to the literate minority in or near the principal cities which was directly affected by newspaper accounts, and these people exerted sporadic but often powerful pressure upon the Russian and Serbian governments. The public opinion of this elite is considered for the most part, though mass attitudes are included whenever possible.

Primary emphasis is placed upon Serbia and its aspirations, so that Belgrade's policies and Serbia's domestic conditions are analyzed at each stage of the Eastern Crisis. Montenegro's role, and its alternating partnership and rivalry with Serbia, is also taken into account. The foreign policies of the great powers are described when they affected the fate of the Serbian people. Considerable attention is given, therefore, to Russian and Austro-Hungarian policy but little to that of Germany, England, and France.

It is hoped that the material in this book will throw some light on many questions: (1) How much did the Serbs rely upon Russian assistance to achieve their emancipation? (2) Was there widespread fear among the Serbs of Russian intervention or domination? (3) How real were the much-vaunted ties of religion, blood, and language between Serbs and Russians? (4) How competent was Serbian leadership and how realistic were its aspirations? (5) Did Serbia or Montenegro genuinely seek to unite all Serbs or to win maximum aggrandizement for themselves? (6) Did the Russian government or the Pan-Slavs truly desire South Slav or Serbian unity or did they seek hegemony in the Balkans? (7) What caused the decline of Russian influence among the Serbs and Serbia's shift into the Austrian sphere of interest in 1878? Final answers, of course, to all these questions cannot be provided even for the limited period under study.

In contrast to previous treatments of the Eastern Crisis, this book examines closely Russia's relations with a single Balkan people and relies primarily upon unpublished materials. B. H. Sumner's admirable *Russia and the Balkans 1870–1880*, while describing the Russian domestic scene and Pan-Slavism at length, concentrates on Russia's relations with other great powers and utilizes only the published Russian and English materials available in the 1930's. David Harris' detailed monograph, *A Diplomatic History of the Balkan Crisis of 1875–1878: The First Year*, also stresses great-power diplomacy. M. Stojanović's *The Great Powers and the Balkans, 1875–78* uses some Austrian and Serbian archival material but likewise deals mainly with European aspects of the crisis. G. H. Rupp's study, *A Wavering Friendship: Russia and Austria 1876 1878*, describes the relations of two great powers; its sections on the South Slavs are brief and often inaccurate. Neither in English nor in the Slavic languages does there exist a thorough treatment of the problems of Serbian-Russian relations in this period. The best Serbian study remains S. Jovanović's excellent general history, *Vlada Milana Obrenovića, 1*. Among Russian accounts S. Tatishchev's *Imperator Aleksandr II, ego zhizn' i tsarstvovanie, 2*, reflects the official tsarist approach. The role of Russian opinion is stressed in S. A. Nikitin's *Slavianskie komitety v Rossii v 1858–1876 godakh*.

Historians, assisted by newly discovered or recently published materials, must continually reassess past events. The complex Eastern Crisis is no exception. Aside from Nikitin's study, at least a generation has passed since the works mentioned above were completed. It seems appropriate to attempt a new interpretation of the Eastern Crisis as it affected Russia and the South Slavs. For the diplomacy of this era the author found the Ristić papers at the Archive of the Historical Institute, Belgrade, to be indispensable; the vast collections of the Austrian State Archives in Vienna and the Public Record Office in London proved extremely useful. Recent Soviet dissertations contain some of the pertinent Russian diplomatic documents; others were found in *Osvobozhdenie Bolgarii ot turetskogo iga*. Valuable original materials pertaining to Russian Pan-Slavism were found in the State Historical

Museum in Moscow and in manuscript divisions of libraries in Moscow and Leningrad. I was able to utilize additional Serbian materials located in the Archive of the Serbian Academy of Sciences and the State Archives of Serbia in Belgrade. Russian and Serbian newspapers of the period provided abundant data on public opinion, and for Russian opinion *Osvobozhdenie* was indispensable. Very useful also were memoirs of Serbian and Russian leaders. From a neutral vantage point I have sought to present their relations dispassionately and objectively.

Two calendars were in use in eastern Europe during the period covered by this book: the western calendar whose dates are often called new style, and the Julian calendar in Orthodox countries such as Russia, Serbia, Montenegro, and Bulgaria, generally referred to as old style. In the nineteenth century the Julian calendar was twelve days behind the western one. In the text new style dates have been used exclusively; in the notes both dates have been given wherever this was pertinent.

During ten years of work on the dissertation and the book I have received much help and encouragement. To Professor Philip Mosely I am deeply indebted for aid in delimiting the topic and for his continuing friendship and advice. Professor Henry L. Roberts encouraged me to persist in my labors and criticized and corrected the manuscript repeatedly. I owe Professor D. Joy Humes my heartfelt thanks for her comments upon the entire book. Professor Dexter Perkins gave me valuable advice, and Mrs. Velma van Buskirk assisted me on stylistic matters. Among foreign scholars, Professor S. A. Nikitin and Dr. V. G. Karasev of Moscow University gave me valuable advice. To Professor W. N. Medlicott and the late Miss Winifred Taffs go my deep thanks for assisting my wife while she gathered materials for me in the Public Record Office. Without my wife's work in England, and her patience and understanding, this book could not have been completed. The library staffs of the Columbia University, Cornell University, Lenin State, New York Public, and Saltykov-Shchedrin libraries gave courteous assistance. Officials of the Austrian State Archives, the Serbian Academy of Sciences, the Serbian State Archives, and the State Historical Museum in Moscow were all helpful in giving me access to needed materials. The Ford Foundation enabled me to do basic research for this study in Austria and Yugoslavia in 1955–1956. Assistance from the Inter-University Committee on Travel Grants in 1958–1959 permitted me to continue my research in the U.S.S.R. The generosity of Wells College in providing funds for summer research here and in Yugoslavia in 1962–1963 allowed me to expand and deepen this study. Grants from the Penrose Fund of the American Philosophical Society in 1964 and from Wells College in 1965 provided necessary assistance in preparing the manuscript for publication.

D. MacKenzie

Aurora, New York
August 1966

CONTENTS

ILLUSTRATIONS

MAPS

PORTRAITS

ABBREVIATIONS

Unpublished Materials

AII, Ban	Arhiv Istoriskog Instituta (Belgrade), Hartije Matija Bana.
AII, Ristić	Arhiv Istoriskog Instituta, Hartije Jovana Ristića.
ASAN	Arhiv Srpske Akademije Nauke (Belgrade).
AVPR	Arkhiv vneshnei politiki Rossii (Moscow).
DAS	Državni Arhiv Narodne Republike Srbije (Belgrade), Poklon i Otkupa.
GIM	Gosudarstvennyi Istoricheskii Muzei (Moscow).
HHSA	Haus-, Hof-, und Staatsarchiv (Vienna).
KZPK	Knjiga zvanične prepiske Kneza (Milana), Arhiv narodne biblioteki u Beogradu (Belgrade), d. 174.
PRO, FO	Public Record Office (London), Foreign Office.
ROBibLen	Otdel rukopisei biblioteki imeni V. I. Lenina (Moscow).
ROBibSS	Otdel rukopisei publichnoi biblioteki imeni M. E. Saltykova-Shchedrina (Leningrad).

Published Materials

Actenstücke	Austria-Hungary. *Actenstücke aus den Correspondenzen des k. u. k. gemeinsamen Ministeriums des Äussern uber orientalischen Angelegenheiten 1* (Vom 16 Mai 1873 bis 31 Mai 1877); *2* (Vom 7 April 1877 bis 3 November 1878). Vienna, 1878.

GIDBiH   *Godišnjak istoriskog društve Bosne i Hercegovine* (Sarajevo).

GIDuNS   *Glasnik istoriskog društva u Novom Sadu* (Novi Sad).

GP   Germany. Auswärtiges Amt. *Die Grosse Politik der europäischen Kabinette*. Berlin, 1922.

Grujić, *3*   Srpska Kraljevska Akademija. "Zapisi Jevrema Grujića," *Zbornik za istoriju, jezik i književnost srpskog naroda*, prvo odelenje, knj. 9. Belgrade, 1923.

IV   *Istoricheskii Vestnik.*

JMH   *The Journal of Modern History.*

KA   *Krasnyi Arkhiv.*

Os. Pr.   *Osobye pribavleniia k opisaniiu russko-turetskoi voiny, 1877–78 gg. na Balkanskom poluostrove.* St. Petersburg, 1899–1903.

OSVOb.   Akademiia Nauk SSSR, Institut Slavianovedeniia. *Osvobozhdenie Bolgarii ot turetskogo iga.* 2 vols. Moscow, 1961–64.

Peredovykh   M. N. Katkov, *Sobranie peredovykh statei Moskovskikh Vedomostei 1863–1887 gg.* 25 vols. Moscow, 1897–98.

RA   *Russkii Arkhiv.*

Ristić   J. Ristić, *Diplomatska istorija Srbije za vreme srpskih ratova za oslobodjenje i nezavisnost, 1875–1878.* 2 vols. Belgrade, 1896–98.

RS   *Russkaia Starina.*

Sb. Mat.   Russia. Voennoe Ministerstvo. *Sbornik materialov po russkoi-turetskoi voine 1877–78 gg. na Balkanskom poluostrove.* St. Petersburg, 1898.

SR   *Slavonic Review.* London.

UZIS   *Uchenye Zapiski Instituta Slavianovedeniia.* Moscow.

Vlada Milana, *1*   S. Jovanović, *Vlada Milana Obrenovića, 1.* Belgrade, 1926.

PRINCIPAL SERBIAN AND RUSSIAN PERSONAGES

I. S. AKSAKOV, chairman of the Moscow Slav Committee.

ALEXANDER II, Emperor of Russia.

R. ALIMPIĆ, Serbian commander of the Drina army, special envoy to Montenegro (1876).

M. BAN, chief of the Serbian Press Bureau, a confidant of Ristić.

V. A. CHERKASSKII, Russian Pan-Slav, attached to Russian headquarters in the Balkans (1876–78) in charge of civil affairs.

M. G. CHERNIAEV, Russian Pan-Slav, commander of eastern Serbian armies in 1876.

M. DESPOTOVIĆ, commander of Bosnian insurgents (1876–77).

R. A. FADEEV, retired Russian Pan-Slav general and publicist.

I. GARAŠANIN, Serbian foreign minister (1842–68), leader of Conservatives.

N. K. GIERS, Russian deputy minister of foreign affairs.

A. M. GORCHAKOV, Russian chancellor and foreign minister.

J. GRUJIĆ, a leading Serbian Liberal, minister of justice (1876–78).

S. GRUJIĆ, Serbian war minister (Sept. 1876–78).

F. HRISTIĆ, Serbian diplomat, a leading Conservative.

N. P. IGNAT'EV, Russian ambassador to Turkey, a leading Pan-Slav.

A. S. IONIN, Russian consul-general in Dubrovnik and Cetinje.

A. G. JOMINI, senior counsellor in the Russian foreign ministry.

Lj. KALJEVIĆ, Serbian Liberal, premier (Oct. 1875–April 1876).

P. KARADJORDJEVIĆ, pretender to the Serbian throne.

A. N. KARTSOV, Russian consul-general in Belgrade (1875–77).

M. N. KATKOV, a leading Russian nationalist, editor of *Moskovskie Vedomosti*.

A. A. KIREEV, prominent Pan-Slav of St. Petersburg.

M. LJEŠANIN, Serbian commander of Timok corps and special envoy.

J. MARINOVIĆ, Serbian premier (1873–74) and head of Conservatives.

V. P. MESHCHERSKII, reactionary Russian editor of *Grazhdanin*.

MIHAILO, metropolitan of Serbia.

Stevča MIHAJLOVIĆ, premier of Serbia (1875, 1876–78).

S. MILETIĆ, editor of *Zastava* and leader of Serbian Liberals in the Vojvodina.

MILAN OBRENOVIĆ, prince of Serbia.

D. A. MILIUTIN, liberal Russian minister of war.

R. MILOJKOVIĆ, a leading Serbian Liberal and follower of Ristić.

NATALIA KESHKO, princess of Serbia.

A. I. NELIDOV, Ignat'ev's assistant in Russian embassy in Constantinople; attached to Russian headquarters (1877–78).

A. P. NIKITIN, Russian general, special envoy to Serbia (Dec. 1876).

NIKOLA I, prince of Montenegro.

T. NIKOLIĆ, Serbian war minister (1875–76).

E. P. NOVIKOV, Russian ambassador in Vienna.

A. I. PERSIANI, Russian consul-general in Belgrade (1877–78).

M. PROTIĆ, Serbian envoy to Russia (1876–78).

S. RADONIĆ, Montenegrin foreign minister (1875–76) and special envoy.

J. RISTIĆ, Serbian foreign minister (1875, 1876–78), leader of the Liberals.

P. A. SHUVALOV, Russian ambassador in London.

A. I. VASIL'CHIKOV, large Russian landowner, chairman of St. Petersburg Slav Society (1876–78).

V. VIDOVIĆ, Bosnian insurgent leader.

THE SERBS AND
RUSSIAN PAN-SLAVISM
1875–1878

CHAPTER I

THE SERBS AND
RUSSIA BEFORE 1875

FOR thirteen centuries the Serbian people have inhabited the northern
and western reaches of the Balkan peninsula, contesting their homeland
with Byzantine Greeks, Bulgarians, and later with the Turks. In the
mid-fourteenth century, Stevan Dušan, the greatest Serbian medieval
ruler, united most ethnically Serbian regions into an empire and advanced toward Constantinople. After his death in 1355, the empire
declined, but his goal of a great Serbian state remained.[1]

The Ottoman Turks, smashing Serbian resistance at Kosovo in 1389,
swept over the Balkan peninsula, destroying the Bulgarian and Serbian
kingdoms. By 1500, except for a handful of hardy mountaineers in
Montenegro, the Balkan Slavs were subjected to Turkish rule. For
three centuries they remained isolated, physically and culturally, from
the rest of Europe.

Turkish power in the northern Balkans began to recede after an
unsuccessful siege of Vienna in 1683; Austrian and Russian influence
increased. The Austrian Hapsburgs had ruled the Slovenes and the
Croats since the sixteenth century, and at the Peace of Karlowitz in
1699, Austria extended its Hungarian domains and absorbed the Serbs
of the Vojvodina. Since 1500, the Russians had maintained sporadic
contacts with Orthodox Slavs in the Balkans. At the Karlowitz settlement, Russia demanded religious freedom for all Turkish Christians

---

[1] On early Serbian history see H. V. Temperley, *A History of Serbia* (London,
1919), and K. Jiriček, *Istorija Srba*, 4 vols. (Belgrade, 1922–23).

and became their champion at the Porte. In 1710, Peter the Great, launching a campaign against Turkey, exhorted the Balkan Christians to rise against the infidel. The leaders of unconquered Montenegro responded enthusiastically. Declared their ruler, Prince-Bishop Danilo, "We are with the Russians who are of the same blood and religion." [2] There was no Balkan insurrection, and the Russian campaign failed, but Montenegrin leaders continued to proclaim loyalty to Russia and readiness to follow her in war. They repeatedly requested St. Petersburg to establish a Russian protectorate over their tiny country. Prince-Bishop Petar I, who succeeded Danilo, declared, "My heart beats for Russia; what is good for her is also good for us." [3]

By the late eighteenth century, Russia had taken over the main burden of fighting the Turks. At issue in frequent Russo-Turkish conflicts were control of the Black Sea and its exits and predominance in the Balkan peninsula. Growing Russian influence among the Balkan Christians served often as a pretext for war. Sometimes Russia fought alone, sometimes in alliance with Austria. In 1783, to delimit spheres of influence, Catherine II and Joseph II agreed secretly that Russian influence would extend over the Turkish Straits and eastern Balkans and Austria would influence the western portion, including most Serbian lands. The Balkan Christians, prior to the nationalist revolts of the nineteenth century, were treated as pawns in the powers' plans for dynastic aggrandizement.

Emergence of the Serbs

The French Revolution and Napoleonic conquests in the Balkans aroused South Slav nationalism. In 1804, the Serbs of the Belgrade region, restive under corrupt and oppressive Turkish overlords, revolted. Led by Karadjordje (Djordje Petrović), a bold pig dealer, the first Serbian insurrection (1804–1813) developed into a national movement to liberate and unify all Serbs.[4] It threatened Turkish rule in the

---

[2] J. Jovanović, "Veze Crne Gore sa Rusijom od druge polovine XVI vijeka do danas," *Istoriski Zapisi*, 1 (1948), knj. 2, sv. 3–4, p. 147.

[3] *Ibid.*, sv. 5–6, p. 251. See also R. Lalić, "O tradicionalnim vezama izmedju Crne Gore i Rusije," *Istoriski Zapisi*, 4 (1951), knj. 7, sv. 7–9, pp. 273–81.

[4] See G. Jakšić, *Evropa i vaskrs Srbije (1804–1834)* (Belgrade, 1927), and L. Arsenijević, *Istorija srpskoga ustanka, 1804–1813*, 2 vols. (Belgrade, 1898). See M. Djordjević's survey of the insurrection, *Politička istorija Srbije XIX i XX veka, 1* (Belgrade, 1956).

Balkans and raised embarrassing issues for Russia and Austria. Could these multinational empires tolerate the emergence of a powerful Serbian nation?

The Serbian rebels, after initial military successes, sought foreign assistance against the Turks. Karadjordje sent an envoy to Vienna, but Austrian leaders, anxious to avoid international complications, declined to provide assistance.[5] In June 1804, Metropolitan Stratimirović, spiritual leader of Orthodox Serbs in the Hapsburg Empire, appealed to the Russian government to dispatch troops to aid the insurgents. He even suggested that a Russian grand duke rule over a liberated Serbia.[6] But a Serbian delegation in search of assistance was received coolly by the Russian government. Foreign Minister Adam Czartoryski told the delegates that the insurrection seemed premature, Serbia was far away, and Russia was bound by treaties of friendship with Turkey.

But Russian private citizens sent money to the Serbs and urged St. Petersburg to act,[7] and in 1806, when Russia went to war with Turkey, she established firm links with Karadjordje's insurgents, who requested money, weapons, and engineers from the Russian army.[8] Regular diplomatic relations were inaugurated in August 1807, when K. Rodofinikin, the first Russian envoy to Serbia, reached Belgrade. A formal treaty placed Serbia under Russian tutelage, and Rodofinikin acquired such influence there that Karadjordje declared in October, "Now the entire fate of the Serbs depends upon our tsar, Alexander I." [9]

The insurrection of 1804 threatened to involve all Serbs, as young Serbian men from Austrian and Turkish lands joined Karadjordje's troops. In 1805, Petar I of Montenegro hailed the revolt and promised to supply as much aid "as our little strength will permit." [10] Austrian leaders, aware that the insurgents wished to liberate the Serbs of their empire, as well as those in the Ottoman Empire, realized that Serbian

---

[5] M. Gavrilović, "Spolašnja politika Srbije u XIX veku," *Srpski književni glasnik, 3*, 13–16; N. Iakovkina, "Russko-serbskie otnosheniia, 1804–1812" (unpublished Ph.D. dissertation, Leningrad State University, 1950), p. 29.

[6] N. Popov, *Rossiia i Serbiia* (Moscow, 1869), *1*, 28–31.

[7] See A. Pypin, *Panslavizm v proshlom i nastoiashchem* (St. Petersburg, 1913), pp. 75, 77.

[8] Iakovkina, "Russko-serbskie otnosheniia," p. 85.

[9] Popov, *Rossiia, 1*, 65; Jakšić, *Evropa*, pp. 82–89.

[10] J. Jovanović, *Stvaranje crnogorske države i razvoj crnogorske nacionalnosti* (Cetinje, 1947), p. 188.

unification was incompatible with their interests. In Vienna some even advocated preventive war to suppress Serbian nationalism.[11]

But conditions were not yet ripe for the liberation of the Serbian people. Karadjordje was unable to establish lasting ties with the Serbs of Montenegro, Bosnia, and Hercegovina; after 1809 the Serbian national movement waned. Sporadic Russian military assistance proved insufficient to bring victory to Karadjordje. The Treaty of Bucharest (May 1812), which ended the Russo-Turkish war, stipulated only domestic autonomy for Serbia. And when Russia became absorbed in the struggle against Napoleon, Karadjordje's policy of reliance upon St. Petersburg proved disastrous. In 1813, the Turks overwhelmed his forces and re-established full control over Serbia. Montenegro, despite loyal co-operation with Russia against the French, learned that its chief prize of war had been assigned to Austria. In dismay Petar I wrote Alexander I, "The Montenegrin people, hearing . . . that the neighboring lands of Bokeljska [the Kotor region] have been ceded to Austria, has lost all the hopes which it has placed in Russia since ancient times."[12] An aspect of Russian policy was revealed which caused repeated anguish to the South Slavs in the nineteenth century: great power interests were favored over claims of small Slav states.

In April 1815, a second insurrection began in Serbia. Miloš Obrenović, a rival of defeated Karadjordje, gained several victories over local Turkish forces. Then Miloš, realizing Turkey's superior power, wisely concluded a compromise peace which assured Serbia considerable domestic autonomy.[13] At home, after arranging the assassination of Karadjordje in 1817, Miloš established a personal autocracy. Abroad, he moved cautiously, obtaining piecemeal concessions from Turkey with Russia's diplomatic support. By the Akkerman Convention in October 1826 the Porte promised to respect Serbia's autonomy and restore to it six districts seized in 1813. In September 1829, after Russia's defeat of Turkey, the latter reaffirmed these pledges in the Treaty of Adrianople but failed to carry them out. Only a successful revolt in the six districts, instigated and supported by the army of Miloš, and Russian diplomatic pressure, finally induced the Porte to

---

[11] V. Čubrilović, *Istorija političke misli u Srbiji u XIX veku* (Belgrade, 1958), pp. 87–94.

[12] V. Djordjević, *Crna Gora i Austrija, 1814–1894* (Belgrade, 1924), pp. 4–5. Djordjević calls Kotor's loss "the greatest misfortune to befall Montenegro since Kosovo."

[13] Jakšić, *Evropa*, pp. 239–43; Čubrilović, *Istorija*, pp. 197–204.

yield. In 1830, Serbia became a hereditary principality with complete domestic autonomy. That its vassalage to Turkey continued, however, was indicated by annual tribute payments and by the presence of Turkish garrisons in key fortresses.

Russia's relations with Prince Miloš deteriorated once Serbia's autonomy was won, although the Serbian public attributed the liberation to Russian efforts. Dedication to legitimacy and conservative monarchy prevented Emperor Nicholas I of Russia from supporting Serbian nationalism. Until the Crimean War, Serbia and Montenegro remained isolated and weak, while Turkey and Austria continued to rule the other Serbian lands. Russian diplomacy supported an aristocratic faction calling itself "the defenders of the constitution" (of 1838). This group induced first Miloš, then his son, Michael, to abdicate and brought Alexander Karadjordjević to the throne in 1842. During the era of the pro-Russian "defenders" (1838–1858), the bases of modern Serbia were built. The emergence of Serbo-Croatian as a literary language permitted closer ties with European thought and created a foundation for Serbian, and Yugoslav, nationalism. The ensuing "bourgeois renaissance," utilizing the heritage of the revolutions of 1789 and 1848, inbued the small Serbian intelligentsia with concepts of national self-determination and popular sovereignty.[14]

In 1844, Foreign Minister Ilija Garašanin, Serbia's first genuine statesman, had outlined in "Načertanije" the guiding principles of its foreign and national policy. He urged the Balkan peoples to join in liberating the peninsula from Turkish control. Serbia's mission was to prepare and direct the campaign of national liberation against Austria and Turkey, her natural and permanent enemies. Russia would be an ally if it did not demand Serbia be subservient. Garašanin explained:

It would be easiest for Serbia to achieve her goal in agreement with Russia, but this would be true only if Russia accepted completely the conditions set by Serbia. . . . An alliance between Serbia and Russia would be the most natural one, but its achievement depends upon Russia; Serbia should accept it with open arms if she is sure that Russia is proposing it seriously and sincerely.[15]

[14] See S. Jovanović, *Ustavobranitelji i njihova vlada, 1838–1858* (Belgrade, 1925), and Popov, *Rossiia,* 2.

[15] I. Garašanin, "Načertanije," in *Zbornik za istoriju jezik i književnost srpskog naroda,* prvo odelenje, *23* (Belgrade, 1923), 358ff.

Garašanin foresaw possible Serbo-Russian rivalry once Turkey had been defeated.

Garašanin was a Greater Serbian nationalist, although he paid lip service to the Yugoslav idea of forming independent national states. His goal was re-creation of Stevan Dušan's glorious empire in the form of a Greater Serbian kingdom. His appeal was to "historic right" and ancient Serbian tradition. Bosnia, Hercegovina, Old Serbia, and Montenegro, all overwhelmingly Serbian and Orthodox, would be annexed to the existing Serbian state. Garašanin constructed a network of agents in these lands to prepare a national insurrection and propagate the idea of Serbia's leadership. During the Revolution of 1848–1849 his agents operated in all South Slav areas (including Croatia, Dalmatia, and Bulgaria), but Prince Alexander refused to involve Serbia. Garašanin concentrated his subsequent efforts in Montenegro and in Serbian areas under Turkish rule. His program in "Načertanije" served Serbian statesmen as a primer until 1914.[16]

During the Crimean War (1853–1856), Serbia and Montenegro, despite Russia's appeals to join forces with her, wisely avoided a premature conflict with Turkey. Nicholas I regarded the Serbian states as mere instruments of Russian policy, ignored their interests, and overestimated their willingness to obey Russia.[17] A memorandum of Jovan Marinović, Garašanin's understudy, expressed Serbia's attitude:

I would not promise the Russians either volunteers or any participation in the war. . . . I would tell them frankly that we cannot allow them in our country . . . so as not to compromise ourselves with Austria and the Porte either legally or in fact. . . . We cannot sacrifice our entire existence for the small benefit which might come from participation.[18]

The Serbian government shared Marinović's belief that a Russian victory in the war was unlikely. Prince Danilo of Montenegro reached the same conclusion, and though his people were ardently Russophile, he kept his country neutral. Danilo realized that if he joined with Russia, Austria would occupy Bosnia and Hercegovina. Abstention from the Crimean conflict enhanced the Serbian principalities' independence. After Russia's defeat, Prince Danilo turned toward France and Austria, temporarily abandoning Montenegro's traditional reliance on Russian

---

[16] Čubrilović, *Istorija*, 186–87, 191–93.

[17] S. Nikitin, "Russkaia politika na Balkanakh i nachalo Vostochnoi Voiny," *Voprosy Istorii* (1946) no. 4, pp. 23–29.

[18] *Ibid.*, p. 24; Popov, *Rossiia*, 2, 360–64.

protection.[19] And the Treaty of Paris (March 1856) removed Serbia from exclusive Russian protection and placed it under the guarantee of the European powers—Austria, France, Great Britain, Prussia, Russia and Sardinia (later Italy).

Serbia as Piedmont, 1860–1868

During the 1860's and 1870's, Serbian and Russian statesmen and publicists proposed various programs to end Serbian disunity and subjugation. Leaders from Serbia such as Ilija Garašanin, Prince Michael Obrenović, and Jovan Ristić urged that the principality become the Piedmont of the South Slavs or at least of the Serbs. Prince Nikola of Montenegro appeared willing at times to accept this; at other times he aspired to lead the Serbian national movement himself. Liberal and radical leaders from other Serbian lands, especially the Vojvodina, distrusted what they considered autocratic regimes in Belgrade and preferred to work for a democratic federation. During Michael's reign in Serbia, the Russian government and the Pan-Slavs gave support to the Piedmontese solution. In the 1870's, these two groups fluctuated between ardent support of Serbia and equally strong support of Montenegro; by 1878 they were favoring Bulgarian claims.

Serbia's campaign for the liberation and unification of the South Slavs was revived by Prince Michael Obrenović, who became prince in 1860, two years after the overthrow of Alexander Karadjordjević. During his exile, Michael had established ties with radical nationalists such as Mazzini and Kossuth. He rejoiced at the Franco-Piedmontese victory over Austria in 1859. Once in power, he began to prepare Serbia to lead a war of national liberation. He viewed his country as a Balkan Piedmont which would attract support from other Serbs and South Slavs in the struggle against Turkey. Adopting the "Načertanije" program, Prince Michael wished to create a greater Serbian state dominated by Serbia and his Obrenović dynasty.[20]

Matija Ban (1818–1903), chief propagandist of Michael's government, described Serbia's goals and her relationship with Russia. The aim of Serbia and its network of agents in Serbian lands was "to deliver from the Ottoman yoke the provinces inhabited by the Serbian race in order to form by their admission to the Principality of Serbia a state

[19] V. Djordjević, *Crna Gora*, pp. 94–101.
[20] S. Jovanović, *Druga vlada Miloša i Mihaila 1858–1868* (Belgrade, 1923), pp. 89–90; Čubrilović, *Istorija*, pp. 222–28.

. . . sufficient to aid efficaciously in the accomplishment of Slav destiny in southern Europe." [21] The minimum objective, Ban wrote later, was to revive the fourteenth-century Serbian state; the maximum aim was a Yugoslav federation. Both goals could be achieved only by war against Turkey. He distrusted the Russian government and the "Moscow national party" and wished Serbia to play an independent, Piedmontese role. Ban believed that, ever since the first Serbian insurrection, Russia had pursued a selfish policy toward the Serbian states, but he concealed these suspicions from the Pan-Slavs and advocated a Yugoslav federation which might join a future all-Slav confederation. A Moscow-Belgrade-Zagreb alliance could assist in achieving Slav unity, wrote Ban, if Russia did not attempt to dominate it.[22] Nevertheless, he feared that Russia's real aim was to divide or even absorb the South Slavs rather than to promote their unification. Ban rejected Metropolitan Mihailo's suggestion that South Slav unification be based upon Orthodoxy. That would exclude Croats, Slovenes, and even some Serbs from a future Yugoslav state and would resemble, he felt, "some sort of Russian agency for the East." "In Belgrade we must not raise the banner of Orthodoxy, but the banner of the Yugoslav people. With the former we are in the hands of the Russians; with the latter we shall remain independent." [23]

During Michael's reign, both the Russian government and the Pan-Slavs favored Serbia's leadership of the Balkan Christians.[24] Foreign

---

[21] AII, Ban 17/6, "Plan general," Sept. 19/Oct. 1, 1860; 5/23, Ban to Garašanin, Jan. 3/15, 1867; 5/13, Ban to Aleksandar Karadjordjević, n.d. Both old and new style dates will be used where pertinent; elsewhere only new style dates will be given.

[22] ROBibSS, Fond I. S. Aksakova, d. 64, Ban to Aksakov, Dec. 28, 1860.

[23] AII, Ban 5/23, "M. le Senateur," Jan. 5/17, 1867. Russian efforts to divide the South Slavs at this time are described also in Ban to Garašanin, Jan. 12/24 and Feb. 17, 1867.

[24] See M. Petrovich's distinction between Slavophilism and Pan-Slavism in *The Emergence of Russian Panslavism 1856–1870* (New York, 1956). Slavophilism—a product of Russian romanticism—developed during the 1830's but lacked definite organization or a well-defined political program. It was the philosophy of a handful of Russian intellectuals, including A. S. Khomiakov, I. V. Kireevskii, and K. Aksakov, who believed western Europe was doomed and that only Russian Orthodoxy could lead men to salvation. Believing in a separate, superior Slav culture, Slavophiles abjured violence and primarily addressed their own countrymen, stressing domestic affairs. Pan-Slavism in Russia, however, was a political outgrowth of Slavophilism after the Crimean War. Borrowing many Slavophile tenets, Pan-Slavs like N. Ia. Danilevskii and I. S. Aksakov transformed them into a

Minister A. M. Gorchakov [25] deplored Turkish oppression, emphasized Russia's humanitarian concern, and denied she had territorial ambitions in the Balkans.[26] Anxious to rebuild Russian influence and prestige there, Gorchakov gave Serbia strong diplomatic support. In November 1860, he informed his consul in Belgrade; "Serbia, from force of circumstances and as a result of her exceptional position, has become the center and point of support for other Slav areas of Turkey." In 1866, Gorchakov, in a dispatch to his consul in Bucharest, reaffirmed this policy:

Bearing in mind that our policy in the East is directed mainly toward strengthening Serbia materially and morally and giving her the opportunity to stand at the head of the movement in the Balkans, the [Foreign] Ministry has decided to subordinate to this plan all of its further activities in regard to arming the Slav peoples in Turkey.[27]

Pan-Slavs in and out of the Russian government acquiesced in Serbia's leadership. Count N. P. Ignat'ev, ambassador to Constantinople,[28]

---

dynamic program of intervention in the affairs of other Slav peoples. As B. H. Sumner notes (p. 57), Pan-Slavism was the link between Slavophilism and Pan-Russianism.

[25] Aleksandr Mikhailovich Gorchakov (1798–1883), a scion of the lesser nobility, received an excellent education at the lycée at Tsarskoe Selo. After lengthy obscurity in the lower reaches of the diplomatic service, he became foreign minister in 1856 and chancellor in 1867. His greatest triumph was in ridding Russia of the humiliating Black Sea clauses of the Treaty of Paris in 1870–71. For general accounts of his career see C. de Grünwald, *Trois siècles de diplomatie russe* (Paris, 1945), pp. 200ff., and Sumner, *Russia and the Balkans, 1870–1880* (Oxford, 1937), pp. 20–23. There is no adequate biography of Gorchakov. Klaczko's *The Two Chancellors* is flamboyant but often inaccurate. F. Charles-Roux, *Alexandre II, Gortchakoff et Napoléon III* (Paris, 1913), covers the period to 1871. Recent Soviet treatments—S. Bushuev, *A. M. Gorchakov* (Moscow, 1944) and S. Semanov, *A. M. Gorchakov, russkii diplomat XIX veka* (Moscow, 1962) are excessively laudatory and brief.

[26] J. Klaczko, *The Two Chancellors: Prince Gortchakof and Prince Bismarck* (New York, 1876), p. 89; S. Goriainov, *La Question d'Orient à la veille du Traité de Berlin (1870–1876)* (Paris, 1948), p. 13.

[27] A. Popov, "Russkaia politika na Balkanakh, 1860–1878 gg," *Avantyury russkago tsarizma v Bolgarii* (Moscow, 1935), pp. 197–98.

[28] Nikolai Pavlovich Ignat'ev (1832–1908), following a successful military career, turned to diplomacy. After his mission to Peking (1859–60), he became director of the Asiatic Department (1861–64), then ambassador to Constantinople (1864–78). On one of Ignat'ev's trips to St. Petersburg, Gorchakov asked him half seriously: "Vous venez me prendre mon portfeuille?" Iu. Kartsov, "Za kulisami diplomatii," *RS, 133* (1908), 90.

urged: an immediate solution of the Eastern Question by Russia and the
Balkan peoples; after Turkey's defeat, a Serbo-Bulgarian state should
be formed, under Russian guidance, ruled by Prince Michael; Bosnia
could be annexed to Serbo-Bulgaria, and Hercegovina by Montenegro.[29] I. S. Aksakov of the Moscow Slav Committee exhorted Serbia
to lead the fight against Turkey. "On Serbia," he wrote in 1862, "are
fastened the glances of all Slav peoples groaning under the Turkish
yoke. . . . Let her unfurl the banner of insurrection and Slavs in
Turkey will rise as one man. Truly it is most convenient [for South
Slavs] to group themselves around the Serbian people." [30]

Russian Pan-Slavs often adopted a tone of superiority that antagonized the Serbs. *The Epistle to the Serbs from Moscow* (1860), warning them not to adopt west European institutions, urged the Serbs to
follow their "elder brother" and adhere to the true path of Orthodoxy.[31] Serbian newspapers denounced *The Epistle* as a "new Musco-
vite gospel" sowing discord between Orthodox Serbs and Catholic
Croats.[32] After a trip through the Balkans, the conservative Aksakov
expressed dismay at the "European poison" infiltrating the Serbian
states. He was revolted by the French atmosphere of the Montenegrin
court, and he considered Serbia's adoption of parliamentary institutions
an attempt "to imitate the external forms of European civilization." [33]
Subsequently, despite this "French influence," Montenegro's patriarchal conservatism appealed to the Russians more than Serbian
parliamentarism. At the Moscow Slav Congress (1867), Professor V. I.
Lamanskii urged that Russian be used as the common Slav language,
while M. N. Katkov called upon Russia to unite the Slavs as Prussia
was uniting the Germans.[34] But Vladan Djordjević, a Serbian delegate,
opposing Russian as the Slav literary tongue, emphasized his people's
desire to share the benefits of European civilization. *Vidov Dan* of

[29] N. Ignat'ev, "Zapiski Grafa N.P. Ignat'eva, 1864–1874," *Izvestiia Ministerstva
Inostrannykh Del* (1914), no. 1, pp. 93ff.

[30] I. Aksakov, *Polnoe sobranie sochinenii I. S. Aksakova* (Moscow, 1886), *1*,
23–24.

[31] *Poslanie k serbam iz Moskvy.* Reprinted in *Polnoe sobranie sochinenii A. S.
Khomiakova* (Moscow, 1900), *1*, 377–79.

[32] E. Mijatović, "Panslavism: Its Rise and Decline," *The Fortnightly Review,* 20
(1873), p. 107; Pypin, *Panslavizm,* pp. 160–61; Petrovich, *Emergence,* 96–102, 129ff.

[33] Aksakov, *Sochinenii, 1,* 23–29; M. Pokrovskii, *Diplomatiia i voiny tsarskoi
Rossii v XIX stoletii* (Moscow, 1923), pp. 250–51.

[34] M. Pogodin, "Zapiski," RS (1874), no. 5, p. 128; H. Kohn, *Pan-Slavism: Its
History and Ideology* (*Notre Dame,* 1953) pp. 142–43.

Belgrade denounced as absurd the Pan-Slav aims of the Congress.[35] During the 1860's only a few isolated figures in Serbia and Montenegro, such as Metropolitan Mihailo and Jovan Sundječić, supported the Pan-Slav program.[36] And Russian Pan-Slavs, with inadequate funds and poor organization, could merely exhort their government and the Serbs to fight Turkey.[37]

Even with Russian backing, Serbia's aspirations to liberate the South Slavs could not be realized. Prince Michael, though inbued with the romantic spirit of 1848 and believing fervently in Serbia's mission, worked to consolidate his personal autocracy and build an effective army. Garašanin revitalized his network of secret agents in Bosnia and Hercegovina (mostly merchants and Orthodox priests), but was too conservative to attempt to enlist their discontented peasantry. In 1861, Matija Ban informed the Russian consul that Prince Michael had abandoned plans to foment rebellion in the two provinces.[38] The prince realized that Serbia was unprepared to fight Turkey. In 1862, Luka Vukalović led a peasant revolt in Hercegovina, and Prince Nikola, who had succeeded Danilo, led Montenegro to war with the Porte; but Serbia, to Prince Nikola's disgust, remained neutral. Only the Powers' mediation saved Montenegro from conquest.[39]

In 1866–1867, Serbia resumed intensive preparations for war. With Russia's encouragement, a Balkan League was formed around Serbia; Michael's prestige soared. A Serbo-Montenegrin military alliance (1866) provided for military and financial aid to Montenegro; in case of victory, national unification was to be achieved under a prince elected by the entire Serbian people. The league was completed by a Serbian military alliance with Greece, a pact of friendship with Ru-

---

[35] Mijatović, "Panslavism," p. 111.

[36] Metropolitan Mihailo was Russophile throughout his career, though he rejected for Serbia the concept of subordination of church to state. See A. Mousset, *La Serbie et son église, 1830–1904* (Paris, 1938,) pp. 246–47. In 1871, Jovan Sundjecić, later Prince Nikola's private secretary, wrote in *Crnogorac,* "Our salvation lies in a federation [of Balkan states] under the hegemony of Russia." J. Skerlić, *Omladina i njena književnost (1848–1871)* (Belgrade, 1906), p. 258.

[37] S. Nikitin, *Slavianskie komitety v Rossii v 1858–1876 godakh* (Moscow, 1960), p. 85; *Ivan Sergeevich Aksakov v ego pis'makh* (Moscow, 1896), 4, 52–53.

[38] AII, Ban 17/29, Ban to Vlangali, April 30/May 12, 1861. Ban noted that this was merely a temporary interruption in the activities of Garašanin's organization; M. Ekmečić, "Nacionalna politika Srbije prema Bosne i Hercegovine i agrarno pitanje, 1844–1875," GIDBiH, *10* (1959), 204–08.

[39] V. Čubrilović and V. Ćorović, "Srbija od 1858 do 1903," *Srpski narod u XIX veku,* knj. 3 (Belgrade, n.d.), pp. 27–28.

mania, and informal ties with Croatian and Bulgarian groups. Here was a basis for a South Slav war against Turkey and Serbian unification.[40]

Russia, whose previous loan offer (1861) had been rejected by Michael, now subsidized Serbia's war preparations. In May 1867, a Russian military mission, dispatched at the prince's request, arrived in Belgrade. To the Russian officers, Serbian War Minister M. Blaznavac boasted of Serbia's strength, and his government declared it expected to be ready for war the following spring. But the Russians soon reported to their War Ministry that their recommendations were being ignored and that Serbia's military resources were inadequate. Though Garašanin's alliance system was nearly complete, Serbian rearmament stagnated. Two of the Russian officers departed much disillusioned. The one remaining officer reported that Garašanin and most of the Serbian public remained warlike but that the prince and Blaznavac had changed their minds.[41]

Austrian policy, as well as Serbia's unpreparedness, caused Prince Michael to hesitate on the brink of war. Since the first Serbian insurrection, Austria had opposed a revolutionary solution of the Eastern Question and become a major obstacle to the liberation and unification of the Serbs. Viennese diplomacy had worked persistently to prevent the union of Serbia and Montenegro or their pursuit of a common foreign policy. Austria's defeat by Prussia in 1866 increased Vienna's fear of strong Slav states in the Balkans. Baron F. Beust explained:

The creation [of such states] on the basis of the national principle along our frontiers would create new centers of attraction which would naturally arouse the inhabitants of our southeastern provinces who are of the same nationality and often of the same faith, and this . . . would create great dangers to the vital interests of the Monarchy.[42]

Out of weakness and calculation the newly formed Austro-Hungarian government sought to emasculate the Balkan League. In August 1867,

[40] For the history of this Balkan League see L. S. Stavrianos, "Balkan Federation: A History of the Movement toward Balkan Unity in Modern Times," *Smith College Studies in History*, 27 (Oct. 1941–July 1942). V. Djordjević, *Crna Gora*, pp. 242–43.
[41] ROBibLen, Fond D. A. Miliutina, no. 169, k. 11, d.8 1867, "Dela Serbskie." The Russian military mission is described and analyzed by S. Nikitin, "Diplomaticheskie otnosheniia Rossii s iuzhnymi slavianami v 60-x gg," *Slavianskii Sbornik* (Moscow, 1947), pp. 285–87.
[42] Beust to Filipović in Zadar, March 11, 1867, cited in V. Djordjević, *Crna Gora*, p. 245.

Prince Michael conferred with the Hungarian leader Count Julius Andrassy,[43] who offered him Bosnia and the Dual Monarchy's support if Serbia would abandon Garašanin's program and its ties with Russia. This tempting offer made Michael hesitate. Andrassy would sacrifice Bosnia to eliminate South Slav opposition to formation of a dual monarchy.[44] Genial and artful Andrassy was to become foreign minister of Austria-Hungary and a leading architect of the future of the Serbs.

Michael did not accept the offer, but the Serbian princes, without repudiating the cause of national liberation or their commitments to St. Petersburg, drew back from war. Prince Nikola of Montenegro feared that Serbia and Russia planned to oust him and unite the Serbian lands under his Obrenović rival. Pressure from Russia and Serbian nationalists had frightened Nikola into co-operation with Belgrade, but he no longer favored war.[45] Serbian diplomacy, exploiting Austro-Turkish preoccupation elsewhere, secured the evacuation from Serbia of the remaining Turkish garrisons in March 1867. This success aroused Nikola's jealousy. After Michael's return from Hungary, the Austrophiles in Serbia gained in influence. In November, Garašanin, the principal proponent of war in the cabinet, was dismissed. Interpreting this as a reversal of Serbian policy, Russia promptly suspended war credits.[46] Russian hopes of an effective Balkan alliance under Serbia's leadership were dashed months before Prince Michael's assassination in May 1868. His death merely confirmed the end of an era of close Serbo-Russian collaboration.

Meanwhile, the indecision of the Serbian princes had encouraged their liberal opponents to assert leadership of the national movement. In August 1866, at Novi Sad in the Vojvodina,[47] some five hundred

[43] Andrassy, a prominent Hungarian nobleman, became premier of Hungary in February 1867. From 1871 to 1879 he served as foreign minister of Austria-Hungary, devoting much effort to blocking Serbian unification.

[44] Čubrilović and Ćorović, "Srbija," pp. 43, 49. The Austrian Compromise (Ausgleich) of 1867 established the dual monarchy of Austria-Hungary.

[45] V. Djordjević, Crna Gora, pp. 253–56, based on the report of Prokesh-Osten of Nov. 12, 1867.

[46] A. Popov, "Russkaia politika," p. 203; S. Jovanović, Druga vlada, pp. 224–26.

[47] A territory lying north of the Danube opposite Belgrade, the Vojvodina had been an integral part of the Kingdom of Hungary since 1860. The Serbian majority there, long free from Turkish rule and enjoying ready contact with central Europe, developed more rapidly culturally and politically than Serbs south of the Danube. Novi Sad, site of the Matica Srpska library, became known as the

delegates from all Serbian lands had established the United Serbian Omladina, ostensibly to promote cultural development.[48] Omladina belonged to the European liberal and national movements, inspired by the Revolution of 1848 and Italian unification. Omladinists agreed that the Serbs could not be emancipated or unified until a liberal government in Serbia led the way. Their chief ideologist was Vladimir Jovanović (1833–1922), a vehement opponent of absolutism, whether Serbian or Russian.[49] Svetozar Miletić (1826–1901), defender of Serbian liberties in the Vojvodina against the Hapsburgs, became their inspirational leader. In 1866, Miletić founded the newspaper *Zastava* as a center of liberal opposition to Prince Michael; Jovanović, exiled from Serbia, joined its staff. In 1867–1868, *Zastava* accused Prince Michael of blocking unification of the Serbs by his cautious foreign policy and autocratic methods at home. Repudiating Michael's monarchy, *Zastava* preached a war of national liberation. Garašanin's agents in the Serbian lands sought advice from Miletić and Omladina as Belgrade grew more hesitant.[50]

At first Omladina was a brilliant success. Local groups sprang up everywhere; early issues of its newspaper, *Mlada Srbadija*, were read enthusiastically, especially in Montenegro and Dalmatia. Omladina established ties with Mazzini and Garibaldi, who wished luck to the Serbian national cause.[51] But subsequent meetings of Omladina revealed deep rifts and failed to construct a definite program of action or a sound organization.[52] Faced with hostility from conservative regimes in Serbia, Montenegro, and Hungary, it split, and by 1871 its local units

---

"Serbian Athens." From the Vojvodina, the literature of Dositej Obradović and other Serbian writers was transmitted to the Serbian principality after the insurrection of 1804.

[48] The nature and significance of Omladina have been debated by Serbian and Yugoslav historians. Jovan Skerlić in his *Omladina i njena književnost*, characterizing it as a national-liberal movement to emancipate Serbdom, considered Omladina analogous to the Tugendbund and Young Italy. He emphasized its deep romanticism and indebtedness to priestly leadership. More recently, Kosta Milutinović in "Crna Gora i Primorje u Omladinskom pokretu," *Istoriski Zapisi*, 6, knj. 9, sv. 1–2 (Jan.–Feb. 1953), 1–46, emphasized the growing influence within Omladina of the socialist ideas of Svetozar Marković and Vaso Pelagić.

[49] For Jovanović see Čubrilović, *Istorija*, pp. 249–55; and W. McClellan, *Svetozar Marković and the Origins of Balkan Socialism* (Princeton, 1964), pp. 35–38.

[50] S. Jovanović, *Druga vlada*, pp. 231–34; Čubrilović, *Istorija*, pp. 247–48.

[51] Milutinović, "Crna Gora," pp. 3, 13–17.

[52] Skerlić, *Omladina*, pp. 124–32; Vlada Milana, I, 133.

had withered. Nevertheless, the ideological preparation for the Serbian national struggle of 1875–1878 was largely Omladina's work.

The Regency Era, 1868–1873

In the years following Michael's murder, the Serbian states were absorbed in domestic problems. A regency of M. Blaznavac, Jovan Ristić, and J. Gavrilović ruled Serbia for the boy-prince, Milan Obrenović. Emphasizing reform at home rather than foreign adventure, the regents promulgated the Constitution of 1869, which affirmed full Serbian autonomy and inaugurated "an hereditary [Obrenović] constitutional monarchy with popular representation." The prince's powers, though, were ill defined. Three quarters of the deputies to the unicameral Assembly (Skupština) would be elected under a restricted suffrage; one quarter would be chosen by the crown. Whether the prince or his ministers would actually rule the country was uncertain, since the constitution stipulated neither the right of legislative initiative nor ministerial responsibility.[53] Despite its shortcomings, the new constitution permitted political parties to grow and provided an arena in which they could contend. In October 1870, a semiliberal press law was approved. Police repression was somewhat reduced, although the minister of interior retained extensive powers.[54]

Montenegro, secularized by Prince Danilo, became an absolute monarchy. His successor, Prince Nikola I, ruled "by grace of God" and controlled all organs of state administration. Former tribal loyalties were being superseded by a new national political mentality. By 1870, Montenegro was building schools, a bureaucracy, and a more modern army. Prince Nikola consulted periodically with representatives of a populace of some 200,000 shepherds and mountaineers, but he declared that his subjects were not ready for a constitution. No political parties existed in this minute replica of autocratic Russia. And Nikola asserted that his domestic policies were brilliantly successful.[55]

---

[53] On the Constitution of 1869 see Ž. Živanović, *Politička istorija Srbije* (Belgrade, 1923), *1*, 231–44; and J. Prodanović, *Istorija političkih stranaka i struja u Srbiji* (Belgrade, 1947), pp. 317–23.

[54] Prodanović, *Istorija*, pp. 328–32. McClellan mistakenly dates the press law as Oct. 1871. Živanović dates it Oct. 1870. *Istorija*, *1*, 249.

[55] Nikola I, "Stanje Crne Gore po ratu 1862," *Zapisi*, 8, sv. 1 (Jan. 1931), 28–29, and "Crna Gora i kretanje u narodu srpskom . . ." sv. 6 (June 1931), 348–61. V. Djordjević's negative account of Nikola's reign in *Crna Gora*, pp. 116ff., is an antidote for the prince's laudatory interpretation.

Abroad, Prince Nikola aspired in his cautious way to lead the South Slav movement. In 1871–1872 his newspaper, *Crnogorac*, seeking to steal Omladina's thunder, preached the unification of Serbdom.[56] He visited St. Petersburg, overcame previous Russian suspicion, and became Alexander II's protégé. Russia now regarded Montenegro as its most reliable foothold in the Balkans.[57] But Nikola relied upon Austrian as well as Russian subsidies to supplement his meager revenues. Montenegro's access to the outside world depended largely upon Austrian good will. Of necessity the Black Mountain balanced uneasily between St. Petersburg and Vienna. And Nikola's ambitions contributed after 1868 to the deterioration of his relations with Serbia. He complained of "Serbian deceitfulness" and declared he would never submit to Serbia's leadership of the national movement.[58]

Belgrade's pre-eminence among the Serbs was eroded under the regency. As Serbia's relations with Prince Nikola and Russia cooled, particularism increased among the Serbs. Montenegro and Novi Sad in the Vojvodina emerged as rival centers of the national movement. Ties linking the Serbs with other Yugoslavs (Croats and Bulgarian exiles) weakened. Serbian unity appeared to be disintegrating. Although Ristić, Serbia's foreign minister during the regency, proclaimed his loyalty to the national mission of liberation and unification, Garašanin's Balkan League dissolved. Serbia's partners resumed independent foreign policies. Ristić blamed the undeniable decline in Serbia's prestige upon an unfavorable European political climate and Russian hostility toward the regency.[59] Completion of Italian and German unification and the loss of French support for a Balkan war of liberation helped compel Ristić to renounce a bellicose foreign policy.

---

[56] *Crnogorac*, founded in 1871 was the semiofficial organ of the Montenegrin government and that country's first and only newspaper. Banned by Austrian and Turkish authorities for its nationalist propaganda, in 1873 it was promptly renamed *Glas Crnogorca* and its political articles grew milder. Nikola's claims of leadership in the South Slav movement are as overblown as his assertions of brilliant domestic successes. See D. Vuksan, *Pregled štampe u Crnoj Gori u 1834–1934* (Cetinje, 1934), pp. 31–35.

[57] Nikola I, "Stanje Crne Gore," pp. 24–28; M. Vukčević, "O politici grafa Andrašija prema našem narodu u oči istočne krize," *GIDuNS*, 5, sv. 13 (1953), p. 407.

[58] Rodich to Andrassy, April 10, 1872, cited in V. Djordjević, *Crna Gora*, pp. 345–47.

[59] Čubrilović, *Istorija*, pp. 329–32.

A divided regency and competition between Austrophile and Russophile factions in Serbia also weakened Belgrade's position. While Ristić
made overtures to St. Petersburg, his fellow regent, M. Blaznavac,
sought rapprochement with Austria-Hungary, assuring Benjamin Kallay, the Austrian consul, that Serbia wished to escape Russian influence.
Kallay reported home that Serbia would not sacrifice itself on a Pan-
Slav altar if an alternative were provided.[60] Count Andrassy, now
foreign minister of Austria-Hungary, again tempted Serbia to renounce its Pan-Slav mission, this time offering Old Serbia and parts of
Bosnia and Hercegovina. Belgrade rejected this proposal since the
regents knew these territories could be acquired only by war with
Turkey.[61]

At first Ristić's personal policy of friendship with Russia was a
dismal failure. Foreign Minister Gorchakov, still furious at Garašanin's
dismissal in 1868, reacted coldly to Ristić's overtures. Adoption of the
liberal Constitution of 1869 and Serbian negotiations with Vienna
deepened the rift. Russian consuls in Belgrade, Sarajevo (Bosnia), and
Novi Sad aided the opposition to the regency; there was even some
Russian support for Prince Nikola's claims to the Serbian throne.[62]
Russia's unfriendly attitude and its support of Montenegro seriously
weakened Serbia.

Both official Russia and the Pan-Slavs promoted fragmentation of the
South Slav movement. Ambassador N. P. Ignat'ev, to magnify his own
and Russia's influence at Constantinople, supported Bulgarian aspirations to a separate exarchate. To divide the Balkan peoples, the Porte
granted the Bulgars terms even more favorable than those Ignat'ev
proposed. The Bulgarian Exarchate drove a wedge among Bulgars,
Serbs, and Greeks, deepened subsequently by a cultural and political
struggle over Macedonia.[63] At first neither the regency nor leaders of
the Serbian church realized the danger to South Slav unity posed by
the Bulgarian Exarchate, but the paths of Serbs and Bulgars now

[60] R. Seton-Watson, "Les relations de l'Autriche-Hongrie et de la Serbie entre
1868 et 1874: La mission de Benjamin Kallay à Belgrade," Le monde slave (Feb.-
March 1926), pp. 221ff.
[61] J. Ristić, Spolašnji odnošaji Srbije novijega vremena (Belgrade, 1901), 3,
140–42.
[62] Čubrilović and Ćorović, "Srbija," pp. 61–62.
[63] G. Trubetskoi, "La politique russe en Orient, le schisme bulgare," Revue
d'histoire diplomatique, 21 (1907), 185ff.

diverged rapidly. Russia fostered Bulgarian separatism and Montenegrin rivalry with Serbia.[64]

While the Serbian states, divided by mutual jealousy, remained inactive in foreign affairs, the radical opposition resumed efforts to achieve Serbian unification by revolution. Though many liberals accepted the regency,[65] others looked to Svetozar Miletić of Novi Sad, who proclaimed that only a reformed Serbia could become the South Slav Piedmont. Miletić adopted a broad Yugoslav approach and worked to promote Serbo-Croatian harmony. He accused the regency of taking a bureaucratic, narrow Serbian view of the national question and of overlooking golden opportunities for war against the Porte. Indignant at Blaznavac's negotiations with Austria-Hungary, Miletić asserted that the regency would sacrifice the Serbian future in order to annex Bosnia. He urged revolutionary action, and even war, to achieve Serbian unity. He shared Mazzini's belief in *fare da se;* therefore, he opposed accepting Russian military aid in a war of liberation for fear Russia might establish a protectorate afterward and stifle a democratic Serbian state at birth. Miletić favored only diplomatic and moral assistance from abroad; he was confident that Serbia's leadership in war would attract support from all South Slavs.[66]

Miletić deemed the Franco-Prussian War (1870–1871) a fine opportunity to emancipate Bosnia and Hercegovina. A national revolutionary organization was required to replace the fading and divided Omladina. At Miletić's initiative, the Society for the Liberation and Unification of the Serbs (Družina za oslobodjenie i ujedinjenje srpsko) was founded in Cetinje, Montenegro, in the summer of 1871. It was designed to prepare a secret uprising in Bosnia and Hercegovina that would fuse a national insurrection in 1872 and drag the Serbian princes into war with Turkey. The society's leaders found three main obstacles blocking the road to Serbian unity: the form of a future state, the question of Serbia's or Montenegro's predominance, and leadership of the military forces in the struggle for liberation. They decided to leave

---

[64] Vlada Milana, *1*, 125; Mousset, *Serbie*, p. 292.

[65] Jovanović and his followers did so. Jovanović asserted that achievement of the national mission of unification and liberation of the Serbs must precede establishment of a democratic regime in Serbia.

[66] M. Klicin, "Život i rad Dr. Svetozara Miletića," *Spomenica Svetozara Miletića* (Novi Sad, 1926), pp. 26–29, 48–50; see N. Radojčić, "Svetozar Miletić o jugoslovenskom jedinstvu—1870 god," GIDuNS, *1* (1928), 92ff.

the dynastic issue and institutions of the future state to a constituent assembly of the Serbian people after liberation. The society appealed to the Serbian states to conclude a military alliance against Turkey.[67]

Svetozar Marković (1846–1875) and his socialist followers joined Miletić's liberals in this attempt to prepare a national insurrection.[68] Marković, after three years in Russia on a Serbian state scholarship, went to Geneva and attacked the regency in pamphlets and newspaper articles. Until Serbia had instituted fundamental democratic and social reforms, he argued, it could not lead a national movement. In *Serbia in the East* (1872) he denounced Ristić's Greater Serbian program, claiming it would antagonize other South Slavs. He advocated instead a democratic Balkan federation. Marković, despite his differences with Miletić, went to Novi Sad and joined his campaign to organize a Serbian revolutionary insurrection.[69]

The regency and St. Petersburg, alarmed at this revolutionary challenge, achieved rapprochement late in 1871, although the Serbo-Russian intimacy of 1866–1867 was not recaptured. When Alexander II agreed to receive Prince Milan at his palace in Livadia, Ristić saw a chance to win Russia's support for the Obrenović dynasty. Blaznavac became reconciled with the Russian consul and accompanied the prince. The tsar's warm reception of the Serbian leaders bolstered the regency and occasioned anger in Vienna.[70] Despite Russia's support, the regents still worried about revolutionary activity and Miletić's growing influence. Unless Belgrade could reclaim leadership of the national movement from the radicals, wrote Ristić (December 1871), the regency and perhaps the dynasty would fall.[71]

The regents delayed a national insurrection for three years, but

[67] D. Vuksan, "Jedan memorandum Družine za oslobodjenje i ujedinenje srpskoga naroda," *Zapisi*, 2 (Jan.–June 1928), 49–51. All Serbian lands were represented in this organization.

[68] For Marković's life and ideology see McClellan, *Marković*; J. Skerlić, *Svetozar Marković: njegov život, rad i ideje* (Belgrade, 1910); V. G. Karasev, "Serbskii revoliutsionnyi demokrat, Svetozar Markovich," *UZIS*, 7, (1953), pp. 348–77; *Vlada Milana, 1*, 139–52.

[69] Čubrilović, *Istorija*, pp. 336–38; McClellan, *Marković*, pp. 178–79.

[70] M. Vukčević, "O politici," p. 112; J. von Reiswitz, *Belgrad-Berlin, Berlin Belgrad, 1866–1871* (Munich and Berlin, 1936), pp. 203–04.

[71] "Pisma Jovana Ristića Filipu Hristiću," *Zbornik za istoriju jezik i književnost srpskog naroda*, prvo odeljenje, *20* (Belgrade, 1931), 82–86; Milutinović, "Crna Gora," pp. 38–42.

gained no further successes in foreign policy. Russia favored Montenegro and the Bulgarians while Austro-Serbian relations deteriorated.[72] The Schönbrunn Convention, concluded between Russia and Austria during the tsar's visit to Vienna in June 1873, signified the rapproachement of the two powers. It provided for mutual consultation in case the interests of the two states came into conflict, but the Austrians refused to add a military convention in case either was attacked by a third power. Germany was asked to join and when it did so this loose, defensive alignment was known as the Dreikaiserbund. The erection of this apparently imposing barrier to change put the troublesome Eastern Question on ice.

Serbia and Russia in the mid-1870's

Domestic conditions in Serbia and Russia influenced their foreign relations profoundly in the 1870's. Serbia, despite its emancipation from Turkish feudalism, remained a primitive, preindustrial country. There was no sizable urban working class, and most of Serbia's meager industry consisted of handicrafts carried on in peasant cottages. Recent Marxist accounts emphasize the development of capitalism in Serbia,[73] but the vast majority of the population were smallholding peasant proprietors raising their pigs and corn in the traditional way.[74]

Serbia, landlocked and without railroads or an adequate road network, was not a major trading nation in 1875.[75] Over the previous three decades, about 80 per cent of its imports had come from the Hapsburg monarchy and almost 70 per cent of its exports had gone there. Serbia's trade with Russia was negligible; its foreign commerce was almost wholly in Austrian hands. The Hapsburgs' merchants, with greater capital resources and superior goods, undermined Serbian handicrafts; their government, through customs treaties, sought economic domination over the Balkan states. Conservative Serbian governments favored

[72] E. Wertheimer, Graf Julius Andrassy, sein Leben und seine Zeiten (Stuttgart, 1910–13), 2, 42–44.

[73] D. Janković's O političkim strankama u Srbiji XIX veka (Belgrade, 1951), pp. 129–31, stresses the disintegration of communal families (zadrugas) and the spread of a money economy in the countryside in the 1870's but fails to provide figures for peasant indebtedness prior to 1890. See McClellan, Marković, pp. 20–24.

[74] V. Karić, Srbija: opis zemlje, naroda i države (Belgrade, 1888), pp. 337–71; V. Karasev, "Osnovnye cherty sotsial'no-ekonomicheskogo razvitiia Serbii v kontse 60-kh-nachale 70-kh godov XIX v.," UZIS, 5 (1951), 206ff.

[75] In 1875, Serbia's exports were 35,014,874 dinars and its imports 31,219,242 (Janković, O političkim, p. 135).

an Austro-Serbian customs agreement to safeguard Serbian trade and free the country from Turkish tutelage, while liberal and nationalist regimes opposed dependence upon the Monarchy and advocated increasing Serbian tariff rates. After Prince Milan dismissed the regency in 1873, the conservative Marinović government drafted proposals for a customs treaty which were received favorably by Count Andrassy, but the latter wished first to conclude a treaty with Rumania, whose trade was more vital to the Monarchy. Austro-Serbian economic negotiations were broken off in 1875—to the Russians' profound relief—because of the revolts in Bosnia and Hercegovina and because Ristić, now very influential, opposed a customs treaty.[76]

Serbia's population of 1,372,741 (1875) was very homogeneous and overwhelmingly rural, though urbanization was beginning.[77] Belgrade, the Serbian capital and principal city, resembled a Russian provincial town, while life in Kragujevac and the smaller towns was freer and more stimulating because their inhabitants were less affected by governmental repression.[78] In Belgrade lived a largely western-trained group of intellectuals and bureaucrats. In the absence of a native aristocracy, this intelligentsia constituted the social and political elite. A smaller merchant class and the better-off peasant proprietors (*gazda*) were the basis for a Serbian bourgeoisie.[79] An extremely low literacy rate and lack of schools revealed Serbia's backwardness. But in the cities a secular, materialistic approach gained ground, while the social role of the Orthodox church declined steadily.[80]

The country was politically unstable and immature. Serbia suffered

---

[76] Karić, *Srbija*, pp. 432–35; D. Djordjević, "Trgovinski pregovori Srbije i Austro-Ugarske, 1869–1875," *Istoriski glasnik Narodne Republike Srbije, 3–4* (1958), 51–73.

[77] The population was 90.26 per cent Serbian. Even in 1884 the urban percentage was only 12.5. The largest towns then were Belgrade (34,864), Niš (16,178), Leskovac (10,870), Požarevac (9,394), Šabac (9,206), and Kragujevac (9,083). Karić, *Srbija*, pp. 234–42.

[78] On Belgrade see P. Rovinskii, "Belgrad, ego ustroistvo i obshchestvennaia zhizn'," *Vestnik Evropy* (April 1870), pp. 530–79 and (May 1870), pp. 132–88, and V. Milenković, *Ekonomska istorija Beograda* (Belgrade, 1932). On Kragujevac see D. Janković, "Prve radničke demonstracije u Srbiji," *Istoriski časopis, 3* (1951–52), 157ff.

[79] Karić, *Srbija*, p. 436; J. Tomasevich, *Peasants, Politics and Economic Change in Yugoslavia* (Stanford, 1954), p. 206.

[80] In 1874, the literacy rate was 6.7 per cent (33.6 per cent in towns and 3.7 per cent in villages). Higher education was limited to the Velika Škola (later Belgrade University). Karić, *Srbija*, pp. 247–61.

greatly from the Obrenović-Karadjordjević dynastic feud. The Obrenović had been in power since 1858, but Pretender Petar Karadjordjević resided in Austria, and his adherents in Serbia constantly agitated for his return. The vague claims to the throne of Prince Nikola of Montenegro, at times backed by Russia, further complicated the picture. Prince Milan Obrenović was largely responsible for his family's insecure position. Dismissing the regency in 1873, he failed to provide firm leadership. He could not gain the confidence of the bureaucratic elite nor acquire mass support and had to rely upon his small professional army. Milan's personality was deterimental to his country. He possessed great intelligence and analytical ability, but customary indolence and permanent immaturity rendered him powerless to handle Serbia's ruthless politicians. Prince Milan, restive at limitations on his power, often reacted to political crises with infantile rage or withdrawal to his bed.

A system of political parties, impossible under Michael's absolutism, developed in the 1870's. During the regency, parties were still hampered severely by the police, but after 1873 conditions for partisan activity grew more favorable. Political groups often constituted an outstanding politician's personal following rather than parties united by definite ideologies, thus contributing to the turbulence of Serbian politics. Prince Milan preferred the Conservatives, who were supported by well-to-do merchants, landowners and bureaucrats. They advocated princely absolutism and opposed the Constitution of 1869.[81] After Ilija Garašanin's death in 1873, the Conservatives were led by Jovan Marinović,[82] a man of integrity but too passive and hesitant to command respect from the Assembly. His ineffectiveness promoted the rise of a "Young Conservative" faction, under Aćim Čumić, with a more dynamic, nationalistic program.

The Liberals, the other major party, were plagued by factional rivalries and ideological differences. Jevrem Grujić, an ardent nationalist, headed the "Liberals of 1858." In the Assembly he built an enthusiastic following of "pure" liberals seeking full parliamentary sovereignty.[83] Jovan Ristić led the more conservative, opportunistic

[81] HHSA, Kallay to Andrassy, July 21 and Dec. 9, 1874; L. Kaljević, *Moje uspomene* (Belgrade, 1908), pp. 23–25.

[82] Marinović (1820–1893), a close friend of Garašanin, was his natural heir as leader of the Conservatives.

[83] S. Jovanović, *Druga vlada*, pp. 95–98.

Jovan Ristić (1831–1899), Regent 1868–1872, Foreign Minister of Serbia, 1875, 1876 1880.

Ilija Garašanin (1812–1874), Foreign Minister of Serbia, 1852–1853, 1861–1867, author of "Načertanije" and architect of Serbian foreign policy in the nineteenth century.

"Liberals of 1868." [84] Another group of young, idealistic liberals followed Ljubomir Kaljević. A bitter feud between Ristić and Grujić hampered the Liberals until 1875, when Stevča Mihajlović assumed leadership. Both rivals could serve without loss of prestige under the titular chairmanship of this venerable peasant leader. Mihajlović, consistently loyal to the Obrenović family, enjoyed wide popularity and gave his party a measure of unity and respectability. In the early 1870's, it attracted some support from lower-class elements in town and country, but its bulwarks were lesser merchants, the *gazda* group of richer peasants, army officers, clergy, and lesser bureaucrats. As defenders of the political and social status quo, the Liberals lost mass support, as dissatisfaction with existing conditions grew in the countryside. [85]

Jovan Ristić, the outstanding Serbian statesman of the 1870's, shared the conservative political orientation of many Liberals. [86] He had obtained an excellent higher education in western Europe on a state scholarship, married into the family of a wealthy Belgrade merchant, and rose rapidly in government service. At thirty, having overcome his humble origin, Ristić represented Serbia in Constantinople. He proved his diplomatic ability by securing the evacuation of Turkish garrisons from Serbian cities in 1867. Becoming second regent in 1868, he gradually assumed the principal role in foreign and domestic affairs and drafted the Constitution of 1869. He demonstrated repeatedly his ability to control the Assembly and govern firmly. Ristić was proud and egotistical, cold and reserved; he gained a large political following but few friends. His hauteur so antagonized Milan that the prince resolved to prevent Ristić from becoming premier. [87] Nonetheless, the Liberal leader exercised great influence. He cloaked authoritarian policies with liberal slogans and asserted that his ideal was the golden mean. "Moderation is the shield which guards freedom," he declared. "I always took the middle path myself." [88] By ability and skill, this Serbian Guizot became the dominant figure in Liberal governments from 1875 to 1880.

Radical groups, with growing support from the peasantry, were beginning to challenge the major Serbian parties. Svetozar Marković, a

---

[84] The "Liberals of 1858" had forced the abdication of Aleksandar Karadjordjević; the "Liberals of 1868" supported Ristić and the regency.

[85] Janković, *O političkim*, pp. 197–98.

[86] For Ristić's career see B. Petrović, *Jovan Ristić* (Belgrade, n.d.), Ž. Živanović, *Jovan Ristić* (Belgrade, 1929), and *Vlada Milana*, *1*, 12–20.

[87] Kaljević, *Moje uspomene*, pp. 24–25.

[88] Janković, *O političkim*, p. 185.

convert to the Russian socialism of N. G. Chernyshevskii,[89] blamed the Belgrade bureaucracy for impoverishment of the peasantry and urged its replacement by a federation of agricultural communes.[90] Marković, who died early in 1875, laid a basis for both Serbian socialism and the Radical party. Adam Bogosavljević, his disciple, became immensely popular with the poorer peasantry. From 1874 to 1880 he led an expanding faction of peasant delegates in the Assembly against Conservative and Liberal governments.[91] Unlike the theoretical Marković, Adam spoke a language readily comprehensible to the peasants who, despite police pressure, elected him repeatedly. Adam declared, "As long as the bureaucratic system lasts here, all governments will be the same." His Radicals gradually abandoned socialist ideology and dedicated themselves to drastic social reform by parliamentary means.[92]

In the post-regency era, the fledgling Serbian constitutional system functioned badly. The Conservative governments of Marinović and Čumić (November 1873–January 1875), despite Prince Milan's support, could not maintain domestic order or obtain Assembly backing. Marinović was highly regarded in St. Petersburg and Vienna,[93] but he was not energetic enough, nor was he seconded strongly enough by Russia, to win concessions from the Porte. The Turks refused to surrender the disputed village of Mali Zvornik despite Milan's personal appeal to the tsar for diplomatic assistance. Much discomfited, Marinović denounced Count N. P. Ignat'ev, the Russian ambassador in Constantinople, for abetting Turkish interests. But Marinović's government was soon toppled.[94] The Čumić cabinet which followed failed to obtain

[89] Yugoslav historians have differed sharply over influences upon Marković's ideology and the significance of his contribution. Skerlić in *Svetozar Marković* stressed the influence of Chernyshevskii upon him, whereas I. Stanojčić emphasized the impact of Marxism. See Čubrilović, *Istorija*, pp. 274–77. For an objective recent appraisal of ideological influences upon Marković see McClellan, *Marković*, pp. 59–63.

[90] Vlada Milana, *1*, 139–52.

[91] Jovanović stated incorrectly that there were only two Radical Socialists in the Assembly of 1874–75; McClellan notes there were four plus several sympathizers. *Ibid*. Vlada Milana, *1*, pp. 228–32; McClellan, *Marković*, pp. 254–55.

[92] Janković, *O političkim*, pp. 227–30.

[93] Gorchakov regarded him as the only gentleman among Serbian leaders. *Vlada Milana*, *1*, 179. Kallay, the Austrian consul in Belgrade, reported that Marinović was Russophile but peaceable and honest. Andrassy warmly supported the Marinović government. HHSA, Kallay to Andrassy, Nov. 15, 1874, no. 49.

[94] HHSA, Kallay to Andrassy, June 2, 1874, no. 35; Jan. 6, 1875, no. 3.

Austrian or Russian approval. Chancellor Gorchakov warned that Marinović had enjoyed full Russian support; Čumić could acquire it only by pursuing his predecessor's policies.[95]

The Liberals profited from their rivals' embarrassment. *Istok*, a newspaper reflecting Ristić's views, began to beat the war drums. It reproached the Conservatives for passivity and failure and urged Serbia to "carry the torch of freedom to the enslaved [Serbian] brethren." Continued *Istok*, "To wait means a certain grave for us. Our goal must be to free ourselves as soon as possible. . . . Many, many favorable moments have been missed. . . . Let us not sell our national mission for the sake of Mali Zvornik. . . . In the interests of her own survival, Serbia must undertake the role of Piedmont."[96] Austria and Russia, the newspaper asserted, were plotting to deprive the Serbs of Bosnia and Hercegovina. The Conservatives' inactivity was ruining Serbia's standing abroad. "Serbia thus must definitely adopt the role of Sardinia-Piedmont; its regime must be *national* and *liberal* like Cavour's."[97] The Ristić Liberals sought to oust the Conservatives from power and maintain control of the national liberation movement.

Their tactics succeeded brilliantly. Čumić resigned and was succeeded by Danilo Stevanović's caretaker regime (January–August 1875). This cabinet, too feeble and inept to obtain Assembly backing or inspire confidence in St. Petersburg, prepared the way for the Liberals' assumption of power. Russia now was committed to the Obrenović dynasty, but continued to insist that Marinović be returned to the premiership.[98] Prince Milan shared the Dreikaiserbund's predilection for Marinović's Conservatives, but the Assembly and the Serbian public favored the Liberals' vehement demands for action.

These aspirations were not supported by St. Petersburg largely because of conditions in Russia.[99] The emancipation of the peasantry in the 1860's had touched off liberal reforms in local government, the

[95] *Ibid.*, Feb. 2, 1875, no. 5.
[96] *Istok* (Belgrade), April 8/20, 1874, no. 35, lead article.
[97] *Ibid.*, June 6/18, 17/29, June 22/July 4, nos. 54, 59, 61.
[98] HHSA, Kallay to Andrassy, April 20, 1875; Cingria to Andrassy, June 20, no. 31.
[99] These can only be summarized here. For lengthier accounts see W. Mosse, *Alexander II and the Modernization of Russia* (New York, 1958), and S. Tatishchev, *Imperator Aleksandr II: ego zhizn' i tsarstvovanie*, 2 vols. (St. Petersburg, 1903).

judiciary, the army, and the censorship, contributing to modernization. Nevertheless, in 1875 the reforms were incomplete. Russia, the most backward of the great European powers, was only slightly more advanced than Serbia in its economic and social development.

Of a population of some 86,000,000, less than one million were engaged in manufacturing, mining, or metallurgy. Most Russians were engaged in agriculture. Perhaps 85 per cent of the populace lived in small isolated villages, producing little more than was required for their subsistence. Despite the abolition of serfdom, the inefficient three-field system prevailed; machinery and fertilizers were little used.[100] Yet Russia's credit abroad depended upon grain exports, derived from larger estates and dispatched through the Turkish Straits. These exports financed purchases of machinery and manufactured goods from western Europe and the United States. Russian industry, protected by rising tariffs and stimulated by state sponsored railway construction, was expanding slowly, but it was outpaced by the advanced industrial economies of western Europe.[101]

Russian society was gradually severing the bonds of the caste system, inherited from old Muscovy. The privileged nobility and higher clergy were in decline, the middle class was growing, and differentiation was beginning among an egalitarian-minded peasantry. The nobility was selling its lands to townspeople and peasants.[102] The peasantry, though free from personal bondage, suffered from high taxation, redemption payments, and overpopulation. Peasants, unlike other classes, were still subject to the poll tax, corporal punishment, and passport restrictions.[103] In 1870, the urban population exceeded 10 per cent, but most of the seven hundred cities of the Empire were little more than overgrown villages. In Great Russia, St. Petersburg (670,000) and Moscow

---

[100] A. G. Rashin in *Naselenie Rossii za 100 let (1811–1913 gg.)* (Moscow, 1956) gives the population of the Russian Empire, excluding Poland and Finland, as 69,959,500 in 1863 and 98,650,500 in 1885 (p. 26). After including a reasonable population figure for Central Asia, omitted by Rashin for 1863, and calculating the average annual increase, the present author reaches his estimate of 86 million for the Empire without Poland and Finland. For Russian agricultural conditions in this period see G. T. Robinson, *Rural Russia under the Old Regime* (New York, 1932), pp. 94–116.

[101] In October 1876, 17,658 versts (10,654 miles) of railway lines were open to traffic, exclusive of Finland. Tatishchev, *Imperator*, 2, 215.

[102] M. Florinsky, *Russia: A History and an Interpretation* (New York, 1953), 2, 929, citing N. Oganovskii, *Sel'skoe khoziastvo Rossii v XX veke* (Moscow, 1923).

[103] For the peasants' plight see Robinson, *Russia*, pp. 117–28.

(c. 400,000) were the only major urban centers.[104] Modest progress in education occurred under Alexander II (1855–1881), but illiteracy still predominated in rural areas.[105]

In theory the emperor remained an unlimited autocrat. Thus Alexander II,[106] deciding that serfdom should be abolished, forced through the emancipation despite opposition from much of the nobility. But thereafter, avoiding unpleasant issues, the emperor stayed generally in the background, spending much time on the parade ground. Alexander, distrusting powerful advisers, preserved his authority by retaining in office both liberal and conservative ministers. Unlike other rulers of his time, he was neither bound by a constitution nor embarrassed by a parliament. No national representation or political parties were permitted to develop. The ministers, unco-ordinated by cabinet or premier, were responsible to the emperor alone. Limited district and provincial self-government had been established, but by the mid-1870's the central bureaucracy interfered frequently in its work.[107] Neither liberals in the *zemstvos* nor revolutionary populists (*narodniki*) were sufficiently organized to threaten the emperor's rule.

During this era of profound change, the Russian bureaucracy contained few outstanding figures. Count P. A. Shuvalov, who had provided strong conservative leadership as chief of police, lost the emperor's favor in 1874 and was sent into semiexile as ambassador to London. Shuvalov's disgrace was a victory of D. A. Miliutin, liberal minister of war, who was completing thorough reform of the Russian army. But Miliutin's liberal course was vigorously opposed by officials of the Ministry of Interior and by the reactionary minister of education, Count D. A. Tolstoi. They sought to muzzle the press, which had been partially liberated from censorship during the 1860's. After July 1873, the minister of interior could suspend for three months any

---

[104] The only other cities with more than 100,000 people in 1870 were Warsaw, Odessa, and Kishinev; eleven others contained 50,000–100,000 people. S. Pushkarev, *The Emergence of Modern Russia 1801–1917* (New York, 1963), p. 151, citing A. Suvorin, ed., *Russkii Kalendar' na 1872 god* (St. Petersburg, 1879), pp. 326, 332–47.

[105] Florinsky, *Russia*, 2, 1046–1047.

[106] Biographers of Alexander II have been hampered by the destruction of most of his private papers, apparently upon instruction of his heir, Alexander III. The best recent treatment is E. M. Almedingen's *The Emperor Alexander II* (London, 1962). The most complete study of his reign is still Tatishchev's work.

[107] See Pushkarev, *Emergence*, pp. 148–50. These organs of self-government were called *zemstvos*. The authoritative work on the *zemstvos* is B. B. Veselovskii, *Istoriia zemstva za sorok let*, 4 vols. (St. Petersburg, 1909–1911).

publication which discussed state affairs in a manner displeasing to the government.[108]

In foreign affairs Alexander made the chief decisions. Almost since his accession, the Foreign Ministry had been directed by Prince A. M. Gorchakov. By 1875, Gorchakov was losing his physical, and some claimed, his mental vigor. Earlier he had gained popularity for his successful defense of Russian national interests, and he was renowned for his French phrases. The old chancellor, as rumors spread about his imminent resignation, guarded his high office jealously against his rivals, N. P. Ignat'ev and P. A. Shuvalov. The resignation of P. N. Stremoukhov, Gorchakov's chief adviser on Balkan problems, under fire from the emperor and a pro-German clique at court, revealed how shaky was the chancellor's position.[109]

Within the Foreign Ministry a rift widened between the Europe-oriented Diplomatic Chancellery, which filled the chief ambassadorial posts, and the nationalistic consular officials of the Asiatic Department.[110] Since 1873 the Chancellery faction, led by Gorchakov and E. P. Novikov, ambassador to Vienna, had advocated co-operation with Austria and maintenance of the Balkan *status quo*. A rival Pan-Slav group, largely from the Asiatic Department, advocated intolerant Russian nationalism and a unilateral solution of the Eastern Question. Ignat'ev, its spokesman, frequently pursued an independent course in Constantinople, and for years he had opposed bitterly any rapproche-

[108] The Ministry could also fine publishers of newspapers and magazines and issue warnings. To ban a publication permanently, consent of the Senate was required. From 1865 to 1880, 177 warnings and 52 orders to cease publication were issued. Pushkarev, *Emergence*, 161–62; I. Grüning, *Die russische öffentliche Meinung und ihre Stellung zu den Grossmächten, 1878–1894* (Berlin, 1929), pp. 11–13.

[109] HHSA, Langenau to Andrassy, April 1875, private letter.

[110] The Diplomatic Chancellery remained the main avenue to advancement in the Russian diplomatic service: its men represented Russia in Vienna, Paris, Berlin, and London in the 1870's. Gorchakov, despite his promises to remove "foreigners" from the service drew from the Chancellery two of his principal advisers, A. G. Jomini and A. F. Gamburger. The Asiatic Department, which dealt with European Turkey as well as Asia, was staffed by pure Russians. It contained most experts on Balkan affairs and supplied most of the consuls for that region. The department's prestige waxed under Ignat'ev's and Stremoukhov's (1864–Dec. 1875) leadership, and waned under N. K. Giers, who ran it for the rest of the Balkan Crisis. For more on the organization and personnel of the Foreign Ministry see *Ocherk istorii ministerstva inostrannykh del, 1802–1902* (St. Petersburg, 1902), and Sumner, *Russia*, pp. 18–35.

ment with the German powers.[111] At times the emperor was strongly influenced by Ignat'ev.

In eastern Europe, as the summer of 1875 began, the forces favoring peace and stability predominated. The Dreikaiserbund, firm if untested, was wedded to the *status quo*. The Russian government, despite Ignat'ev's pleas, pursued a pacific, Austrophile policy. The threat of a Turko-Montenegrin war over the Podgorica affair had been averted.[112] The Franco-German war scare subsided in May. Advocates of drastic change or revolution—Serbian liberals and radicals, Bosnian nationalists, and Russian Pan-Slavs—lacked power and co-ordination.[113] The Balkans appeared unusually peaceful. It was a deceptive calm.

[111] G. de Wesselitsky-Bojidarovitch, *Dix mois de ma vie, 1875–1876* (Paris, 1929), pp. 17–19.

[112] See M. Vukčević, *Crna Gora i Hercegovina u oči rata, 1874–1876* (Cetinje, 1950), pp. 46–95.

[113] For example, Serbian revolutionaries in Bosnia and Hercegovina believed they had been abandoned by both Serbia and Montenegro. Premier Marinović had declared on November 27, 1874, "Serbia cannot be the hinge of Serbdom [or] the refuge of revolutionary activities." Quoted by M. Ekmečić, *Ustanak u Bosni 1875–1878* (Sarajevo, 1960), p. 52.

CHAPTER II

THE REVOLTS IN
HERCEGOVINA AND BOSNIA

Reactions to the Hercegovina Revolt

IN early July 1875, the Christians of Gabela in southern Hercegovina revolted against the Turks; this was followed by a larger uprising at Nevesinje further to the north.[1] By mid-August a large part of Hercegovina was aflame and outbreaks were spreading northward into Bosnia. The Turkish government, hoping local officials could suppress the Hercegovina risings, at first denied they were serious, then ordered its troops to crush the insurrection. When initial Turkish military measures proved ineffective, the Porte and the Powers were confronted with a major crisis.[2] The emancipation movement in Hercegovina threatened to become a national struggle to liberate and unify all Serbs. Austria-Hungary was directly challenged; and relations between Russia and the Serbs again became highly significant.

[1] Apparently the movement at Gabela began on June 21/July 3. Skirmishes with the Turks started on June 27/July 9 at Krekov in the Nevesinje district of central Hercegovina. See Vukčević, *Crna Gora*, pp. 100–04; V. Čubrilović, *Bosanski ustanak, 1875–1878* (Belgrade, 1930), pp. 52–55; G. Vuković, *Hercegovački i Vasojevički ustanak* (Sarajevo, 1925). The English correspondent Stillman, wrote, "The insurrection in its early stages was mainly among the Catholic population of Popovo and Gabella. . . . The insurrection spread because the whole country was ripe for it and because the military conduct of the Turks was inefficient and unintelligent." W. J. Stillman, *Hercegovina and the Late Uprising* (London, 1877), p. 3.

[2] For the Turkish reactions see D. Harris, *A Diplomatic History of the Balkan Crisis of 1875–1878: The First Year* (Stanford, 1936), pp. 63–66, and for the Powers', pp. 66ff.

During the following months Serbia and Montenegro were placed in difficult positions. Their princes wished to annex the insurgent provinces; generally Hercegovinians wished to join Montenegro and Bosnians Serbia. Public opinion pressured both princes to support the insurgent cause even to the point of war, while Russia and Austria insisted upon their neutrality.

Many contemporaries ascribed the Hercegovina revolts to foreign instigation and intrigue. Russian leaders blamed Austrian or German machinations.[3] The Serbs considered the Austrian military clique responsible for the Gabela uprising.[4] Youthful Montenegrins believed their own government was involved. In western Europe, Russia was suspect.[5] Foreign agents were operating in Hercegovina, but there is no evidence that the insurrection was organized or directed by an outside power. On the contrary, it appears the revolts were spontaneous protests by Christian merchants and peasants against heavy taxation and oppressive rule by local Turkish authorities.[6] In 1874, an Ottoman official, Dr. Josef Koetschet, finding deep discontent among the peasantry of Bosnia and Hercegovina, warned his colleagues of impending disaster.[7]

[3] Chancellor Gorchakov believed Germany might have been responsible. Kartsov, "Za kulisami" *RS*, *133* (1908), 341–42. Ignat'ev attributed the revolts to Austrian intrigue. IV, *135* (1914), 441–42.

[4] M. Alimpić, *Život i rad generala Ranka Alimpića u svezi sa dogadjajima iz najnovije srpske istorije* (Belgrade, 1892), p. 599. Ban was certain that the Hercegovina uprisings had been instigated by Austria. AII, Ban 17/43, "Moj predlog Ristiću," Aug. 12/24, 1875.

[5] Vukčević, *Crna Gora*, p. 99; M. Stojanović, *The Great Powers and the Balkans, 1875–1878* (Cambridge, Eng., 1939), p. 15.

[6] Čubrilović and Ćorović, *Srbija*, pp. 74–75. The *Manchester Guardian's* correspondent, denying that the insurrection was caused by foreign agitators, wrote that "the outbreak took . . . the Omladina itself by surprise." The Nevesinje insurgents demanded security against Turkish violence and abrogation of unjust taxes and forced labor. Moslem landlords (*begs*) had prevented reform; it was largely against their exactions that the Catholic peasantry of the Narenta district had risen in revolt. A. Evans, *Through Bosnia and Hercegovina on Foot during the Insurrection August and September 1875* (London, 1876), pp. 333–58.

For economic and cultural conditions in Bosnia and Hercegovina see V. Skarić, "Iz prošlosti Bosne i Hercegovine XIX vijeka," GIDBiH, *1* (1949), 19ff., and V. Bogičević, "Stanje raje u Bosni i Hercegovini pred ustanak 1875–1878 godine," GIDBiH, *2* (1950), 148–83.

[7] J. Koetschet, *Aus Bosniens letzter Türkenzeit* (Vienna, 1905), pp. 1–6. The official Turkish census for 1874 gave the population of "Bosnia" (including Hercegovina and Novi Pazar) as 1,216,846, including 576,756 Orthodox, 442,050 Moslems, 185,503 Roman Catholics, 3,000 Jews, and 9,537 gypsies. The Turks were

The Hercegovina revolt had an immediate and powerful impact upon other Serbian lands. In Serbia proper, Stevanović's weak cabinet held office pending mid-August elections. Promoting Serbia's national mission, Belgrade authorized private recruitment of volunteers, publication of proinsurgent appeals in the press, and dispatched Mićo Ljubibratić to his homeland to lead the insurrection.[8] Prince Milan agreed that Serbia should provide unofficial aid, but neither he nor his government adopted a definite policy. Instead the prince departed for Vienna on July 30. His trip, emphasizing Serbia's reliance on the Powers, forestalled an independent course by Belgrade.[9]

Milan's avowed purpose was to confer in Vienna with Austrian and Russian leaders, but because of his financial difficulties, he was more concerned to arrange his marriage to a wealthy Rumanian heiress, Natalia Keshko.[10] Foreign Minister Andrassy, seconded by Russian Ambassador E. P. Novikov, urged him to keep Serbia neutral. Milan agreed not to intervene in Hercegovina unless Montenegro did.[11] The prince left Vienna determined to maintain Serbian neutrality and the Dreikaiserbund's support.

During his absence, the Stevanović government was borne along on a tide of sentimental nationalism. Committees to aid the insurrection, financed by rich merchants, sprang up throughout Serbia. Public subscriptions helped in recruiting and equipping volunteers who were organized into bands and sent across the frontier. To insure that this assistance remained unofficial, Serbian citizens were forbidden to participate. When the Russian consul, A. N. Kartsov, warned Foreign

---

noted for exaggerating the Moslem population and underestimating the number of Christians. Evans, *Through Bosnia*, p. 265. See also F. Schmid, *Bosnien und die Herzegowina unter der Verwaltung Österreich-Ungarns* (Leipzig, 1914), p. 5; A. von Mollinary, *46 Jahre im österreich-ungarischen Heere, 1833–1879* (Vienna, 1905), *2*, 290–91.

[8] DAS, 132/83, D. Stevanović, "Šta je srpska vlada uradila." According to S. Ljubibratić and T. Kruševac, Mićo Ljubibratić acted in Hercegovina entirely on his own, not on orders from Belgrade. He was a native of Hercegovina who had since early youth devoted himself to the cause of Serbian liberation and unity. S. Ljubibratić and T. Kruševac, "Prilozi za proučavanje hercegovačkih ustanaka, 1857–1878 godine," GIDBiH, 7 (1955), 185–204; *8* (1956), 301–40.

[9] Ekmečić, *Ustanak*, pp. 120–21.

[10] Natalia's father was a Russian colonel with large estates in Rumania; her mother was from the Rumanian aristocracy. *Vlada Milana*, *1*, 245–46; Harris, *History*, p. 104.

[11] HHSA, Varia Turquie I, 1875, "Extrait d'un compte rendu d'une conférence à Vienne le 5 août."

Minister Milan Bogičević that official aid to the insurgents might cost Serbia European protection, the Serb replied that the *entraînement générale* was so powerful that he doubted even the prince could master it.[12]

The only newspapers permitted to publish in Serbia were *Srpske Novine* (official), *Vidov Dan* (Conservative), and *Istok* (Liberal). The first two minimized the insurrection's importance. But *Istok*, blaming it on Turkish misrule, declared: "If the uprising should spread and Montenegro intervenes, and Serbia should look on with folded hands, then Serbia's future would be lost once and for all." [13] The government confiscated an issue advocating Serbian aid to the insurgents. But the very next day *Istok* quoted an appeal by the insurgents from a Czech newspaper: "Now or never! Help brothers!" [14] Accusing *Vidov Dan* of passivity in foreign affairs and of advocating absolutism at home, *Istok* asserted:

Now is a relatively favorable time to fulfill the national mission. Austria in agreement with Russia is unfriendly toward Turkey; Germany is paralyzed by France. Montenegro is always ready to shed blood for national liberation. . . . Piedmont would never have achieved her task if all Italians had not supported her morally and in fact. . . . Serbia, the Piedmont of Serbdom and Southern Slavdom must not abandon to others the leadership in the cause of national liberation and unification. Serbia must be larger in order to secure her future!! [15]

With naïve confidence, it predicted success in the coming inevitable conflict with the Porte and urged Prince Milan to lead a Serbian advance to Kosovo: "Serbia alone is a handful for Turkey which because of its financial weakness cannot conduct real war. The inter-

---

[12] *Osvobozhdenie Bolgarii ot turetskogo iga* (Moscow, 1961), *1*, 56–57, Kartsov to Jomini, Aug. 7/19. (Hereafter referred to as OSVOb.) Milan told Kartsov on August 15, "Vous connaissez trop bien la situation du moment pour ne pas apprécier la terrible position où je me trouve depuis mon retour de Vienne. D'une part—impossibilité absolue de maîtriser le mouvement national en faveur de l'insurrection en Herzégovine; de l'autre l'abdication . . . qu'en ce moment de crise j'envisagerais comme une lâcheté à laquelle je préférerais même une mort violente. Le seul parti qu'il me reste donc à prendre c'est de céder à l'entraînement général et de me mettre à la tête de mon peuple." See also Vlada Milana, *1*, 245.

[13] *Istok*, July 5/17, no. 59, lead.

[14] *Ibid.*, July 13/25 and 14/26, nos. 62, 63; HHSA, Cingria to Andrassy, Aug. 6, no. 51.

[15] *Istok*, July 23/Aug. 4, no. 66, lead.

vention of Serbia [would] signify *the igniting of the East!* It is up to Serbia therefore to sing the funeral hymn of the half-moon." [16]

Istok's exhortations reflected the bellicose views of the intelligentsia. It was the most influential newspaper in Serbia, and *Vidov Dan* was a feeble competitor for control of public opinion. Since Belgrade was the only large urban center, "public opinion" was produced mainly by the politicians, journalists, and students who met in its numerous cafés. *Istok*'s articles roused excitable, unruly elements; skeptical, realistic voices were drowned out. The Belgrade intelligentsia was mostly war-like and "burned with patriotism." [17] A Serbian district official wrote, "Now or never we must show the world we are capable of living as a free people and not as the sons of slaves!" [18] But this vocal minority found it difficult to convince peasants raised in peace and relative prosperity that it was their duty to fight.[19]

Prince Milan, returning to Belgrade (August 12), heard the shouts of a volunteer detachment in the streets: "Long live the king of Serbia. . . . At the Turks! Give us war!" [20] Though Stevanović's secret encouragement of unofficial aid to the insurgents had not yet committed Serbia irrevocably to a bellicose policy, it placed Milan in an awkward position. He had assured Austrian diplomats that volunteer bands were not coming from Serbia. In the Council of Ministers he demanded, as Novikov had urged, that recruitment and dispatch of volunteers be halted immediately since, in case of war, Serbia would be isolated. Stevanović replied that any sudden cessation of aid would be difficult

[16] *Ibid.*, July 30/Aug. 11, no. 69. On August 2/14, *Istok*, reiterating that Serbia alone could stand up to Turkey militarily, took great comfort from a statement by *Sankt Peterburgskie Vedomosti*: "Serbia and Montenegro can count on Russia unconditionally and at any time." *Istok* interpreted this to signify that no matter how a Serbo-Turkish war turned out, Serbia could lose nothing.

[17] Kaljević, *Moje uspomene*, p. 7; L. Lazarević, "Pred rat: sećanje na 1875–76," *Zapisi, 2* (1928), 209–10.

[18] OSVOb., *1*, 52–53, V. Živanović to L. Karavelov, Aug. 2/14, 1875.

[19] Lazarević, "Pred rat," p. 209.

[20] *Vlada Milana, 1*, 246; Alimpić, *Život*, pp. 497–500. Ranko Alimpić, appalled at the disorderly mob he observed passing the Terazije in Belgrade singing warlike songs, went to Premier Stevanović and told him, "If the government finds that it is the time to work for the expansion of Serbian frontiers, it must take matters into its own hands and carry out preparations . . . without attracting the attention of diplomacy. . . . If this is not the time, the rising [in Hercegovina] should be ended and the people pacified as soon as possible." Alimpić added that bands should only be sent across the frontier with proper leaders. Serbia's goal should be to liberate Old Serbia, Macedonia, and Bosnia; Hercegovina should be left to Montenegro so as to prevent friction between the two Serbian states.

and dangerous because of public sentiment in Serbia. Milan stormed out of the meeting. Three days later the government submitted its resignation.[21] But volunteer bands continued to cross the frontier with Milan's knowledge. Only decisive action by the prince could stop Serbia's drift toward war.

The Hercegovina revolt caught the tiny Montenegrin capital by surprise. Cetinje, wrote W. J. Stillman, contained a single, wide street with about forty one-story stone houses on either side. Prince Nikola's palace was merely the largest of these. Opposite the palace stood the seminary, converted into a hotel for visitors whose ground floor housed government offices. Prince Nikola administered justice beneath the elm tree outside his palace. The simple, dignified Montenegrins reminded Stillman of Scotch Highlanders. Cetinje's population, swollen by chiefs from various parts of the country, awaited impatiently a decision for war or peace. Caring little what Europe did, Montenegrins counted upon Serbia to lead the struggle for national liberation.[22]

Montenegro had long exercised strong influence in Hercegovina; its prince could not renounce this now. In late 1874, after restraining Hercegovina's chiefs from armed action, Nikola had promised never to abandon them. With but few exceptions they awaited his orders.[23] Since most of the leaders of the July insurrection had recently been in Montenegro, it appeared to some that Nikola had arranged the revolt. And Montenegrin aspirations in Hercegovina were evident. In April 1875, Petar Vukotić, Nikola's closest adviser, had told the Austrian chief of staff, General Beck, "We live up there in a rocky desert [Felswüste] and look down upon the green plains of Hercegovina. We want to acquire enough pasture land to nourish our stock." [24] Yet Nikola was ignorant of the insurgents' plans. From Cetinje the Russian consul, A. S. Ionin, wrote, "Here we were almost the last ones to learn what had happened in that province [Hercegovina]." And at first Nikola considered the Nevesinje rising an insignificant local putsch.[25]

[21] DAS 132/82, "Šta je srpska vlada uradila."

[22] Stillman, *Herzegovina*, pp. 18–21.

[23] Nikola I, "Stanje Crne Gore," pp. 27–28; D. Tunguz-Perović, "Uloga Knjaza Nikole od početka Nevesinjske puške do stupanje službene Crne Gore u rat," *Zapisi, 3* (1928), knj. 3, p. 260.

[24] E. von Glaise-Horstenau, *Franz Josephs Weggefährte* (Vienna, 1930), pp. 182–83.

[25] OSVOb., *1*, 27–30, Ionin to Jomini, June 25/July 7; *ibid.*, p. 66, Aug. 12/24; Koetschet, *Bosniens*, p. 14.

Montenegro adopted initially a surprisingly passive policy toward the insurrection. The chiefs of Hercegovina were ordered "to abstain from the rising since the time for that has not yet come." [26] The Montenegrin government decided to guard the frontier to prevent volunteers from slipping into Hercegovina. [27] Financially dependent upon Russia, the prince heeded its advice to remain neutral. Neither Russia nor Serbia, Nikola believed, was now likely to fight Turkey; a better opportunity should be awaited. [28] With Montenegro seeking pacification, the revolt, asserts Stillman, could have been stopped promptly had the Turks shown the slightest disposition toward conciliation. [29]

Nikola soon renounced his pacific policy in the face of manifold pressures. He was caught by his aspirations in Hercegovina, nationalist agitation, and the Powers' insistence upon Montenegrin neutrality. His subjects, and some of his advisers, urged him to make war or at least to permit volunteers to join the insurgents. And the impatient Serbs of the Vojvodina criticized his willingness to parley with the Turks. The prince's organ, *Glas Crnogorca*, responded, "There is no price nor offer of the Porte which can bind us to true neutrality. The very thought contradicts the past of Montenegro and the patriotism of Prince Nikola." [30]

As the insurrection spread and Turkish military operations increased, Nikola realized that unless he assisted it, the rising would be crushed by the Porte or pre-empted by Austria or Serbia. The fate of Montenegro and Hercegovina had become indissolubly linked. Especially disquieting for Nikola was the news that pro-Serbian Mićo Ljubibratić had become the principal leader of the Hercegovina insurrection. Entering the province from Serbia, Ljubibratić issued proclamations "To the Serbs of Turkey," and "To brother Serbs of the Moslem faith," urging co-operation in a national liberation movement. He sought to convene an assembly, choose a provisional government, organize a Hercegovinian army, and appeal to the Powers for aid. Prince Nikola, fearing extension of Serbia's influence and anxious to obtain complete control of the insurrection himself, opposed Ljubibratić's efforts. Ionin, the

---

[26] Nikola I's letter to Petar Vukotić cited in Vukčević, *Crna Gora*, p. 108.
[27] *Russkii Mir* (St. Petersburg), July 11/23, no. 96.
[28] Tunguz-Perović, "Uloga," p. 261.
[29] Stillman, *Herzegovina*, pp. 11–13.
[30] Nikola I, "Hercegovački ustanak," *Zapisi, 8*, knj. 13 (March 1935), p. 138.

Russian consul in Cetinje, reinforced Nikola's suspicions. The prince intrigued against Ljubibratić and sent an aide, Peko Pavlović, to undermine his position. Ljubibratić wrote to Nikola on July 29 explaining that his goal was a national insurrection, but his efforts to co-operate with the prince were rebuffed and he was forced to leave Hercegovina.[31] Through Petar Vukotić the prince's orders were conveyed to the Hercegovina chieftains. He had resolved "either to sustain the movement until the situation became clarified and avert surprise on the part of Austria, or . . . to strengthen or accelerate the movement and hold it firmly in his hands to guard it from foreign influence."[32]

Prince Nikola thus established his pre-eminence in Hercegovina, but his problems mounted. His tiny principality was being inundated with refugees. Reports reached him that volunteers from Austrian Dalmatia were joining the insurgents. Stillman accurately described Nikola's response:

The personal tendencies of the Prince, unlike his predecessors, were to attain his ends by patience and peaceful appliances it possible, but his people have a very different way . . . and the most that could be done was the least possible to the national feeling, but without losing sight of the national aspirations. . . . It would have been unsafe and futile for the Prince to have attempted to cut off all aid for the insurgents.[33]

Despite Nikola's caution and desire for peace, by early August it was doubtful whether he could preserve neutrality. And if Montenegro intervened, could Serbia lag far behind?

The Serbs of the Vojvodina strongly backed their brethren in Hercegovina. Committees formed in all the larger centers to collect contributions and volunteers. The entire region boiled with excitement.[34] In *Zastava*, Svetozar Miletić hailed the insurrection: "Twice it has come about that in the breasts of all Serbdom, and in our own, hope has been kindled by the heroism of the Hercegovinians . . . and by the enthusiasm with which the poeple of Serbia, this focus and mainstay of Serbdom, reacted to the insurrection."[35] Though worried by

---

[31] Ljubibratić and Kruševac, "Prilozi," pp. 301–09.

[32] Nikola I, "Hercegovački ustanak," *Zapisi*, 11 (Nov. 1932), 253, 263; Vukčević, *Crna Gora*, p. 108; Harris, *History*, pp. 125–26.

[33] Stillman, *Herzegovina*, pp. 22–23.

[34] J. Radulović, "Političke veze izmedju Hercegovine i Vojvodine u drugoj polovini prošlog vijeka," *Istoriski Zapisi*, 3, knj. 6 (Oct.–Dec. 1950), pp. 419–20.

[35] *Zastava* (Novi Sad), Aug. 4, 1875, cited by Radulović, *ibid.*, p. 419.

Serbia's conservatism and suspecting that Austria was planning to annex Bosnia and Hercegovina, Miletić was heartened by public sympathy for the insurgents in all Serbian lands. He urged the Powers not to
intervene. "It would be in the interest of both Russia and Austria to
adopt the position: 'The East belongs to the Christian peoples.'"
Miletić, though unsure that the insurrection would spread or the
Serbian states intervene,[36] nevertheless prepared his people for sacrifices
in the national cause:

> If ever a war breaks out for the liberation of the Serbian people in Turkey,
> the duty of Serbs on this side [of the Danube and the Sava rivers] will be to
> concentrate all their strength to assist this liberation and contribute at least a
> tenth of their property, or at least sacrifice their profits [prihod] on the
> altar of the Serbian state in the Balkan peninsula.[37]

Other Austrian Slavs also responded warmly. Committees to aid the
insurgents were established throughout Croatia and Slavonia, although
the authorities prohibited enrollment of volunteers. Obzor (Zagreb),
the principal Croatian newspaper, claimed Russia favored the insurrection and that it was "the duty of the knightly Prince Nikola to fulfill
his pledged word that there will not be peace until the last Serb is
liberated; the Obrenović dynasty has the duty to execute the mission
which it began heroically. . . . Let this autumn be the last before the
promise [of liberation] becomes a reality."[38] Warned Bishop Juraj
Štrosmajer, Croatian champion of the Yugoslav idea, "If Serbia and
Montenegro strike, it will not be possible to restrain the Croats either
from at least sending volunteers."[39] But the Austro-Hungarian authorities proved equal to the challenge. They curtailed discussion of the
revolt in the Croatian Sabor and issued orders preventing proinsurgent
demonstrations.[40] Croatian support for the rising was short lived, and
Vienna kept its Slav subjects under control.

Austro-Hungarian policy had been formulated at a crown council in
January. Andrassy, who had opposed adding South Slav territories to
the Monarchy for fear the Slav population would become excessive,
now acquiesced to a future annexation of Bosnia and Hercegovina,

---

[36] Zastava, July 25/Aug. 6, no. 86, "Varnica ili plamen?"
[37] Quoted in V. Stajić, Svetozar Miletić (Belgrade, n.d.), p. 143.
[38] Nikola I, Zapisi, 8, knj. 13 (Feb. 1935), pp. 79–80.
[39] Vukčević, Crna Gora, p. 155. See Harris, History, p. 67, for Croatian
reactions.
[40] Ekmečić, Ustanak, pp. 125–26.

provided disorder there created a suitable pretext and Europe was persuaded that the Monarchy was merely safeguarding its legitimate interests. Thus Andrassy had partially yielded to the military clique which had long urged annexation to protect Dalmatia. But Andrassy argued that parts of Bosnia and Hercegovina should be ceded to Serbia and Montenegro, if they won a war with the Porte, since "otherwise these lands could be compared with a volcano which would be as unpleasant and dangerous for us as they are now for Turkey." [41] Later, Andrassy would abandon these sensible reservations and surrender completely to the demands of the kaiser's generals.

The Austrian military clique regarded the Hercegovina revolt as a heaven-sent opportunity to intervene, but Andrassy, worried about European reaction to any sudden move, upheld official Austrian neutrality. Frontier authorities were instructed to admit individual refugees, but not armed bands, into the Monarchy, and Andrassy assured the Porte that Austria-Hungary would consider the insurrection a Turkish matter. [42] The Monarchy would only intervene militarily, declared the kaiser (July 30), if Turkey could not maintain control of the two provinces, "since it cannot be allowed that these provinces in question fall into other hands than ours." [43] Andrassy instructed Baron Rodich, governor of Dalmatia, that the insurgents should not be assisted; all Slav units in Austrian service were withdrawn from the frontier. [44] On August 12, the foreign minister defined Austrian objectives as: to maintain good relations with Turkey and with the Powers, who were against intervention; "prevent the Serbian states from controlling the insurgent areas; prevent any final solution of the Eastern Question; and retain the sympathies of the Christian inhabitants of the East and make it clear to them that they can expect a final settlement of their fate only from us." [45] It seemed doubtful that these objectives could be achieved.

The Russian government was taken wholly unawares by the insurrection. Chancellor Gorchakov was taking the baths in Switzerland. The tsar feared that the Serbian princes would be overthrown if they

[41] HHSA, Protocol of Jan. 29, 1875, appended to Vukčević, "O politici."
[42] Actenstücke, *1*, Herbert to Andrassy, July 3 and 10.
[43] Von Mollinary, *46 Jahre*, *2*, 288.
[44] Andrassy to Rodich, July 21 and Aug. 10, cited in Vukčević, *Crna Gora*, pp. 117, 123–24.
[45] "Politische Instruction für den Statthalter Baron von Rodich," cited by Ekmečić, *Ustanak*, p. 124, and Harris, *History*, p. 71.

prevented their aroused subjects from joining the insurgents, but he believed the Dreikaiserbund could restore peace.[46] He referred to the insurgents as "bandits" (*razboiniki*),[47] but he contributed to a private fund to aid the wounded and refugee families in Hercegovina.

Gorchakov had left Baron A. G. Jomini in charge of the Foreign Ministry.[48] He informed A. I. Nelidov, Ignat'ev's assistant in Constantinople, that the emperor desired peace and would deplore any crisis in the Balkans.[49] Peace could best be maintained if the Dreikaiserbund exerted diplomatic pressure upon both Turks and insurgents. The moderate leadership of Russia and Austria, Jomini felt, could discover "un juste milieu." [50] The baron proposed that the Dreikaiserbund establish a "centre d'entente" in Vienna. A peaceful settlement could be reached, he suggested, if the insurgents submitted to the Porte, the Serbian states remained neutral, and the Turks introduced reforms.[51]

The Russian ambassadors in Vienna and Constantinople, for different reasons, deplored the insurrection. Suspecting Serbian nationalists of instigating it, Novikov warned Belgrade not to support the rising. Until Russia can unite the Slavs as Bismarck had the Germans, declared this advocate of the *status quo*, an insurrection is premature. A South Slav federation born of a Christian revolution against Turkey, he feared, might be anti-Russian.[52] In Constantinople, Count Ignat'ev, always seeking the limelight, felt that the Powers should exert strong pressure upon Turks and Christians to end the bloodshed.[53] From Paris, a Russian diplomat cautioned Marinović, the leader of the Serbian Conservatives, "For a good solution of the Eastern Question it is

---

[46] HHSA, Langenau to Andrassy, July 23/Aug. 4, no. 39E.

[47] GIM, f. Cherniaeva, Avtobiografiia M. G. Cherniaeva, p. 8.

[48] Aleksandr Genrikhovich Jomini (1814–1888), senior counselor in the Foreign Ministry (1856–1888), was a typical product of the Diplomatic Chancellery. He was noted for his fine French style and for loquacity.

[49] Jomini declared that the emperor "est bien éloigné de vouloir provoquer une crise en Orient. Au contraire Sa Majesté dirige toute sa politique vers l'apaisement général."

[50] However, Jomini believed only a temporary solution was possible to maintain the Ottoman Empire, as the following declaration reveals: "Ce travail de Sisyphe, ces efforts continuels pour boucher des flessures d'un édifice vermoulu pour retarder ou amorter sa chute, ne constituent pas une tâche séduisante, mais elle est indispensable." Jomini to Nelidov, July 12/24, 1875, OSVOb., *1*, 34.

[51] Jomini to Le Flo, Aug. 2, cited by Tatishchev, *Aleksandr II, 2,* 293.

[52] M. Piročanac, *Beleške povodom jedne diplomatske istorije* (Belgrade, 1896), pp. 14–15.

[53] Ignat'ev, IV, *135* (1914), 447–50.

essential that all these little insurrections be pacified. Believe me that the time is not yet propitious and when one harvests the fruit before it matures, one runs the risk of getting none." [54] But time was short.

The Russian military attaché in Constantinople reported that the Turkish Empire was being seriously undermined. If the Turks, while they possessed the strength, sought to settle accounts with the Serbian states, a general explosion was likely.[55] Generally, official Russia reacted cautiously and negatively to the insurrection. No drastic program of action came from St. Petersburg.

Russian public opinion, later very significant in the crisis, responded sluggishly to initial reports from Hercegovina. The Slav committees remained dormant. Ivan Aksakov of the Moscow Committee at first considered the insurrection an Austrian plot to gain influence in the Balkans at Russia's expense.[56] The St. Petersburg Committee took no action until October.[57] Most Russian intellectual life centered in the two capitals, and since provincial newspapers were closely supervised by the authorities, the Moscow and St. Petersburg press enjoyed a virtual monopoly in forming public opinion. This was expressed mainly by Russian "society" (*obshchestvo*), a literate and favored minority of perhaps a half million persons. Hindered though they were by a capricious censorship, Russian daily newspapers were rapidly expanding their circulation and coverage of events.[58] The authorities allowed them considerable latitude in discussing Balkan questions.[59]

A sampling of press reaction reveals great diversity. The first Russian newspaper to report the revolt, moderate *Odesskii Vestnik*, compared

[54] ASAN, no. 8823, A. Vlangali to Marinović, Aug. 8, 1875 (from Paris).

[55] OSVOb., *1*, 44–47, A. S. Zelenoi to D. A. Miliutin, July 31/Aug. 12.

[56] I. Aksakov to E. A. Cherkasskaia, July 22–24, *Slavianskii Sbornik*, ed. I. Koz'menko (Moscow, 1948), p. 142.

[57] *Pervye 15 let sushchestvovaniia S.-Peterburgskago Slavianskago Blagotvoritel'-nago Obshchestva* (St. Petersburg, 1883), p. 331.

[58] From 1855 to 1875 occurred a fourfold increase in the number of Russian periodical publications; the number of individual copies sold also increased substantially. Semiofficial *Golos*, the newspaper with the greatest circulation during the 1870's, reached a peak of 22,632 copies daily in 1877. Among journals the most widespread was *Novoe Vremia* (liberal) which claimed 20,000 subscribers. The dull, official government newspaper, *Pravitel'stvennyi Vestnik*, had 11,181 subscribers in 1879. *Vestnik Evropy*, a solid liberal monthly, sold about 6,000 copies in the mid-1870's. Grüning, pp. 13, 19, 44; *Istoricheskie ocherki Rossii so vremeni Krymskoi voiny do zakliucheniia Berlinskogo dogovora, 1855–1878* (Leipzig, 1878–79), *2*, 143–74.

[59] Wesselitsky-Bojidarovitch, *Dix mois*, p. 38.

it with a thundercloud threatening universal destruction. Both the conservative *Moskovskie Vedomosti* and liberal *Russkie Vedomosti* promptly advocated autonomy for Bosnia and Hercegovina. *Birzhe-viye Vedomosti*, chief commercial organ, suggested that the two provinces be allowed to select their own provisional administration, then either remain with Turkey or join Serbia, Montenegro, or Austria-Hungary.[60] The official newspaper, *Pravitel'stvennyi Vestnik*, published brief, noncommittal accounts of the revolts.[61] Semiofficial *Golos* attempted to set the tone for the Russian press. Happy that Serbia and Montenegro were avoiding involvement, it predicted that if they remained neutral, the insurrection would die naturally. *Golos* was confident that Serbia could be restrained.[62]

Among Russian newspapers, *Russkii Mir*, a Pan-Slav organ, gave immediate sympathy to the South Slav cause. Serbia, it declared, was destined to become a Balkan Piedmont and unify the Turkish Slavs. It shared and perhaps reinforced the absurd overoptimism of the Serbian Liberals:

Turkish fortified camps offer no terrors for the Serbian heroes. . . . To breach this chain and, linking hands with their brethren in Hercegovina and Bosnia, smash the poorly disciplined Turkish horde . . . will not be very difficult for the considerable Serbian army, . . . armed with new rifles and artillery and in which every soldier thirsts to gain revenge for ancient wrongs.

Only British hostility and Austrian economic threats, concluded *Russkii Mir*, prevent Serbia from helping to free her brethren.[63] But even this Pan-Slav newspaper did not yet demand Russian intervention in Hercegovina.

Russian socialists sent the first volunteers but were split by the Hercegovina revolt.[64] After some hesitation, S. M. Stepniak-Kravchinskii, a leading Narodnik (agrarian socialist) went there as a volunteer. The insurgents, he wrote, are fighting for political independence

---

[60] Akademiia Nauk SSSR, Institut Slavianovedeniia, *Obshchestvenno-politicheskie i kul'turnye sviazi narodov SSSR i Iugoslavii*, ed. S. A. Nikitin and L. B. Valev (Moscow, 1957), pp. 7–8.

[61] See *Pravitel'stvennyi Vestnik* (St. Petersburg), July 9/21 and 11/23, nos. 151, 153.

[62] *Golos* (St. Petersburg), nos. 186, 188, 201, 204.

[63] *Russkii Mir*, July 15/27, no. 100.

[64] See J. Billington, *Mikhailovsky and Russian Populism* (Oxford, 1958), pp. 99–100.

which must precede social revolution. "As long as a people suffers under foreign rule and a foreign faith, the social question for it takes second place." In Hercegovina, Russian socialist volunteers could establish intimate ties with the Serbian revolutionary youth.[65] P. L. Lavrov's Narodnik faction disagreed sharply. To be sure, the insurrection had been caused by economic factors, but national, racial, and religious antagonisms now predominated. "A struggle for the independence of one or another national territory is a waste of strength for the exploited masses," warned *Vpered!* Exploiters, it declared, were leading this struggle. Characteristically underestimating the significance of Balkan nationalism, Lavrov declared, "For us there is only one holy war: the war of labor vs. capital." [66]

Initial South Slav reactions to the Hercegovina revolt were enthusiastic, suggesting that a movement for Yugoslav unity, against both Turkey and Austria, might develop. But the Serbian and Montenegrin governments, virtually compelled by public sentiment to permit unofficial aid, hesitated and remained neutral. Austria-Hungary struck a pose of benevolent neutrality. A confused Russian government and public spoke in many discordant voices.

Interregnum in Belgrade and Revolt in Bosnia

In mid-August, the Balkan crisis suddenly deepened. The Serbian government resigned, revolts broke out in Bosnia, and Montenegro decided to provide major support to the insurgents in Hercegovina. With Serbia and Montenegro apparently on the verge of war, the South Slav insurrections threatened to join in a single, cataclysmic Balkan revolution against Turkey. The Powers, especially Austria and Russia, were confronted with difficult decisions.

In Serbia, Stevanović and most of his ministers had adopted a bellicose policy, but this shift came too late to save the cabinet. On August 15, national elections were held in an atmosphere of crisis. Despite vigorous efforts by the authorities,[67] the Ristić-Grujić Liberals scored a decisive victory. All candidates for the Assembly who advocated a bellicose foreign policy triumphed. Prince Nicholas Wrede, the new

---

[65] OSVOb., *1*, 48–50.

[66] *Vpered!* (Geneva), August 15/27, "Istoricheskii fatalizm," OSVOb., *1*, 72–76.

[67] The Radical newspaper, *Oslobodjenje* (Kragujevac), reported the re-election of its deputies to the Skupština despite police interference and violent accusations by *Vidov Dan. Oslobodjenje*, Aug. 10/22, 1875.

Austrian consul, reported sadly, "The Omladina and its hangers-on fully control the country now and hold the Assembly entirely under their influence." Stevanović agreed to remain in office only until another cabinet could be formed.[68]

The election results clearly indicated a Ristić government, but Prince Milan, intensely disliking the Liberal leader, desperately sought another solution. During the second half of August, Serbian politics grew extremely fluid. Jovan Marinović refused to attempt a Conservative ministry despite Milan's entreaties and was unable to construct a coalition cabinet.[69] Other moderate politicians tried and failed. In deep perplexity the prince took to his bed with nervous prostration and spoke of abdication.[70]

From right to left the Serbian press urged warlike action. Abandoning its old passivity, *Vidov Dan* declared that Serbia should utilize the revolts in Bosnia and Hercegovina to fulfill her national mission. Serbs should bury political differences.[71] *Istok* reiterated that if the Serbian states went to war, Russia would not permit Austrian intervention. "Sardinia put Napoleon III to the test. Serbia must do likewise to Alexander II. . . . From Russia we expect no more than the observation of Austria. With Turkey we shall deal by ourselves." [72] Emerging briefly from the oblivion of suspension, leftist *Oslobodjenje*, although vaguer than its fellow newspapers, called the insurrections "A social struggle of a brother people against Turkish oppression. . . . Let the fighters for freedom be recruited from the Serbian people, let the revolution form its legion." [73] Across the Danube, *Zastava* hailed Stevanović's downfall and agreed Serbia should compel Alexander II to commit himself. On August 25, it thundered: "Forward Serbia! Russia will not wish to and Austria-Hungary will not dare to stand in your way." [74]

Serbian foreign policy remained uncertain, though Prince Milan yielded somewhat to the public clamor for war. Foreign Minister Milan Bogičević aptly described the basic dilemma to Russian Consul

[68] HHSA, Wrede to Andrassy, Aug. 19, no. 56; PRO, FO 78/2399, White to Derby, Aug. 17; Harris, *History*, pp. 107–08.
[69] HHSA, Wrede to Andrassy, Aug. 19, no. 57.
[70] *Ibid.*, Aug. 24, no. 62.
[71] *Ibid.*, Aug. 22, no. 61.
[72] *Istok*, Aug. 10/22, no. 73.
[73] *Oslobodjenje*, Aug. 10/22.
[74] *Zastava*, Aug. 10/22, 13/25, nos. 93, 95.

Kartsov: "Son Altesse apporte la paix et trouve ici la guerre." [75] A few hours in Belgrade convinced the prince how totally his engagements to the diplomats in Vienna conflicted with the aspirations of public opinion. His audience with Kartsov, on August 15 confirmed a dramatic change in his attitude. "You know," he announced to the startled envoy, "that I am preparing for war with Turkey." Either he would lead the war party or be forced to abdicate. He pretended to be patriotic:

In all sincerity I dare not condemn this enthusiasm, for if ever Serbia wishes to adopt the role of a Slav Piedmont, a role for which Providence seems to have designed her, she could not choose a more favorable moment. In letting it escape this time too, she would without question be judged unworthy of national existence by this same Europe which so unanimously today has urged upon this country a neutrality which would be political suicide for it.

A Bosnian revolt was imminent, added Milan, and would still further complicate his position. The prince asked Kartsov: would Russia, in case of a Serbo-Turkish war, permit the Dual Monarchy to occupy Serbia?[76]

While St. Petersburg pondered this query, Milan's prediction about Bosnia came true with startling swiftness. During the night of August 15–16 the oppressed Bosnian peasantry, led by nationalistic merchants and clergy, revolted in the Kozar region; other risings followed in the south. The movement spread with lightning speed. Bands of insurgents were soon operating over much of the Bosnian countryside.[77]

The Bosnian rebels were as closely associated with Serbia as the Hercegovinian insurgents were with Montenegro. Peasants, merchants, and Orthodox priests were virtually unanimous in desiring annexation

[75] HHSA, Wrede to Andrassy, Aug. 19, no. 57.

[76] OSVOb., *1*, 56–57, Kartsov to Jomini, Aug. 7/19.

[77] Evans, *Through Bosnia*, p. 260. The chief studies of the Bosnian insurrection are Čubrilović's *Bosanski ustanak* and the recent Marxist account, Ekmečić's *Ustanak u Bosni*. Christian dissatisfaction with an expensive Ottoman administration and inferior social and economic status was intense in 1875. Reforms sponsored by the authorities in Constantinople in the years after 1850 had destroyed the old feudal structure in Bosnia but had not consolidated a new, effective Turkish administration. Moslem landowners (*begs*) stubbornly resisted these efforts at reform (Čubrilović, pp. 3–7). Ekmečić, describing the revolt as a "class war of the peasantry . . . [to] divide up the beg lands," admits that the merchant class directed it because of its conflict with the Turks over trading rights and local self-government. Ekmečić, *Ustanak*, pp. 32–35.

to Serbia. In 1870, the regency had requested the Porte to entrust Bosnia to Serbian administration in exchange for increased tribute payments.[78] When this approach failed, Belgrade had revived its political activity in Bosnia, appealing to the entire populace on a national basis irrespective of creed or social status. In 1873, a Bosnian delegation was invited to Belgrade, as Ristić explained, in order "to get people used to our advice, and so as not to let them go to any other quarter." Serbian leaders feared already that if they failed to act, Vienna might become predominant in Bosnia.[79] Bosnian émigrés in Serbia, in close touch with the Serbian government, had helped prepare the insurrection. One of their spokesmen, Vaso Vidović, realizing the Bosnian Serbs could not defeat the Turks unaided, hoped to involve Serbia once the revolt had spread over the entire province.[80]

It soon became evident that nearly all the insurgent leaders in southern Bosnia would follow Belgrade's directions. And in the north the majority of chiefs proclaimed their loyalty to Serbia; Vaso Vidović, their principal leader, promptly journeyed again to Belgrade, where Milan received him warmly. "Just do not forget that you are Serbs, and I shall do what I can for you," declared the prince.[81] Bosnian leaders differed as to how annexation to Serbia should be carried out but agreed it should be done. From Belgrade's viewpoint the only disquieting factor was the appearance on the Austro-Bosnian frontier of Petar Karadjordjević, the Serbian pretender. "Mrkonjić," as he called himself, having considerable financial backing and military experience, expected some Bosnian chiefs to select him as their commander. In a September proclamation to the Serbian people, Karadjordjević declared that he would fight as an ordinary soldier to liberate Bosnia. Aware that he coveted the Serbian throne, Belgrade's agents helped induce the chiefs to disregard "Mrkonjić." [82] The Bosnian socialists Pelagić, Ugrinić, and Horvačanin obtained the allegiance of a few Bosnian chiefs, but they also advocated Bosnia's unification with Serbia.[83]

Until the Bosnian outbreak, Prince Nikola, although he could not

---

[78] Ristić, *Spolašnji odnošaji*, 3, 305–25.
[79] AII, Ristić 17/415, Ristić to (Dučić), Oct. 28, 1873.
[80] Čubrilović, *Bosanski ustanak*, pp. 61–67.
[81] *Ibid.*, p. 76.
[82] Ekmečić, *Ustanak*, pp. 119, 148–50.
[83] For their program, which emphasizes the necessity of eliminating Ottoman rule, see *Zastava*, Jan. 1/13, no. 1.

prevent individual Montenegrins from going to Hercegovina, maintained Montenegro's neutrality.[84] When the Bosnians rose, the excitement intensified, and Nikola's efforts to restrain it infuriated his subjects. Ionin reported, "Le Monténégro est effectivement en effervescence." Even the prince's palace guards were slipping across the frontier into Hercegovina. Nikola feared his army would melt away just when he needed it most.[85]

Under this intolerable pressure Prince Nikola decided to act. On August 20, he met on Mount Lovčen with the Hercegovina chieftains and promised them support. If their rising should fail, Montenegro would go to war with Turkey to free Hercegovina; he would not permit the insurrection to be crushed.[86] Nikola left Peko Pavlović and Petar Vukotić to lead the Montenegrin troops in Hercegovina and coordinate insurgent operations. The situation there changed fundamentally. Until the Lovčen meeting each chieftain had done as he pleased; now the insurgents became a united, organized force directed by Montenegrins and receiving weapons and instructions from Cetinje. Nikola I had taken full charge of the Hercegovina rising.[87] At Cetinje a committee was formed to aid refugees from Hercegovina, and Prince Nikola appealed to Austria and Russia to supply grain to feed them.[88]

Montenegro impatiently awaited formation of a new cabinet in Belgrade. Apparently seeking to overcome the coolness between the two principalities and encourage Serbia to go to war, *Glas Crnogorca* declared, "Our duty is to aid the Hercegovinians, not just sympathize with them. And our aid must not only be extensive but general. . . . Our national future demands that we now demonstrate we are all for one."[89]

---

[84] As late as August 10 the Turkish Grand Vizir praised Prince Nikola for his correct attitude toward the insurrection in Hercegovina and suggested that a *modus vivendi* had been worked out between the Porte and Montenegro. Čubrilović, *Bosanski ustanak*, p. 59.

[85] OSVOb., *1*, 64–67, 77–81, Ionin to Jomini, Aug. 12/24 and 19/31.

[86] Curiously, Nikola dated the Lovčen meeting incorrectly as July 26/Aug. 7. He says little in his memoirs about the Hercegovina insurrection until after the meeting. See Nikola I, *Zapisi*, 8, knj. 13 (April 1935), pp. 238–51; Čubrilović, *Bosanski ustanak*, p. 60; G. Vuković, *Hercegovački*, p. 45; Vukčević, *Crna Gora*, p. 131.

[87] Nikola I, "Crna Gora i Hercegovina," *Zapisi*, 7, sv. 1 (July 1930), pp. 101–02; Čubrilović, *Bosanski ustanak*, p. 60.

[88] Nikola I, "Hercegovački ustanak," *Zapisi* (April 1935), p. 252.

[89] *Ibid.*, p. 256.

As August ended, Prince Nikola warned the Dreikaiserbund's consuls that unless immediate steps were taken to halt the insurrections in Bosnia and Hercegovina, Montenegrin neutrality could probably not be preserved for long. Ionin was told by the president of the Montenegrin Senate that the Bosnian revolt and rising excitement among the Austrian Slavs and in Serbia, had transformed a local uprising into a national struggle. The Montenegrins could not permit Serbia to preempt their military role in Hercegovina. "If Serbia should declare war," Nikola announced, "or if its participation in the struggle in Bosnia should become predominant and resolute," Montenegro would have to enter the war. Neutrality under such circumstances would bring Montenegro's disintegration without contributing to pacification. Nikola believed that his position was more difficult than Milan's.[90]

Meanwhile, Alexander II and Baron Jomini had concluded that Prince Milan's query about Russia's attitude toward an Austrian occupation of Serbia was a *ballon d'essai* to test the solidarity of the Dreikaiserbund. They agreed that Milan could be restrained from war if he were compelled to take full responsibility for his actions.[91] The tsar warned a Serbian officer in St. Petersburg that Serbia must refrain from war. Russian leaders, convinced that Montenegro, and perhaps Greece, would follow Serbia and raise the Eastern Question in all its gravity, were determined to keep Belgrade neutral.[92]

Austria-Hungary clarified its position before Russia responded to Milan's *démarche*.[93] Andrassy opposed an Austrian occupation of Serbia since the Dual Monarchy would then be branded a Turkish gendarme. "Not just Serbia but also Montenegro, Hercegovina, and Bosnia would attribute the destruction of their hopes primarily to us," he wrote Emperor Franz Josef. Instead, Andrassy recommended awaiting the results of Russian pressure upon Serbia, joining a Russian *démarche* only upon request.[94] He evaded Novikov's suggestion that the members of the Dreikaiserbund present to Serbia identical notes against war.[95] Sharing Jomini's conviction that the Serbian query was a trial balloon, the Austrian foreign minister affirmed that "the revolutionary party" (*sic*) of Ristić-Grujić sought war in order to achieve power; Milan

[90] OSVOb., *1*, 80, Ionin to Jomini, Aug. 19/31.
[91] HHSA, Langenau to Andrassy, Aug. 16, telegram, and Aug. 19, no. 41B.
[92] *Ibid.*, Aug. 16, no. 40E, Aug. 19, no. 41C.
[93] For details see Harris, *History*, pp. 114–16.
[94] HHSA, Andrassy to Emperor Franz Josef, Aug. 17.
[95] *Ibid.* (Andrassy) to Hoffmann, Aug. 19, telegram.

favored peace and would be buttressed by a firm Russian reply.[96] Andrassy, while supporting a Russian *démarche*, ducked responsibility for restraining Serbia.

Meanwhile Alexander II moved to stop Serbia. On August 19, he instructed the Russian consul, Kartsov, to warn Prince Milan that if Serbia attacked the Porte, Russia would abandon it and its prince to their fate. Ignat'ev simultaneously urged moderation upon the Turks.[97] Precisely how Kartsov executed these instructions remains obscure. The Austrian Consul Wrede asserts that although Kartsov delivered St. Petersburg's warning, he advised Prince Milan privately that immediate war was Serbia's only recourse; evidence suggests that Ignat'ev pressured Kartsov to encourage the Serbs into war.[98] Ignat'ev denied this and claimed he tried to dissuade the principalities from action because he realized that they could not defeat the Porte.[99] Nevertheless, it appears probable that Ignat'ev encouraged Serbia and Montenegro at least to prepare for war.

Prince Milan's response to Austro-Russian pressure was most equivocal. When Wrede informed him on August 19 of Montenegro's reiteration of neutrality, the prince retorted that the Bosnian insurrection and the election of an Omladinist Assembly greatly complicated his situation. Refusing to commit Serbia to neutrality, Milan stated that his country's course had not yet been charted. He added, "It is a mistake to believe that the excitement in Serbia is only produced by a wish to aid our brethren in Hercegovina oppressed by the Moslems. If the Serbian nation is inciting an action policy, it *is on its own account*" ("si la nation serbe pousse à une politique d'action, *c'est pour son propre compte*.") Wrede concluded that personally the prince still opposed

---

[96] *Ibid.*, Andrassy to Langenau, Aug. 17, telegram.

[97] *Ibid.*, Langenau to Andrassy, Aug. 19, telegram no. 28.

[98] Wrede reported he had learned reliably that Kartsov's private advice to Prince Milan was diametrically opposed to his official statements. Ostensibly, the Russian consul had told Milan and his ministers that he regarded war as a necessity for Serbia and in his view the sooner it was started, the better. In a marginal comment on this letter, Andrassy agreed that this strange advice had resulted from Ignat'ev's pressure. *Ibid.*, Aug. 14/26, Privatschreiben. The British and Italian consuls in Belgrade shared Wrede's doubts about Kartsov. PRO, FO 78/2399, White to Derby, Aug. 22, no. 37. Indirect corroboration of Wrede's accusations against Ignat'ev is provided by the subsequent testimony of Serbian Colonel Catargi, aide to Prince Milan. M. Hasenkampf, *Moi dnevnik 1877–1878 gg.* (St. Petersburg, 1908), p. 470.

[99] IV, *135* (Feb. 1914), 445–46.

involvement in war, but the Serbian situation was "very serious" because of Milan's precarious position.[100]

The tsar's warning, though weakened by Kartsov's private statements, helped restrain the principalities from immediate action. Serbia's political turmoil, disunity, and military unpreparedness made war extremely risky in any event. And without Serbia, Prince Nikola would not fight. Serbia's internal disorder and rivalry with Montenegro were the primary explanations for their failure to fight Turkey in August 1875.

Russia and the First Ristić Cabinet

Serbia's paralyzing interregnum ended as fighting intensified between the Turks and insurgents in Bosnia and Hercegovina. On August 31, Prince Milan, bowing to the victorious Liberals, approved a cabinet headed by Stevča Mihajlović but dominated by Jovan Ristić, Jevrem Grujić, and Radivoj Milojković.[101] The formation of this "action ministry," backed by a solid majority in the new Assembly, caused *Istok* to rejoice. "Its members are heart and soul members of the national party. It is the surest guarantee of freedom and progress." [102] But the Rumanian consul, noting Milan's open hostility to the new government, reported that the desperate prince contemplated a *coup d'état* or immediate war.[103] Asserting that liberal legislation favored by the Assembly majority would produce anarchy, Milan referred to it as a collection of subversives. The prince remarked privately that he was merely awaiting a suitable opportunity to rid himself of both the new cabinet and the new Assembly.[104]

To bolster his position, Foreign Minister Jovan Ristić avoided rash acts and sought to win Austro-Russian support for the government.[105]

---

[100] HHSA, Wrede to Andrassy, Aug. 19, no. 57.

[101] *Ibid.*, Aug 30, no. 66. The members of the "action cabinet" were: Stevča Mihajlović, premier and minister of public works; Jovan Ristić, foreign minister; Jevrem Grujić, interior minister; Radivoj Milojković, minister of justice; Kosta Jovanović, minister of finance; Tihomir Nikolić, war minister; Alimpije Vasiljević, minister of education and religious affairs. Grujić, *3*, 108.

[102] *Istok*, Aug. 20/Sept. 1, no. 78.

[103] *Aus dem Leben König Karls von Rumänien: Aufzeichnungen eines Augenzeugen* (Stuttgart, 1897–1900), *2*, 458, D. Sturdza, Rumanian envoy in Belgrade, to Prince Charles, Aug. 20/Sept. 1.

[104] HHSA, Wrede to Andrassy, Sept. 2, 8, nos. 70, 72.

[105] His confidant, Matija Ban, chief of the Serbian Press Bureau, had submitted a comprehensive plan for Serbia's leadership of a war of national liberation, asserting that the Bosnian revolt presented Ristić with a wonderful opportunity to

Denying he had instigated earlier Omladinist agitation in Croatia, he pledged friendship with the Dual Monarchy. His government, promised Ristić, would do its utmost to calm public excitement and prevent warlike outbursts in the Assembly. The Austrian consul, impressed by Ristić's overtures, reported that he was probably the only Serbian leader able to halt the country's drift toward war. But Andrassy did not hasten to embrace the Liberal leaders, and St. Petersburg was unfriendly.[106] Unsupported by Milan and the Dreikaiserbund, the Ristić cabinet had to rely upon the Assembly and the excited public opinion it represented.

The vital issue of war or peace remained to be decided. The new Assembly convened September 1 at the provincial city of Kragujevac. At first Milan peevishly refused to open it formally.[107] On September 10, he finally shouldered his responsibility and delivered a "throne speech" to the delegates. Seeking to satisfy everyone, Milan referred sympathetically but cautiously to the revolts in Bosnia and Hercegovina, protested his loyalty to the Sultan, and expressed support for the Powers' efforts at pacification.[108] Milan's moderation pleased the Powers, but his failure to recommend definite policies left matters to the Assembly and the "action ministry."

The Assembly selected a large committee to draft a reply to Milan's speech. After bitter debate, it voted twenty-one to twelve to aid the insurrections regardless of consequences. The committee's majority report to the Assembly emphasized that failure to assist its brethren would condemn Serbia to its present narrow boundaries and cause the permanent loss of Bosnia. Eventually, Serbia itself would succumb to a powerful neighbor (clearly Austria-Hungary). The minority, agreeing that the Serbian people favored aiding the insurgents, recommended merely that Serbia's frontiers be guarded and the Powers' demands for neutrality be obeyed.[109]

"clear the air inside Serbia" and extend its frontiers to the south, west, and southeast. AII, Ban 17/43, "Moj predlog Ristićcu," Aug. 12/24. *Ibid.*, Aug. 26, 27, Sept. 3, nos. 64, 65, 71.

[106] *Ibid.*, Mayr to Andrassy, Aug. 29/Sept. 10, no. 47A.

[107] The prince explained to Wrede that he did not wish to go there to discuss the war question. Already he was deeply at odds with his ministry: "Je m'en lave entièrement les mains et je les laisse faire jusqu'au jour où ils auront une minorité d'une voix dans l'assemblée. Je leur demanderai alors leur démission." *Ibid.*, Wrede to Andrassy, Sept. 2, no. 70; Harris, *History*, p. 110.

[108] See Ristić, *1*, 45–48; Harris, *History*, p. 110.

[109] AII, Ristić 27/172, Ristić to Milan, Sept. 3/15. The committee's minority was

Ristić addressed the Assembly on September 16. Never one to take hasty action, he adopted a neutral stand on the war issue which threatened to split his cabinet. Ristić had learned that Colonel A. Orešković, responsible for preparing war plans, believed that the Serbian army could not be ready for action before December. Orešković advised postponing war with the Porte until spring but supporting the insurgents through the winter.[110] Sobered by this report and the responsibilities of government, Ristić stated privately, "As a Serb I favor war; as a minister I am opposed to it." [111] Surveying Serbia's diplomatic position, he told the delegates that the Powers had strongly urged neutrality. Serbia could not afford to flout their wishes since only Montenegro could be counted on to fight. On the other hand, declared Ristić replying to a question, an Austrian move to crush the insurrections or occupy Serbia was unlikely because Vienna would require German and Russian consent. Russia, which had played such a significant role in Serbia's rebirth, would scarcely permit Austria to invade it. At a secret session, Ristić recommended assistance to the insurgents, since abandoning them would compromise Serbia's future, but he left the decision on war or peace up to the Assembly.[112]

On September 18, the draft reply to Prince Milan, reflecting the views of the committee's moderate majority, was presented to the entire Assembly. A united Conservative-Radical opposition, composed partly of the prince's own delegates, demanded whether aid to the insurgents would involve Serbia in war. The ministers reasserted evasively, "Our duty is to help our brethren wherever this may lead." [113] The Assembly voted seventy-seven to thirty to aid the "insurgent breth-

divided between wealthy urban representatives, such as Simo Nestorović, who opposed aid unconditionally, arguing it would lead to a war without allies and to Serbia's destruction, and others, including radical deputies, who favored assistance to the insurgents if the Skupština rather than the government were entrusted with it in order to prevent officials and rich merchants from profiting from the war. Grujić, *3*, 109–14; Vlada Milana, *1*, 251–52.

[110] AII, Ristić 26/699, Ban to (Ristić), Sept. 1/13.

[111] *Gertsegovinskoe vosstanie i vostochnyi vopros* (St. Petersburg, 1876), pp. 43–46.

[112] Grujić, *3*, 121–22; Ristić, *1*, 51–53. Ranko Alimpić received select instructions from the government early in September to take charge of volunteer bands in the Užiće and Šabac areas of Serbia and send them into Bosnia. Alimpić, *Život*, pp. 504–06.

[113] Pera Todorović, *Odlomci iz dnevnika jednog dobrovoljca* (Belgrade, 1938), p. 136; OSVOb., *1*, 97–98, Kartsov to Jomini, Sept. 10/22.

ren."[114] Its public response to the throne speech was only a paraphrase of the original, but secret additions, adopted upon the insistence of the ministers by a vote of sixty-seven to thirty-nine, authorized the government to borrow 3,000,000 ducats[115] for "aid to the insurrection to liberate our brethren in Turkey" and Serbian rearmament.[116] The Assembly, contrary to Prince Milan's expectations, had supported the "action cabinet."

A crisis promptly developed between Milan and his government. The Assembly delegation bearing the reply to the throne speech was rudely received by the prince. Milan declared: "I do not approve of the work of the Ristić government. It wishes to drag the country into war and I will not allow that unless absolutely necessary because I do not want to put at stake this bit of bloodily acquired land and throne which I inherited from my glorious ancestors." Surely Ristić must realize, added Milan, the power of Turkey and the weakness and unpreparedness of Serbia.[117] But Ristić, backed by his ministers, urged the prince to approve the Assembly's decisions and emphasized how moderate they were.[118] On September 24, Milan claimed that the establishment of a permanent committee by the Assembly was unconstitutional; Ristić must come to Belgrade to discuss the legislature's recent decisions.[119] With the blessing of the Council of Ministers, Ristić proceeded to the capital either to obtain Milan's signature to the Assembly's measures or if the prince refused, to submit the cabinet's resignation.[120] On September 27, after two lengthy conferences with Milan, Ristić telegraphed his colleagues that the differences between the Prince and the cabinet remained profound.[121] An impasse resulted within the Serbian government which only external factors could resolve.

The continuing war fever in Serbia, fostered by *Istok* and *Zastava*, appeared to favor the "action ministry." But *Istok* grew impatient as

---

[114] Grujić, *3*, 126. Harris (*History*, p. 111) suggests incorrectly that the Assembly majority voted for a declaration of war and wrongly dates the plenary session as September 20.

[115] This is equivalent to 36,000,000 dinars.

[116] Grujić, *3*, 125, 130.

[117] Kaljević, *Moje uspomene*, p. 8.

[118] AII, Ristić 27/190, 191, Ristić to Milan, Sept. 10/22 and 11/23.

[119] *Ibid.*, 27/193, Milan to (Mihajlović), Sept. 12/24.

[120] Grujić, *3*, 149.

[121] AII, 27/196, Ristić to (Mihajlović) Sept. 15/27.

the Ristić government hesitated on the brink of war. Appealing to the cabinet on September 10 not to bow to diplomatic pressure, it claimed that Serbia had almost 200,000 men under arms and was fully prepared for war. "Now there is no longer any excuse" for inaction. The Powers will merely talk.[122] Montenegro would surely join the struggle to liberate and unify the Serbs as soon as Serbia declared war. *Istok* rejoiced at the tone of the Assembly's reply to Milan and the angry reaction of the Hungarian press. In its desperate impatience *Istok* asserted on September 30 that Russia was abandoning Austria and supporting the insurgents.[123]

Zastava, unrestricted by Serbian censorship, castigated Belgrade for its indecision. Miletić, though unenthusiastic about the liberalism of the Ristić cabinet, urged Serbia to declare war immediately. All conditions favor a national Serbian war, he asserted; the Dreikaiserbund has lost its significance. *Zastava*'s article (September 17) entitled: "Serbia must go forward, cowards to the rear," noting an alliance offer from Montenegro and an alleged free hand from Europe, criticized Belgrade's delay.[124] By early October *Zastava* blamed Milan personally for Serbia's failure to move. Montenegro, the Ristić ministry, and the Assembly favor war, claimed Miletić, only Milan does not. "He [Milan] wants to halt the course of the history of the liberation of the Balkan Serbs." If Milan acts as Andrassy's viceroy, concluded *Zastava*, let Montenegro lead the way.[125]

And Montenegro? In Cetinje, news of the "action ministry's" accession was well received, although Ristić personally was regarded as an opponent by Montenegrin leaders.[126] Ristić planned to send an envoy to negotiate political and military agreements with Montenegro, but apparently Milan vetoed that idea. Nikola declared that in case of war, Montenegro would stand by Serbia. "Our ruler's view," telegraphed Cetinje, "is that in no case should the opportunity to fight Turkey be let slip." [127] The Montenegrins, according to Nikola, had resolved upon war and only required a similar decision from Serbia; [128] *Glas Crno-*

---

[122] *Istok*, Aug. 29/Sept. 10, no. 81.

[123] *Ibid.*, Sept. 7/19, no. 85; Sept. 11/23, no. 86; Sept. 14/26, no. 87; Sept. 16/28, no. 88; Sept. 18/30, no. 89.

[124] *Zastava*, Aug. 27/Sept. 8, no. 103; Aug. 31/Sept. 12, no. 105; Sept. 5/17, no. 108.

[125] *Ibid.*, Sept. 24/Oct. 6, no. 119.

[126] Vukčević, *Crna Gora*, p. 146.

[127] OSVOb., *1*, 91–92, Ionin to Gorchakov, Aug. 31/Sept. 12; Vukčević, *Crna Gora*, p. 146.

[128] Nikola I, *Zapisi*, *11*, sv. 6 (Dec. 1932), 308.

gorca stated that the only way to liberate Serbian lands in Turkey was by immediate action.[129] But Montenegro still would not take the initiative; that would be left to Serbia. Nikola was bellicose for domestic purposes, reasonable in his conversations with European correspondents.[130]

During September, the South Slavs' military situation deteriorated. Neither in Hercegovina nor in Bosnia did the insurgents gain. The Turks seized a boatload of arms and ammunition sent from Belgrade to northern Bosnia, crushed the main body of insurgents there and killed Petar Pečija, their ablest leader. The north Bosnian insurgents, seriously weakened by this disaster (September 10), could operate henceforth only in small bands, shielded by the mountains.[131] Large concentrations of Turkish troops near Niš worried the Serbs. War with Turkey would clearly be no picnic.[132] By late September it was evident to Belgrade and Cetinje that the anticipated general South Slav insurrection had not materialized.

Austro-Russian distaste for the Liberals weakened the "action cabinet" and encouraged Prince Milan to unseat it. Official Russian spokesmen were virtually unanimous in their disapproval. Alexander II had disliked Ristić since their meeting in St. Petersburg years before.[133] He and Gorchakov regarded Grujić and Ristić as dangerous radicals and warmongers. Alexander II declared that he would not deal with this "revolutionary party." [134] Baron Jomini noted that Serbia, unlike Montenegro, possessed every prerequisite for prosperity; it need only abandon plans of aggrandizement and develop its resources. Austria-Hungary naturally could not tolerate a turbulent, expanding Serbia under "radical" control. Serbia could not claim to be an "eastern Piedmont," Jomini told Mayr, the Austrian chargé d'affaires in St. Petersburg, until it had a stable government.[135] While the "action cabinet" retained power, St. Petersburg feared a revolutionary war in the Balkans.

Russia's leading Balkan diplomats, temporarily at least, were working

---

[129] *Istok*, Sept. 23/Oct. 5, no. 91, "Pregled novina."

[130] See Harris, *History*, pp. 129–30, for an appraisal of Nikola's policy by a correspondent for the London *Times*.

[131] Čubrilović, *Bosanski ustanak*, pp. 77–82; Harris, *History*, p. 108.

[132] HHSA, Wrede to Andrassy, Sept. 2, no. 70.

[133] *Ibid.*, Mayr to Andrassy, Aug. 10/22, no. 42.

[134] *Ibid.*, Sept. 10, no. 47B. The tsar told Jomini, referring to Serbia: ". . . quelles que soient ses sympathies pour les Slaves, il ne voulait avoir rien de commun avec le parti révolutionnaire qui y tient le pouvoir entre ses mains."

[135] *Ibid.*, Sept. 5, no. 46; Sept. 10, no. 47D.

for peace. During September, Ignat'ev advised both Serbs and Turks to be peaceful.[136] Ignat'ev, convinced that his Foreign Ministry would repudiate any forward policy in the Balkans, refused to take independent action in behalf of the Christians.[137] And Alexander II, as the ambassador had surmised, strongly supported the Austrophile orientation of Gorchakov and Novikov.[138] Kartsov likewise adopted a pacific approach, exhorting the Serbs to remain neutral and emphasizing Austro-Russian harmony.[139]

The Russian press and public, unlike the government, displayed strong sympathy for the South Slav struggle. General M. G. Cherniaev, the Pan-Slav editor of *Russkii Mir*, predicted in August that the insurgents, assisted by Serbia and Montenegro, could liberate the Balkan Christians and that the Powers' efforts to preserve the *status quo* were doomed.[140] *Russkii Mir* commiserated with the Serbian states, forced to stand by while the fate of Serbdom was being decided. Since Serbia lacked leadership, the newspaper for a time expected Montenegro to lead the Balkan liberation movement.[141] *Russkii Mir*, violently Austrophobe, ardently backed Ristić and called Serbian Omladinists "fiery patriots" comparable to the Italian Carbonari.

For us [Russia] successes by Serbia and Montenegro and their expansion would be desirable because they would shield us from Austria which by entering Bosnia and Hercegovina would place itself in the very center of the Eastern Question. If the principalities are defeated, a united Europe, if it wishes, could always stop Turkish advances and save them from ruin.[142]

The newspaper predicted that conflict between the Slav states and Turkey was inevitable, despite the Powers' diplomatic efforts.[143]

[136] *Ibid.*, Sept. 10, Privatschreiben, and no. 47A.

[137] A. Nelidov, "Souvenirs d'avant et d'après la guerre de 1877–78," *Revue des deux mondes* (May 1915), pp. 305–06.

[138] Kartsov, RS, *133* (1908), p. 348. The emperor covered Novikov's Austrophile reports with flattering comments.

[139] HHSA, Mayr to Andrassy, Sept. 10, Privatschreiben; Wrede to Andrassy, Sept. 8, no. 73; OSVOb., *1*, 97–102, Kartsov to Jomini and Ignat'ev.

[140] *Russkii Mir*, Aug. 1/13, no. 117. For the career of Mikhail Grigorevich Cherniaev see D. MacKenzie, "Panslavism in Practice: Cherniaev in Serbia (1876)," *JMH, 36* (Sept. 1964), 279–83.

[141] *Russkii Mir*, Aug. 8/20 and 17/29, nos. 124, 133. When liberation had been completed, Bosnia, Hercegovina, and Bulgaria should become autonomous principalities or be annexed to Serbia and Montenegro. *Ibid.*, Aug. 19/31, no. 135.

[142] *Ibid.*, Aug. 29/Sept. 10, no. 145.

[143] *Ibid.*, Sept. 16/28, no. 163.

Some liberal organs also supported the Serbs. The respectable and influential *Vestnik Evropy* in its September issue stressed Serbia's readiness for war and urged Russia to grant her at least moral assistance. Russia, not the western powers, it asserted, helped create Serbia and should now protect it.[144]

But most leading Russian newspapers backed the official policy of a peaceful, European solution. M. N. Katkov's *Moskovskie Vedomosti* favored autonomy for Bosnia and Hercegovina. Meshcherskii's reactionary *Grazhdanin* expected the Powers to calm this "untimely excitation" of the Eastern Question.[145] Mildly liberal *Golos*, subsidized by the Foreign Ministry, echoed official concern by denouncing the appearance of "revolutionary" volunteers in the insurgents' ranks as a threat to the Balkan social order.[146] In early September, *Golos* declared that with Ristić in office, war between Serbia and Turkey was almost inevitable. But ten days later, claiming that Milan's throne speech revealed Serbia's helplessness, it predicted that the two Serbian states probably would not act.[147] *Golos* sought to explain:

Much to the peoples' amazement, despite the election of a warlike Assembly and ministry, the latter is indecisive and hesitant. Why such a rapid change in spirit? Clearly something unusual occurred; not only were the Serbs warned not to move, but it was possible to convince them even that war with Turkey would be harmful to them.[148]

On October 1, questioning the official nonintervention policy, *Golos* published a lead article sympathetic toward the South Slavs:

Nonintervention is a fine principle, but to let the Turks do as they wish in the Balkans would remove any reason to restrain Serbia and Montenegro. . . . Who, following the principle of nonintervention, can stop the natural expression of Slav indignation at Turkish barbarism, this sympathy for their brethren? . . . Why should not the Slav nations be allowed to free themselves from foreign rule as Germany and Italy did?[149]

---

[144] *Vestnik Evropy*, Sept. 1875, and *Russkie Vedomosti*, Sept. 7/19, cited by S. Nikitin, "Russkoe obshchestvo i voprosy balkanskoi politiki Rossii, 1853–1876" (unpublished doctoral dissertation, Moscow, 1946), pp. 911–12.

[145] P. Miroshnichenko, "Otnoshenie russkogo obshchestva k balkanskim sobytiam, 1875–1878 gg" (unpublished doctoral dissertation, Stalino, 1946), 2, 5–6.

[146] *Golos*, Sept. 12/24, no. 252.

[147] *Ibid.*, Aug. 28/Sept. 9, no. 237; Sept. 7/19, no. 247.

[148] *Ibid.*, Sept. 10/22, no. 250.

[149] *Ibid.*, Sept. 19/Oct. 1, no. 259.

Such statements in the semiofficial press encouraged the Serbian war faction to expect Russian assistance in a conflict with Turkey.

The Slav committees had become more active. The St. Petersburg Committee requested permission to collect contributions for Hercegovina throughout the empire. The tsar had consented (August 4), provided the money went exclusively to civilian victims.[150] From Moscow, Ivan Aksakov wrote enthusiastically to the Pan-Slav V. A. Cherkasskii:

We may be on the eve of great events. . . . I am sure Serbia and Montenegro will not stay neutral—the cup of patience is brim full so that the slightest drop will cause it to overflow. What then? Can Russia allow Austria to occupy Serbia with her armies? That would be the beginning of Russia's fall. So unless diplomacy can maintain the status quo, there will be thunder and lightning. Now it is very essential to excite public opinion here in Russia.[151]

The Pan-Slavs sought to aid the insurgents militarily. In September, General Cherniaev, conqueror of Tashkent, proposed recruitment of a volunteer detachment for Hercegovina. He obtained Aksakov's support but could not induce Moscow merchants to finance his scheme. Alarmed by Cherniaev's plans, which conflicted with Russian policy, the tsar forbade him to travel to Hercegovina and had the Third Section place him under surveillance.[152] Public sympathy, though diverging from official policy, was not yet intense enough to bring large-scale financial or military assistance to the South Slavs.

A showdown occurred between Prince Milan and the "action cabinet" against a background of insurgent setbacks, Austro-Russian disapproval of Ristić, and the war chants of the Serbian press. The dispatch of Serbian troops to the frontiers without Prince Milan's consent ignited the crisis. On September 29, Kartsov sent an alarming report to St. Petersburg:

Serbian militia mobilized and sent to frontier districts; regular army occupies some frontier positions. These orders were issued by the Assembly contrary to the prince's wishes.[153] The Turkish army is also moving for-

---

[150] OSVOb., *1*, 88, Mel'nikov to I. P. Kornilov, Aug. 25/Sept. 6; Nikitin, *Slavianskie komitety*, p. 271.

[151] Aksakov to Cherkasskii, Sept. 21/Oct. 3, *Slavianskii Sbornik*, p. 145.

[152] OSVOb., *1*, 182–83; Nikitin, *Slavianskie komitety*, pp. 273–75.

[153] According to Milan, the order was given by the war minister and he had learned of it through the newspapers. A certain Pavlović told Wrede that the troops had been sent in response to threatening moves by the Turks and violations of the Serbian frontier. HHSA, Wrede to Andrassy, Sept. 25 and 26, nos. 87, 88.

ward. Only energetic diplomatic action can save the situation and peace. Prince Milan, ready to do anything to this end, has asked Marinović to return to Belgrade . . . to save the country. The cabinet is imposing on the prince revolutionary and warlike measures which he has decided to reject at all costs considering them to be directed against his person.

Jomini, transmitting this telegram to the tsar, awaited authorization for immediate action.[154] Suggesting that Turkey might be permitted to occupy Serbia to eliminate "republican-socialist elements," Jomini hailed Austria's declaration that it would not enter that country without the Powers' prior approval.[155] Russia and Austria agreed that the Dreikaiserbund should restrain Serbia.

On October 6, the Dreikaiserbund announced, "Any passage of armed bands from Serbian territory into Ottoman territory would be considered [by the Powers] an act of aggression." Deploring the concentration of Serbian troops on the frontiers, it urged the militia be restored to a peacetime footing.[156] This *démarche* followed Ristić's fall, but Austrian and Russian pressure had stiffened Milan's resolve to oust Ristić and his cabinet. On October 1, several days before its resignation, Kartsov was told to inform Belgrade, "The Guarantor Powers of the Treaty of Paris [the Great Powers of Europe] will find it impossible to preserve the Principality from a Turkish occupation if the Serbian government resorts to aggressive acts against the Porte." The next day Andrassy instructed Wrede to join this Russian step.[157] Milan was in close touch with both consuls and undoubtedly knew of the Powers' impending formal action before he removed Ristić.

On October 4, the prince dramatically confronted his cabinet. That morning he had learned that the ministers were intriguing to turn the army against him. He decided to go personally to the Assembly, which had just reconvened in Belgrade.[158] To the amazement of Kaljević, the Assembly's president, Prince Milan, accompanied by a single adjutant and dressed in hunting costume, suddenly appeared at the door and demanded to be shown to the ministers' chamber. Ristić, seeing the prince, turned pale as death. Milan declared:

[154] *Ibid.*, Mayr to Andrassy, Sept. 17/29, telegram no. 34.
[155] PRO, FO 181/531, Doria to Derby, Sept. 28; HHSA, Mayr to Andrassy, Sept. 17/29, no. 49B.
[156] *Ibid.*, Wrede to Andrassy, Oct. 7, no. 96.
[157] *Ibid.*, Mayr to Andrassy, Oct. 1, telegram no. 35; Andrassy to Wrede, Oct. 3.
[158] *Ibid.*, Wrede to Andrassy, Oct. 5, no. 95. The Assembly had been transferred to Belgrade and this was one of its first sessions.

I have come to settle accounts with you and talk with the delegates. . . .
You are arousing the people against me. You are preparing street demonstrations to compel me to bow to your intentions. . . . If I permitted
people to act this way toward me, I would not deserve to remain on the
throne. Thus I am going into the Assembly to tell the people what you are
like and to discuss the question of war and peace.

A shocked Ristić wrote out the cabinet's resignation; Milan seized the
document and angrily stuffed it in his pocket. The prince explained to
a hushed Assembly that despite its sympathy for the insurgents, Serbia
could not fight because the Powers were opposed and the country was
unprepared. He advocated military preparation and neutrality, then
called upon the delegates for their views. A majority shouted, "We
want peace." [159]

Not yet satisfied, the prince summoned the Assembly delegates to his
palace. He told them that, contrary to Ristić's assurances, Serbo-Montenegrin relations were strained and that no uprisings had been prepared in Bulgaria and Old Serbia. [160] Milan questioned each deputy
about his views on war. A few voted definitely for war or peace, but
most responded, "For war, but only if possible, Sire, that is if we are
prepared, let us march, if not let us be silent." Afterward the Prince
told Kaljević, "See how smart and sly the peasant [delegate] is. He
brags in warlike fashion in the streets and cafés, praises the Novi
Sad [Zastava] articles which incite war, but when you push him in a
corner and ask him a clear question about it, he finds some formula
which won't give off an odor. This is their 'if possible, Sire.' " [161]

Thus Ristić's "action cabinet" fell, and the Assembly yielded to
Milan's arguments in favor of peace. The usually indecisive prince,
backed by Austro-Russian diplomacy, for once had acted resolutely.
However, the consuls' reports which had provoked the Dreikaiserbund's démarche, exaggerated the war danger. Neither Ristić nor the
Assembly majority had favored immediate conflict with Turkey. Milan
had merely utilized a pretext to rid himself of a cabinet which he
detested. But Ristić's fall did reduce Serbo-Turkish tension. Until
spring, Serbia's official neutrality seemed certain. Since Belgrade remained the key to the Eastern Crisis, the Serbs' struggle for liberation
had at least been postponed.

[159] Ibid.; Kaljević, Moje uspomene, pp. 9–11.
[160] Todorović, Odlomci, pp. 137–38.
[161] Kaljević, p. 13; Vlada Milana, 1, 258–59.

CHAPTER III

PRELUDE TO THE
SERBO-TURKISH WAR

THE fall of the Ristić cabinet in early October brought temporary *détente* to the Balkans. There could be no war of liberation while Serbdom remained politically divided and militarily unprepared. European diplomats could continue seeking a peaceful solution of the crisis. But *détente* did not signify abandonment of the struggle by the South Slavs; public pressure upon the Serbian states to intervene openly persisted. Although Russian official policy remained oriented toward Europe, in spite of strong Pan-Slavic protests, Serbia and Montenegro became increasingly committed to war as the winter passed.

Winter Détente

On October 9, the colorless Kaljević government assumed power in Serbia. After ousting Ristić, Prince Milan had urged the Assembly's president to become premier. Kaljević, protesting inexperience, nonetheless conferred with leaders of all political factions; most of them supported his candidacy. Backed by a majority of the Assembly, Kaljević formed a cabinet of second-rank Liberals.[1] The new government emphasized domestic reform, worrying conservatives. When Kaljević presented Milan with liberal legislation relating to the press

---

[1] Milan vetoed Kaljević's nomination of Vladimir Jovanović, the outstanding ideologist of the Liberal Party. For the cabinet's composition see Vlada Milana, *1*, 263.

and the police, the prince declared sadly, "I am signing the misfortune of this country." On second thought he added,

Who knows what is good? Perhaps the people will rejoice so at these reforms that they will forget the Hercegovina insurrection and free me from the heavy responsibility which confronts me of either entering a war unprepared and against the will of the great powers or opposing the belligerent current.[2]

Kaljević argued that his cabinet's pacific foreign policy was realistic. Greece and Rumania could not be counted upon to fight; Bosnia and Bulgaria were incapable of a general insurrection. At home, concluded Kaljević, aside from the intellectuals, there was little enthusiasm for war.[3] His cabinet readily agreed to Milan's request to comply with the Powers' "advice." Kaljević instructed Ranko Alimpić to prevent the departure of volunteers for Bosnia and to convert them into frontier guards during the winter. War Minister Nikolić merely told Alimpić that the Bosnian rising must be kept alive until spring. Serbian rearmament and secret aid to the insurgents continued. Belgrade could afford to do no less.[4]

Prince Milan's position between the Powers and Serbian interventionists was most insecure. Agitation increased in Serbia to replace him with Prince Nikola or Petar Karadjordjević.[5] Personal timidity and the perpetual threat to his dynasty kept Milan from espousing peace too ardently. Instead, the prince soon relapsed into his customary indolence and indecision.

Serbian politicians wrangled bitterly over the war question. Patriots such as Alimpić were dismayed at their narrow partisanship. Conservatives reiterated a selfish, hands-off policy: "The insurgents should not have risen against their rulers. . . . Serbia should not allow itself to become involved; we do not need the crags of Hercegovina nor the bare rocks of Bosnia, for which Serbia would impoverish and ruin itself. . . . Let us leave the insurgents to their fate whatever it may be." The Ristić Liberals responded, "Now or never has come the time to liberate our brethren." Kaljević and his followers steered between

[2] *Ibid.*, pp. 264–69; Kaljević, *Moje uspomene*, pp. 12–17.
[3] *Ibid.*, p. 19.
[4] Alimpić, *Život*, pp. 512–20; PRO, FO 260/1, White to Elliot, Oct. 11, no. 82.
[5] HHSA, Wrede to Andrassy, Oct. 10, 19, Nov. 11, nos. 101, 108, 111.

them. Unless Serbs rallied to the national cause, predicted Alimpić, the country would be defeated in a future war.[6]

Liberal and radical newspapers reinforced the war party. *Istok*, blaming "reaction" for Ristić's ouster, added that reaction "cannot make an Assembly majority into a minority." For *Istok* the vital question was whether the Assembly was warlike. It accused the new Conservative-Radical coalition of blind partisanship and "political immorality" in opposing war. Must Bosnia and Hercegovina emancipate themselves and cast eternal shame upon Serbia?[7] In *Zastava*, Miletić attacked Milan for undermining a warlike Assembly and cabinet and seeking to transform his country into a "Serbian Naples." "It would be shameful if a youngster [*dečak*] like Milan could divert the country from its holiest goal."[8] Prince Milan, declared Miletić, must either strike at Turkey, or at his own people: either war or civil war.[9] *Zastava* likewise denounced Kaljević's "two-faced liberalism" and predicted that Serbia's warlike enthusiasm would revive when fighting in Bosnia intensified.[10]

The Radicals' new organ, *Staro Oslobodjenje*, also summoned the Serbs to act. In October, it claimed that Ristić's cabinet had fallen because it was "incapable of either 'external action' or 'internal freedom.'" Kaljević's fears about Serbia's unpreparedness were groundless.[11] A Turkish violation of the Serbian frontier provoked the paper to proclaim that a national war of emancipation was beginning despite bureaucratic opposition. But success in the struggle could be achieved only if the Serbian parties co-operated and the princes renounced their selfish claims. "The form of the future Serbian state must be left to the entire Serbian people."[12] In February, *Staro Oslobodjenje* advocated a more ambitious program:

It is time for the organization of . . . a general Balkan movement against the Turkish state. . . . The best way is through the agreement and co-operation of all the peoples of Turkey in the Balkans. . . . Then there would be no need for them to beg the aid of Serbia, Montenegro, or some

[6] Alimpić, *Život*, pp. 521–24.
[7] *Istok*, Oct. 10/22, 12/24, 14/26, 17/29, nos. 98–101.
[8] *Zastava*, Oct. 21/Nov. 2, no. 134.
[9] *Ibid.*, Jan. 9/21 and Jan. 22/Feb. 3, 1876, nos. 5, 12.
[10] *Ibid.*, Oct. 21/Nov. 2, 1875, no. 134; Jan. 25/Feb. 6, 1876, no. 14; Feb. 8/20, no. 22, "Dopisi."
[11] *Staro Oslobodjenje* (Kragujevac), Oct. 24/Nov. 5, 1875, no. 30.
[12] *Ibid.*, Oct. 12/24, 17/29, nos. 25, 27.

other "Piedmont" against Turkey. Their strength alone would be sufficient to destroy the Turkish state. . . . The aid of neighboring states could be limited to giving arms, munitions, and sending skilled leaders among the insurgents. . . . It is not possible to achieve this now; thus it is the duty of the peoples of Serbia, Rumania, and Greece to agree to undertake a revolutionary role in Turkey. . . . An alliance of the peoples of Serbia, Rumania, Greece, and Montenegro before the struggle would be a guarantee that afterward would be formed a federation of the free peoples of the Balkan peninsula.[13]

This nebulous peoples' alliance, adopting Miletić's naïve doctrine of *fare da se*, explicitly rejected Obrenović leadership of the national liberation movement.

Belgrade's absorption with domestic matters allowed Montenegro to assume temporarily a position of national leadership. On October 17, Prince Milan, oblivious to events abroad, marched to the altar with Princess Natalia. The Montenegrins' dismay at Ristić's fall and Kaljević's pacifism was expressed by Cetinje's *Glas Crnogorca*: "Should we force others into war? To us this does not seem worthy of the Serbian name which is renowned for its martial qualities." [14] Not until late November did Milan respond, reluctantly at that, to pressure for action from Montenegro and the Serbian public. He sent Filip Hristić to Cetinje with a draft of a Serbo-Montenegrin alliance and a letter from the Foreign Ministry suggesting that the two countries "exchange ideas and information about the present general position of our people in order to reach a genuine and complete agreement . . . about conditions and methods which would most reliably guarantee the success of our great national mission." [15]

Perhaps the Hristić mission found Montenegro more responsive than Milan had hoped. It failed to bring about an immediate alliance but laid the groundwork for a subsequent one. No definite agreements were reached in Cetinje, though Hristić reported that Montenegro was willing to join a Serbian war against Turkey. Nikola recommended that the two states aid the insurgents, then make war in the spring unless the Porte allowed them to administer Bosnia and Hercegovina. After victory, declared Nikola, Montenegro would annex most of Hercegovina; Serbia could absorb the remainder, plus Bosnia and Old

[13] *Ibid.*, Feb. 6/18, 1876, no. 19.
[14] *Istok*, Oct. 10/22, no. 98, *Glas Crnogorca*.
[15] OSVOb., *1*, 154–56; Nikola I, *Zapisi*, 15, 171, 176; Vukčević, p. 189.

Serbia. The Montenegrin prince demanded prompt conclusion of political and military agreements and suggested an early meeting with Milan to arrange them.[16] But Prince Milan delayed a reply, then announced that Montenegro had blocked agreement. Actually, his pathological suspicion and timorous vacillation prevented an alliance in 1875. *Zastava* angrily accused Milan of cowardice and deceit. "Montenegro . . . is playing her role better than her sister, Serbia. Montenegro is the only Slav land which enjoys the general love and respect of all other Slavs." [17]

The insurgents, though sustained by the Serbian states, were adversely affected by the *détente*. In Bosnia, Vaso Vidović's efforts to construct a centralized national movement failed.[18] Lacking were able military leaders and sufficient ties between the chiefs and the peasantry. Belgrade's parsimony and inconsistency demoralized the rebels. An assembly at Jamnica resolved upon a major winter campaign against the Turks, but its decision would not be executed.[19] Mićo Ljubibratić, the ablest insurgent leader in Hercegovina, was arrested by the Austrians while traveling in January, leaving the movement there in Prince Nikola's hands.[20]

Turkish officials such as Dr. Koetschet and Reouf Pasha realized that the pacification of the two provinces depended upon Montenegro. In January 1876, Koetschet conferred with Nikola in Cetinje. The prince, claiming that he preferred concessions gained peacefully to entire provinces won in a dangerous war, agreed to support pacification provided Turkey recognized Montenegrin sovereignty, ceded him two seaports and the right bank of the Morača River, and compensated him for maintenance of refugees from Hercegovina.[21] Nikola told the Turkish official, "I shall try in the future too to remain neutral. If the Porte agrees to make me large territorial concessions, I can crush the Herce-

---

[16] For Hristić's report of Nov. 24/Dec. 6 see Vukčević, *Crna Gora*, pp. 190–92, and Čubrilović, *Bosanski ustanak*, pp. 196–97.

[17] *Zastava*, nos. 152, 168; Vukčević, *Crna Gora*, pp. 192–93.

[18] Vidović's program of Dec. 18/30 advocated creation of Bosnia-Hercegovina as an independent province which would subsequently join a Greater Serbia. *Zastava o Bosne i Hercegovine* (Sarajevo, 1956), *4*, 8–11.

[19] Ekmečić, *Ustanak*, pp. 165–66, 190.

[20] Nikola I, *Zapisi*, *8*, knj. 13 (Jan. 1935), 12–13. From Dubrovnik, Ljubibratić exhorted his countrymen to continue the struggle. When he attempted to proceed to Bosnia, he was arrested and interned by the Austrian authorities. Ljubibratić and Kruševac, "Prilozi," GIDBiH, *9* (1957), 267ff.

[21] Koetschet, *Bosniens*, pp. 22–36.

govina revolt in three days." [22] But the Porte was deaf to demands which Koetschet considered reasonable, and Nikola rejected the minor concessions it did offer. In mid-January, Nikola permitted his subjects to join the insurgents. The failure of Turko-Montenegrin negotiations undermined the *détente*.

In Serbia, too, it could scarcely outlast the winter. Prince Milan, the bulwark of peace, gradually shifted into the war party. Domestic and foreign pressures, and personal insecurity, caused him to renounce a peaceful course.[23] In November, Milan yielded to pressure and consented to rapid rearmament to enable Serbia to strike in the spring.[24] In December, Jovan Marinović, a leading opponent of war, withdrew temporarily from politics. He wrote Andrassy that in Serbia emotion had overcome logic; the public believed Russia would rescue the country from an unsuccessful struggle. Marinović predicted Serbia's defeat in a war with Turkey, but he noted that only strong European pressure could prevent a conflict. His withdrawal left Milan helpless before the Ristić Liberals.[25] In early January, the prince named a commission of staff officers to plan a spring campaign. He shook off his lethargy, participated in its discussions, and conferred frequently with his ministers. When Kartsov praised his new vigor, Milan responded:

What do you expect? In the advice you give me there is something for all tastes, and consequently we are preparing. In your eyes these preparations are simply measures of internal organization because you are sure we will not budge without the consent of Russia. But your colleagues will not judge it that way when they have discovered the secret and now I expect you will be the bearer of a new collective note seeking to calm my bellicose ardor.[26]

---

[22] V. Djordjević, *Crna Gora*, p. 375.

[23] Piročanac (*Beleške*, p. 34) ascribed Milan's shift primarily to Russian influence as did many foreign observers in Belgrade (see HHSA, Wrede to Andrassy, Nov. 23, 1875, no. 112). The British consul attributed it to pressure of nationalist opinion (*Istok*, *Zastava*, etc.) and unfavorable comparisons it made between Milan and Nikola. *Das Staatsarchiv, 30*, 205–06. Kaljević, ascribing Milan's shift to both of these factors, notes that the memorandum of Stojan Bošković, one of his ablest ministers, made a deep impression on the prince. It urged him to decide upon a prompt declaration of war in his and Serbia's interest.

[24] HHSA, Wrede to Andrassy, Nov. 23, no. 112.

[25] *Ibid.*, ad Dec. 19, no. 121, Marinović to Andrassy, Dec. 6.

[26] OSVOb., *1*, 165–66, Kartsov to Gorchakov, Dec. 27/Jan. 8. The reports of Kartsov to Gorchakov at this time (end of 1875) appear to show that he was confused and unclear about Russian policy. Thus he advised Milan to press forward with rearmament but pointed out the grave dangers of war for Serbia. Kartsov was not a decisive, aggressive individual and wished to avoid antagonizing

Wrede reported that if the insurrection revived in the spring, fear of losing his throne would induce Milan to act. In February, the prince told the Greek consul, "Ma décision est prise et la guerre est inévitable." [27]

Milan now stressed preparedness, but he retained the Kaljević cabinet in office.[28] The Council of Ministers approved increased military and financial aid to the insurgents and ratified Milan's decision to send Ranko Alimpić to conclude a military alliance with Montenegro.[29] When Wrede, reaffirming the Powers' wish that Serbia remain quiet, protested against Serbian rearmament, Milan retorted that Serbia must be ready for war, but it would fight only if the insurgents resumed operations, Montenegro went to war, and the Powers did not intervene.[30]

Serbian nationalists speculated anxiously about Russia's attitude. The Serbian correspondent of *Russkii Mir* declared, "We [Serbs] would like the Russian government to declare officially that it will not permit the annexation of Bosnia and Hercegovina to Austria since that would antagonize all the Slav and Orthodox peoples of Turkey." [31] In an impassioned Pan-Slav appeal for a crusade against Turkey, he predicted:

Speak but one word, Russia, and not only the entire Balkan peninsula, . . . but all the Slav peoples . . . will rise in arms against their oppressors. . . . In alliance with her 25,000,000 fellow Orthodox, Russia will strike fear into all of western Europe and no one can withstand such an alliance.[32]

Istok, wondering what the Powers would do, asserted that the Serbian states were preparing "to cut the Gordian knot of the Serbian future." It continued,

---

either the Europe-oriented Russian diplomats or Pan-Slav diplomats like Ignat'ev. Kartsov attempted to maximize his and Russia's influence in Serbia by cultivating close relations with Prince Milan, but he apparently had no policy of his own.

[27] HHSA, Wrede to Andrassy, Jan. 15 and Feb. 25, nos. 3, 19.

[28] Kaljević, *Moje uspomene*, pp. 20–21.

[29] Grujić, *3*, 151.

[30] Milan told Wrede, "Je ne suis nullement de ceux qui veulent la guerre *à tout prix*. . . . Je n'ai pas la présomption d'entreprendre à *moi seul* la lutte avec la Turquie. . . . Mais si l'insurrection en Herzégovine continue ou bien si elle éclate avec vigueur sur d'autres points, si le Monténégro entre ouvertement en lice et si j'ai enfin l'assurance que les Puissances n'interviendront pas *activement* pour nous en empêcher, je considerai le moment venu pour prendre de mon côté part à la lutte." HHSA, Wrede to Andrassy, Feb. 25, 1876, no. 19.

[31] *Russkii Mir*, Nov. 15/27, no. 223, report from Belgrade of Nov. 6/18.

[32] *Ibid.*, Jan. 1/13, 1876, no. 1, report from Belgrade of Dec. 21.

Last fall Russia tied the hands of Serbia and Montenegro. Will she do so in the spring? . . . If the Turks do not accept the [Andrassy] reforms, . . . we shall be on the verge of war under the protection of brother Russia. War by Serbia and Montenegro is inevitable. . . .[33]

Russia, Austria, and the Andrassy Plan

What were Russia's views at this time on the South Slav question? During October and November, Novikov, who supported the Andrassy Plan, and Ignat'ev contended for the emperor's support, and Russian consuls and Serbian officials reached varying conclusions about St. Petersburg's objectives. Official Russian policy was unclear until December, when Gorchakov accepted the Andrassy Plan.

Ambassador Ignat'ev wished to negotiate a solution in Constantinople in direct talks between the Dreikaiserbund's envoys and the Turks. He relied heavily upon his influence at the Porte and his domination of Count F. Zichy, the Austrian ambassador.[34] Ignat'ev sought to restore peace in the Balkans through a Russo-Turkish entente, camouflaged by the adherence of the Dreikaiserbund. To benefit the South Slavs, he recommended

the annexation of the southern part of Hercegovina . . . as far as Stolac and Nevesinje to Montenegro . . . and recognize over this new territory the suzerainty of the Sultan. . . . This would . . . allow Montenegro to extend its actual control and the power of Prince Nikola would soon be established in all of Hercegovina. . . . This would be the point of departure for the formation of an independent Serbian state whose core would be Montenegro. . . . The reforms conceived by Turkey would have to be introduced simultaneously into the rest of Hercegovina and Bosnia. Inasmuch as Serbian envy would not allow only Montenegro to gain advantages, Serbia must be granted [Mali] Zvornik.

Ignat'ev assured Gorchakov that the Porte and the insurgents would accept this, but if the winter passed without a settlement, the Serbian states and probably Rumania would make war.[35] This solution would establish Montenegro as the South Slav Piedmont and exacerbate its rivalry with Belgrade. Posing as a friend of the Serbs, Ignat'ev's main concern was to insure his future in Constantinople.

Count Andrassy, on the other hand, sought to keep the negotiations

[33] *Istok*, Jan. 18/30, no. 7.
[34] HHSA, Jomini to Ignat'ev, Sept. 1875; Ignat'ev, IV, *135* (Feb. 1914), 444–45; Nelidov, "Souvenirs" (May 1915), p. 308.
[35] Ignat'ev, IV, *135* (Feb. 1914), 827–32.

in Vienna and prevent Russian or South Slav domination of the insurgent provinces. He opposed Ignat'ev's suggestions and submitted his own plan to St. Petersburg. The Porte should be allowed to administer all of Bosnia and Hercegovina provided it granted religious equality, eliminated tithes, and the corvée and abolished tax farming. Andrassy quickly rejected Gorchakov's proposal of full autonomy for the two provinces. He elaborated his program in his November 16 dispatches to St. Petersburg. In contrast to Ignat'ev, Andrassy wished to preserve the *status quo* and prevent the emergence of a large South Slav state. Novikov, Russian ambassador in Vienna, accepted Andrassy's approach completely. A bitter opponent of Ignat'ev and Balkan nationalism, he also wanted negotiations held in Vienna and urged his government to adopt Andrassy's plan.[36]

In Gorchakov's absence, Alexander II conducted negotiations with Turkey and the Powers, avoiding full commitment to either Ignat'ev or Andrassy.[37] In late October, Ignat'ev went to Livadia to win the emperor's support. He warned that Andrassy's approach would destroy Russian influence at the Porte and lead eventually to a Russo-Turkish war. Although swayed by some of Ignat'ev's arguments, Alexander declared that a direct Russo-Turkish agreement was incompatible with the Dreikaiserbund. The count returned to Constantinople deeply disappointed. In a lengthy report to the emperor in November, he asserted that he had prevented an attack upon Serbia by Hussein Avni's "Young Turks." The Ottoman Empire, he reiterated, could best be preserved by a Russo-Turkish entente.[38]

Baron Jomini, acting chief of the Foreign Ministry, adhered like the emperor to a middle course. He refused to participate in the polemics between Ignat'ev and Novikov and withheld their most violent letters from his sovereign.[39] Jomini's moderate views were reflected by an important declaration (October 29) in the official newspaper, *Pravitel'stvennyi Vestnik*, reiterating Russia's adherence to the Dreikaiserbund but encouraging the South Slavs:

[36] HHSA, Andrassy to Mayr, Oct. 2, 10, Nov. 16; Mayr to Andrassy, Oct. 8 and 9/21, Privatschreiben. For details see Harris, *History*, pp. 140–45, 151–53.

[37] HHSA, Mayr to Andrassy, Oct. 8. To Jomini's dismay, the tsar issued instructions to Ignat'ev and Nelidov directly rather than entrusting their execution to him. Miliutin, *Dnevnik* (Moscow, 1947–50), *1*, 225.

[38] Ignat'ev, IV, *135* (Feb. 1914), 456–60; (March 1914), 805–07; HHSA, Langenau to Andrassy, Jan. 5, 1876; Harris, *History*, pp. 146–47.

[39] HHSA, Mayr to Andrassy, Oct. 5, 8, 9/21, Privatschreiben.

By participating in that alliance, Russia has not sacrificed the sympathies which it has continually had for the oppressed Christian population of Turkey. . . . The sacrifices which the Russian people has made in behalf of the Turkish Christians are so great that they give Russia the right to announce this sympathy to all Europe. . . . The Imperial Cabinet . . . cannot remain a passive and inactive observer of the events unfolding in Hercegovina which threaten to involve Serbia and Montenegro in an unequal struggle. . . . In any case, one can rest assured that the sad state of affairs which up to now has damaged the interests of the Porte, the Christians, and Europe will be brought to an end.[40]

But Andrassy's dispatches of November 16 convinced Jomini that Ignat'ev's plan would destroy the Dreikaiserbund; to preserve it, he favored adopting Andrassy's program.[41]

Returning to St. Petersburg on December 3, Chancellor Gorchakov supported the Austrian proposals. Though convinced by some of Ignat'ev's arguments, the chancellor demanded a European solution of the crisis and determination of Russian policy in St. Petersburg. "Gorchakov," commented Ignat'ev bitterly, "decisively rejected any idea of preferring a direct agreement with Turkey to follow blindly the fantasies and plans of Andrassy." [42] The Andrassy Plan, drafted with Novikov's assistance, was accepted by Alexander II on December 28.[43] St. Petersburg had bowed to Vienna; in the Foreign Ministry the Austrophiles had defeated the Pan-Slavs. Official Russia had opted for pacification after a hesitation which created doubts about its sincerity.

Gorchakov expressed confidence that the Andrassy Plan would pacify Hercegovina provided the Porte promptly executed the reforms it contained.[44] He admonished Veselicki-Bojidarović, Hercegovina's unofficial spokesman:

Return to them [insurgents] as soon as possible and explain to them the importance of the protection they can find in the benevolent support of the

[40] *Pravitel'stvennyi Vestnik* (St. Petersburg), Oct. 17/29; Tatishchev, *Aleksandr II, 2*, 296–97.

[41] HHSA, Langenau to Andrassy, Nov. 24, telegram 48; Harris, *History*, p. 154.

[42] Ignat'ev, IV, *135* (Feb. 1914), 463.

[43] HHSA, Varia Turquie I, 1875, Gorchakov to Novikov, Nov. 26/Dec. 8; Langenau to Andrassy, Dec. 28, telegram 60 and Dec. 19/31, no. 71A-B; Harris, *History*, p. 167.

[44] HHSA, Varia Turquie I, 1875, Langenau to Andrassy, Feb. 4/16, 1876, no. 9B; Nelidov, "Souvenirs," p. 309.

great powers and the danger of further stubbornness which might deprive them of such protection. . . . Try to get them to accept these Andrassy reforms and subordinate themselves to the will of Europe.[45]

Gorchakov assured Vienna that Ignat'ev now would follow instructions,[46] but he refused to consider what might happen should the insurgents refuse to lay down their arms.[47] Jomini had strong doubts about Andrassy's plan, and P. N. Stremoukhov, the retired Balkan expert, predicted that the peninsula would be aflame by spring since Serbia and Montenegro would not be restrained.[48]

Consul Kartsov's inability to obtain clear instructions revealed the Ministry's persistent doubts about the Andrassy Plan. Confused by the Ignat'ev-Novikov feud, he had gone to St. Petersburg in late November to discover official policy. Kartsov characterized Andrassy's scheme as an impotent palliative and warned, "The position of Prince Milan is becoming more difficult by the day. I fear that he will be unable to follow the advice of the Powers and will end by giving in to the [war] movement. Spring comes early in the Danubian area; events can flare up unexpectedly. What do you expect me to do? What is our program?" Gorchakov merely snapped his fingers, and Jomini told Kartsov confidentially on the stairs, "Que voulez-vous? Il n'a pas de programme." [49]

More puzzled than ever, the consul returned to Belgrade, where Milan and his ministers awaited him with extreme impatience. "The prince, especially," reported Kartsov, "hoped naïvely I would be the bearer of *un mot d'ordre* which he would merely have to obey in order to make a victorious exit from the crisis." Great was his dismay when instead Kartsov inquired how Serbia could achieve its vast ambitions. Milan showed him Hristić's report about a possible alliance with Montenegro. But Kartsov disapproved strongly of "this plan to inflame the insurrection which the great powers are seeking on the other hand to pacify, this ultimatum which the two principalities are preparing to present to Europe." Instead, Kartsov advised the prince to cultivate

[45] Akademiia Nauk. *Obshchestvenno-politicheskie i kul'turnye sviazi narodov SSSR i Iugoslavii*, ed. S. Nikitin (Moscow, 1957), p. 27.

[46] HHSA, Langenau to Andrassy, Jan. 7/19, 1876, no. 5.

[47] Jomini to Ignat'ev, IV, *136* (April 1914), 51.

[48] HHSA, Langenau to Andrassy, Dec. 19/31, Privatschreiben.

[49] Kartsov, RS, *133*, 348–49.

good relations with his neighbors and avoid aggressive action. In December, the consul sent to the Ministry a copy of Hristić's report and requested new instructions.[50]

To discover the Foreign Ministry's attitude toward Serbian rearmament, Kartsov then inquired of N. K. Giers,[51] "Does your ministry approve of the fact that while trying to convince the Serbs of our unity with Austria in seeking to achieve peace, you at the same time advise them to prepare themselves in case those aspirations prove fruitless?" Giers replied that the tsar had consented to secret Serbian rearmament. But in mid-February he declared in another letter, "Acceptance by the Porte of the Andrassy Note [February 13] and her expressed readiness to introduce the demanded reforms, forces us to put pressure now on the insurgents as well as on Serbia and Montenegro for the pacification of the area." Giers added that Serbian rearmament could continue but more cautiously than before. Kartsov was "completely baffled." [52] Was the Ministry suggesting the Andrassy Plan might fail and that Serbia must consequently rearm in secret?

Officially, Gorchakov strongly backed the Andrassy Plan. On February 15, disturbed that Alimpić was on his way to Cetinje to form a military alliance between Serbia and Montenegro,[53] he instructed his envoys Kartsov in Belgrade and Ionin in Cetinje to warn that the Serbian states would receive no Russian support should they endanger the peace. Since Kartsov had advised rearmament and the dispatch of Alimpić, Milan reacted to this message with confusion. Did Russia have one policy in Belgrade, another in Constantinople, a third in Vienna, and still another in St. Petersburg? On February 17, Andrassy sent a yet sterner warning, but Milan, awaiting word from Alimpić, refused to halt rearmament or pledge neutrality.[54] Justifying his policy, he told Kartsov:

Russia has always advised Serbia and Montenegro to maintain friendly relations with one another. The present moment is very favorable for the

[50] OSVOb., *1*, 163–64, Kartsov to Gorchakov, Dec. 24/Jan. 5, 1876.

[51] Nikolai Karlovich Giers (1820–95), assistant minister for foreign affairs (Dec. 1875–82); foreign minister (1882–95). He pursued in 1875–76 a cautious policy of balance between Pan-Slavs and Austrophiles in the Foreign Ministry.

[52] Kartsov, RS, *133*, 564–65, 570–71.

[53] See—pp. 79–81.

[54] Harris, *History*, pp. 381–82, citing M. Stojanović, "Serbia in International Politics from the Insurrection in Herzegovina (1875) to the Congress of Berlin (1878)" (unpublished Ph.D. dissertation, University of London, 1930), p. 87.

conclusion of a treaty of alliance. Also [Alimpić's] plan relates only to the possibility of war, and this certainly cannot change the benevolence of Russia since it is consistent with the general nature of her advice: prepare for all eventualities.[55]

Gorchakov's support of pacification had been weakened again by the absence of a clear, unified Russian policy, but, as we shall see, Russian pressure on Princc Nikola helped delay a Serbo-Montenegrin alliance.

Growing public sympathy in Russia produced sizable contributions to the South Slavs. By January 6, 1876, almost 360,000 rubles had been sent to Hercegovina by Slav committees, the Red Cross, newspapers, and other unofficial organizations. Almost two thirds of this sum came from the common people and a considerable portion from the provinces.[56] In the pro-Slav movement in the capitals students played a prominent rolc, and some intellectuals planncd to participate in the insurrection.[57]

Most active in gathering contributions were the Slav committees, though their members disagreed how the funds should be utilized. The committees arranged that appeals for aid from the Serbian and Montenegrin metropolitans be read in churchcs and published by the press.[58] Some members of the St. Petersburg Committee, such as the Kireev brothers, advocated direct financial and military aid for the insurgents. Chairman A. I. Vasil'chikov declarcd, "I have no intention of deciding the Eastern Question apart from the European Powers." His recommendation to limit assistance to noncombatants was approved by the committee, but its independent Commission for the Collection of Contributions solicited aid for the insurgents themselves.[59]

Slav committee representatives in the Balkans found their role misinterpreted. Prince P. A. Vasil'chikov, heading a Red Cross medical dctachment while doubling as a Committee envoy, discovered that people in Hercegovina and Montenegro believed that he had a political mission. He was accosted in the streets of Dubrovnik by individuals

[55] Kartsov, "Za kulisami," pp. 565–66.

[56] Aksakov, *Sochineniia, 1*, 228; *Bratskaia pomoshch postradavshim semeistvam Bosnii i Gertsegoviny* (St. Petersburg, 1876), pp. 486–92; Nikitin, *Slavianskie komitety*, pp. 276, 286.

[57] T. Snytko, "Iz istorii narodnogo dvizheniia v Rossii v podderzhku bor'by iuzhnykh slavian za svoiu nezavisimost' v 1875–1876 gg." in *Obshchestvennye . . . sviazi*, pp. 89–91; OSVOb., *1*, 190, Agent's report to III Section, March 12/24, 1876.

[58] *Bratskaia*, pp. 486–92.

[59] A. Golubev, *Kniaz A. I. Vasil'chikov* (St. Petersburg, 1882), pp. 112–13.

seeking rifles to fight the Turks. Vasil'chikov joined the Benevolent
Society of Cetinje, but he could not control its expenditures. "I am
definitely a member of an insurrectionary committee, which disturbs
me greatly since I consider it my duty to refrain from direct aid to the
insurrection and limit myself to direct benevolent work by aiding only
émigrés." [60]

Leading Serbian nationalists solicited aid from the Slav committees.[61]
Metropolitan Mihailo's vast influence among the Serbs made his letters
especially important. Mihailo, thanking Aksakov for supporting refugees from Bosnia and Hercegovina, contrasted Russian generosity with
European callousness. He added a Pan-Slav appeal: "Russia, which has
twice borne conflicts with Europe, must clash with it a third time. And
we hope, we pray to God, to aid her emerge victorious in this desperate struggle of the southern Slavs who see their salvation only in
Russia, and expect from her sincere brotherly aid." [62] Writing Nil
Popov (February 1876), he criticized European diplomacy and predicted war in the spring. "Please solve the Eastern Question as soon as
possible," begged Mihailo, "later it will be more difficult and dangerous
for us both." [63]

Russian public sympathy for the South Slavs confronted the tsar
with difficult problems. To forbid unofficial assistance and suppress the
committees would alienate the public; to encourage the insurgents
would antagonize the Powers. And the emperor, the heir, and Gorchakov all sympathized privately with the insurgents' cause.[64] When the St.
Petersburg Committee tried to involve the zemstvos in gathering contributions for the Slavs, the government forbade state employees to
participate. Raising money in private homes and in public prayer
services for this purpose was also forbidden. One Russian wrote indignantly, "There is no limit to the contempt with which Russians react
to the present policy of their monarch." [65] Though the government

[60] ROBibLen, Dnevnik P. A. Vasil'chikova, 3/5, pp. 166–67; Nikitin, *Slavianskie
komitety*, pp. 278–80. Stojanović asserts (*Great Powers*, p. 82) that the Moscow
Slav Committee "directed in fact the whole action in Hercegovina." There is no
evidence from Russian sources to confirm this.

[61] ROBibLen, f. Nil Popova, "Moskovskii Slavianskii Blagotvoritel'nii Komitet,
Opis' Bumagi, 1868–1877 gg."

[62] OSVOb., *1*, 146–47, Mihailo to Aksakov, Oct. 30/Nov. 11, 1875.

[63] ROBibLen, f. Popova, Mihailo to Nil Popov, Nov. 4/16, Jan. 23/Feb. 4 and
Jan. 28/Feb. 9, 1876.

[64] *Ibid.*, Dnevnik F. V. Chizhova, Jan. 15/27, 1876, p. 9 back.

[65] Snytko, "Istorii," p. 82; Nikitin, *Slavianskie komitety*, p. 276.

restricted pro-Slav agitation which it incorrectly associated with the revolutionary movement, the cumbrous wheels of bureaucracy moved slowly. In December, the Slav committees were put under the Ministry of Interior, but in January a member of the St. Petersburg Committee reported that Baron Jomini had said, "Faites tout pourvu que nous n'en sachions rien." [66] Apparently, aid to the insurgent Slavs would be tolerated if the government were not involved.

Veselicki-Bojidarović's visit to Russia (January 1876) revealed strong public support for the Slav cause. Captivated by an enthusiastic welcome in St. Petersburg, this champion of Hercegovina wrote smugly, "The whole Russian people saw in me the incarnation of its supreme will: to liberate the Slavs and the Orthodox." He expressed concern lest extreme Pan-Slav statements in the press hinder the achievement of an autonomous Hercegovina. In Moscow, he met leaders of the nobility and was flattered by Aksakov's enthusiastic words, "your initiative has clarified our views; your acts and words have put new life in our hearts." [67] The Slav committee gave him 90,000 rubles to buy arms for the insurgents, but even Aksakov could not induce the Moscow merchants to open their pocketbooks.[68]

The Russian press now expressed unanimous sympathy for the South Slavs but differed over Russian policy. Semiofficial *Golos*, sharing Gorchakov's pacific approach, relied more than other newspapers upon a diplomatic solution. Rejoicing at Ristić's fall, A. A. Kraevskii complimented Prince Milan for frustrating the warmongers and praised the Kaljević cabinet. Serbia should abandon temporarily its national dreams.

We are ready to recognize the full legitimacy of the aims of Serbian leaders as well as the sympathy in our society for these aims. But we deny categorically that the present is the time to realize such ideas. In our view neither internal conditions nor the material strength of Serbia itself nor the present political situation [in Europe] give the Serbs the least hope of constructing on the ruins of Turkey any large or unified Slav state.[69]

[66] ROBibLen, Dnevnik A. A. Kireeva, *6*, 114.

[67] Wesselitsky-Bojidarovitch, *Dix mois*, pp. 105, 114–17; Nikitin, *Slavianskie komitety*, pp. 283–84.

[68] Aksakov wrote to the Moscow Merchants' Society: "New dramatic expressions of sympathy are needed in behalf of the Hercegovinians not only because they are of solace to our unfortunate coreligionists who put all their hopes in Russia, but also because the Russian government itself needs these expressions of sympathy for the success of diplomacy." OSVOb., *1*, 181–82.

[69] *Golos* (St. Petersburg), Sept. 30/Oct. 12, 1875, no. 270.

Just before the government's October 29 declaration of support for the Dreikaiserbund and sympathy for the Turkish Christians, *Golos* greeted the Russian public's sympathy for the Slavs, predicting that it would aid the diplomats to achieve a peaceful solution.

We do not complain of this rise of feeling since it is necessary to stir our society into action. In any case, the strongest possible excitation of public feeling and thought in Russia on such a question as the Eastern is desirable and in favor of the insurgents' struggle, the only struggle outside our borders to which we cannot be inactive spectators as we must not lose our most reliable and close allies: the Slav peoples. . . . Who is interested in a diplomat's words unless the country stands behind him? Our diplomats need public evidence of warm sympathy for Hercegovina to carry through their negotiations.

Kraevskii believed that Russia must defend Slav interests, but had no duty to unify the Slav world as Piedmont had united Italy.[70]

The diplomats' prospects of success diminished, *Golos* admitted, as fall gave way to winter. In November, it predicted that the insurrection would survive until spring, and neither Russia nor their princes could prevent Serbia and Montenegro from fighting then. Since Russia could not be expected to restrain them by force, the Powers and the Porte must solve the crisis quickly. The Andrassy Note was "a significant step forward," but the diplomats underestimated popular excitement in the Balkans.[71]

Other newspapers suggested more drastic policies. *St. Petersburgskie Vedomosti* and *Russkie Vedomosti*, both liberal nationalist organs, concluded by December that force was required "to smash the charmed circle" of the Hercegovina impasse.[72] Left-liberal *Nedelia* proposed complete liberation of the Balkan Slavs. The legal left was less militant: *Delo* advocated their liberation but opposed a Russo-Turkish war; *Otechestvennye Zapiski* mildly suggested the neutralization of Bosnia and Hercegovina under Turkish suzerainty pending complete independence.[73]

Most vehement and closest to the Serbian Liberals was *Russkii Mir*.

[70] *Ibid.*, Oct. 15/27, no. 285.

[71] *Ibid.*, Nov. 12/24 and Dec. 6/18, nos. 313, 337; Jan. 6/18, 10/22, Jan. 28/Feb. 9, 1876, nos. 6, 10, 28.

[72] Nikitin, "Russkoe obshchestvo," p. 922.

[73] Miroshnichenko, "Otnoshenie russkogo obshchestva k balkanskim sobytiiam, 1875–1878 gg. (Stalino, 1946), 2, 30–31, 34.

To avoid suspension, Cherniaev moderated his editorials but still asserted that the Porte, not the Christians, had benefited from European diplomacy. Henceforth Russia should not follow behind Austria on Balkan questions; the insurrection must be allowed to spread. Since Vienna would not fight to save the Porte, Russia could foster South Slav emancipation.[74] Cherniaev urged Russia to adopt an energetic, nationalist Balkan policy. Throughout the *détente, Russkii Mir* printed bellicose reports of its Belgrade correspondent. In January, Cherniaev declared Russia should follow Prussia's example by liberating and unifying the South Slavs.[75] He predicted failure for the Andrassy Plan and sought to calm Belgrade's fears of a possible Austrian occupation of Serbia. Russia, he declared, would never permit that to occur.[76] The Serbian war party could rely upon *Russkii Mir*'s warm support.

Russian revolutionaries remained deeply divided. Tkachev's *Nabat* called the insurrection "a purely governmental, diplomatic question" without benefit to socialism.[77] But in a letter to Lavrov's *Vpered!* a leftist volunteer in Serbia asserted that this "is a war conducted by slaves . . . against their ancient oppressors." As a socioeconomic revolt against feudalism, and not primarily a religious or national conflict, it merited socialist support. *Vpered!*'s editors were unconvinced: "We cannot agree that *now* the struggle is being fought for social revolution. . . . We shall continue to pursue socialist agitation among the South Slavs so that the seeds already sown will grow under more favorable circumstances." The journal would support only those Slavs who fought against landowners and capitalists.[78] Lavrov and Tkachev grossly underestimated the strength of South Slav nationalism.

Despite a capricious censorship, the Russian press kept the public abreast of Balkan events. It reinforced Russian sympathies for their South Slav brethren and influenced the actions of Serbian and Russian leaders as the snows melted in the Balkans.

Rising Tension, March–April 1876

With the coming of spring, tension between the Serbian states and the Porte rose rapidly. The insurgents renewed their attacks while

---

[74] *Russkii Mir,* Sept. 24/Oct. 6 and Sept. 30/Oct. 12, 1875, nos. 171, 177.
[75] *Ibid.,* Nov. 5/17, Dec. 23/Jan. 4, 1876, nos. 213, 261.
[76] *Ibid.,* Jan. 10/22, Jan. 27/Feb. 8, Feb. 12/24, nos. 9, 26, 42.
[77] *Nabat,* no. 1, Dec. 1875, cited by Nikitin, "Russkoe obshchestvo," p. 949.
[78] *Vpered!,* Nov. 3/15, in OSVOb., *1,* 130–32.

Serbia sought alliances with Montenegro, Greece, and the Bulgarian exiles. However, the Dreikaiserbund's pressure induced Montenegro to consent to a final attempt at a compromise settlement between the insurgents, the Powers, and the Porte. The breakdown of the Sutorina negotiations in April and Cherniaev's arrival in Belgrade made war inevitable.

Political chaos and rising Moslem fanaticism in Constantinople also contributed to the coming of war. The arbitrariness, extravagance and incompetence of Sultan Abdul Aziz (1861–May 1876) finally caused his overthrow. On May 11, 1876 a progressive "Young Turk" faction, led by the energetic Midhat Pasha achieved power after a series of mass demonstrations, and on May 29 Abdul was deposed and replaced by Murad V. This well-intentioned but weak-minded ruler was immediately induced to announce a program of reform. On June 16 Hussein Avni, the strongest military leader, was killed by a fanatic and Midhat, intensely Russophobe, became preeminent in Constantinople. The turmoil in the Turkish capital and the massacres of Christians in Bulgaria helped doom attempts by the Powers to arrange a peaceful solution to the Balkan crisis.

In Serbia bellicose pressures within the Assembly and intelligentsia were increasing, and no major faction advocated a peaceful solution. Even the Conservatives' *Vidov Dan* yielded to the war mood:

There are questions on which we are all agreed: such a question is war with the Turks. Any government which wants to decide upon it in a sensible way can be sure of our support. But does the government believe the time has come for such a decision? Does it find present European conditions favorable? Does it consider our armed forces ready? We just do not know about this. . . . Uncertainty ruins our tradespeople and all of our economic life. To fulfill our patriotic duty we would be ready to sacrifice everything, but our task must be defined. The government should declare what it wants: war or peace.[79]

Liberal newspapers openly favored war. *Zastava* pleaded, "If Serbia does not utilize the present opportunity to achieve her mission in the Balkans, she will have lost her future forever." [80] *Istok*, rejecting Ignat'ev's stingy offer of Mali Zvornik, proclaimed that "only an aggrandized, powerful Serbia will possess the requirements for independent

---

[79] *Pravitel'stvennyi Vestnik*, April 1/13, 1876, no. 64, quoting *Allgemeine Zeitung* (Augsburg).

[80] *Zastava*, April 14/26, no. 57.

national life. What we want is the unification and liberation of the Serbian people in Turkey into a *single national* state." Serbia faced these alternatives: "War, with all its horrors but from which we can emerge with our national existence assured, or peace, a cowardly peace in which the body of our state will suffer from incurable ailments until a bigger crisis kills it. . . . The choice does not seem difficult to us." [81]

Alimpić's mission to Montenegro revealed Prince Milan's conversion to the war party. He departed on February 12 bearing letters and instructions from the prince.[82] Arriving in Cetinje February 23, Alimpić discovered hidden obstacles to a Serbo-Montenegrin military and political alliance. Prince Nikola told him next day:

> You see, the Montenegrin people are poor and if they spend much on preparations, it may not come to war. I had some offers from Turkey,[83] and others may be made. Before I decide on any step, I want to know definitely whether or not Serbia will fight in the spring. I now control the Hercegovina insurrection and could acquire there some benefits for Montenegro and thus would not wish to abandon that for something uncertain with Serbia.[84]

Russia's opposition helped block an alliance. Consul A. S. Ionin warned Prince Nikola that unless Montenegro followed its advice, Russian aid would be suspended. Ionin added, "I do not counsel you to crush the uprising, but refrain from participating in it while not losing your rights in the diplomatic field. Do not bind your hands at all, but simultaneously agree with Serbia in case of eventualities." The Russian consul also told Alimpić bluntly, "Russia does not want war, and you [Serbia] are incapable alone [of fighting] since you would succumb. Russia is far away; she cannot help you." Following Russian advice closely, Prince Nikola informed the Serbian envoy, "We are preparing for war, but I do not believe it will come to that. We cannot do so against Russia's will." [85] The prince equivocated and awaited further offers from the Turks.

Vienna now sought to convert Prince Nikola to the Andrassy Plan

---

[81] *Istok*, March 14/26, no. 30.

[82] Alimpić, *Život*, pp. 527–28; Grujić, *3*, 151. For texts of the letters of Milan to Nikola and Pavlović to Petrović of Jan. 30/Feb. 11 see "Prepiska izmedju Crne Gore i Srbije u godini 1876," *Zapisi*, *4* (April 1929), 240–41.

[83] In December 1875, Konstant Effendi had offered Montenegro the port of Spić (Spizza) and other minor advantages; in January, Dr. Koetschet came to Cetinje, suggesting the Porte was ready to negotiate.

[84] Alimpić, *Život*, p. 530.

[85] *Ibid.*, pp. 533–40.

and forestall his alliance with Serbia. On March 2, Andrassy sent Baron Rodich to Cetinje to disrupt the Alimpić mission. Rodich, seeking to insure Montenegro's neutrality, argued that if Cetinje intervened in the insurrection, Turkey would attack and the Powers would abandon Nikola to his fate. If the prince proved unco-operative, Austria would have to sever economic aid and hold up arms shipments. On the other hand, if Montenegro helped pacify Hercegovina and broke off negotiations with Serbia, the Powers would urge the Porte to offer the prince substantial territorial concessions. Clearly tempted by such prospect of bloodless aggrandizement, Nikola asked Alimpić, "Why can we not agree with Austria in our affair? Then we could perhaps achieve it peacefully." But the envoy replied that their common objective was the liberation of the Serbs and that the Austrians were merely seeking to divide and eventually swallow them.[86] Nikola decided to reject Andrassy's offer.

The prince's suspicion of Serbia irritated Alimpić profoundly. Nikola accused Belgrade of seeking control of the Hercegovina revolt and of leaking news of their negotiations to Andrassy. The Serbs, he asserted, had reneged on previous treaty commitments. Might not a Serbo-Montenegrin treaty be repudiated by a new Serbian cabinet? Declared Nikola, "It will be hard to reach agreement. You do not accept my demands and I cannot agree to yours. Finally, who can trust you Šumadijans that you will not bargain with the treaty and acquire new benefits for Serbia, and Montenegro will again be left out." Alimpić retorted testily that Montenegro's parleying with Austria could be interpreted as betrayal of Serbdom. The alliance would be between rulers, not their ministers. He regarded Nikola's reproaches and minor objections to the proposed treaties as mere pretexts to avoid agreement.[87]

Alimpić returned to Belgrade without the Montenegrin alliance, but his mission laid the bases for it and clarified Serbia's objectives. Before the envoy departed, Prince Nikola had accepted a political convention (March 17) though he refused to sign it. He pledged that as soon as a *casus belli* arose, Montenegro would enter the war. On the way home, Alimpić explained Belgrade's aims to Consul Ionin:

[86] *Ibid.*, p. 536; V. Djordjević, *Crna Gora*, pp. 379–81; Jovanović, *Stvaranje*, p. 313.

[87] Alimpić, *Život*, pp. 530–38; HHSA, Wrede to Andrassy, March 1, no. 23.

The Serbian . . . question can be separated from the Eastern Question and settled without involving Russia in war. In the Eastern Question we Serbs do not dream of competing with Russia nor hindering her because we have no pretensions to the Straits. We wish only to liberate the Serbian areas from Turkey. I feel that we could free ourselves from the Turks if Russia aided us financially. Our success would be beneficial to Russia in the Eastern Question because liberated Serbdom would become a strong barrier which once and for all would block the road into the Balkan peninsula to the Austro-Germans.

Ionin responded warmly to this statement.[88]

Prince Milan, spurred on by a socialist demonstration at Kragujevac and Petar Karadjordjević's activities in Bosnia, sought to build a Balkan coalition.[89] Belgrade sent Major J. Dragašević to Bucharest to arrange common action with the Bulgarian exiles. He assured them that Russia secretly supported Serbia's war plans. However, the Russian envoy warned Dragašević and the exiled Bulgarians that "having decided to pursue the work of pacification, the Imperial [Russian] Government could only condemn any undertaking tending to impede its success." [90] Milan urged Greece to abandon its passivity and openly support the Balkan Slavs, but Athens refused to receive a Serbian envoy. M. Garašanin, sent there as a private observer, reported that there was little prospect of Greek aid.[91] Milan lacked the persuasiveness of a Prince Michael.

About March 12, Prince Milan told a gathering of Serbian leaders that Serbia must either complete her war preparations or adopt a pacific policy and delay indefinitely an attempt to unify Serbdom. The assembled leaders agreed to hasten war preparations, though some military experts warned of possible defeat. Mastering his own doubts, Milan resolved to intensify military preparations.[92]

Serbia's warlike moves cracked Dreikaiserbund unity. Official Russia refused to adopt strong measures to restrain Serbia again. The emperor

---

[88] Alimpić, Život, pp. 543, 545.

[89] HHSA, Wrede to Andrassy, March 2, no. 25; Piročanac, Beleške, pp. 36–37.

[90] Grujić, 3, 151; OSVOb., 1, I. Zinov'ev to Gorchakov, March 11/23 and 13/25. The Bulgarians—reported Zinov'ev—would rally enthusiastically to a Serbian-led war of liberation.

[91] Stojanović, Great Powers, p. 82; HHSA, Wrede to Andrassy, March 14, no. 28.

[92] Harris, History, p. 384.

opposed risking Russian lives in a Balkan conflict, but he remained sympathetic toward the South Slavs; the empress advocated expelling the Turks from Europe.[93] Aware that the Serbian states were concocting "bloody drama . . . for the spring," War Minister Miliutin worried lest Russia, by restraining them, discredit herself before Slav opinion. On March 12, he wrote:

Gorchakov already believes that European diplomacy will not succeed in holding back Serbia, Montenegro, and perhaps Rumania from open intervention in the struggle. If, in the spring, all the Slav provinces of Turkey take up arms, our chancellor would propose to leave both sides to the dictates of fate: let arms decide which side will triumph.[94]

Gorchakov refused to deny a British report that Russian consuls were encouraging insurgent resistance,[95] but he affirmed that St. Petersburg's policy was "clear and open as noonday" and that "the most stringent counsels had been given both to the Prince of Serbia and the Prince of Montenegro [not to intervene]."[96] Count Ignat'ev warned that Austrian attempts to prevent an alliance of the Serbian states were detrimental to Russian interests; Slavdom must be on guard against Vienna's intrigues.[97]

Austria moved unilaterally to restrain Serbia. Though professing satisfaction with Nikola's peaceful assurances, Andrassy was alarmed by Serbia's military preparations and defiant attitude, and called its rearmament provocative. Unless Milan promised to be peaceful, Austria might occupy Serbia.[98] On March 16, Consul Wrede dropped a "bomb": Milan must pledge that Serbia would remain at peace unless Montenegro declared war. The prince, though shaken, refused to follow "in the wake of Montenegro"; he would consult Russia before

[93] HHSA, Langenau to Andrassy, March 1/13, Privatschreiben.

[94] Miliutin, *Dnevnik*, 2, 24-25.

[95] *Das Staatsarchiv* (Leipzig, 1878), *30*, 205, Elliot to Derby, Feb. 14. Elliot wrote, "The Russian consulate [at Dubrovnik] is the open resort of the insurgent chiefs; their correspondence is sent to the Consul [A. S. Ionin] who is a party to all their projects. . . . It is not surprising that the insurgents should suppose their attempt to be fully approved by the Russian government."

[96] *Ibid.*, p. 208, Loftus to Derby, Feb. 29.

[97] Kartsov, RS, *133*, 564, 567. "Vienna's object is very clear," Ignat'ev wrote Kartsov. "It wishes to undermine our influence and the importance of . . . Belgrade and Cetinje in order to replace them with Austrian influence. In Petersburg and Vienna [Ambassador Novikov] they do not see this."

[98] HHSA, Wrede to Andrassy, Feb. 25 and March 9; Andrassy to Wrede, March 12.

announcing Serbia's policy.[99] He urged Kartsov to discover St. Petersburg's attitude and reminded him that Serbian rearmament was proceeding at Russia's recommendation.[100]

Gorchakov, though displeased at Austria's unilateral step, responded to Andrassy's request for support. He composed appropriate instructions to Kartsov, then canceled them when he learned, late on March 19, of Alimpić's recall. The chancellor refused to compromise himself needlessly before the Russian public with another stern warning to Serbia. Andrassy, disliking his hesitation, wrote Baron Langenau in St. Petersburg that Russia's silence would confirm Milan's belief in Dreikaiserbund disunity and weaken his resistance to the warmongers. "Intervention cannot and must not come about," wrote Andrassy, "but it is essential that the threat of it be held like the sword of Damocles over the Serbian Government or all of our actions will be useless." Gorchakov agreed grudgingly to support "la bombe Wrede," but he deplored threats against Serbia which would never be executed.[101] A small but significant difference persisted in Austrian and Russian views of the Serbian question.

Awaiting Russian encouragement, Serbia delayed its reply to Austria as long as it dared. But Russia's silence eventually compelled Pavlović to declare (March 25):

The Serbian government has no intention of attacking Turkey or of interfering in any way with the pacification work of the great powers which would invite their collective intervention. Military preparations which have been made to date are merely the completion of a military organization much retarded in recent years.

From this equivocal statement Wrede concluded that Russia's silence had shocked Serbia into a peaceful course.[102] *Istok* was puzzled and disquieted by apparent Austro-Russian collaboration, but it predicted bravely that Russia would soon revert to its traditional pro-Slav policy.[103] Only *Zastava* perceived that Austrian diplomacy had floundered until Russia came belatedly to its rescue.[104]

---

[99] *Ibid.*, Wrede to Andrassy, March 17, no. 29.
[100] *Ibid.*, Kartsov, RS, *133*, 568–69.
[101] HHSA, Andrassy to Langenau, March 17, 23; Langenau to Andrassy, March 19, telegrams 21, 22, March 25, no. 14A-B.
[102] *Ibid.*, Wrede to Andrassy, March 25, nos. 35, 36.
[103] *Istok*, March 14/26 and 19/31, nos. 30, 32.
[104] *Zastava*, March 11/23, no. 40.

Austrian and Russian leaders concluded from this March crisis that if they remained united, Milan would resist the war party. Andrassy and Gorchakov now proposed strong action against Omladinist elements in Serbia and Austria-Hungary.[105] Austrian pressure had helped delay the Montenegrin alliance without which Serbia could not make war, but Milan and his ministers did not contemplate immediate action. Russia had not rescinded its advice to rearm; and Kartsov's uncertainty and St. Petersburg's delay had suggested differences which the Serbs might exploit. The Serbian governments knew of the pro-Slav enthusiasm in Russia. Russian pressure had been too weak to dash their hopes of Russia's support in case of war. Their drift toward conflict had not been halted, much less reversed.

The Powers attempted once again to pacify the insurgent provinces. Ambassador Novikov had rebuffed the Bosnian rebels' appeal for Russian aid in January and told their envoys bluntly that Bosnia could "in no case go to Serbia now." They returned to Bosnia disillusioned and angry. The insurgents' funds were almost exhausted, the chiefs could not be controlled, and the Austrian authorities were arresting Bosnian leaders.[106] Despite their considerable number,[107] the Bosnian rebels were too poorly organized really to threaten Turkish control. In April, Russia was prepared to permit an Austrian occupation of Bosnia provided Turkey granted autonomy to Bosnia and Hercegovina, territorial concessions to Montenegro, and guaranteed the safe return home of Slav refugees.[108] Austria opposed these concessions to the South Slavs but strongly favored pacification. Austrian optimism about a peaceful solution had reached its height a month before when Baron Rodich reported that Prince Nikola also had been converted to pacification.[109] However, Dr. Koetschet, who had seen Nikola in January, warned that only if the Porte accepted Montenegrin demands,[110] would the prince co-operate.

Negotiations at Sutorina in early April dispelled hopes of an early

[105] PRO, FO 65/931, Loftus to Derby, March 28, no. 115; HHSA, Andrassy to Langenau, March 27. Neither statesman specified what "action" should be taken.
[106] Ekmečić, Ustanak, p. 195.
[107] PRO, FO 78/2489, Freeman to Derby, April 21. Freeman estimated them at 10,000–12,000 in north Bosnia alone.
[108] Miliutin, Dnevnik, 2, 40–41. Convinced by now that the Andrassy Plan would not solve the crisis, Alexander II hoped Andrassy would agree to full autonomy for Bosnia and Hercegovina. HHSA, Langenau to Andrassy, April 6/18, no. 20.
[109] HHSA, Andrassy to Wrede, March 6.
[110] Koetschet, Bosniens, pp. 40–46.

peace. At Gorchakov's request, Veselicki-Bojidarović had sought the adherence of Montenegro and the insurgents to a modified version of the Andrassy Plan. Prince Nikola had consented, but asserts that he did so only to demonstrate good faith toward Austria. Veselicki and Božo Petrović met with the insurgent chiefs at Sutorina on April 3 but failed to reach agreement with them.[111] Three days later Baron Rodich arrived bearing Andrassy's latest proposals to the insurgents which called upon them to accept Turkish promises of reform and lay down their arms. After the baron attempted in vain to undermine the insurgents' faith in Prince Nikola, the chiefs countered with demands of their own, calling virtually for liquidation of Turkish rule in both provinces.[112] The outcome was a total deadlock.

The fiasco at Sutorina was a sharp setback to Austrian diplomacy and increased Austro-Russian differences. The insurgents, refusing to follow Andrassy, remained loyal to Prince Nikola. The latter, no longer hoping to acquire territory by negotiation, promptly increased his aid to the insurgents and reverted to the idea of an alliance with Serbia.[113] Gorchakov's growing support during March and April for autonomy of the insurgent provinces and territorial increases for Montenegro enhanced Russia's prestige in the Serbian lands. *Istok* rejoiced at Russia's "liberation" from Vienna: "The Andrassy diplomacy has failed. *Now Russia is speaking for herself* and has promised the rayahs this will be the end of their unbearable situation." [114]

After Sutorina, Gorchakov backed Montenegrin claims to part of Hercegovina and a seaport as the best means to settle the crisis. The chancellor, rather than impose Andrassy's terms, defended the insurgents' Sutorina counterproposals demanding withdrawal of most Turkish troops from Bosnia and Hercegovina and refusing to lay down their arms until the promised reforms had been fully implemented.[115] When the Turkish ministerial council rashly decided (April 20) to launch preventive war against Montenegro, Gorchakov warned that

[111] Nikola I, *Zapisi, 8*, knj. 13 (March 1935), pp. 139–40. The prince asserted he had arranged the April 3 meeting so that it would fail.

[112] On the insurgent demands see Djordjević, *Crna Gora*, p. 386; Čubrilović, *Bosanski*, pp. 124–25; *Zastava o B. i H.*, 4, 44–46, no. 38.

[113] Vukčević, *Crna Gora*, pp. 247–49.

[114] *Istok*, April 9/21, no. 38.

[115] HHSA, Langenau to Andrassy, March 30/April 11, no. 18C; *Staatsarchiv, 30*, 235, Loftus to Derby, April 14. For the counterproposals see Harris, *History*, p. 255.

such an attack would bring on a Balkan conflagration. When the Powers supported Russia, the Turks abandoned plans to assault Montenegro. Prince Nikola had indeed become "l'enfant chéri de la Russie, auquel on n'ose pas toucher." [116] The prince, deeply beholden to Russia, for the next months conferred with Consul Ionin before reaching decisions.[117] Russo-Montenegrin relations became warm and intimate.

Belgrade, though jealous, rejoiced at emphatic Russian support for Montenegro and the postponement of war. The Serbs welcomed even indirect Russian backing. A rock-throwing incident at the Austrian consulate in Belgrade on April 9 had revealed the deterioration of Austro-Serbian relations. Andrassy's aide, Baron Hoffman, declared pessimistically, "It is unfortunately true that the revolutionary party [Liberals] is endeavouring to drive the country into war, and that as great excitement prevails throughout the principality, it is doubtful that Prince Milan will show sufficient firmness in resisting it." [118] Prince Charles of Rumania pleaded with Milan to avoid rash decisions, but the Serbian prince replied that further opposition to the war current might cause revolution.[119]

The sudden arrival of General Cherniaev in Belgrade on April 28 heightened bellicose enthusiasm there. His newspaper, *Russkii Mir*, had popularized the Slav struggle in Russia and had urged the Serbian states to go to war. He shared the Serbian Liberals' dream of a Greater Serbia ruled by the Obrenović dynasty.[120] Frustrated in earlier attempts (1867, 1875) to reach Serbia, Cherniaev had arranged his trip with the assistance of the Moscow Slav Committee. In response to its overtures, Serbian leaders wrote that they would welcome Cherniaev properly, though they preferred General R. A. Fadeev. Cherniaev, bribing a passport official, left Russia without the consent of the tsarist government.[121]

Cherniaev's coming deeply affected Serbian-Russian relations. Barely

[116] HHSA, Langenau to Andrassy, April 26, no. 22 A-C; April 15/27, Privatschreiben.

[117] PRO, FO, Gonne to Buchanan, April 22.

[118] *Ibid.*, FO 78/2486, White to Derby, April 28, no. 36; White to Elliot, April 21, no. 28; HHSA, Wrede to Andrassy, April 30, no. 55, April 12, nos. 46, 47.

[119] *Aus dem Leben König Karls von Rumänien* (Stuttgart, 1897–1900), 3, 15, 21–22.

[120] GIM, f. Cherniaeva, Cherniaev to G. Vul'fert [1879?].

[121] N. Durnovo, "K istorii serbskoi-turetskoi voiny 1876 g.," IV, 75 (1899), 533–34; D. MacKenzie, "Panslavism in Practice: Cherniaev in Serbia (1876)," JMH, *36* (Sept. 1964), pp. 281–82.

Milan Obrenović (1854–1901), prince (1868–1882), then king (1882–1889) of Serbia.

Mikhail Grigorevich Cherniaev (1828–1898), Russian conqueror of Tashkent (1865), commander-in-chief of the Morava-Timok armies in Serbia in 1876.

a month after Russia's reluctant support of the "bombe Wrede," a leading Pan-Slav general arrived, seemingly with St. Petersburg's tacit approval. Cherniaev's boastful disclosure that he was corresponding with an aide of the Russian heir reinforced this impression. Serbian leaders quickly grasped how valuable the general could be in their war plans.[122] His arrival nullified Russia's earlier support of Andrassy and tilted the scales further in favor of war. Through negligence, official Russia once again had encouraged a Serbo-Turkish conflict which its policies had sought to avert.

On the Eve of War, May–June 1876

Only a week after Cherniaev's arrival, Kaljević's moribund cabinet resigned. Prince Milan reluctantly permitted the return of Mihajlović's "action ministry," dominated as before by Ristić and Grujić.[123] Although the Serbian public regarded it as a war cabinet, Wrede believed Ristić might first try diplomacy and seek to lessen Serbia's dependence on Russia by repairing relations with Vienna. Indeed, Ristić promptly announced that Serbia had no aggressive intentions toward Turkey and promised to restrain popular excitement. He declared that Serbian national interests, not foreign advice, would determine his cabinet's policy. Frontier authorities received strict orders to avoid trouble with the Turks and prevent the passage of volunteers.[124] However, the more pacific ministers fell silent. Wrede reported on May 25, "Within the cabinet the more moderate Ristić has already been overshadowed by J. Grujić, who must be regarded as the actual head of the present government and who definitely pursues warlike aims. Any other policy would cost the government its popularity and perhaps lead to its immediate fall." Only the threat of direct intervention by the Powers, he concluded, could restrain Serbia.[125]

Behind a diplomatic smoke screen the new government rushed military and political preparations for war. A Military Council, formed in April, debated Serbian strategy. The majority supported the plan of Major Sava Grujić which advocated a southeastward offensive against the main Turkish forces and defensive operations elsewhere. Only if

---

[122] Aksakov, *Sochineniia, 1,* 220; Kartsov, RS, *134* (1908), pp. 69–70.

[123] For the cabinet's composition see Grujić, *3,* 157.

[124] HHSA, Wrede to Andrassy, May 6, 10, 22, nos. 57, 61, 68; PRO, FO 78/2486, White to Elliot, May 10, no. 51.

[125] HHSA, Wrede to Andrassy, May 25, no. 70.

this Niš army were destroyed, argued Grujić, could the Serbian territories of the Porte be annexed. A minority, supported by the ministers,
favored defensive warfare in the east while Bosnia, the principal political objective, was seized. Prince Milan sided with the majority of his
military specialists, and the Grujić plan was adopted on May 14.[126] The
Council of Ministers resolved (May 13) "to assist the emancipation of
our brethren in Turkey and as far as possible achieve the unification
of the Serbian people in the Turkish Empire." Bosnia and Old Serbia
should be annexed to Greater Serbia.[127]

Meanwhile, Cherniaev had inspected the Serbian army and found it
woefully unprepared. He told the prince that the soldiers were so
apathetic that Serbia might lose an offensive war. Cherniaev wrote
home that the Serbs expected miracles from him, but he added, "The
[Bulgarian] populace awaits merely the signal from Serbia to begin
war." [128] He wished to give that signal himself. At War Minister
Nikolić's suggestion, Cherniaev was proclaimed a Serbian citizen and
commander of the eastern armies on May 24.[129]

Serbia desperately needed funds to finance the war. Cherniaev requested the Slav committees to loan Serbia at least 500,000 rubles and
offered its mines and forests as collateral. The general stressed that
Serbia would thus become an economic dependency of Russia.[130] Metropolitan Mihailo appealed to Aksakov for financial aid to Serbia,
promising, "The Serbian people will not depart from the bases of the
Slav way of life." [131] Aksakov replied that the committees lacked
money. The Serbian cabinet then decided to send Mihailo to Russia to
obtain money from the government or private banks. But on June 6,
Ristić informed his ministers that the tsar had vetoed this mission.
Instead, Milosav Protić of the Court of Cassation (the highest court of
appeal in Serbia) was dispatched to St. Petersburg to explain Serbia's
financial plight and seek assistance while Milovan Janković visited
Serbian areas of Austria-Hungary. Metropolitan Mihailo, in a letter to

[126] N. Rakočević, *Ratni planovi Srbije protiv Turske* (Belgrade, 1934?), pp.
115–25; Grujic, 3, 159–60; S. Grujić, *Operacije Timočko-Moravske vojske* (Belgrade, 1901–02), *1*, 45, 55. For the military plans see DAS 29, "Operacioni plan"
(signed by Orešković), April 19/May 1, and "Natsrt ratne operacije protiv
Turske" (signed by S. Grujić and R. Alimpić), May 10/22.
[127] Grujić, 3, 159.
[128] GIM, Avtobiografiia Cherniaeva, p. 9.
[129] HHSA, Wrede to Andrassy, May 25, no. 70.
[130] ROBibSS, f. Aksakova, no. 387, Cherniaev to Aksakov, April 29/May 11.
[131] OSVOb., *1*, 225–27, Mihailo to Aksakov, May 19/31.

N. Durnovo, a member of the Moscow Slav Committtee, supported the Protić mission, adding:

Everything points to the beginning of action. Whether this is beneficial or not, results will reveal. We cannot retreat because we have gone too far. Therefore, I ask you to do everything that is required in the present situation. We count on the love of Russia and brotherly sympathy for Orthodox and Slav sufferers. . . . We have come too far to turn back, and you, if you leave us to our fate, know well that it is your own cause.[132]

The Ristić government, realizing that alliances with Greece or Rumania were unlikely because of the uncertainty of a war with Turkey, believed that when Serbia struck, insurrections would erupt in Old Serbia and spread in Bulgaria. But an immediate military alliance with Montenegro was vital. Ristić telegraphed Cetinje that the Serbian states should decide when to begin war.[133] At first Prince Nikola refused to negotiate, but Britain's rejection of the Berlin Memorandum and the Powers' espousal of nonintervention finally convinced him that conflict was inevitable.[134] On May 30, when Ristić reiterated Serbia's determination to fight and proposed an alliance, Nikola agreed. On June 16, a treaty of alliance and a military convention were signed in Fiume.[135] Serbia and Montenegro pledged to enter the war in their own manner within ten days of ratification. Belgrade would supply its partner with a monthly subsidy. In case of victory Bosnia would join Serbia, and Hercegovina unite with Montenegro; the Narenta and Drina rivers would separate the two Serbian states. Realizing that St. Petersburg, which had saved him from the Turks in April, desired peace, Nikola did not reveal his negotiations with Serbia to Ionin, who had lately been his confidant. Later he told Ionin, "It was not a question of asking Russia's advice, but of virtually announcing a *fait accompli*." To Ionin's warning that aggressive war would antagonize Europe, Nikola declared that he and Milan preferred censure to being "roti au petit feu." [136]

As soon as the treaties with Montenegro had been signed, Milan

[132] Durnovo, IV, 75 (1899), 536–37; Grujić, 3, 166–69, 173.

[133] *Ibid.*, pp. 160–61; AII, Ristić 13/39, May 4/16; "Prepiske," *Zapisi*, 5 (July–Aug. 1929), pp. 98–99.

[134] OSVOb., 1, 262–64, Ionin to Gorchakov, June 27/July 9.

[135] AII, Ristić 13/40, May 18/30, telegram. The correspondence pertaining to negotiations for the alliance is in "Prepiske," pp. 100–03, and (Oct. 1929), pp. 250–51. For the alliance text see Grujić, 3, 170–73.

[136] OSVOb., 1, 262–64, Ionin to Gorchakov, June 27/July 9.

informed General Cherniaev that war was certain. The prince declared that he had decided upon war months before; only recently had the "less belligerent ministers" reached the same conclusion. Without a firm commitment from Montenegro, it had been doubtful that Serbia could make war.[137]

Foreign diplomatic reports confirmed the imminence of conflict. On May 29, Sir William White, British consul in Belgrade, wrote, "I am assured that the military authorities are of the opinion that preparations for war with the Porte are so far completed that they see no objection to commence hostilities as soon as the Government may feel disposed to do so." [138] Andrassy believed that Serbia would soon declare war, but he noted that Montenegro remained pacific. However, on June 3, Rodich reported the closing of all Montenegrin schools, suggesting that war was about to begin.[139]

Ristić launched a final diplomatic salvo. He requested the Porte, in return for increased tribute payments, to entrust Bosnia's administration to Serbia and Hercegovina's to Montenegro. Turkish and Montenegrin opposition doomed this plan.[140] Prince Milan, pessimistic about Ristić's scheme, explained, "We feel that it would not be proper to attack Turkey like bandits without having brought about a proper rupture on diplomatic grounds." [141]

The Turks were more concerned about a rumored Serbo-Russian alliance. The Porte announced that if Russian troops joined the Serbs on the Danube, Turkey would immediately invade Serbia. Constantinople pressed Filip Hristić for an explanation.[142] But it was much too late for this, though Belgrade wished the rumors were true! Before leaving Belgrade for the front, Prince Milan explained to the tsar why Serbia had decided on war contrary to official Russian advice; he pleaded for the emperor's benevolent protection:

Since without being at war, the principality has been forced for a year to endure . . . the consequences of one, I came to the conclusion that it was

---

[137] A. Cherniaeva, "K. M. G. Cherniaevu," RA (1914, no. 1), pp. 34–38, Milan to Cherniaev, June 5/17.

[138] Staatsarchiv, 30, 287, White to Derby, May 29.

[139] Actenstücke, 1, no. 377, p. 255, Andrassy to Zichy, May 29, no. 438, p. 284, June 9.

[140] AII, Ristić 12/40, Plamenac to Ristić, June 6/18; Grujić, 3, 177; Ristić, 1, 91–92.

[141] Milan to Cherniaev, June 5/17, RA (1914, no. 1), p. 37.

[142] DAS, 26/274, 275, Hristić to Ristić, June 12/24 and 13/25.

better for it to accept the intolerable situation imposed upon her [by Turkey] and lacking any other solution, to resort to arms . . . I realize, Sire, that I have no right to count on the support of Your Majesty, my decision not conforming to the advice which You never ceased giving me through the intermediacy of Your representative, M. Kartsov.[143]

Milan and his cabinet continued to expect support from St. Petersburg nonetheless.

During these final prewar weeks, the Serbian press redoubled its demands for prompt action. As soon as Ristić resumed power, *Istok* called for immediate war. With the Bulgarians in revolt, "are we going to wait for the Eastern Question to be decided without Serbia?" Serbs must bury their political differences and co-operate with other South Slavs, then the flames of insurrection would spread to all of European Turkey.[144] The Serbian people, declared *Zastava* in mid-June, has crossed its Rubicon: neither threats nor force can restrain it.[145]

The Serbian papers regarded Russia with alternating hope and dismay. During the emperors' May meeting in Berlin, *Istok* remained confident that Russia would not betray its traditional pro-Slav policy and asserted that Andrassy had gone to Berlin to get his orders from Germany and Russia; the Berlin Memorandum was Gorchakov's ultimatum to Turkey.[146] But *Zastava* was pessimistic about the Berlin meeting and Russia's Balkan policy:

Instead of the Slavs benefiting from Russia's greatness, often Russia has extracted benefits by dividing them with its neighbors. . . . The Russian tsar believes that other Slavs, especially Orthodox ones, will automatically cry out in their sufferings: hurrah for the tsar! . . . This suffering gives the Turkish Christians the right to put Russia's friendship to a real test. . . . The meeting of the emperors in Berlin is only a new trap for the insurrection. . . . We hope that the Serbian princes and people will no longer allow themselves to be misled by diplomacy even if the Russian emperor himself stands at its head.[147]

Early in June *Istok* asserted that Russia, backed by Germany, would override Andrassy's objections and decide upon a "drastic policy."

---

[143] AII, Ristić 18/1, Prince Milan to Alexander II, June 15/27. A draft apparently prepared by Ristić and without the prince's signature.
[144] *Istok*, April 28/May 10, May 2/14, 9/21, nos. 46, 48, 51.
[145] *Zastava*, May 5/17, June 4/16, nos. 68, 83.
[146] *Istok*, April 23/May 5, April 25/May 7, nos. 44, 45.
[147] *Zastava*, April 25/May 7, no. 63, "Berlinski sastanak."

"Tsar Alexander does not need to call upon Serbia and Montenegro as Nicholas I did during the Crimean War. Serbia and Montenegro stand like loaded cannon which will burst into flame if that is the request of Slav Russia." [148] But on June 25, sharing some of *Zastava*'s pessimism about Russia's policy, *Istok* cried bitterly:

Russia, if she does not assist us, already thereby hinders us. Long ago we would have obtained our freedom had we not been regarded as the advance post of Pan-Slavism. . . . This has made our position more difficult not only toward Europe and the Powers, but toward the Balkan states which should work together since they have the same troubles and enemies.[149]

"Courageous statements of the Russian press" in behalf of the Serbs, though, heartened the Serbian papers somewhat.[150]

On the eve of war, official Russian policy toward the Serbs remained indecisive. Unconvinced by the empress' anti-Turkish tirades, Alexander II wished to preserve the Ottoman Empire and a Balkan *status quo amélioré* in partnership with Germany and Austria. He deplored rebellion and considered peace essential for Russia. Gorchakov, urging autonomy for the insurgent provinces and pressure on Turkey, refused to restrain the Serbian states until the Porte carried out its promises to the insurgents. Alexander wished to preserve ties with Austria, but if they broke he was confident of German support.[151]

In Berlin, Gorchakov had yielded once more to Andrassy's blandishments. The chancellor suggested using the insurgents' Sutorina proposals as a basis for pacification and establishing an international commission to supervise their execution. Pending a settlement, Austria and Russia should occupy the two provinces.[152] Andrassy, rejecting such coercive measures, persuaded the chancellor to accept instead a two-month armistice while Turkish reforms were carried out. A decision on compensation for Montenegro was postponed, and Gorchakov abandoned objections to an eventual Austrian annexation of "Turkish Croatia." [153] To save the Dreikaiserbund, Gorchakov temporarily re-

[148] *Istok*, May 21/June 2, May 23/June 4, nos. 55, 56.

[149] *Ibid.*, June 13/25, no. 64.

[150] *Zastava*, June 4/16, no. 83.

[151] Miliutin, *Dnevnik 2*, 43, 46; HHSA, Langenau to Andrassy, June 1, no. 30; May 2, no. 23; S. Goriainov, *Le Bosphore et les Dardanelles* (Paris, 1910), p. 316.

[152] HHSA, Varia Russie, 1876, "Original des ursprünglichen Vorschlages, welcher vom Fürsten Gortschakoff in Berlin gemacht wurde und in Namen der 3 Mächte den Grossmächten mitgeteilt werden sollte."

[153] *Ibid.*, Andrassy to Franz Josef, May 10, telegram.

scinded his pro-Slav stand and laid the basis for the Budapest Conventions of 1877. He was not a Pan-Slav, he told Lord O. Russell, British ambassador to Germany, but a Russian desirous of peace, progress, and order.[154] When Britain rejected the Berlin Memorandum—the outcome of the Dreikaiserbund's deliberations—Gorchakov urged the other Powers to get Turkey to accept it anyway.[155]

Official Russia's vacillations enhanced the role of its Balkan consuls as war approached. Some diplomats asserted that Gorchakov was unable to hold them to their instructions. A. S. Ionin's pro-Slav views were notorious, but the chancellor refused to disavow them as he might easily have done.[156] In late May, Consul Kartsov, still perplexed about Russian aims, met with the tsar and Gorchakov at Ems. Alexander II was furious at Cherniaev's secret trip and acceptance of a Serbian command. Upon the advice of chancellor and consul, he renounced his intention to strip Cherniaev of his military decorations, but Kartsov was ordered to sever relations with him and prevent Serbia from going to war. However, Gorchakov told the consul confidentially, "Despite all this, do not forget that although the tsar is opposed to war, his son, the heir to the throne, stands at the head of the [Slav] movement." Kartsov left Ems as confused as before.[157]

Kartsov's statements revealed Russia's dual policy. He warned Andrassy that, despite Russian objections, a Serbo-Turkish war was probable because Omladinists controlled the Serbian government.[158] But he informed Novikov, "As far as human beings can foresee, I can say definitely that peace will not be disturbed." This vacillation showed the contest between the heir's "war party" and a peace faction led by the tsar and Novikov; Gorchakov shifted uneasily between them.[159]

[154] PRO, FO 641/852, Russell to Derby, May 15, no. 209, cited in Harris, *History*, p. 453.

[155] HHSA, Andrassy to Karolyi, June 6, telegram 8; Harris, *History*, p. 340.

[156] For example, the Russian diplomat, Vlangali, wrote, "One cannot expect anything else as long as the chancellor, whom I consider has reverted to infancy [tombé dans l'enfance] is in charge of affairs. He is moved now by only two sentiments: egoism and vanity." Earlier he wrote, "Much trouble in the East comes from . . . the consuls. It is so unusual to come across a consul who is reasonable and who shares the views of his government." ASAN, no. 8823, Vlangali to Marinović, May 28 and June 22, 1876; HHSA, Langenau to Andrassy, June 1, no. 30.

[157] Kartsov, RS, *134*, 70–71.

[158] HHSA, Andrassy to Wrede, May 29.

[159] Kartsov, p. 71.

The divergence of views weakened the Foreign Ministry's efforts to restrain Serbia.

Nonetheless, some final attempts were made. N. Lodyzhenskii, the chargé d'affaires in Belgrade, reiterated Russia's opposition to Serbian aggression, and on June 7 Kartsov informed Milan and Ristić that if Serbia

either directly or indirectly committed aggression against Turkey, she would be completely abandoned to her fate by Russia . . . and could not count on sympathy or aid from that Power in case of defeat, and that Austria-Hungary would be perfectly free to take whatever measures against the Principality she would consider necessary.

The Serbs replied evasively that Serbia had no aggressive intentions and would remain at peace as long as possible.[160] "The prince," noted Consul White, "has not even promised any delay but merely to do his best." [161] At this time, of course, Ristić was vigorously trying to persuade Nikola to join a military alliance.

Kartsov, though still supporting Serbian rearmament, now feared Russian involvement in a Balkan conflict as deeply as the tsar. He returned from Ems and wrote Ignat'ev that he was profoundly convinced that "our direct and most holy interests demand that we, so far as possible, reject any solidarity with the Slav movement. In truth, is it worthwhile for us to inspire against ourselves a coalition of all of Europe and perhaps . . . risk a repetition of the unhappy year, 1853?" Svetozar Miletić's visit to Belgrade (June 6–10) caused him worry that "the Serbian movement might turn into a purely revolutionary South Slav one." He continued, "I shall do what is possible to restrain the Serbs from war." [162] Ristić informed Wrede that Kartsov supported unequivocally the Powers' demand that Serbia remain at peace. "The sudden realization of being left wholly in the lurch by Russia," reported Wrede, "has made the Belgrade cabinet hesitate in the eleventh hour." Some Serbs even called Kartsov's latest advice treason to the Slav cause.[163]

Chancellor Gorchakov, though he supported a peaceful solution to

[160] Tiutin, p. 171; HHSA, Wrede to Andrassy, June 7, no. 81; June 8, no. 83.
[161] PRO, FO 78/2486, White to Derby, June 8, nos. 57, 59.
[162] OSVOb., *1*, 241–42, Kartsov to Ignat'ev, May 31/June 12. However, Miletić in conferences with Serbian leaders merely sought to arrange material aid by the Serbs of the Vojvodina for the Serbian cause.
[163] HHSA, Wrede to Andrassy, June 14, no. 86.

the end, repudiated his concessions to Andrassy in Berlin. Adhering closer to Ignat'ev's approach, he reiterated on June 17 support for autonomy of the insurgent provinces and cession to Montenegro and Serbia of parts of Hercegovina and Mali Zvornik respectively.[164] Gorchakov had already repudiated his concessions to Andrassy in Berlin. But foreseeing Serbia's destruction in war, he instructed Ignat'ev (June 24) to seek to avert it by all means. He ordered Kartsov:

Warn Milan vigorously of the danger of attack on his part for which the Turks are waiting and bind him to remain on the defensive. If [Serbia] is subjected to an attack by the Porte, try to get your colleagues to protest on the basis of the [Paris] treaty. If, contrary to our advice, the struggle breaks out, and especially on the part of Serbia, the Powers will announce complete nonintervention.[165]

Such a pledge, however, would encourage rather than dissuade the optimistic Serbian leadership.

On June 27, Gorchakov finally admitted that a local Balkan conflict was inevitable. Blaming other powers for this outcome, he denied indignantly, but unconvincingly, that Russia had been pacific in London and bellicose in the Serbian capitals: [166]

The character of the emperor and of his whole reign refute this gratuitous insult. Our representatives are too disciplined [*sic!*] to permit themselves to deviate. The Christian powers have delayed too long to disarm the insurgents by granting an autonomy offering the best chance of pacification. Kartsov has once again been instructed to protest against any attack on the part of Serbia, but the latest news indicates that Milan has been overcome [*débordé*] and that a struggle is inevitable.

Unless the Turks attacked, Russia would remain neutral.

Unofficial Russian views of the South Slav question now varied from mild sympathy to demands for an anti-Turkish crusade. General Fadeev's June memorandum expressed the extreme Pan-Slav approach: Russia's influence in Constantinople has been undermined; she must abandon pacification since the Ottoman Empire is collapsing. Allied with Germany and the South Slavs, Russia should solve the Eastern Question by seizing the Straits and establishing control over the Bal-

---

[164] HHSA, Varia Turquie I, Gorchakov to Shuvalov, June 5/17.

[165] Tiutin, "Politika," p. 171, citing AVPR, Konstantinopel 1876.

[166] R. Seton-Watson, "Russo-British Relations during the Eastern Crisis," SR, *3* (1924), 680, Gorchakov to Shuvalov, June 15/27.

kans.[167] Fadeev's plan, though, was incompatible with the aims of Serbian nationalists who rejected Russian hegemony.

The Slav committees disagreed sharply over the Serbian question. A. S. Ionin, backed by Ignat'ev, favored annexation of Hercegovina to Montenegro; he gave Prince Nikola funds designated by the committees for Hercegovina's wounded and refugees. Such favoritism toward Montenegro, feared N. A. Kireev, a member of the St. Petersburg Committee, would ruin the committees' relations with other South Slavs. He advocated closer co-operation with Metropolitan Mihailo's Belgrade Committee and increased aid to Bosnia and Bulgaria. Veselicki-Bojidarović, who desired an independent Hercegovina, accused Ionin of undermining his position. But Aksakov, convinced that Veselicki wished to rule Hercegovina, deplored his feud with Ionin and warned the St. Petersburg chairman of Veselicki's exaggerated ambitions.[168]

The Slav Committees and the Russian government had discussed the desirability of inciting a Bulgarian insurrection. In April 1876, N. A. Kireev and Bulgarian exiles had urged major support for a Bulgarian rising while most members opposed it. Chairman A. I. Vasil'chikov argued that lives would be sacrificed in vain: "To incite the poor, defenseless Bulgarians to armed insurrection, when they lack arms and when neither Serbia nor Russia has promised them aid, would be to condemn them to inevitable destruction. I positively refused any participation of the [St. Petersburg] Slav Committee in such an undertaking." [169]

In May, a Bulgarian uprising did break out.[170] N. A. Kireev, rejoicing at what he supposed was the long-awaited hour of Slav liberation, rushed off to Bucharest to join the Slav ranks and asked the St. Petersburg Committee for funds and weapons. His older brother, A. A. Kireev, and Aksakov seconded his efforts.[171] Even A. I. Vasil'chikov now reversed his stand:

You know that this spring I was of the opinion that until Serbia and Montenegro entered the struggle, it would be unwise to instigate and allure

[167] Os. Pr., no. 1, pp. 45ff., Fadeev to Giers, May 28/June 9.

[168] *Slavianskii sbornik*, pp. 108–09, N. A. Kireev to A. A. Kireev, May 11; OSVOb., *1*, 205–07, Aksakov to A. I. Vasil'chikov, April 29/May 11.

[169] Golubev, *Vasil'chikov*; pp. 114–115; I. S. Ivanov, "Bolgarskoe opolchenie i ego sformirovania v 1875–1879 gg.," RS, *66* (1890), p. 117.

[170] For reports of its outbreak see OSVOb., *1*, nos. 97, 100.

[171] *Slavianskii sbornik*, pp. 102–03; OSVOb., *1*, nos. 96, 112.

the Bulgarians. . . . Now, on the contrary, the time has come to act energetically. . . . But the main thing is funds. Whatever sums remain at our disposal should be sent to V. S. Ionin via Odessa to the Russian consulate in Galatz.[172]

But N. A. Kireev failed to achieve genuine Serbo-Bulgarian co-operation against Turkey. Aware of the antagonism between Serbs and Bulgarians, he tried in vain to persuade them to divide regions liberated from the Porte. Accompanied by I. Ivanov, a Bulgarian in close touch with the Russian Slav Committees, he went to Belgrade in June to obtain weapons for Bulgarian refugees in Serbia, but Milan refused to arm them or even to allow them to cross into Bulgaria to aid the uprising.[173] Prior to the Serbo-Turkish War, hamstrung by internal quarrels and meager funds, the Slav committees gave conflicting advice but little aid to the South Slavs.

The Russian government, aware that the committees were buying weapons for Balkan insurgents, tolerated their activities as "the affair of private persons." Their slender purses and the sympathy of high officials for the Slav struggle largely accounts for this lenient attitude.[174] But the authorities rejected Colonel Kishel'skii's requests for leave to join the Bulgarians, forbade General Fadeev to go to the Balkans, and issued a directive recalling General Cherniaev.[175] Officialdom permitted monetary contributions for the Slavs but tried to prevent Russian officers from joining the fray while a peaceful solution in the Balkans appeared possible.

The Russian press debated Cherniaev's trip and the Serbian states' drift toward war. *Russkii Mir* asserted that the Serbs' adoption of Cherniaev revealed the intimacy between Russians and South Slavs. Cherniaev explained that he had accepted a Serbian command to demonstrate belief in the Slav cause. To the Russian public, he described Serbian strength in glowing terms, asserting "every Serb understands that war is necessary for Serbia's moral position." [176] *Novoe Vremia* considered his trip significant because Serbia was of crucial importance in the Eastern Crisis. Later it advocated a Russian volunteer movement

---

[172] *Ibid.*, pp. 245–46, A. I. Vasil'chikov to I. K. Iankulio, June 4/16.

[173] I. Ivanov, "Bolgarskoe opolchenie i ego sformirovania v 1875–1879 gg.," RS, *62* (1889), 137–41.

[174] ROBibLen, Dnevnik Kireeva, *6*, 122.

[175] Miliutin, *Dnevnik 2*, 41; Nikitin, *Slavianskie komitety*, p. 289; OSVOb., *1*, nos. 113, 117.

[176] *Russkii Mir*, May 25/June 6, no. 142, date-lined Belgrade, May 16 [28].

to aid the South Slavs: "We express our sincere sympathy to all Russians not bound by duties of service who set forth to fight for the holy cause of the liberation of Slavdom from the Turkish yoke. There in the common struggle with the Ottomans will be forged the firmest bonds between Russian society and the self-liberating Slav world." [177] Such statements heartened Serbian leaders. Even *Golos*, though warning against ambitious *condottieri*, wished Cherniaev success.[178]

After Britain's rejection of the Berlin Memorandum, most of the press accepted the probability of a Serbo-Turkish conflict. *Moskovskie Vedomosti* declared that the Powers should no longer hinder the Serbian states from aiding their brethren even if this meant war. This English action, agreed *Novoe Vremia*, placed the fate of the Slavs squarely in their own hands.[179] *Russkii Mir* hinted that Russia would support even a Serbian war of aggression:

Serbia, with truly heroic self-sacrifice, remained on the sidelines as long as there was still the slightest chance of the pacification of the neighboring Slav provinces by diplomatic measures. Now . . . Serbia can only cross herself and throw herself into the holy struggle which alone can now solve the question of the future fate of Turkish Christians. . . . As for Russia, her role toward Serbia is no longer open to the doubts which still seemed possible a few months ago.[180]

Golos' appeals to the Serbs to avoid aggressive action and rely upon the Powers stood in sharp contrast with other newspapers. In mid-June, paralleling Gorchakov's final peace efforts, *Golos* reiterated Russia's support of pacification and warned the Serbs:

The Montenegrin and Serbian governments have shown themselves willing to obey reasonable advice even at serious risk to themselves. . . . Conflict with Turkey would *only* obtain European sympathy if a declaration of war, or its equivalent, is made by Turkey. . . . The only possible course for them is to avoid any act which would put the blame for conflict on them.[181]

Golos then reaffirmed "the sincere sympathy of the Russian people" for the Serbs.[182]

The Serbs regarded the entire first year of the Balkan crisis as a

[177] Nikitin, "Russkoe obshchestvo," p. 973.
[178] *Golos*, May 30/June 11, no. 148.
[179] Nikitin, "Russkoe obshchestvo," p. 973.
[180] *Russkii Mir*, June 17/29, no. 165.
[181] *Golos*, June 1/13 and 2/14, nos. 150, 151.
[182] *Ibid.*, June 8/20, no. 157.

prelude to war with Turkey. Serbia's political instability and economic hardships and Montenegro's increasing commitment to the Hercegovina insurgents were primary causes of conflict. Neither in Russia nor in Serbian lands did a mass movement espouse a South Slav war of liberation. The bellicose views of the Serbian and Russian press reflected only a vocal, educated minority in the principal cities.[183] In Serbia this element, backed by Montenegro and the press, twice swept the Ristić Liberals into power and committed them to a war program. The pressure upon Prince Milan, despite his doubts that war would bring victory, overcame his modest powers of resistance. Milan concluded, and the diplomats agreed, that he would lose his throne if he persisted in a pacific policy.

Russia shared responsibility for the coming of war. To be sure, the tsar and Gorchakov, fearing the revolutionary implications of the South Slav upheaval and distrusting the Serbian "action cabinet," supported a peaceful, diplomatic solution to the end. But the grave split within the Russian leadership and its secret sympathies for the Slavs deprived Gorchakov's diplomacy of clarity and authority. Pan-Slav diplomats attacked with impunity the official doctrine of co-operation with Austria and advocated unilateral solutions of the Eastern Question. General Cherniaev, through the negligence rather than the connivance of Russian officialdom, made his crucial journey to Belgrade. Confused by conflicting currents in the top echelons of leadership, Kartsov hesitated between the Pan-Slavs and the tsar. The independence and lack of discipline of his agents helped to nullify Gorchakov's sincere efforts to avert conflict.

Perplexed though they were by contradictory Russian advice in 1875–1876, the leaders of Serbia and Montenegro ultimately concluded that neither Russia nor Austria would intervene to prevent their war with Turkey. But Russia did not push them into the struggle. The war party in Serbia, buoyed by unreasoning optimism, assessed the military and political situation inaccurately. Once Cherniaev had arrived, the Serbian extremists concluded that official Russia could be dragged into a war to free the South Slavs and aggrandize the Serbian states.

[183] OSVOb., *1*, 246–47.

CHAPTER IV

THE SERBO-TURKISH WAR

ONCE their military alliance had been signed (June 16), the Serbian states were determined upon war despite the Powers' efforts to restrain them. In mid-June the Serbs sent their militia to the frontiers; on June 22 the Ristić cabinet made its final decision for war. The Serbian government, attempting to cloak aggression with diplomacy, dispatched a lengthy letter to the Porte explaining that Serbia would occupy Bosnia "to assure the tranquillity and integrity of Turkey." [1] On June 29 Prince Milan, accompanied part way by his ministers, proceeded to army headquarters. The next day his war proclamation appeared and on July 2 Serbian and Montenegrin forces crossed the Turkish frontiers.

The Serbian states' declarations of war inaugurated a critical phase in Russia's relations with the Serbs. Their attempt to smash Turkish rule in the Balkans, aided by unofficial Russia, put St. Petersburg in an embarrassing position between pro-Slav Russian public opinion, which urged intervention, and the Powers, who insisted on neutrality. For the Serbs, the decision for war represented a desperate gamble that would succeed only if Russia were drawn in. Serbia's military forces were clearly inferior to those of Turkey and during the four months of war Serbian leaders intermittently sought a truce. When the Serbs faced certain disaster, Russia finally intervened to force an armistice on the Porte.

The Serbian Offensive and Reichstadt

On June 30, Prince Milan issued a war proclamation which sought unsuccessfully to satisfy both the Serbian people and European opinion. Serbia, it declared, had striven mightily to avert war; now she must

---

[1] AII Ristić 18/31, Prince of Serbia to Grand Vizir, June 10/22, copy.

act in self-defense. Brother Serbs in neighboring Turkish provinces awaited deliverance, but, and this was to reassure Europe, this would not be a revolutionary war.[2] Montenegro's war proclamation, on the other hand, called forthrightly for the liberation and unification of the Serbian people.[3]

As Serbian and Montenegrin troops crossed the Turkish frontiers, General Cherniaev issued a manifesto (July 2) exhorting the Balkan peoples to rise against Islam: "We are fighting . . . for the holy cause of Slavdom, . . . for freedom . . . , for the Orthodox cross. . . . Long live the unity of the Balkan peoples!"[4] Expecting a general Bulgarian insurrection and support from the Russian public, Cherniaev hoped to reach Sofia, liberate Bulgaria, and perhaps even solve the Eastern Question.[5]

Prince Milan, who became a close friend of the conservative General Cherniaev, urged the Serbian states to unite their forces and crush Turkey,[6] but not all Serbian leaders were so optimistic or ambitious. Ristić did not expect to defeat the Porte or fight a lengthy war. Rejecting the concept of *fare da se*, Ristić wished Serbia to act as a Slav vanguard to lead Russia into the war. But his policy was more audacious than Cavour's. Unallied with Russia, he relied more heavily upon Serbian nationalism than had the Piedmontese statesmen upon the Italian National Society.[7] Nor did he renounce the weapons of diplo-

[2] Matija Ban, Milan's chief propagandist, later asserted Serbia had not sought to destroy the Ottoman Empire's integrity but merely to defend itself and improve the Christians' status. Turkey had provoked the war by concentrating troops along the frontier and violating Serbian territory. Surrounded for a year by "a circle of fire," its agriculture and trade ruined, Serbia, claimed Ban, had had no choice but to respond finally to its brothers' cries of distress. See AII, Ban 4/9, "Mémoire adressé à la conférence de Constantinople." Since the Belgrade government had planned a war of aggression, Ban's arguments are unconvincing.

[3] For the texts of the war proclamations see H. Schulthess, *Europäischer Geschichtskalender 1876* (Nördlingen, 1877), p. 508.

[4] Schulthess, *Europäischer*, p. 510.

[5] ROBibSS, f. Aksakova, no. 387, Cherniaev to Aksakov, Sept. 24/Oct. 6, 1876.

[6] AII, Ristić 18/752, Milan to Ristić and Cherniaev, July 2/14. The intimate relationship between Cherniaev and Prince Milan is reflected in their extensive correspondence during and after the campaign. See "Pis'ma vlastitelei Serbii . . . ," in RA (1914), no. 1, pp. 25–65, 182–96.

[7] Piročanac (*Beleške*, pp. 4, 5, 68, 69) accused Ristić of involving Serbia recklessly in a hopeless war without considering the Powers' attitudes. Actually, Ristić appears to have weighed the alternatives carefully. He wrote: "Serbia, if she remained a passive observer of the Slav uprisings around her . . . would lose her position in the east, would renounce her mission and become an object of scorn to her jealous rivals and merit the contempt of the whole Slav world. . . . A great policy cannot be pursued without great risk." Vlada Milana, *1*, 309–12.

macy. Before the first important battle, he suggested that Belgrade was willing to negotiate whenever the Porte desired. Then the Powers, led by Russia, might mediate a settlement beneficial to the Serbs.[8] Subsequently, Ristić described Belgrade's expectations:

Serbia counted most on the participation of her oppressed Slav brethren with whose help she hoped to achieve some successes on the battlefield, then through the diplomatic mediation of the tsarist Russian government obtain confirmation of these results. *But the participation of the Christians, particularly of the Bulgarians, failed in a manner which amazed everyone.*[9]

If Serbia were victorious, Ristić told a French journalist, it might annex Old Serbia and enter a confederation with Montenegro and the insurgent provinces, but it would remain under Turkish suzerainty if the Powers desired.[10]

Ristić's prompt moves to calm Austrian fears revealed a realistic sense of proportion. Serbia, he assured Wrede, wished to maintain friendly relations with Austria-Hungary; no hostile acts against the Monarchy would be permitted.[11] To a Hungarian journalist he denied that Belgrade coveted any Austro-Hungarian territory:

The natural frontiers between Serbia and the neighboring Monarchy are the Danube and the Sava. For us to cross these frontiers would be tantamount to suicide. Before our eyes there is sufficient territory [Old Serbia] for the expansion of our state and to fulfill its civilizing mission to the south and east. [Austria] will have in us a true and satisfied neighbor.

Dependent upon Austrian friendship for its well-being, Serbia would not attempt to unite all Serbian speaking people.[12]

Serbia's declaration of war stirred Bosnia. Under Belgrade's supervision a proclamation of union with Serbia was drawn up, signed by most insurgent leaders[13] and issued on July 2. This revived sagging insurgent

[8] HHSA, Wrede to Andrassy, July 5, no. 104.

[9] Ristić, *1*, 197–98, 208–09.

[10] AII, Ristić 18/170, E. Poirier, "En Serbie," *L'Ordre* (Paris), Aug. 5, 1876. Serbian objectives are outlined in *ibid.*, Ban 11/16, (Ban) to Farley, Aug. 20/Sept. 1. In concealed form, this was the program of Greater Serbia.

[11] HHSA, Wrede to Andrassy, July 1, no. 101.

[12] *Moskovskie Vedomosti*, July 2/14, no. 166, interview with the editor of *Budapester Korrespondenz*; *ibid.*, July 8/20, no. 172, Ristić's interview with a correspondent of *Wiener Presse*.

[13] There was some opposition to such a union, especially by Vaso Pelagić, who considered annexation to Serbia premature. He advocated Bosnian independence

morale and undermined Petar Karadjordjević's position. On July 27, Serbia announced "the formal unification of Bosnia with Serbia."

Belgrade's object was to intensify the insurrection, and it had sent the Serbian forces at the Drina River, under Alimpić, into Bosnia, but the offensive was too feeble and too poorly co-ordinated with the insurrection to succeed. Alimpić had warned Prince Milan on June 27: "Bosnia is our *primary* objective. We should strike as powerfully as possible into Bosnia to achieve real success there. . . . Instead the weakest army has been sent to the Drina." Crossing the Drina (July 3), Alimpić, joined by some 5,000 Bosnians, attacked Bjelina on the road to Sarajevo, but the Serbian militia was no match for the Turks, whose strength Belgrade had underestimated. The utter failure of Alimpić's offensive seriously undermined the Bosnian insurrection.[14]

Belgrade then sent Colonel Mileta Despotović to unify and direct the disparate Bosnian bands.[15] Arriving early in August at insurgent headquarters, Despotović at first won wide support. Later, obsessed like Cherniaev with his own image, he began to consider himself *le prince régnant* of Bosnia.[16] Adopting the techniques of a Russian autocrat, he reduced the movement to a mere adjunct of the Serbian war effort and lost the backing of the Bosnian people.[17]

Vienna, determined to prevent Serbia's annexation of Bosnia, instructed its officials in Dalmatia to inform the Bosnian population that "we will not permit such a unification." The Austrian consul in Sarajevo was to foster protests against a Bosnian union with Serbia. But little support for the Monarchy developed even among the Catholic minority. Prodded by Austrian agents, a few Orthodox refugees petitioned Franz Josef to occupy Bosnia, but among the insurgents there were no avowed adherents of an Austrian occupation. And the failure

---

and a "brotherly and free alliance with Serbia." Pelagić, *Istorija Bosanskog ustanka*, pp. 187–88, cited by Čubrilović, *Bosanski*, pp. 207–08. The proannexation element, led by Vaso Vidović, obtained the support of the vast majority of the chiefs and the Bosnian populace. *Ibid.*, pp. 208–09; Ekmečić, *Ustanak*, pp. 232–33.

[14] Alimpić, *Život*, pp. 551–70; AII, Ristić 18/515, Vidović to Ristić, July 4/16; Ekmečić, *Ustanak*, pp. 256–58.

[15] Despotović, born in Serbia, served in the Russian army, rising to the rank of colonel. Already retired from Russian service at the outbreak of the Serbo-Turkish War, he re-entered the Serbian army. His Pan-Slav views are revealed in letters to Kartsov and Ristić. AII, Ristic 18/508, Despotović to Ristić, June 30, Čubrilović, *Bosanski ustanak*, p. 210; Ekmečić, *Ustanak*, pp. 236–38.

[16] A. Evans, *Illyrian Letters* (London, 1878), pp. 21–22.

[17] Ekmečić, *Ustanak*, pp. 236–41.

of Alimpić's offensive obviated any further Austrian action for the time being.[18]

Andrassy worried less about Montenegro.[19] Although Prince Nikola promptly advanced into Hercegovina with his main forces and was elected prince by the insurgent chiefs, he declared that he would accept this honor, and Hercegovina's union with Montenegro, only if the Powers approved. His army, swelled by eager Hercegovinian battalions, advanced almost to Mostar, ostensibly "to join up with the Serbian army." But instead of launching a co-ordinated attack upon Sjenica to sever the insurgent provinces from the rest of the Ottoman Empire, as Belgrade desired, Nikola's army assaulted blockhouses near Podgorica and repelled minor Turkish attacks.[20]

Vienna, promising financial and diplomatic support and eventual territorial concessions to Cetinje, prohibited further Montenegrin advances in Hercegovina. Lieutenant Colonel Thömmel was sent to warn Prince Nikola to take no action contrary to Austrian interests. "As victor or vanquished," Andrassy wrote Baron Rodich, "Nikola will need our support." [21] Thömmel informed the prince that in no case would Serbia acquire Bosnia, but by co-operating with Vienna, Nikola could obtain a slice of Hercegovina. On July 15, Nikola declared he would act *de concert* with Austria, and Thömmel predicted that he would rely upon Austria, not Serbia: "The alliance with Serbia does not appear to be very firm and it will not be difficult to paralyze it. . . . The prince thinks Russia would not hinder us from taking Bosnia, especially if we gave a slice each to Serbia and Montenegro." Andrassy pledged to close the ports of Kotor and Klek to Turkish shipping, pay Nikola a yearly subsidy, and support him diplomatically in case of defeat. In return the prince promised to follow Vienna's instructions. Thömmel telegraphed triumphantly, "Any [Montenegrin] intention of direct co-operation with Serbia in the direction of Sjenica probably [has been] definitely abandoned." [22] Exploiting Montenegro's economic weakness, Andrassy prevented the Serbian states from linking forces or annexing the insurgent provinces.

---

[18] *Ibid.*, pp. 245–47; Djordjević, *Crna Gora*, p. 391.

[19] See Prince Nikola's letter to Emperor Franz Josef quoted by J. Ćetković, *Ujedinitelji Crne Gore i Srbije* (Dubrovnik, 1940), p. 34.

[20] Djordjević, *Crna Gora*, pp. 387–93. See "Prepiske," *Zapisi*, 5 (Dec. 1929), 363–65.

[21] Actenstücke, *1*, 342.

[22] Djordjević, *Crna Gora*, pp. 392–95.

The Serbian July offensive was doomed when the general Balkan insurrection, anticipated in Belgrade, failed to develop. Assisted by about 1,500 Bulgarians from Serbia, Cherniaev's main forces captured Babina Glava inside Bulgaria, but the Bulgarian insurrection failed to revive.[23] The initial skirmishes with the Turks revealed to Cherniaev how imperfect an instrument was his militia army.[24] News of the Timok army's defeat at Veliki Izvor on July 18 caused Cherniaev to abandon his offensive and retire ingloriously into Serbia. After only two weeks of war, his forward strategy was a failure.[25] The Serbs, considering their inexperience in war, had performed satisfactorily under fire and the artillery had revealed excellent qualities. Nor does lack of Serbian patriotism account for the retreat. In both urban and rural areas Serbian civilians displayed admirable unity and self-sacrifice.[26] Serbia's resources were simply inadequate for offensive warfare.

The Russian government, displeased at the outbreak of war, would not permit pro-Slav opinion to force it into the conflict. St. Petersburg refused official aid to the Serbian states and adopted a policy of nonintervention. The emperor, instructing the Third Section to recall Cherniaev,[27] stated that since Serbia had disregarded his advice, Russia could not be blamed for abandoning it to its fate.[28] War Minister Miliutin, though asserting that Russia was fully ready to fight, opposed war vigorously. "It is my conviction that war for us would be a terrible misfortune. . . . Our diplomacy is so conducted that in case

[23] Cherniaev had authorized V. S. Ionin and P. Enchev to organize Bulgarian detachments in eastern Serbia to assist his offensive. OSVOb., *1*, 248, "Polnomochie," June 20/July 2. On the strength of Bulgarian volunteers and insurgents at this time see *ibid.*, pp. 268–70.

[24] AII, Ban 11/51, "Srpsko-turski rat."

[25] Vlada Milana, *1*, 319–20. Rupp (*A Wavering Friendship*, pp. 129–30), states incorrectly that Cherniaev captured Niš on July 4 with the Turks withdrawing beyond the city.

[26] Confirming the Serbs' *élan patriotique*, Kartsov noted the abundance of voluntary gifts to the government and that of a population of about 1,200,000 almost 220,000 men were in the army. The whole question for the Serbs, he wrote, was money, rifles, and ammunition. Kartsov to Gorchakov, Kartsov to Ignat'ev, July 8/20, OSVOb., *1*, nos. 155, 156, pp. 285–91.

[27] Kartsov showed Wrede a "secret" document signed by General Potapov to this effect. HHSA, Wrede to Andrassy, July 10, no. 107.

[28] The tsar's written comments on intercepted letters during July and August reveal his opposition to aiding the Serbian states. He agreed with the author of a letter to A. A. Kraevskii of *Golos* who stated that as far as the government was concerned, the Turks could crush the insurrection. Snytko, "Iz istorii," pp. 79–80.

of war we inevitably would be isolated." [29] The emperor and leading Russian diplomats, fearful of arousing a European coalition, favored nonintervention. Even before Serbia's weakness became apparent, the Russian government desired a European conference to end the fighting and work out peace terms. Russian envoys abroad were instructed to sound out the other Powers.[30]

The Serbo-Turkish War severely tested the Dreikaiserbund. For months Russia and Austria had quarreled over autonomy for Bosnia and Hercegovina and Montenegro's territorial gains. Half-measures, wrote Gorchakov, would no longer suffice. Frank Austro-Russian discussions, replied Andrassy, might produce agreement. Their parley at Reichstadt on July 8, vital for Russia's future relations with the South Slavs, was the result.[31]

At Reichstadt, important oral agreements were reached on various possible outcomes of the Serbo-Turkish conflict. Gorchakov and Andrassy reaffirmed publicly their policy of nonintervention. In secret they agreed that their governments would regulate any postwar settlement. If the Serbian states triumphed, they would be permitted significant territorial increases; if the Turks won, the two Powers, intervening to prevent massacres of Christians, would insist upon the territorial *status quo ante* for Serbia and Montenegro. Turkish fortresses were not to be re-established on Serbian soil. Montenegro would maintain her independence, but Serbia, while retaining her autonomy, would remain a tributary vassal to Turkey. Should either side gain an overwhelming victory, the two Powers would conclude another agreement before acting.

Written interpretations of the Reichstadt agreements differed over the disposition of Turkish territory if the Slavs triumphed. According to the Russian version, Austria would obtain only "Turkish Croatia" and some parts of Bosnia contiguous to Austria. Belgrade would acquire "some parts of Old Serbia and Bosnia"; Montenegro would be granted all of Hercegovina and an Adriatic seaport. Andrassy's draft, however, reserved to the Monarchy *all* of Bosnia and Hercegovina

[29] Miliutin, *Dnevnik, 2,* 51–54, 64–65.

[30] Tiutin, p. 21.

[31] HHSA, Andrassy to Novikov, July 7. For the details and European implications of Reichstadt see G. Rupp, "The Reichstadt Agreement," *American Historical Review, 30* (April 1925), 503–10, and Rupp, *A Wavering Friendship,* pp. 111–51; Sumner, *Russia,* pp. 172–76. For an Austrian interpretation see Wertheimer, *Graf Julius Andrassy, 2,* 296–330.

except small portions reserved for the Serbian states. Serbia could expect a slice of Bosnia along the Drina but not enough to threaten Dalmatia. Montenegro might obtain adjacent portions of Hercegovina and the port of Spič. The Serbian states could partition the tongue of land lying between them (the "Enclave") and establish a common frontier on the Lim River.[32] Thus the Russian version specified more for Montenegro and far less for the Monarchy than Andrassy's.

Further interpretations of the oral agreements followed. Gorchakov's *pro memoria* (July 10) stipulated a benevolent neutrality toward the Serbs not excluding unofficial Russian aid. Austro-Russian intervention might be required in case of a stalemate or a decisive military victory by either side. If the Christians won, continued Gorchakov, "since Austria-Hungary excludes a large Slav state and Russia a Greek empire, it would seem that the most rational solution would be the creation of little independent states, each in the territorial bounds where history has placed it, and connected with a federal tie."[33] Andrassy's instructions to Thömmel (July 27) reveal how much Gorchakov's plan deviated from Austrian designs. Austria, anxious to maintain the *status quo* in European Turkey as far as possible, would await the outcome of the war. If Turkey won, the Powers' intervention would prevent loss of territory by the defeated Serbian states. Should Serbia and Montenegro be victorious, "we must prevent them at any cost from becoming masters of Bosnia and Hercegovina." Thus they might obtain only portions of the insurgent provinces not required for Austrian security. The Monarchy would pursue this course even if it caused an open breach with Russia.[34]

The Reichstadt discussions affected deeply the course of the Serbian national movement. Reaffirmation of nonintervention allowed the Serbo-Turkish War to be fought to a decision without much fear or hope of unilateral Austrian or Russian interference. St. Petersburg, renouncing support for a large Slav state, abandoned without apparent regret an opportunity to become the Napoleon III for a Slav Piedmont.

---

[32] For the Austrian version see A. Pribram, *The Secret Treaties of Austria-Hungary* (Cambridge, Mass., 1920), *2*, 188–90 and Sumner, *Russia*, pp. 584–85. The Russian version is in *Krasnyi Arkhiv, 1*, 36–38, and Sumner, pp. 586–87.

For the rest of 1876, Gorchakov and Andrassy disputed whether Hercegovina had been included in the Austrian sphere. Rupp, *A Wavering Friendship*, pp. 139–44; Harris, *History*, pp. 437–38.

[33] KA, *1*, 40–42; Sumner, *Russia*, pp. 587–88.

[34] Ekmečić, pp. 252–53.

Opposing war, Gorchakov could be well satisfied with his version of Reichstadt. Apparently, he had yielded wholly neither to Andrassy nor the Pan-Slavs. He returned to Russia convinced he had preserved the Dreikaiserbund and obtained all of Hercegovina for his protégé, Montenegro, and parts of Old Serbia for Serbia. Concealing Reichstadt's secret clauses from Ignat'ev, the chancellor, lest Belgrade draw incorrect conclusions, hastened to inform Protić (July 22): "I tell you that you will not get Bosnia no matter what you do, since I must admit to you that Count Andrassy at the Reichstadt meeting declared that the interests of the Austrian monarchy will not permit the existence of a powerful Serbia." If Serbia triumphed, added Gorchakov ten days later, it might obtain a rounding of its frontiers, but not Bosnia.[35] For the sake of co-operation with Vienna, Russia had made a partial surrender of Slav interests in the Balkans.[36]

The favorable reactions to Reichstadt of Russian Pan-Slavs and the Serbian nationalist press revealed their ignorance of the secret agreements. Rejoicing at the public reaffirmation of nonintervention, Count Ignat'ev predicted that Serbia could achieve its most cherished goal. "If victory is on the side of the Serbs, then a *fait accompli* will occur in their behalf. . . . Andrassy raves when anyone even hints to him of the necessity of the annexation of Bosnia to Serbia." [37] Nonintervention, declared *Istok*, guaranteed a localized war which was precisely what Serbian patriots desired. Serbia needed only the assistance of the Balkan Christians to end Turkish misrule. At Reichstadt, Austria had yielded completely to Russia's wish to end the Christians' unbearable plight. The Serbo-Turkish war would inevitably be followed by an Austro-Russian conflict. "We doubt that the Austrian government will ever decide to annex Bosnia and are convinced that Russia would not allow it anyway." [38] *Zastava* was equally confident that the Serbians would

---

[35] DAS, 29/98-XI, Protić to Ristić, July 21/Aug. 2, telegram. Added Protić, "It is believed in St. Petersburg that we can obtain Novi Pazar and perhaps Niš or Vidin but nothing more."

[36] Tiutin ("Politika," p. 137) provides this Soviet interpretation: "The Reichstadt Agreement was a betrayal by tsarism and the Hapsburg monarchy of the insurgent Bosnians. The Russian and Hungarian governments betrayed precisely those Slav peoples for whose liberation they had supposedly carried out their aggression in the Balkans. As a result of this deal for the division of the Balkans, Russian tsarism counted on strengthening its position in the approaches to the Straits."

[37] Kartsov, RS, 134, 74–75.

[38] *Istok*, June 30/July 12, July 2/14 and 18/30, nos. 70, 71, 78. *Istok* had now attained the unprecented total for a Serbian newspaper of 2,000 subscribers. AII, Ristić, Mijatović to [Ristić?], July 1/13, 1876.

win and that the diplomats would bow to *faits accomplis*. If Austria did not interfere with the natural process of Serbia's triumphs, the resulting greater Serbia would not threaten the Monarchy's legitimate interests.[39] Profound disillusionment awaited these enthusiastic advocates of Serbian unity.

Much would depend upon the military showing of the Serbian states, but the guidelines of their future had been laid at Reichstadt. Eventually Gorchakov would have to admit publicly that he had chosen Vienna instead of Belgrade. Because of the vociferous and influential pro-Slav element in Russia, this admission would cause him genuine agony.

Some Pan-Slav officials, on the other hand, desired immediate Russian intervention in behalf of the Serbian states. Although convinced that a volunteer movement would involve Russia in war eventually, Ignat'ev in Constantinople urged his government to dispatch a Russian army of 200,000 to aid Serbia, arguing that Turkey would be caught unawares and quickly defeated.[40] To Belgrade's delight he kept it informed of Turkish troop dispositions.[41] Younger members of Ignat'ev's embassy staff, fretting at St. Petersburg's passivity, greeted Cherniaev's early "victories" enthusiastically and favored direct Russian intervention. Wrote A. I. Nelidov, "We openly supported the Serbian cause."[42]

Unofficial Russia, unrestrained by diplomatic realities, responded sympathetically to the Serbian states' declarations of war. Ivan Aksakov, leader of the Pan-Slavs, wrote happily to Prince V. A. Cherkasskii, "Everything depends now upon the successes of Cherniaev . . . but in any case it appears we will not avoid war next year either in the event of victory or defeat for Serbia."[43] Cherkasskii, deploring Russia's nonintervention and alignment with the Dreikaiserbund, replied, "I cannot look at our . . . useless and stupid policy without deep indignation."[44] Typical of the Pan-Slav view of conflict as a crusade against Islam was the prediction of A. A. Kireev: "Either he [Cherniaev] will defeat the Turks or lay down his life for the just Slav cause."[45]

[39] *Zastava*, June 22/July 4, July 7/19, 9/21 and 14/26, nos. 92, 101, 102, 105. HHSA, Langenau to Andrassy, July 7/19, Privatschreiben.
[40] Ignat'ev, IV, *136* (April 1914), p. 56; Nelidov, "Souvenirs" (May 1915), p. 319.
[41] Grujic, *3*, 185–87.
[42] Nelidov, pp. 334–36.
[43] Aksakov to Cherkasskii, June 24/July 6, *Slavianskii sbornik*, pp. 148–49.
[44] ROBibSS, f. Aksakova, no. 386, Cherkasskii to Aksakov, July 8/20.
[45] ROBibLen, Dnevnik Kireeva, *6*, 124, June 22/July 4.

The Russian press mostly agreed that the Serbian war had been justified by Turkish provocations and England's rejection of the Berlin Memorandum. Since European diplomacy could not improve the Christians' status, declared Professor D. Ilovaiskii, the South Slavs must secure their rights in a desperate struggle.[46] Serbia is merely guarding its frontiers and protecting its trade, stated *Novoe Vremia*, and the South Slavs are fighting to guarantee human rights and defend civilization and Orthodoxy.[47] Only semi-official *Golos* questioned Serbia's wisdom in declaring war. "The Serbian government began military operations precisely when the Porte was most conciliatory. This gives the enemies of Serbia a pretext to call her a disturber of the peace. . . . Our government cannot approve of the breach of the peace by Serbia."[48] Under public pressure even *Golos* soon agreed that the Serbian states, after exhausting diplomatic means, had been compelled to take up arms to defend their rights.[49]

The press, because of its optimistic assessment of the Serbs' chances, at first supported official nonintervention. Let events take their course, *Russkii Mir* admonished the Powers. "A great task now devolves upon the little Serbian principality but one not beyond the Serbs' profound courage and determination to overthrow the Moslem yoke or die."[50] *Moskovskie Vedomosti*, accusing England and Austria of aiding the Turks, agreed that Russia could not participate, but advocated unofficial assistance to the Serbs.[51] Russia would not intervene now, but "it still has the power to place its sword, so to speak, on the threshold of the battlefield and declare it will not permit the participation of any other power hostile to the Slavs." Meanwhile Russian society had a perfect right to act.[52] Only if defeat threatens the Serbian states, declared *Russkoe Obozrenie*, will Russia join the conflict. "War in behalf of the Slavs," warned *Sankt Peterburgskie Vedomosti*, "will always be the most popular, national war."[53]

Some nationalist newspapers urged unofficial Russian aid to hasten a Slav victory. Declared one, "We will help our oppressed brethren

[46] *Russkii Mir*, June 27/July 9, no. 175, letter of July 5.
[47] *Novoe Vremia*, June 28/July 10, cited in Miroshnichenko, "Otnoshenie," 2, 52.
[48] *Golos*, June 23/July 5, no. 172.
[49] *Ibid.*, July 24/Aug. 5 and Aug. 11/23, nos. 203–20.
[50] *Russkii Mir*, June 20/July 2, no. 168.
[51] *Moskovskie Vedomosti*, July 3/15, no. 167.
[52] *Sankt Peterburgskie Vedomosti*, July 3/15, no. 181.
[53] Nikitin, "Russkoe obshchestvo," p. 975.

with everything possible because this is not merely in our interests but is our duty . . . because on the side of the Slavs is historic truth and legality." [54] And *Novoe Vremia* issued a significant appeal to the Russian public:

> Upon Russian society there lies a sacred obligation to assist with all its means, principally with money, these heroic fighters. The Serbian loan must be subscribed by our resources so that in the history of this struggle the Russian name will play the proper part even if Russia itself does not take a more active part in it. . . . Nothing can prevent noble sacrifices on the part of society itself if only it can be profoundly inspired to help the fighters for freedom. We helped Garibaldi and the Italians; can we not even help the Slavs free themselves from slavery? I am convinced that Serbia will not be allowed to perish even if Turkey should turn out to be the victor.[55]

In July, neither Russian press nor public anticipated Serbia's defeat. Exaggerated reports from Cherniaev's headquarters suggested a great Slav triumph was imminent. During the first week of war, claimed *Novoe Vremia*, Cherniaev had won major victories and the Bulgarians were rising *en masse;* if the Turks were sensible, they would retreat to Adrianople.[56] On July 15, several St. Petersburg newspapers placed Cherniaev near Niš "on the road to Constantinople." Though skeptical of this, *Golos* predicted the Slavs might win after a difficult struggle.[57]

The press debated solutions to the Eastern Question. Conservative organs, formerly advocates of Russia's seizure of the Straits and hegemony in the Balkans, temporarily adopted the language of national liberation. Declared *Grazhdanin*, "Russia will not conquer the East but will liberate it . . . from the yoke of Asiatic despotism." The Eastern Question would be solved in accordance with Russia's interests which coincided with those of the South Slavs. "On the day when the Porte perishes, Russia will leave the Slavs to decide their own fate without interfering in their internal affairs." [58] Most conservative newspapers hinted that Bosnia and Hercegovina might go to the Dual Monarchy in return for Russian occupation of Bulgaria,[59] but *Russkii Mir* insisted they be given to the Serbian states:

---

[54] *Sankt Peterburgskie Vedomosti*, June 23/July 5, no. 175.

[55] *Novoe Vremia*, June 27/July 9, no. 117 in AII, Ristić 18/364. Sections of this article were underlined in red, presumably by Ristić, who considered this indication of unofficial Russian support for Serbia to be very significant.

[56] *Ibid.*   [57] *Golos*, July 4/16, 5/17, and 14/26, nos. 183, 184, 193.

[58] Miroshnichenko, "Otnoshenie," 2, 73–75.   [59] *Ibid.*, p. 163.

Our diplomacy must seek merely to add Greece and Rumania to the cause of driving out Turkish rule, undertaken by Serbia, and practically the whole Eastern Question will be solved without any serious sacrifices by us [Russia]. We must follow in Turkey only one great objective with all our strength: the complete liberation of the rayahs by the annexation of Bosnia to Serbia and Hercegovina to Montenegro, Thessaly and Epirus to Greece and the formation of a separate Bulgarian state. . . . The Magyars can in any case remain calm: Bosnia will go to no one else except Serbia.[60]

Russia's future lies in the south, declared *Novoe Vremia;* only when Constantinople is in Slav (presumably Russian!) hands, could Russia become a true world power. After Turkey's defeat, a great Slav federation might be established. Liberal *Nedelia,* considering the South Slav cause the most progressive national movement of its generation, advocated unification of the freed Slavs.[61]

Tied to official apron strings, *Golos* sought vainly to moderate this Pan-Slav fervor. It admitted that South Slav liberation was a progressive movement deserving Russian society's sympathy, but it favored a moderate solution of the Eastern Question without significant territorial gains for the Serbian states. Regardless of the war's outcome, *Golos* would support their independence. But because of the Powers' opposition, Belgrade should not expect to win Bosnia, and Montenegro's claims in Hercegovina might have to be reduced. Russia itself sought no territory or advantage, claimed *Golos.*[62]

Serbian Reverses and Unofficial Russian Assistance

A month after launching a war to liberate and unite the Serbs of Turkey, Serbia appeared on the verge of defeat, while Montenegro gained victories. As the Serbian offensives failed, the armies retreated into Serbia. Belgrade's urgent pleas to Montenegro to relieve Turkish pressure and occupy the territory between their armies were ignored by Prince Nikola, who gave little help to the Serbs. General Cherniaev, reporting that his militia was fleeing the battlefield, warned Belgrade

---

[60] *Russkii Mir,* July 3/15, no. 181.

[61] Miroshnichenko, "Otnoshenie" 2, 74–79. Declared *Novoe Vremia,* Sept. 12/24, "The Slavs must unite like the Germans—no longer will there be Serbs, Bulgarians, Montenegrins, or Hercegovinians." Whether Russia would play Prussia's role in the process of unification was not stated, but both liberals and conservatives clearly expected Russia to take a vital part in fostering Slav unity.

[62] *Golos,* June 2/14, July 10/22 and 16/28, July 29/Aug. 10, Aug. 2/14 and 5/17, 1876.

that unless peace were concluded promptly, the Turks would invade Serbia and massacre its inhabitants.[63]

Gloomy reports from the front transformed Prince Milan's initial optimism into fear and despair. Without significant aid from a Bulgarian insurrection or from Montenegro, the war was becoming unbearable for Serbia. On July 24, Milan asked his government to consider an appeal to the Powers for an armistice. But the cabinet, citing Count Ignat'ev's assurances of Russian diplomatic or military aid if Serbia resisted another two months, urged continuation of hostilities in the form of a co-ordinated Serbo-Montenegrin offensive in the west and holding operations in the east. Metropolitan Mihailo should go to Russia to secure a government loan and volunteers. Were peace concluded now, argued Ristić and Grujić, the Porte would demand removal of the Obrenović dynasty. Much alarmed, Milan bowed to their arguments and abandoned thoughts of peace. But the military situation continued to deteriorate. Early in August, the Turks captured Zaječar and Knjaževac and occupied most of eastern Serbia. Undismayed, Ristić claimed that the withdrawal was deliberate, and declared that his government would resist to the end.[64]

While the Serbian press asserted bravely that the army had not yet been defeated and that Russian assistance was imminent,[65] there was public discouragement over military reverses and Russia's failure to intervene. Serbia had intended a political demonstration, reported Kartsov, not to engage in a grueling war. "Serbia was like a duelist who had informed the police about the duel but arrived at the dueling ground to discover with horror that the police were not coming." [66] Protić expressed the disillusionment of many Serbs when he wrote Ristić from St. Petersburg: "We have been completely deceived by the Bulgarians and left entirely to our own fate by Russia." A few days later he recommended concluding a separate peace.

When we are without allies and lacking everything, when we are betrayed by the miserable Bulgarians . . . to work for a separate peace is a matter of patriotism. . . . The aim of some Bulgarians and Russians was merely to

[63] AII, Ban 11/51; Grujić, *3*, 193–95; Piročanac, *Beleške*, p. 63; *Vlada Milana, 1*, 319–20, 324; Vuksan, *Pregled*, p. 20.

[64] Ristić, *1*, 125–218. But Ban claimed that Lješanin had received orders to hold Zaječar "à outrance." AII, Ban 11/51; Grujić, *3*, 193–98.

[65] *Istok*, Aug. 1/13, 6/18, 12/24, nos. 83, 85, 87; *Zastava*, July 30/Aug. 11, no. 114.

[66] Kartsov, RS, *134*, 308.

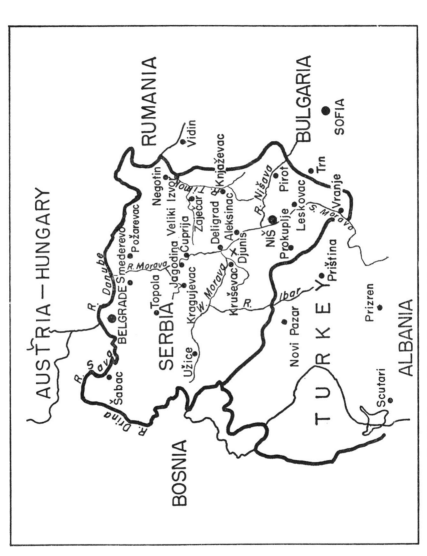

Serbia (heavy line indicates Serbian frontiers as of July 1878).

involve us in a war . . . so the Bulgarians could acquire an easy autonomy, and we would have to involve Russia to retain what we have and give the Russians occasion to acquire greater influence for themselves. . . . . Russian diplomacy has been completely discredited here [Russia] and abroad. In our behalf the court will not declare war even if all of Serbia should become a wasteland. Consequently, do not be carried away by the loud sympathies and monetary sacrifices of the Russian people.

Gorchakov and the tsar, warned Protić, merely wish to use Serbia for selfish purposes.[67]

Meanwhile, dramatic newspaper accounts of the war, sent from Cherniaev's headquarters, aroused the sympathies of the Russian public.[68] "If the Serbs are not strong enough to free their brethren," threatened *Russkii Mir*, "the task by the nature of things is shifted into stronger hands." Russia should prepare itself for action:

The approaching intervention in the Serbo-Turkish war will be diplomatic in character only if Serbia is successful militarily. The defeat of Serbian arms would bring an immediate intervention of another [military] type. . . . If a Russian army corps entered Bulgaria now, all of Europe would breathe easier [*sic!*] . . . No one in the entire Christian world would oppose the unanimous outburst of a great people [Russians], wishing at any cost to save its brethren from destruction.[69]

Even *Golos*, which reacted to Serbian reverses by urging European diplomatic intervention, warned, "Russia will never permit the destruction of Serbia whose status can be altered only with the Powers' permission." [70] Protić had been overly pessimistic!

The pro-Slav movement in Russia reached its climax that summer. "It seized hold of all layers of society," wrote Professor A. D. Gradovskii, "and thrust all other interests into the background." [71] *Golos* noted that even the children were playing a game called "the Eastern Question," and all wished to be Cherniaev.[72] "Such a general popular [*vsenarodnoe*] movement has scarcely been seen before in the history

[67] AII, Ristić 26/715, Protić to Ristić, July 21/Aug. 2; 26/716, July 25/Aug. 6.
[68] *Russkii Mir*, nos. 206–08.   [69] *Ibid.*, Aug. 13/25, no. 222.
[70] *Golos*, Aug. 20/Sept. 1. See also issues of July 23/Aug. 4, July 25/Aug. 6, July 31/Aug. 12, Aug. 4/16, 8/20, 1876.
[71] A. D. Gradovskii, *Sobranie sochinenii*, 6 (St. Petersburg 1901), 227. Reported *Novoe Vremia*, July 19: "All the attention of our society has been attracted by the Hercegovinians, Montenegrins, Serbs, and Bulgarians." Cited in Miroshnichenko, "Otnoshenie," 2, 56–59.
[72] *Golos*, July 11/23, no. 190.

of the Russian people," asserted Prince A. I. Vasil'chikov.[73] Tsarist police reports confirm the widespread nature of pro-Slav enthusiasm in the provinces.[74] The sympathy of the Russian people for the embattled Slavs was general, agreed General A. L. Potapov.[75] A letter intercepted by the police revealed how bellicose some Russians had become: "A declaration of war [by Russia] is expected here any day. You cannot imagine what enthusiasm has seized everyone here. . . . Wherever one goes, they talk only of the poor Slavs." [76]

Skeptics and opponents of aid to the South Slavs were drowned out by the clamor. No educated person, declared an anonymous letter to *Golos,* believes the protestations of mass sympathy for the Slavs which fill the Russian press. "Ask this multimillion mass: what are the Slavs? All will stare goggle-eyed. . . . The newspapers can speak in the name of a certain social circle, but to refer to the 'people' [*narod*] they cannot." [77] Ambassador Novikov called the Slav struggle "a filthy fight." "I shall cry out to all of Russia that she is helping the evil passions of revolutionaries." He rejoiced at each Serbian defeat, but Russia was deaf to his cries.[78] Ambassador P. A. Shuvalov in England and high police officials shared Novikov's fear of revolution.[79]

[73] *Pervye 15 let,* pp. 379–80. Wrote Meshcherskii in *Moi vospominaniia* (St. Petersburg, 1898), *2,* 281, "At the end of the summer in Russia everything else was put aside and only the Slav question occupied all minds to the point where there was no corner of Russia in which the Slav question did not burn."

The death of N. A. Kireev (July 18), writes Devollan, was the spark which awakened Russian society. G. Devollan, "Nedavniaia starina," RA (1879), no. 7, pp. 340–41.

[74] In Simbirsk province, reported an amazed police official in August, enthusiasm for the Slavs was great among all social groups except merchants. Commoners could frequently be overheard expressing hatred toward the Turks. From Riazan' came the report that "among all classes of the population of the province is manifested a hot sympathy for the Slav cause. . . ." In Pskov province peasants and townspeople were responding with warm sympathy to the Slav cause. OSVOb., *1,* nos. 185, 187, 242, 243, pp. 316, 317, 370, 371.

[75] *Ibid.,* pp. 316–17, A. L. Potapov to A. B. Lobanov-Rostovskii, deputy minister of internal affairs, July 31/Aug. 12.

[76] *Ibid.,* p. 365, letter of Aug. 29/Sept. 10 from Moscow province.

[77] *Ibid.,* p. 328, intercepted letter of Aug. 5/17 to A. A. Kraevskii. The tsar commented, "Much truth in this." Available evidence suggests that information about the South Slavs definitely reached the masses and aroused intense interest and sympathy among them.

[78] Jelavich, *Russia in the East,* pp. 163–64, A. Krupenskii to Giers, July 28/Aug. 9.

[79] A. Porokhovshchikov, "Zapiski starozhila," IV, 67 (1897), 10. Timashev, the minister of internal affairs, who considered the Slav movement childish, was annoyed that it throve despite his censors' efforts. General Mezentsov told

Pro-Slav enthusiasm was fostered and led primarily by the Slav committees of Moscow and St. Petersburg.[80] They provided significant financial, medical, and military aid to the Serbian cause. Hitherto small and conservative organizations, their membership now included liberals such as A. A. Kraevskii, G. Devollan, and A. D. Gradovskii, despite protests from old-guard Slavophiles.[81]

Ivan Aksakov, chairman of the Moscow Committee, was the unquestioned leader of the Slav movement throughout the war. More dynamic than any of the St. Petersburg Pan-Slavs, he became the inspiration and embodiment of the movement.[82] It was Aksakov who had encouraged Cherniaev to go to Serbia; now he directed the collection of contributions and recruitment of volunteers. Aware of the inadequate organization and resources of the committees, Aksakov saw them merely as intermediaries between the Russian public, the government, and the South Slavs. He denied that the committees could direct the war against the Turks, though he rejoiced at the unprecedented public agitation. Aksakov explained to Cherniaev, "By sending you to Serbia and later sending volunteers, I had it in mind to cause *the official participation of Russia* and never believed in the possibility of having the committees alone solve the matter." [83]

Aksakov attempted to avoid personal disputes between adherents of a particular South Slav country, but nonetheless he clashed repeatedly

---

Porokhovshchikov in September that the conservatives' plan to wreck the Slav movement was to proclaim Cherniaev a traitor and expel Aksakov from Russia. See also Meshcherskii, *Moi vospominaniia, 2,* 284; Nikitin, "Russkoe obshchestvo," p. 1017.

[80] For the most authoritiative analysis of their role see Nikitin, *Slavianskie komitety,* pp. 271–342.

[81] ROBibLen, Dnevnik Kireeva, *6,* 125; Miroshnichenko, "Otnoshenie," *2,* 62–65; Nikitin, *Slavianskie komitety,* p. 311.

[82] Meshcherskii (*Moi vospominaniia, 2,* 81) called him "a virtual popular dictator" with tremendous public support, but this represents one of his typical exaggerations.

[83] GIM, Aksakov to Cherniaev, Sept. 7/19, Nov. 1/13. In a letter to K. P. Pobedonostsev, Aksakov emphasized the need for the Russian government to assist Serbia and the Russian volunteers: "Now for Serbia, the Serbian government and the Russians fighting there money is needed most of all, but money in amounts exceeding the resources of all the committees and commissions for collection established in almost all the cities of Russia. Millions are required. . . . The Serbian cause has become the Russian cause, Russian blood is flowing, Russians are fighting and cannot lay down their arms without ruining Russian honor, until they have obtained something for Serbia." "Pis'ma I. S. Aksakova k K.P. Pobedonostsevu," RA (1907), no. 3, pp. 165–66, Aug. 6/18, 1876.

with Cherniaev and Fadeev, who set narrower goals for the pro-Slav movement. In vain he warned Cherniaev not to adopt Serbian views, especially in regard to Bulgaria. "You are a Russian and we Russians must stand above Bulgarians and Serbs and adopt a broader view. For Russia, Bulgarians and their independence is no less dear than the Serbs and their independence." [84] Cherniaev's *idée fixe* was that his Serbian army, supported by unofficial Russia, could solve the Eastern Question without involving the Russian government. Aksakov attacked this view:

In the first place, in no case can *Serbia* stand at the head of *Russian* society, and certainly Russian society cannot follow behind Serbia's tail. It appears that even *together* they cannot prevail. The Serbs have not matured enough for that. In no event is Serbia capable of solving the Slav question. She is not in a condition to attain even a national idea because the phrasemakers educated in Paris [the Serbian statesmen] cannot serve as a criterion for the local national political ideal, they cannot go beyond the "greater Serbian idea." In the second place, only Russia can solve the Slav question, not even Russian society . . . but Russia as a whole, as a *state* organism *headed by the government.*

Aksakov believed that only Russian power could liberate the Slav peoples and allow them to develop under its benevolent protection. Cherniaev's dream of leading the way to Constantinople with a Serbian army was nonsense, but Aksakov continued to assist him.[85]

Loyalty to Cherniaev and his volunteers contributed to Aksakov's sharp conflict with General R. A. Fadeev, who proposed in July to divert the efforts of unofficial Russia to the liberation of Bulgaria. Pointing to Serbo-Bulgarian rivalry, Fadeev characterized as fantasy Cherniaev's plan to advance into Bulgaria with a Serbian army. Fadeev sought to tap the resources of Moscow merchants to finance a Bulgarian volunteer army and obtained unofficial support from the tsar and the heir. If this force were supported by Russian society, the government would eventually assist a Bulgarian insurgent movement.[86] Because of their dynastic aims, argued Fadeev, neither Serbia nor Montenegro

---

[84] *Ibid.,* Sept. 7/19.

[85] *Ibid.,* Nov. 1/13. The St. Petersburg Committee likewise backed Cherniaev.

[86] Fadeev claimed the tsar had approved, declaring on July 28, "I expect much from such a manifestation of public activity as long as it can remain *unofficial,* without betraying the government." Fadeev to Aksakov, July 17/29, OSVOb., *1,* 300–02, "Pis'ma Aksakova," RA (1907), no. 3, p. 166, Sept. 20/Oct. 2.

could solve the Slav question. Russia, to achieve its broader objectives in the Balkans and the Straits, should concentrate on Bulgaria. Otherwise, he warned, the Serbs would dominate the Balkans, preventing Russia from solving the Eastern Question in her own interests. Aksakov agreed with most of Fadeev's arguments, but he objected that such a scheme would require long preparation and vast sums which private persons could not provide. Furthermore, Fadeev's primary aim seemed to be to control the entire Bulgarian venture for his personal glory.[87] Rebuffing Fadeev's challenge to his leadership, Aksakov retained control of the Slav movement. The Moscow merchants contributed some 150,000 rubles for a Bulgarian army, but they entrusted its expenditure to a new commission of the Moscow Committee under Aksakov's direction.[88]

The Slav Committees, despite these internal quarrels, helped arrange a substantial Russian loan to Serbia. In June, Protić arrived, seeking assistance for the Serbian war effort, but he could achieve nothing through official channels.[89] Ristić promised, "If a loan is arranged and the rifles from Berlin are received, the most brilliant victory will be achieved over the Turks." Then Metropolitan Mihailo appealed to Aksakov for aid.[90] Aksakov's letters of introduction to the heir and the empress' lady-in-waiting opened the necessary doors to Protić. The government agreed to underwrite a loan to Serbia if it were handled by private banks. After meeting with E. L. Lamanskii, director of the State Bank, eight private Russian bankers consented to arrange a loan. Wrote Aksakov:

The loan, or more accurately subsidy to Serbia from the State Treasury of 4,000,000 rubles, has been approved in principle, but under the greatest

[87] GIM, Aksakov to Cherniaev, Sept. 7/19. Aksakov instead advised Cherniaev to take control of the preparation of Bulgarian cadres himself, "for this affair can be beneficial *to Russia itself* and the interest of Russia takes precedence over everything else, for that which benefits Russia is also beneficial to the Serb, the Bulgarian, and all of Slavdom."

[88] Nikitin, *Slavianskie komitety*, pp. 338–39.

[89] Gorchakov told Protić, "Conduct your affairs as best you can and if you obtain not six but one hundred million rubles, we will be pleased, but the government itself will not give you one penny since you began the war against our advice." ROBibSS, Aksakov Papers, no. 280, Protić to Aksakov, July 7/19.

[90] OSVOb., *1*, 275–76, Mihailo to Aksakov, July 1/13; Protić to Aksakov, July 7/19, ROBiSS, Aksakov Papers, no. 280. "I shall do whatever you say," wrote Protić, "since the quickest financial aid is essential." F. F. Trepov, police chief in St. Petersburg, told Protić, "We will not let you leave without the money; it would be shameful for Russia if that happened."

secrecy and upon condition that it be masked by private banks and persons. The tsar finally waved his hand saying: do whatever you want if only the government is not involved officially.[91]

Serbia's treasury was empty. The cabinet decided to accept the Russian terms, although they were not especially generous,[92] and Protić was empowered to open a public subscription in Russia. The Assembly approved, Prince Milan signed the loan contract, and the Russian banks agreed to advance 500,000 rubles on account.[93] However, the Russian loan helped less than its size suggests. The subscription lagged in Russia, and most of the money did not reach Serbia until after the campaign. The camouflaged state loan encouraged Belgrade to continue the war and demonstrated Pan-Slav influence in Russia, but left the Serbian treasury desperately short of funds.[94]

In Russia, the Slav committees, the Red Cross, and the Orthodox Church solicited contributions to assist South Slav refugees and wounded. With official sanction, public appeals for funds to assist civilians were made in the press and from the pulpit. Here too the Slav committees played a leading role.[95] Newspaper accounts of the Slavs' sad plight stimulated urban contributions; the clergy and Slav committee agents roused the rural masses. Small contributions from the lower classes predominated. Aksakov wrote, "Contributions were in inverse proportion to the social ladder, though there were exceptions. Our wealthy citizens did not participate to any great extent." Two thirds of the money received by the Moscow Committee "came from our poor, burdened ordinary people and each kopeck therefore has great moral significance." [96]

Unofficial Russian financial aid to the South Slavs was substantial but

---

[91] Nikitin, *Slavianskie komitety*, pp. 297–98; Grujić, *3*, 197–98.

[92] The Russian bankers recommended a public subscription for a loan of 3,750,000 paper rubles at 6 per cent annual interest with repayment to begin in November 1877, although the Skupština had desired repayment to start five years after signature of a loan agreement.

[93] The banks included the International Commercial Bank of St. Petersburg, the Bank for Foreign Trade, and Volga-Kama Commercial Bank.

[94] Grujić, *3*, 203–05, 209–10; *Vlada Milana, 1*, 313; Nikitin, *Slavianskie komitety*, pp. 298–99.

[95] Aksakov to N. P. Giliarov-Platonov, Aug. 8, *Ivan Aksakov v ego pis'makh, 4*, 282.

[96] Aksakov, *1*, 226–29. Sumner (*Russia*, p. 188), citing Pokrovskii's biased and inaccurate *Russkaia istoriia s drevneishikh vremen* (Moscow, 1913), *4*, 253, gives the misleading impression that merchants were prominent contributors.

insufficient to satisfy their needs. After the Serbo-Turkish war, Aksakov announced that total funds expended by the Slav committees and other private organizations on the South Slavs from July 1875 through October 1876 approximated 3,500,000 rubles, including about 500,000 rubles worth of contributions in kind.[97] Only a fraction of the money was dispatched by the committees to the Serbian and Montenegrin governments, but considerable sums were expended in indirect support of their war effort, especially to transport and maintain Russian volunteers.[98] This relieved the overburdened Serbian treasury and preserved the unofficial character of the aid.

Russian society, through the Slav committees and Russian Red Cross, provided significant medical assistance to the South Slavs during the war. The Army's medical administration gave permission for doctors, nurses, and medical supplies to be sent to Serbia. Near the front a Slav committee hospital was established and staffed with Russian personnel. The Old Believer community in Moscow contributed a one-hundred-bed hospital for Serbia, fully staffed and equipped, out of its own resources. Proportionately, even more was done for Montenegro.[99]

The Slav committees' most demanding task was to recruit and dispatch volunteers to Serbia.[100] Organized recruitment began in July, reached its peak in August, then gradually declined. Aksakov originally believed that the Moscow and St. Petersburg committees could handle this task alone.[101] But when thousands of persons from all parts of Russia sought to volunteer, the Slav societies in Kiev and Odessa assisted, and additional recruitment centers were established in the provinces.[102] Aksakov recounted, "All of Russia was ready to cover itself with branches of the Slav Committee, but to our sorrow we could not

[97] Aksakov, *Sochineniia*, 1, 226–29.

[98] *Pervye 15 let*, pp. 414, 537–47; Aksakov, *Sochineniia*, 1, 230–31. The Moscow Committee spent about 140,000 rubles to transport volunteers to and from Serbia, 80,000 to support Cherniaev's army, and 20,000 on Novoselov's Ibar army. A substantial sum, admitted Aksakov, went to cover Cherniaev's personal debts.

[99] Aksakov, *Sochineniia*, 1, 232–33; *Pervye 15 let*, pp. 386, 540–41; OSVOb., 1, 453–55; Nikitin, *Slavianskie komitety*, p. 307.

[100] For a detailed treatment see Nikitin, *Slavianskie komitety*, pp. 314–27.

[101] Aksakov, *Sochineniia*, 1, 222–24; *Pervye 15 let*, p. 386. In Moscow the Slav Bazaar was utilized with A. Porokhovshchikov, aided by some retired generals, handling recruitment; in St. Petersburg General V. D. Dandevil' conducted recruitment. Meshcherskii wrote of these hectic days in Moscow: "In Aksakov's reception room my head ached from the mass of people of every calling who flooded into the parlor like the tide." *Moi vospominaniia*, 2, 281–82.

[102] Nikitin, *Slavianskie komitety*, pp. 308–10.

satisfy these insistent demands because a decision for the establishment of a section [but not a temporary recruitment center] depends upon the Ministry of Interior." [103]

Recruitment in the capitals was generally done carefully and according to definite criteria; elsewhere, it was often haphazard. Aksakov ordered that priority be given to commissioned and noncommissioned officers, but ordinary soldiers with experience in battle were acceptable. Civilians and applicants with dubious motives were to be rejected.[104] Nevertheless, even the Moscow recruiters enlisted adventurers and drunkards.[105] The Odessa bureau, which sent as many volunteers as either capital, recruited most of the city's wastrels. Recruitment of Don Cossacks was handled in a chaotic, improvised manner by the local newspaper editor.[106]

Bands of volunteers proceeded to Serbia throughout the summer and early fall. How many left Russia and arrived in Serbia cannot be determined precisely. The Slav committees, according to their official figures, sent 4,303 volunteers. Since others traveled independently, Professor Nikitin's estimate of 5,000 volunteers sent appears reasonable.[107] On the other hand, the number of Russians serving in the Serbian armies never exceeded 3,000.[108] About 2,000 recruited volunteers never reached the front. Some spent their allowance money and remained in Russia; others enjoyed life in Rumanian or Serbian cafés.[109]

What were the volunteers' motives? A few officers, such as N. A. Kireev, who died heroically on July 18 leading his troops, were idealistic Pan-Slavs with a sincere desire to liberate the Slavs. A larger

---

[103] Aksakov, *Sochineniia, 1,* 224.

[104] OSVOb., *1,* 297–98, Aksakov's memorandum.

[105] Meshcherskii, *Pravda o Serbii* (St. Petersburg, 1877), pp. 42–45.

[106] On provincial recruitment and its inadequacies see OSVOb., *1,* nos. 211, 213, 219, 220, 226. They confirm the all-class character of the volunteer movement. Also Nikitin, *Slavianskie komitety,* pp. 316–19.

[107] See *ibid.,* p. 320 for a breakdown of volunteers sent by the Slav committees. For the total sent by the Moscow and St. Petersburg committees respectively, see Aksakov, *1,* 227, 233, and *Pervye 15 let,* p. 541. Both Meshcherskii's *Pravda o Serbii,* p. 90, and A. Khvostov, *Russkie i serby v voinu 1876 g.* (St. Petersburg, 1877), p. 38, estimated that 5,000 volunteers had been dispatched from Russia.

[108] General Cherniaev calculated that at the end of the campaign, 1806 enlisted men and 646 officers (Russian) were under his command. In GIM, Avtobiografiia, p. 9, he states, "In all there were 2,645 volunteers with me and they were heroes." According to Ristić (*1,* 154), Russian volunteers in the Serbian armies never exceeded 3,000.

[109] Nikitin, *Slavianskie komitety,* p. 320.

contingent of reserve officers volunteered primarily because war was their profession. Generally, these elements arrived in Serbia early in the campaign. Of them Meshcherskii boasted, "All the volunteers seemed heroes, bearers of a holy idea, a new type of crusader going to die for the oppressed brethren." [110] Professor Nikitin concludes, on the basis of numerous volunteer declarations, that the ordinary Russian soldiers pursued no selfish aims and wished no harm to the Serbian people; they went to liberate.[111] Many Russians aroused by reports of Turkish atrocities, went simply "to smite the Turks." [112] But later came less desirable types: adventurers, fortune hunters, and riffraff. With good reason, Gleb Uspenskii attributed much of the poor behavior, drunkenness, and immorality of the rank and file to the heritage of serfdom.[113]

St. Petersburg's relationship with the volunteer movement and the Slav committees remained ambiguous throughout the war. Official Russia lacked a definite policy or the will to enforce one. Although angry at Cherniaev's disobedience, the tsar neglected to insist that he return to Russia. Neither did he muzzle the Pan-Slav press or close down the Slav committees.[114] During July and August, the latter were free to collect contributions and dispatch volunteers.[115] On August 8, the tsar legalized the temporary retirement of Russian army officers to enable them to proceed to Serbia; they were promised readmission to their regiments without loss of seniority at the end of the campaign. This action encouraged more officers to serve with Cherniaev.[116]

Indeed, the court was displaying unmistakable sympathy for the Slav struggle. Emperor and empress encouraged all private efforts in their behalf. As head of the Russian Red Cross, the empress assisted the

---

[110] Meshcherskii, *Moi vospominaniia*, 2, 280–81.

[111] Nikitin, *Slavianskie komitety*, p. 324.

[112] *Ibid.*, p. 321; OSVOb., *1*, 429–31, *Vpered!*, Sept. 28/Oct. 10, 1876.

[113] *Otechestvennye Zapiski*, no. 12, p. 180, cited by Nikitin, "Russkoe obshchestvo," p. 1008.

[114] HHSA, Langenau to Andrassy, Sept. 8, telegram 72. F. F. Trepov, commandant of St. Petersburg, had proposed reimposition of full censorship for six months, but the tsar and his ministers rejected his suggestion.

[115] Some provincial officials, however, hindered Slav committee efforts, and Moscow's governor general, V. A. Dolgorukov, forbade a prayer service in the Iverskaia Cathedral upon the departure of a nurses' detachment. But he drew upon himself the wrath of the empress and refrained henceforth from such measures. ROBibLen, Dnevnik Chizhova, *6*, 113–14; Nikitin, *Slavianskie komitety*, p. 308.

[116] Miliutin, *Dnevnik*, 2, 62, 66, 67; OSVOb., *1*, 315–16.

dispatch of medical detachments. The court preferred undefeated Prince Nikola to Milan, suspected of being "in the hands of the Omladina," but reacted strongly to Serbian victories and defeats. Deep gloom prevailed at court, confided Miliutin, during the Serbian retreat. Confidence in the preservation of European peace was shaken; Gorchakov "talks in a sort of whisper, frowning." [117] In contrast, when Cherniaev's reports of the Šumatovac victory were received (see below, p. 130), the Austrian ambassador noted "qu'elle joie immense cette nouvelle avait produit partout à Zarskoe." [118] So closely was the court cooperating with the St. Petersburg Slav Committee at this time, noted Prince A. I. Vasil'chikov, that "here the popular agitation has taken on an official look." No sooner were volunteers enrolled, than the authorities provided them with leave papers and foreign passports. [119]

The government, unwilling to stifle the pro-Slav movement and unable to lead it, allowed the Slav committees' influence to expand. To Cherniaev, Aksakov described the excitement and turmoil of these eventful summer days:

You cannot imagine how much work I have, or the Slav committee has, what it means to stand face to face with an all-popular [vsenarodnym] movement! One must talk daily with hundreds of persons and receive daily over 100 letters. . . . There has taken place and is taking place an unprecedented affair. War is being conducted apart from the government by the Russian people itself (literally the people which merely asks: why is not the tsar sending us!) and the Slav Committee of Moscow which is treasury and commissariat for you. I began recruitment without any permission and finally society won for itself this right. . . . [120]

The government was under intense public pressure to abandon its policy of nonintervention. At a theatrical presentation in St. Petersburg, reported an agent of the Third Section, the audience, after contributing generously to the Slav cause, "openly and sharply criticized the government for its passive relationship toward the Slav movement." [121] Public dissatisfaction was intense, wrote General F. F.

---

[117] HHSA, Langenau to Andrassy, Aug. 2, Aug. 1/13, nos. 44B, 45E; Miliutin, Dnevnik, 2, 60, 67, 68.

[118] HHSA, Langenau to Andrassy, Aug. 30, no. 49 A-F. This Serbian "victory," affirmed Miliutin (2, 70), was the exclusive topic of conversation at Court for several days.

[119] Golubev, Vasil'chikov, pp. 116–17.

[120] GIM, Aksakov to Cherniaev, Sept. 7/19.

[121] OSVOb., 1, 317–18, report of July 31/Aug. 12.

Trepov (August 20), when the police forbade a departing volunteer from reading an appeal for contributions to the Serbs.[122] Another agent reported growing conviction among students and factory workers that St. Petersburg should adopt the public's pro-Slav attitude. What are the diplomats doing to halt Turkish atrocities in Bulgaria? Aksakov asked Giers. Russia would have to feed all eight million Balkan Christians unless its policy became more forceful. The Foreign Ministry should realize how aroused Russian society had become over events in the Balkans.[123] The liberal editor of *Novoe Vremia*, A. S. Suvorin, supported Pan-Slav efforts to alter governmental policy: "Whatever the government is like, I am ready to sacrifice my soul to it if it proceeds to liberate the Slavs and drive the Turks from Europe. . . . That is why I seek to arouse the public: I am seeking to separate its aspirations from official ones; I want it to demonstrate its independence." [124]

In response to this pressure, Gorchakov asserted that the government's course would not be determined by public agitation, but some foreign diplomats believed that officialdom, and the chancellor himself, were being converted by the Pan-Slavs.[125] Alarmed at Vienna's protests against violent anti-Austrian articles, the authorities did suspend temporarily some of the more extreme newspapers.[126] St. Petersburg, although it gained little public support for its official diplomacy, would not tolerate press attacks upon its allies. General Fadeev was put under police surveillance, and the Orthodox clergy was instructed to refrain from pro-Slav agitation.[127] To prevent the loss of essential officers to the volunteer movement, the tsar prohibited their transfer to retired

[122] *Ibid.*, p. 333, Aug. 9/21. Trepov was receiving anonymous letters expressing anger at Russia's passivity. *Ibid.*, pp. 319–20, Aug. 1/13.

[123] *Ibid.*, pp. 333–34, Aug. 9/21; pp. 374–76, Aksakov to Giers, Sept. 1/13.

[124] Nikitin, *Slavianskie komitety*, p. 327.

[125] PRO, FO 65/939, Loftus to Derby, Aug. 16, no. 366. Reported White from Belgrade, "The Servians see in this sympathy evinced to their cause in high [Russian] quarters quite sufficient encouragement to protract the war and abundant reason to hope for ultimate support on the part of Russia." *Ibid.*, FO 78/2487, White to Derby, Aug. 29, no. 122.

[126] For repeated attacks on Austrian policy, *Russkii Mir* was forbidden temporarily to make street sales (mid-August); it was suspended altogether for one month (early September) for urging Russia to enter the war. *Grazhdanin*, for its lead, "Slavianskaia letopis" (Aug. 1/13), advocating immediate Russian entry, was supended for two months. HHSA, Langenau to Andrassy, Sept. 2, telegram 71; Aug. 28/Sept. 9, no. 50C; OSVOb., *1*, 322–23; Nikitin, *Slavianskie komitety*, p. 323.

[127] OSVOb., *1*, 423, Mezentsov to Lobanov-Rostovskii, Sept. 23/Oct. 5.

status "until the clarification of the situation," although only a month earlier he had sanctioned these transfers.[128] Belatedly, Miliutin sought to halt departures of regular Cossacks and to discover how many had already left to serve with Cherniaev.[129] But these restrictive measures were halfhearted.

St. Petersburg could have suppressed the pro-Slav movement in Russia, but it merely curbed its excesses. Both government and public opinion favored Serbian liberation, though differing over Russia's orientation in foreign affairs and means of promoting a Slav victory. Divided Russian officialdom [130] contributed as before to the duality and passivity of the government. Astounded at the tsar's leniency toward unauthorized departures of volunteer officers, Miliutin wrote:

It is clear that in this whole affair of the volunteer movement to Serbia the tsar himself has acted in a dual manner [*dvoistvenno*] and partly himself contributed to the spread of the conviction that the government encourages this movement. Everyone knows that the heir took and continues to take a most active part in the Slav cause. Unfortunately, adventurers such as Fadeev ingratiate themselves into his confidence. The agitation issuing from Anichkov Palace [the heir's residence] goes entirely counter to the accepted official policy; the tsar knows this (sometimes even himself seems to sympathize) and closes his eyes to it. With such duality can there be any definite system in our actions or any clear plan?[131]

Only when compelled by Serbia's defeat to exercise decisive leadership would St. Petersburg rein in the Slav committees, forcing them, and Russian opinion, into traditional subservience.

Russia and the Debate over a Serbo-Turkish Armistice

The question of an armistice between Turkey and the Serbian states arose after the initial Serbian offensive failed. Periodic efforts to arrange a truce, coinciding generally with Serbian setbacks, continued until Serbia's defeat at Djunis on October 29 finally provoked a Russian

---

[128] Miliutin, *Dnevnik*, 2, 70; OSVOb., 1, 366.

[129] OSVOb., 1, nos. 272, 276, 285, 290, pp. 413, 418–19, 425–26, 429; Miliutin, *Dnevnik*, 2, 84; Nikitin, *Slavianskie komitety*, pp. 329–30.

[130] These divisions are revealed clearly in A. Porokhovshchikov's "Zapiski starozhila," pp. 9ff., a rather sensational account of his "mission" to Livadia. However, Miliutin (*Dnevnik*, 2, 83–84) generally corroborates Porokhovshchikov's assertions.

[131] *Ibid.*, 2, 85–87, Sept. 23/Oct. 5. This was written just after Porokhovshchikov's interview with the tsar at Livadia.

ultimatum to the Porte. A recurring debate over an armistice involved all parties to the Serbo-Turkish conflict and promoted discussion of bases of peace. Because Russian leaders devoted such attention to the truce question, it became a significant factor in Russia's relations with the Serbian states.

The Serbs themselves initiated the debate. Encountering a better armed and more numerous foe, Serbia's peasant soldiers lost all enthusiasm for war. In late July, Prince Milan, and for a time even General Cherniaev, favored a cessation of hostilities. Opposing an armistice were the more bellicose Serbian ministers, the intelligentsia, and the arriving Russian volunteers. Between these factions stood Ristić, advocating continuation of the war, since his government and political future would be discredited by a hasty, abject plea for peace.[132] If Serbia admitted defeat while Montenegro won victories, could Belgrade retain leadership of the national movement? Would not Piedmont's mantle pass to the Black Mountain? Ristić's war policy was based upon the premise that Russia must be drawn into the conflict or at least mediate a Serbo-Turkish settlement. If peace were concluded now at Serbia's request, his objectives would not be achieved. Would the Serbian people, after sacrificing blood and treasure, accept a peace based on the *status quo ante*? Cherniaev too, recovering from initial panic, realized that his future was at stake in the war. To beg for peace would be dishonorable and make his presence in Serbia superfluous. Such considerations help explain Belgrade's hesitations and Cherniaev's abrupt reversals on the truce question. Whenever military success appeared possible, Cherniaev and the Serbian government opposed concluding an armistice.

Early in August, while Prince Milan still led the peace faction, two unidentified Serbs sounded out Consul White about possible British mediation. They were told that until Serbia admitted defeat and responsibility for the war and appealed openly to the Powers, no mediation could occur.[133] The Serbian militants argued that continuing the war would harden the militia, expose Turkish barbarism, and win European and Russian sympathy. The tsar might be induced to intervene officially. The partisans of war *à outrance*, though alarmed at Turkish occupation of eastern Serbia, still counted on Greek or Rumanian participation. White concluded, nonetheless, that if the Belgrade

---

[132] Ristić, *1*, 125–28; DAS 151/455, Ristić to Protić, Aug. 11/23.
[133] *Staatsarchiv, 31*, 83, White to Derby, Aug. 5, 1876.

government sought peace, it would be supported by the Serbian people.[134] By mid-August, Ristić, dissuading Prince Milan from hasty surrender, suggested to foreign consuls that Serbia was willing to conclude an armistice. But if the Porte refused the *status quo ante* as the basis of peace, resistance must continue to the bitter end.[135]

Responding to Ristić's hints, some Powers offered to mediate a settlement. The Italian consul intimated that Italy would support the *status quo ante*.[136] The French and British governments would mediate if Belgrade requested it.[137] Vienna, however, insisted that since Serbia had been the aggressor, it must express a desire to lay down its arms; Turkish victories made a return to the *status quo ante* unlikely. Andrassy reaffirmed support for the Obrenović dynasty, but he suggested that the Ristić government be sacrificed to demonstrate that Serbia had attacked against the prince's wishes.[138]

Ristić ascertained the Russian attitude before responding to the Powers' overtures. Kartsov had intimated a week earlier that no diplomatic action to end the war could be taken prior to a decisive battle.[139] Giers now told Protić that Russia awaited overtures from one of the belligerents. Should Serbia win a substantial victory, Russia herself would seek an armistice. But now, without a formal request from Belgrade, she would not act for fear of compromising Serbia's chances of victory. (A Serbian victory, of course, would make Russia's hand stronger at the peace talks.) If Serbia formally requested Russia to mediate an armistice, Serbia might expect the *status quo ante*. But what would Russia do, asked Protić, should the Porte press unacceptable demands upon Serbia? "Since we are protecting you," responded Giers, "we will not abandon you so easily." Unless Serbia could secure its frontiers and thereby eliminate Turkish suzerainty, he added, it was pointless to continue the struggle.[140] Chancellor Gorchakov and the tsar both advised Prince Milan to agree to an armistice.[141]

---

[134] *Ibid.*, pp. 89–91, Aug. 14.

[135] AII, Ristić 18/46, Ristić to Protić, July 30/Aug. 11, telegram and 18/264, Aug. 1/13, draft of Ristić's views.

[136] *Ibid.*, 18/66, 70, Aug. 12, drafts by Ristić; 18/93, Joannini to Ristić; HHSA, Wrede to Andrassy, Aug. 16, no. 130.

[137] Grujić, *3*, 205.

[138] HHSA, Wrede to Andrassy, Aug. 16, Privatschreiben, Aug. 17, telegram.

[139] *Ibid.*, Aug. 10, No. 125.

[140] AII, Ristić 26/718, Protić to Ristić, Aug. 1/13.

[141] *Ibid.*, 18/58, Ristić to Protić, Aug. 19; DAS 151/455, Ristić to Protić, Aug. 11/23; HHSA, Langenau to Andrassy, Aug. 4/16, no. 46 A-C.

On August 18, just before the Battle of Alexinac, Cherniaev opposed an armistice: "Our military situation is better than ever before"; he telegraphed Ristić. The latter replied that the tsar and the Powers advised conclusion of a truce, but he would avoid any commitment pending receipt of a more definite estimate of the military situation from Cherniaev.[142]

As the military situation at Alexinac deteriorated, Ristić believed that if Russia realized Serbia's desperate situation, it might provide major assistance. The cabinet agreed that Protić should explain Serbia's plight and appeal for aid. "Serbian and Russian blood is now mixing to cement our solidarity," Ristić wrote Protić, "but only a Russian army corps can prevent an eventual Turkish breakthrough." Abandoned by the Bulgarians, Serbia was bearing the entire burden of Slavdom's war with the Crescent:

If we do not get help from somewhere . . . we must make peace. . . . We again turn our eyes to powerful Russia. . . . If she does not encourage the Greeks and reverse the attitude of the Rumanian government so we can obtain more weapons, we have no alternative but peace at any price. . . . We have not promised the consuls anything but are holding the question open; . . . we will follow the advice of the Russian government. . . . Maintain friendship and brotherhood with the Russians; we must stick with them through thick and thin.[143]

Cherniaev's telegram of August 23 persuaded Belgrade to seek a truce. His troops at Alexinac were reeling under the Turkish assault. The army, discouraged and exhausted, must soon yield.[144] The Council of Ministers, after a debate of many hours, resolved to accept mediation. On August 24, Prince Milan, somewhat embarrassed, explained to the consuls that the indecisiveness of the Alexinac fighting and Turkey's refusal to recognize Serbia's rights as a belligerent had delayed his decision. Continuation of the war, added the prince, would merely result in useless slaughter.[145]

Official Russia hailed Milan's announcement. Gorchakov emphasized that an armistice must apply to all belligerents. Despite rising public enthusiasm in Russia for the Serbian cause, he pledged that the tsar and

---

[142] AII, Ristić 18/56, 58, Cherniaev to Ristić, Aug. 18, Ristić to Cherniaev, Aug.
[143] DAS 151/455, Ristić to Protić, Aug. 11/23.
[144] AII, Ristić 18/262, Cherniaev to Milan, Aug. 11/23.
[145] *Ibid.*, 18/72, (Ristić) to Cherniaev, Aug. 12/24; Grujić, *3*, 211; HHSA, Wrede to Andrassy, Aug. 25, no. 135.

the nation would persist in a pacific course. Russia would oppose any Turkish demand for a war indemnity from Serbia.[146]

Meanwhile, Prince Nikola, despite recent victories over the Turks and promises of Russian financial assistance, was not averse to an armistice. A. S. Ionin's pressure upon him for more active collaboration with Serbia had been of little avail. Informed by Ristić of the Powers' mediation offers, Prince Nikola replied (August 18) that although Montenegro's military position was favorable, if Serbia desired an armistice it should accept one for both principalities. At first, Nikola said that Prince Milan could speak in Montenegro's name as well as Serbia's,[147] but then Vienna reminded Prince Nikola that independent Montenegro should not request an armistice through vassal Serbia. Nikola decided to appeal directly to the Powers, but he reminded Andrassy that because of its victories, Montenegro was entitled to much better terms than Serbia. Feigning generosity, Nikola declared he would agree to peace because his Serbian ally was "no longer capable of maintaining itself in the field." [148] Austria again had exploited the rivalry between Belgrade and Cetinje.

Sharp fluctuations in Serbia's military situation endangered armistice negotiations. On August 25, two days after his despairing telegram, Cherniaev wrote Ristić that by repulsing all Turkish attacks on Šuma-tovac his army had scored a glorious victory. Russian officers, he informed Belgrade, were arriving en masse; Serbian morale was high. Armistice negotiations should be delayed until the situation was clari-fied.[149] Cherniaev's optimism proved contagious. Prince Milan, evading the consuls' queries about a truce,[150] wrote Cherniaev on August 30

---

[146] *Staatsarchiv, 31,* 98, Loftus to Derby, Aug. 25. Gorchakov told the British ambassador, "Nous nous sommes abstenus de toute initiative; nous avons laissé faire; nous avons attendu que l'Europe agit; mais si rien ne se fait, si cette effusion de sang continue, et si l'Empereur . . . me commande de prendre la plume en main, je vous garantis qu'elle sera trempée dans une encre qui comporterait avec la dignité et la puissance de l'Empire." The chancellor added hastily, "Mais ce ne serait pas la guerre."

[147] Vuksan, "Crna Gora i Srbija u god 1876," *Zapisi, 4* (April 1929), 229; "Prepiska," *6* (Jan. 1930), 43–44; AII, Ristić 18/1, 3, 4, Ristić to Radonić, and Radonić to Ristić, Aug. 15/27, 18/30; Djordjević, *Crna Gora,* pp. 396–97.

[148] *Ibid.,* pp. 397–98. Djordjević ascribes Nikola's decision primarily to Austrian pressure; *Staatsarchiv, 31,* 102, Buchanan to Derby, Aug. 20.

[149] AII, Ristić 18/80, Cherniaev to Ristić, Aug. 25.

[150] HHSA, Wrede to Andrassy, Aug. 29, no. 137.

that "the noble Slav cause" required Serbia to fight on. "An armistice would be good for reorganization of the army, but I feel it would be difficult to obtain and could lead us to peace whether we want it or not. Upon your answer depend my futher actions—the *démarche* I made to the Powers [on August 24] does not as yet impose any obligations on me." [151] Once again Milan placed his country's fate squarely in the Russian general's hands. When the Turks captured Adrovac on September 2 and approached the Serbs' last defense line in the Morava Valley, Cherniaev telegraphed Milan to negotiate an immediate armistice. The Council of Ministers promptly empowered Protić to seek Russian mediation. [152]

With Serbia facing defeat, Sir Henry Elliot, British ambassador at the Porte, presented English proposals for a peaceful settlement (September 3–4). These "English bases" called for an armistice of at least one month, restoration of the *status quo ante* in Serbia and Montenegro, local administrative autonomy for Bulgaria and the insurgent provinces, and Turkish execution of the Andrassy reforms. [153] Turkey replied that it would conclude an armistice if the Serbian states accepted the following peace preliminaries: (1) restoration of Turkish garrisons in four Serbian fortresses; (2) limitation of the Serbian army to 10,000 men; (3) payment by Serbia of a war indemnity or increased tribute; and (4) the *status quo ante* for Montenegro. [154] Only a completely defeated country could accept such terms.

Serbia's request for an armistice after serious military setbacks placed Russia in a difficult diplomatic position. On August 21, before Milan had called for the truce, A. I. Nelidov had written Ignat'ev, "If the Serbs are decisively beaten, as one must soon anticipate, our position here [Constantinople] will become even more difficult than at present because all the threads of our influence will be broken by such a defeat of Cherniaev and we would have to create everything anew." [155] As the

[151] RA (1914) no. 1, p. 42, Milan to Cherniaev, Aug. 18/30.
[152] Ristić, *1*, 135; Grujić, *3*, 213–14. Protić asserted Austria-Hungary wished to give the Turks time to crush Serbia.
[153] W. Wirthwein, *Britain and the Balkan Crisis, 1875–1878* (New York, 1935), pp. 104–06.
[154] W. Langer, *European Alliances and Alignments, 1871–1890* (New York, 1956), pp. 95–96; Grujić, *3*, 220–21.
[155] Ignat'ev, IV (May 1914), p. 431, letter of Aug. 9/21. Miliutin (*Dnevnik*, *2*, 73) felt the Serbs' retreat cast gloom over the Slavs' prospects.

Turkish army multiplied its victories, Baron Jomini predicted Turkish evasion of efforts to restore peace; he feared Russia would be drawn into the war: "A lengthy and successful defense by the Serbs alone could save us [from war]. Alas, this is most improbable! Today's news reveals that despite their efforts, the poor Serbs will succumb to superior numbers."[156] The Turks had put a high price on an armistice, and the tsar found their demands upon Serbia wholly unacceptable.[157] Chancellor Gorchakov, stressing Russia's determination to halt the bloodshed, accepted the "English bases," but with reservations. Russia would agree to: (1) an unconditional armistice *"pur et simple"*; (2) the *status quo ante* for the Serbian states, while foreseeing inevitable territorial increases for Montenegro; (3) liberal local or administrative autonomy for the insurgent provinces. The Powers, urged Gorchakov, should impose these terms upon the Porte.[158]

Gorchakov's concessions to London signified rejection of the proposals which Ignat'ev had made in August for a Balkan settlement. Then the count had favored a Russian ultimatum to Turkey followed, if necessary, by the Powers' military action.[159] About September 10, an Ignat'ev memorandum, setting forth a different set of territorial changes, warned, "Russia cannot permit the destruction of the Slavs even if other Powers are willing to look on."[160] Montenegro, he contin-

---

[156] Jelavich, *Russia in the East*, pp. 21–22, Jomini to Giers, Aug. 21/Sept. 2.

[157] "I hope the Great Powers do not yield [to Turkish demands]. I see no other way out than a breach of diplomatic relations and then war, but of course I would first make an agreement with England and Austria . . . to put an end to the war in Serbia." Tiutin, "Politika," pp. 219–20. These penciled comments, which Miliutin (*Dnevnik 2*, 77) believed the tsar had erased, reveal, Tiutin claims, how weak were Alexander's nerves. That they did not constitute any final directive for war with Turkey is confirmed by Giers's statement to Langenau that Russia would not go to war immediately even should the Porte refuse an armistice or gain decisive victories over the Serbs. HHSA, Langenau to Andrassy, Sept. 9, no. 56 A-F.

[158] *Ibid.*, telegram 73; Tatishchev, *Aleksandr II, 2*, 324; *Staatsarchiv, 31*, 114, Derby to Loftus, Sept. 13. Tiutin, "Politika," p. 214.

[159] Ignat'ev, IV (April 1914), pp. 58–59. Temporarily abandoning his unilateral approach toward a solution of the Eastern Question, Ignat'ev was, in August, prepared to trade Austrian occupation of most of the insurgent provinces for Russian control of Bulgaria. The rest of Hercegovina would go to Montenegro but no increase was provided for Serbia.

[160] *Ibid.*, pp. 59–61. From the start of the war Ignat'ev had urged maximum Russian aid to Serbia. On August 10, he had written Kartsov that if the Serbs could hold out for two more months, their cause would triumph. "We must aid Serbia in every way in order to avoid being drawn into the mess ourselves." Kartsov, RS, *134*, 72–74.

ued, must be given important increases of territory.[161] Serbia could be mollified with a slice of Old Serbia and a "correction of frontiers" near Niš.[162] Only "Turkish Croatia" need be offered Vienna in compensation; the remainder of the insurgent provinces and Novi Pazar (the "Enclave") could be given autonomy or at least local self-government. An autonomous Bulgaria, including two thirds of Macedonia, should be created under Ottoman suzerainty and the Powers' supervision. Vienna, urged Ignat'ev, might accept his plan since no large Slav state would be established, the Bosnian question would remain unresolved, and Montenegrin aggrandizement would create a counterpoise to Serbia. Gorchakov, however, found his solution incompatible with the Reichstadt agreement. After Russia accepted the "English bases," Ignat'ev urged unilateral Russian military action if the Porte rejected an armistice. He argued that Russia's military position would improve less during the winter than Turkish defenses, and delay might allow Turkey to crush the Serbian states and obtain European allies.[163]

Meanwhile Russian leaders had obtained indications of German support. Emperor William I wrote the tsar in early September, "The memory of your attitude toward me and my country from 1864 to 1870/71 will, whatever may come, determine my policy toward Russia." Alexander interpreted this, and explanations provided by von Manteuffel, a special envoy of William I, as German encouragement of a Russo-Turkish war.[164] Von Manteuffel talked with the tsar, then reported that unless the Balkan Christians' security were guaranteed, Russia would fight.[165] These German assurances bolstered the tsar's position when he took decisive steps at Livadia the following month.

The Porte rejected an unconditional armistice, but on September 15 instructed its commanders to suspend hostilities temporarily. Belgrade too was in a receptive mood, as Consul White reported:

[161] Montenegro, wrote Ignat'ev, should acquire Spič and Spuž, the part of Hercegovina between the Narenta River and a line from Nevesinje to the junction of the Piva and Tara rivers. If necessary, Prince Nikola could hold these areas as a vassal of the Porte paying annual tribute; otherwise Montenegro would be recognized as independent.

[162] Ibid., p. 65. With Belgrade facing defeat, Ignat'ev was prepared to concede it almost as much territory as he would later at San Stefano when the Serbs were victorious.

[163] Ibid., pp. 65–66, 70–73, 75–77.

[164] Briefwechsel des Botschafters General v. Schweinitz (Berlin, 1928), pp. 115–16; Sumner, Russia, pp. 202–04.

[165] GP, 2, nos. 231, 232, pp. 40, 44–45.

All the influential public men of Servia have arrived at the conviction that unless Russia comes openly to declare war against the Porte the Principality is in extreme peril of being overrun. . . . They admit that Servia alone and unassisted cannot accomplish any practical result. . . . Hence a general desire amongst these gentlemen to accelerate the cessation of hostilities.[166]

Kartsov advised Serbia to abstain from offensive operations, and the Council of Ministers authorized Prince Milan to halt hostilities.[167] As a truce took effect (September 15), it appeared that the armistice debate was over, that peace was imminent, and that official Russia, eschewing intervention, was promoting a peaceful solution.

Russian Volunteers and Serbia's Defeat

The diplomats' progress was imperiled again by General Cherniaev's actions. He and his Russian volunteers, welcomed in Serbia as Russia's vanguard,[168] played a key role in Serbian-Russian relations. As a Russian commanding Serbia's main army, Cherniaev at first possessed tremendous authority and prestige. Friction mounted as Serbian hopes of victory dwindled and as undesirable elements followed the dedicated Russian heroes of early summer. Cherniaev's irresponsible Pan-Slav policies and Serbia's defeat exploded the myth of Slav solidarity and brotherhood.

Cherniaev was as responsible as anyone for the deterioration of Serbo-Russian relations during the war. To his delusions of grandeur he was prepared to sacrifice thousands of Serbian lives. Many high-ranking Serbian officers lost confidence in him during the opening offensive.[169] Never before in command of more than a few thousand men, Cherniaev proved unable to co-ordinate or discipline his motley forces. Unwillingness or inability to select a competent staff multiplied his troubles; his Russian subordinates were mostly petty, incompetent adventurers.[170] Except for a few extreme conservatives, Cherniaev's Russian contemporaries considered him impractical and egotistical, a

---

[166] *Staatsarchiv, 31,* 121, White to Derby, Sept. 14.   [167] Grujić, *3,* 217–18.

[168] N. Maksimov in *Dve voiny, 1876–1878* (St. Petersburg, 1879) asserted (p. iv) that arriving volunteers were greeted warmly: "Everyone wanted to help. The reception was most joyous." Khvostov agreed (*Russkie i serby,* p. 5) but added that Cherniaev promoted the belief among the Serbs that all of Russia stood behind him.

[169] For details on Cherniaev's military role in Serbia see MacKenzie, "Practice," pp. 282–83.

[170] Khvostov, *Russkie i serby,* p. 44; Maksimov, *Dve voiny,* pp. 55–68.

poor tactician, and a man absorbed in intrigue.[171] After his abortive July offensive, Cherniaev sought to preserve his army pending massive unofficial Russian aid or official intervention.

To win the Russian public's support, Cherniaev established a Correspondence Bureau at his Deligrad headquarters which enforced strict controls on newspapermen and "improved" the war news. The Bureau systematically deceived the Serbian and the Russian public. "Not a single honest line could reach the Russian press from the battlefield," declared P. A. Viskovatov of *Golos*. At first only correspondents from pro-Cherniaev newspapers such as *Russkii Mir* and *Moskovskie Vedomosti* were allowed at headquarters. After repeated protests to Prince Milan, other newspapermen were finally permitted to stay near by. Only with great difficulty did the International Telegraphic Agency obtain uncensored reports from correspondents reaching Semlin, Austria, but these were denounced as fabrications by pro-Cherniaev organs. The Correspondence Bureau, glorifying the exploits of Cherniaev's forces, aroused sympathy and excitement in Russia. To explain early setbacks, the Bureau asserted falsely that large numbers of Austrian troops, dressed as Turks, were fighting for the enemy. Cherniaev's retreat into Serbia was "voluntary." "Victories" were reported from areas where no fighting had occurred; minor skirmishes were magnified into major Slav triumphs. The Bureau accused the Turks of bestial atrocities against Russian and Serbian wounded. As *Golos* explained subsequently, "The Bureau was really a weapon of political blackmail of the most criminal kind. By means of lies and deception, it hoped to involve Russia in a war with Turkey." [172] The Bureau successfully promoted Cherniaev's popularity and stimulated Russians to contribute money to the Slav cause.

General Cherniaev preserved his image in Serbia as Russia's spokesman by maintaining sporadic contact with official Russia. After his success at Šumatovac on August 25, he telegraphed the tsar of his "glorious victories." Later he sent Prince Milan this indication of official Russia's support: "Prince Gortchakoff remercie Tchernaieff pour ses sentiments déposés aux pieds de l'Empereur . . . et ne cesse

---

[171] Khvostov, *Russkie i serby*, pp. 26–27; Miliutin, *Dnevnik*, 2, 97–98; Meshcherskii, *Moi vospominaniia*, 2, 292ff.

[172] *Golos*, Nov. 7/19, Nov. 26/Dec. 8, Dec. 8/20, 1876, nos. 308, 327, 339. During the war, confirmed *Golos*' editor, only one of Viskovatov's dispatches from Serbia was cleared by Cherniaev's censorship.

pas de prendre vif intérêt aux succès de l'armée serbe et aux destinées de la nation [serbe]." [173] Though the tsar's anger at the general was waning, Cherniaev's pride prevented him from seeking forgiveness. It was primarily through the heir, consistently sympathetic toward the volunteer movement, that he maintained links with official Russia.[174]

Most of Cherniaev's support came from the Russian public. At times he received over three hundred letters daily. After Šumatovac, came a flood of congratulatory telegrams from various parts of Russia.[175] Cherniaev corresponded largely with the Slav committees, which he showered with requests for money, volunteers, and clothing for his troops. Aksakov chided him for ingratitude and inept handling of the volunteers, but he supported him fully to the end of the campaign. It was from the Slav committees that Cherniaev continued to seek assistance.[176]

Cherniaev's attempts to reshape Serbia's political institutions to suit his conservative convictions undermined his relations with Belgrade. He relied heavily upon Prince Milan, who admired him and shared his dislike of parliamentary government. Avoiding a showdown with Ristić, Cherniaev feuded with War Minister Nikolić, the official with whom he came into closest contact. Nikolić, a tireless and dedicated patriot, co-operated with the volunteers, but he criticized Cherniaev's offensive strategy and the Correspondence Bureau, accusing him of ruining the Serbian army's morale. Cherniaev declared, "It is easy to sit in Belgrade and criticize actions at the war front." [177] Their quarrel deepened as Cherniaev usurped functions of the war ministry. With

---

[173] DAS, 29/100–1, Cherniaev to Milan, Sept. 1/13. This message had been transmitted to Cherniaev by Consul Kartsov.

[174] V. Djordjević, Srpsko-turski rat (Belgrade, 1907), 1, 410. Aksakov urged Cherniaev to beg Alexander II's forgiveness but to no avail.

[175] AII, Ristic 18/118, Aug. 26/Sept. 7, and 18/116, 120, Filipov and Aksakov to Cherniaev.

[176] ROBibSS, f. Aksakova 18, no. 387, Cherniaev to Aksakov, Sept. 2/14, 3/15, Oct. 2/14; GIM, Aksakov to Cherniaev, Sept. 7/19.

[177] AII, Ristić 18/63, Cherniaev to Nikolić, Aug. 10/22. According to most Serbian and Russian contemporary accounts (see Khvostov, pp. 54ff.; Maksimov, Dve voiny, p. 136; S. Grujić, Operacije, 1, 56, Golos, Nov. 5/17, 16/28, 1876, nos. 308, 317), Nikolić was able, honest, and dedicated. With a meager staff and budget, he had prepared Serbia for war. Upon Cherniaev's arrival, Nikolić provided him with full information about the Serbian army. Only Meshcherskii (Pravda o Serbii, pp. 175ff.) supported Cherniaev's allegations that Nikolić was a petty intriguer, jealous of him and the volunteers.

Milan's permission, he promoted and decorated noncombatant members of his staff, paid them generously from Slav committee funds and imposed punishments forbidden by Serbian law.[178]

As soon as the truce became operative, Cherniaev provoked a crisis. He instructed his subordinates to organize a "spontaneous" movement to proclaim Serbia an independent kingdom.[179] Then he telegraphed Prince Milan on September 15 that sentiment in the army in its favor was irresistible. "To restrain the movement is no longer in my power. Any attempt to do so would destroy all authority in my army." [180] But he told Dr. Vladan Djordjević that he had arranged the proclamation to forestall a Serbo-Turkish peace and compel Russia to enter the war.[181] To Aksakov he explained:

In Belgrade . . . the view prevailed that the war could not be continued. The ministers were disturbed by the fact that power had passed out of their hands and into those of Cherniaev, and they joined the general chorus for peace. This general pressure on Milan for peace made him hesitate. . . . It was essential to indicate a goal which would flatter everyone, unite all parties and force them to desire continuation of the struggle.[182]

Domestic and external considerations induced Prince Milan to refuse promptly a title he greatly coveted. "I feel it would be very sad," he telegraphed back, "if movements in the army should dictate my internal and foreign policies." [183] The prince wished to become king of an independent country, but he feared foreign reactions:

The proclamation of Serbian independence would alienate all the Powers. . . . As for Russia it is questionable whether she would recognize Serbia's new status and thus be dragged into the war. Despite the strength of public opinion in Russia, it must be remembered that it is the tsar who decides serious questions such as this. The tsar is friendly toward Serbia, but if all of

[178] *Golos,* Nov. 16/28, no. 317, report from Belgrade of Nov. 9; Todorović, *Odlomci,* pp. 72–73. Cherniaev's brutal tactlessness helped induce Major Velimirović, a brave and respected Serbian officer, to commit suicide (pp. 65–71).

[179] The fullest discussion of the "Deligrad event" is in Vlada Milana, *1,* 445–50. Jovanović concludes correctly that the royal proclamation was Cherniaev's idea and that he sought thereby to make a Serbo-Turkish peace impossible.

[180] AII, Ristić 18/159, Cherniaev to Milan, Sept. 3/15.

[181] Djordjević, *Srpsko-turski rat, 1,* 409–11.

[182] GIM, Cherniaev to Aksakov, Oct. 2/14.

[183] AII, Ristić 18/159, Sept. 3/15, telegram.

Europe pronounces itself opposed to a Russo-Turkish war, I do not believe he would risk it.[184]

Cherniaev and his entourage had been awaiting an opportunity to seize control of Serbia.[185] Now, pressing Milan to accept a crown, Cherniaev asked permission to send to Belgrade an army "delegation" four battalions strong to "lay at the feet of Your Majesty the feelings of fidelity and devotion of their constituents." This force, claims Ristić, had orders to overthrow the government and constitution.[186] This was the crucial moment for the Ristić regime. Never had Russian influence in Belgrade been "so open, so direct, and so decisive," confirmed the foreign consuls. Prince Milan, however, supported his ministers; their reply to Cherniaev refused to accept the royal title. Ironically, Nikolić conveyed the government's response to Cherniaev: obey the cabinet or leave Serbia.[187]

Negative foreign reactions to Cherniaev's royal proclamation poured into Belgrade. Official Russia condemned it promptly and unaminously. Gorchakov called it folly; Miliutin feared this "stupid undertaking" would "greatly complicate our diplomacy." [188] A government-inspired article in *Golos* (September 19) denounced Cherniaev's action for obstructing a peaceful settlement.[189] The proclamation, reported Ćukić

---

[184] RA (1914), no. 1, p. 44, Milan to Cherniaev, Sept. 3/15.

[185] Before leaving Russia, Cherniaev had denounced Serbian parliamentarism and hinted it should be abrogated—*Russkii Mir*, April 7, 1876, no. 72. According to Protić, one of Cherniaev's cronies wrote early in the war that the Assembly should be abolished and a *coup d'état* executed as soon as enough Russian officers had arrived in Serbia. AII, Ristić 26/717, Protić to Ristić, July 26/Aug. 7. In an undated wartime telegram Cherniaev wrote Aksakov how Serbia would benefit from a coup: "The influence of Russia upon Serbia would be real and rest on firm foundations. The chief of state and the entire people sympathize with Russia. The ministers gradually could be named from Russians. Hostile parties would disappear and one of the Slav states would become *de facto* a Russian province." Nikitin, "Russkoe obshchestvo," p. 1025. Cherniaev scarcely needed to add that he would become its ruler.

[186] DAS, 29/100–11, Cherniaev to Milan, Sept. 5/17; Ristić, *1*, 140–41; Vlada Milana, *1*, 449–50.

[187] PRO, FO 78/2488, White to Derby, Sept. 17, no. 135. HHSA, Wrede to Andrassy, Sept. 13, no. 146. Ristić told Wrede that Cherniaev was changing from a Serbian general into a Russain dictator and that his government was "*débordé*." "The proclamation," added Ristić, "merely confirmed how correct I was." *Ibid.*, Sept. 19, no. 151. Milan's reply was drafted at a cabinet meeting.

[188] Miliutin, *Dnevnik*, *2*, 79, Sept. 6/18; Grujić, *3*, 219.

[189] *Golos*, Sept. 7/19, no. 247; HHSA, Mayr to Andrassy, Sept. 15/27, no. 52B.

from Vienna, had endangered Serbia's chances to obtain the *status quo ante* and must be disavowed publicly before peace efforts could resume.[190] Refuse the kingship, Andrassy warned Milan, or lose Austria-Hungary's support.[191]

Milan hastily assured Austria and Russia that he would not change his mind and accept the royal title.[192] He had written Cherniaev on September 18 that unless the proclamation were withdrawn, the Powers might recall their consuls or even authorize Austria to occupy Serbia. Instead of drawing Russia into war, the army's action would bring the country a humiliating peace.[193] Cherniaev, discovering that he could not compel Belgrade to submit, merely declared that the proclamation could not be withdrawn. He requested time to ascertain its effect on Russian opinion, threatening otherwise to launch a desperate assault against the Turks and either perish or return to Russia with his volunteers.[194] Neither Cherniaev nor Belgrade wished to provoke a complete breach. Indeed, Milan requested of Cherniaev (September 24) a sizable personal loan and accepted his offer of 40,000 rubles. In an order of the day (September 26), Milan thanked the army for its loyalty but did not accept the royal title.[195] The proclamation remained in effect in Cherniaev's command, but it was ignored in Belgrade.

Through the Correspondence Bureau's efforts, Cherniaev's proclamation stirred up Russian public opinion. *Moskovskie Vedomosti* interpreted it as a genuine Serbian popular manifesto:

In the chivalric outburst of the Serbian army was manifested the feeling animating the entire Serbian people protesting against the vassal relationship with the Porte. The proclamation has been approved by the Assembly [*sic!*] and a petition to the prince urging acceptance of the kingly title was signed by all but two of its members.[196]

---

[190] AII, Ristić 18/163, Ćukić to Ristić, Sept. 10/22.

[191] HHSA, Andrassy to Wrede, Sept. 26. While Serbia was under Russian tutelage, Andrassy opposed Milan's aspirations to kingship; once the country was under Austrian domination, Vienna encouraged them.

[192] HHSA, Wrede to Andrassy, Sept. 23, no. 154; Oct. 5, no. 158.

[193] RA (1914), no. 1, pp. 46–48, Milan to Cherniaev, Sept. 6/18; Grujić, *3*, 217.

[194] *Ibid.*, pp. 224, 227; Djordjević, *Srpsko-turski rat*, *1*, 432.

[195] RA (1914), no. 1, pp. 50, 52, Milan to Cherniaev, Sept. 12/24 and 15/27.

[196] *Moskovskie Vedomosti*, Sept. 7/19, 14/26, nos. 228, 234. *Sankt Peterburgskie Vedomosti* and *Russkie Vedomosti* likewise interpreted the proclamation as a sign of the determination of the Serbian army to continue the war. Nikitin, "Russkoe obshchestvo," p. 1026.

Russkii Mir asserted that it reflected the wishes of the Serbian army and the Belgrade government.[197] The public reaction, though sufficient to alarm the Austrian chargé d'affaires,[198] did not alter official policy. Even Aksakov considered the proclamation a blunder.[199] *Golos,* with the Foreign Ministry's support, launched a vigorous counterattack against pro-Cherniaev newspapers.[200] The general's grandstand play had failed.

Among Serbian newspapers, *Istok* featured reports from the Correspondence Bureau and supported Cherniaev loyally during the campaign, but it omitted all mention of his proclamation and carefully denied that Pan-Russianism had support in Serbia.[201] *Zastava,* urging Milan to accept kingship because the entire Serbian people favored it, beat the drums for the proclamation: "When a united kingdom of Serbia is a *fait accompli,* Europe will have to abandon talk of the integrity of Turkey." [202] Miletić viewed Cherniaev's pronunciamento as a step in liberating and unifying Serbdom.

The abortive royal proclamation reduced Cherniaev's political influence in Serbia, but militarily he remained pre-eminent. No sooner had the ten-day truce begun than he complained of Turkish violations and claimed that such a short truce benefited only the Turks.[203] Instead, Cherniaev advocated a lengthier, demarcated armistice during which he could visit Russia to seek massive assistance.

The armistice debate promptly reopened in Belgrade. Kartsov officially advised the Serbian ministers to adhere to the truce despite Turkish violations, although apparently he was unofficially holding out the prospect of Russian intervention.[204] When the Porte unilaterally

[197] *Russkii Mir,* Sept. 22/Oct. 4, no. 229, "Za tridtsat dnei." This was the first issue following a month's suspension.

[198] HHSA, Mayr to Andrassy, Sept. 15/27, no. 52B.

[199] GIM, Aksakov to Cherniaev, Sept. 6/18.

[200] *Golos,* Sept. 7/19, 9/21, nos. 247, 249. "King making" in tiny Serbia was called ridiculous. "We had not heard that a military dictatorship reigned in Serbia and that the army had been granted a decisive voice in political and state questions."

[201] *Istok,* July 16/28, Oct. 24/Nov. 5, nos. 77, 115.

[202] *Zastava,* Sept. 17/29, Sept. 19/Oct. 1, Oct. 3/15, nos. 142, 143, 151. "Only opponents of a better Serbian future can belittle or overlook the significance of that vital act [proclamation] . . . which corresponded to general popular wishes." *Ibid.,* no. 143.

[203] DAS, 29/100–IX, Cherniaev to Milan, Sept. 8/20; Grujić, *3,* 219–20.

[204] Kartsov, caught between St. Petersburg's pacific admonitions and Ignat'ev's bellicose exhortations, apparently was again playing a dual role. To the Serbs he

announced a week's extension of the truce, Belgrade's dilemma deepened. Cherniaev, claiming his military position was superior to the Turks', opposed any armistice shorter than six weeks. Some Serbian ministers (Ristić, Grujić, and Milojković) argued that Cherniaev was too optimistic in believing that the war should continue either immediately or after six weeks. They preferred to end the war with the Powers' assistance on the basis of the *status quo ante;* the remaining ministers agreed with Cherniaev. Prince Milan broke the deadlock on September 26 by siding with the war faction.[205] Belgrade rejected the truce's prolongation and Cherniaev resumed offensive operations.

Cherniaev sought revenge upon the Ristić government by resuming his feud with Nikolić and accusing him of attempting during his visit to Deligrad "in every way to reduce my authority." His army had been inadequately supplied because of "the ignorance and incapacity of the [war] ministry." "In any other country," Cherniaev asserted, "Nikolić would not rise by ability above the rank of battalion commander." Henceforth, he would deal directly with Prince Milan.[206] The War Ministry sent a sharp attack upon the Russians' behavior: "From all sides both from the city of Belgrade and the provinces come to me complaints against the Russian volunteers, who overindulge in spirits and in a drunken state commit scandalous acts in hotels, cafés, and the streets." The Serbian government, grateful for Russian aid, would use force to compel volunteers to obey the laws of the land only as a last resort, but if necessary it would expel guilty ones from Serbia.[207]

---

hinted unofficially, claims Wrede, that Russian armed aid was imminent. HHSA, Wrede to Andrassy, Sept. 13, no. 146. Later Wrede reported, "Kartsov's attitude and speech have been a major hindrance to the quick conclusion of peace and are becoming more pronounced. . . . His statements openly suggest the prospect of armed [Russian] intervention in behalf of Serbia. Whereas earlier he held himself aloof from the Russian volunteers, . . . now he is constantly with the new Russian arrivals and the Russian consulate has become their headquarters." *Ibid.,* Sept. 19, no. 148; Grujić, *3,* 220–21; Ristić, *1,* 142.

[205] Kartsov, pleading lack of instructions, refused to advise the Serbs. The war faction, claims Ristić, accepted Cherniaev's statement that he was closer to the Balkans than the Turks were to the Morava. Had Serbia made peace at this time, Ristić adds, it would have been spared the worst horrors of war. Ristić, *1,* 144–45, 152–53; Grujić, *3,* 222–26; Vlada Milana, *1,* 342–44.

[206] AII, Ristić 18/165, Cherniaev to Jovanović, Sept. 18/30, telegram.

[207] *Ibid.,* 18/363, Nikolić to Cherniaev, Oct. 1/13. Although signed by Nikolić, this letter was written by a certain Beker, a subordinate official, claims Colonel

In an indignant reply (October 18) Cherniaev demanded a full
apology and brought the dispute to the point of crisis. To Ristić he
wrote, "Take into consideration that once the Russian officers and I
have left and the [Nikolić-Beker] letter has been communicated to
the Slav committees, you cannot expect any more moral or material
assistance from the Russian people.[208] After the ministers had discussed
the letter, Ristić expressed to Cherniaev his government's regret at the
incident.[209] But Nikolić stubbornly refused to apologize and accused
Cherniaev of usurping his powers and misusing Russian funds. Nikolić,
supported by his colleagues in the cabinet, remained in office.[210] Once
again the Ristić government had survived a struggle with Cherniaev.

Cherniaev was unable to abide competitors and feuded constantly
with Russian diplomats and military leaders. From the beginning he
had disliked Kartsov, viewing him as a rival for Prince Milan's favor.
Kartsov's official reports exposed the general's Pan-Slav activities. After
the royal proclamation, he and Wrede urged the prince to repudiate
Cherniaev altogether.[211] Complaining of Kartsov's intrigues, the general
appealed to Aksakov to secure the consul's recall.[212] In late September,
a retired Russian general, S. K. Novoselov, assumed command of the
Ibar army at Belgrade's request. He infuriated Cherniaev by establishing friendly relations with Kartsov and the Serbian government. Some
Russian volunteers were attracted to Novoselov's army; Cherniaev
promptly demanded that all arriving volunteers proceed directly to his
headquarters and sought unsuccessfully to subordinate Novoselov to
his orders.[213]

As Belgrade's resources neared exhaustion, Serbian leaders grew disil-

---

Catargi. Great damage would be done to the Serbian cause, he warned, unless
Beker were dismissed as satisfaction to Cherniaev. DAS, 29/101–5, Catargi to
Milan, Oct. 6/18.

[208] Ristić 18/363, Cherniaev to Ristić, Oct. 6/18.

[209] *Ibid.*, Ristić to Cherniaev, Oct. 23. Ristić concluded, "Incidents such as
these . . . cannot in any way damage the recognition by the Serbian people of the
great services you are rendering to their country."

[210] HHSA, Wrede to Andrassy, Nov. 7, no. 172, citing confidential report of
Oct. 28; Grujić, *3*, 233.

[211] Kartsov, RS, *134*, 70–71, 311; OSVOb., *1*, 384.

[212] GIM, Cherniaev to Aksakov, Oct. 2/14.

[213] DAS, 29/101–3, Cherniaev to Milan, Oct. 4/16. For Novoselov's version see
OSVOb., *1*, 427–28. Although Novoselov did not meddle in Serbian politics,
neither was he an effective military leader. See M. Petrović, *Ratne beleške 1876,
1877 i 1878 g.* (Čačak, 1955), *1*, 214, 224.

lusioned with unofficial Russian aid they knew was insufficient to bring victory.[214] Milan wrote Cherniaev that without much greater assistance Serbia could not continue the war.[215] "Only official Russia can give things a different turn," Ristić wrote on October 4, "and until she is in a position to do so, it would be better for us to await it in a truce status rather than suffer great losses without prospect of greater success." [216] The Serbian people and government, reported Wrede, are ready to make peace, but until Prince Milan liberates himself from Cherniaev's influence, they cannot do so.[217]

Cherniaev appealed to Aksakov to secure major and immediate aid for Serbia. With typical exaggeration he declared: "The Serbs have already gained a three-quarters victory over Turkey, but in this struggle they have exhausted their last penny and put forward their last man. Now has come the critical time to aid them *fundamentally*, all at once. . . . The first and principal step in this sense would be the realization of the loan." He requested also 10,000 volunteers, 1,500 Cossacks, 25,000 rifles, 25,000 overcoats, 10,000 pairs of boots, and six long-range batteries. If the Slav committees supplied these items promptly, Cherniaev pledged he would reach Sofia by January, bid farewell to the triumphant Serbs, and take charge of the Bulgarian forces.[218]

Instead of disciplining unruly volunteers, Cherniaev expected the Slav committees to do so. They finally selected General V. D. Dandevil' to supervise Russians in Serbia and provide new arrivals with money and equipment. He was to expel those who "have conducted themselves in a manner unworthy of a Russian soldier" and enlist aid from the Serbian authorities if police measures were required.[219]

[214] HHSA, Wrede to Andrassy, Sept. 19, no. 151. Ristić, Milojković, and Metropolitan Mihailo, claiming unofficial aid was inadequate, all asked insistently when Russia would intervene officially. Meshcherskii, *Pravda o Serbii*, pp. 142ff.

[215] RA (1914) no. 1, pp. 56, 58, 62, Milan to Cherniaev, Sept. 22/Oct. 4, Sept. 26/Oct. 8. Serbian troops, wrote the prince, lack warm clothing, ammunition, and the treasury is empty.

[216] DAS, 151/455, Ristić to Protić, Sept. 22/Oct. 4.

[217] HHSA, Wrede to Andrassy, Oct. 5, no. 159.

[218] ROBibSS, f. Aksakova, Cherniaev to Aksakov, Sept. 24/Oct. 6 (completed Oct. 2/14). He would need only 10,000,000 rubles to achieve victory, claimed Cherniaev, whereas it would cost official Russia at least 800,000,000 rubles. "Turkey is at its last gasp!" concluded Cherniaev.

[219] *Pervye 15 let*, pp. 539, 540, 545. For instructions to Dandevil' by the St. Petersburg Commission on collections, see OSVOb., *1*, 382–83.

Dandevil' established good relations with Belgrade, but there was no committee representative at the frontier to greet arriving volunteers. V. Iasherov, a volunteer, noted that his group wandered aimlessly about the frontier town of Kladovo and finally had to pay for private transportation to Belgrade.[220] Not until early October was a Benevolent Committee established in Belgrade to co-ordinate unofficial aid to Serbia and "dispel the already developing dissatisfaction between Serbs and Russians." [221] Composed of both Serbs and Russians under Metropolitan Mihailo's chairmanship, this committee did much to aid Serbian war victims,[222] but it was created too late to insure harmonious Serbo-Russian relations.

Serious friction between Serbs and Russians developed during the latter stages of the campaign. A Serbian major, violently denouncing Cherniaev, warned Ristić against this "Russian madman." [223] An anonymous Serb told Prince Meshcherskii, "It was nice of Cherniaev to come to Serbia; . . . but we did not think he would arrive with such an assortment of Russians to conquer our country. Look at what surrounds him: uncivilized elements, drunkards, and not a single Serb on his staff." [224] Russian officers confirmed that poor behavior by volunteers often caused friction. According to Major Khvostov, volunteers "sought to seize as much power as possible and meanwhile, when failures occurred, threw the entire blame on Serbian commanders or army." So widespread was moral license among them that the Serbs ceased to trust the honorable ones. By the war's end, "indignation against us was so great that [the Serbs] would not give us anything even for money." [225] Another volunteer officer, N. V. Maksimov, was even more emphatic:

We proudly, confidently appeared in Serbia as saviors in the conviction that without us Serbia would perish. All of us from generals to sergeants were little Pompadours, adopted the role of dictators, and did not hesitate to

[220] DAS, 151/455, Ristić to Protić, Sept. 22/Oct. 4; V. Iasherov, "V Serbii, 1876–1877," *Russkii Vestnik, 133* (Jan. 1878), pp. 203ff.; Khvostov, *Russkie i serby,* p. 13.

[221] OSVOb., *1,* 441–42, Filippov to Aksakov, Sept. 17/29. The Slav committees agreed to let Dandevil' handle the volunteers' military affairs.

[222] For the Benevolent Committee's work see *ibid.,* p. 455, Kartsov to Asiatic Department, Oct. 14/26, and p. 531, Mihailo to Aksakov, Nov. 25/Dec. 7.

[223] AII, Ristić 26/734, Bogičević to (Ristić), Oct. 1/13. "I can tell you that you will see black days and great humiliation with this Russian madman."

[224] V. Meshcherskii, *Odin iz nashikh Mol'tke* (St. Petersburg, 1890), pp. 343–44.

[225] Khvostov, *Russkie i serby,* pp. 35, 43, 45, 60.

dominate the Serbs and reproach them simultaneously for accepting money and clothing from Russia. It was only natural that Serbian pride was injured.

Ignoring Serbian law and acting as they pleased, Russian officers showed little interest in the Serbs and failed to curb misbehavior.[226]

Nor were the Serbs blameless for the deterioration of relations. Raw militia units often fled the battlefield, sometimes firing upon Russian officers who sought to restrain them. Many Serbian soldiers inflicted slight wounds upon themselves to escape action. Uninspired by an apathetic prince, exhausted in an unequal struggle, the militia virtually ceased to fight weeks before the end of the campaign.[227] An army of slackers, mostly wealthy peasants and merchants, obtained profitable posts behind the lines and were held in justifiable contempt by the Russian volunteers. Serbian merchants, according to Russian accounts, often took financial advantage of volunteers.[228] Unless guaranteed payment Serbs often refused to care for wounded Russians. But the belief of some Russian officers that Serbs were cowardly was denied by other observers and refuted by the magnificent showing of the small regular army and artillery units.[229]

Divergent cultures and national outlooks separated Serbs from Russians. The chief philosopher of Russian Pan-Slavism, N. Ia. Danilevskii, attributing differences among the Slavs primarily to west European influences, had predicted that they would disappear in a common struggle against non-Slavs: "Therefore the open struggle which will awaken both on our part and on that of the [other] Slavs powerful sympathies of a common faith and origin [*edinoplemennosti*], hidden in the depths of the soul of the popular masses themselves . . . will quickly turn all the advantages to our side." [230] But after the campaign, G. Devollan, a Slav committee envoy, realized that social differences

---

[226] Maksimov, *Dve voiny*, pp. 21, 132–35.

[227] Khvostov, *Russkie i serby*, pp. 61, 66. Matija Ban confirmed that Serbian infantry became dispirited and passive by mid-September. "The Russian volunteers alone continued to fight. . . ." AII, Ban 11/51.

[228] Maksimov, *Dve voiny*, p. 118; Devollan, *Serbskii vopros*, p. 10; Meshcherskii, *Pravda o Serbii*, p. 85.

[229] Khvostov, *Russkie i serby*, p. 21; Maksimov, *Dve voiny*, p. 4; Meshcherskii, *Moi vospominaniia*, 2, 302. Devollan stated (*Serbskii vopros*, pp. 5, 10) that it was foolish to accuse an entire people of cowardice when every Russian knew the Serb militia was inexperienced and had done its best. More Serbs than Russians had been killed in the campaign.

[230] N. Danilevskii, *Rossiia i Evropa* (St. Petersburg, 1871), p. 460.

had promoted Serbo-Russian antagonism. "In Serbia collided two wholly different social structures and there was no connecting element which could facilitate their understanding of one another." [231] To his amazement, Maksimov discovered he had nothing in common with his Serbian soldiers: "All these assurances of our brotherhood with the Slavs, all this nonsense about our blood relationship . . . is fine in the mouth of a politician or historian, but it is purely fiction in the sense of natural human feelings. . . . Serbia is for me a land of different views, manners, habits, convictions, education, and direction." [232] Prince Meshcherskii, dismayed at the decline of Orthodoxy and the lack of interest in Russian language and culture, concluded pessimistically that west European influence had triumphed in Serbia.[233] Many volunteers were disillusioned by the discovery that Serbian peasants lived as well as some Russian landowners. "The poor country of our oppressed brethren," wrote Maksimov, "was a place where the peasants drink wine and live off the fat of the land." [234]

Disgruntled Pan-Slavs drew unwarranted conclusions about unofficial Russia's role in the Serbian war. "Before the war," wrote Khvostov, "the Serbs did not know us and loved us; now having become acquainted, they hate us."

Between us has opened a veritable abyss, and until Serbian wounds heal and perhaps longer, the Russian name will be pronounced with hatred. All our sacrifices add up to nothing, and the general devastation brought on the Slav peoples is the only common denominator. Should the Serbs be thankful to us for their destruction? [235]

Ivan Aksakov was equally gloomy:

I cannot regard except with sadness and a heavy heart the results of all my personal activity and in general all our efforts in 1876. Instead of saving Serbia, we almost ruined her; one third of her territory is in enemy hands; exhaustion, destruction, and humiliation; instead of "brotherly love" virtually "brotherly hatred" since the mass of returned volunteers has spread all over Russia such a scorn for the Serbs that most of the contributions arrive with the inscription: "only not for the Serbs." . . . The charm of the

---

[231] Devollan, *Serbskii vopros*, pp. 15, 19–20.

[232] Maksimov, *Dve voiny*, p. 131. But, he added (pp. 132–33), friendly, natural relations were often established between ordinary Serbian and Russian soldiers.

[233] Meshcherskii, *Pravda o Serbii*, pp. 201–03.

[234] Maksimov, *Dve voiny*, p. 35.

[235] Khvostov, *Russkie i serby*, introduction and p. 78.

Russian name has been destroyed both in Serbia and throughout the Slav world, yet outside of Russia there is no future for Slavdom. Finally, Russian society is losing faith in its . . . independent activity.[236]

G. A. Devollan, reaching a more balanced verdict, predicted correctly that once the volunteers had departed, the Serbs would forget "the refuse in the cafés" and "recall the great sacrifices made for them by the Russian people." [237] Nonetheless, the relationship between Serbs and Russians was touchier and more complex than either had expected.

The growing prospect of Serbian defeat compelled official Russia to clarify its Balkan policies, as Russian diplomats put forth their views. From Livadia, the tsar sought Austrian support for a peaceful settlement or, failing that, for joint military action against the Porte. He sent General Sumarokov-Elston to Vienna on September 27 to convey to Emperor Franz Josef, Alexander's proposals for energetic European action to obtain "un armistice réel et immédiat." The tsar's letter stated that Russia opposed creation of a large Slav state in the Balkans, but favored genuine autonomy for the insurgent provinces and Bulgaria. In case the Porte rejected this, the Powers should impose a solution. Austria would occupy Bosnia, Russia move into Bulgaria, and the Powers make a naval demonstration at the Bosphorus. If the Ottoman Empire collapsed as a result, the Reichstadt agreements would be invoked.[238] Turkish rejection of the English bases, Jomini wrote to Giers, should be followed by a Russian ultimatum to the Porte. Sumarokov-Elston's mission was Russia's attempt "sortir du chaos." [239] Diplomacy, warned Miliutin, might fail to resolve the crisis. "A very categorical question" had been put to Vienna. "In case it turns out finally that we are unable to proceed further with Austria-Hungary and England, war [with Turkey] will become unavoidable." He foresaw full Russian mobilization if one or more nations assisted Turkey.[240]

The Austrian emperor's reply, on October 3, was not encouraging. Fearing eventual creation of a powerful Serbian state, he opposed genuine autonomy for the insurgent provinces. Austria would not support Russia militarily if the Porte rejected the English bases. In case

[236] GIM, Aksakov to Cherniaev, Jan. 4/16, 1877.

[237] Devollan, *Serbskii vopros*, p. 21.

[238] The tsar stated repeatedly that force would probably be necessary to secure the Porte's compliance. HHSA, Alexander II to Emperor Franz Josef, Sept. 11/23, 1876; Tiutin ("Politika," p. 226) cites Gorchakov's letter to Andrassy.

[239] Jelavich, *Russia in the East*, p. 26, Jomini to Giers, Sept. 9/21.

[240] Miliutin, *Dnevnik*, 2, 80; OSVOb., *1*, 396–97, Miliutin, to Reitern, Sept. 14/26.

Russian forces entered Turkey, the Monarchy would occupy Bosnia and Hercegovina.[241] Austria, commented Jomini, sought gains without taking risks and desired either a *replâtrage* or Ottoman dissolution. But unless Russia permitted Austrian occupation of Bosnia, she must face the intolerable threat of an Anglo-Austrian-Turkish coalition. Jomini hoped enough reinforcements could be sent to Cherniaev to prevent a decisive Turkish victory over Serbia. Then the diplomats could take charge and spare Russia the danger of war against a coalition.[242]

Heeding Miliutin's objections to an autumn campaign, the tsar agreed not to utter the dread word "mobilization" unless armed intervention became inevitable. But Franz Josef's refusal to join in military action convinced Alexander that unilateral Russian force would probably be required.[243] On the other hand, he reproached Gorchakov for suggesting that large reinforcements of volunteers be sent to Serbia, and he criticized Guards' officers, and indirectly the heir, for encouraging officers to join Cherniaev. Pan-Slav agitation, noted Alexander, was hampering his efforts to end the Serbo-Turkish war. If force were required, the Russian government would control it.[244] The tsar sought to calm English fears over the volunteer movement. Lord Derby, the British foreign secretary, believed that each additional Russian volunteer strengthened the Serbian war party and undermined the Powers' peace efforts.[245] Later, Derby complained that the influx of Russian volunteers was blocking a peaceful settlement. He wrote Ambassador Loftus in St. Petersburg:

The presence of Russian officers and soldiers in the Servian army has assumed proportions which fall little short of national assistance. It is stated that upwards of 15,000 Russian subjects have now joined the Servian

[241] HHSA, Emperor Franz Josef to Alexander II, Oct. 3.

[242] Jelavich, *Russia in the East*, pp. 28–30, Jomini to Giers, Sept. 23/Oct. 5, and Sept. 25/Oct. 7.

[243] Miliutin, *Dnevnik*, 2, 83–84, 87, entries of Oct. 4 and 7.

[244] *Ibid.*, pp. 87–90. Giers commented, "Having wisely awaited the favorable moment to leave our apparent inaction, we are finally raising our strong voice. . . . Whatever happens henceforth it will be the government itself which will act openly and not the Slav committees which so easily go astray: this will be more respectable and less dangerous." Jelavich, *Russia in the East*, p. 144, Giers to Jomini, Sept. 16/28.

[245] *Staatsarchiv, 31*, 139–40, Derby to Loftus, Sept. 27. Shuvalov explained that because of the excited state of Russian opinion, the tsar could not halt the volunteer movement.

cause. . . . If the Emperor of Russia is as sincerely desirous of a speedy and peaceful termination of the present disastrous struggle as His Majesty's government believe him to be, he can scarcely be insensible to the difficulties which are thus thrown in the way of a settlement.[246]

Russia, though pushing war preparations, continued to advocate a Serbo-Turkish armistice to reassure the Powers. On October 10, Alexander wrote the Austrian emperor that the Powers should agree to a truce of at least one month and broad autonomy for the Christian provinces. Again he suggested a secret Austro-Russian agreement to fight Turkey in the spring should diplomatic action fail.[247] The tsar continued to co-operate with the Powers, as Shuvalov suggested, on the basis of the English proposals. But Russia would not accept the restrictive, non-political type of autonomy for the Christian provinces which was favored by Austria and England.[248] When Serbia had resumed fighting after the recent truce, further attempts for a truce were made; Gorchakov favored a short truce, arguing that the six-month truce now proposed by Turkey would impose unnecessary hardships upon the Serbian states.[249] The chancellor telegraphed Shuvalov, "The Imperial Government cannot be indifferent to bloodshed in the Balkan peninsula. The emperor proposes to the Guarantor Courts to stop bloodshed by imposing immediately upon both sides an armistice of six weeks to give the cabinets time to agree on the solution of unresolved questions." [250] Russia's obstinacy on the truce question, enhanced by the desire to obtain Serbian support in a winter campaign, helped insure Serbia's defeat.

In mid-October, Alexander II summoned his ministers to Livadia to a series of crucial meetings. Finance Minister M. Reitern, a strong partisan of peace, noted in his diary, "The general atmosphere of Livadia

---

[246] *Ibid.*, pp. 166–69, Oct. 11. Derby's figures grossly exaggerated the extent of unofficial Russian aid to Serbia. See *supra*, p. 122.

[247] HHSA, Alexander II to Franz Josef, Sept. 28/Oct. 10.

[248] OSVOb., *1*, 393–94, Shuvalov to Gorchakov, Sept. 11/23; *ibid.*, pp. 415–16, Gorchakov to Shuvalov, Sept. 21/Oct. 3.

[249] Gorchakov to Shuvalov, Oct. 1/13, 2/14, SR (June 1925), pp. 192–93; HHSA, Varia Russie 1876, Gorchakov to Novikov, Oct. 3/15, telegram.

Serbia and Montenegro opposed the six months' truce, proposed by Turkey, but were willing to accept the shorter one supported by Russia. See Serbo-Montenegrin telegraphic correspondence on the truce question in *Zapisi, 6* (Jan. 1930), 46–47, and (Feb. 1930), p. 108.

[250] HHSA, Gorchakov to Shuvalov, Oct. 1876.

was extremely warlike." Gorchakov was unusually bellicose, Ignat'ev favored war, and the tsar doubted the efficacy of peaceful methods.[251] War fever was increasing in Russia, reported Loftus, and might force her into military action.[252] Reitern's memorandum, opposing military involvement on financial grounds, was not supported by other ministers and was criticized severely by the tsar,[253] who had just read General N. N. Obruchev's war plan. Obruchev predicted that except in winter, Russian armies could occupy Constantinople within three months and forestall formation of a European coalition.[254]

A Jomini-Gorchakov memorandum, submitted to the ministers on October 15, advised continued co-operation with the Powers. It considered unilateral Russian military action as a last resort. But if deemed necessary, it must be undertaken quickly. A November invasion of Bulgaria would catch the Turkish forces arrayed against the Serbian states between two fires: within a month the Porte would be defeated. Ignat'ev should return to Constantinople to hasten negotiations while Russian forces mobilized. Turkey's refusal of a six weeks' armistice could be used as a pretext for war.[255] Despite scattered objections and Miliutin's warning against a winter campaign, the memorandum was approved. Unless peace was achieved quickly, Russia would break relations with Turkey and mobilize (about November 13). If necessary, war would begin in mid-December.[256]

The Foreign Ministry, while bellicose, was not particularly favorable to Serbia. The chancellor, apparently considering Belgrade guilty of aggression against Turkey did not even instruct Ignat'ev to demand for it the *status quo ante*. Serbia, in return for guarantees to the Porte

[251] Extracts from M. Reitern's diary in RS, *143* (July 1910), pp. 39-40. Present at the Livadia meetings were the tsar, the heir, Gorchakov, Reitern, Miliutin, Adlerberg, and Ignat'ev.

[252] *Staatsarchiv, 31,* 183, Loftus to Derby, Oct. 17.

[253] S. Valuev, *Dnevnik, 1877–1884* (Moscow, 1961), pp. 291–92.

[254] Miliutin, *Dnevnik, 2,* p. 92. For the text see M. Hasenkampf, *Dnevnik,* annex no. 1. Nelidov telegraphed from Constantinople that the Turkish army was so weak it would not even be able to hold out against the Serbs during the winter. Rejecting Obruchev's proposal to seize Constantinople, the tsar wrote, "The political aim of the war must be exclusively the temporary occupation of Bulgaria." Tiutin, "Politika," p. 242.

[255] Ignat'ev, IV, *136* (May 1914), pp. 432–39; Goriainov, *Bosphore,* p. 325. Thus the Foreign Ministry shared Cherniaev's optimism and seriously underestimated Turkish strength. Gorchakov assumed that Serbia and Montenegro would still be fighting in mid-November.

[256] Miliutin, *Dnevnik, 2,* 93–95, Oct. 4/16.

against resumption of war, would obtain Mali Zvornik, but would have to pay more tribute if the Turks demanded. On the other hand, Montenegro would receive a considerable increase in territory. A curious reluctance to support Serbia coincided with bellicose statements by the Ministry's spokesmen. Jomini wrote Giers:

> The Rubicon will be crossed. Ignat'ev leaves tonight. He will present our claims, then an ultimatum, then break relations! . . . I only fear that Europe . . . will come forward with mediation proposals. There is no more time to lose. If we wait beyond the end of November [old style], the opportunity to crush Turkey will be lost.

But Jomini realized that unless Austria's attitude were clarified and Germany's moral support obtained, war would have to wait until spring.[257] Gorchakov, too, was resolute: "We are at the height of the crisis. Our decisions have been made. We will continue to be impartial and moderate in our views. But we will be unshakable in our determination not to be satisfied with sterile phrases to improve the conditions of the Christians."[258] This "improvement" did not include betterment of Serbia's position.

The Turks, unable to remove the Serbian states from the war through diplomacy, resumed the offensive. Osman Pasha, forcing back Serbian Colonel Horvatović (October 19–21), approached the Djunis heights, guarding the Morava Valley. In dismay, Ristić requested Ignat'ev to arrange an immediate armistice.[259] On October 29, disaster struck Cherniaev's army. In a sudden assault, the Turks captured the Djunis positions; the Serbs, abandoning weapons and equipment, fled the battlefield while Russian volunteers suffered grievous losses. The Serbian army was demoralized and the road to Belgrade lay open. At 3 P.M., Cherniaev asked Milan to telegraph the tsar that only an immediate armistice would save Serbia. Russian leaders were informed at once of the country's desperate plight.[260]

Russia reacted promptly and dramatically. Receiving Kartsov's dispatches describing the Turkish advance (October 30), Gorchakov

---

[257] Ignat'ev, IV, *136* (May 1914), pp. 440–41; Jelavich, *Russia in the East*, p. 31, Jomini to Giers, Oct. 5/17.

[258] *Ibid.*, pp. 30–31, Gorchakov to Giers, Oct. 5/17.

[259] AII, Ristić 18/74, draft of a memorandum by Ristić, handed to Kartsov on Oct. 12/24; Grujić, *3*, 234; Ristić, *1*, 148–50. Thus five days before the fatal encounter at Djunis, Belgrade was suing for peace.

[260] Vlada Milana, *1*, 348; Grujić, *3*, 235.

took them to the tsar. An hour later Alexander was conferring with his ministers. At this meeting Gorchakov allegedly declared, "Your Majesty, now is not the time for words, not the time for sympathy: the hour for action has come. Here is my telegram, already prepared, to our ambassador in Constantinople." Unless the Turks halted within twenty-four hours, stated this ultimatum, Ignat'ev would leave Constantinople and war would follow. Gorchakov asserted that they accepted his proposal, the ultimatum was sent, and Serbia was saved.[261] The tsar claimed that, learning of Serbia's defeat, he decided to send the ultimatum to prevent further bloodshed since the Turks might massacre Serbian civilians.[262] But Ignat'ev's version was that he had persuaded the Porte to accept a six weeks' armistice before the ultimatum arrived. The Turkish government, thunderstruck by it, yielded power to Midhat Pasha's war faction. Ignat'ev asserted that he had saved Serbia and that Gorchakov's ultimatum provoked the subsequent Russo-Turkish war.[263]

The Russian ultimatum was effective regardless of individual responsibility. Turkey immediately accepted a two months' armistice which even allowed Russian munitions and volunteers to enter Serbia and Montenegro.[264] Acting unilaterally without consulting the Powers, Russia imposed a truce favorable to the Serbian states.

The Serbo-Turkish war deeply affected relations between Russia and the Serbs. The Ristić Liberals had been encouraged by Pan-Slav leaders to make war, then to continue it after prospects of victory disappeared.

---

[261] M-skii, "Kniaz' A. M. Gorchakov," RS, 40 (Oct. 1883), 178–79. Gorchakov claimed that his prompt action prevented Serbia's destruction and that even Miliutin had not recommended decisive action. His version is substantiated somewhat by Miliutin's silence about his role at the Oct. 18/30 meeting. After learning of Djunis, he merely wrote, "Such a situation is no longer tolerable. It is essential to adopt a decisive tone." Miliutin, *Dnevnik*, 2, 102, Oct. 18/30.

[262] Having done his utmost to promote peace, he must now act alone unless Europe agreed to energetic measures. He pledged not to occupy Constantinople and denied any intention of making Serbia and Rumania into kingdoms. Interview of Loftus with Alexander II on Nov. 2, 1876, cited in Tatishchev, *Aleksandr II, 2*, 330–31; *Staatsarchiv, 31*, 209–10, Loftus to Derby, Nov. 2.

[263] Ignat'ev, IV, *136* (May 1914), pp. 448–52. Ignat'ev most unfairly attributed the ultimatum to Gorchakov's desire to undermine his position in Constantinople. Before the ultimatum's arrival, however, Ignat'ev had written Gorchakov that his negotiations with the Turks were doomed to failure. A week after the ultimatum's presentation, Ignat'ev boasted to Kartsov: "My ultimatum [*sic!*] saved Serbia from final destruction when everything collapsed." Tiutin, "Politika," pp. 245–46.

[264] Vlada Milana, *1*, 353.

During the struggle the pro-Slav movement in Russia, led by the Slav committees, reached its peak and provided enough financial and military aid to keep the Serbian states fighting. Russian public opinion diverged sharply from the official position. Unofficial Russia, led by Aksakov and Cherniaev, fought Turkey while St. Petersburg, unwilling to antagonize the Powers, sat on the sidelines. Lack of strong leadership and definite official policy permitted the Russian public to play an unprecedented political role. But the campaign revealed that unofficial aid and Serbo-Montenegrin strength could not defeat Turkey. Volunteer misbehavior and Cherniaev's attempts to dominate Serbia cooled the Serbs' enthusiasm, although Ristić recognized the importance of unofficial Russian aid: "It helped significantly to lighten the sufferings and misfortunes of war. . . . There are few comparable cases in history of such sympathetic participation as was shown by the Russian people toward the Serbian people during its struggle." [265]

The Battle of Djunis, revealing the futility of unofficial Russian efforts, forced Cherniaev and the Belgrade government to appeal to official Russia, whose advice they had spurned in making war. The basic decision to adopt a forceful Balkan policy had already been made at Livadia. The ultimatum to Turkey reasserted official leadership, relegating the Slav committees and the press to relative obscurity. The prestige of Cherniaev and the committees was damaged beyond repair, but they had triumphed indirectly. By assuming control of the situation, St. Petersburg committed itself to decisive action it had hitherto avoided. The Russian ultimatum and partial mobilization, barring total surrender by the Porte, made a Russo-Turkish war inevitable. Ristić's gamble to compel Russia to become Serbia's Napoleon III might yet succeed. And the ultimatum, revealing Russia's concern for the fate of the South Slavs, assuaged Serbian resentment at volunteer misbehavior.[266] The Serbs continued to look to Russia for salvation, no longer to the Slav committees or retired generals, but to the Russian government.

[265] Ristić, *1*, 156–57. Thanking a crowd in Russia for its contributions to the Serbs, Protić declared they "will never forget this since all hope of their deliverance from the Turkish yoke is placed solely on the Russians." Snytko, "Iz istorii," p. 103. For other Serbian statements of thanks to the Russians see OSVOb., *1*, nos. 215, 238, pp. 344, 367–68.

[266] Devollan, *Serbskii vopros*, p. 21.

CHAPTER V

BETWEEN TWO WARS

THE Djunis disaster produced panic in Serbia, but the Russian ultimatum brought relief and rejoicing. Turkey's prompt acceptance of the ultimatum ended the fighting until January 1, 1877, but left many vital questions unresolved. The Serbian states were suspended between war and peace, a status they could ill afford, and the future of the Russian volunteers was uncertain. Would official Russia support or recall them? Russia's prestige in Serbia was restored by the ultimatum, but the relationship of the two countries required clarification. Could Russia and the Porte work out satisfactory terms before the armistice expired? Could Serbia afford to go to war again? Were peace concluded, could the Ristić cabinet survive? During the months prior to the Russo-Turkish War, most of these questions were settled.

Liquidation of the Volunteer Episode

Cherniaev and his staff had been caught unprepared by the Turkish assault. After Djunis, he distributed Serbian military decorations lavishly, then abandoned his army and returned to Belgrade.[1] Even in defeat he possessed considerable power and influence in Serbia. Though still at odds with the Ristić government, Cherniaev was cheered by crowds in the streets of the capital. He received petitions from Belgrade intellectuals expressing warm thanks for the volunteers' sacrifices.[2] He had timed perfectly his reappearance in Belgrade, benefit-

[1] ROBibLen, Dnevnik Chizhova, 7, 4; Aksakov queried, "Why did everyone lose his head after the Djunis disaster and your entire staff scurry off to Belgrade without worrying about a more orderly withdrawal of the army?" GIM, f. Cherniaeva, Aksakov to Cherniaev, Jan. 4/16, 1877.

[2] A. Fel'kner, *Slavianskaia bor'ba, 1875–1876* (St. Petersburg, 1877), pp. 287–88.

ing from the Serbs' enthusiasm at the Russian ultimatum. Many Serbs believed that Russia was about to invade Turkey.[3]

Cherniaev, taking up residence in a Belgrade hotel, minimized Serbia's defeat. He wrote to Prince Milan:

The first phase of this war has just ended. . . . Although the results obtained are not decisive, . . . it is unquestionable that this struggle of a country of 1,300,000 inhabitants against the entire Moslem world has elevated Serbia from a moral standpoint and completely changed its situation vis-à-vis the Powers and the entire world.

The general declared that Colonel Horvatović could act as commander-in-chief while he sought aid in Russia to resume the war.[4] He admitted that his army had been overwhelmed by numerical superiority, but he added that Serbia would soon be prepared to resist the foe. Cherniaev told his volunteers that he had achieved his objective of repelling the Turks temporarily. The general sought to transform Djunis into a moral victory in order to retain his position in Serbia and attract more Russian assistance.[5]

But Russia shattered his hopes. Though the Serbs agreed that he should travel to Russia to obtain aid, the tsar forbade his trip. To exonerate himself, Cherniaev wrote Alexander that Serbia had taken up arms only because its existence was threatened. "My modest task was merely to hold back the Moslem pressure on a country which had entrusted its defense to me until your majestic word was spoken." Serbia had finally bowed to overwhelming force when official Russian aid had failed to arrive. Although physically and financially exhausted, "at Your first word, Your Majesty, the Serbian people will exert itself to the utmost to participate . . . in the execution of Your great goal [of liberation]." Cherniaev signed the letter "Your faithful servant" and volunteered to lead Russian forces in Serbia in a Russo-Turkish war. Commented the tsar, "Whose faithful subject? The King of Serbia's?"[6]

The general, rebuffed by St. Petersburg and criticized by the Slav

[3] *Golos,* Nov. 2/14, no. 303, report from Čačak, Nov. 3.

[4] DAS 29/101–21, Cherniaev to Milan, Oct. 23/Nov. 4, telegram.

[5] *Russkii Mir,* Nov. 11/23, no. 279, report from Belgrade, Nov. 9/21.

[6] Os. Pr., no. 1, pp. 70–72, Cherniaev to Alexander II, Nov. 17/29. On this letter are angry comments by the emperor and Miliutin. "What right," asked Miliutin, "does Cherniaev have to speak in the name of the Serbian people?"

committees, could not maintain his position in Serbia. He had removed control over the volunteers' affairs from Dandevil's capable hands and gave inconsistent, confusing orders. Many volunteers remained loyal, but disobedience and disorder flourished among them.[7] Cherniaev, failing to win Prince Milan's support for a *coup d'état*,[8] realized that his role in Serbia was played out. He left Belgrade at the end of November.

The volunteers' plight grew more perilous as Russian and Serbian officers exchanged bitter accusations. The Serbs, accused of cowering in the cornfields while the Russians fought, were held responsible for Djunis.[9] In his Kremlin speech on November 10, the tsar, crediting reports of returning volunteer officers, compared the Serbs' military showing unfavorably with that of the Montenegrins.[10] The Serbian public, shocked by the tsar's derogatory remarks, reacted angrily. Denying allegations of cowardice, Ristić complained privately that the tsar was wrong to insult the entire Serbian army, but in public he criticized neither tsar nor volunteers. Ristić told Wrede that Serbian officers from the Morava army claimed that Russian officers had been the first to abandon their posts at Djunis.[11] Colonel Orešković asserted that the Russians alone were responsible for the Djunis defeat: Colonel Mezheninov, commander of the Russian brigade, had left the battlefield and Cherniaev had not appeared until the battle was over.[12]

[7] OSVOb., *1*, no. 407, P. Tolstoi to Aksakov, Feb. 1/13, 1877; Fel'kner, *Slavianskaia*, pp. 286–87.

[8] Iasherov, p. 20; Khvostov, p. 49; PRO, FO 78/2488, White to Derby, Nov. 24, no. 209.

[9] Tiutin, "Politika," p. 237; Nikitin, "Russkoe obshchestvo," p. 1021.

[10] Declared the emperor: "In this unequal struggle the Montenegrins revealed themselves always as real heroes. Unfortunately, one cannot give the same praise to the Serbs." HHSA, Langenau to Andrassy, Nov. 11, ad no. 56; Tatishchev, *Aleksandr II, 2,* 335–36.

[11] HHSA, Wrede to Andrassy, Nov. 12 and 17, nos. 175 and 176.

[12] AII, Ristić 18/187, Orešković to War Minister, Oct. 29/Nov. 10. A report from Protić to Ristić (DAS 27/137) revealed growing antagonism between Serbian officials and Russian Pan-Slavs. Aksakov asked Protić how vassal Serbia dared hand out military decorations (Order of Takovo) to highly placed Russians. He warned of foolish Serbian pride. Protić confided that his reply would not have been to Aksakov's liking. Below were comments, apparently by Ristić: "From this letter can be seen what fools [*ludaci*] were the Russian Slavophiles, who in fact were not Slavophiles but true Russophiles who regarded small Slav peoples as nice mouthfuls to satiate Russian insatiability. Especially the Serbs displease them, since only the Serbs have never attempted to flatter and give way to the Russians as the Bulgarians have done on every occasion until the Russians liberated them."

These charges, whatever their merits, temporarily poisoned relations between the Serbs and Russian volunteers. From the Ibar army, Russian Colonel N. Sytenko wrote General V. D. Dandevil': "The inhabitants [Serbs] have begun to act impudently [*derzko*] toward our Russians so I had to issue a strict order to the people of Čačak under threat of military punishment to act more decently toward our officers." [13] Colonel Mezheninov submitted his resignation, complaining that Serbs had treated him and other Russians with disrespect.[14] Dandevil' reported to the St. Petersburg Committee that he and the volunteers were being ostracized by the Serbs.[15] Other Russian officers demanded that their men be rescued from "a terrible position." [16] And some Serbs realized that Cherniaev had deceived them and Russian aid was not coming. Others, desiring to fight to the bitter end, still looked to Russia for "great and rich gifts." [17]

Confused and exposed to Serbian criticism, many volunteers applied for return to Russia. But St. Petersburg, contemplating a winter campaign against Turkey, opposed their immediate repatriation and decided to transfer capable ones to Russian service.[18] But Cherniaev, without consulting the Russian commander-in-chief in the Balkans, Grand Duke Nikolai Nikolaevich, telegraphed Aksakov that if Serbia were threatened anew with invasion, the volunteers would be withdrawn to prevent their destruction. This contradicted official policy directly and angered both Aksakov and official Russia.[19] Then on December 13 the Serbian War Ministry ordered many of the volunteers placed under Serbian commanders. Members of two Russian battalions declared that they would return to Russia rather than serve under Serbian command. Execution of this order, warned Kartsov, would cause most volunteers to depart. The Council of Ministers instructed War Minister S. Grujić to rescind it. By late December,

[13] K. Pushkarevich, "Balkanskie slaviane i russkie 'osvoboditeli,' " *Trudy instituta slavianovedeniia Akademii Nauk SSSR, 2* (1934), 213.

[14] OSVOb., *1*, 584, Tolstoi to Aksakov, Feb. 1/13, 1877; DAS 29/101, Mezheninov to Dokhturov, Oct. 30/Nov. 11, 1876.

[15] GIM, f. Cherniaeva, Dandevil' to Vul'fert, Nov. 4/16, telegram.

[16] OSVOb., *1*, 466–67, 477. After Kartsov had transmitted home the numerous complaints of Russian volunteers, Minister of Interior A. E. Timashev ordered Aksakov to take immediate steps to improve their position in Serbia.

[17] *Golos*, Nov. 4/16, 1876, no. 305, report from Belgrade of Nov. 8.

[18] For Nikitin mission see pp. 165f. Kartsov had Prince Milan informed that it was the emperor's will that volunteers capable of service should remain in Serbia. KZPK, Kartsov to Lodyzhenskii, Nov. 17/29.

[19] GIM, f. Cherniaeva, Aksakov to Cherniaev, Jan. 4/16, 1877.

friction and recriminations were waning and Serbs and Russians were again on friendlier terms.[20]

The Slav committees, unable to support the volunteers financially, persuaded the Russian government to accept responsibility for them. The War Ministry agreed that on January 1, 1877, all volunteers wishing to remain in Serbia would be transferred into active Russian service. Aksakov explained that this would induce the government "to take action and become involved in the Serbian cause."[21] He warned that only volunteers who returned immediately to Russia would receive expense money from the committee.[22]

In late December, the Russian volunteers awaited impatiently the coming of General A. P. Nikitin, the War Ministry's representative, expecting him to remove uncertainty and restore discipline. Djunis had not cooled the volunteers' ardor. In the streets of Belgrade they marched singing harmoniously.[23] Reviewing the Russian volunteer division on December 25, Nikitin reported that despite tattered uniforms and a shortage of rifles, its morale remained high. He promptly enforced the volunteers' complete subordination to the Serbian authorities and reduced some officers with battlefield promotions to the ranks.[24] Most volunteers then decided to return home at committee expense. They departed on ships of the Danube Steamship Company, chartered by Kartsov. The Slav committee representatives liquidated their affairs in Belgrade also.[25] Serbian officials and friendly crowds bade good-bye to the volunteers. In a message to "the brother Russians," Prince Milan wished them well, declaring that the Serbs regarded Russia as the guarantor of their future.[26]

[20] Iasherov, "V Serbii," pp. 58–59; *Golos*, Dec. 10/22, no. 341, report from Belgrade, Dec. 11; Fel'kner, *Slavianskaia*, p. 286.

[21] GIM, f. Cherniaeva, Aksakov to Cherniaev, Jan. 4/16. In case of a Russo-Turkish war, Aksakov argued, there would be a Russian vanguard already in Serbia; if the Serbo-Turkish truce were extended, such a force would preserve Russian influence there.

[22] Aksakov to Naryshkin, Dec. 4/16, RA (1897), no. 2, pp. 257–61.

[23] OSVOb., *1*, 584–85, Tolstoi to Aksakov, Feb. 1/13, 1877. The volunteer division then numbered 187 officers and 3,024 men, including 1,524 Russians.

[24] *Ibid.* Most observers agreed that Nikitin handled the volunteers awkwardly. Iasherov states (pp. 58–59) that volunteers who accepted government money from Nikitin could leave Serbia without official permission. Hearing this, many Russians decided to return home immediately. See also GIM, f. Cherniaeva, Aksakov to Cherniaev, Jan. 4/16, 1877; HHSA, Wrede to Andrassy, Jan. 12, no. 4.

[25] *Ibid.*; Sb. Mat., no. 8, pp. 76–77, 87–88.

[26] Fel'kner, *Slavianskaia*, p. 287; Devollan, *Serbskii vopros*, p. 21; DAS 29/67, Milan to "Brother Russians," n.d.

The episode of the Russian volunteers in Serbia was virtually complete. Less than one hundred, paid by the Russian government, remained behind. They included Colonel A. M. Miloradovich and eighty-two officers "counting on the aid of God, the Slav committees, and Russian society." The 2,000-man detachment they commanded consisted of Bulgarians, Albanians, Old Serbs, and Montenegrins, most of whom could not return home. Without their Russian officers, who refused to abandon them, these volunteers would have been in a desperate situation. N. I. Brailko, chief of staff of this Russo-Bulgarian brigade, appealed successfully to unofficial Russian organizations for assistance.[27] But the volunteers' departure from Serbia contributed to a sharp decline of Russian interest in the principality.

Belgrade's Appeal: The Marinović Mission

When the armistice was concluded, it seemed doubtful that Serbia could resume the war. In contrast with Montenegro, it had been invaded, had suffered heavy losses in blood and resources, and had earned Russia's reproaches. Would Serbia now place its national mission above survival? The country, Wrede reported, was totally exhausted and war-weary, its militia would fight no more. Ristić reputedly favored a separate peace based on the *status quo ante;* Milan, still dependent upon Russia, would follow its desires.[28]

As soon as the fighting ceased, the Serbian cabinet discussed its future course and probed Russian intentions. The ministers, in a memorandum for the prince on November 4, emphasized the need to acquaint the tsar with Serbia's situation and requirements. They proposed sending a cabinet member, preferably Ristić, to Russia. Serbia's present military and financial condition, the ministers argued, required restoration of peace; however, Serbia could resume the struggle subsequently in return for: (1) Russian assurances that war would achieve South Slav liberation; (2) participation of Russia in the conflict; (3) annexation to Serbia of Bosnia and Old Serbia creating a Serbian kingdom under the Obrenović dynasty; and (4) a Russian loan of 12 million rubles and about 100,000 breech-loading rifles. Unless these conditions

---

[27] Sb. Mat., no. 8, p. 77; OSVOb., *1*, 591–92; *ibid.*, p. 611, Giers to Miliutin, Feb. 23/March 7.

[28] Wrote Wrede, "His Highness . . . obeys blindly every wink from St. Petersburg. He is no longer Prince of Serbia, but has become completely a Russian governor-general." HHSA, Wrede to Andrassy, Nov. 2.

were satisfied, Serbia must conclude immediate peace.[29] The cabinet agreed that most of Hercegovina should be reserved to Montenegro. If Russia responded favorably, Serbia could raise fifty battalions of infantry and twenty-five batteries. The cabinet believed that a Russo-Turkish war was inevitable and that Serbia should participate to recoup its wartime losses.[30]

On November 14, Gorchakov replied that he would receive with real satisfaction only Jovan Marinović, the Conservatives' leader. Ristić, defending his cabinet's wartime achievements, promptly submitted the government's resignation. However, the prince would not accept it without an alternative cabinet to take charge of the government. Sava Grujić replaced Nikolić as war minister, but otherwise the cabinet remained unchanged. Ristić consented reluctantly to send Marinović to Russia.[31] St. Petersburg was seeking to intervene in Serbian politics and undermine the Ristić ministry.

Marinović accepted a vital mission from a government he detested. Ristić's instructions to him repeated that Serbia could not resume war alone. It would make peace if Russia so advised, leaving the question of compensation for war damage up to Russia. Marinović was to thank the tsar for the Russian ultimatum. The Serbs' present low spirits would be revitalized should Russian banners appear in the Balkans:

With the prospect of the powerful protection of the tsarist eagles freeing their oppressed brethren and the expectation that Serbs in Hercegovina would be joined to Montenegro and Serbs in Old Serbia and Bosnia joined with Serbia, the Serbian people would develop new energy and would be prepared to enter the battle behind the glorious flags of the tsar.

Marinović's confidential instructions described Serbia's needs and her potential contribution.[32]

Prince Milan secretly gave the envoy another set of instructions. Overjoyed at St. Petersburg's request for Marinović ("because of your patriotism and devotion *to me*"), Milan told him to assure the tsar that he would abide loyally by Russia's advice in the future. Blaming the

---

[29] For the various drafts of the cabinet's position see DAS 39/165, Nov. 4; AII, Ristić 18/5 and 192 of Nov. 5 and 14. In his Nov. 5 draft Ristić declared that Serbia could not resume war with unofficial Russian aid even if 20,000 volunteers were provided; resumption would necessarily be a matter of life or death.

[30] Ristić, 2, 1–3; Grujić, 3, 245–46.

[31] DAS 39/178, Mihajlović to Gorchakov, n.d.; Ristić, 2, 3; AII, Ristić 18/192, (Ristić) to Milan, Nov. 2/14; Grujić, 3, 247.

[32] Ristić, 2, 5–12.

war upon the intrigues of the Ristić government and deploring his past reliance upon the Slav committees and General Cherniaev, the prince declared, "Today I wish to rely upon the Imperial Cabinet [Russia] which knows much better the interests of Serbia." Implied was a plea for official Russian support for Marinović's Conservatives. Serbia, materially and morally exhausted, could participate in war only when Russia led the way. If the Russians intended using Serbia as a base of operations against Turkey, the Serbs could aid them to cross the Danube. If Austria also fought Russia, Serbia's position would become most perilous. Milan denounced the Ristić constitution:

Unscrupulous politicians, profiting from my minority, imposed a constitution upon the country in open contradiction with the moral and intellectual level attained by the people. . . . Tell the Imperial Cabinet formally that I consider the present political organization of the country to be the main cause of the calamities which face it today. . . . I solicit the support of the Imperial Cabinet to extract Serbia *from the abyss* toward which she is moving steadily. . . . For my part I would be happy if the Imperial Government judged it expedient to contribute to a political reorganization of Serbia.[33]

The prince was calling for Russia to undermine his government!

Marinović, though warmly welcomed in the Russian capital, could not obtain the definite commitments Belgrade required. The tsar merely declared that if Russia did not fight, Serbia could make peace on the *status quo ante;* in case of war, it would receive military and financial support for participating and territorial increases in case of victory. Reported Marinović:

On the question of a territorial increase, he [the tsar] told me very convincingly that he cannot say anything definite now since, first, he does not know whether or not there will be a war, and second, it is unknown now what the aim of such a war would be: merely to improve the condition of the Christians or to change the territorial status of Turkey. In the latter case he would be entirely disposed to grant us some increase in Old Serbia.[34]

Dissatisfied with this vague reply, Ristić instructed his envoy to stress Serbia's need of prompt Russian aid for military preparations. He must ascertain precisely which territories Serbia would acquire; its

[33] KZPK, 74–83, "Instructions secrètes données à Marinović lors de son départ pour Pétersbourg."

[34] AII, Ristić 18/328, Protić to Ristić, Nov. 16/28; 332, Marinović to Ristić, Nov. 23/Dec. 5.

communications with Russia must be guaranteed in the event of a Turkish attack. But Marinović telegraphed on December 2 that the principality could expect no money for rearmament; Kartsov would answer Ristić's other questions. Then, to Ristić's indignation, the envoy confided that he had let the tsar and Gorchakov read all his instructions! Despite this, Marinović learned merely that Russia counted on Serbian military assistance in event of war and would send a military mission to Belgrade. Russia would not promise territory until war became certain.[35]

Kartsov, having antagonized many persons in Belgrade,[36] accompanied Marinović to St. Petersburg partly to safeguard his position as consul. At a conference of top Russian leaders on November 28 Kartsov proposed sending two Russian divisions to Serbia to protect it from the Turks. His plan was rejected, but the consul achieved his purpose. The tsar placed the Nikitin military mission under his supervision, and Marinović's criticisms of him were received unsympathetically by Russian officials.[37]

Marinović unconditionally opposed Serbia's resumption of the war, and he intentionally sabotaged his mission by his statements in Russia. If war were resumed, he told A. A. Kireev, Serbia could raise only 10,000 men.[38] He informed foreign ambassadors that Serbia could make no significant military contribution and that a Turkish attack would compel it to sue for peace immediately. His objectives, reported English consul, Loftus, were a Serbo-Turkish peace on the *status quo ante* and the Serbian premiership.[39] Marinović had a vested interest in the failure of his mission.

Russian leaders were amazed, Marinović reported on December 5, at Serbia's claims to major territorial gains in return for joining a Russo-Turkish war. He advised Ristić, because of uncertain Russo-Turkish relations, to prepare for a defensive war and await the outcome of the Powers' deliberations in Constantinople. So anxious were Russian lead-

---

[35] *Ibid.*, Ristić 18/328–333; Ristić, *2*, 13–14.

[36] OSVOb., *1*, 586, Tolstoi to Aksakov, Feb. 1/13, 1877. "The behavior of Kartsov outrages not only the ministers but the entire Serbian intelligentsia."

[37] HHSA, Wrede to Andrassy, Nov. 18; AII, Ristić 18/332, Marinović to Ristić, Nov. 23/Dec. 5; Kartsov, "Za kulisami," pp. 471–73.

[38] ROBibLen, Dnevnik Kireeva, 7, 19–20, Nov. 23/Dec. 5.

[39] PRO, FO 65/942, Loftus to Derby, Dec. 6, no. 583; HHSA, Langenau to Andrassy, Dec. 6, telegram 9; Dec. 9, no. 64B.

ers to avoid a conflict, continued his report, that peace was much more likely than war.[40]

But the Serbian cabinet resolved to reach agreement with Russia on military co-operation. When pressed by Ristić (December 17), Kartsov agreed to request a "volunteer" division and an extension of the armistice until March 1, but he explained that Russia, during the truce, could not send regular troops or rifles to Serbia. In a Russo-Turkish war, the Serbian army must hold back the Turks for about two weeks to permit Russian forces to reach the battlefield. Officially, Kartsov could not even pledge that Russia would regard a Turkish attack upon Serbia as a *casus belli*; privately, he assured Ristić that this would draw Russia into the war. Serbia's war effort would be subsidized by St. Petersburg. Kartsov announced that General Nikitin was bringing one million rubles to prepare the Serbian army for action. Unspecified territory in Old Serbia would be its reward for fighting.[41] Ristić, still distressed at the vagueness of the Russian proposals, pressed Marinović to obtain firm commitments on as many issues as possible. The Serbian cabinet, however, confident that Russia would in no case abandon Serbia, decided to accept St. Petersburg's terms for military co-operation.[42]

In the midst of these negotiations occurred an incident threatening Austro-Serbian relations. On December 19, the "Maros," an Austrian monitor, approaching unusually close to the Serbian side of the Danube, was fired upon from the Belgrade fortress. An explosion on board the vessel caused some casualties; the Austrian and German consuls in Belgrade were passengers.[43] Exaggerated accounts of the affair produced intense excitement in Belgrade. Russian correspondents there claimed that Wrede had arranged the incident to enable Austria to occupy Serbia and oust the Ristić government.[44] The Dual Monarchy, asserted *Golos*, had staged it to demonstrate indirect support of Tur-

---

[40] AII, Ristić 18/332, Marinović to Ristić, report of Nov. 23/Dec. 5.

[41] Grujić, *3*, 253–54; Ristić, *2*, 13–15.

[42] AII, Ristić 18/335, Ristić to Marinović, Dec. 5/17; Grujić, *3*, 254.

[43] According to Jovanović, it was Wrede's idea to have the monitor maneuver between Belgrade and Zemun. The accidental shots from the fortress led the consul to the false conclusion they were directed at him. *Vlada Milana*, *1*, 361.

[44] HHSA, Wrede to Andrassy, Dec. 19, no. 187, *Russkii Mir*, Dec. 19/31, no. 304, report from Belgrade, Dec. 9/21; *Golos*, Dec. 18/30, no. 349, reports from Belgrade, Dec. 19, 20; Dec. 19/31, no. 350.

key. *Golos* warned bluntly, "Vienna should realize that the Russian ultimatum of October 30 expressed our firm determination not to permit foreign troops, whether Austrian or Turkish, to occupy Serbia. An Austrian incursion into Serbia would be considered just as incompatible with the views of Russia as a Turkish one." [45]

The "Maros" incident caused a temporary upset in the Serbian government. As soon as he heard the news, and without Austrian prompting, Prince Milan told Wrede that he would demand Ristić's resignation and relieve the fortress commander. Wrede, upset by rising anti-Austrian feeling and Belgrade's inability to control it, urged Vienna to occupy the fortress. [46]

The Ristić ministry resigned the same day and the prince accepted its demission. The incident, Milan wrote Stevča Mihajlović, had placed Serbia in a position which only the cabinet's resignation could relieve. Praising the ministry's wartime services, he asserted that satisfying Austria was his sole aim. [47] But the prince was being untruthful. The same day he appealed to Marinović, who was still in Russia:

To save the country from very dangerous consequences which could stem from this [incident], I have gone to meet possible demands by providing Austria in advance with striking satisfaction by approving the ministry's resignation. I count upon your devotion and patriotism and appeal to your heart to take on the premiership and foreign ministry in these difficult circumstances.

Milan proposed that Marinović lead a Conservative cabinet, confer with Russian leaders, and press for prolongation of the armistice. Marinović replied timorously that resignation of the ministry was excessive satisfaction for such an incident. Even under ordinary circumstances he could scarcely form a Conservative ministry; in wartime, it would be impossible. [48]

It had been Kartsov, still at odds with Ristić, who urged Milan to oust

---

[45] *Ibid.*, Dec. 10/22, no. 341, Dec. 12/24, no. 343, lead articles.

[46] HHSA, Wrede to Andrassy, Dec. 19, no. 187.   [47] KZPK, Dec. 8/20.

[48] *Ibid.*, Milan to Marinović, Dec. 8/20; Marinović to Milan, Dec. 9/21. Protić wrote: "Les tendances belliqueuses se sont emparées de la Serbie à un tel point, que Marinović se juge impuissant de l'arrêter sur cette pointe. S'il survenait une guerre, il y verrait une douloureuse preuve par laquelle devrer passer la Serbie pour se débarrasser de cette surexcit et redevenir apte à être dirigée par un gouvernement honnête et raissonnable. Le retour de Marinović au ministère hâterait la crise que pourrait être fatale au Prince. La conscience de Marinović lui défend d'encourager le Prince à s'engager dans cette voie." DAS 29/76.

the cabinet. The prince had complied, believing Kartsov was acting upon instructions. But when Gorchakov learned of the consul's unauthorized step, he telegraphed, "Do not interfere in the least with the composition of the ministry." Milan was informed that Russia would not dictate his choice of cabinet.[49] All his efforts to build a new government failed. The deeply embarassed prince finally had to reconfirm the Ristić ministry in office in late December.[50] Meanwhile Andrassy rebuked Consul Wrede for suggesting that Austria occupy the fortress and instructed him to accept conventional reparation. Vienna refused to request Ristić's ouster and renounced interference in Serbia's domestic affairs.[51] Thus the "Maros" affair ended without a change of ministry or a breach in Austro-Serbian relations. But Kartsov had fatally antagonized Ristić and lost much prestige.

Marinović remained in St. Petersburg to obtain money for rearmament and a truce extension. His tactless criticisms of Russia's war preparations antagonized government leaders. Marinović failed to realize that ultrapacifism would undermine his position. The tsar, hearing of Marinović's comments, ordered him to leave Russia. The envoy returned hastily to Belgrade, bearing Prince Milan a letter from Alexander:

My views have not changed toward you or the Serbian nation. . . . I still hope that peace will emerge from the present negotiations. I shall try to make it [peace] as favorable as the military situation of Serbia suggests. It is up to you to prepare the Serbian nation either for energetic co-operation in case of war or to profit from peace in order to restore order and prosperity to the country.[52]

Russia desired military co-operation with Serbia only if negotiations with Turkey failed and Belgrade prepared itself. But Marinović's blunders had strengthened the Ristić government.

The Russian Response: The Nikitin Mission

In the winter of 1875–1876, the Russian government continued to ponder possible military collaboration with the Serbian states. Much depended upon its assessment of their capabilities and upon Austrian

---

[49] KZPK, Marinović to Milan, Dec. 12/24; Kartsov, "Za kulisami," p. 305.
[50] HHSA, Langenau to Andrassy, Dec. 22, telegram 120; Wrede to Andrassy, Dec. 25; KZPK, 95–97.
[51] *Ibid.*, Andrassy to Langenau, Jan. 4, 1877; Andrassy to Wrede, Jan. 17.
[52] KZPK, p. 124; Vlada Milana, *1*, 357.

reactions. Could the Serbian contribution, so soon after Djunis, justify expending Russian funds and risking Austrian hostility? In December, St. Petersburg dispatched the Nikitin mission to Serbia to ascertain the facts.

Many Russians were disillusioned with the Serbs at this time. The tsar's Kremlin speech was a case in point. Gorchakov had reminded Marinović that Serbia was no longer the focus of Russian attention and that its leaders should abandon false dreams of glory.[53] Colonel A. S. Zelenoi, Russian military attaché in Constantinople, after inspecting the Drina front, advised his government not to rely upon Serbian military co-operation or fight a winter campaign. And Kartsov sent back pessimistic reports about Serbia's preparedness. Since Djunis, the Serbs had made no military preparations:

Extreme distaste for war has developed among them, and now they could be called to arms only by positive assurances that Russia would enter the struggle simultaneously. . . . The prince affirms that a two week extension of the armistice would help the cause. From other sources I see that this is clear self-deception. Chaos and disintegration are complete.

Kartsov concluded that Serbia should seek a separate peace or a lengthy prolongation of the truce. "For now I repeat we should expect nothing in the way of co-operation from Serbia." [54] Grand Duke Nikolai Nikolaevich wrote the tsar that the Serbian army probably would not fight when the armistice expired. Alexander II replied that in case of war the grand duke might have to dispatch an army corps to prevent Serbia's destruction.[55]

Among unofficial spokesmen, Aksakov, formerly Serbia's champion, now denounced it bitterly: "Serbia will attract to herself indignation and scorn in Russia. The blood of thousands of Russians, sacrificed for your ministers . . . , demands loud satisfaction and exemplary punishment. The Serbs must justify themselves before Russia." [56] Though Aksakov deplored the tsar's public criticism of Serbia, he believed that it accurately reflected Russian sentiment. He wrote Cherniaev, "One needs a truly Russian patience and magnanimity to avoid spitting in the face of the Serbian government and intelligentsia and leaving them to their fate." [57]

---

[53] HHSA, Wrede to Andrassy, Dec. 15, no. 184.

[54] OSVOb., 1, 529, 561–62.   [55] Os. Pr., no. 3, pp. 8, 9, 35, 36.

[56] Aksakov to Protić, Oct. 22/Nov. 3, 1876, cited in Nikitin, "Russkoe obshchestvo," p. 1035.

[57] GIM, Aksakov to Cherniaev, Nov. 7/19, 1876.

The press generally echoed these criticisms. The Belgrade govern-ment, declared *Birzhevye Vedomosti*, persuaded many Russians to go to "certain and useless death" in Serbia.[58] *Russkii Mir* admitted that the Serbs had been unprepared for war and were not as brave as their leaders had claimed. Russian efforts had been concentrated too exclu-sively in Serbia: "brilliant Montenegrin victories" needed reward. Nonetheless, *Russkii Mir* continued to defend Belgrade, denouncing what it interpreted as Austrian threats to Serbian autonomy in the "Maros" crisis.[59] *Golos* declared (November 8) that the Serbian ques-tion had become secondary, and that Serbia could defend itself if attacked. But on November 26 it proclaimed with a confidence un-shared by officialdom that in event of war 80,000 Serbs, 30,000 Mon-tenegrins, plus insurgents and Greeks would assist Russia against the Porte.[60] Though wishing Russia to protect the Serbs pending solution of the Balkan crisis, *Golos* still criticized Belgrade for launching war against Turkey.[61]

Russian public opinion favored greater assistance to the Slavs even if it led to war. Mezentsov, the chief of the Third Section, who had requested his subordinates to assess public views toward the South Slavs and a possible Russo-Turkish conflict, informed the tsar (No-vember 24) that in Russia proper there was widespread pro-Slav sym-pathy. Government employees were making generous financial con-tributions. Some nobles were contributing, but most were apathetic. Less affluent merchants (*meshchane*) were sacrificing, whereas rich merchants refused to give. The peasantry, at first ignorant of Balkan events, now believed in the holiness of the Slav cause. All elements had responded favorably to the tsar's Moscow speech, and a more decisive policy would obtain overwhelming Russian support.[62] A. I. Koshelev

[58] Oct. 23/Nov. 4, no. 243, cited in Nikitin, "Russkoe obshchestvo," p. 1030.

[59] *Russkii Mir*, Oct. 26/Nov. 7, Oct. 28/Nov. 9; Dec. 10/22, 1876, nos. 263, 265, 296; Jan. 1/13, 1877, no. 1.

[60] *Golos*, Oct. 27/Nov. 8, Nov. 1/13, 14/26, nos. 297, 304, 315. This latter statement may have been designed to obtain diplomatic concessions from the Turks.

[61] *Ibid.*, Nov. 7/19, Nov. 25/Dec. 7, Dec. 19/31, nos. 308, 326, 350.

[62] Mezentsov's November 3 circular posed these questions: (1) are all social strata in the province sympathetic to the Balkan Slavs and how strong and conscious is this sympathy? (2) how has it been manifested concretely? (3) if Russian armed intervention proves necessary, what private co-operation can the government expect from Russian social groups? OSVOb., *1*, 459.

In response the St. Petersburg police reported the strongest pro-Slav sympathy among the uneducated rural population. The Montenegrins were more popular than the Serbs, who were accused of cowardice. A police report from Pskov testified that, during the winter, news from the Balkans absorbed everyone's attention in Moscow; never had there been so many Slavophiles in Russia.[63]

St. Petersburg and the Slav committees were shifting their attention from Serbia to Bulgaria. At Livadia (October 1876) War Minister Miliutin supported formation of an auxiliary Bulgarian militia in case of a Russo-Turkish war.[64] Bulgarian battalions in Serbia were to be reorganized by I. Ivanov, aided by the Moscow Committee. General N. G. Stoletov, chosen to command this force in war, arranged for its maintenance in Kishinev.[65] An influential Pan-Slav, Prince V. A. Cherkasskii, was appointed (November 9) to head the civil administration in Bulgaria in case of a Russian occupation.[66] By December the Slav committees, too, decided to concentrate upon Bulgaria, and money was no longer sent to Serbia.[67] In a war with Turkey, Bulgaria would become the focus of Russian efforts.

Nevertheless, St. Petersburg could not permit destruction of Serbia. Convinced by Kartsov's reports of the country's desperate plight, the tsar empowered the War Ministry to send General Nikitin to Belgrade.[68] Nikitin received precise instructions from the General Staff (December 5) to sort out the volunteers, gather full information about the Serbian army, and plan its reorganization with the Serbian War

---

emphasized the feverish expectations there (c. November 1) of a Russian war declaration—this would have been very popular. A police report from Iaroslavl estimated that contributions to the Slavs had come from the peasantry (80 per cent), service class (15 per cent), and nobility and merchants (5 per cent). In Moscow province, pro-Slav feeling was most intense among the upper classes and clergy in urban areas. These findings were summarized (Nov. 12/24) in a report by Mezentsov to Alexander II. *Ibid.*, pp. 463–65, 467–70, 485–87, 506–08.

[63] A. I. Koshelev, *Zapiski* (Berlin, 1884), p. 228.

[64] I. Koz'menko, "Iz istorii bolgarskogo opolcheniia, 1876–1877," *Slavianskii sbornik*, pp. 121–23.

[65] Ivanov, "Bolgarskoe," pp. 145–46.

[66] D. G. Anuchin, "Kniaz Vladimir A. Cherkasskii kak ustroitel' Bolgarii," RS, 59 (July 1888), 210.

[67] Aksakov explained, "If our resources permitted, we would organize benevolent aid there [in Serbia] but meanwhile we must shift the main center of our activities into Bulgaria. It is more important to us and for the Slav future than Serbia." "Nakanune . . . ," RA (1897), no. 2, p. 261, Dec. 4/16, 1876. See Aksakov to Pobedonostsev, Nov. 21/Dec. 3, RA (1907), no. 3, pp. 168–69.

[68] Former chief of staff of the Vilna military district, Nikitin was recommended by Miliutin "as the person most capable for the proposed mission to Serbia in order to help the government there organize its armed forces." Miliutin, *Dnevnik*, 2, 111–14.

Ministry. He was given a million rubles to cover aspects of rearmament and preparation which Serbia could not finance.[69] A Serbian corps was to defend the lower Timok-Danube region until a Russian division could cross into Serbia. Since the armistice would expire January 1, Nikitin was instructed to establish quickly a Danube crossing at Kladovo, obtain adequate supplies, and arrange Serbian forces in defensive positions there.[70]

Nikitin reached Belgrade on December 24 and promptly corroborated Kartsov's pessimistic reports. To his amazement, the Serbs had made no serious military preparations and only about 9,000 men remained under arms. Mobilization of the militia was ordered only after he conferred with Prince Milan (December 25). The Kladovo area had not been fortified nor could it possibly supply food for a Russian division.[71] The Serbs, confident that the armistice would be prolonged, were passive. Kladovo's defense depended on 3,000 Russo-Bulgarian volunteers and some 2,000 Serbian regulars.[72]

Nikitin's mission failed dismally, but the reasons were hotly disputed. He blamed the Serbs. He claimed that War Minister Grujić, asked to submit a list of his army's requirements, had purportedly demanded large sums to purchase food. Nikitin asserted that Belgrade wished to pay off old debts and administrative expenses with his money. When the truce extension was confirmed at the end of December, Prince Milan suspended Serbian mobilization and the War Ministry sank into complete apathy. Nikitin informed Russian headquarters (January 6) that Serbian forces could not be reorganized into an effective army. A new, extravagant list from Grujić convinced him it was pointless to remain in Serbia, especially since most Russian volunteers had decided to return home. At a final audience, added Nikitin, the prince admitted that his government wished to use Russian money to meet its regular financial obligations. Milan declared that Russia should not count on Serbian forces; if led into battle again, they would

[69] Sb. Mat., no. 8, pp. 59–61, "Instructions of the General Staff to General Nikitin," Nov. 23/Dec. 5, 1876.

[70] Ibid., pp. 63–65, "Report of General Nikitin to the War Minister," Feb. 2/14, 1877.

[71] Sb. Mat., no. 8, p. 61, Nikitin to Nepokoichitskii, Dec. 7/19 (?). Since by his own account Nikitin reached Belgrade on December 24, this letter should probably be dated Dec. 17/29. Nikitin's pessimistic reports to St. Petersburg, according to Kireev, caused much of the tsar's dissatisfaction with Serbia. ROBibLen, Dnevnik Kireeva, 7, 118, Feb. 28/March 12, 1877.

[72] Nikitin to Geiden, Dec. 18/30, OSVOb., 1, 567–68.

probably surrender or flee. Nikitin was recalled at his own request (January 8) and left Belgrade two days later.[73]

Most other accounts criticize Nikitin. Kartsov wrote that when dealing with Serbian officials, he "acted like a subordinate." The Serbs, exploiting Nikitin's gullibility, spent his money as fast as possible while he sought a Serbian military decoration.[74] The commander of the Russo-Bulgarian brigade asserted that War Minister S. Grujić was co-operative and pro-Russian. Nikitin's refusal to honor his legitimate requests placed Grujić in an awkward position and threatened to throw Serbia into the arms of Russia's rivals.[75] Foreign Minister Ristić complained of Nikitin's belated arrival and his inadequate funds.[76] Grujić protested that he had provided requested information and attempted to prepare for war. He wrote Nikitin that without additional money Serbia could not be made ready. But Nikitin had already departed and other members of his mission refused to accept the letter.[77] Actually, both sides contributed to a fiasco which repeated the Cherniaev-Nikolić quarrel of 1876. Nikitin's incompetence, naïveté, and profound suspicion of Serbian leaders virtually insured his failure.

His sudden departure with most of the million rubles shocked and perplexed the Serbs. "Is Russia abandoning us?" inquired Premier Mihajlović and Metropolitan Mihailo. Prince Milan wondered why the Russians were leaving and how he should react to Turkish peace overtures.[78] Following Nikitin's departure, Milan received the tsar's letter which proposed military co-operation, but the disastrous Marinović and Nikitin missions had undermined such prospects. Without Russian money the Serbs could not rearm. A second wrangle between a Russian general and a Serbian war minister frustrated their governments' desire to assist each other against Turkey.

The Budapest Conventions

Austro-Russian negotiations, culminating in the Budapest Conventions of 1877, further circumscribed any potential alliance between

---

[73] Sb. Mat., no. 8, p. 73, Nikitin to Miliutin, Feb. 2/14; p. 62, Nepokoichitskii to Giers, Dec. 27/Jan. 8: HHSA, Wrede to Andrassy, Jan. 12, no. 4; Nikitin to Geiden, Dec. 21/Jan. 2, OSVOb., *1*, 570–71.

[74] Kartsov, "Za kulisami," p. 304.

[75] (Miloradovich) to Moscow Slav Committee, Jan. 22/Feb. 3, RA (1897), no. 2, pp. 276–77.

[76] DAS, no number, Ristić to Protić, Dec. 17/29.   [77] Grujić, *3*, 263–65.

[78] Sb. Mat., no. 8, p. 87. "Confidential memorandum of Colonel Snesarev about the situation in Serbia and the Russian volunteers." Feb. 8/20, 1877.

Russia and the Serbian states.[79] Russia required a precise agreement with Vienna before fighting Turkey. St. Petersburg's hopes of joint military action had been dashed by the abortive Sumarokov-Elston mission to Vienna in October.[80] In November 1876, the tsar, fearing imminent war, had resolved to conclude an arrangement with Vienna which would protect the Russian flank. Chancellor Gorchakov proposed that Austria pledge neutrality in a Russo-Turkish conflict and renounce any extension of its military influence to Rumania, Serbia, Montenegro, and Hercegovina which would comprise "une zone continue, destinée a préserver de tout contact les armées des deux empires." Vienna could occupy Bosnia at will provided it did not hinder operations by Russia and its potential Balkan allies.[81] This would enable Russia to lead a South Slav coalition against Turkey and occupy Bulgaria without fear of European interference.

Austria would not accept such terms. In reply, Andrassy reaffirmed the Monarchy's right to occupy Hercegovina as well as Bosnia. Both Powers should keep their forces out of Serbia and Montenegro, which would be neutralized and compelled to abstain from a Russo-Turkish war. Afterward, Serbia could be compensated in the insurgent provinces and Montenegrin gains would be regulated by a subsequent Austro-Russian agreement.[82] Andrassy would permit Russia to occupy Bulgaria as part of a European effort to improve the Christians' status, but he opposed a South Slav–Russian alliance:

At the moment . . . when Russia places herself during the struggle against Turkey at the head of these [Christian] peoples, the affair takes on different colors. . . . Russian co-operation with Serbia and Montenegro transforms a European action into a Slav movement, a Christian and humanitarian undertaking into an exclusively Orthodox one, and the war into a revolution.

Did Russia wish to share the odium of Serbian aggression against Turkey by allying herself with Belgrade? asked Andrassy. Even with

[79] For a general description of the negotiations see Rupp, *A Wavering Friendship*, pp. 173–82, 275–303; Sumner, *Russia*, pp. 275–89.

[80] See *supra*, pp. 147–48.

[81] HHSA, Geheimakten, *1*, rot 453, Gorchakov to Novikov, Oct. 21/Nov. 2. Under the influence of the excitement prevailing in Livadia at the time of the ultimatum, the chancellor wrote that Russia was too deeply moved by events in the Balkans to await quietly the dissolution of Turkey. "L'Empereur est decidé d'en finir, Sa Majesté n'a plus de confiance dans la diplomatie européenne . . . et est résolu à agir seul et sans retard."

[82] Letter of Nov. 16/28, cited in Goriainov, *Le Bosphore*, p. 331. Novikov wrote Gorchakov on December 5 that the Austrian counterproposals were "très raides pour les Serbes." SR (Dec. 1925), p. 44, no. 102.

Russian subsidies, he argued, the Serbs could contribute little. Alone, Russia could make peace with Turkey unhindered; then Austria and Russia could win the Balkan states' gratitude with territorial compensation. But if the Serbian states participated in a war of annihilation against the Porte, they would press exaggerated claims at the peace settlement. Russian leadership of such a revolutionary coalition, concluded Andrassy, would undermine the Dreikaiserbund's principles and threaten the internal stability of its members.[83]

St. Petersburg made concessions, while insisting upon its right to obtain the military aid of the Serbian states. Gorchakov consented reluctantly to an eventual Austrian occupation of Hercegovina, provided the "Enclave" of Novi Pazar would be included in the proposed neutral zone. Argued the chancellor:

Had Austria-Hungary accepted common action against Turkey . . . it would have been natural to keep Serbia as well as Montenegro neutral. The two powers could have decided the political and military attitude of those countries. But the moment we have to act alone, it would be impossible for us to deprive ourselves of the co-operation of these two countries as bases of operations and as effective diversions. [Commented Andrassy: "Böses Unsinn. Divergence bleibt!"] Besides . . . no one could prevent them from taking up arms again the day of our entry into Turkey, and from the moment of their participation in the war, it would be indispensable, particularly in Serbia, to supervise and organize their military activities. Besides, we could not exercise there any more influence than that required by military necessity, and it is probable that once the war began, the Serbian forces would move outside the principality. [Andrassy commented: "Also keine Russen."]

Gorchakov added that Russia would avoid a clash with Austrian forces by staying out of western Serbia, but it required the Serbian states' co-operation in war and could not permit any extension of Austrian influence there.[84] Ambassador Novikov reasserted Russia's rights to operate within Serbia, and the tsar rejected Vienna's efforts to bar Russian operations from the western Balkans.[85]

The two governments gradually compromised their differences. Gorchakov suggested that Russia mainly desired co-operation with the Serbian states *outside* their borders. Andrassy still opposed any occupa-

[83] HHSA, Geheimakten, *1*, rot 453, Andrassy to Langenau, ad Dec. 26.

[84] *Ibid.*, Gorchakov to Novikov, Nov. 23/Dec. 5.

[85] Goriainov, *Le Bosphore*, p. 332, Novikov to Gorchakov, Nov. 23/Dec. 5. On this dispatch the tsar commented, "Tout cela ne peut être admis."

tion of Serbia by Russia or its use as a military base, but he told Novikov, "If the pursuit of the enemy caused Russian troops to cross into Serbian territory, on condition that this was not a movement planned to effect an occupation of the principality, especially at the beginning of the campaign, the Vienna cabinet would make no protest." [86] This concession lifted the despondency in St. Petersburg.[87] The tsar now was convinced that if "Turkey pursued the war in Serbia or continued to occupy Serbian territory, Russian troops could not be prevented from fighting the enemy on that territory." Novikov and Andrassy drafted a military convention and signed it on January 15.[88]

A political convention concerning the postwar settlement took two additional months to negotiate. Until it was signed on March 18, Austria was not squared, and uncertainty about its attitude persisted in St. Petersburg.[89]

Russian plans to protect Serbia were altered by the Austro-Russian agreements. Nikitin had sought to arrange a Russian crossing of the Danube at Kladovo, but Russian headquarters learned that Austria would not permit this. Novikov reported that a Russian invasion of Turkey through Serbia would provoke an Austro-Russian war. Only Russian military missions and volunteers could visit Serbia, not regular army units.[90] Grand Duke Nikolai Nikolaevich feared that Serbia, unless Russian forces were stationed there, would conclude a separate peace, depriving Russia of a pretext for war and allowing Turkey to concentrate its forces against her. Recognizing Serbia's potential military value, the grand duke recommended that its rearmament be as-

[86] HHSA, Geheimakten, *1*, rot 453, report of Dec. 5/17. Apparently this was written by Novikov after a conversation with Andrassy.

[87] Miliutin, *Dnevnik*, 2, 117–18, entries of Dec. 2/14, 6/18.

[88] HHSA, Geheimakten, *1*, rot 453, Gorchakov to Novikov, Dec. 15/27. Andrassy, however, refused to incorporate Gorchakov's statement in the military convention. His interpretation was: "I told Novikov orally that if unforeseen war events . . . should cause Russian troops to cross momentarily the frontiers of the neutral zone formed by Serbia, the Kaiser would appreciate this eventuality fairly and . . . would not consider it under such circumstances as an act hostile to Austria-Hungary." *Ibid.*, Andrassy to Langenau, Jan. 24, dispatch no. 1.

[89] Drafts and counterdrafts of the political convention were exchanged between Vienna and St. Petersburg during January and February. Only on March 12 did Gorchakov authorize Novikov to complete the negotiations. Sumner, *Russia*, p. 279. For the text of the Budapest Conventions see A. Pribram, *Secret Treaties*, 2, 192–95.

[90] Os. Pr., no. 5, pp. 156–61, Parensov to Levitskii, Dec. 15/27; D. Naglovskii, "Kishinevskoe sidenie," RS, *112* (1902), 257–58, entry of Dec. 24/Jan. 5.

sisted by Russia. The tsar, however, still considered Serbia's role insignificant.[91]

The Budapest Conventions, by restricting potential co-operation between Serbia and Russia, loosened their political ties. Andrassy warned Belgrade that Russian use of its territory as a base would violate the Treaty of Paris and might provoke an Austrian occupation.[92]

Russia was paying a stiff price for Austrian neutrality. Vienna could occupy Bosnia and Hercegovina, the Serbian states' primary objectives, and Russia had to renounce attempts to extend its influence in the western Balkans. Without military effort, Austria could prevent creation of a greater Serbian state. In return Russia merely secured Austrian neutrality and the right to co-operate militarily with the Serbian states outside their frontiers.

The Constantinople Conference and the Serbian States

The October ultimatum had produced a bellicose mood at the Russian court and among the public,[93] but by late November Russian leaders grew more anxious for a peaceful settlement. Their willingness to parley with the Turks and the Powers averted a fall campaign.[94] While the Russians were trying to secure Austrian neutrality through the Budapest Conventions, Russian diplomats worked with the Powers at the Constantinople Conference, in December and January; Bulgaria was a principal topic for debate. St. Petersburg's pacific approach enhanced Langenau's optimism about prospects for a Balkan settlement, and Baron Jomini admitted that some Russian leaders regretted the Moscow speech and the hasty mobilization.[95]

[91] Sb. Mat., no. 14, pp. 25–26, Nikolai Nikolaevich to Alexander II, Dec. 26/Jan. 7. The tsar's comment was: "We know definitely that we cannot count on any help from Serbia and that the Serbian government definitely does not wish to continue the war."

[92] Kartsov, "Za kulisami," pp. 473–74, 477.

[93] For Russian public opinion between the wars see infra, pp. 166ff. The tsar, until after the Moscow speech (Nov. 10) and his order for partial mobilization, was determined to act alone if necessary to protect the Balkan Christians. GP, 2, no. 254, p. 85; no. 255, pp. 86–87; SR (June 1925), pp. 195–97, Gorchakov to Shuvalov, Oct. 22/Nov. 3.

[94] SR (Dec. 1925), Gorchakov to Shuvalov, Oct. 24/Nov. 5 and Oct. 28/Nov. 9, nos. 94, 95, pp. 433, 434, Gorchakov to Ignat'ev, Nov. 15/27, no. 127, p. 451. Ignatev, IV (May 1914), pp. 463–64, Jomini to Ignat'ev, Dec. 5/17.

[95] HHSA, Langenau to Andrassy, Nov. 10/22, 60A and Privatschreiben and Nov. 11/23, no. 61. The tsar, Langenau learned, had issued the mobilization decree

Russia, in spite of earlier friendly assurances from Germany, had been unable to obtain definite German support against Turkey and Austria-Hungary. Bismarck had urged a Russian attack on Turkey, but he advised St. Petersburg to conclude an agreement with Vienna first.[96] The Foreign Ministry, unwilling to risk a conflict with an Anglo-Austrian-Turkish coalition, insisted upon guarantees of Austrian neutrality before approving war. If Russia could make a settlement at the Constantinople Conference, she would not have to meet the severe Austrian demands being worked out by the Budapest Conventions and fight a costly war with Turkey which might benefit Russia very little.[97] Thus St. Petersburg protracted its negotiations with Austria until the failure of the conference compelled acceptance of Vienna's conditions.

Russia's proposals at the conference were primarily Count Ignat'ev's. His maximum plan advocated indefinite occupation of Bulgaria by Russia and of other Turkish territories by the Powers until reforms had been executed; his minimum called for Bulgarian autonomy backed by nonmilitary guarantees.[98] Gorchakov instructed Ignat'ev to present his maximum first, but he added that acceptance of the minimum would still spare Russia a ruinous war. To Ignat'ev's query whether he should insist upon Russian occupation of Bulgaria, the tsar wrote no. "Ignat'ev must understand that we wish to attribute serious significance to the conference and come to an agreement if this is possible."[99] At the conference, Ignat'ev sought to obtain a large autonomous Bulgaria while avoiding a breach with the Powers.

At preliminary talks with the Powers' envoys (December 11–22) and at the conference itself (December 23–January 20) the future of Bulgaria was the principal subject. At Austrian insistence, Ignat'ev abandoned insistence upon a Russian occupation and agreed to split

---

with tears in his eyes. "I have worked for the maintenance of peace for twenty years, and now I am supposed to make war," he lamented. *Ibid.*, Dec. 8/20, Privatschreiben.

[96] GP, *2*, nos. 256–59, pp. 89–98; Čubrilović, *Bosanski ustanak*, p. 285.

[97] Ignat'ev, IV, pp. 463–67; *ibid.*, pp. 462–63: Tiutin, "Politika," p. 278.

[98] Ignat'ev informed Gorchakov on Nov. 4/16 that he had outlined a maximum plan and that Prince A. N. Tseretelev and Eugene Schuyler, American consul in Constantinople, had drafted a minimum proposal. OSVOb., *1*, 487–88; 489–95; Tiutin, "Politika," p. 269; Sumner, *Russia*, p. 234.

[99] SR (Dec. 1925), nos. 98, 125, pp. 435, 450–51, Gorchakov to Shuvalov, Nov. 6/18, Gorchakov to Ignat'ev, Nov. 12/24; AVPR, Konstantinopel 1876, d. 35, 1. 466, cited in Tiutin, "Politika," p. 269.

Bulgaria longitudinally, but he won the Powers' assent to an auton-omous state including the sandjak of Niš and most of Macedonia. Neither Austria nor England objected at this time to a large Bulgaria on ethnic grounds.[100] Ignat'ev obtained the Powers' acquiescence to most of his minimum, but his proposed Bulgarian frontiers were certain to antagonize Belgrade.

Serbia, expecting Ignat'ev to defend its interests at the conference, at first took no initiative to secure representation. *Istok* declared on November 12, "The powerful hand of Russia has taken up our cause as her own. We are more than satisfied to be represented by her. We have no doubt that she will defend us . . . and is acting in our interests." Serbs could face the future confidently, stated *Istok*, since a Russian war on behalf of the Slavs would follow the conference.[101] Only when Gorchakov advised the Serbian states to seek admission to the confer-ence did Ristić, with Montenegro's approval, submit a formal request (December 13).[102] When the Powers rejected it, Ristić entrusted Ser-bia's case to Ignat'ev: "Knowing of your sympathy and devotion to the Serbian nation, I need not urge you to protect our interests at the conference." Prince Milan sent the Frenchman, Grignan, to Constan-tinople as an unofficial observer.[103]

[100] Andrassy believed, however, that Ignat'ev's maximum would be the first step toward the decomposition of the Ottoman Empire. "The geographic partiality of the [Ignat'ev] scheme . . . is directed against the future development of the Greek population and is merely intended to promote Pan-Slavist and Russian interests." *Staatsarchiv, 31,* 260, 269, Salisbury to Derby, Nov. 29, Buchanan to Derby, Dec. 11, telegram; Sumner, *Russia* pp. 239-40; Cecil, *Life of Robert, Marquis of Salisbury* (London, 1921), *2,* 108ff.

[101] *Istok,* Oct. 31/Nov. 12, Nov. 10/22, nos. 117. *Zastava* called for Serbdom to be represented at the conference if Turkey were given a vote. Otherwise the Slavs should rely upon Russia to represent them (Nov. 3/15, no. 168). Ristić wrote, "We know that we have in you our best advocate." AII, Ristić 18/191, (Ristić) to Ignat'ev, Nov. 9/21.

[102] *Ibid.,* 13/45, 46, 47, Ristić to Radonić, Nov. 21/Dec. 3, Nov. 25/Dec. 7, Nov. 29/Dec. 11, Nov. 30/Dec. 12; 18/197 Ristić to Ignat'ev, Dec. 1/13. Ristić wrote Radonić (Dec. 7), "Even though we are convinced our request [for repre-sentation] will be rejected, I feel we should persist in our effort and claim our rights so that if we are turned down, we shall have more basis to turn to the conference in writing. Serbia and Montenegro, after four months of war, should not act as if the matter did not concern them." Prince Milan explained to his foreign minister the same day why he opposed a Serbian request for admittance. Ristić retorted, "I am responsible for foreign affairs. Only one minister disagreed with me on this." KZPK, pp. 18-22.

[103] AII, Ristić 18/199, Dec. 7/19, draft; 18/200, Ignat'ev to Milan, Dec. 8/20; 19/65, Grignan to Ristić, Dec. 11/23.

But Ignat'ev treated the Serbian question as secondary. Instead of pressing the Porte for substantial concessions, he merely proposed that Serbia and Turkey evacuate occupied territory and restore the *status quo ante*. The villages of Mali Zvornik and Zagora were to go to Serbia on the ground that Turkey held them in violation of the Treaty of Adrianople (1828).[104] On behalf of Montenegro, Ignat'ev argued stubbornly for contiguous parts of Hercegovina and three Adriatic seaports. He yielded to Austro-Italian objections to Montenegrin access to the sea only upon instruction from St. Petersburg.[105] Ignat'ev was influenced by Montenegro's superior military position, but again Serbia was treated as a poor relation.

Belgrade's unofficial envoy, Grignan, warned of Ignat'ev's hostility toward Serbia. Irritated at Belgrade's aspirations to a major Balkan role and at its disregard for Russia's advice in 1876, Ignat'ev considered Serbia's defeat a salutary lesson. He castigated "soi-disants grands hommes [apparently Ristić and J. Grujić] qui ont engagé ce malheureux pays dans une guerre où il ne pouvait rien gagner." Grignan concluded from Ignat'ev's derogatory remarks that "one would have to close one's eyes to consider him a friend of the Serbs." The count stated that Russia would not have objected to Turkish imposition of severer terms upon Serbia. Grignan telegraphed Ristić: "You can be absolutely certain that there is no question of giving you anything at all beyond the *status quo*. Russia is the power least favorable to you. [Ignat'ev] speaks of Serbia as if it were his enemy."[106]

[104] To his dispatch of Nov. 29/Dec. 11 on the tasks of the conference, Ignat'ev appended his "Esquisses des conditions de paix." Since the campaign had turned out badly for the Serbs, "on pourrait difficilement donner suite au désir de la principauté de faire rectifier sa frontière du côté de l'ancienne Serbie." But, he went on, one must consider that the occupation of eastern Serbia, involving its complete devastation, had cost Serbia huge losses. Thus, in fixing conditions of peace, it is essential: (1) to give Serbian and Turkish troops only eight to ten days to withdraw from occupied territory; (2) to arrange an exchange of war prisoners; (3) that the Porte grant an amnesty to Turkish subjects involved in the war of 1876; (4) to leave Mali Zvornik to Serbia. The bed of the Drina should constitute, in accordance with the hatti-sherif of 1833, the Bosnian-Serbian frontier. OSVOb., *1*, 542. At the conference Ignat'ev argued in favor of these minor rectifications in favor of Serbia, and Salisbury agreed they would not violate the principle of the integrity of Turkey. *Staatsarchiv, 31*, 330-39, Protocol 2 of the Constantinople Conference, Dec. 16/28.

[105] *Staatsarchiv, 31*, 333; Sumner, *Russia*, pp. 242-43.

[106] AII, Ristić 19/67, 68, 81, Grignan to Ristić, Dec. 13/25, 17/29, 18/30. These reports are collected in a folder entitled, "Tourret," which was Grignan's pseudonym.

Grignan's reports suggest that Ristić was prepared for rapprochement with Turkey if Serbia were properly compensated. The envoy sounded out Foreign Minister Safvet Pasha unofficially about a Serbo-Turkish entente which would end Serbia's dependence on Russia. When the Turks pressed him to name the price, Grignan hinted at cession of Mali Zvornik and territory near Alexinac and cancellation of arrears of tribute. The Turkish foreign minister, though much interested, replied that Turkey could yield no more than Mali Zvornik to a defeated vassal.[107] Belgrade did not pursue these overtures, but Grignan's letters indicate that the Serbs were considering alternatives to alignment with Russia. But officially Serbo-Turkish relations remained frigid.[108]

Neither Ignat'ev nor his government, despite their dislike for Ristić, would abandon Serbia to the Turks. Indeed, at this time the count opposed war partly because of Serbia's defenselessness. He warned the Porte emphatically that Russia might consider an attack upon Serbia or Montenegro a *casus belli*.[109] Ignat'ev, executing Gorchakov's instructions of December 23, sought to extend the Serbo-Turkish armistice. Gorchakov knew that if war came the Russian right flank would be exposed if the Serbian army were eliminated. He concluded, "C'est indispensable pour sauver la Serbie."[110] Under Russian pressure, Turkey on December 28 prolonged the armistice until March 1.

The demands of the Constantinople Conference—a reduced version of Ignat'ev's minimum—were rejected immediately by the Porte.[111] The Serbs did not regret the failure of the conference, as Protić's account of his conversation with Ignat'ev attests:

I could not help but remark to him that it was shameful to me as a Serb to see Niš, Skoplje, and Prizren districts placed by Russia under Bulgaria since they had comprised part of the Serbia of Nemanja and of the glory of the Serbian past. . . . I demonstrated to him that the Serbian language prevails there . . . and that what was done with these Serbian lands [at the confer-

---

[107] *Ibid.*, 19/65, 66, Dec. 11/23.   [108] Ristić, *1*, 220–23.

[109] Ignat'ev, IV, *136* (May 1914), pp. 457–460; AII, Ristić 18/341, Marinović to Ristić, Dec. 18/30.

[110] SR (Dec. 1925), no. 143, pp. 454–55, Gorchakov to Ignat'ev, very secret.

[111] They included creation of a large autonomous Bulgaria, a united Bosnia-Hercegovina with local autonomy under Ottoman suzerainty and provided significant gains for Montenegro and the *status quo* for Serbia. Ignat'ev, IV, *136* (May 1914), p. 457; OSVOb., *1*, 553. Sumner (*Russia*, pp. 243–46) stresses the important role played by the Turks in reducing the Powers' demands and imperiling their preliminary agreements.

ence] was unjust. . . . He [Ignat'ev] justified himself by saying that it was the fault of the English since in their program, that area was left to Bulgaria, and that he could not depart from this program.[112]

Ignat'ev's proposals revealed his, and his government's, preference for Bulgaria and Montenegro. Serbia's treatment at the conference fore-shadowed her fate at San Stefano a year later.

The Serbian States Negotiate for Peace

The armistice extension and the collapse of the conference left the Serbian states in limbo between war and peace. Confronted with a superior foe and unable to reorganize its shattered forces, Serbia needed peace more urgently than victorious Montenegro. Marinović urged Belgrade to make peace regardless of Russia's future course, but he admitted that the prince would not so readily separate himself from Russia.[113] Turkish rejection of the conference proposals forced Serbia to reassess its policy. The ministers decided (January 22) that unless Russia sent financial aid, Serbia must conclude peace. In no case could she fight unless Russia first went to war.[114]

A Turkish offer to negotiate directly with Belgrade, on January 25, compelled a quick decision. The Russian Foreign Ministry advised acceptance of any reasonable overture.[115] The Turks' initial demand for a guarantee against resumption of the war alarmed the Serbs, but they finally consented to parley. No definite commitments would be made, however, until clarification of Russian policy toward Turkey and the Serbian states.[116]

On February 6, Milan explained to the tsar that to resist a March invasion Serbia must mobilize but lacked money even to maintain the army's truce strength of 30,000 men. The prince's letter continued:

Only your advice can prescribe the course I should adopt. . . . If war between Russia and Turkey can be predicted, I shall be happy to co-operate in it energetically, but I must inform Your Majesty that I could not do this without financial means. . . . If, on the other hand, war is improbable or must be delayed until after the month of February, please advise me as to

---

[112] AII, Ristić 22/274, Protić to Ristić, March 8/20, 1877.
[113] HHSA, Wrede to Andrassy, Jan. 17, no. 6.   [114] Grujić, 3, 266.
[115] AII, Ristić, 22/27, Protić to Ristić, Jan. 13/25; Ristić, 1, 232; Grujić, 3, 267.
[116] Ibid., pp. 268–71; KZPK, Milan to Stevča Mihajlović, Jan. 14/26.

the means to follow to arrive at the conclusion of peace. . . . Whatever may be the advice of Your Majesty, I shall be happy to follow it faithfully.[117]

Austro-Russian support facilitated conclusion of a Serbo-Turkish peace. By early February, Ristić learned that both Gorchakov and Andrassy approved of negotiations. Russian leaders advocated a separate peace because Serbia was unprepared for war. The tsar favored it "since we cannot count on the co-operation of [Serbia], and Montenegro . . . would join us anyhow in case of war." [118] When Prince Milan learned officially from Kartsov (February 12) that Russia still preferred a peaceful solution, he telegraphed the Grand Vizir that Serbian envoys would come to Constantinople for peace negotiations.[119]

The political situation in Serbia was confused. From the November armistice until March 1877, the Ristić Liberals faced powerful opposition from a war-weary people and from rival political parties which condemned the government's conduct of the war.[120] In its defense the cabinet claimed that Serbia had fought bravely in a necessary war and must pursue the national cause with Russia's help. *Istok* wrote:

Serbia succumbed but drew Russia out of her reserve and Serbia stands as the harbinger of the Slav future. . . . Even if Serbia itself gains nothing, if our brother Bulgarians, Bosnians, Hercegovinians, or Montenegrins do, we also have gained. The Italians shed much blood before the Italy of Garibaldi and Cavour was built.[121]

The Serbian princes must join with Russia to expel the Turks from Europe, declared *Istok*, "for now it is certain that the great Tsar

[117] AII, Ristić 18/34. Milan to Alexander II. Internal references indicate this draft in Ristić's hand was written on Jan. 10/22.

[118] AII, Ristić 26/13, 18, Protić to Ristić, Jan. 15/27; Jan. 23/Feb. 4; Os. Pr., no. 3, p. 9, Alexander II to Nikolai Nikolaevich, Jan. 18/30; Grujić, *3*, 275; HHSA, Andrassy to Wrede, Feb. 5.

[119] Ristić, *1*, 237–38; Grujić, *3*, 227–78.

[120] Here is a sample of the opposition arguments: "Never has the [Serbian] people felt greater need to tell its feelings to the prince than now. The people believe in you but has no faith in your present ministers who took an unprepared Serbia into a war without allies and frivolously engaged her in a struggle with an empire twenty times stronger, ministers who led prince and people to a new Kosovo at Djunis. The Serbian people needs peace to bind up its wounds. . . . The people asks that a *special commission* examine all the work of these ministers for the vast damage they have done." ASAN no. 9536, "Pretstavka Knjazu Milanu," n.d.

[121] *Istok*, Jan. 1/13, no. 1.

Liberator will be for the Serbs what Napoleon III was for the Italians, and perhaps even more." A separate peace would be abdication of national leadership. Would anyone in Serbia be satisfied with the *status quo ante* after such heavy sacrifices? [122] According to *Istok*, the Serbo-Turkish War had (1) reasserted Serbia's national role, (2) acquired European recognition and sympathy, (3) hardened the Serbian people, and (4) opened the Eastern Question.[123] *Zastava*, favoring resumption of the war, generally defended the Ristić government. Under Ristić the Serbs would fight until their objectives had been achieved. Peace now would be betrayal of the Serbian cause and block creation of a greater Serbian state south of the Sava.[124] Both newspapers counseled perseverance.

The opposition to Ristić appeared overwhelming, but it was frag-mented. Prince Milan, Kartsov, and Marinović, all anxious to oust the Liberals, exploited strong pacific feeling. On January 26, the day after the Turkish offer to negotiate, the prince demanded convocation of a Great Assembly to debate the peace issue. The cabinet, fearing the worst, bowed to Milan's threats. In the February 20 elections the opposition obtained a majority and anticipated a final reckoning with the Ristić government. But the prince was alarmed by the gains regis-tered by anti-Obrenović groups, and just before the Great Assembly met, he decided to abandon Marinović and Kartsov. In a typical burst of opportunism, he reached sudden agreement with the Ristić Liber-als.[125]

Peace could now be concluded by the Ristić cabinet. To remove Serbia from the war, the Porte renounced demands for a guarantee against its re-entry. Serbian and Turkish envoys quickly agreed to restore the *status quo ante*. The Great Assembly was convened Febru-ary 26, two days before expiration of the armistice. Ristić, with the prince's support, insisted that the Assembly vote first on the proposed peace treaty and provided this evaluation of the situation:

Russia stands ready with a powerful army to fight Turkey. But we do not know whether Russia really intends to fight or when, nor what gains Serbia

---

[122] *Ibid.*, Jan. 14/26, no. 5, "Dopisi lz Sarajaeva," Dec. 31/Jan. 12; Jan. 19/31, no. 7.

[123] *Ibid.*, Jan. 26/Feb. 7, no. 10. The negative aspects of the war were not enumerated!

[124] *Zastava*, Dec. 19/31, 1876, no. 102; no. 20, Feb. 6/18, 1877.

[125] Vlada Milana, *1*, 362–69; Živanović, *Politička istorija, 1*, 344.

could expect in the event she participated. If we conclude peace and Russia soon afterward goes to war, we might regret not having participated, but also expecting Russia to do so without our having any prospect of the prolongation of the truce would place us in a dangerous position if we had to face the renewal of the unequal struggle after so much sacrifice. At this critical moment the prince wishes to hear the voice of the people on the proposals which the Porte has made to us.

The delegates voted almost unanimously to approve the treaty, then were dismayed to learn that the Assembly had been dissolved. The opposition, unable to censure the government, was dispersed by force. Milan's new alliance with the Liberals was confirmed and Kartsov lost his last shreds of influence.[126] On March 1, Serbian envoys were instructed to sign the treaty.

Serbia's withdrawal, as Vienna expected, worsened Serbo-Montenegrin relations, which had been deteriorating since Djunis. Belgrade asserted that it could not provide Prince Nikola with a subsidy.[127] Thömmel telegraphed Vienna (November 1), "The armistice provides us [Austria] with an opportunity to drag Prince Nikola further away from his alliance with Serbia." On January 25, he reported triumphantly, "Montenegro no longer attributes any importance to solidarity with Serbia." [128] The Serbo-Turkish peace undermined Montenegro's bargaining position. Prince Nikola declared that Belgrade's action had abrogated the Serbo-Montenegrin alliance of 1876. Ristić replied that Serbia had had no alternative. Agreeing that their mutual obligations had ceased, he nonetheless hoped the two states would afford one another moral support.[129]

Far greater difficulties stood in the way of a Turko-Montenegrin settlement. In late January, Prince Nikola agreed to negotiate directly but, conscious of his relatively favorable military position, he insisted upon important Turkish concessions. He told English Consul E. Monson before negotiations began that he doubted their success. Nikola

[126] HHSA, Wrede to Andrassy, Feb. 19, no. 18; March 3, 29, nos. 26, 34; Ristić, 1, 274–75, speech of Feb. 16/28 to the Great Assembly. For a defense of the sudden dissolution, see Ristić to Hristić, March 18/30, *Pisma Ristića*, p. 242; AII, Ban 6/45, "1877-Journalisme"; Vlada Milana, 1, 371–72.

[127] KZPK, Nikola to Milan, Oct. 15/27 and Nov. 19/Dec. 1 and Milan to Nikola, Nov. 21/Dec. 3, 1876.

[128] Djordjević, *Crna Gora*, pp. 401, 404–05.

[129] For these exchanges between Serbia and Montenegro, see AII, Ristić 13/58–60, 64; DAS, 26/196, 197, 200–03.

believed that Montenegro should continue the war rather than sign an inglorious peace. Russian grain would supply it for years, and his people could resume the struggle at any time. "You know," the prince told Monson, "that in fact the tranquillity of those regions [Bosnia and Hercegovina] depends upon Montenegro and that as long as we remain dissatisfied and disappointed in realizing aspirations we consider just, this will react upon our neighbors." Unless a peace settlement benefited the insurgents, Nikola believed, he would be compromised in their eyes.[130]

Montenegro's behavior was much affected by Russian and Austrian policy. Russia's warm support was suggested in a Gorchakov memorandum:

It is not merely out of sympathy for those brave mountaineers . . . that we insist upon the opportunity for a territorial increase in their favor. . . . We believe it indispensable that Montenegro be granted conditions of existence which will permit it to become a state offering guarantees of peace and stability. Montenegro has demonstrated that it possesses the elements of order and discipline necessary to this end.[131]

Rather than urge Cetinje to yield to the Porte, Gorchakov telegraphed Nelidov, "If the Montenegrin representatives consult you, advise them to be moderate." In perplexity, Nelidov inquired whether he should tell them to make specific concessions, but Gorchakov replied evasively.[132] He wished apparently to preserve his mediatory role and a Russian pretext for war. Vienna, on the other hand, flatly opposed some of the Montenegrin territorial claims (to Zupac and Sutorina), threatening to suspend its road subsidy and occupy the disputed areas if Cetinje persisted. Unwilling to alienate Austria, Prince Nikola reluctantly renounced the two regions.[133]

For six weeks Turko-Montenegrin negotiations dragged on without

[130] *Staatsarchiv, 32,* 90, Monson to Derby, Feb. 1, 1877.

[131] HHSA, Geheimakten, *1,* Aide-mémoire, Feb., 1877; *ibid.,* Gorchakov to Novikov, Feb. 28. Gorchakov had accepted in substance a pro-Montenegrin memorandum composed by A. S. Ionin. See Os. Pr., no. 1, "Proposals for territorial changes in the Balkan peninsula," Jan. 18/30.

[132] AVPR, Konstantinopel 1877, d. 22, l. 595, 671, cited in Tiutin, "Politika," p. 375; HHSA, Langenau to Andrassy, March 7/19, no. 110; Miliutin, *Dnevnik, 2,* 152; Nelidov to Giers, Feb. 21/March 5, in Jelavich, *Russia in the East,* p. 157. Gorchakov persisted in his exhortations for moderation after prospects of a Montenegrin and Turkish settlement had virtually disappeared.

[133] Djordjević, *Crna Gora,* pp. 407–08. See especially telegram of Thömmel to Andrassy, Feb. 23.

success. Though the Porte increased its territorial offers somewhat and Prince Nikola abandoned claims to part of the area his troops had conquered, deadlock resulted. The Montenegrins stubbornly demanded the fortress of Nikšić, and Monson primarily blamed the Turks for refusing to yield what to them was essentially worthless territory. Turkish obduracy brought collapse of the negotiations in mid-April, when the armistice with Montenegro expired.[134]

The Serbo-Turkish peace undermined Belgrade's influence in the insurgent provinces and demoralized the Bosnian rebels. In Constantinople, the Serb delegates had agreed to prevent formation of volunteer bands in Serbia. Belgrade advised insurgent leaders in Bosnia to cease operations, since they could not succeed. Ristić told their envoy that he could not assist them and that the insurrection no longer benefited Serbia.[135] But the Bosnian insurgents had dreamed so long of unification with Serbia that many of them could conceive at first of no other course. "When Bosnian refugees in Austria-Hungary heard that Serbia had made peace with Turkey," wrote a Bosnian merchant, "they were struck dumb, as if a thunderbolt had fallen from the sky."[136] Unaware of Serbia's exhaustion and dependence upon the Powers, insurgent leaders accused Belgrade of betraying the common cause. *Zastava*, echoing their complaints, advised them to turn to Russia or Montenegro: "Serbia this time was unable to pursue that holy mission [of liberation and unification], so nothing binds us any longer to Serbia." The Bosnian chiefs, claimed *Zastava*, would go to Cetinje and offer Prince Nikola leadership of the insurrection.[137]

Serbia sought to maintain some influence in Bosnia through its agent, Colonel Despotović. Upon instructions from Belgrade, he arranged a

[134] *Ibid.*, pp. 409-10, *Staatsarchiv*, *32*, 127, 139, Monson to Derby, March 16, March 25. Nelidov reported to Gorchakov (April 5), that he had urged the Turks to accept the reduced Montenegrin demands, but Safvet Pasha replied that the Porte could not yield Nikšić, Kolačin, and Kući. It was Nelidov's opinion Savfet would have consented had he not been under intense pressure from the Turkish war party. OSVOb., *1*, 624-25; *ibid.*, p. 637, Nelidov to Gorchakov, April 4/16. It seems that the main obstacle to conclusion of peace was not the territorial dispute but the Porte's desire to impose vassal status on Montenegro.

[135] AII, Ristić 18/675, (Ristić) to Skobla, telegram, n.d.; Ekmečić, *Ustanak*, pp. 288-89; Čubrilović, *Bosanski ustanak*, pp. 263-64; Grujić, *3*, 276, 285.

[136] Some insurgent leaders such as Simo Bilbija were so disillusioned they began to agitate against the Serbian government. AII, Ristić, 18/263, Babić to Vasi, Feb. 15, 1877. G. Muir-Mackenzie and P. Irby, *Travels in the Slavonic Provinces of Turkey in Europe*, 4th ed. (London, 1877), p. 35, cited in Ekmečić, *Ustanak*, p. 292.

[137] *Zastava*, March 13/25, no. 40.

de facto truce with the Turks. The colonel still commanded a sizable force of insurgents, but his authority declined further.[138] Arthur Evans, a British correspondent who visited western Bosnia at this time, was impressed with the insurgents' courage and determination, but not with Despotović. "Nothing is wanting to the insurrection but a leader," he wrote. Colonel Despotović's autocratic ways antagonized the freedom-loving Bosnians, many of whom broke away from his authority. He was "a man of spruce and bovine presence who swaggered up clinking his spurs"; he greeted Evans in French and served him Russian tea and sponge cake *glacé*. Over some choice Dalmatian wine, Despotović told him, "Voyez-vous, que je ne suis pas seulement commandant de l'armée bosniaque—je suis chef du peuple bosniaque." "In fact," replied Evans, "this is your Montenegro, and you are its Nikola." "Precisely," said Despotović, "J'y suis le Prince Régnant." [139]

In Bosnia, Russian influence was replacing Serbian. Though the insurgents were unsuccessful in efforts to obtain financial aid from the Russian court,[140] the Slav committees responded warmly to their appeals and with official approval tried to revive the rebellion. In March, an agreement was concluded in Belgrade between Naryshkin and insurgent leaders: a new rebel offensive would be co-ordinated with Russia's attack upon Turkey. Almost 10,000 rubles were given Despotović by the St. Petersburg Committee to make preparations. Russian agents sought to form volunteer bands in western Serbia to aid the insurgents, but General Alimpić dispersed them, denouncing such activity because it cast doubt upon Serbia's peaceful intentions.[141] Serbia's estrangement from the Slav committees and from the Bosnian insurrection was evident.

[138] OSVOb., *1*, 558. Reports of A. N. Kudriavtsev, Dec. 2/14, and 9/21, 1876; Ekmečić, *Ustanak,* pp. 268–69. Evans estimated in February 1877 that the insurgents numbered only about 2,000 (*ibid.,* p. 271), whereas Kudriavtsev's estimate was 5,000.

[139] Evans, *Illyrian Letters,* pp. 21–22, 39–40.

[140] Two Bosnian envoys had gone to Russia with Belgrade's blessing. Ristić told them "they could explain to the tsarist government the situation in which Bosnia finds itself and discover a way which would be best to aid their country." Ristić to Cukić, Jan. 25. The envoys proceeded via Bucharest and Odessa. AII, Ristić 17/253, Skulić and Škorić to Ristić, Jan. 29. For details see Ekmečić, *Ustanak,* p. 297.

[141] HHSA, Wrede to Andrassy, March 16; Ekmečić, *Ustanak,* pp. 293–96; AII, Ristić 19/609, Despotović to Ristić, n.d., 180. HHSA, Wrede to Andrassy, March 16. Despite this, Bosnians entertained boundless hope now in their "northern uncle."

In March, Belgrade acted to restore Serbia to a peacetime footing. At the request of local Serbian commanders, the government ordered liquidation of the Russo-Bulgarian volunteer brigade at Kladovo. With a Russo-Turkish conflict imminent, Ristić wished to eliminate any Turkish pretext to occupy that Danube city.[142] He was deeply concerned by Serbia's vulnerability, as his letter to Filip Hristić reveals:

Our position is bleaker, more dangerous and more delicate than it was on the eve of our war. We must be cautious and restrained. . . . A Russo-Turkish war could bring complications which could bring into question the very existence of our principality. We hope that Russia will respect the peace we concluded with Turkey since she was not opposed to that peace. What is more, she advised us to conclude it. It would not be in keeping with a great power like Russia after such conduct to be the first to violate such a peace.[143]

Consul Wrede predicted correctly that Belgrade, now cautious and pacific, would re-enter the war only after major Russian victories.[144]

Meanwhile Ristić obtained the removal of the Russian consul. He did not know that after the "Maros" affair Kartsov had requested transfer to Paris.[145] Anxious to settle accounts with him, Ristić in mid-March sent Protić a memorandum accusing Kartsov of anti-Obrenović activity, secret encouragement of Belgrade to make war in 1876, and plotting to overthrow the Ristić cabinet. The memorandum stressed the consul's alleged dealings with Serbian socialists. "Since all of these proceedings have been of a nature to encourage the elements of disorder, which unfortunately are to be found in every country, it should be sufficient to bring them to the knowledge of His Imperial Maj-

[142] DAS, 13/77, Commander of the Timok Corps to Supreme Command, Belgrade, Feb. 18/March 2; PRO, FO, St. John to Derby, April 16, no. 126; Grujić, 3, 288. Ristić denied any intention of collaborating with Russian forces at Kladovo. Staatsarchiv, 32, 207, St. John to Derby, April 20.

[143] Pisma Ristića, pp. 243, 245, Ristić to Hristić, March 12/30 and April 6/18. Hristić was instructed to pledge Serbia's neutrality unless its frontiers were violated by Turkey.

[144] "All signs lately point to the sincere will of the Serbian government to maintain the peace following the decisive vote by the Great Assembly showing clearly the opposition to war here. Even if Russia declares war on Turkey, Serbian action is not to be feared. Only if the tsar's army succeeds during the war in dealing crushing blows against Islam, only if Europe's attitude permits Russia a free hand in the Balkans, only then could Serbian chauvinism gain the upper hand again and induce Serbia to go to war to obtain its share of the spoils." HHSA, Wrede to Andrassy, March 12, no. 29.

[145] Kartsov, RS, 134, 304.

esty."[146] Ristić, in an accompanying letter, explained to Protić that Prince Milan had approved the memorandum after the consul had defended the activities of the disreputable Russian Colonel Markov.[147]

But officials of the Russian Foreign Ministry blamed Ristić for the Kartsov affair. Admitting that the consul had departed occasionally from his instructions, they defended most of his actions and pledged that he would observe orders strictly in the future. Giers observed that the Eastern Crisis was too grave for the Ministry to deal with trivial Serbian complaints. Nonetheless, Russian leaders were dismayed at Kartsov's complicity with Serbian socialists. Protić reported that the memorandum had done its work and that Ristić need worry no longer about the consul. "Let him be irritated. His teeth are drawn." Indeed they were. Kartsov's value to his government had depended upon a close relationship with Prince Milan, which had been shattered irretrievably.[148] Concluding that he was no longer useful, the Ministry relieved him of his post.[149] The disconcerting independence of the Ristić government had been demonstrated once again.

Russian Policy and Attitudes on the Eve of War

With the coming of spring, Russia grew more bellicose. Failure of the Constantinople Conference, signature of the Austrian political con-

[146] AII, Ristić 22/301, March 5, 1877; DAS, Ristić to Protić, Dec. 17/29, 1876; Vlada Milana, *1*, 373–74.

[147] For antidynastic statements, Markov was requested in mid-March to leave Serbia, but he flatly refused and had to be deported forcibly. Kartsov demanded an explanation from Ristić, hinting that the Russian press reaction might damage Serbia. Ristić replied that Markov's intolerable behavior justified his deportation. Ristić asserted that he had previously refrained from expelling misbehaving Russians in order not to antagonize St. Petersburg and Russian public opinion. DAS, 151/455, Ristić to Protić, March 9/21, April 4/16; PRO, FO, St. John to Derby, April 4, no. 40.

[148] DAS, 151/455, Ristić to Protić, April 4/16; AII, Ristić 22/277, Ristić to Protić, March 25/April 6. Declared Giers sadly to Protić, "The task of a Russian consul in Belgrade is an extremely difficult one." *Ibid.*, 22/275, Protić to Ristić, March 18/30.

Kartsov's nephew asserted that Belgrade accused Kartsov falsely of absconding with funds from the Belgrade Benevolent Society. Many years later in Paris, Milan explained to the former consul why he had acted to remove him, "Eh, bien, franchement, mon cher Kartzov, j'en avais assez de votre joug et de votre tutuelle, qui me pesaient par trop et je vous ai imaginé cette crasse, spéculant sur votre nervosité qui vous amenerait à quelque coup de tête." Kartsov, "Za kulisami," pp. 305, 477–78.

[149] St. Petersburg, to save face, at first gave Kartsov a long leave and the chargé d'affaires, N. Lodyzhenskii, ran the consulate until September when Persiani, a conciliatory individual, formally replaced him. Vlada Milana, *1*, 374.

vention, and Turkish rejection of Montenegro's territorial claims convinced St. Petersburg that war was inevitable and perhaps desirable. With Serbia at peace, the government and Pan-Slavs gave increased support to Montenegro and the Bulgarians.

Until the political agreement with Vienna was complete, Russian leaders had stressed diplomacy. In January, Baron Jomini had asserted that the time for war had passed, and that Russia had been abandoned by its allies: "Russia saved Serbia from destruction and forced the Powers to agree to collective action in the Conference. We have done our duty. . . . If Europe agrees to consider itself impotent, that is its affair. We will stay at home." [150] Ignat'ev claimed Russia had triumphed at the Constantinople Conference because its minimum program had been adopted; he advised collaboration with the Powers. Russia, he felt, should go to war only if compelled to, but Russo-Turkish differences could yet be settled peacefully.[151] The tsar and Gorchakov had concluded that Russia in a war with the Porte could not count on support from any of the Powers.[152] The chancellor's circular to the Powers (January 31) had revealed continued adherence to a European approach. Fearing a coalition war, he appeared ready for peace at almost any price. Never in all its history, lamented Miliutin, had Russia's foreign policy been so aimless and uncertain.[153]

At a series of late February meetings, though, the tsar rejected the peace faction's program. Ministers Reitern, Valuev, and Timashev opposed war unconditionally, and Gorchakov suggested that Russia demobilize and proclaim "freedom of action." [154] But Alexander accepted an Obruchev-Miliutin memorandum barring demobilization until Turkey made major concessions. The emperor agreed that peace at any price was incompatible with Russia's honor. Any thought of

[150] Jomini to Ignat'ev, Jan. 7, Ignat'ev, IV, *136* (May 1914), p. 467.

[151] *Ibid.*, pp. 456ff. The latter suggestion was an attempt by the ambassador to regain his influence at the Porte by reverting to a bilateral (Russo-Turkish) basis for negotiations.

[152] SR (March 1926), no. 177, pp. 744–45. Shuvalov to Gorchakov, January; Miliutin, *Dnevnik, 2,* 132.

Just before the declaration of war, Gorchakov told Alexander II, "More than ever I am convinced that Your Majesty should count only on God and your sword." Replied the tsar, "No one is more convinced of this than I." AVPR, Doklades, April 10/22, quoted in Goriainov, *Le Bosphore,* p. 344.

[153] Miliutin, 2, *Dnevnik,* 133, 136, entries of Jan. 13/25, Jan. 25/Feb. 6 and Jan. 29/Feb. 10. It should be repeated that Miliutin was a bitter opponent of the old chancellor, whose policy was by no means as "aimless" as Miliutin suggested.

[154] *Ibid.*, p. 138, Feb. 8/20; Ignat'ev, IV, *136* (June 1914), pp. 840–41; Reutern-Nolcken, pp. 133–43.

immediate disarmament was abandoned.[155] Instead, Ignat'ev would visit European courts to obtain speedy replies to Gorchakov's circular. If the Powers accepted it, a protocol containing the proposals demanding implementation of the reforms they had agreed to at the Constantinople Conference, could be presented collectively to the Porte. Only should the Turks accept such a protocol and promptly execute its provisions could Russia demobilize; otherwise there would be war. Ignat'ev departed early in March.[156]

St. Petersburg shifted sharply toward war once Austria had been squared (March 18). The tsar, characterizing the Porte's demands on Montenegro as impertinent and unacceptable, favored decisive action and considered war inevitable.[157] Signature of the London Protocol (March 31) by all six Powers left him unmoved.[158] "We can consider ourselves secure from Germany and Austria-Hungary," he wrote Nikolai Nikolaevich, "but it is hard to guarantee that in the future. So we must begin military operations as soon as possible."[159] Russia would not demobilize, Langenau was told, unless Turkey executed the Protocol and made peace with Montenegro. Russia's refusal to compel Nikola to accept Turkish terms suggested that it no longer desired peace.[160] The Russian decision to declare war was reached April 11, and the Porte's rejection of the Protocol (received April 12) was merely a boon to Russian diplomats seeking to justify the war.[161]

[155] Miliutin, *Dnevnik*, *2*, 138–40, Feb. 8/20, 10/22, 12/24. This memorandum began by stating that war must be avoided because of the internal and foreign situation, but ended by insisting that Russia act either with the Powers to execute the reforms agreed to at the Constantinople Conference, or, if the Powers demurred, issue an ultimatum to Turkey and go to war if it were rejected. "I am certainly with Miliutin," the tsar told Reitern, Feb. 23, "there are moments in the life of states, as of individuals, when it is necessary to forget everything save the defense of honor." Reitern, RS, *143*, 43–44; Sumner, *Russia*, pp. 258–59.

[156] Ignat'ev, pp. 854–59; HHSA, Langenau to Andrassy, March 26/April 7, no. 14 A-E, Réservé; Sumner, *Russia*, p. 260.

[157] Os. Pr., no. 3, p. 14, Alexander II to Nikolai Nikolaevich, March 8/20.

[158] For the negotiations leading to the Protocol's conclusion see Sumner, *Russia*, pp. 260–70. The final document was a greatly watered-down version of Ignat'ev's draft and was not received enthusiastically by St. Petersburg.

[159] Os. Pr., no. 3, p. 14, Alexander II to Nikolai Nikolaevich, March 19/31.

[160] HHSA, Langenau to Andrassy, March 30, telegram, no. 29; March 28/April 9, no. 15; *Staatsarchiv*, *32*, 146, Shuvalov's declaration before signing the London Protocol. Within the Foreign Ministry, P. A. Valuev wrote March 27, Jomini and some of his colleagues now desired war and the failure of the Protocol. Valuev, *Dnevnik*, p. 8.

[161] Tiutin, "Politika," p. 393. For this justification see *Staatsarchiv*, *32*, 204, Gorchakov to Russian envoys, April 7/19.

The Russian public, not opposed to a defensive war were becoming increasingly reluctant to fight for Serbia's sake. Comments such as the following were reported by Novgorod's chief of police (on February 19, before Serbia had signed the peace with Turkey):

Which war and for whom? For Serbia? But are there genuine reasons for that? Let us admit that the affairs of [Serbia] are unenviable, but who produced that if not Serbia herself? Yes, and who will believe that . . . the principality entered the war unselfishly? The Serbs have been drawing away from Russia for a long time and are much more attracted to the West. . . . To spill Russian blood for them would be a lot to ask.[162]

Even before the Serbs had made peace the Pan-Slavs had ignored desperate Serbian pleas and concentrated on Bulgaria and Montenegro. In vain the commander of the Russo-Bulgarian brigade had urged Aksakov to renew unofficial aid to Serbia. "It is wicked," he wrote, on February 3, "to deceive their [Serbs'] expectations and throw them so to speak into the embraces of our enemies." [163] While Metropolitan Mihailo sought reconciliation with the Slav committees, Pan-Slavs such as Prince V. P. Meshcherskii sowed discord with anti-Serbian diatribes like *Pravda o Serbii*. The metropolitan concluded, "Russia does not require our aid [in war] to be sure, but to strengthen mutual brotherly relations, one should not neglect a people which sacrificed so much . . . for its brethren." [164] Such appeals went unheard.

After the Serbian peace, Veselicki-Bojidarović advised the Slav committees to help Montenegro achieve South Slav aspirations and establish a powerful Slav-Orthodox committee in Cetinje "to resist the slander coming from the West." [165] Aksakov declared that Serbia's conclusion of peace "proved to the whole world that the heroic self-sacrifice of the Russian people had served no purpose." [166] "The Slav Committee," wrote its chairman, "now has a single objective: the regeneration of Bulgaria." [167]

Even *Russkii Mir* abandoned Serbia. On March 3, it violently at-

---

[162] OSVOb., *1*, 594–95, Report to Third Section from Novgorod's police chief, V. I. Zholobov, Feb. 7/19.

[163] Miloradovich to Moscow Slav Committee, Jan. 22/Feb. 3, "Nakanune . . . ," RA (1897), no. 2, pp. 276–77.

[164] ROBibLen, f. Nil Popova 13/48, Mihailo to Popov, Feb. 5/17.

[165] *Ibid.*, 6/22, Veselicki-Bojidarović to Popov, March 8.

[166] Aksakov, *Sochineniia*, *1*, 240–41, speech of March 6/18.

[167] GIM, Aksakov to Cherniaev, April 12/24.

tacked Serbian leaders and institutions and denied the principality any
further role in the Eastern Question:

Slavdom, represented by Serbia, bowed its head among the masses of the
victorious enemy and the intrigues of native officialdom. . . . Serbian officials, calling themselves "ministers," played again . . . a quasi-constitutional
comedy with the participation of the inevitable "political parties." . . . We
have nothing in common with the Serbian administration, built on west
European models and wholly unsuited to a small, patriarchal country. The
Belgrade "intelligentsia" has perhaps much more in common with the
Austrian Germans than with its own Serbian people. . . . Serbia departs
from the scene to give place to more powerful actors to whom the small
principality would be a hindrance rather than a useful auxiliary. One way
or another the Eastern Question must be solved . . . and for the achievement of this common goal, the participation of Serbia has become superfluous.

Later, *Russkii Mir* asserted that Serbia's separate peace was treason
against the Slav cause. "The defection of Serbia makes Montenegro . . . the principal bearer of the Slav idea." [168]

Most Pan-Slavs now were ready to sacrifice the western Balkans to
Austria in exchange for a Russian occupation of Bulgaria and domination over the Straits. General Fadeev, renowned for bitter Austropho-
bia, astonished Wrede by declaring that Russia's only correct policy
was co-operation with Vienna; he proposed partition of the Balkans
into Austrian and Russian spheres.[169] Two Bosnian delegates (S. Škorić
and J. Skulić) were told by Professor V. I. Lamanskii that an Austrian
occupation of their homeland was necessary and would be beneficial.
The Dual Monarchy might even occupy Serbia. Overhearing this,
Protić commented, "Such rascals our Slavophiles—to sacrifice all of
Serbdom to Austria in order to seize the Balkans." [170] Countess Bludova,
confirming Protić's version, explained to Metropolitan Mihailo the Pan-
Slavs' amazing reversal:

Here, unfortunately, some of the best fighters of Slavdom are prepared to
give Austria part of Bosnia and Hercegovina, believing this increase in Slavs
will contribute to the quicker dissolution of Austria. This is also being
preached in the Foreign Ministry and by the tsar himself. One reason for
this was the attitude taken by your intelligentsia and ministers—their

---

[168] *Russkii Mir*, Feb. 19/March 3, March 5/17, nos. 47, 61, leads.
[169] HHSA, Wrede to Andrassy, April 18, no. 43.
[170] AII, Ristić, 22/274, Protić to Ristić, March 8/20.

attitude of superiority and considering themselves like Frenchmen, causing Russians to laugh at their Piedmontese pretensions.[171]

This explanation placed unfair blame on the Serbs and omitted any mention of the Pan-Slavs' imperial lust. They and St. Petersburg were prepared to sacrifice the Serbian people to the Dual Monarchy.[172]

The Pan-Slavs were being closely supervised by the government. In November 1876, Prince A. I. Vasil'chikov, complaining that his St. Petersburg Committee's responsibilities exceeded its resources, requested the authorities to define its realm of activity. In case of war he merely desired a position at headquarters for the committees comparable to that of the Red Cross.[173] After Ivan Aksakov's speech (March 18, 1877) which criticized sharply official passivity on the Slav question, Pan-Slav agitation was drastically curtailed. Copies of newspapers containing the speech were confiscated. So severe grew the censorship that articles of some prominent Pan-Slavs could not be published. Among the ministers, Valuev led the attack against the Slav committees, while Miliutin defended them. The tsar called Aksakov "un enfant terrible," and though he did not close down the Moscow Committee, Aksakov's friends realized his political role had ended for the time being.[174] Unofficial organizations had to subordinate themselves to official direction.

As war approached, the Russian press, except for *Golos,* became bellicose. *Golos* greeted Serbia's separate peace and denounced advocates of a war "to clear the air." Until the second week in April, it preached peace and defended diplomatic efforts to avert a conflict.[175] *Moskovskie Vedomosti,* on the other hand, considered war the only

---

[171] *Ibid.,* 26/746, Bludova to Mihailo, March 18/30.

[172] But not all pro-Slav newspapers. *Istok* reprinted a "very interesting article" from *Russkie Vedomosti,* no. 32, dated Feb. 4/16. It stated, "Russian society has made it clear it would be contrary to the dignity, honor, and interests of Russia to cede to Austria even the smallest piece of Serbian territory. And truly if the Austrians were let into Bosnia and Hercegovina, not only they but also Serbia and Montenegro would be lost to Slavdom and Russia . . . would lose her influence." "If Russia tells Austria to keep hands off Bosnia and Hercegovina, she [Austria] will have to do so." *Istok,* no. 25, March 4/16.

[173] OSVOb., *1,* 554–556, memorandum of A. I. Vasil'chikov to A. V. Adlerberg, Court Minister, November.

[174] ROBibLen, Dnevnik Chizhova, 7, 38, March 11/23 and 14/26; Dnevnik Kireeva, 7, 38–41; ROBibLen, f. Aksakova, no. 195, Lamanskii to Aksakov, March 13/25; *Slavianskii sbornik,* pp. 161–63, Cherkasskii to Aksakov, March 24/April 5.

[175] *Golos,* Jan. 18/31, Feb. 2/14, April 10/22, nos. 19, 33, 98.

solution.[176] *Grazhdanin,* openly favoring war and Slav liberation, espoused Russian seizure of the Straits and driving the "enemies of civilization" from Europe. Liberal *Novoe Vremia* advocated liberation of Bulgaria and all South Slavs.[177] The flag of emancipation first unfurled in Serbia, predicted *Russkii Mir,* would soon wave over a larger field.[178]

Between the wars, Russia's relations with the component parts of Serbdom varied widely. Its ties with Serbia became cool and official while whose with Montenegro remained warm and intimate. As the Pan-Slavs' influence declined in Russia, the government utilized them to foster its own policies. Thus the Slav committees ceased aid to Serbia but helped organize a Bulgarian militia and revive the Bosnian insurrection as preludes to a Russo-Turkish war. St. Petersburg's suspicion of Ristić and its conviction that Serbia was no longer a serious military factor obstructed closer Serbo-Russian relations. A military alliance could scarcely be built upon Kartsov's intrigues, Marinović's pacifism, or Nikitin's ineptitude. And Ignat'ev's espousal at the Constantinople Conference of Bulgarian and Montenegrin claims, and his neglect of Serbia's interests, added to Belgrade's reservations about co-operation with Russia. The Austro-Russian conventions suggested that Russia placed collaboration with the Dreikaiserbund ahead of assistance to the South Slavs. Official and unofficial Russian statements hinted that the Serbs might be sacrificed to insure Russian hegemony in the eastern Balkans. Austria-Hungary once again exploited intra-Serbian differences, and those between Serbs and Russians, to fragment the Serbian national movement.

[176] *Moskovskie Vedomosti,* Feb. 1/13, 2/14 and 17/29, cited in Miroshnichenko, "Otnoshenie," 3, 210–12.

[177] *Ibid.,* pp. 213–14, 222.   [178] *Russkii Mir,* Feb. 18/March 2, no. 46.

CHAPTER VI

SERBDOM AND THE RUSSO-TURKISH WAR

RUSSIAN troops were crossing Turkish frontiers in the Balkans and the Caucasus when Alexander II issued his long-anticipated war manifesto from army headquarters in Kishinev on April 24. In response to Austrian requests, this document contained nothing to incite a South Slav revolution. Emphasizing Russia's long but unavailing efforts to improve the status of the Balkan Christians by peaceful means, the manifesto was vague as to war aims.[1] The emperor appeared resolved to win the war without encumbering alliances with Balkan states which might disturb Austro-Russian relations. The Turks' response (April 26) accused the Slav committees of instigating the risings in Bosnia and Hercegovina and blamed Russia for the evils which had afflicted the Ottoman Empire the past two years. Without Russian intervention, claimed the Porte, the Serbian states could not have defied the Sultan.[2]

Public Reaction to the War Manifesto

The Russian public reacted enthusiastically to the war proclamation. Foreign diplomats in St. Petersburg, suspicious of the Pan-Slavs and

[1] In the manifesto the tsar stated, "Notre désir d'améliorer et de garantir son [Christians'] sort a été partagé par la nation russe toute entière, qui se montre aujourd'hui prête à porter de nouveaux sacrifices pour alléger la position des chrétiens dans la presqu'île des Balkans." For the full text see *Staatsarchiv, 32,* 218-19. HHSA, Andrassy to Langenau, April 16; Langenau to Andrassy, April 19, 1877.

[2] *Staatsarchiv, 32,* 235-39. "Tous les maux qui ont affligé depuis deux ans cette partie de l'Empire sont dus a l'action ostensible ou occulte, mais toujours présente de la Russie."

ignorant of provincial feeling, concluded incorrectly that bellicose sentiment was largely restricted to Moscow.[3] A French envoy, E. M. de Vögué, reported St. Petersburg's mood: "The city is calm and dead. . . . No enthusiasm, lassitude and fatalism." But he noted that the tsar's entry into Moscow occurred amidst "une foule en délire." [4] Russian contemporaries present a different picture. When war was proclaimed, noted A. I. Koshelev, "The general enthusiasm was boundless; zemstvos, cities, private persons, even peasant societies contributed according to their capacities more or less significant sums for military expenses and also to aid the Slavs either directly or through the Slav committees. The general enthusiasm was such as to recall 1812." [5] Other official spokesmen emphasized more explicitly than had the tsar that this would be a war of liberation, not of conquest.[6] Police reports affirmed strong approval of the tsar's action by all social groups and major regions.[7]

The Pan-Slavs, though disappointed at the manifesto's moderation, rejoiced at Russia's entry into war and rallied behind the government. "Finally we can breathe freely," declared A. A. Kireev. "The emperor is a fine fellow [*prosto molodets*]. He writes and speaks like a true-blooded Russian." [8] Although less enthusiastic, Ivan Aksakov urged his colleagues to back the war effort: "It does not correspond in tone to the public mood, but that is not essential. Anyway it is a victory of

---

[3] Ambassador Langenau, for example, found "enthousiasme indescriptible" in Moscow and agreed the press was "très sympathique" to the war manifesto (HHSA, Langenau to Andrassy, April 27, telegram no. 51), but nonetheless concluded there was no general sentiment in Russia favoring war, that the "more level-headed part of society" was unsympathetic and the army not war-minded." *Ibid.*, April 27/May 9, no. 24 A–D.

[4] *Journal du Vicomte E. M. de Vögué*, pp. 37–39, entries of April 24, May 4, 5.

[5] Koshelev, *Zapiski*, p. 228.

[6] In the declaration of Count Bobrinskii, a spokesman for the nobility, to the tsar was the assertion Russia was fighting "pour l'affranchissement de nos frères opprimés." Wrote the mayor of Moscow, Russia fought "not to win a vain glory, but in the name of Christ for our Slav brethren who have suffered so much, . . . to implant liberty and well-being, to call upon congeneric races to enter a new life." HHSA, Langenau to Andrassy, ad no. 23, April 24/May 6, excerpts from declarations in *Pravitel'stvennyi Vestnik*.

[7] OSVOb., 2, nos. 24, 29, pp. 44, 47–48. According to a Moscow report, approval of the war declaration was evident among all classes. Upper-class leaders emphasized the necessity to preserve Russian influence over the South Slavs, whereas commoners regarded the war as just punishment of the Turks for their misdeeds. General confidence in the military outcome was coupled with strong Anglophobia.

[8] ROBibLen, Dnevnik Kireeva, 7, 46, 48, April 24/May 1.

national [*narodnaia*] feeling over the powerful insensitivity of Petersburg circles." [9] Aksakov told his Moscow Committee that official Russia had finally adopted the Slav cause and was fighting "for the liberation of the enslaved and oppressed Slav brethren." Content now to
operate under official supervision, the Moscow chairman stated, "We
do not treasure independent action . . . but wish to serve Slav interre-
lations [*vzaimnosti*] by all reasonable means." [10]

The role of the Slav committees (now called "benevolent societies")
during the war was modest. With a common representative at Russian
army headquarters at Kishinev, they emphasized regeneration of Bulgaria or, in Aksakov's words, "renewing in Slav lands, occupied by our
armies, a correct national life" based on spiritual values. The Bulgarians
must be kept from the false path which had led Serbia and Greece to
ruin. Selfishness, neglect of Orthodoxy, and adoption of poisonous,
western parliamentarism had alienated Serbia from Russia and brought
it under baneful Austrian influence. Similar dangers in Bulgaria could
be scotched by resolute action:

I hope that Prince Cherkasskii [head of the Russian civil administration for
occupied Bulgaria] will sweep away all this filth (especially the radical
"Young Bulgarians"). . . . If only Bulgaria could become for about fifty
years a province with Russian governor-generals, . . . she would become
strong, would be alien to politicking, and would approach closer to Russia,
where lies the spiritual salvation for all Slav peoples.[11]

The St. Petersburg Society, incorrectly predicting an expanded wartime role, publicly stressed restoration of Orthodox churches and care
of the indigent.[12]

The Slav societies acted as obedient auxiliaries of the government.
Aksakov, confirming his society's impotence, abdicated to Prince Cherkasskii control over weapons obtained earlier for the Bosnian insurgents. In July, unable to communicate effectively with his agents at
headquarters, Aksakov requested plaintively that the prince utilize
them as his "loyal helpers within their sphere" rather than let them
stagnate. Concluded the Moscow chairman, "The Slav committees
represent Russian public opinion on the Eastern Question, and in the

[9] GIM, Aksakov to Cherniaev, April 12/24.
[10] Aksakov, *Sochineniia*, *1*, 251ff., speech of April 17/29.
[11] ROBibSS, Aksakov papers no. 21, Aksakov to Naryshkin, April 13/25; GIM,
Aksakov to Cherniaev, April 12/24; Aksakov, *Sochineniia*, *1*, 260–61.
[12] OSVOb., *2*, no. 35, p. 54, April 27/May 8.

solution of that question a true governor, with which the government must cope, is public opinion alone." [13]

Pan-Slav generals, so prominent during 1876, occupied obscure positions in the Russo-Turkish conflict. General Cherniaev offered his services to Serbia but received no encouragement.[14] Instead, the tsar assigned him and his colleagues to distant and subordinate posts. Aksakov lamented, "In general it is extremely strange that the entire ready contingent of people who acquired experience in war in those [Balkan] countries are not to be used in action." [15] General Fadeev requested the Serbian government to place him in charge of an invasion of Old Serbia. But Ristić, learning he had no official backing, rejected his overtures, and St. Petersburg urged him to leave Serbia. The Foreign Ministry's prompt repudiation of Fadeev, and Belgrade's refusal to employ him, reassured Vienna and London.[16] Belgrade wished to cooperate with official Russia and would not hire Pan-Slavs if St. Petersburg disapproved.

News of the outbreak of war brought rejoicing to Serbia. Reported F. Georgiević, who had strong Russian sympathies: "This day produced indescribable enthusiasm by all Serbs. . . . Belgrade took on a holiday air about noon [April 25]. . . . Loud shouts of 'Long live the Russian tsar!' were heard in all the streets. . . . Now our fate is in the hands of Russia and we can regard the future with complete confidence." [17] Istok responded joyfully with a fervent Pan-Slav statement:

We live, and shall live, in a single great family which has a single Slav policy. . . . The great historic Slav idea hastens to its fulfillment. Tsar Alexander, with the aid of the Slav God, will free twelve million Christian slaves as he freed the serfs in Russia. The Balkans will become the model for the future regeneration of the rotten West. . . . And for all this we have now to thank in advance the holy and powerful mother of Slavdom, Russia.[18]

[13] *Slavianskii sbornik* (1948), pp. 166–67, Aksakov to Cherkasskii, April 24/May 6.

[14] GIM, Cherniaev to Milan, spring 1877, Belgrade.

[15] *Slavianskii sbornik* (1948), pp. 167–68, Aksakov to Cherkasskii, April 25/May 7.

[16] HHSA, Wrede to Andrassy, May 1, no. 47. Langenau rejoiced (May 1/13, no. 26E) at the recall of "ce panslaviste enragé." PRO, FO 65/966, Loftus to Derby, May 23, no. 265; Kartsov, RS, *134*, 479, Giers to Kartsov, April 24/May 6. Fadeev remained hopeful he could later return to Serbia. AII, Ristić 22/279, Fadeev to Vlajković, May 13/25.

[17] *Russkii Mir*, April 20/May 2, no. 104, report from Belgrade, April 13/25.

[18] *Istok*, April 15/27, no. 42, lead.

Serbia—Neutrality or War

Istok believed that the diplomats were keeping Serbia neutral. Russia could accomplish Slavdom's mission, but the time might come when Serbia's voice would again be heard.[19] Proclaimed *Zastava*, "With its declaration of war Russia redeems the tsar's words in the Kremlin and reaffirms her mission as a great Slav state. The heirs of Peter and Catherine . . . have not forgotten the way to Tsarigrad." It hoped that the Russians would cross the Danube at Kladovo and drag Serbia into the war. European diplomacy would not dare oppose the Russian campaign or Slavdom's liberation. For the present Serbia must remain neutral; later it should occupy Bosnia and Old Serbia.[20] Unlike *Istok*, Miletić's organ could be unrestrained in efforts to involve Serbia in the Russo-Turkish War.

Belgrade sought Russia's advice before deciding its course. Colonel Dj. Catargi was sent to Russian army headquarters in Kishinev bearing letters to the tsar and to Ignat'ev in Constantinople. Prince Milan placed himself at the emperor's disposal and greeted Russia's declaration of war as "a new generous decision in behalf of the oppressed Slavs." Since Serbia would require Russian aid to renew the war, "I am resolved to undertake nothing without the advance approval of His Majesty." But must Serbia, he asked Ignat'ev, remain a spectator of "this general movement of Orthodox Slavs?"[21]

The Serbian cabinet was divided on the war issue. Premier Mihajlović, J. Grujić, and a minority within the army advocated prompt action; Ristić and Milojković favored continued neutrality. If Russia won important victories, predicted Consul Wrede, the Serbian peace faction would be overborne.[22] Already suspecting the truth about the Budapest Conventions, Ristić doubted that Serbia would obtain sufficient territory to compensate it for renewed sacrifices. If necessary, he would renounce Bosnia but would not join Russia merely for glory and to win Bulgarian autonomy. "If Bosnia must be omitted from Russian plans because of Austria," he wrote Protić in St. Petersburg, "it

[19] *Ibid.*, April 20/May 2, no. 44, lead.

[20] *Zastava*, April 15/27, no. 58, lead. *Ibid.*, April 20/May 2, no. 61; April 22/May 4, no. 62, lead.

[21] AII, Ristić 22/240, 241, Milan to Alexander II and Ignat'ev, April 12/24, copies in Ristić's handwriting.

[22] HHSA, Wrede to Andrassy, April 27, no. 44.

would be desirable for us to be given Vidin, Niš, and Old Serbia." [23] When Protić asked about Serbia's future frontiers, Ignat'ev scowled at mention of Vidin and refused to promise Niš or Old Serbia. The Foreign Ministry, reported the envoy, had been antagonized by Belgrade's methods in ousting Colonel Markov; Giers regarded Ristić as a base individual and a Russophobe.[24] The Ministry's attitude toward the Serbs was further warped by Kartsov's tendentious reports.[25]

Vienna moved quickly to insure Serbian neutrality. Andrassy warned Belgrade that a breach of the peace, unless justified by Turkish aggression, would antagonize the Powers. Implied was a threat to occupy the principality should it enter the war.[26] Simultaneously, Andrassy warned the Porte not to occupy Kladovo from a neutral Serbia and pledged that the Russians would not cross the Danube there. The Turks agreed to refrain from such action. Wrede informed Belgrade of these Austrian steps, noting that they rendered Serbian military preparations superfluous.[27] Austria-Hungary wished to prevent any extension of the conflict which might increase Serbia's dependence upon Russia and further arouse its own Slav subjects.

Meanwhile, the initial response to Serbian overtures at Russian army headquarters was favorable. Russian leaders, reported Catargi, were well disposed and anxious to forget previous misunderstandings. Headquarters would accept Serbia as a partner in war and protect it against reprisals by other Powers or the Turks. Serbian forces would be subordinated to Russian headquarters but commanded by Prince Milan. Belgrade could expect territorial compensation in Old Serbia in case of

---

[23] DAS, 151/455, Ristić to Protić, April 14/26. Protić replied: both Bosnia and Hercegovina would probably be occupied by Austria-Hungary. AII, Ristić 26/28, Protić to Ristić, April 15/27, telegram; Grujić, 3, 290.

[24] AII, Ristić 22/278, Protić to Ristić, April 24/May 6. In confirmation of Protić, Giers told Kartsov, "The action of the Serbian government in regard to Markov is truly disgusting . . . and I expressed my anger at Ristić. In other circumstances we would have been much more outspoken, but now we do not wish to increase Prince Milan's difficulties." Kartsov, RS, *134*, 480. See *supra*, Ch. V, n.147, on Markov's ouster.

[25] Kartsov telegraphed the Ministry April 15/27: "Prince Milan and Ristić, to save their extremely shaky position in Serbia, intend to propose military co-operation with us. . . . Personally I continue to think that we should not expect benefits from co-operation with that government." There is nothing to suggest that the cabinet's position was insecure at that time. OSVOb., 2, no. 5, pp. 21–22.

[26] HHSA, Wrede to Andrassy, May 1, no. 47; Vlada Milana, *1*, 380–81.

[27] Actenstücke, 2, nos. 7, 8, 13, 14, 21, 26, pp. 1–17.

victory; military and political details could be settled subsequently. Ignat'ev promised one million rubles for war preparations.[28]

The Russian leaders' written replies to Belgrade avoided definite commitments but suggested that headquarters desired Serbian participation. The tsar's letter to Milan, counseling prudence and patience, breathed good will:

It is painful for you to be a simple spectator to a struggle which I have been compelled to undertake in defense of the most sacred interests of our coreligionists in Turkey. Realizing the difficult position of Serbia under present circumstances, I advise you to maintain a cautious attitude since my troops are not as yet able to protect the principality effectively.

Ignat'ev urged neutrality until Russian troops were massed along the Danube.[29] Headquarters initially decided to send General A. K. Imeritinskii to Belgrade with one million rubles to supervise Serbia's rearmament.[30] Catargi left Kishinev confident he had fulfilled his mission.

But headquarters, at the request of moderate Russian ministers, renounced temporarily its plan to co-operate with Serbia. Chancellor Gorchakov opposed participation by the Balkan states as complicating a peace settlement with the Porte and increasing danger of European intervention. Alexander II accepted Gorchakov's view that the war should be localized and fought for limited objectives.[31] In Kishinev (May 8) the tsar, Miliutin, Gorchakov, and Reitern agreed it was "more convenient, at least at first, that Serbia remain a neutral zone . . . which avoided the drawback that the Viennese court probably would have been extremely alarmed and dissatisfied by the rearmament of Serbia with our open co-operation." On the same day, Turkey declared war on Rumania; Russian leaders decided to satisfy Rumania's urgent requests for a subsidy and advise Belgrade to remain passive.[32]

[28] AII, Ristić 22/256, Catargi to Milan, telegrams of April 19/May 1 and April 21/May 3; Grujić, 3, 290–91; Ristić, 2, 35–36; Vlada Milana, 1, 381–83.

[29] AII, Ristić 22/244, 242, Alexander II and Ignat'ev to Milan, April 19/May 1.

[30] Miliutin, Dnevnik, 2, 161: Ignat'ev, IV, 137 (July 1914), pp. 60–61. Indeed, the tsar told Catargi that unless Serbia fought, it would sign its death warrant. Ibid., p. 60, Nelidov to Ignat'ev. Sumner, however, concluded incorrectly (Russia, pp. 328–29) that Imeritinskii actually went to Belgrade.

[31] Tatishchev, Aleksandr II, 2, 384. In Gorchakov's view, after two or three Russian victories, peace could be concluded with Turkey.

[32] Miliutin, Dnevnik, 2, 161, 164, entry of April 26/May 8. On the Russian relationship with Rumania in 1876–1877, see Sumner, Russia, pp. 290–301. The tsar's reaction to Rumanian demands was: "On voit . . . qu'ils ne pensent qu'à nous soutirer de l'argent sous prétexte de coopération *dont nous pouvons parfaitement*

Nikolai Nikolaevich canceled Imeritinskii's proposed mission to Belgrade. Alexander II, commending his brother's action, wrote, "At the present moment the most important thing is that the Serbs *not undertake* anything, inasmuch as they cannot be of great benefit to us and by premature intervention they could get us involved in a quarrel with Austria, which, by not permitting the Turks to enter Serbia, has performed us a significant favor." [33] Ignat'ev believed that renunciation of collaboration with Serbia would hinder the Russian offensive in the Balkans; [34] however, at this time the adherents of limited war prevailed.

Shortly after receiving Catargi's optimistic report about military cooperation with Russia, the Serbian cabinet received Gorchakov's telegram: "The will of His Majesty the Emperor is that Serbia remain on the defensive and abstain from any aggressive or provocative act. It will be up to the prince [Milan] to judge what measures he should adopt in conformity with his resources and on his own responsibility." [35] On May 11, Consul Kartsov, dressed in full uniform, delivered the tsar's advice in person to Prince Milan. Announcing his recall, he hinted that it demonstrated Russia's dissatisfaction with Serbia. Milan could not conceal his dismay. [36]

Belgrade sought clarification of Russia's attitude. Perplexed at apparently conflicting advice from the diplomats and the military, the Serbian cabinet sent Catargi back to headquarters with letters from Milan and Ristić. The prince noted that he had taken initial steps to insure preparedness, but that Gorchakov's telegram had compelled him to suspend them. [37] Ristić declared, "We shall resign ourselves to abstention [from war] as long as the considerations prevail which have produced the advice we have received from St. Petersburg, and we like to hope that these considerations will not persist for long. In any case we will subordinate ourselves to the decisions and the will of His Majesty, the Emperor Alexander." Ristić hoped that the tsar would

---

nous passer [italics mine]." OSVOb., 2, no. 47, pp. 67–68, Alexander's comment on report of Nelidov to Gorchakov, May 7/19.

[33] Os. Pr., no. 3, p. 16, Alexander II to Nikolai Nikolaevich, April 27/May 9.

[34] Ignat'ev, IV, *137*, 60.

[35] AII, Ristić 22/245, Gorchakov to Kartsov, April 26/May 8, telegram, copy by Ristić.

[36] HHSA, Wrede to Andrassy, May 13, no. 48; PRO Blue Book XCII 1877, White to Derby, May 15, no. 24; Pisma Ristića, p. 248, Ristić to Hristić, May 10/22.

[37] AII, Ristić 22/247, Milan to Nikolai Nikolaevich, April 30/May 12, copy.

accept Belgrade's co-operation since *"absolute* abstention by Serbia would be its condemnation to death."[38]

The second Catargi mission also failed. Russia definitely opposed Serbia's involvement for the time being and rejected similar overtures from Rumania and Greece.[39] Nelidov explained why:

The desire [of Serbia] to act was inspired more or less artificially and the offensive capabilities of Serbia are negligible, so I will not conceal from you my joy at the inactivity of Serbia. On the other hand, there was danger of provoking Austria, and although our [Budapest] convention with Austria does not prevent the movement of Serbs beyond the Danube, the situation in Hungary has become critical, and the Vienna government would certainly have been induced to take action hostile to us.[40]

Alexander II wrote his brother, "The advice we gave to Serbia [to remain passive] created the very best impression in Vienna," frustrating efforts to create an Anglo-Austrian-Turkish coalition against Russia.[41]

Belgrade complied reluctantly with Russian advice. The Serbian envoy in Vienna was instructed to deny that Belgrade contemplated war and to state that it was concentrating on domestic tasks because of "circumstances outside of Serbia's control." [42] Ristić declared that Serbia would remain quiet unless it were evident that Rumanian independence or Bulgarian autonomy would result from the war; then Serbia would join the conflict. Only strong Austrian pressure, concluded Wrede, could then keep Serbia neutral.[43]

During May 1877, Russian leaders were preoccupied far more with general policy than with the small Balkan states. London warned Russia (May 6) not to endanger British interests at Constantinople and the Straits, or England would renounce its neutrality. This thinly veiled threat was accompanied by British efforts to conclude a military alliance with Austria against Russia.[44] These moves greatly alarmed P. A. Shuvalov, Russian ambassador in London. After conferring with Bis-

[38] *Ibid.,* 22/246, Ristić to Khitrovo, April 30/May 12, draft by Ristić.

[39] Stojanović, *Great Powers,* pp. 151–52; Grujić, *3,* 292.

[40] Ignat'ev, IV, *137* (July 1914), 65, letter of May 27.

[41] Os. Pr., no. 3, p. 18, Alexander II to Nikolai Nikolaevich, May 16/28.

[42] HHSA, Ćukić to Orczy, May 11/23; Actenstücke, *2,* Zichy to Andrassy, May 23, telegram.

[43] HHSA, Wrede to Andrassy, May 21, no. 51; PRO, Blue Book XCII 1877, White to Derby, May 20, no. 25.

[44] For details see Rupp, *A Wavering Friendship,* pp. 390–99.

marck, he returned to St. Petersburg in late May to urge a compromise peace. Supported by Ambassador Novikov, Shuvalov advised the tsar to avert conflict with England by concluding peace when Russian armies reached the Balkan Mountains.[45] Alexander and Gorchakov accepted Shuvalov's arguments, and the chancellor gave him confidential instructions (May 30) outlining a "petite paix aux Balkans" which Russia would accept if Turkey requested peace before Russian forces crossed the mountains. This compromise settlement called for an autonomous Bulgaria extending southward only to the Balkans; for Montenegro and Serbia "an increase of territory in conformity with the interests of general stability and which will be decided in common"; for Bosnia and Hercegovina "des institutions jugées d'un commun accord compatibles avec leur état intérieur et propres à y assurer une bonne administration indigène." Russia would compensate Austria in the two provinces.[46] This proposal, vague on vital questions, left much of a Russo-Turkish settlement to agreement by the Powers while excluding the small Balkan states from the war and the peace settlement.

Russian army headquarters were now in Ploesti in Rumania, and when, toward the end of May Belgrade learned that the tsar would rejoin his army there, its hopes revived. Reports circulated in the Serbian capital that Prince Milan, facing a deteriorating position at home while his country remained inactive, wished to visit the emperor.[47] Ristić believed that if Alexander came to Ploesti, the prince must go to greet him. "The tsar is one of our guarantors. . . . We dare not expose ourselves to the consequences of inattention."[48] Just before he left St. Petersburg, Alexander indicated he would permit Milan's trip, although he doubted that the prince should leave his unstable country. Langenau found the tsar's remarks about Serbia "most ungracious"; the tsar had said that Milan was surrounded by "traitors" and that Serbian military co-operation would be useless.

[45] Goriainov, Le Bosphore, pp. 345–46, memorandum of Shuvalov, May 10/22.

[46] SR (Dec. 1926), no. 228, pp. 433–37, Gorchakov to Shuvalov, May 18/30.

[47] White reported: "The presence of the Emperor Alexander in his army surrounded . . . by so many of his Slavophile advisers is perhaps the last favorable opportunity . . . for Milan to induce his imperial patron to reconsider his views and intentions with regard to Serbia." PRO Blue Book XCII 1877, White to Derby, May 21, no. 26.

[48] Pisma Ristića, p. 248, Ristić to Hristić, May 10/22. Catargi was instructed to suggest such a visit to Russian leaders. HHSA, Wrede to Andrassy, May 24, telegram.

Nonetheless, the tsar reminded the ambassador that the Budapest Conventions permitted Serbian co-operation.[49] At army headquarters, Catargi sought to win the grand duke's good will and approval of Milan's trip and undercut the Rumanians, whose demands were regarded there as most unreasonable.[50] But not until June 11 could Milan announce that the emperor would receive him.[51] The prince, Ristić, and Serbian military leaders went to Ploesti to obtain financial aid and permission to re-enter the war.

Headquarters' approval of the prince's visit signified another shift in Russian policy. On June 2, the tsar left St. Petersburg for the army; Shuvalov departed next day for London, bearing Gorchakov's conciliatory instructions. Once at headquarters, Alexander abandoned the idea of halting at the Balkans. Military operations, argued Ignat'ev at a war council of June 6, should not be subordinated to diplomacy or the Powers' wishes. A pledge not to cross the Balkans would retract the tsar's promise to liberate the eastern Christians and sacrifice Bulgaria, Serbia, and Rumania to the Porte. Miliutin and Cherkasskii supported his vehement opposition to splitting Bulgaria at the Balkan Mountains. The tsar was converted,[52] and Gorchakov had to yield. From Bucharest Baron Jomini reported: "Une demi-paix aux Balkans est repoussée a l'unanimité, on nous là reprôche comme un crime. L'Empereur lui—même regrette d'avoir laissé partir Schouvalow et ne veut entendre parler d'aucun obstacle à sa marche en avant." Most top leaders now advocated a great, undivided Bulgaria extending to the Aegean and establishing Constantinople as a free city.[53] Convinced that Gorchakov's May 30 proposals—delivered on June 8 by Shuvalov in London —would hinder military operations, Alexander II ordered the chancellor to telegraph new ones to Shuvalov. Russia would not be bound by

[49] Ibid., Langenau to Andrassy, May 22/June 3, Privatschreiben, Geheim.

[50] AII, Ristić 22/288, Catargi to Milan, n.d.; telegram of May 26, Catargi reported, "Il parait que la Russie est fatiguée de toutes les prétentions du Prince Charles [of Rumania] qui veut jouer le premier rôle . . . ne cesse de créer un million d'embarras aux Russes. J'ai profité de cette situation pour attirer l'eau sur les moulins." His tactic, he noted, was successful.

[51] HHSA, Wrede to Andrassy, June 14, no. 59; Grujić, 3, 292.

[52] Ignat'ev, IV, 137 (July 1914), pp. 67–70. Also present at the meeting were the heir, Nikolai Nikolaevich, and Nepokoichitskii. Skalon (Moi vospominaniia, p. 115) states this first meeting was held on June 6. Ignat'ev fails to date it. Rupp concludes incorrectly (A Wavering Friendship, p. 332) that it occurred on June 13, which is impossible since Jomini reported the results on June 9.

[53] Jelavich, Russia in the East, p. 37, Jomini to Giers, May 28/June 9.

the letter of May 30. "After ripe reflection," wrote Gorchakov, "we cannot consent to a separation of Bulgaria into two parts; it must be united and autonomous." [54]

When the tsar abandoned the Foreign Ministry's moderate program, Serbia's position changed. Prior to the June 6 meeting the Ministry had advised the Serbs to remain quiet.[55] Ignat'ev, on the other hand, had consistently urged that Serbia and Rumania be brought into the war.[56] The Foreign Ministry was powerless to pursue a neutral policy for Serbia without the emperor's support; Jomini feared the gravest consequences.[57] Semiofficial *Golos*, immediately reflecting the new bellicose policy, declared that Russia need not take the Powers' views into account.[58]

When the Serbian delegation arrived at Ploesti on June 16, Russian diplomats who had opposed Serbia's participation in the war were in full retreat. Meeting with Serbian leaders next day, Gorchakov advised neutrality for the time being, since Serbia's entry now might be misinterpreted in Vienna. Later, if Belgrade's participation appeared desirable, Andrassy's approval might be obtained.[59] The chancellor told Ristić (June 20), "I have always regarded Serbia as the point of departure for the resurrection of the East. It must maintain this position by wise conduct. I regret the tsar's words in Moscow about the Serbs. I have always regarded the Serbs as brave people. Those words were spoken in a moment of dislike." Russia would not interfere in Serbia's internal affairs, though it disapproved of the course taken "by the younger generation" of Serbian leaders.[60] Coming so soon after the bitter disputes over Kartsov and Markov, Gorchakov's statements were viewed by Ristić as genuine concessions.

---

[54] *Ibid.*, p. 38, May 31/June 12; Skalon, *Moi vospominaniia*, pp. 133–34; Ignat'ev, IV, *137* (July 1914), pp. 58–59; OSVOb., *2*, no. 77, p. 107, Gorchakov to Shuvalov, May 30/June 11, telegram.

[55] "They [the Serbs] would only make difficulties for us in our political relations," Giers wrote A. S. Ionin, May 23/June 4. "They would be of little use militarily." *Ibid.*, *2*, no. 67, p. 97.

[56] Ignat'ev, IV, *137* (July, 1914), pp. 70–71.

[57] However, Giers now concluded that a smashing Russian military victory would ease the diplomats' task in making peace. Jelavich, *Russia in the East*, pp. 38–39, 146, Jomini to Giers, June 4/16 and 6/18, Giers to Jomini, June 4/16.

[58] *Golos*, June 3/15, no. 112.

[59] Hasenkampf, *Dnevnik*, pp. 37–38, Jomini's memorandum of June 17.

[60] Ristić, *2*, 39–42; Grujić, *3*, 293. Declared Gorchakov, "One should retain old customs and institutions."

The emperor, though friendly with Milan, was hostile toward Ristić and his government. At their first meeting, Alexander refused his hand to Ristić and informed the prince that he had no confidence in his cabinet. The tsar was still displeased at Serbia's unauthorized declaration of war in 1876. "At dinner," noted Miliutin, "Ristić sat like a man condemned to death." Prince Milan accepted the tsar's advice as meekly as a small son from an imperious father.[61] Alexander, assuring the prince that Russia would not abandon him, declared that when the Russian army crossed the Danube, Serbia could enter the war. When Ristić inquired whether this advice was compatible with Gorchakov's telegram of May 8, the emperor explained, "Prince Gorchakov cannot advise you any differently than I am advising you now. If, after the crossing of the Danube you join the Russian armies, you need not fear that Austria will attack you. . . . Until the Russian army crosses the Danube, remain quiet and afterwards you may enter if you wish." [62] Serbian offensive operations, cautioned the Russian leaders, should be confined to Bulgaria and Old Serbia. Only Ignat'ev held out prospects of Russian financial assistance during the war.[63]

At Ploesti, while barring immediate action by Belgrade, the Russians outlined possible subsequent collaboration against Turkey. But Serbian and Russian public statements contained no hint that the principality would eventually enter the war. Serbian leaders emphasized to foreign consuls that the tsar had advised continued neutrality.[64] Even well-informed observers concluded that Russia had rejected Serbian offers of military co-operation.[65] Russia and Serbia sought to disarm Austrian suspicions.

Returning from Ploesti, Prince Milan opened the Assembly in Kragujevac with a vague, cautious speech (July 2):

After conclusion of a Serbo-Turkish peace, I informed my people that the fate of the Eastern Christians lies in stronger hands [Russia's]. We could interrupt the war for the holy cause without danger. Events have borne out my words. Not far from our frontiers wave the victorious standards of the tsar. His arrival at headquarters in Rumania gave me a desired opportunity

[61] Miliutin, *Dnevnik*, 2, 176–78.

[62] Later Alexander repeated to the Serbian leaders, "Je ne vous engage pas, je ne vous force pas, mais vous pouvez [entrer] si vous voulez." Ristić, 2, 38–39.

[63] *Ibid.*, pp. 43–44; Grujić, 3, 293.

[64] HHSA, Wrede to Andrassy, June 23 and 28, nos. 60, 63.

[65] Hasenkampf, *Dnevnik*, p. 471; HHSA, Wrede to Andrassy, June 28, no. 62.

to express thanks to him for the powerful protection given during the events of last year. He . . . assured me of his future concern for Serbia and the Serbian nation.

The delegates could concentrate on domestic matters, though "the events which are occurring around us . . . require the greatest watchfulness on our part." [66] The parliamentary opposition promptly accused the government of involving Serbia in war prematurely in 1876. Condemning the Ristić cabinet for using police tactics and failing to respond to popular will, most opposition delegates resigned (July 9) after declaring, "The actual situation suggests that we are isolated. We have no ties [veze] with anyone. Despite so many sacrifices we stand isolated. The Eastern Question is developing without us. Such state sagacity should be condemned." The Ristić government responded by holding new elections to fill their seats and denying requests for freedom of the press.[67]

Istok reflected Belgrade's cautious policy. In mid-May it had declared that Serbia "will act as its interests demand." Deprecating possible Rumanian participation in the war, it had asserted that Russia could defeat the Turks unaided. Therefore, rumors of an imminent Russo-Turkish peace were ridiculous. Russia would dictate a settlement from Adrianople or Constantinople.[68] *Istok* interpreted the tsar's friendly attitude at Ploesti as confirming Serbo-Russian solidarity. "There are misunderstandings in every family, and Russia and her emperor are mother and father to all Slavdom." [69]

On June 1, *Zastava* had urged Serbia to enter the war immediately and confront Russia with a *fait accompli*. "Serbia is summoned to follow war events. But emancipation cannot occur if Serbia and the East remain peaceful. Without Serbia and the other eastern peoples, Russia cannot liberate the Slavs but could merely divide up the East with other Powers." Belgrade need not await a Russian summons nor accept Russian promises to remember it at the peace table. "Serbia must outwit Austria, enter Bosnia and Old Serbia. . . . Serbia must fight Turkey so that official Russia will accept the war goals of Serbia as the war goal of Russia." [70] After Milan's meeting with the tsar, *Zastava* believed that the Ploesti meetings had refuted reports that Russia

---

[66] *Staatsarchiv, 32*, no. 6477, pp. 324–25.   [67] Prodanović, *Istorija*, pp. 410–12.
[68] *Istok*, May 1/13, May 10/22, 15/27, May 29/June 10.
[69] *Ibid.*, June 1/13, 8/20, 10/22, 12/24.
[70] *Zastava*, May 20/June 1, no. 77, lead "Rusko-turski rat i Srbija."

barred Serbia's entry because of Vienna. It predicted Serbia's imminent entry into the war.[71]

Ploesti planted the seeds of future co-operation, despite the Russians' negative assessment of Serbia's military capabilities. Serbian officers who accompanied Prince Milan were dismayed at Russian contempt for their army. One complained:

Our army is being judged by the results of the last war, forgetting that against our small principality were directed . . . the entire regular forces of the Ottoman Empire. . . . Now that we have rested, we possess an active army of 65,000 men with 300 cannons. . . . Despite some financial exhaustion, we are nevertheless in a position to do our duty.

The Serbs, he concluded, could not be prevented from joining the war.[72] Nor was Russian headquarters seeking to do so. Immediately after Ploesti, the emperor approved a memorandum stating that Serbian forces would probably soon be summoned to enter the struggle. They would operate in Old Serbia and western Bulgaria, or in one of those theaters. If the Serbs could prevent Turkish forces near their frontiers from opposing the Russians in Bulgaria, they would perform a valuable service.[73]

The Russian nationalist press vainly urged the government to reject its "European" approach and adopt an uncompromising "Slav" program. Pan-Slavs advocated Rumanian and Serbian participation in the war on military and political grounds. M. N. Katkov deplored the neutrality of Serbia and Greece and Rumania's inactivity. "Can it be that we reject these peoples, who are anxious to fight, in order to please diplomacy?" Serbia should participate and if Austria interferes it might have to fight Russia.[74] Austrian diplomatic pressure was preventing Russian forces from crossing Serbia and by-passing the Balkan Mountains: "To keep our armies out of these or other routes, which could lead them more surely to victory, means to aid the enemy. . . . Whoever wishes to thus aid our enemy is his ally and our opponent." [75] After Rumania declared its independence (May 21), *Russkii Mir* urged

---

[71] *Ibid.*, June 5/17, 12/24.

[72] *Russkii Mir*, June 17/29, no. 161, report from Bucharest, June 8/20. This assessment of Serbian capabilities was grossly overoptimistic. Among the Serbian officers in the Ploesti mission were Colonels Lješanin and Horvatović. *Istok*, June 8/20, no. 63.

[73] Sb. Mat., no. 8, pp. 85–96.   [74] Peredovykh, May 26/June 7, no. 127.

[75] *Ibid.*, June 23/July 5, no. 155. See also July 3/15, no. 164.

Serbia to follow suit and enter the war: "Is it conceivable that the Serbian people . . . can remain a passive observer? . . . The Serbian people possesses the indisputable moral right to participate in the general denouement of the great cause it first raised. . . . An independent Rumania presupposes an independent Serbia; Belgrade cannot remain behind Bucharest." Austria could not compel the Serbs to sit with hands folded.[76] Aksakov, ascribing Montenegrin setbacks during June to Serbia's enforced neutrality, wrote, "And why can Rumania proclaim its independence and not the Serbs? This is an affront to Slav honor, was carried out more or less on behalf of Austria and causes disgust in our country." [77] When the Turks invaded Montenegro, even *Golos* urged Serbia to join the war once Russian troops had crossed the Danube. By restricting the war theater, "Austria *ipso facto* violates the neutrality she promised to observe." [78] But when the threat to Montenegro subsided, *Golos* resumed its pacific stance:

Serbia clearly does not intend to take the step [entry into war] which would lead to misunderstanding between Vienna and St. Petersburg [*sic*]. Trusting firmly in Russia, Serbia must await calmly the fulfillment of the "brilliant hopes" opened for her. . . . Either the necessity of self-defense will enable Serbia to take an active role, or by remaining neutral, Serbia will render service to Russia.[79]

Official Russia continued to consider Serbian participation in the war unnecessary and undesirable.

Montenegro and the Insurgents in the Russo-Turkish War

Montenegrins responded joyfully to Russia's declaration of war on Turkey. In Cetinje were heard happy shouts of "Long live the Russian tsar!" Declared the official *Glas Crnogorca*, "Italy had her angel protector in France; we have one in the Russian people." After the Turko-Montenegrin truce expired on April 19, there was no legal obstacle to resumption of the struggle. A council of war in Cetinje on April 25 decided to fight until Montenegro had secured a tolerable existence. Cetinje's objectives included acquisition of the section of Hercegovina

[76] *Russkii Mir*, May 22/June 3, no. 135, report from Bucharest May 2/14; June 10/22, no. 154, lead; June 16/28, no. 160.
[77] *Slavianskii sbornik*, pp. 174–76, Aksakov to Cherkasskii, June 4/16 and 7/19. A. A. Kireev echoed these sentiments. ROBibLen, Dnevnik Kireeva, 7, 56.
[78] *Golos*, June 7/19, 16/28, nos. 116, 125.   [79] *Ibid.*, June 23/July 5, no. 132.

around Nikšić, extending like a wedge into Montenegro; control of northern Albania, especially the seacoast; and formal recognition of Montenegro's independence by the Porte. On April 26, Prince Nikola announced resumption of hostilities. He complied reluctantly with the advice of the Austrian envoy, Lieutenant Colonel Thömmel, to omit "meaningless" phrases such as "liberation and unification of the Serbian people." The prince telegraphed Alexander II that Montenegro was proud to fight at Russia's side. Responded the tsar, "May God aid our *common* work in achieving our holy mission." [80]

Despite Serbia's neutrality, Montenegro's position was better than in 1876. There were more trained troops, a greater number of rifles, and sufficient money and provisions for the campaign. The men of Cetinje, marching against the foe, reputedly told their commander, "We go to certain victory, we now are armed as never before." [81] Prince Nikola was quick to mend his diplomatic fences. Two envoys, Božo Petrović and Stanko Radonić, were dispatched from Constantinople to Kishinev to present to the tsar Montenegro's aims and seek his aid to achieve them. Later they traveled to Vienna to give assurances that Montenegro, relying upon Austrian support, would co-operate on the Bosnian question. [82]

At first Montenegro's army remained passive. Assuming a defensive posture along the frontiers, Nikola's army sought to blockade Nikšić and the Duga forts, islands of Turkish territory jutting into Montenegro. The prince, awaiting additional equipment, wished to lure the

[80] *Istok*, April 17/29, April 20/May 3, April 27/May 9. Peredovykh, April 7/29, no. 91B, report from Cetinje, April 14/26; Djordjević, *Crna Gora*, pp. 411–13.

[81] Peredovykh, April 17/29, no. 91B. According to the correspondent for *Politische Correspondenz* (Vienna), first-class Montenegrin troops numbered 15,-804 at the start of the campaign (13,600 in July 1876) and were aided by 2,060 second-line troops and 6,890 Hercegovinians (compared with 5,400 in 1876). Russia's military representative in Montenegro, Colonel A. A. Bogoliubov, reported that "thanks to the aid of our government, preparations for the resumption of war could be carried out on rather a large scale." The combined Montenegrin-Hercegovinian forces, he estimated, numbered 17,000. Bogoliubov, however, believed Montenegro's economic position to be weaker than in 1876. Os. Pr., no. 5, "Doneseniia voennykh agentov," Bogoliubov to Miliutin, June 4/16, pp. 1–9.

[82] "Montenegro," telegraphed Thömmel to Andrassy April 25, "has taken on no obligations toward Russia in the matter of operations. Also Russian aid consists solely of food and medical supplies." On April 29, Thömmel could report to Andrassy Prince Nikola's promise, in case of an Austrian occupation of Bosnia, to serve as its flag bearer (*Fahnenträger*). Djordjević, *Crna Gora*, pp. 412–13.

enemy into the mountains.[83] To a Russian officer he remarked, as they observed military supplies arriving from Kotor, "Look at that! We have powder and grain; that is all we need. You will see now how we will thrash them [the Turks]. We shall let them enter our country, then we will beat them." [84]

Early in June, the Turks launched a massive three-pronged offensive to crush Montenegro before the Russians crossed the Danube. Montenegrin commanders quarreled among themselves; their forces suffered repeated setbacks and heavy losses. If the Turks could unite their forces and advance on Cetinje, reported A. S. Ionin on June 21, their triumph was probable.[85] Prince Nikola, in apparent desperation, appealed to Austria-Hungary for assistance.[86] Andrassy informed Nikola that the Monarchy would not permit Montenegro's integrity to be endangered.[87] Austria and Italy offered to mediate an armistice, but Prince Nikola refused to negotiate.[88]

Russia reacted sympathetically to Montenegro's plight. Giers promised that four cannon would be dispatched to Cetinje without involving the Russian government directly.[89] The St. Petersburg Slav Society sent money to aid the wounded and the needy.[90] "All glance with

---

[83] On May 19, the "Vicenza" arrived in Kotor with 2 cannon, 3,000 rifles, and 800 grenades. Largely because of Nikola's co-operative attitude, the Austrian authorities speeded their unloading, and all of the equipment reached Cetinje. Djordjević, *Crna Gora*, p. 414.

[84] Evans, *Illyrian Letters*, pp. 154–55.

[85] OSVOb., 2, no. 87, pp. 112–13, Ionin to Giers, telegram June 9/21.

[86] Evans, *Illyrian Letters*, p. 160; Djordjević, *Crna Gora*, p. 415. Colonel Bogoliubov estimated that the Turkish attackers numbered 52,000, outnumbering the defenders three to one. But he attributed Montenegrin reverses primarily to Nikola's penchant for assigning key posts to his relatives and to lack of discipline in the army. "Now as before I repeat that the Montenegrins are incapable of any serious offensive operations; their sphere is defense and raids." Os. Pr., no. 5, pp. 17–18, Bogoliubov to Miliutin, June 20/July 2, July 6/18.

[87] Djordjević, *Crna Gora*, p. 415.

[88] OSVOb., 2, no. 95, pp. 121–23, Ionin to Gorchakov, June 15/27.

[89] Giers wrote, "C'est avec un intérêt douloureux . . . que nous suivons la lutte sanglante en Monténégro qui semble tourner au désavantage de cette principauté malgré ses efforts héroiques." The cannon arrived in Montenegro August 23 and were used in the reduction of Nikšić. OSVOb., 2, no. 88, pp. 113–15, Giers to Ionin, June 11/23 and notes.

[90] The committee agreed to dispatch 20,000 rubles to the prince via A. A. Naryshkin to assist families of dead and wounded Montenegrins. After Chairman K. N. Bestuzhev-Riumin read A. S. Ionin's letter to Aksakov of June 21 about the Montenegrins' situation, the meeting voted 21,500 rubles for Montenegro, 25,000

anxious concern at Montenegro," wrote Katkov. He blamed Austrian diplomacy: "Only thanks to the measures adopted by Austria toward Serbia and the Bosnian insurrection did the Turks have the opportunity to send 60,000 men against invincible Montenegro." [91]

But the tide of battle had already turned in Montenegro's favor. Two of the invading columns were defeated; the third and largest, that of Suleiman Pasha, was checked on June 25. By June 28, the Turkish invasion was over, and Prince Nikola's forces were heartened by the Russian crossings of the Danube. Requiring troops in Bulgaria, the Turkish command withdrew Suleiman's army, leaving the Montenegrins in a favorable position. [92]

But Nikola remained cautious. The prince, reported Evans to the *Manchester Guardian*, "perceived Italian susceptibilities in Albania and Austrian zones in Hercegovina and forebore to threaten either Mostar or Skutari." Nor would Nikola risk his mountaineers in the Drin Plains, despite his dream of liberating Old Serbia. For the time being, "the policy chalked out for the Montenegrin government . . . was masterly inactivity." [93]

Meanwhile the Bosnian insurrection waned. Early in 1877, claims M. Ekmečić, it ceased to be a revolution and became a political and military auxiliary of Russia. "The aim," Despotović wrote later, "was to maintain the insurrection in Bosnia until Russia began war against Turkey and took Slav interests under its protection." [94] Montenegro initially hoped Despotović could undertake a diversionary operation toward Mostar. Prince Nikola promised him financial aid and contemplated sending advisers under Mašo Vrbica "to take if possible the

---

for Ionin, and 4,000 for P. A. Vasil'chikov for distribution to needy Montenegrins. *Pervye 15 let*, pp. 464, 470–71.

[91] Peredovykh, June 2/14 and June 23/July 5, nos. 134, 155.

[92] OSVOb., 2, no. 95, pp. 121–23, Ionin to Gorchakov, June 15/27; Hasenkampf, *Dnevnik*, p. 51; Evans, *Illyrian Letters*, p. 160.

[93] Evans, *Illyrian Letters*, pp. 162–64. "The political caution of the Prince makes him averse to attempting too great things with his small means. He perceives, or thinks he perceives, that little that Montenegro can at present do, will have any great influence in making the ultimate readjustment of her frontiers more favourable. The great service has been performed. 60,000 Turkish regulars, who might have turned the scale against Russia at Simnitza were drawn off from taking part in the Danubian operations, at the critical moment. Russia has already contracted her debt of honour to the Principality [Montenegro]" (p. 162).

[94] HHSA, Despotović to Andrassy, Nov. 3, 1877, quoted in Ekmečić, *Ustanak*, p. 299.

entire insurrection in hand." Despotović expressed readiness to co-operate with Prince Nikola "since I knew this was necessary in our common interests." [95] Such a link with the insurgents would have enhanced Montenegro's influence in Bosnia and Hercegovina and strengthened its aspirations to Serbian leadership. But Andrassy, insisting that Nikola limit himself to minor aid to the insurgents, forbade the Vrbica mission on the ground that it would infringe Austrian interests.[96] Austria-Hungary would tolerate neither Serbian nor Montenegrin control of Bosnia. But Vienna's efforts to win the allegiance of Bosnia insurgent leaders were unsuccessful.[97]

During the spring, military operations in Bosnia were indecisive and small scale.[98] In mid-May, Ismet Pasha undertook an offensive against Despotović but abandoned it when the insurgents scattered. During June, a series of raids and minor attacks by bands under Despotović's command caused the Turks some concern. In July, the insurgents attempted in vain to capture the small Turkish fortified towns of Čelebić and Ključ. Believing his forces were too undisciplined to undertake major operations, Despotović awaited the solution of the Bosnian question by a Russian victory over Turkey.[99]

---

[95] AII, Ristić 17/258, Despotović to Ristić, May 20.

[96] HHSA, Andrassy to Thömmel, April 24, cited by Ekmečić, *Ustanak*, pp. 301–02.

[97] Petar Uzelac and Lazar Miodragović were apparently pro-Austrian (see HHSA, Wrede to Andrassy, March 16; Ekmečić, *Ustanak*, pp. 302–03), but the only chief to co-operate closely with Vienna was Ivan Musić, who sought unsuccessfully to increase Austrian influence in the insurrection. Although he retained his ties with Montenegro and obeyed Nikola's military commands, Musić was regarded with suspicion both in Cetinje and in Bosnia and remained an isolated figure. See Ekmečić, "Uloga Ivana Musića," GIDBiH, 7, 154–59.

[98] Dr. Svetozar Teodorović, Austrian consul in Sarajevo, estimated Despotović's forces numbered about 1,500 in May and 3,000 in July. (Ekmečić, p. 307.) Gerent Depolo, Austrian vice-consul, reported from Banjaluka on May 26 that Despotović had concentrated 3,000 to 4,000 men around Tiskovac and Grahovo. But during Ismet Pasha's offensive, the insurgents split into small bands and fled into the forests or into Dalmatia. Actenstücke, 2, no. 58, pp. 35–36, Depolo to Wassitsch in Sarajevo.

[99] Ekmečić, *Ustanak*, pp. 308–11; Čubrilović, *Bosanski ustanak*, pp. 267–72. In defense of this viewpoint one insurgent chieftain wrote "that Despotović did not do more no one could demand since why shed blood of people in vain when it is known that Russia is fighting for Bosnia, as well as for Bulgaria." AII, Ristić 17/28, Babić to Ristić, Aug. 11: Another viewpoint was: "Entirely absorbed in administration," Despotović was unable to win "any sympathy either among the leaders or their men." *Ibid.*, 17/25, M. Baić to Ristić, July 6/18.

An influential insurgent faction, headed by the Bilbija brothers,[100] wished to remove Despotović and establish a Bosnian provisional government. V. S. Ionin, the Russian Slav societies' envoy, dissatisfied with Despotović's passivity, agreed with the dissidents. Ionin conferred at Knin (July 8) with Despotović and the Bosnian chiefs. Convinced he would be chosen president of a provisional regime, Despotović agreed to consult the chiefs, but he added, "I must warn you, by the way, that since I am recognized as ruler of Bosnia not only by Serbia and Montenegro but also by the Russian tsar, no temporary government can have more significance and trust [*doveria*] than I." When the chiefs decided not to choose him president, Despotović threatened to leave Bosnia. Retorted the chiefs, "Go wherever you wish, you have no legitimate claim to be ruler of Bosnia but were imposed on us by Serbia and have proved both cowardly and incompetent." After long debate, however, they agreed that Despotović could retain his posts pending arrival of sufficient funds to finance a provisional government. Despotović had won a reprieve. But Ionin reported that the Bosnians hated Despotović, resented his autocratic ways, and criticized the Slav societies for assisting him.[101]

In August 1877, the Turks succeeded with Austria's co-operation in virtually crushing the Bosnian insurrection. Since Bosnia would be theirs under the Budapest Conventions, the Austrians considered the insurrection a nuisance. A. von Mollinary, governor of the Croatian Military Frontier, rejected military collaboration with the Porte, but Baron Rodich, Dalmatia's governor, closed the border and forbade shipment of grain to the insurgents. Deprived of his Dalmatian sanctuary, Despotović was pinned down at Crni Potoci in mid-August, his army was defeated and dispersed, and he was interned by the Austrians.[102] Despotović's defeat was attributed by his supporters to a

---

[100] According to Čubrilović, other leaders of this faction included Simo Čavka and the merchant Božo Ljubojević and Ilija Bilbija. Čubrilović, *Bosanski ustanak*, pp. 401–02.

[101] Pushkarevich, pp. 220–22. A. S. Ionin to A. I. Vasil'chikov, July 3/15. This letter is dated May 3/15 which is surely an error since he arrived at Knin about June 26/July 8.

[102] When Despotović's request to proceed to Russia was rejected by Ambassador Novikov, he was interned at Linz, Austria. Withdrawing from the insurrection, he declared its purpose had been achieved since Russia was now involved in war and leading the Slav cause. HHSA, Despotović to Andrassy, Nov. 3, 1877, Linz. On details of the Crni Potoci operations see Čubrilović, *Bosanski ustanak*,

conspiracy by Bosnian chiefs co-operating with Vienna.[103] Actually, Despotović had lost the chiefs' backing and popular support.[104]

Militarily, the debacle at Crni Potoci dealt a mortal blow to the Bosnian insurrection. With the Austrian frontier tightly closed, it became virtually impossible to re-equip Bosnian bands. Most of the leaders were interned by Austria or fled to Serbia. When Golub Babić appeared in Bosnia to revive the rising, he could gather only a small band which operated in the mountains. In the southwest and north the insurrection smoldered on without threatening Turkish control. Aid no longer came from Russian Slav societies, which were no longer interested in the rebels' cause. In desperation the remaining chieftains turned again to Belgrade, but Ristić claimed that Serbia was too exhausted to provide assistance. The insurgents felt abandoned, isolated, and betrayed.[105]

After Despotović's internment, V. S. Ionin persuaded the insurgent chiefs to establish a provisional government. A meeting (*skupština*) attended by some 200 persons was held at Kravljak on October 11. According to Ionin, its delegates included all the important insurgent chiefs.[106] Anxious to forestall Austrian annexation by having the Bosnians demonstrate capacity for independent political life, Ionin told the assembly:

Brothers, your fight must not be without a goal or out of personal hatred for your enemy. Your aspirations need to be expressed in the interests of your homeland and all of Slavdom. . . . Hurry then to fulfill your national duty and it will not be shameful if poorly armed bands succumb to the blows of a force one hundred times stronger, but it would be an eternal

---

pp. 274–75; Ekmečić, *Ustanak*, pp. 314–17. After his release, Despotović went to Russia and worked on behalf of the Bosnian cause at the Berlin Congress.

[103] A priest, A. Kolundžić, claimed that dissident elements had disobeyed Despotović's orders at the crucial point in the battle at Crni Potoci and had abandoned their positions in disorder. The revolt against Despotović he attributed to the selfishness and lack of patriotism of men such as Petar Uzelac. *Zastava o B. i H., 4*, no. 133, Aug. 28/Sept. 9.

[104] Čubrilović, *Bosanski ustanak*, p. 276; Ekmečić, *Ustanak*, pp. 219–320.

[105] *Ibid.*, pp. 321–22; Čubrilović, *Bosanski ustanak*, p. 276.

[106] Other conservative chiefs, especially Vaso Vidović, denounced the provisional government, claiming it had not been selected with popular consent. His group would consider no step which threatened renunciation of Serbia's support. AII, Ristić 17/157, Vidović to Toskić, Nov. 15. Later he demanded inclusion of some north Bosnian leaders in the government.

shame if, while under arms, you failed to utilize your opportunity to declare before the world the wishes of your people.[107]

Ionin was named president of a fourteen-member government, but he resigned when Jovo Skobla threatened to break up the new regime.[108] The provisional government declared that Bosnia had never wished annexation to an outside power, but desired liberation from Turkish slavery and unification with other Serbian lands. If the Powers blocked unification of Serbdom, Bosnia desired complete self-government until unification could be achieved.[109] Above all, Bosnian leaders opposed absorption by Austria-Hungary.[110]

The provisional government in vain sought outside financial and diplomatic support. J. Bilbija and Skobla requested aid from Prince Nikola to "benefit our liberation and the emancipation of Serbdom." Refusing assistance, he referred to the provisional government as "the newest Serbian comedy," apparently believing that Belgrade had staged the whole affair.[111] But in Belgrade, the Bosnian envoys were informed that Serbia was no longer interested in the insurrection.[112] Fear of Austria-Hungary dissuaded the Serbian states from assisting the Bosnians.

Austria-Hungary, backed by official Russia, acted to crush the provisional government. Officials were ordered to arrest its leaders on sight. Simo Čavka and Trivun Bundalo, members of the Bosnian regime, were seized and interned. Since no foreign state offered encouragement, these Austrian measures rendered operation of the provisional government almost impossible; its influence waned steadily.[113]

Nonetheless, it did express the widespread opposition in Bosnia to

[107] *Zastava o B. i H.*, 4, no. 159, Oct. 12/24.

[108] Ionin's statement of resignation, dated Knin, Oct. 3/15, is in *ibid.*, no. 160, Oct. 14/26. For Skobla's threats see no. 165, Oct. 23/Nov. 4, and V. S. Ionin to A. I. Vasil'chikov, Oct. 16, in Pushkarevich, "Balkanskie slaviane," pp. 223–25. Ionin, stressing Skobla's pettiness, described the provisional government's financial needs and submitted a list of those who, receiving aid simultaneously from Belgrade, continually sought to promote discord and damage Russian interests.

[109] *Zastava o B. i H.*, 4, no. 159, Oct. 12/24.

[110] The members of the government planned at first to include a statement against annexation by Austria-Hungary, but this was toned down in the published version. AII, Ristić 17/27, "Predlog izjave privremene Bosanske Narodne Vlade," appended to J. Bilbija to Ristić, Aug. 6.

[111] HHSA, Thömmel to Andrassy, Oct. 27 and 30, in Ekmečić, *Ustanak*, pp. 330–31.

[112] HHSA, Wrede to Andrassy, Dec. 25.

[113] Ekmečić, *Ustanak*, pp. 330–32.

replacement of effendis in turbans by gentlemen in top hats (Austrians). In mid-November, the Bosnian insurgents declared, "The guarantee of our national program we find first of all in brotherly Serbia and in no case in Croatia or in Austria-Hungary. Any countryman of ours will be proclaimed a traitor if he thinks differently." They demanded: (1) destruction of the *spahija* (large feudal estates) without compensation, (2) tax exemption of the insurgent areas for ten years (except school taxes), and (3) vesting supreme power in a national assembly elected by all adult males.[114] This program reflected the views of the more radical element among the insurgents. The feeble regime continued to appeal for support and recognition. "We can entrust our national cause," it declared in December, "only to our born brethren, the Serbian principalities . . . and to great and holy Russia." [115]

The siege of Nikšić provided an outlet for the Montenegrins' martial ardor. From late July until its surrender on September 4, it was the focal point of their military effort. Prince Nikola, husbanding manpower, avoided frontal assaults. The timely arrival of Russian cannon speeded the reduction of the fortress. News of its capture caused unrestrained rejoicing in Cetinje. "People surged along the street," wrote Evans, "firing, shouting, singing, leaping with joy. It was an enthusiasm, an ecstasy, unintelligible, impossible in a civilized country." There was cause for celebration. Nikšić had been a Turkish gateway into Montenegro. Acquisition of the city and the rich plains around it would enhance Montenegro's security and double its wealth.[116]

The fall of Nikšić relieved Montenegrin forces for an advance into Hercegovina. "One must see the neglected state of Nikšić's fortifications," reported Thömmel, "to understand the collapse of a state." Except for a few weakly held Turkish forts, he warned, there was nothing to stop Nikola's advance to Mostar. Capturing strong points in Hercegovina, often by offering their garrisons generous terms, Montenegrin forces penetrated regions regarded by Vienna as its sphere of interest. To set his "standard-bearer" straight, Andrassy reminded Prince Nikola of the demarcation line they had agreed upon. "It seems to me," he

---

[114] This program, reprinted in *Zastava*, appeared originally in *Schlesische Zeitung*, which obtained it from a correspondent in Belgrade. Its authenticity is somewhat doubtful, but it reflects some insurgent aspirations. *Zastava o B. i H.*, 4, no. 178, Nov. 16/28.

[115] *Ibid.*, no. 187, Dec. 4/16, OSVOb., 2, no. 250, Sept. 29/Oct. 11.

[116] Evans, *Illyrian Letters*, pp. 164–88.

wrote Thömmel (September 28), "that it is already time for the prince to rest upon his laurels." Nikola protested the Austrian veto, but had to withdraw from Bileća and conclude his fall campaign in Hercegovina.[117]

The Russian leadership, cognizant of Nikola's problems, continued to give him generous support. Although Novikov in Vienna was displeased that Montenegro had not prevented transshipment of Suleiman's army to the Bulgarian front, Russian headquarters realized that this was impossible. In fact, Grand Duke Nikolai Nikolaevich and the tsar congratulated him on the end of the military threat to Montenegro.[118] Official Russian financial aid both for war purposes and postwar development continued.[119] The St. Petersburg Slav Society dispatched sizable sums to support families of dead and wounded Montenegrins.[120] Russian assistance enabled Montenegro to remain somewhat independent of Austria-Hungary, but failed to inspire strong pro-Russian sentiment there. The Russians' patronizing ways were resented by sturdy mountaineers who also disliked autocracy.[121]

In December and January, Prince Nikola concentrated his operations in the Morača Valley and on the Adriatic coast. The fertile Morača Valley, guarded by Turkish forts at Spuž, Podgorica, and Žabljak, was coveted for its arable land, fisheries, and its access to Lake Skutari. Possession of the coastal strip from the Dalmatian frontier to the Bojana River would boost Montenegrin commerce. When the Montenegrins besieged Bar (Antivari), Thömmel feared that they might seize the

[117] *Ibid.*, pp. 208–15; Djordjević, *Crna Gora*, pp. 419–21.

[118] *Ibid.*, 418–19.

[119] OSVOb., *2*, no. 104. A. S. Ionin to Gorchakov, June 25/July 7, requesting 500,000 rubles for an offensive into Old Serbia was approved. *Ibid.*, no. 266, Oct. 21/Nov. 2, Giers to Gorchakov, telegram, confirmed the tsar's consent to cover Montenegrin war expenses beginning November 1/13 and to grant Cetinje a five-year loan to purchase grain. See also *ibid.*, no. 292, A. S. Ionin to Gorchakov, telegram, Nov. 12/24.

[120] *Ibid.*, no. 215, Aug. 30/Sept. 11, Prince Nikola to Aksakov, telegram. For details of the St. Petersburg Society's contributions to Montenegro see *Pervye 15 let*, p. 464.

[121] Evans wrote from Cetinje on Sept. 6, "They [the Russians] cannot understand the egalitaire spirit of the Montenegrins. They come here with a general air of patronage, thinking that the mountaineers will fawn upon their benefactors, and are unpleasantly deceived. . . . Montenegro is willing enough to accept Russian help, but she certainly has given a quid pro quo and does not choose to be treated as a pensioner. Nor can the Montenegrins forget how often Russia in her Turkish war has made [Montenegro] a cat's paw, and left it in the lurch when the day of settling came." Evans, *Illyrian Letters*, p. 174.

entire coast line. The Austrian consul in Bar refused to leave, and according to Thömmel (December 2), 95 per cent of the population was opposed to Montenegrin rule. Andrassy promptly instructed him to warn the prince about military operations on the coast. Nikola's request for written description of Austrian coastal interests was rejected, but Thömmel declared that Montenegro could not retain the port of Spič. Having abandoned his offensive in Hercegovina at Vienna's behest, Nikola claimed that his alliance with Russia obligated him to attack the Turks elsewhere. Andrassy should raise objections in St. Petersburg, not in Cetinje. The Montenegrin advance, retorted Thömmel, imperiled Austrian interests and could be regulated only by Vienna and Cetinje.[122]

Despite Austrian admonitions, the Montenegrin advance continued. The peace settlement, wrote Andrassy (December 21), would not depend upon Montenegro's wartime gains; only Austrian financial aid had enabled Nikola to besiege Bar. Austro-Russian relations, added Andrassy, could not be disturbed by Montenegro's claims. Russian headquarters, however, urged Nikola to occupy a maximum amount of territory and confront the peacemakers with *faits accomplis*, and the Russian press emphasized Montenegro's right to an Adriatic port.[123] Bar capitulated January 10, Ulcinj ten days later, and the island forts of Lesendra and Vranjanina on January 30; Podgorica was besieged. When hostilities ceased, the Montenegrins were in possession of a sizable coastal strip and the agricultural land they had long desired.[124]

However, despite Russian victories, Turkish rule was largely preserved in the western Balkans. Austro-Turkish pressure virtually destroyed the Bosnian insurrection, and most of Hercegovina was denied to Montenegro. Austrian power, poised on the frontiers of the insurgent provinces, kept the Serbian principalities artificially separated. Only on the Adriatic Montenegro stood triumphant and aggrandized, posing a threat, in Andrassy's view, to Austrian hegemony. The extent of Montenegrin gains would be a troublesome question for the peacemakers.

Russian Reverses and Summons to Serbia (July–November 1877)

In June and early July 1877, Russian forces in the Balkans advanced rapidly, carrying all before them. Turkey's doom appeared imminent

---

[122] *Ibid.*, pp. 214–15; Djordjević, *Crna Gora*, pp. 422–24.
[123] Peredovykh, Dec. 1/13, no. 297B; Nov. 10/22, no. 279.
[124] Djordjević, *Crna Gora*, pp. 425–26.

and inevitable. Generals Skobelev and Gurko, seizing the Balkan passes, surged beyond the mountains toward Adrianople. The moment of the complete liberation of the Turkish Christians seemed nigh. Would Serbia, Rumania, and Greece now enter the conflict either at Russia's request or to achieve aggrandizement and independence?

After the Ploesti meetings,[125] Russian headquarters repeatedly demanded immediate Serbian entry into the war. With his forces safely across the Danube (June 28–29), Grand Duke Nikolai Nikolaevich desired the Serbian army to secure his right flank. On July 5, as his army swept ahead, came the first Russian summons. The grand duke urged Belgrade to declare war and proclaim Serbian independence. When Catargi objected that without funds this would be impossible, the Russian commander pledged one million rubles once Serbian forces were massed on the Turkish frontier. "Do not lose a moment," Catargi advised Prince Milan, "the emperor is counting on you." Returning to Kragujevac for instructions, the envoy was told to inform Russian headquarters that without money Serbian forces could not even be prepared for war. Besides a million for preparations, Belgrade wanted a million rubles per month during Serbia's participation. Four or five weeks after receiving the initial million, Serbia could join the fight.[126]

Catargi departed for headquarters on July 20, the day of the first unsuccessful Russian assault upon Plevna. By the time he arrived, the grand duke, searching everywhere for reinforcements, desired immediate Serbian and Rumanian, and, if possible, Greek participation in the war. He wrote the emperor: "In view of the significant assistance which a movement of the Serbs into Turkish territory could provide for our army at the present time, I consider it would be extremely desirable to grant them financial aid as soon as possible for their immediate entry into action." [127] Informing his government that it would obtain the money it requested, Catargi transmitted the tsar's message:

[125] See *supra*, pp. 203–08.

[126] AII, Ristić 19/113, Catargi to Milan, July 5, telegram, copy by Ristić; 22/238, "Aide-mémoire pour le Colonel Catargi," July 3/15; 19/1, Milan to Nikolai Nikolaevich, July 4/16; Grujić, 3, 294.

[127] Os. Pr., no. 3, pp. 53–54, Nikolai Nikolaevich to Alexander II, July 13/25. For a discussion of the question of direct Rumanian participation see Sumner, *Russia*, pp. 324–27, and for overtures to Greece, *ibid.*, pp. 331–34.

The grand duke requested his brother to authorize immediately dispatch of the million rubles to Belgrade which the Serbs needed for war preparations. The tsar empowered War Minister Miliutin to so instruct the Ministry of Finance. Skalon, *Moi vospominaniia*, pp. 211, 213.

Tell Milan I love him like a son, that he can count on my protection under any circumstances, and that Serbia's national future depends on her participation. . . . *If Serbia does not cross the frontier within a twelve-day period, she is lost and her national future will be forever compromised.* . . . Tell the prince that if he enters the war within twelve days, he will be doing me a real service and I will take account of it. You have nothing to fear from Austria.[128]

This statement, contrasting sharply with his advice at Ploesti a month previously, reflected the changing situation on the Balkan front.

The Serbian leadership, noting the Russians' initial reverse at Plevna, responded evasively. Although Prince Milan apparently wished to comply with the emperor's request, his divided cabinet adopted a wait and see attitude. Dissatisfied that headquarters had not offered a monthly subsidy, it decided (July 30) to await Catargi's formal report and arrival of the million rubles before taking action.[129] Following the second abortive assault on Plevna (July 30), headquarters promised Serbia an additional subsidy during its participation. But Ristić emphasized that until the million rubles arrived, Serbia could not rearm, much less march. He inquired repeatedly of his agent in Bucharest when and how the million would be sent. Preoccupation with the growing Turkish counteroffensive, responded Petronijević, had delayed Russian action on this matter.[130] Distraught over a burgeoning military crisis, headquarters had the chargé d'affaires in Belgrade, N. N. Lodyzhenskii, rouse Prince Milan from his slumbers (August 14) and urge him to mobilize immediately. Next day the grand duke informed the prince that Serbia must move, "every hour is precious."[131] A. I. Persiani, formerly Russian consul in Athens, was named to the Belgrade post vacated by Kartsov.[132] Russia's need of Serbia had never been greater.

Serbia's indecision stemmed from domestic considerations as well as Russian reverses. The Ristić government was preoccupied with rising political opposition in the Assembly. Only by imposing rigorous cen-

[128] AII, Ristić 19/3, Catargi to Milan, July 15/27, telegram; Ristić, *2*, 62–63; Grujić, *3*, 295.

[129] Grujić, *3*, 296; Ristić, *2*, 63–64: Vlada Milana, *1*, 385, note, Ministers V. Jovanović and A. Vasiljević favored immediate response to headquarters' request, but Ristić, J. Grujić, and S. Grujić argued for delay. *Zastava*, Nov. 11/23, no. 175, report from Belgrade, Nov. 4/16.

[130] Ristić, *2*, 63; AII, Ristić 18/9, 19/10, 12, 16, 21, 22 Ristić-Petronijević telegraphic exchanges; Jelavich, pp. 165–66, Gamburger to Giers, July 28/Aug. 9.

[131] AII, Ristić 19/14, Nelidov to Lodyzhenskii, Aug. 3/15; HHSA, Wrede to Andrassy, Aug. 21, 25, nos. 87, 90, Grujić, *3*, 297.

[132] AII, Ristić 19/13, Gorchakov to Lodyzhenskii, Aug. 4/16.

sorship, which isolated Kragujevac from the rest of Serbia, and filling seats vacated by the opposition could the cabinet force through its program. The Assembly then dutifully thanked Russia for past assistance and expressed willingness to make new sacrifices if necessary. Early in August, the Assembly was dissolved permitting the cabinet to return to Belgrade. Ristić then submitted its resignation to Prince Milan (August 7), but he persuaded it to remain in office. Ristić's popularity was waning—he had bested the opposition only by using strong-arm tactics. Bitter political schism continued to wrack the country.[133]

Intense popular opposition to resumption of the war persisted in Serbia until Russia's military fortunes improved. Serbian public opinion, reported White, "condemns both the way the last war was brought about and conducted and any secret designs of renewing it." How could we desire war, one Serb asked General Fadeev, when "the first condition is that we must renounce all hope of [acquiring] Bosnia."[134] Wrede reported that both Belgrade and rural areas opposed reentry, that the militia would flee at the first sight of the enemy. On August 27, he wrote:

The opposition of the Serbian people to the renewal of military undertakings is so great that the government did not dare raise the war issue even in the last Assembly packed with its supporters. . . . People are so upset here . . . that only a determined leader is needed to bring them to open rebellion. Whereas last year there was in some places a certain enthusiasm for a fight with Turkey and many greeted it with enthusiasm, this is today *nowhere the case.*[135]

Serbian leaders admitted, especially after the third Russian defeat at Plevna, that their countrymen were pacific and depressed and would oppose war.[136]

---

[133] HHSA, Wrede to Andrassy, nos. 68, 70 of July 14; no. 85, Aug. 13; Grujić, *3*, 296–97; Vlada Milana, *1*, 377, 380.

[134] PRO, FO 78/2613, White to Derby, Aug. 23, no. 128.

[135] HHSA, Wrede to Andrassy, Aug. 10, 21, 27, nos. 82, 88, 91. Later Wrede wrote, "All reports from the interior agree about the terrific opposition to the war plans of the government. *Ibid.*, Sept. 12, no. 95.

[136] AII, Ristić 26/755, Bogičević to Ristić, Sept. 14/26; PRO, FO 78/2613, White to Derby, Oct. 3, no. 161. Thus the assertion by *Russkii Mir's* correspondent that the "Serbian people warmly desire to fight side by side with the Russians against the Turks" is refuted by all other evidence. *Russkii Mir*, July 31/Aug. 12, report from Belgrade, July 23/Aug. 4, no. 205.

During the Russian reverses at Plevna, *Istok* reflected official caution. After the second Russian assault, it worried lest Russia might have to abandon all its wartime gains; however, it dismissed as ridiculous talk of a Turkish victory, emphasizing that reverses were strengthening the Russian people's determination to achieve victory.[137] But after the third setback, *Istok* feared a possible Russo-Turkish peace which would be "burial for Slavdom," since the Balkan Christians could not be liberated. Doubtful that the Russians could reach Constantinople in 1877, *Istok* resigned itself to a probable second campaign. It noted that Russian military prestige could not be fully restored until Plevna fell, and it conveyed the impression that until then Serbia would not fight.[138]

Istok reaffirmed the importance of Slav unity and Serbia's role. "All Slav peoples can and must live in their ethnographic unity, all equally free and bound by moral ties, and if need be with the physical support which their survival requires." National unions of Serbs, Croats, or Bulgarians were insufficient to provide security. "The Slavs indeed are great, but great is the number of their enemies, and their only salvation is in unity, a well-contrived Slav union [*zajednica*]." Threats to the spirit of unity included Croatian separatism and Western ideas:

The Serbian areas—Bosnia and Old Serbia—must be united with the principality of Serbia since the Serbs who live there have always desired it and lately have announced it to the whole world. And that our defender, Russia, wants this there is no doubt because only thus can be secured the higher cultural and political interests of Russia and Orthodox Slavdom.[139]

Not until Plevna's fall appeared imminent did *Istok* suggest Serbia's possible re-entry. A cautious statement appeared November 25: "Should the fate of our brethren and the interests of our dear homeland require that Serbia renew the war with the Turks, we would greet this wholeheartedly since we are sure that the enthusiasm, devotion, and patriotism of Serbia would mean that the outcome of the war would be wholly different now." Three days later it declared that Serbia must participate, not to refurbish military honor, but to fulfill the mission of liberating her brethren. On December 2, Ristić's organ finally declared

[137] *Istok*, July 27/Aug. 8, "Rat," p. 2; July 31/Aug. 12, Aug. 3/15 and Aug. 28/Sept. 9.
[138] *Ibid.*, Sept. 4/16, 18/30; Oct. 9/21.
[139] *Ibid.*, July 15/27, 17/29, Aug. 14/26, Oct. 5/17.

that since the Serbian states wished to help solve the Eastern Question, "therefore we should realize that it is essential for us to create a *fait accompli*" by proclaiming independence and occupying Turkish territories.[140]

Serbia's relationship with Russia was treated in a significant lead article (November 30). Stressing a common interest in liberation, *Istok* assessed realistically their divergent viewpoints:

No one could seriously believe that Russia, upon conclusion of peace, would risk her prestige and interests solely for the sake of certain desires of Serbia, no matter how justified they may be. Their spheres of action are different; Russia has moral obligations toward Europe which she must fulfill; Serbia's situation gives her some freedom. But Russia and Serbia have in common a mutual, strong, inseparable aim which unites them as brothers: the liberation of the Slav people under Turkey. Russia desires this liberation on principle; Serbia for its own sake; Russia to maintain her prestige in Europe and because of her human feelings and sympathies toward the oppressed Christian peoples; Serbia for the actual liberation of its brethren so they will not perish physically beneath the Moslem sword. Russia is the fighter for freedom on principle; Serbia is the actual executor.

The enemies of Slavdom, continued the article, had failed to sow discord between Serbia and Russia, but Serbia must enter the war or risk losing her rightful reward at the peace settlement. Then came a warning which was noticed immediately by the Austrian consul:

No matter how one assesses the actions of Russia in past centuries, even admitting that Russia often, upon conclusion of peace, left out of account the interests of Serbia and handed her over to the overwhelming power of Turkey, it must be admitted that this was done out of necessity. On the other hand, should such necessity prevail [now] for Russia, Serbia has the right to secure itself from the repetition of such an eventuality.

Therefore, Serbia should help solve the Eastern Question "and thus assure [to Serbia] the foundation stones of Dušan's empire, Bosnia and Old Serbia." [141]

Zastava, repudiating *Istok's* caution, steadily urged Serbian participation in the war. After the second Plevna setback, deploring Russia's

---

[140] *Ibid.*, Nov. 13/25, 16/28, Nov. 20/Dec. 2.

[141] *Ibid.*, Nov. 18/30, no. 129. Wrede enclosed translations of the lead articles in nos. 128 and 129 of *Istok* noting the increasing bellicosity and confidence of this semiofficial organ.

"wholly official manner" of conducting the war, *Zastava* declared, "This situation must end once and for all. Russia should unfurl all the flags at her disposal. Why should Gorchakov disdain the aid of the Balkan Slavs, especially Serbia, when Bismarck made an alliance with revolutionary elements against Austria?" [142] Serbia, predicted *Zastava*, would soon attack Osman Pasha, the Turkish commander at Plevna, from the rear. Russia might not require Serbian assistance, but it would have vast political significance and considerable strategic importance. A Serbo-Montenegrin offensive into Bosnia and Hercegovina combined with a Russian advance to Constantinople would achieve a better future for the Slav peoples. [143] Unless Serbia joined the struggle soon, other states (unnamed) might usurp her rightful role in Bosnia: "The most favorable opportunity has come for Serbia to end what it began. Without Russia, Serbia could not reorder the East; without Serbia, Russia cannot do so now, since she is advancing in Bulgaria and the lands on that side of the Balkans; on this side of the Balkans, the lands await their deliverer which is Serbia." [144] Even after the third Plevna, which disheartened Russians and Serbs elsewhere, *Zastava* remained confident of Russian victory in 1877, if Serbia were unleashed. [145] Serbia will enter the war, asserted the newspaper, not at Russia's behest but to guarantee the liberation and unification of Serbdom, that is in its own interest. It advocated a Serbo-Montenegrin invasion of Bosnia and Hercegovina and defensive operations elsewhere. [146] *Zastava*'s Belgrade correspondent reported that Serbia could not fight unless Russia wholeheartedly adopted a Slav program and allied itself with the principality:

Serbia must be assured as to what she will obtain or at least that Russia will adopt the goal of the unification of the Serbian people as her own cause. Serbia cannot enter the war emptyhanded. A band of insurgents can, but not a government which is responsible to its people for its action. . . . We will not pull out chestnuts for others—that is, acquiring Bosnia for Austria.

[142] *Zastava*, July 26/Aug. 7, no. 115, "Sa bojnog polje."
[143] *Ibid.*, Aug. 7/19, "Položaj i značaj Srbije," no. 122.
[144] *Ibid.*, Aug. 19/31, no. 128, "Na Srbije je red!"
[145] *Ibid.*, Sept. 11/23, no. 141, "Bojno polje."
[146] *Ibid.*, Oct. 19/31, no. 163, "Učešče Srbije u ovom ratu." Clearly such a war strategy would benefit Russian operations very little and would be intolerable to Austria-Hungary. *Zastava* explained: "It would today be a wholly un-Slav, inimical policy . . . if Serbia once again fought as she did last year. Such political warfare of going in all four directions at once would not bring important results in any of them; that would be in foreign interests, not in those of Serbdom."

In close connection with Russia we must fight; otherwise not. *We want war because Bosnia is not yet Serbian*, but official Russia must be won over to our program.[147]

Zastava dismissed fears that Austria might intervene or Serbia become the tool of a victorious Pan-Slav Russia.[148]

A realistic view of Russian aims is taken by the confidential "Memoir to White," written by a Ristić confidant. Phrased to win support in England for Serbian aspirations, the memoir emphatically rejected Pan-Slavism. Russia, assured of victory, was co-operating closely with the Bulgarians, most subservient of the South Slavs. For thirty years St. Petersburg had sought "to divide and paralyze the Serbian race and oppose it to the Bulgarian race, compact and aggrandized." At the Constantinople Conference, Russia had favored Montenegro and an autonomous Bulgaria dependent upon it. Should Turkey survive the war, enlarged vassal principalities—Serbia, Greece, Rumania, and Bulgaria—should be created. Serbia would obtain Old Serbia, northern Albania, and Bosnia unless Austria objected. If the Ottoman Empire collapsed, Turkish Slavs should be united under one dynasty, presumably the Obrenović. As a minimum, independent Serbian, Rumanian, and Greek kingdoms could be set up if Turkey fell, interallied for "the common defense of Europe." The Serbian kingdom, federated with Slav Macedonia and Bulgaria, should include Vidin, Sofia, and Durazzo. Vienna could be offered "Turkish Croatia" as compensation. Concluded the memoir, either Serbia must be independent or "bien russe." [149] The memorandum sought to exploit British fears of a Russian-dominated Bulgaria, but neither Russia nor Austria could accept its proposal of a Yugoslav federation dominated by Serbia.

Vienna, after Russia's initial reverse at Plevna, abandoned its opposition to Serbia's participation, whereas England continued to oppose it vigorously. Andrassy instructed his consul in Belgrade (July 25): "In

---

[147] *Ibid.*, Oct. 23/Nov. 4, no. 165, "Dopisi," Belgrade, Oct. 14/26. The censorship in Belgrade, added the correspondent, barred discussion of this issue in Serbian papers.

[148] *Ibid.*, Nov. 8/20, no. 174, "Austro-Ugarska naprema ratovanje srpskih kneževina"; Nov. 4/16, no. 172, "Rusko-turski rat i narodi Balkanskog poluostrva-II." Serbia and Rumania, noted the latter article, after achieving full independence, "will conduct their affairs solely in their own interests."

[149] HHSA, Memoir to White, Aug. 1, copy enclosed with Wrede to Andrassy, Oct . 7, no. 100. Its author was Matija Ban. Andrassy expressed dissatisfaction with the Serbian goals it expressed and at Austria's "compensation."

the present situation, it is not in our interest to prevent the further development of the crisis." [150] Vienna dropped broad hints that it would not prevent Serbia from joining the war unless its troops sought to enter Bosnia.[151] When Marinović urged Andrassy to restrain Serbia by threatening to occupy it, the foreign minister declined to reply and informed his consul that the Monarchy would not threaten Belgrade.[152] Only if the Serbs launched "une guerre révolutionnaire," Andrassy informed Derby, would Austria move into Bosnia.[153] Rejoicing at this reversal, Prince Milan declared, "I see with satisfaction that [the Austrians] are . . . gradually getting used to the idea of Serbia's entry into action." [154] On the other hand, London, anxious to spare the Porte additional burdens, warned Belgrade against abandoning neutrality. Reported White,

I at once spoke to Ristić in very strong terms and told him that his country reminded me of a man who wanted to commit suicide and was once prevented from effecting this object through the interposition of powerful friends . . . who might look on quietly the next time he was about to make a similar attempt.

Nothing could injure Serbia's future more, warned the consul, than a conviction by neutral powers that it was a perpetual disturber of the peace and a willing instrument in Russia's hands, a conviction which would result from repeating its aggression of 1876.[155] Reinforcing this admonition, the British foreign secretary, Lord Derby, wrote that in England's view "an unprovoked violation of the engagements then [March 1877 in the Serbo-Turkish treaty] entered into by Serbia would be a breach of faith, not only towards the Porte but towards England and would render it impossible for the Government of the

---

[150] *Ibid.*, Andrassy to Wrede, July 25.

[151] PRO, FO 7/904, Buchanan to Derby, Aug. 6 and 10, telegrams 656, 673.

[152] HHSA, Varia Belgrad 1877, Marinović to Andrassy, date illegible but enclosed with Wrede to Andrassy, Aug. 15, Privatschreiben; Andrassy to Wrede, Aug. 27.

[153] OSVOb., *2*, no. 179, p. 223, Shuvalov to M.I.D., Aug. 2/14.

[154] *Russkii Mir*, Aug. 23/Sept. 4, no. 228, report from Belgrade of Aug. 22.

[155] *Staatsarchiv, 33*, no. 6556, pp. 135–36, White to Derby, Aug. 22. White had been sending reports home about Serbian rearmament, and he stated that Russia was considering making full use of Serbia in the war. The Serbs, he felt, were increasingly responsive, and he noted a statement of the tsar when he was pressed to guarantee Serbia territorial advantages at the peace settlement, "How can I do this unless Serbia is in possession at the time of something she claims." PRO, FO 78/2613, White to Derby, no. 117, Aug. 16. See also nos. 112, 113, Aug. 7, 8.

Queen to support the claims of Serbia in any discussions which may take place at the end of the present war." [156] Although English pressure perhaps delayed Serbia's entry, what Belgrade had really feared was Austrian action. Now the Serbs concluded correctly that this would not occur unless they invaded Bosnia.

Toward the end of August, Russian headquarters dispatched M. A. Khitrovo and Prince A. N. Tseretelev to Belgrade to deliver the initial subsidy and obtain a Serbian commitment to join the conflict soon. Khitrovo, despite his friendship with Ristić, failed to extract any promises from the Serbs, since headquarters had not empowered him to conclude a formal convention. He returned to headquarters with the news that Serbia would participate under the right circumstances but needed additional weeks for preparation.[157] Tseretelev, who delivered 500,000 rubles to Belgrade (August 25) proved to be a deplorable envoy. He reported pessimistically:

Here all admit that Serbia is extremely exhausted and weary but understand the inevitability of war. Within the Ministry there is no agreement. It is sluggish, unpopular. Ristić, apparently, wishes while obtaining money, to wait until every danger has passed and dreams of a [Russo-Serbian] convention. I am seeking to hasten the time of action.[158]

His method of "hastening . . . action," claims Ristić, was attempting to persuade the prince to oust the Ristić government and declare war immediately. Exaggerating the opposition's influence, Tseretelev wrote, "Essential is the rapprochement of all parties, possible only with the open participation of the Imperial Government. Otherwise the passive resistance of the people can ruin the whole affair." This attempt to revive Cherniaev's policy of 1876 antagonized the Serbian government. Leaving Belgrade amidst the bitterest recriminations, Tseretelev informed headquarters that it was impossible to deal with the Ristić cabinet and that the Serbs could not enter the war.[159]

[156] *Staatsarchiv, 33*, no. 6557, pp. 136–37, Derby to White, Aug. 23.

[157] AII, Ristić 18/15, Khitrovo to Ristić, n.d.; HHSA, Wrede to Andrassy, Aug. 25, Aug. 27, nos. 90, 91; Skalon, *Moi vospominaniia*, p. 276; Ristić, *2*, 64–65.

[158] OSVOb., *2*, nos. 195, 196, pp. 236–37, Nelidov to Tseretelev, Aug. 14/26 and Tseretelev to Nelidov, Aug. 15/27. Tseretelev did report that Milan promised to cross the frontier within a month and he urged the immediate dispatch of the second half million rubles.

[159] *Ibid.*, no. 200, p. 237, Aug. 16/28; no. 201, p. 239, Aug. 17/29. Nelidov transmitted this negative assessment to the emperor. Ristić, *2*, 64–65; Hasenkampf, *Dnevnik*, p. 471.

Tseretelev's negative reports and Serbia's passivity brought relations between Russian headquarters and Belgrade to their nadir. Noting strong anti-Ristić sentiments at headquarters, Catargi telegraphed Milan, "Grand Duke Nikolai Nikolaevich advises you in your own interest and that of Serbia to declare war immediately and cross the frontier with 20,000 men. The emperor will be overjoyed at this." [160] Tseretelev's findings, the emperor told Catargi, suggested that Serbia could not co-operate militarily. The Serbian cabinet, he continued, had deceived him and Prince Milan about prospects of entering the war. Unable to convince the tsar of Ristić's sincerity, Catargi reported sadly that headquarters would send no more money until 20,000 Serbian troops had crossed the Turkish frontier.[161] Ties with headquarters were also threatened by General Fadeev's sudden reappearance in Belgrade. The Serbs wisely gave the Pan-Slav general no encouragement. Giers assured Vienna that official Russia had not sanctioned his mission, and General M. D. Skobelev, at the grand duke's request, urged Fadeev to leave Serbia.[162]

The Russians' desperate need of Serbian military assistance induced headquarters and the Foreign Ministry to try again. Dissatisfied with Tseretelev's report, Nelidov in a memorandum to the grand duke (August 30), recommended further study of the muddled situation in Serbia by a trusted officer. He opposed immediate Serbian entry since it might provoke complications with Vienna and bring defeat to the principality's disorganized army. Anxious to relieve Turkish pressure on his overtaxed army, Nikolai Nikolaevich accepted this memorandum, which served as the basis for the Bobrikov mission to Serbia.[163]

With some misgivings, Russia's diplomats finally withdrew objections to Serbian participation once it became evident this would not endanger Austro-Russian relations. Baron Jomini's letter of August 7 had revealed their fears and defective knowledge of Serbian conditions: "If they [the Serbs] are unleashed with the Omladina at their

[160] AII, Ristić, 19/29, Catargi to Milan, Aug. 23/Sept. 4, telegram.

[161] *Ibid.*, 19/37, Sept. 2/14, telegram.

[162] HHSA, Wrede to Andrassy, Aug. 27, nos. 91, 92. Jelavich, *Russia in the East*, p. 57, Jomini to Giers, Aug. 21/Sept. 2. Hasenkampf (*Dnevnik*, p. 95) contains the text of Skobelev's blunt letter to Fadeev. For his part, Ristić informed Hristić (Aug. 16/28), "Fadeev intended nothing less than to enter our military service but was *immediately and decisively* refused. Even if we had not had bad experience with Cherniaev, we could not accept him since he is *persona non grata* with the Austrians." *Pisma Ristića*, p. 251.

[163] Hasenkampf, *Dnevnik*, pp. 95–96.

head, the Slav question will be raised, and if Andrassy is overborne [*débordé*] in his turn and persuaded to come out against us, . . . hundreds of millions of lives will be endangered." A Foreign Ministry official at headquarters, A. F. Gamburger, believed that "miserable allies" like Serbia and Rumania were costly and had proven their military incompetence.[164] But, by August 17, Jomini no longer opposed Serbian involvement as long as the Budapest Conventions were observed. "I do not believe this [Serbian participation] will create trouble for us since Plevna has reassured our good friends." However, he doubted Serbia would join the war. "They [headquarters] do not wish to realize that those people [the Serbs] are making fun of us and do not dream of dying for us. They did so last year only to drag Russia in and they succeeded. Now they will let her [Russia] do the job without compromising themselves." After talking with Catargi, Jomini was convinced that Belgrade had renounced its ties with the Slav societies[165] and would follow a prudent course based on self-interest.[166] Giers, informing Loftus that no alliances had been made with Serbia or Rumania, added that Russia had told Belgrade to act freely in accordance with its interests.[167]

While preparing a third assault upon Plevna, the grand duke dispatched Colonel G. I. Bobrikov, one of his favorites, to Belgrade to "discover precisely whether the Serbs desire and are able to fight. . . . We are held up at Plevna . . . , and it would be extremely helpful to

---

[164] Jelavich, *Russia in the East*, p. 165, Jomini to Giers, July 26/Aug. 7; Gamburger to Giers, July 28/Aug. 9.

[165] A. A. Naryshkin, pleading for the retention of the Slav societies' links with Serbia, wrote A. I. Vasil'chikov July 19/31, "Doubtless there is no point in our direct activity in Serbia now. But inasmuch as Serbia will always retain its importance in the Slav world, we should maintain continual ties with her. . . . I am certain that the coolness toward Serbia, manifested not only in Russia but among all other Slavs who participated in last year's war, soon will yield to a juster appraisal of the unenviable, but far from useless role which fell to her to play in the present great struggle . . . When the principality begins once again to exert influence on other branches of the Serbian people . . . then we should make use of our influence in order to unite its aspirations and tendencies around the goal which Russia sets. . . . We should not neglect a single opportunity to give the Serbs our fatherly patronage, especially at a moment bitter for them. It is not for us, partly having encouraged them to begin the war in 1876, to tell them now: 'vac victis.' " ROBibSS, Aksakov Papers, no. 595.

[166] Jelavich, *Russia in the East*, pp. 54–55, 57, Jomini to Giers, Aug. 5/17 and 7/19, Aug. 21/Sept. 2.

[167] *Staatsarchiv*, *33*, no. 6575, pp. 155–56, Loftus to Derby, Sept. 12.

us if the Serbs succeeded in drawing off part of the Turkish army."
Bobrikov was provided with written instructions (September 2) outlining various alternatives:

It is very important and necessary to determine on the spot how soon . . .
and with what forces the Serbs can begin war . . . without military support from us. . . . If the Serbs are ready for this, the strongest pressure
must be applied to bring them into war immediately. . . . If it turns out
they are unable to do so, it would be preferable, given the lateness of the
season, to ask them not to declare war . . . until they get further orders
from the Imperial Government, but . . . with the second half million
establish observation detachments along the Turkish frontier . . . and thus
draw off part of the enemy strength.[168]

The grand duke's letter to Prince Milan read, "The co-operation of the
Serbian army would be particularly useful to me at the present moment."[169] Bobrikov departed for Belgrade after hearing numerous admonitions about the problems of working with the Serbs.[170]

Serbian leaders welcomed Bobrikov enthusiastically. Unable to conceal his joy, Milan displayed greater interest in rubles than in war.
Large sums would be required, explained the prince, to re-equip and
mobilize his army; however, he hastily assured Bobrikov of his devotion to the tsar and his willingness "to enter the struggle immediately
to fulfill my holy duty." Repelled by Milan's greed and insincerity,
Colonel Bobrikov was favorably impressed with Metropolitan Mihailo
and War Minister Sava Grujić. When Ristić declared that Serbia
would invite destruction by entering the war before spring, Bobrikov
replied that in that case the Serbs might be left out of it altogether.
Nonetheless, the envoy appreciated Ristić's frankness. Without it, he
wrote later, his mission could not have succeeded. After conferring

---

[168] For the full text see G. Bobrikov, *V Serbii*, pp. 13–17, or his *Zapiski*, pp.
41–45.

[169] AII, Ristić 19/27, Nikolai Nikolaevich to Milan, Aug. 21/Sept. 2.

[170] For example, Nelidov warned, "The Serbs themselves are a fine people and
devoted sincerely to us, but the unfortunate representative form of government
has produced among them the most impossible political parties. . . . Try to agree
with one faction and tomorrow you will have all the remaining ones against
you. . . . It is essential to act independently and firmly. That it is difficult to
work there is proven by the examples of all your predecessors." Tseretelev
predicted that the Serbs would await the spring, then enter the war merely to
share in the spoils. *Ibid.*, 19/37, Catargi to Milan, Sept. 2/14; Bobrikov, *Zapiski*, pp.
43–48.

with Serbian leaders, he reported to headquarters that until its forces had been re-equipped, Serbia would not fight.[171]

On September 12, a third massive Russian assault on Plevna was repulsed by Osman Pasha's army with frightful losses for the Russians. Pessimism and despair enveloped Russian leaders. The emperor reportedly prayed and cried alternately from anxiety. Grand Duke Nikolai Nikolaevich even suggested withdrawal beyond the Danube but was dissuaded by the emperor and Miliutin. The grand duke and Miliutin argued over responsibility for the defeats.[172] Russian diplomacy was in equal disarray. Lacking real authority, Gorchakov refused to deal with daily diplomatic problems; Giers remained in St. Petersburg in virtual ignorance.[173] The active diplomats in the Balkan theater were prone to pessimism and even cowardice. Nelidov advised the tsar that if the Powers proposed mediation, Russia should accept even a disadvantageous peace. Neither a winter campaign nor wintering over in Bulgaria would be feasible; Russia would have to accept peace terms within a few weeks. Baron Jomini was almost equally gloomy.[174]

The Russian public reacted to the Plevna defeats with indignation and dismay. After the second Plevna, wrote a French diplomat, E. M. de Vögué, Russians called the grand dukes commanding their armies "tas d'imbéciles." [175] Pobedonostsev wrote the heir, "Here we are in a terrible condition, in unimaginable agitation and fear as a result of the unexpected reverses at Plevna and particularly because of the complete lack of news from the army. Bad rumors are flying." [176] Following the third Plevna defeat, D. Ilovaiskii, a prominent Pan-Slav journalist, wrote: "the nervous mood of Russian society reached an extreme degree." [177] The harsh words uttered in Moscow about the Serbs were regretted; Russia now would be glad of their assistance.[178]

---

[171] *Ibid.*, pp. 47–48.

[172] Hasenkampf, *Dnevnik*, pp. 108–09, 118; Tatishchev, *Aleksandr II, 2*, 401–03; Jelavich, *Russia in the East*, pp. 58, 62.

[173] PRO, FO 65/938, Loftus to Derby, Sept. 12, no. 493; HHSA, Langenau to Andrassy, Aug. 22/Sept. 3, Privatschreiben.

[174] Miliutin, *Dnevnik, 2*, entry of Sept. 30/Oct. 12; Jelavich, *Russia in the East*, pp. 58–62.

[175] *Journal de Vögué*, p. 47, Aug. 19.

[176] *Pisma K. N. Pobedonostseva*, pp. 67–68. On September 29, he wrote of the general disillusionment and that Giers was "beside himself in desperation." *Ibid.*, pp. 69–74. For more about popular reactions see *Russland . . .*, pp. 343–51.

[177] D. Ilovaiskii, "Poezdka pod Plevna v 1877 g.," RS, 37 (1883), p. 351.

[178] ROBibLen, Dnevnik Kireeva, 7, 77–78, Sept. 6/18.

The Russian press debated Serbia's neutrality and its possible entry into the war. Katkov in *Moskovskie Vedomosti* considered Serbia's forced inactivity highly detrimental to the Russian war effort and attributed to it "all the difficulties on our right flank." Russian public opinion, declared Katkov, regretted that diplomatic considerations had prevailed over military ones: "We definitely do not see what considerations could hinder . . . the emergence of Serbia from her forced neutrality. Even less can we understand why Russia should alienate her natural allies in the common cause in the East, which for Serbia is her own cause." Russia should not disdain the assistance of a considerable army, hardened in battle: "The more troops, the less bloodshed and the more decisive the results." [179] *Russkii Mir's* editors realized, however, that Serbia and Greece could not join the conflict until Osman had been defeated. "Their role as auxiliaries will begin when it is merely a question of hastening the denouement." Serbian and Montenegrin forces, stated *Russkii Mir*, could draw off important Turkish forces "and after the capture of Plevna, they will open for us a broad theater of action on the right flank." [180]

Most inconsistent about Serbia was the Foreign Ministry's *Golos*. Before the third Plevna, it suggested Belgrade should hasten to fight since Vienna no longer opposed its entry. Afterward, it admitted the Serbs could not do so until Plevna fell. Later, as Serbia prepared to fight, *Golos* warned Belgrade:

Serbia knows what program she must adhere to in order not to complicate eastern events. . . . Nothing has been said about Turkish territories other than Bosnia, so the acquisition of Vidin or Niš would not be regarded by Austria as a violation of its "direct interests." This may not satisfy extreme Serbian patriots, but it is still worth while for the Serbs to take up arms. . . . Events in the east are taking such a turn that further inactivity by Serbia could only damage her.[181]

On the eve of Serbia's entry into the war, *Golos* had made contradictory statements about Serbian assistance,[182] whereas *Russkii Mir* de-

[179] Peredovykh, nos. 182, 193, 213, 230.
[180] *Russkii Mir*, Aug. 31/Sept. 12 and Sept. 4/16, nos. 236, 240.
[181] *Golos*, Aug. 31/Sept. 12, Sept. 9/21, 13/25, Nov. 5/17, nos. 201, 210, 214, 267.
[182] *Ibid.*, Nov. 17/29, 1877, no. 279. The lead asserted that Serbia's entry would "finally give the war the character of a Slav struggle against the Moslem yoke." This was as close to a "Slav position" as *Golos* ever came. But by December 7 it had reversed itself, claiming that Serbian participation might seriously inconven-

clared loyally, "We see no reason not to consider the Serbs true friends and allies in the cause they entered first." [183] As in 1876, encouragement by friendly Russian newspapers undoubtedly reinforced Belgrade's desire to enter the war.

Headquarters, after the third Plevna, pressed harder for Serbian co-operation. The grand duke inquired whether and when Serbia would join the war. Milan responded that it would enter as soon as possible; he denounced Tseretelev's negative reports. The Ristić cabinet could not deceive either him or the tsar "since military affairs and war preparations are being carried out under my personal direction." Bobrikov, concluded Milan, would testify to Serbia's good faith and desperate need of money.[184] Aware now that the principality could not declare war immediately, headquarters urged establishment of an observation corps on the southeastern frontier promising to send the other half million rubles to Belgrade when 30,000 elite troops were in position.[185]

During October, headquarters' request was obeyed. When Ristić informed the cabinet (October 3) of the grand duke's statement that Serbia would endanger its future unless it co-operated, the ministers agreed to mobilize enough men for an observation corps but demanded a monthly subsidy of one million rubles for Serbia in case of war.[186] Assessing the Serbian army's potential rather favorably, Bobrikov asked headquarters for more money.[187] When a corps of 25,000 Serbs had been concentrated near the border, Bobrikov advised headquarters (October 11) to send the other 500,000 rubles, though he rejected as

---

ience Russia. "Other participants in the war can congratulate themselves that they do not have an ally like Serbia. Russia can get along without the aid of the Serbian militia." See nos. 287, 288, 290.

[183] *Russkii Mir*, Nov. 27/Dec. 9, no. 324. See also Nov. 29/Dec. 11, no. 326.

[184] AII, Ristić 19/37, Catargi to Milan, Sept. 2/14, telegram; 19/39, Milan to Catargi, Sept. 6/18; Bobrikov, *Zapiski*, p. 50.

[185] Reporting headquarters' more favorable attitude toward Serbia, Catargi pleaded, "If you do this [establish an observation corps] quickly, the emperor will be most thankful. . . . It is the only way to re-establish good relations and rehabilitate the Serbian ministry in Russian eyes." AII, Ristić, 14/41, Catargi to Milan, Sept. 9/21, telegram; 19/58, Nelidov to Lodyzhenskii, Sept. 11/23; Bobrikov, *Zapiski*, p. 50.

[186] Grujić, *3*, 301.

[187] Reported Bobrikov to the chief of staff: "Given small amounts of money and a short time, she [Serbia] can fill her magazines [*zapasa*] and prepare for war with prospects of success." Os. Pr., no. 5, pp. 127–29, Bobrikov to (Nepokoichitskii), Sept. 24/Oct. 6.

unwarranted Belgrade's demand for a large monthly subsidy.[188] The grand duke authorized dispatch of the half million, and it arrived in Belgrade October 26.[189] Russia had expended a million rubles to prepare Serbia for war.

Turkish threats could not forestall Serbo-Russian co-operation. As the observation corps occupied its positions, Foreign Minister Server Pasha warned that if Serbia again went to war and suffered defeat, it could not obtain the *status quo ante*.[190] The Serbs turned to Russia for advice. Responded headquarters: avoid a conciliatory reply which would permit Turkey to reduce its forces opposite Serbia. Utilize the presence of the Turkish concentrations to justify Serbian military preparations.[191] A few days later, Server Pasha, asserting that Serbia swarmed with Russian agents and gold, warned, "We have innumerable ways [to injure Serbia] without even being formally at war with you." Ristić, following Russian advice, claimed that Serbia was merely guarding its frontiers. From their Vienna embassy, the Turks supplied money and arms to Petar Karadjordjević, in Austrian territory, hoping to foment revolt in Serbia.[192] These attempts failed, and Serbia prepared for direct involvement in the Russo-Turkish war.

Victory of Russia and the South Slavs (December 1877– January 1878)

When Serbia finally joined Montenegro, the insurgents, the Bulgarians, and Rumania, the war took on aspects of an Orthodox war against Islam and a Slav revolt against the Porte. Greece, however, failed to join the fight, and Russia's military co-operation with the Serbian states was restricted by the Budapest Conventions. This helps account for Vienna's equanimity and continued neutrality.

The Russians brought in General Totleben to direct a siege of Plevna. As it neared success, headquarters formally summoned Serbia into war. When Milan sent congratulations at recent Russian victories, the emperor replied (October 29), "I wish that the princely [Serbian] army

---

[188] Bobrikov, *Zapiski*, pp. 50–51. On the basis of his reports, headquarters agreed to provide Serbia with 150 rubles daily for each 1,000 men operating in Turkish territory, when their number exceeded 25,000.

[189] AII, Ristić 19/45, Catargi to Milan, Oct. 1/13; Ristić, *2*, 70; Grujić, *3*, 302–03.

[190] DAS, 26/300, Hristić to Ristić, Sept. 13/25; Ristić, *2*, 43.

[191] *Ibid.*, Grujić, *3*, 301–02; AII, Ristić 19/46, Nelidov to Persiani, Oct. 4/16, copy by Ristić.

[192] *Ibid.*, 19/139, Hristić to Ristić, Oct. 7/19; Ristić, *2*, 46, 54–57.

were taking part." On November 12, the grand duke instructed the Serbs to cross the Turkish frontier at his signal; he assured Belgrade it would receive money during the fighting.[193] While Plevna resisted, Belgrade haggled over a definite subsidy and awaited a peremptory summons. As late as November 20, Ristić declared equivocally, "It is possible we will enter the campaign, but it is also possible that Serbia will not be called upon to take up arms." [194]

On November 23, headquarters instructed Serbia to enter the war within ten days. Even then Prince Milan, stingy and fearful, wished to wait "until clarification of the situation at Plevna." He replied with cabinet approval that Serbia required promise of a subsidy. The Russians refused such pledges and pressed for a definite response.[195] Determined upon war at last, Ristić persuaded his colleagues and the prince to begin war without a subsidy, but he sent Milosav Protić to headquarters to resolve the troublesome financial issue.[196] From headquarters, Khitrovo, chief of the grand duke's diplomatic chancellery, pleaded with Ristić "to strike while the iron is hot" and rejoiced at the prospect of Serbia's entry:

> I never understood how Serbia could remain passive in the present events. I understand even less now how [the defeat of Turkey] can be accomplished without the active and immediate co-operation of all the elements for whose benefit they are being carried through. . . . I would like to see Serbian blood flow beside ours . . . for I believe this to be indispensable . . . in the interests of Serbia as well as for the cause we have served so long, in our common Slav interest.[197]

But the Serbs did not enter Turkey until Plevna had fallen. This belated action would cost Serbia territory and prestige. Ristić's assertion that its entry was delayed by Karadjordjević threats and the army revolt at Topola is unconvincing.[198] Instead it was due to the cabinet's caution and the prince's infantile fears. It was no coincidence that the

---

[193] AII, 19/50, Catargi to Milan, Oct. 31/Nov. 12, telegram; Grujić, *3*, 303–04; Bobrikov, *Zapiski*, pp. 54–55.

[194] HHSA, Wrede to Andrassy, Nov. 22, no. 114.

[195] Bobrikov, *V Serbii*, pp. 60–61; AII, Ristić 22/350, Catargi to Milan, Nov. 13/25, telegram.

[196] In his letter to the grand duke, taken by Protić, Milan argued that without a monthly subsidy the Serbian army would not even have the essentials for warfare. AII, Ristić 19/52, Milan to Nikolai Nikolaevich, Nov. 17/29, draft by Ristić.

[197] *Ibid.*, 22/360, Khitrovo to Ristić, Nov. 20/Dec. 2.

[198] In support of his allegation, Ristić cited Ćukić's telegram from Vienna of December 8. *Ibid.*, 19/149. However, this dispatch reached him only a day or two

declaration of war was approved December 11, the day *following* Plevna's fall. By then Milan had learned from his envoy that the tsar had declared, "Tell Prince Milan that he can count on me." [199]

Meanwhile, the Russian leadership had drafted bases of peace. With the Foreign Ministry in eclipse, official policy was determined mostly at headquarters. Baron Jomini, the Ministry's principal spokesman, advocated a moderate settlement without major territorial gains for the Turkish Christians. An advance on Constantinople, he feared, would induce other powers to intervene.[200] Nelidov and Miliutin desired to bypass the Ministry altogether, but the emperor insisted that it be consulted. Therefore, Nelidov, in collaboration with Gorchakov and Ignat'ev, drafted letters to the German and Austrian emperors explaining Russia's proposed peace terms.[201] These letters, signed by Alexander II, were dispatched December 9, just before Plevna's capitulation. Nelidov's accompanying "Notice" outlined conditions of peace based on the proposals of the Constantinople Conference.[202] Bulgaria, to be occupied by Russia for two years, would become autonomous with boundaries approximating those set at Constantinople. In Bosnia and Hercegovina, to be organized as the conference had recommended, Austria-Hungary could "assume participation and control analogous to that of Russia in Bulgaria." The independence of Serbia, Montenegro, and Rumania would be recognized. Serbia would obtain Mali Zvornik, and "the Powers would consider the possibility of a greater correction of frontiers on behalf of this state," a vague statement committing Russia to nothing. Montenegro would be compensated territorially in accordance with wartime successes.[203]

---

before Plevna's surrender. HHSA, Wrede to Andrassy, Dec. 16, no. 121; Ristić, *2*, 76–78.

On December 7, a battalion of Serbian troops near Kragujevac mutinied, proceeded to Topola and controlled that town until December 11, when other army units arrived from Belgrade and crushed the mutineers, but Serbia could have entered the war well before this outbreak. See Djordjević, *Srpski-turski rat*, *2*, ch. iii; *Vlada Milana*, *1*, 391–92, 402; Grujić, *3*, 307–08.

[199] *Ibid.*, p. 307.

[200] Jelavich, *Russia in the East*, pp. 64–70, Jomini to Giers, Oct. 23/Nov. 4, Dec. 14/26.

[201] Miliutin, *2*, 241–44; Tatishchev, *Aleksandr II*, *2*, 425–526. Few changes were made in Nelidov's original draft.

[202] See *supra*, pp. 174–79.

[203] HHSA, Alexander II to Franz Josef, Nov. 27/Dec. 9 and attached "Notice"; SR, *6*, no. 254, p. 428, Gorchakov to Shuvalov, Nov. 20/Dec. 2, très secrète. Jomini

Plevna's fall prodded Russian ambitions. The December 12 war council, over objections, resolved that the army should immediately advance on Constantinople. Russian troops, argued Ignat'ev, should at least reach Adrianople and the Straits before an armistice. Impressed with recent military successes and by the ambassador's pleas, the emperor had him draft revised bases of peace.[204] Ignat'ev's proposals, drawn up before any significant Serbian military action, offered considerably larger gains to the Balkan Christians, except the Serbs, than had Nelidov's. Bulgaria's frontiers were to be drawn ethnically. Montenegro's territorial acquisitions must equal the area conquered by its armies. Rumania would obtain a significant increase of territory, whereas Serbia's frontiers would merely be corrected. Serbia, agreed the war council, unlike Montenegro and Rumania, had contributed nothing to the Russo-Turkish War, and Austria would oppose any major increase in its favor. Ignat'ev's plan urged administrative autonomy for Bosnia and Hercegovina without reference to Austrian rights. Russia would be compensated for all wartime expenses by an indemnity or with additional Turkish territory.

The emperor objected that Gorchakov (and presumably the Powers) would never accept such a drastic settlement. Ignat'ev was ordered to return to his estate near Kiev and await instructions.[205] Had Serbia abstained from the Russo-Turkish War, it could have expected little at a peace settlement under the Nelidov or Ignat'ev proposals.

Prince Milan congratulated the Russians over the capture of Plevna and prepared to depart for the front. Telegraphed the tsar in reply, "I cannot conceal my regret that you did not follow sooner the example of the Rumanians, who have shed their blood with ours for the holy cause we fight for." Milan's war proclamation (December 13) explained that Turkish threats and violations of the peace had compelled Serbia to fight: "Although the great and brave Russian army could achieve victory without our help, nothing in the world can remove

---

concurred with these proposals, whereas Ignat'ev warned the tsar (December 6) that they signified abandonment of traditional Russian goals in the Balkans. Jelavich, *Russia in the East*, p. 68, Jomini to Giers, Nov. 21/Dec. 3 (?); Ignat'ev, IV, *137* (July 1914), 73.

[204] At the war council were the emperor, grand duke Nikolai Nikolaevich, Miliutin, Obruchev, Totleben, Nepokoichitskii, Skobelev, and Imeritinskii. Skobelev recommended wintering over in Sofia and broadening the front when Serbia and Greece entered the war. Skalon, *Moi vospominaniia*, pp. 40–42; Ignat'ev, IV, *137* (July 1914) 75–76.

[205] *Ibid.*, pp. 76–81.

from us our duty as a member of the Christian community of nations and the duty Serbia and the Serbian race must perform. Peoples can obtain freedom only through sweat and if necessary through blood."[206] The Porte responded with a declaration angrily denouncing Serbia and proclaiming Milan's deposition.[207]

The Serbian public resigned itself to war while the government and the press whipped up a largely synthetic enthusiasm. In Belgrade a popular demonstration was organized before Milan's palace. There were loud cries of "Long live the Emperor of Russia," reported the new Russian envoy, Persiani.[208] *Istok* published reports from the interior asserting that Serbs were rallying enthusiastically around their prince to complete the liberation of Serbdom.[209] On December 21, its editors announced, "We have guarantees from the exalted Russian tsar that Serbdom will be wholly liberated from the Turkish yoke."[210] In Novi Sad, *Zastava* gave its blessing to a reassertion of Serbian leadership:

There has been fulfilled what was so long anticipated and so desired by the Serbian people. . . . The law of self-preservation and the securing of its future today sends Serbia into war. Serbia will reveal itself again in its proud role as the first defender of the freedom of its oppressed brethren. As such, Serbia stands on high with bright banners and its enemies can only look up from the filth below. . . . Serbia is repaying what it owed to its heroes who fell last year.[211]

Meanwhile Milan hid timidly behind the Russian eagle. Fearing responsibility for a war which might yet fail, Milan declared that he was merely executing Russia's orders and kept its military envoy, Colonel Bobrikov, constantly at his elbow.[212]

---

[206] AII, Ristić 19/95, Milan to Alexander II, Nov. 30/Dec. 12, telegram, draft copy by Ristić; 19/96, Alexander II to Milan, Dec. 2/14.

[207] Actenstücke, 3, no. 80, p. 55, Server Pasha to the Porte's representatives abroad, Dec. 19.

[208] AII, Ristić 19/101, Persiani to Gorchakov, Dec. 3/15, telegram. Of the Serbs conscripted into the army before the outbreak of war only 3 per cent failed to appear. *Ibid.*, 22/357, Ristić to Catargi, Nov. 18/30, telegram. *Pisma Ristića*, p. 261, Ristić to Hristić, Nov. 8/20. Wrede confirmed the demonstration but believed it had been staged, rather clumsily at that, by the Ristić government. HHSA, Wrede to Andrassy, Dec. 15, no. 125.

[209] *Istok*, no. 137, Dec. 6/18, "Dopisi," pp. 1–2. See also no. 139, Dec. 11/23, "Dopisi," Zaječar, Dec. 4/16, pp. 2–3.

[210] *Ibid.*, no. 138, Dec. 9/21, lead.

[211] *Zastava*, Dec. 6/18, no. 188, "Rat i nezavisnost srpska."

[212] Bobrikov, *V Serbii*, p. 64.

Russians reacted favorably, especially at headquarters, to Milan's proclamation, despite Serbia's lateness in joining the war.[213] For the Pan-Slavs, A. A. Kireev claimed that Serbian participation had transformed the war into one between Slavs and Turks, Christians and Moslems. "Thus Serbia, which we held so long in disgrace, which we handicapped to Austria's benefit, enters the fight."[214]

Vienna responded mildly, emphasizing it would remain neutral unless the Serbs threatened its interests in the western Balkans. Austrian leaders, reported a Russian correspondent, would permit Serbian independence and gains in Old Serbia if Bosnia were untouched.[215] Andrassy, warning Gorchakov against a Serbian move toward Bosnia or Ada Kala (in the Danube), called Belgrade's entry "an ambush." "The decision of the Serbian government to intervene has created general indignation here [Austria]." Russia, he predicted, would derive little benefit from Serbian military assistance and might face political difficulties at the peace settlement. But if St. Petersburg observed the Conventions, the Monarchy would not hinder utilization of Serbian forces.[216]

Ristić hastily reassured Vienna of his disinterest in Bosnia. General Alimpić had strict orders to remain inactive on the Drina front unless the Turks attacked from Bosnia. The Serbian cabinet agreed not to raise the issue of Bosnia's future although it refused to renounce claims to the province. Belgrade asserted that Serbian operations east of the Lim River in the Novi Pazar (the "Enclave") region would not injure Austrian interests. Wrede replied, however, that Novi Pazar had belonged to Bosnia-Hercegovina for centuries. He would consult with Vienna to determine whether Serbian attacks there would be permitted.[217]

Russia reinforced Austrian warnings. Persiani, since his arrival as

[213] AII, Ristić 19/53, Petronijević to Ristić, Dec. 12/24, telegram. On the other hand, there were indications that the emperor and Foreign Ministry were unenthusiastic. HHSA, Langenau to Andrassy, Dec. 14/26, no. 70B.

[214] ROBibLen, Dnevnik Kireeva, 7, 94-95. Katkov warmly supported Serbia's entry into the fight. Peredovykh, no. 307.

[215] Golos, no. 297, Dec. 5/17, telegram from Vienna of Dec. 4/16; no. 301, Dec. 9/21, report from Vienna of December 14.

[216] HHSA, Andrassy to Langenau, Dec. 20 and 23.

[217] Ibid., Andrassy to Wrede, Dec. 22; Wrede to Andrassy, Dec. 25, nos. 125 and 128; Grujić, 3, 311. Grand Duke Nikolai Nikolaevich and Gorchakov doubted that Serbian operations in Novi Pazar would be compatible with the Budapest Conventions, whereas Miliutin was confident they would be and the emperor accepted his view. Miliutin, Dnevnik, 2, 261.

consul, had urged Belgrade to maintain good relations with the Monarchy. Russia, he informed Ristić, would disapprove of Serbian action in the Austrian sphere of interest; Belgrade must bear the consequences of any such move. Gorchakov, too, strongly advised the Serbs not to infringe Austrian interests. Headquarters had already made a similar plea. Prince Milan hastily promised to comply.[218] Russia's loyalty to the Budapest agreements reassured Vienna.

Blocked in Bosnia and restricted in Novi Pazar by Austrian vetoes, the Serbian command concentrated its efforts in the southeast. Russian headquarters had instructed the Serbs to advance toward Pirot and Sofia.[219] They were to engage Turkish forces on the frontier, safeguard the Russian right flank, and liberate Serbian territory. On December 15, the Serbian offensive corps, completely reorganized and re-equipped since Djunis, crossed into Turkey.[220]

Serbia proved a useful ally. Drawing off considerable Turkish forces, the Serbs eased General Gurko's passage of the Balkans. By December 28, they had joined Russian troops (at Sveta Nikola), and captured Ak Palanka and Pirot, cutting communications between Niš and Sofia.[221] Congratulating the Serbs for executing all his instructions precisely, the grand duke wrote the tsar, "The Serbs have surpassed all my expectations. . . . In two weeks they have achieved very important results." [222] So impressed was the grand duke by Serbian successes that he telegraphed St. Petersburg asking that his instructions for the preliminaries of peace be changed to read "an increase of territory" for Serbia instead of a "correction of frontiers." [223]

These promising initial gains, partly the product of Bobrikov's able

[218] HHSA, Wrede to Andrassy, Dec. 25, no. 128; Langenau to Andrassy, Dec. 26, telegram 99; AII, Ristić 19/62, Milan to Ristić, Dec. 7/19 and 16/28, telegrams.
[219] *Ibid.*, 19/93, Nelidov to Persiani, Nov. 18/30, telegram copied by Ristić. Bobrikov cautioned his superiors not to expect a bold or massive Serbian offensive. Os. Pr., no. 5, pp. 43–45, Bobrikov to Nepokoichitskii, Nov. 23/Dec. 5. Nearly all Serbian military experts favored a southward advance into Old Serbia and Bosnia (Kosovo, Sjenica, Skoplje) but had to bow to Austrian and Russian desires. Rakočević, *Ratni planovi*, pp. 140–41, 148.
[220] Five corps totaling 81,000 men had been formed by War Minister Sava Grujić and represented a combination of regulars and militia. Three corps (47,000 men and 128 cannons) advanced toward Niš; the rest were assigned to defend the frontiers. For a detailed breakdown of the Serbian forces see Vlada Milana, *1*, 403.
[221] Bobrikov, *Zapiski*, pp. 70–71, Vlada Milana, *1*, 404–05.
[222] AII, Ristić 19/218, Milan to Ristić, Dec. 21/Jan. 2, telegram; Os. Pr., no. 5, pp. 123–124, Nikolai Nikolaevich to Alexander II, Dec. 20/Jan. 1; Hasenkampf, *Dnevnik*, pp. 267–68.
[223] *Ibid.*, p. 318, Jan. 2/14, 1878.

advice, were not exploited by the Serbs. Out of greed and ambition, Prince Milan, bypassing his Russian adviser, assumed personal command of the eastern sector. Milan gained headquarters' approval of a poorly conceived operation against Hafiz Pasha's forces. His troops captured Niš and reached Slivnica, but this strategy prevented conquest of all of Old Serbia before the armistice.[224] The six-week campaign revealed the Serbs' endurance and bravery and the competence of their commanders.[225] But tactical errors probably reduced Serbia's gains at San Stefano.

During the campaign Ristić maintained firm control of Serbia. The grand duke urged Milan to rid himself of parliamentary institutions, but there were no overt attempts by Russian officers or diplomats to oust the cabinet. General Belimarković, a protégé of Milan, emerged as a potential strongman, and opposition to the government persisted, but Ristić was equal to the challenge.[226] Ristić's *Istok* glorified military victories: "Even our enemies admit Serbian heroism." [227] It hailed the capture of Niš as opening a new and brilliant era for Serbia. *Istok* then quoted Milan's exhortation to drive onward: "Although Serbian banners wave over Niš, sorrowful Kosovo is not yet avenged!" [228] It rejoiced at Serbia's revived partnership with Russia, the true pillar of Orthodox Slavdom: "Under her flag have gathered all Orthodox Slavs, and especially the Serbian people which has fought as the vanguard of Orthodox Slavdom and began the holy struggle and has now entered for a second time into the fight." [229]

Zastava likewise hailed Russia's role as a liberator preparing a solution of the Eastern Question in a spirit of humanity and in accordance with

---

[224] After capturing Niš, asserts Jovanović, the Serbs should have moved southward into Macedonia or southwest to Novi Pazar. Vlada Milana, *1*, 411; Bobrikov, *Zapiski*, pp. 80–81.

[225] The campaign lasted from Dec. 15, 1877 to Feb. 3, 1878. Serbian casualties totaled 5,410, including 708 killed, 3,000 wounded, 159 missing, and 1,534 who died of their wounds. The chief commands were given to Prince Milan's cronies, Belimarković, Horvatović, and Lešjanin, and were entirely in Serbian hands. During the second war there was greater harmony within the Serbian command and Serbian officers knew their men and their capabilities better than Cherniaev and his Russian colleagues had known theirs in 1876. See *Ibid.*, pp. 408–10.

[226] Grujić, *3*, 312; Bobrikov, *Zapiski*, p. 64; HHSA, Wrede to Andrassy, Jan. 29, no. 6. Bobrikov, while critical of Ristić's narrow patriotism, scrupulously avoided interference in Serbia's domestic politics.

[227] *Istok*, Dec. 16/28, no. 141.   [228] *Ibid.*, Jan. 1/13, 6/18, 1878, nos. 1, 3.

[229] *Ibid.*, Dec. 25/Jan. 6, no. 145.

nationality.[230] Later came this lyric outburst: "When the Russian eagle proudly waves over Tsarigrad [Constantinople], then must the Serbian banner of independence and unification be unfurled from the Timok to Skadar on the Bojana, from the Sava through Prizren and the field of Kosovo to Šar Planina." [231] Optimism and Serbo-Russian harmony were the order of the day.

Even the subsidy issue was finally settled—although not to Belgrade's full satisfaction—because of Serbian military successes. Belgrade requested full support for its operational corps and a partial subsidy for defensive militia forces. At first headquarters supplied only 60,000 rubles, but later the grand duke, enthusiastic over Serbian victories, authorized payment of the full subsidy for the offensive armies.[232] Headquarters supplied, belatedly at that, only half the money which its own representative had requested.

Serbia's relations with Rumania and Bulgaria deteriorated during the campaign. Disputes over territory and spheres of influence alienated Milan from Prince Charles of Rumania. Although Russian headquarters had authorized the Rumanians to capture the towns of Vidin and Belgradjik, Belgrade sought secretly to acquire them for Serbia. To prevent an open Serbo-Rumanian feud, headquarters instructed Serbian forces to halt at the Adlie River and allow the Rumanians to occupy the two cities.[233] But the Russians failed to demarcate clearly areas of Serbian and Rumanian interest. When a Serbian brigade penetrated Rumanian positions near Belgradjik, Foreign Minister Kogalniceanu threatened to sever diplomatic relations. Ristić, though he made a conciliatory reply, persisted in efforts to win Vidin for Serbia at the peace table.[234] The Serbs watched anxiously lest Rumania seek foreign

---

[230] *Zastava*, Dec. 30/Jan. 11, no. 200.   [231] *Ibid.*, Jan. 13/25, 1878, no. 8.

[232] Originally Belgrade had requested 1,000,000 rubles monthly in support money, but headquarters, refusing any money for the defensive militia, delivered a total of only 270,000 rubles for the six weeks' campaign. This sum represented a month's subsidy for the 60,000 men of the operational corps. Despite this niggardliness, Belgrade expressed its thanks and relative satisfaction. The balance of the Russian money arrived in Belgrade only a week before the armistice. Grujić, *3*, 309–14; AII, Ristić 22/220, Ristić to Milan, Dec. 21/Jan. 2, telegram; 22/373, Petronijević to Ristić, Dec. 19/31.

[233] *Ibid.*, 19/53, Petronijević to Ristić, Dec. 12/24; 19/184, Milan to Ristić, Dec. 13/25, telegram; 22/309, Nelidov to Persiani, Dec. 14/26; Hasenkampf, *Dnevnik*, pp. 251–52. Iorga, *Correspondance diplomatique roumaine*, pp. 299, 308.

[234] AII, Ristić 19/245, 246, Ristić to Milan and Milan to Ristić, Dec. 29/Jan. 10; 19/253, 271, Ristić to Milan, Jan. 3/15 and 4/16.

recognition as a kingdom. Jealousy, not friendship, was the legacy of Serbo-Rumanian wartime partnership.

A graver feud, mainly over frontiers, developed between Serbia and Bulgaria. The ineptitude and pro-Bulgarian bias of responsible Russian officials helped transform a territorial dispute of long standing into deadly antagonism. Aksakov warned the chief of Russian civil administration of Bulgaria, Prince V. A. Cherkasskii, of the Serbs' violent objection to the boundary proposed at the Constantinople Conference. Delimitation of Bulgaria's western frontier, he cautioned, would prove most difficult.[235] But Cherkasskii, before an ethnic survey could be made, supported maximum Bulgarian claims. In a letter to Colonel Bobrikov he referred to the entire area occupied by Serbian troops as Bulgarian, thus assigning the Prizren, Priština, and Niš districts to Bulgaria. Bobrikov deplored this approach to the South Slav question:

> With what a light heart was decided the crucial questions of delimiting the Bulgarian nationality from the Serbian! It was in our interest to prepare the way for their alliance, not to poison their relations, since there is no greater insult than to give one's property to another. . . . Neither ethnic, topographic, nor strategic considerations suggested any necessity to retain unchanged the former frontiers of the Serbian principality.

Cherkasskii's letter, concluded Bobrikov, suggested a settlement with generous rewards for Bulgaria, which had contributed little to the liberation of the Slavs, while treating Serbia very stingily.[236]

Serbian leaders apparently did not realize how partial to Bulgaria were Cherkasskii and Ignat'ev. Metropolitan Mihailo, blaming growing Serbo-Bulgarian antagonism on foreign influences, believed Russia was the only possible arbiter: "Turkish policy . . . and Papal propaganda [he wrote Nil Popov January 29] . . . have derailed the Bulgarian intelligentsia and sown hatred. . . . And many Bulgarians from Russia, out of patriotism, . . . fearing that some village might be wrongly included within the boundaries of Serbia, exploit the good will of the Russians and increase this invented hatred." On the other hand, he asserted, his Benevolent Committee had treated Serbian and Bulgarian refugees in 1876 with complete impartiality. "Our Serbian people," he noted, "regard the Bulgarians as their brothers." But Mihailo, claiming "natural frontiers" for Serbia which included much territory usually considered Bulgarian, contributed nothing to reduce

---

[235] *Slavianskii sbornik* (1948), p. 188, Aksakov to Cherkasskii, Dec. 17/29.
[236] Bobrikov, *Zapiski*, pp. 76–80. He received Cherkasskii's letter on Jan. 4, 1878.

antagonism.[237] Belgrade, confident of Russia's fairness, wished her to represent Serbia at peace negotiations. While Prince Charles made frantic efforts to have a Rumanian envoy admitted to peace discussions, Milan believed Serbia could obtain favorable terms through Consul Persiani.[238] Whereas antagonism between St. Petersburg and Bucharest was rising, Serbian-Russian relations appeared excellent. Belgrade did not fear that its legitimate aspirations would be blocked by Russia.

Meanwhile Russian armies were advancing victoriously everywhere. After General Gurko crossed the western Balkans and occupied Sofia (January 4), Turkish resistance in Europe virtually collapsed. But the Russian war council of December 12 had agreed that no armistice should be accorded the Turks until they had accepted Nelidov's bases of peace. Emperor Alexander's return to St. Petersburg enhanced the confusion during these critical weeks. Telegraphic communications with headquarters, never very rapid or efficient, were complicated still further by the tsar's return and by the precipitous advance of the grand duke's army.[239] Alexander, without a clear policy of his own, vacillated between the "European" and nationalist factions.

An excited public opinion unquestionably influenced his judgment. Ambassador Langenau had been concerned at the increasing chauvinism of the Russian press.[240] He reported on December 4, "Pan-Slavism has been celebrating here for some time real orgies once again. . . . People are mistaken who believe that the Pan-Slavs have become reasonable." Official Russia, he feared, might bow once again to their pressure.[241] On the other hand, Loftus, his British colleague, relying upon the assurances of moderate newspapers, believed Pan-Slavism was a passing phenomenon without significant support from official Russia. Loftus concluded, "The speedy conclusion of the war is desired ardently by the great majority of the educated class in Russia." [242] The Pan-Slavs did remain subdued until late in the fall. Aksakov's incendiary speech (October 8) to the Moscow Slav Society could not be

[237] ROBibLen, f. Popova 13/48, Mihailo to Nil Popov, Jan. 17/29.

[238] *Aus dem Leben, 3*, 429, 437–38; AII, Ristić 19/283, Milan to Ristić, Jan. 10/22, 1878, 19/286, Jan. 11/23, telegram.

[239] For details about the breakdown of communications and its grave results see Sumner, *Russia*, pp. 345–53.

[240] HHSA, Langenau to Andrassy, Oct. 26/Nov. 7, Privatschreiben; Nov. 9/21, no. 63 A.B.

[241] *Ibid.*, Nov. 22/Dec. 4, no. 65 A.G.; Dec. 7/19, no. 69C. Andrassy reacted with equal concern to this growth of Russian chauvinism; stimulated by "the undesirable activities of Aksakov and Co." Andrassy to Langenau, Dec. 20, copy.

[242] PRO, FO 181/560, Loftus to Derby, Nov. 7, 21, nos. 602, 650, 651.

published in Russia.[243] But after Plevna's capture, most of the press became extremely bellicose. *Moskovskie Vedomosti* insisted upon the final solution of the Eastern Question.[244] *Russkii Mir*, scoffing at European threats to intervene, asserted that Russia had destroyed the Treaty of Paris and regained a completely free hand in the Balkans: "We can direct our efforts toward the complete achievement of our aims as freely as Prussia did during the French campaigns [1870–1871]. We can boldly go to Constantinople just as the Germans did to the walls of Paris." "The new peace treaty," it added, "will be dictated by the Russian army and its leaders, perhaps within the walls of Constantinople."[245] Declared *St. Peterburgskie Vedomosti*, "The stubbornness of the Turks . . . will cause a Russian march on Tsarigrad. If the enemy has lost his head and shows complete disorganization, we must take advantage of this and without regard for losses, completely destroy . . . Turkey."[246]

The tsar was carried along by the prevailing mood of popular excitement. Many military men and some of his political advisers agreed with the nationalists that Russia should exploit its advantage fully. When the sultan telegraphed the emperor (January 13) appealing for the cessation of hostilities, Alexander responded that the advance would continue until the bases of peace had been unconditionally accepted by the Porte. He instructed Nikolai Nikolaevich to delay negotiations and press on with military operations.[247]

The Foreign Ministry was preoccupied with European reactions to the Russian surge. Fearing British intervention, Gorchakov requested London to stipulate clearly its interests in the Turkish Straits.[248] And Austrian objections to the bases of peace caused consternation among

[243] For the speech see Aksakov, *1*, 272–75. Wrote A. A. Kireev, "Aksakov can truly speak . . . for the Russian nation." ROBibLen, Dnevnik Kireeva, 7, 83–84. Its publication, however, was prevented by Interior Minister Timashev, and the Russian public learned of the speech only in early November after the *Times* of London published it in translation.

[244] Peredovykh, nos. 311, 319, Dec. 15/27, Dec. 21/Jan. 2.

[245] *Russkii Mir*, Dec. 7/19, no. 334; Jan. 11/23, no. 9. This newspaper attributed great significance to Serbian military co-operation and rejoiced at Serbian victories. See Dec. 16/28, Dec. 22/Jan. 3, nos. 343, 349.

[246] *Istok*, Jan. 14/26, no. 6, "Pregled ruske štampe," p. 2, citing article of *St. Peterburgskie Vedomosti*.

[247] Tatishchev, *Aleksandr II, 2*, 427–29; Ignat'ev, IV, *139* (Jan. 1915), 37–38; Hasenkampf, *Dnevnik*, pp. 339–40.

[248] PRO, FO 65/911, Loftus to Derby, Dec. 25, confidential; HHSA, Langenau to Andrassy, Dec. 29, telegram 102.

Russian diplomats.[249] The Ministry had not yet regained its old authority, but it sought to refute in *Golos* the more extreme nationalist claims. Opposing a march to the Bosphorus, it declared that Constantinople was not Russia's goal and that it did not fear European discussion of a Russo-Turkish peace. *Golos* consistently minimized the wartime role of Russia's small Balkan allies.[250] Continuing rivalry between Gorchakov and Ignat'ev, and the chancellor's disinclination for serious work, reduced the Ministry's effectiveness.

At headquarters, Nikolai Nikolaevich, who had (December 30) favored prompt conclusion of peace and as late as January 20 opposed delaying an armistice, suddenly adopted an uncompromising nationalist program. The capture of Adrianople on January 21 transformed his views. Next day he wrote the emperor, "It is necessary to go to the center, to Tsarigrad and there finish the holy cause you have assumed." Worried lest the Foreign Ministry induce his brother to halt the advance, the grand duke cut telegraphic communications with St Petersburg and advocated seizure of Constantinople and the Straits.[251]

Such an extreme course, which undoubtedly would have provoked war with England, was averted by decisions taken in St. Petersburg. At a crucial meeting of top leaders on January 21, the emperor and Miliutin opposed capture of the Straits for fear of precipitating war with England and Austria-Hungary. Count Ignat'ev, consistent advocate of occupying the Straits, was ordered to leave for headquarters to take charge of peace negotiations.[252] Alexander II telegraphed the grand duke on January 24 to advance pending an armistice without occupying Gallipoli or Constantinople since that would violate Russia's pledges to the British.[253] When the Turks accepted Russian bases of peace unconditionally on January 30, headquarters ordered suspension of hostilities. A triumphant Russia, backed by the resurgent Serbian states, Rumania, and the Bulgarians, faced a prostrate Turkey. There remained the danger of an Anglo-Austrian alliance to restrain them from full exploitation of their successes.

---

[249] See *infra*, pp. 251–52.

[250] *Golos*, Dec. 4/16, 9/21, Dec. 25/Jan. 6, Jan. 15/27, 1878.

[251] Hasenkampf, *Dnevnik*, pp. 342, 360. Hasenkampf considered the grand duke's ideas totally unrealistic. Skalon, *Moi vospominaniia*, 2, 79, 160–66. It is Skalon who notes the grand duke's foolish decision to sever telegraphic communications. *Ibid.*, pp. 148–49. See Sumner, *Russia*, p. 352, for a discussion of this affair.

[252] Ignat'ev, IV, *137* (July 1914), 91; *139* (Jan. 1915), 33–34.

[253] *Ibid.*, pp. 32–33; Hasenkampf, *Dnevnik*, pp. 389–90. This telegram did not reach Adrianople until January 29.

CHAPTER VII

SERBDOM AND
SAN STEFANO

ON January 31, 1878, an armistice was signed at Adrianople ending hostilities between Russia and Turkey. Declared Namyk Pasha desperately, "Your arms are victorious, your ambition is satisfied, but Turkey is lost. We accept everything which you desire." [1] Included in the armistice were bases of peace by which the Porte promised independence to Montenegro, Rumania, and Serbia, and autonomy to a tributary Bulgaria. The insurgent provinces would receive "une administration autonome avec des garanties suffisantes." Whereas Serbia was guaranteed merely "une rectification de frontière," Bulgaria would comprise all areas with Bulgarian majorities, and in no case would its boundaries be less generous than those proposed at the Constantinople Conference. Montenegro would obtain an increase of territory equivalent to its wartime conquests; Rumania was promised "a sufficient territorial compensation." [2]

Signing the armistice, the grand duke ordered Belgrade and Cetinje to cease hostilities immediately. Serbian interests, he informed Milan, had been protected—independence and "des avantages territoriaux" were assured. For details of subsequent peace negotiations, the prince should correspond directly with St. Petersburg. [3] Prince Milan ordered

[1] Hasenkampf, *Dnevnik*, p. 390.

[2] G. Noradounghian, *Recueil d'actes internationaux de l'empire ottoman* (Paris, 1897–1903), *3*, 507–08; Sumner, *Russia*, pp. 625–26.

[3] AII, Ristić 19/327, Nikolai Nikolaevich to Milan, Jan. 19/31; 19/385, Jan. 20/Feb. 1, 1878; Grujić, *3*, 317–18.

the Serbian advance to cease on February 3. "I am particularly touched," he wrote the grand duke, "that the tsar has agreed to take the interests of Serbia under his powerful protection." And Prince Nikola, reassured by prospects of major territorial gains, unhesitatingly confided Montenegro's fate to Russia.[4]

Prelude to Peace

But in both Serbian states there was deep concern over imminent Russo-Turkish peace negotiations. Russia's vast strength, proclaimed *Istok* bravely, guarantees eventual satisfaction of Serbian demands. "With the support of powerful Russia we can calmly await the outcome."[5] But Kosta Ćukić, the Serbian envoy in Vienna, noting that Belgrade was unhappy with the formula, "correction of frontiers," warned that Europe could not afford a disgruntled Serbia.[6] Fearing Russia might repeat Napoleon III's actions at Villafranca,[7] *Zastava* cited reports that Austria would occupy Bosnia. The Slav peoples, it announced, had not fought for independence to become pawns of Austria and Russia. The tsar and the Powers must not interfere with creation of independent Slav states in the Balkans nor with the union of the insurgent provinces with Serbia and Montenegro. *Zastava* found the autonomy proposed for Bosnia and Hercegovina in the Russian bases of peace clearly inadequate and the territorial gains promised Serbia and Montenegro insufficient. "Such a peace cannot satisfy a single Serb." The people of the insurgent provinces would be robbed of their legitimate rights. Warned *Zastava*, "Russia won the East for itself as much with the strokes of the pen of diplomacy as with the sword. Under the influence of this great achievement, the Russians have forgotten one thing and that is to be equally just toward the eastern peoples. . . . Bosnia and Hercegovina could become Russia's Achilles heel."[8] Serbian dissatisfaction with the Treaty of San Stefano was foreshadowed.

---

[4] Skalon, *Moi vospominaniia*, p. 210; Bobrikov, *Zapiski*, p. 82.

[5] *Istok*, Jan. 27/Feb. 8, no. 11, lead.

[6] AII, Ristić 22/329, Ćukić to Ristić, Feb. 2/14.

[7] On July 11, 1859, Napoleon III had concluded with Austria the secret armistice of Villafranca which was most unfavorable to Piedmont's ambitions. The Italian National Society, however, encouraged revolutionary assemblies in central Italy to vote for annexation of their states to Piedmont, upsetting the arrangements of the Powers.

[8] *Zastava*, Feb. 5, 8, 10, 13, nos. 14, 16, 17, 18.

Montenegrins shared some of these doubts. While Prince Nikola sought Austrian and Russian support for his claims,[9] Stanko Radonić urged Montenegro's intimate collaboration with St. Petersburg and submission of its demands directly to the tsar. Although rejoicing that Ignat'ev and Nelidov, both pro-Montenegrin, had been named as Russian negotiators, Radonić warned that everything depended upon the instructions they received from St. Petersburg. "I fear strongly that Russia may seek maximum gains in Asia and give us very little just in order to conclude peace more easily." The Russian negotiators' good will must be obtained so that they would recommend maximum Montenegrin gains to St. Petersburg.[10]

In Russia the armistice pleased the ministers but angered the chauvinists. The sudden cessation of hostilities, asserted Ignat'ev with justification, undermined Russia's military position in the Balkans and reduced his chances of negotiating a successful treaty.[11] Exaggerating Russia's military victory, Katkov emphasized that with most of the Balkans controlled by her and her allies, never had Russia been so powerful. Russia, to isolate England, might permit the Austrians to occupy Bosnia, but should occupy Constantinople and dictate peace:

Russia alone was at war with Turkey; to her alone belongs the right to dispose of what was gained by her arms and blood. Russia, with the rights of the victor, can perhaps include in its peace conditions among others the cession of Bosnia and Hercegovina and then transfer them to Austria-Hungary. This means Austria would receive these provinces as a gift from Russia. . . .[12]

Encouraged by the nationalists' reckless exhortations to seize the Straits, the excited public grossly overestimated Russian strength and regretted that hostilities had ceased without a triumphant occupation of Constantinople.[13] Here was potent support for Ignat'ev.

Russian peace terms, though modified to meet Austrian objections,

---

[9] Nikola I to Emperor Franz Josef, Feb. 3/15, cited in Djordjević, *Crna Gora*, p. 427.

[10] OSVOb., *2*, no. 398, Radonić to Popović, Jan. 19/31.

[11] Ignat'ev, IV, *137* (July 1914), 93; *139* (March 1915), 747–49. The tsarevich, sharing the count's opinion of Grand Duke Nikolai Nikolaevich's ability, was equally displeased.

[12] Peredovykh, Feb. 1, 5, 8, 13, 27, nos. 19, 23, 26, 31, 44.

[13] *Russland vor und nach dem Kriege*, 2d ed. (Leipzig, 1879), pp. 372–73. On the public reaction to the armistice see OSVOb., *2*, Komarov to Mezentsov, Jan. 25/Feb. 6, no. 415.

were largely the work of Ignat'ev, now at the summit of his career. His "maximum" program, submitted to the tsar in mid-January, had called for a fully independent greater Bulgaria, major gains for Greece, large increases for the Serbian states (including division of Old Serbia and Novi Pazar sandjak between them), and Russian control of the Turkish Straits. Alexander had rejected this as too drastic to obtain Europe's approval.[14] Ignat'ev's "minimum," still demanding substantial cessions to the Serbian states, was approved by top Russian leaders almost without comments or objections.[15] Before the final draft of his instructions was prepared, Ignat'ev submitted some important questions to Gorchakov. Would the peace treaty be final or preliminary? If preliminary, the Powers should be allowed to examine only provisions altering previous European treaties. Should Serbia be restricted to a "correction of frontiers"? Could Montenegro be granted most of Hercegovina? [16]

Secret Austro-Russian correspondence had influenced the chancellor's response. On January 8, Emperor Franz Josef, predicting that the Ottoman Empire would not dissolve immediately, had objected to a large Bulgaria or autonomy for the insurgent provinces. If Russia demanded retrocession of southern Bessarabia, lost at the Treaty of Paris (1856), Austria-Hungary must annex Bosnia and Hercegovina.[17] Replying belatedly to the Russian peace proposals of December 9, 1877,[18] Andrassy warned that the Monarchy would consider final neither a Russo-Turkish treaty nor any *faits accomplis* it might contain.

---

[14] Ignat'ev, IV, *139* (Jan. 1915), 51.

[15] *Ibid.*, pp. 44–49; Miliutin, *Dnevnik, 3,* 11. Present at this meeting were the tsar, Miliutin, Gorchakov, Ignat'ev, Giers, and Jomini. According to this "minimum," the Montenegrin frontier would run from the confluence of the Piva and Tara rivers to the Lim River on the Serbian side and to the Drin and Bojana rivers on the Albanian side. Nikšić, Nevesinje, Stolac, Gacko, Spuž, Podgorica, and Žabljak would all go to Montenegro. To Serbia the Porte would cede the region along the Drina to its confluence with the Lim, then the boundary would extend along the Lim to Prijepolje, thence to the Morava River below Leskovac. Bosnia and Hercegovina would be organized according to the Powers' original proposal at the Constantinople Conference.

[16] Ignat'ev, IV, *139*, pp. 38–42.

[17] HHSA, Geheimakten I, rot 453, Franz Josef to Alexander II, Jan. 8. The kaiser affirmed "que le moment de la dissolution de l'Empire Ottoman n'est pas encore arrivé, et que par conséquent l'organisation de la presqu'île des Balkans ne pourra pas aboutir cette fois à un résultat définitif, tel que nous l'avions prévu à Reichstadt." The tsar's reaction to this letter was explosive: "Je suis outré. . . . C'est détestable." Miliutin, *Dnevnik, 2,* 260.

[18] See *supra*, pp. 237–38.

Only if Turkey collapsed would Vienna consent to an independent Bulgaria, and even then it would oppose a Russian occupation there once peace was concluded. Serbia's independence could be recognized, if Austrian commercial interests were protected, but the territorial gains of the Serbian states must be restricted:

We recall that our [Budapest] conventions foresaw the prospect of a territorial increase for Serbia only in case of the dissolution of the Ottoman Empire. We must state that in view of the general indignation provoked by the disloyal attitude of Serbia [by re-entering the war], it would be very difficult for us to get public opinion in Austria to accept an aggrandizement of that principality which would not be justified by the eventuality indicated above.

And barring Ottoman collapse, Montenegro's aggrandizement must not exceed limits set at the Constantinople Conference.[19]

Before receiving this chilling document, the tsar had made concessions to Franz Josef. Alexander did insist upon retrocession of southern Bessarabia, a unified autonomous Bulgaria, and indefinite Russian occupation of that country. But in return the Monarchy could eventually annex the insurgent provinces. After signing a preliminary peace with the Porte, Russia would submit for the Powers' approval all matters of general concern.[20] The Russians, regarding Bulgaria as the key to achievement of their aims in the Balkans, would make concessions at Serbdom's expense. Vienna and St. Petersburg still disagreed on many issues, but the latter had already begun to yield ground.

Therefore, in reply to Ignat'ev's questions, Chancellor Gorchakov emphasized the preliminary character of a Russo-Turkish peace. Montenegrin gains must be limited in the west to win Austrian approval—Ignat'ev should not claim for Cetinje the Nevesinje-Stolac regions of Hercegovina. Evading the question about the Serbian formula, the

[19] HHSA, Geheimakten I, rot 453, "Observations sur les Notices" (Jan. 1878); Andrassy to Langenau, Jan. 15, telegram no. 6. Significantly, at this time Andrassy did not preclude possible access to the sea for Montenegro, but he noted that in such case the Monarchy must obtain guarantees to prevent smuggling.

[20] Ibid., Alexander II to Emperor Franz Josef, Jan. 4/16. On Bosnia and Hercegovina the tsar declared, "En T'offrant la latitude d'occuper temporairement la Bosnie et l'Herzégovine, comme moi la Bulgarie, j'avais en vue de Te laisser le faculté de transformer plus tard cette occupation temporaire en une annexion; même après que Mes troupes auraient évacué la Bulgarie, si Tu trouvais nécessaire à Ta securité."

chancellor merely noted that proper instructions could be supplied later. The small Balkan states, since their independence had not yet been confirmed, could send envoys to defend their interests but would be barred from formal participation in the peace negotiations. Ignat'ev, altering his treaty draft accordingly, departed in great haste for Bucharest on January 25.[21]

Austro-Russian differences narrowed further after he left. On January 26, Emperor Franz Josef consented to an autonomous Bulgaria, occupied temporarily by Russia, within limits established by the Constantinople Conference, and retrocession of southern Bessarabia.[22] And Gorchakov, denying Russia intended to exclude other Powers from a final settlement, welcomed a future European conference.[23] He reminded Ignat'ev that the treaty with Turkey must be labeled preliminary.[24] To meet Austrian objections, Gorchakov (February 12) stated his terms more precisely: Russia desired "une Bulgarie entière, compacte, autonome et tributaire," but Austria could occupy the insurgent provinces and was guaranteed Russian support on that issue at a subsequent European conference. He ignored Bulgarian frontiers and territories to be ceded to the Serbian states.[25]

At Gorchakov's insistence, Ignat'ev stopped over in Bucharest (January 31–February 2) to "elucidate" Russian peace terms. Rumanian leaders, already disgruntled with Russia, were shocked by the count's blunt demand for retrocession of southern Bessarabia.[26] Indignant at

[21] Ignat'ev, IV, *139* (Jan. 1915), pp. 49–51. At the January 24 meeting at which the final draft was approved, only minor objections were raised. Afterward Gorchakov and Jomini supposedly declared, "C'est un chef d'oeuvre, un travail de bénédiction qui n'avait pu être rédigé que par un homme qui possédait entièrement dans son cerveau les archives orientales."

[22] HHSA, Geheimakten I, rot 453, Franz Josef to Alexander II, Jan. 14/26.

[23] *Ibid.*, Langenau to Andrassy, Jan. 29, telegram no. 7, and Jan. 30, Privatschreiben.

[24] Ignat'ev, IV, *139* (March 1915), pp. 765–69; OSVOb., *2*, no. 402, Jan. 20/Feb. 1. "In this situation," wrote Gorchakov, "it seems difficult to maintain integrally the program you drafted for the preliminary peace. Matters of European interest will be submitted to the conference."

[25] *Ibid.*, Gorchakov's memorandum to Ubri, Jan. 31/Feb. 12, no. 438. The same day in a dispatch to Shuvalov, the chancellor, calling the diplomatic situation "incontestablement grave," stressed the importance of maintaining Austro-Russian co-operation. *Ibid.*, no. 437.

[26] Hasenkampf, *Dnevnik*, pp. 469–70. Ignat'ev told Bratianu, "If you do not want to give it back, then we shall take it ourselves."

this demand, and at Ignat'ev's methods, Foreign Minister Kogalniceanu protested vehemently to St. Petersburg.[27] But Rumanian objections were fruitless and merely infuriated Russian nationalist opinion.[28]

Ignat'ev arriving in Adrianople on February 8, conferred with envoys of the Serbian states before negotiating with the Turks. For Montenegro, Radonić claimed western Hercegovina to the Narenta, the Lim River frontier, and a generous stretch of Adriatic coastline. Colonel Catargi presented Belgrade's claims, formulated during January. Serbia's principal political objective was independence.[29] As to territory, the Serbian cabinet had decided (January 15) to demand Old Serbia, Kosovo vilayet, the eastern part of Novi Pazar sandjak, Vidin, and Skoplje. Accompanied by maps and statistics, these claims had been communicated to Russian headquarters and St. Petersburg.[30] Ristić privately expressed confidence that Serbia would at least be allowed to retain territory its troops had occupied, and he hoped to obtain Višegrad (Bosnia) and the Lim frontier on the west.[31] Foreign consuls in Belgrade had reacted variously to these claims.[32] Concerned over its territorial aspirations, the Belgrade cabinet sent Milosav Protić to St. Petersburg to argue its case and discover Russian attitudes. Ristić

[27] Kogalniceanu to Ghika, Feb. 22/March 6 in Iorga, *Correspondance diplomatique roumaine*, no. 688.

[28] For example, see *Grazhdanin*, Feb. 9/21, no. 6, "Rossiia i Rumynia" which accused Bucharest of thanklessness and of becoming an anti-Russian western bastion.

[29] HHSA, Wrede to Andrassy, Jan. 3, no. 2; *Golos*, Jan. 5/17, no. 5, report from Vienna to *Politische Correspondenz;* AII, Ristić 19/254, Milan to Ristić, Jan. 5/17; 19/287, Kogalniceanu to Milan, Jan. 12/24. Earlier Belgrade raised the issue of a Serbian kingdom but dropped it when Prince Charles of Rumania abandoned his claim to kingship. Of the foreign consuls, only pro-Serbian Joannini of Italy backed Milan's aspirations to a kingly title.

[30] *Ibid.*, 19/253, 254, (Ristić) to Milan, Jan. 3/15, 4/16, and Milan to Ristić, Jan. 5/17. Catargi was instructed on January 17 to press these Serbian claims at headquarters. Grujić, 3, 313-15.

[31] HHSA, Wrede to Andrassy, Jan. 26, no. 5. Farther reaching were the claims made by Metropolitan Mihailo. To be stable and prosperous, he argued, Serbia in the east must attain its "natural frontiers," the Isker and Struma rivers, including in Serbia territory almost to the city of Sofia. ROBibLen, f. Popova, Mihailo to Popov, Jan. 17/29.

[32] None of the consuls objected to Serbian independence. Only White of England disputed Belgrade's claims to Old Serbia, and the Austrian and German consuls gave strong unofficial encouragement to Ristić. Persiani of Russia, refusing to commit himself on Serbian territorial claims, told Wrede that some of their hopes might be disappointed. Joannini encouraged the Serbs in their "chauvinistic beliefs." HHSA, Wrede to Andrassy, Jan. 26, no. 5.

instructed him to advocate autonomy for the insurgent provinces to prevent their annexation to Austria-Hungary.[33]

Ignat'ev, though supporting some of the Serbian and Montenegrin demands (he had recommended most of these same increases in his "maximum"), hastened to dash the envoys' more extravagant hopes. Because of Austrian opposition, Montenegro could not obtain much of Hercegovina, and its claims to Skutari and north Albanian territory would provoke conflict with the Albanians supported by Italy and Austria. Otherwise, he would seek to satisfy Cetinje.[34] The count reminded Catargi that initially Prince Milan had disregarded Russian advice to re-enter the war. Joining it belatedly, Serbia then had failed to take decisive action, merely following Russian forces, and had not occupied all of Old Serbia. If the Serbs had seized that region and part of Bosnia, his chances of obtaining a sizable increase for them would be greater. The Turks, warned Ignat'ev, would resist territorial cessions to a country which had "'acted very badly" toward them. As to Vidin, since Serbian and Rumanian claims conflicted and its population was largely Bulgarian, he would seek its inclusion in Bulgaria. Ignat'ev agreed to back annexation of Niš and its environs to Serbia, but he evaded Catargi's other demands.[35] Extremely irritated at the Russian's overbearing manner, Catargi accused him of insulting Rumanians and Serbs, alienating them from Russia by disdain for their national aspirations.[36]

Describing to Gorchakov his meetings with the envoys, Ignat'ev urged again that the centers of the Hercegovina insurrection (Nevesinje-Stolac) be granted to Montenegro despite Austrian objections. The Powers, he argued, had no right to restrict Serbian and Montenegrin gains secured by Russia. Ignat'ev did not recommend major Serbian acquisitions in the east, although he declared: "The annexation of Niš to Serbia I consider wholly justified because of the proximity of the city to the Serbian frontier and because of its capture by the Serbian armies." Telegraphed Gorchakov (February 14): Do whatever is possible for Montenegro, but "because of Austria-Hungary, it is essential

---

[33] *Ibid.*, Feb. 7, no. 12; Grujić, *3*, 316–17; Ristić, *2*, 111.

[34] Ignat'ev, IV, *140* (April 1915), 50.   [35] *Ibid.*, pp. 49–50.

[36] When Catargi noted the major territorial gains claimed by Montenegro in comparison to Serbia, Ignat'ev exclaimed, "Montenegro is another matter. It fought for three straight years, and you? In 1876 you were beaten into the dust, and now you fought some two months almost without having an enemy against you." Hasenkampf, *Dnevnik*, pp. 469–72; Skalon, *Moi vospominaniia*, p. 270.

to avoid extension of Montenegro on the Hercegovina side." Without mentioning Serbia, the chancellor intimated he adhered to the formula, "correction of frontiers," which would merely permit it to acquire Niš. "Especially adhere stubbornly to everything that affects Bulgaria," he ordered, "and hasten peace negotiations so as to confront the Powers with a maximum number of *faits accomplis*." [37] Gorchakov shared Ignat'ev's preference for Bulgaria and Montenegro over Serbia. For his part, Ignat'ev realized he could not fully satisfy the Serbian states: "No matter what concessions we may succeed in extracting from the Turks for the principalities [he wrote Gorchakov, February 15] we can be sure in advance that they will invariably appear insufficient and will not correspond to the hopes and longings of our present allies." [38]

The Serbian States and Russo-Turkish Negotiations

After Safvet Pasha, Turkey's senior envoy, arrived in Adrianople on February 12, peace negotiations began. Ignat'ev, to avoid "unpleasantness" and "irritating explanations," kept the South Slav envoys ignorant of their progress. Such secrecy produced alarming rumors. The Russians, reported Catargi, wish the Porte to cede Niš to Bulgaria and compensate Serbia with Novi Pazar. Deeply concerned, Belgrade dispatched Colonel M. Lješanin to Adrianople. [39] A later Catargi telegram (February 18) allayed Ristić's fears: Niš had been assigned to Serbia, but very little territory would accompany it. [40] Nonetheless, Catargi was instructed to reaffirm Serbian territorial claims and delay settlement of the frontiers until Lješanin arrived. [41]

Colonel Lješanin bore letters from Milan to Ignat'ev and the grand duke. It would be most unjust, declared the prince, to include Kosovo vilayet, and especially Niš, in Bulgaria. Serbia required it for economic development, and it belonged ethnically and historically to the Serbian

[37] Ignat'ev, IV, *139* (Jan. 1915), pp. 58, 62; OSVOb., *2*, nos. 443–45.

[38] Ignat'ev, *139* (Jan. 1915), p. 51.

[39] AII, Ristić 19/349, (Ristić) to Milojković, Feb. 2/14; Grujić, *3*, 317; Ristić, *2*, 113–14.

[40] AII, Ristić 22/321, Catargi to (Ristić?), Feb. 6/18; "La Serbie au Congrès de Berlin," *Revue d'histoire diplomatique*, *5* (1891), p. 484. At one point, according to Ristić, Ignat'ev proposed drawing the frontier two miles from the walls of Niš.

[41] AII, Ristić 19/352, Ristić to Milan, Feb. 7/19. Ristić hoped this would insure for Serbia its minimum territorial objectives in the east, i.e., a frontier from Sveti Nikola via Caribrod and Grdelica and including Ak Palanka and Vlasotinac inside Serbia.

people. The Bulgarians, who had contributed only passive suffering to the Slav cause, would obtain a state extending from the walls of Constantinople to the frontiers of Serbia. Could the Serbs, after sacrificing so much blood and treasure, be deprived of Niš, "a fortress which is indispensable for the defense of our frontier on the southeast and whose Christian population is purely Serbian?" Other Powers might oppose Serbia's annexation of Bosnia, but cession of Kosovo vilayet was fully compatible with a "correction of frontiers." Continued Milan poignantly, "Bosnia and Hercegovina separated from their motherland, Old Serbia mutilated and even our *status quo militaire* in Old Serbia destined to serve Bulgarian interests—that, Your Excellency, is the sad prospect which opens before the Serbian nation despite the heroic struggle, despite unparalleled sacrifices!" Russia must satisfy various interests, but what danger or inconvenience could result from augmenting Serbia's population by a few hundred thousand persons? If Niš were not included in Serbia, concluded the prince, he and his people would be gravely antagonized.[42]

Delivering this message to the Russians (February 22), Lješanin and Catargi reiterated Belgrade's maximum territorial demands.[43] Serbia would not abandon Niš even to Russian threats of force. "We know in advance that the outcome of such a conflict would be unsatisfactory [for Serbia], but the world would glimpse a spectacle unusual between allies." [44] Thus Belgrade was prepared for a breach with Russia and an appeal to world opinion against her. Ascribing some success to Lješanin's efforts, Ristić asserted that the Colonel's *démarche* and the tsar's personal intervention preserved Niš for Serbia. Ignat'ev, concluded Ristić inaccurately, was unconditionally pro-Bulgarian.[45]

Lješanin reported serious disagreement at Russian headquarters over terms to be demanded of the Porte. Nelidov, reflecting the Foreign Ministry's fear of diplomatic isolation, advocated major concessions to Austro-British pressure. "We are doing our best," telegraphed Catargi and Lješanin, "but it is hard to repair what Nelidov has spoiled—he is a

[42] *Ibid.*, 22/498, (Milan) to Ignat'ev, Feb. 2/14. The rough draft is in Ristić's writing with corrections by Milan.

[43] AII, Ristić 22/323. These claims included Višegrad, Nova Varoš, Sjenica, Prijepolje, Novi Pazar, Kosovo, Vranje, Leskovac, Niš, Ak Palanka, Pirot, and Trn. Feb. 16/28, (Milan?) to Ristić.

[44] Ristić, 2, 120; W. Georgewitsch, *Die serbische Frage* (Stuttgart, 1909), p. 51.

[45] *Revue d'histoire diplomatique* (1891), p. 484; C. Busch, "Die Botschafter Konferenz . . . ," *Deutsche Rundschau*, 141 (1909), 368; Ristić, 2, 121.

powerful enemy who does us much harm." Prince Cherkasskii's group, on the other hand, favored reckless exploitation of Russia's victories in behalf of Bulgaria; it was he who wished to hand Niš to the Bulgarians. Ignat'ev, while accepting some of Cherkasskii's views, wavered between the two factions.[46]

Indeed, Ignat'ev had already decided to demand Niš for Serbia, but otherwise he reacted negatively to Lješanin's *démarche*. He would study the Serbian claims carefully, though they appeared exaggerated. Ignat'ev argued that Belgrade's demand for the entire Kosovo vilayet, promised to Bulgaria by the Constantinople Conference, revealed an unfortunate antagonism toward Bulgaria. Serbo-Bulgarian disputes over the Kosovo area could be settled later by negotiation under Russian supervision. This was a Slav family quarrel in which neither Turkey nor the Powers should interfere. The angry Lješanin was given statistical data proving to Ignat'ev's satisfaction that Kosovo vilayet, except for Niš, was predominantly Bulgarian. Besides, argued Ignat'ev, he had already given the Turks a map of Russia's proposed Serbo-Bulgarian frontier, and Safvet Pasha had declared that the Porte would cede no territory to Serbia. The Turks of Novi Pazar would fight rather than be annexed to Serbia. Ignat'ev added that the tsar took these Turkish objections seriously. Only if Serbia remained a vassal of the Porte, might she obtain greater territorial concessions.[47]

Besides Turkish anger, Ignat'ev believed that the main obstacle to satisfaction of Serbian aspirations was the phrase, "correction of frontiers." For this restrictive formula he unfairly blamed Grand Duke Nikolai Nikolaevich:

It was obvious with the opening of hostilities by the Serbs, especially after the capture of Niš by them and the occupation of Turkish territory, as well as the victorious advance of our army to Adrianople, that preliminary conditions of the armistice should have been more severe for the Turks and more favorable to our allies than immediately after the fall of Plevna. But General Headquarters, unfortunately, lost sight of this and unquestionably committed a major and irrevocable mistake in demanding not the aggrandizement [*uvelichenie*] of Serbia but merely a correction [*ispravlenie*] of frontiers.[48]

46 *Ibid.*, HHSA, Wrede to Andrassy, March 22, no. 30.

47 AII, Ristić 22/323, (Catargi) to Ristić, Feb. 16/28, telegram; Ristić, *2*, 120; Ignat'ev, IV, *141* (July 1915), 49.

48 *Ibid.*, p. 44.

The narrower formula had been employed in both Nelidov's and Ignat'ev's December peace proposals.[49] But the grand duke, impressed by Serbian military successes, had telegraphed St. Petersburg (January 14) requesting alteration of his instructions for the peace preliminaries to "an increase of territory" for Serbia. But that very day Alexander II informed him that his instructions would remain unchanged. Gorchakov subsequently confirmed this decision.[50] Austrian pressure upon St. Petersburg, not an oversight by the grand duke, was responsible for the formula which reduced Serbia's gains at San Stefano and contributed to her alienation from Russia.

To explain his failure to satisfy Serbian desires, Ignat'ev emphasized Austrian intrigues and Turkish stubbornness. The Serbs seemed unaware, he reported, that Constantinople and Vienna were selfishly seeking to foment discord among the South Slavs. Only renewal of hostilities would induce the Porte to yield to Belgrade's demands. Anyway, he questioned whether Serbia had earned major territorial acquisitions:

Since now there is no question of the dissolution of the Ottoman Empire, we can obtain territorial compensation [for Serbia] only on the basis of those sacrifices borne by Serbia in the present war and the recognition by the Porte of her full independence. . . . Thus will be accomplished the first and significant step toward the creation in the future of "Greater Serbia," whose achievement I for my part would like to see subsequently.[51]

Ignat'ev posed again as the staunch defender of Serbian interests, hampered only by headquarters' errors and St. Petersburg's regrettable pusillanimity.

Belgrade's hopes that Protić's mission in St. Petersburg might win official Russian favor were disappointed. The top Russian leaders' acceptance of the Order of Takovo, Serbia's chief military decoration, heartened the Serbs as it suggested St. Petersburg's continuing friendship. Rejoicing prematurely over this trifle, Prince Milan wrote the tsar: Serbia "has just obtained, thanks to Your paternal solicitude, its independence and territorial advantages."[52] In the Russian capital,

---

[49] *Supra*, pp. 237–38.

[50] Hasenkampf, *Dnevnik*, pp. 318, 323. Gorchakov telegraphed Ignat'ev (Feb. 7/19): "Adhere to the instructions you brought with you." OSVOb., 2, no. 456, p. 503.

[51] Ignat'ev to Gorchakov, Feb. 26, in Ignat'ev, IV, *140* (April 1915), 47–48.

[52] AII, Ristić, 19/351, Milan to Ristić, Feb. 7/19; 22/396, (Milan) to Alexander II, Feb. 13/25, rough draft.

however, Protić found himself in a false position, since Persiani had reported that he had no political mission. After urging Serbian claims, Protić concluded that Russian leaders were definitely pro-Bulgarian.[53] Jomini warned that unless the Dual Monarchy occupied all of Bosnia and Hercegovina, Serbia could expect only minor gains. Slavdom, argued Protić, requires a strong Serbia to withstand Austrian pressure; Bulgaria cannot perform this vital function. But in St. Petersburg most of Old Serbia, reported the envoy, was known as "Bulgaria." Giers, though distressed at this, was powerless. Protić concluded sadly, "Russia, unfortunately for her, is not seeking to secure Bulgaria from the Turks, but purely to guarantee it from Serbia and the Serbian nationality; Serbian interests are in danger."[54] Giers assured the Austrian ambassador, even before frontiers had been finally determined, that Serbia would obtain no Bosnian territory. Protić's mission won no tangible advantages for Belgrade.[55]

Montenegrin frontiers at first caused little trouble. On February 19, Safvet and Ignat'ev reached agreement on all articles of the treaty pertaining to Montenegro. Unlike his impassioned objections to a large Bulgaria and territorial increases for Serbia, Safvet revealed surprising willingness to make major concessions to the Black Mountain. Ignat'ev ascribed this to Montenegrin valor and the Turks' conviction that Cetinje was indissolubly bound to Russia. To Gorchakov he reported that considerable territory in Hercegovina and a seacoast had been obtained for Montenegro. "We have just signed articles with Safvet on Montenegro," telegraphed Ignat'ev. "The boundary line is drawn according to my plan, approved in St. Petersburg." But the next day (February 20) Safvet recollected that he was not authorized to cede Podgorica or a seacoast. Unless he withdrew his concessions, the Porte would repudiate him. The Russians then agreed to allow a European delimitation commission subsequently to make "modifications" on the spot that it considered necessary and fair to both parties. This formula, pointed out Ignat'ev, satisfied some of Safvet's objections while assuring to Montenegro possession almost intact of the frontiers he had assigned to her. Gorchakov instructed Ignat'ev not to insist upon

[53] *Ibid.*, 22/259, Protić to Ristić, Feb. 8/20, telegram.

[54] *Ibid.*, 19/357, (Ristić) to Milan, Feb. 15/27, citing an undated report from Protić; 22/?, Protić to Ristić, March 2/14.

[55] *Ibid.*, 22/260, Feb. 17/March 1; HHSA, Langenau to Andrassy, March 3, telegram no. 40.

major Montenegrin gains in Hercegovina because of Vienna's attitude. Even with these reductions, Montenegro would be roughly tripled in size.[56]

Progress had been made on Montenegro's western boundaries, but the thorny issues of the Serbo-Bulgarian and Serbo-Montenegrin frontiers remained. When Safvet stalled, the Russians insisted headquarters be moved closer to Constantinople. The Porte bowed reluctantly to this ultimatum, and on February 23 the grand duke's forces advanced to San Stefano, two hours' march from the city. This step, largely a response to Ignat'ev's advice, was designed to overcome Turkish recalcitrance on South Slav frontiers and produce a treaty by March 3, the anniversary of Alexander II's accession to the throne. In San Stefano, Russo-Turkish negotiations were resumed and unresolved issues settled.[57]

Bolstered by the army's advance, Ignat'ev, despite Turkish opposition, won acceptance of most of his Bulgarian program. Though yielding Salonika at the chancellor's request (February 28), he rejected categorically a Turkish proposal to submit Bulgarian frontiers to a special mixed commission after signature of a preliminary treaty.[58] Ignat'ev secured for Bulgaria an Aegean seacoast and most of the region conquered by Serbian armies during the war. Pirot, Trn, and Vranje, and most of Macedonia were to be included in his big Bulgaria.[59]

Russian proposals to reorganize the administration of Bosnia and Hercegovina and to cede some of its territory to the Serbian states was opposed strongly by the Turks,[60] who wished to limit concessions to those proposed by the Constantinople Conference and the London Protocol. The Russian delegates reported: "We succeeded in maintain-

---

[56] Ignat'ev, IV, *140* (May 1915), 407–08, 419–20, 424; Ristić 19/54, Feb. 10/22; OSVOb., *2*, nos. 474, 475, Ignat'ev and Nelidov to Gorchakov, Feb. 14/26, nos. 1, 2; Sumner, pp. 412–13.

[57] Ignat'ev, IV, *140* (June 1915), pp. 773ff.; Sumner, *Russia*, pp. 386–87.

[58] OSVOb., *2*, no. 478, Ignat'ev and Nelidov to Gorchakov, Feb. 15/27, no. 13.

[59] *Ibid.*, no. 492, Memorandum of Ignat'ev, March 1878; Ignat'ev, IV, *141* (July 1915), 40; (Aug. 1915), 364. According to Novikov, "as for the Bulgarian frontiers, we have chosen the principle of the majority of the population." This ethnographic concept, retorted Andrassy, is "le moins heureusement choisi" for purposes of delimiting frontiers. OSVOb., *2*, no. 479, Novikov to Gorchakov, Feb. 15/27.

[60] Sadullah Bey had finally taken his place as second Turkish delegate, replacing Sadyk Pasha, who had declined that dubious honor. OSVOb., *2*, no. 474, Ignat'ev and Nelidov to Gorchakov, Feb. 14/26.

ing for Bosnia and Hercegovina our original demands . . . [for full autonomy]." [61] As to frontiers, Ignat'ev failed to obtain the Lim boundary, partitioning the "Enclave" between Serbia and Montenegro. To join the Serbian states, objected the Turks, would isolate Bosnia and Hercegovina from the rest of the Ottoman Empire, place in Serbian hands strategic towns (Novi Pazar, Sjenica, and Mitrovica) they had not captured, and assure to Serbia control of the proposed Mitrovica-Salonika rail route. The bases of peace mentioned merely a correction of Serbia's frontiers. Turkish national honor would not permit abandonment of unconquered territory to a country which had entered the war following the Porte's defeat. In 1876, only a Russian ultimatum had saved Serbia from just punishment. It was amazing that Russia could assist such a treacherous country. Though unconverted by this flood of rhetoric, Ignat'ev and Nelidov feared that insistence upon their original boundary proposal might foster Austro-Turkish rapprochement and embroil Russia with Vienna.[62]

To break the deadlock over frontiers, the Russians proposed that the Turks retain a corridor through the "Enclave," fifteen to twenty-five kilometers wide, containing the military highway and railroad route. This would guarantee Turkish communications with Bosnia and Hercegovina and separate the Serbian states, though it would leave heights overlooking the corridor to Serbia and Montenegro. Such a solution, confided Ignat'ev, would enable them to dominate the corridor and eventually the insurgent provinces as well but deprive Austria of a pretext to occupy the latter. A tract of land in the Morava valley equivalent to its losses in the corridor would compensate Serbia. On February 28 came the showdown on this new frontier proposal. Mehemed Ali of the Turkish general staff, joining the debate without authorization, sought to expand the corridor and limit Bulgarian boundaries to those of the Constantinople Conference. In response, the Russians staged a walkout and urged the grand duke to end Turkish stubbornness by advancing to the Bosphorus; however, Nikolai Nikolaevich persuaded the shaken Turks to accept Ignat'ev's compromise

---

[61] *Ibid.*, no. 493, Feb. 21/March 5, no. 3.

[62] *Ibid.; ibid.*, no. 486, Ignat'ev to Gorchakov, Feb. 17/March 1, telegram. "Afin de vaincre résistance turque, accélérer la paix et éviter difficultés avec l'Autriche, j'ai du renoncer rendre Montenegro absolument limitrophe avec Serbie"; no. 487, Feb. 18/March 2, no. 15; Ignat'ev, IV, *141* (July 1915), 44–45. Catargi generally confirms Ignat'ev's account of these negotiations. AII, Ristić 22/322, Catargi to Ristić, Feb. 13/25, 19/54, (Catargi and Lješanin) to (Ristić), Feb. 15/27.

proposal unconditionally. The last obstacle to signature of the Treaty of San Stefano had been cleared away.[63]

The Treaty and Initial Reactions

The Treaty of San Stefano, though destined never to be executed, had far-reaching effects upon the South Slavs and their relationship with Russia. Satisfying most of Montenegro's legitimate aspirations, Ignat'ev's treaty, intentionally or not, antagonized Serbia and Rumania. The Bulgarians were jubilant while Bosnians and Hercegovinians were disappointed and worried about the future. Unequal treatment of the Balkan peoples at San Stefano intensified their rivalries and began their alienation from Russia.

The treaty granted Serbia independence but only a fraction of its territorial demands. On the Bosnian side, where expansion was blocked by Austria, only the villages of Mali Zvornik and Zakar were obtained. Turkish resistance, reinforced by Vienna, had reduced Serbia's share of the "Enclave." To the southeast, where the Serbs claimed the entire *vilayet* (province) of Kosovo, San Stefano assigned them only four of its *kazas* (counties) (Kuršumlje, Prokoplje, Niš, and Leskovac). Since it seemed earlier that the whole vilayet would go to Bulgaria, this represented a partial success for Serbia. The remaining kazas (Topolnica, Pirot, Vranje, and Trn), though largely occupied by Serbian troops, were to be Bulgarian. Areas outside the new frontiers were to be evacuated by Serbian troops within fifteen days of the signature of the treaty.[64]

Montenegro was treated much more generously. Its independence was recognized. On the Hercegovina side, although its maximum claims were blocked and Ignat'ev had abandoned the Nevesinje area, the Black Mountain scored major gains: Gačko, Bilek, Nikšić, and the Duga Pass. These would give Cetinje great leverage in Hercegovina. To the northeast most of Novi Pazar sandjak would be obtained giving Montenegro a Drina frontier whence it could influence Bosnia. Substantial acquisitions in the southeast (including Spuž, Podgorica, and Žabljak) would shield the country from Turkish invasion. A substantial

---

[63] OSVOb., 2, no. 489, Ignat'ev to Gorchakov, Feb. 19/March 3; Ignat'ev, IV, *142* (Aug. 1915), 365–70; Hasenkampf, *Dnevnik*, pp. 472–74. Hasenkampf also generally corroborates Ignat'ev's account.

[64] For the text of San Stefano see Noradounghian, *Recueil d'actes, 3*, 509–21. Ignat'ev, IV, *142* (Oct. 1915), 67–69.

coastline, including the ports of Bar, Spić, and Ulcinj, would extend its control to the Bojana River. If San Stefano were executed, Montenegro would be increased threefold, opened to foreign trade, and obtain greater influence in Bosnia and Hercegovina.[65]

Anxious to speed the treaty's execution, Ignat'ev received the envoys of the Serbian states, informed their governments of the peace terms, and provided them with copies of pertinent articles and maps of their proposed frontiers. The count met a negative response from the Serbs:

It cost me considerable effort to make reasonable the representatives of Prince Milan. It was necessary to exhaust all possible arguments to convince them that it had been impossible to acquire for Serbia, at the present moment, more than we obtained in the preliminary treaty. Convinced at last that we had obtained the largest concessions possible under present circumstances, Catargi and Lješanin, however, did not conceal from me that Serbia could not consider itself satisfied unless Austria fails to occupy Bosnia and Hercegovina; if that occupation takes place, then the principality reserves the right to claim additional aggrandizement in Old Serbia.

Radonić, on the other hand, expressed full satisfaction, but since three quarters of the promised territory was in Turkish hands, he expressed concern about its transfer to Montenegro. Both Prince Nikola and A. S. Ionin congratulated Ignat'ev warmly for his efforts at San Stefano.[66]

Official Belgrade's initial reaction was ambivalent. Ristić commented moderately to Catargi:

We were pleased that Niš was assured to us but were dismayed that Pirot and Vranje . . . will not remain to us. I believe that those towns, as well as the rest of Old Serbia which they assign to Bulgaria, will always constitute sore points in our future relations with Bulgaria. The arrangement in that regard is of a nature to inspire fears for the future. Otherwise, it is satisfactory . . . since the extent of territory is greater than originally agreed upon at Adrianople.[67]

[65] *Shornik dogovorov Rossii*, pp. 159–61.

[66] Ignat'ev, IV, *142* (Sept. 1959), pp. 736–37; OSVOb., *2*, no. 495, Ignat'ev to Gorchakov, Feb. 25/March 9.

[67] AII, Ristić 19/108, Ristić to Catargi, March 8/20, draft. After conclusion of the more favorable Berlin Treaty, however, Ristić told the Assembly that Serbia could not rejoice over San Stefano and had been alienated by inadequate territorial compensation in the east. Ever since establishment of the Bulgarian Exarchate (1870), Russia had supported Bulgarian territorial claims, and at San Stefano its attitude toward Serbia had been most unfriendly. "La Serbie . . . ," p. 484; Ristić, *2*, 142–44; Busch, *Deutsche Rundschau, 141*, 368.

But the cabinet, Wrede had reported earlier, would not be content with minor border rectifications.[68] The Council of Ministers resolved unanimously that until a mixed commission delimited the frontier and the Turks withdrew from areas assigned to Serbia, no territory would be evacuated.[69] And in St. Petersburg, Protić claimed an Aegean port for Serbia and told Russian leaders that it was entitled to all lands occupied by its troops and could be expelled by force alone.[70]

Until late March, when San Stefano's terms became known, the Serbian public relied upon Russian support to acquire all of Old Serbia. If most of that province went to Bulgaria, reported F. Georgievič from Belgrade, it would be a more severe blow to Serbdom than the defeat at Kosovo.[71] According to *Istok,* all areas of Old Serbia and most areas of Macedonia contained Serbian majorities.[72] *Istok* hinted that in return for Russia's backing, Serbia would fight loyally at her side should she become involved in war with England or Austria. "Serbia and Russia are indissolubly bound," proclaimed the newspaper. The tsar and the Russian people, aware of Serbia's vast services, would surely reward her:

We have no reasons to doubt that Russia will fulfill her word. . . . We still do not know whether we shall obtain all of Old Serbia or just the territory occupied by our troops, but so much is sure that over the bastions of Niš, the Serbian banner will continue to wave. . . . Thus the fears of Serbian patriots are unjustified. . . . The only thing which could worry us would be excessive extension of Bulgaria which would be, frankly, *undeserved.*[73]

Russia would make no concessions at the expense of the liberated Slavs, concluded *Istok.* "Such a Russia is our ideal." [74]

After such high hopes, disillusionment was severe when the territorial provisions were made public. Shackled by censorship, *Istok* could

[68] HHSA, Wrede to Andrassy, Feb. 11, no. 15.
[69] Grujić, *3,* 318–19; AII, Ristić 22/457, Milan to Ristić, n.d., citing a telegram from Catargi of March 10.
[70] *Ibid.,* Protić to Ristić, March 2/14 and 22/282, April 5/17.
[71] *Russkii Mir,* Feb. 19/March 3, no. 48, report from Belgrade of Feb. 8/20. In 1389, the Serbs were overwhelmingly defeated by the Turkish invaders on the plains of Kosovo.
[72] *Istok,* Feb. 10/22, no. 16, p. 4, "Spisak stanovništva u Staroj Srbiji." The pashaliks of Skoplje, Bitolja, Solun (Salonika), Seres, and Kastorija were said to contain Serbian majorities.
[73] *Ibid.,* Feb. 5/17, 15/27 and Feb. 19/March 3, nos. 14, 18, 20.
[74] *Ibid.,* Feb. 24/March 8, no. 22.

merely declare that "as far as Serbia and Montenegro are concerned, their demands cannot be considered accomplished." [75] *Zastava*, less inhibited, at first could not decide whom to blame—Austria or Russia —for the outcome. It hailed the creation of a big Bulgaria but deplored San Stefano's treatment of the insurgent provinces:

The point of departure in the Eastern Question was that Bosnia and Hercegovina should go to Serbia and Montenegro, but this question remains unsettled since they are only to acquire administrative autonomy. . . . For the sake of Austria, Russia was compelled to deal thus with the Serbian question. Serbs, Bosnians, and Hercegovinians will remember this. San Stefano is the best proof that it is precisely Austria-Hungary which is to blame that only a partial solution was achieved by this peace which contains the germs of further bloody complications . . .[76]

Two days earlier, warning that disunity imperiled the Serbs' future, *Zastava* noted their unfortunate position: "Between the Bulgars and the Croats, or better between Russia and Austria-Hungary, the Serbs must abandon land in the east for the sake of Slav brotherhood and in the west because of some higher political considerations." It pointed an accusing finger at Russia: "We see the Bulgarian people, supported by Russian bayonets and directed by Russian statesmen anxious by means of Bulgaria to achieve Pan-Russian aims . . . seizing that area which by geography and ethnic position belongs to Serbia." But the newspaper ended with an appeal to Russia to remain loyal to its maxim of Slav equality.[77] *Zastava's* editors still hoped Russia would treat the Serbs fairly.

In Serbia popular dissatisfaction with the treaty and the Russians, unable to find adequate outlet in the press, was expressed more strongly in private conversation. According to Jovanović, "our indignation against the Russians after San Stefano was indescribable." Some Serbs characterized Russian policy from beginning to end of the Eastern Crisis as perfidious and insincere. There was a growing conviction that Russia had used the Serbs to create a big Bulgaria and was now discarding them.[78] Noting this unhappy public mood, F. Georgiević, a

[75] *Ibid.*, March 15/27, no. 30. No evidence of such Montenegrin dissatisfaction could be discovered.

[76] *Zastava*, March 12/24, no. 40, "Sveti Stevanski mir."

[77] *Ibid.*, March 10/22, no. 39, "O Slavenskoj, naročito južnoj, solidarnosti."

[78] Vlada Milana, *1*, 412–15. Another writer comments, "It is well known that Serbian public opinion was deeply dissatisfied with the San Stefano Treaty,

profoundly Russophile Serb, sought rather lamely to combat it in order to reassure Russian readers:

To be sure, in view of her vast sacrifices, the rewards in a material sense [of the treaty] cannot satisfy her [Serbia]. But since our aim was much loftier and more moral: to free our brethren, we Serbs can glance happily into the future as members of a great Slav family. . . . Those foreigners who say that Serbia is dissatisfied with the present peace are bitterly mistaken, as are those who claim that the inadequacy of territorial compensation will lead to our alienation from Russia and to mutual hostility and discord.[79]

Within a few months he would have to swallow these words!

Rather then engage in fruitless recriminations with St. Petersburg, the Serbian government simply refused to execute the treaty until the Turks did. Ristić instructed the Serbian chief of staff to retain control of regions occupied by the army until the Porte evacuated areas such as Novi Pazar, designated for Serbia. Ignat'ev's exhortations were in vain. When he urged Belgrade to expel the Turks forcibly if necessary, Ristić retorted that the Russians had concluded the treaty, let them insure its execution. To General Protić he explained:

In my view we could, if the Russians insist, retire back across the Timok but not abandon Trn, Vranje, or Pirot. That entire area should be retained as a pledge for the acquisition of the territory which is to belong to us but is not yet in our hands. Compliance [with Ignat'ev's demands] could be very injurious to us, while a firm stand nowise, since we won those areas with our blood.[80]

To guard its national interests, Belgrade would not hesitate to flout Russian wishes.

The Slavs of Bosnia and Hercegovina also reacted negatively to San Stefano. In Dubrovnik, refugees from Hercegovina expressed dismay that Russia was leaving their homeland in suffering and insecurity when it desired annexation to Montenegro. They resolved firmly not

---

especially with the frontiers of the new Bulgaria." L. J. Aleksić, "Srpska štampa . . . 1875–1878," *Istoriski Glasnik*, 3–4 (1953), 75. The creation of a big Bulgaria, asserted Matija Ban, delivered the first and hardest blow to the Balkan peoples' confidence in Russia and enabled other powers to undermine Russian influence in the peninsula. Ban 19/1, "1877 god."

[79] *Russkii Mir*, March 22/April 3, no. 78, report from Belgrade, n.d.

[80] Ristić to Kosta Protić, March 8/20, cited in B. Petrović, *Jovan Ristić*, pp. 60–61.

to submit to an Austrian occupation.[81] Bosnian insurgents, true to their dream of joining Serbia, were dissatisfied with autonomy and feared occupation by the Dual Monarchy. To the Croats of Zagreb they declared:

Bosnia and Hercegovina rose not to have the crown of Zvonimir thrust upon them but for freedom. We did not make such sacrifices to prepare the way for Austrian annexation but to join with Serbia and Montenegro or to form a separate independent state. We want occupation or annexation by Serbia and Montenegro because they have the same language, customs, and more guarantees of progress. . . .[82]

To counter disillusionment with Russian policy among his countrymen, that loyal Pan-Slav, Mileta Despotović, assured them that only international obligations had prevented Russia from imposing the solution they desired; they must retain faith in the Russians: "I am completely convinced that the Tsar Liberator in this respect did everything that circumstances allowed. . . . Bosnians! Be patient, have faith, be thankful for the benefits obtained for us, since you can be sure that the time is not far off when we will achieve our goal." [83] Indeed, patience was the insurgents' only recourse.

Despite some regret at shabby treatment of Serbia, official Russia rejoiced over San Stefano. The emperor, though happy with the treaty, shared Miliutin's fears that war with an Anglo-Austrian coalition might well result from it.[84] Greater Bulgaria, asserted Gorchakov with an uneasy glance toward Vienna, was the work of the Constantinople Conference, not San Stefano. Giers and Jomini, more concerned than their chief about Serbia's displeasure, assured Protić that only Austrian objections had prevented Russia from backing Serbian claims to Bosnia.[85] Ignat'ev asserted that the treaty represented the fairest settlement possible under the circumstances. The Lim frontier had been abandoned because of Austrian and Turkish opposition, but Serbia had been compensated in the east to match Montenegro's gains

[81] *Zastava*, March 14/26, no. 41, p. 1, "Dopisi" (Belgrade), March 8/20.

[82] *Ibid.*, Feb. 24/March 8, no. 31, "Bosanska izjava Hrvatima." This declaration was signed "Nekoliko Bosanaca" ("a few Bosnians").

[83] *Ibid.*, Feb. 27/March 11, no. 33, "Braci u Bosni."

[84] War Minister Miliutin (*Dnevnik*, 2, 24–27) described the "general joy" in St. Petersburg at news of its signature. Giers told Kireev that the treaty was truly glorious and had exceeded official expectations. ROBibLen, Dnevnik Kireeva, 7, 115.

[85] AII, Ristić 22, Protić to Ristić, March 2/14.

and maintain a balance of power between the Serbian states. He defended the controversial Serbo-Bulgarian frontier:

We were obligated, in creating a Bulgarian principality, to protect it from the excessive claims of its neighbors thus removing also any pretext for an immediate quarrel between Serbs and Bulgarians. And therefore, not permitting too great a development of Serbian aspirations, their unquestioned rights were satisfied by granting to Serbia . . . territories inhabited in actuality by a majority of Serbs.[86]

But Colonel Bobrikov, a dispassionate Russian expert, evaluated San Stefano differently. Ignat'ev's Bulgarian frontier would deprive Serbia of most of its conquests. Did not that curved boundary reflect primarily concern for Austrian rather than Serbian interests?[87] It was clear why the treaty was unpopular in Serbia. Abjuring any aim to benefit all South Slavs, it clearly favored Bulgaria. St. Petersburg was foolish to rejoice at a settlement which could satisfy no one: "By this treaty we armed against ourselves not only the western great powers, but all of the peoples for whose interests we had taken up arms. By the Treaty of San Stefano we laid the basis for quarrels among the peoples of the [Balkan] peninsula and foreshadowed our humiliation at Berlin."[88]

The Pan-Slavs, while hailing the treaty as a worthy settlement fulfilling some Russian national goals, were sharply divided over the proposed Serbo-Bulgarian frontier. V. A. Cherkasskii and V. I. Lamanskii believed that all of Old Serbia belonged with Bulgaria, while Ivan Aksakov strongly opposed such a solution.[89] Serbia was being treated unfairly, noted A. A. Kireev, because of Russia's friendship with Vienna.[90] *Russkii Mir* supported Belgrade and espoused Serbian claims to Vidin and all of Old Serbia. Objecting to Ignat'ev's frontier, the editors asserted that many purely Serbian areas were to be excluded from the principality and warned:

The formation of a stronger Serbia is essential as the bearer of Slav interests on that side of the Danube directly opposite Austria-Hungary, which still intrigues to break our moral ties with the Serbian people. We believe that in the interests of Slavdom and in our own interests, we should seek to create

[86] Ignat'ev, IV, *142* (Oct. 1915), 67–69.
[87] He might better have said Russian interests!
[88] Bobrikov, *Zapiski*, pp. 84–88, 93–94.
[89] Ristić 22, Protić to Ristić, March 2/14; *Slavianskii sbornik*, p. 188, Aksakov to Cherkasskii, Dec. 17/29, 1877.
[90] ROBibLen, Dnevnik Kireeva, 7, 113.

out of the Serbian principality a more solid state body capable of standing by itself.

"For us," declared the paper, "the Bulgarians and the Serbs are equally close, but this requires the greatest possible strengthening of the Serbian principality." [91] Two weeks later, *Russkii Mir* reiterated its warning, "It is essential now to insure that the seeds of discord not be sown by our own hands between the peoples of the Balkan peninsula." [92] When the treaty became public, the editors agreed Russia had achieved the maximum possible, but they added, "Serbia, who aided the most the cause of liberation of the Turkish Slavs by her self-sacrificing campaign . . . received much less than she deserved." [93]

The nationalist press considered San Stefano the absolute minimum a victorious Russia could accept. The treaty, declared *Grazhdanin*, "is far from corresponding to the sacrifices borne by Russia, although it is a glorious one." Its basic inadequacies were its "preliminary" character and its failure to solve the Eastern Question. Constantinople and the Straits remained Russia's fundamental objectives, and the Austrians would go to war only if Russia "alone or with the Serbian principality unites the Yugoslavs into a single organism." Despite these shortcomings, the treaty was glorious "since in fact has been achieved the emancipation of the South Slavs and all the Christians of Turkey." [94] At San Stefano, announced Katkov, Russia had set minimum terms. If a European congress wished to treat the Christians more generously, Russia would rejoice, but the Powers could not deprive them of gains already secured. Only questions left unresolved at San Stefano, such as the future structure of Bosnia and Hercegovina, could be discussed at a congress.[95]

In mid-March, A. A. Maikov wrote a series of articles for *Novoe Vremia* expanding upon *Russkii Mir*'s objections to a big Bulgaria.

[91] *Russkii Mir*, Feb. 11/23 and Feb. 19/March 3, nos. 40, 48, leads.

[92] *Ibid.*, Feb. 22/March 6, no. 51.

[93] *Ibid.*, March 10/22, no. 66. In similar vein *Grazhdanin* declared, "Much is not done which one might expect for Montenegro, Serbia, and especially Bosnia and Hercegovina as if it had been forgotten that it was because of them that the eastern crisis began." March 19/31, nos. 11–12, "Mirnyi dogovor i novaia voina."

[94] *Ibid.; ibid.*, March 7/19, no. 10, "Mir s Turtsieiu, Anglia i Avstriia."

[95] Peredovykh, March 2/14, no. 57, and March 9/21, no. 64. In the latter editorial, Katkov, avoiding taking sides in the Serbo-Bulgarian frontier controversy, wrote, "Serbia received less than the sacrifices she made last year and this one entitled her to, but the blame for this falls on Austria which jealously exerted pressure [on Serbia] forbidding her to advance in various directions."

According to Protić, they caused a "sensation" and helped swing public support to Serbia.[96] Accusing the Bulgarians of "Bulgarizing" Serbs in the disputed frontier zone, Maikov stated, "It is the duty of Russia, and her direct interest, once and for all to nip this in the bud." Russians should pay special attention to the Serbs because of their honorable nature, repeated assistance to the Russian army and "their deep . . . devotion to the Russian tsar and to Russia." All of Old Serbia was purely Serbian in tradition and should be annexed to the principality. A strong Serbia would block Austrian expansion, but if the Serbo-Bulgarian boundary were unfairly delimited, Russian influence might be undermined.[97]

Belgrade, though grateful for such support, apparently attached more significance to a report to the *London Times* (March 22) on Russian attitudes. The correspondent wrote that San Stefano's provisions for Serbia had amazed the Russian public by their stinginess when compared with Bulgarian and Montenegrin gains, but most official and unofficial circles approved of them. Recalling the volunteer episode, most Russians believed Serbia's aspiration to become the South Slav Piedmont was incompatible with Russian policy. So intense was the Serbo-Bulgarian rivalry that Russia had been compelled to adopt Bulgaria as its protégé. The Pan-Slavs believed that the Serbs had succumbed to heretical west European doctrines while Bulgaria, adhering to traditional Slav values, remained Russia's natural tool in the Balkans.[98] St. Petersburg's lack of real concern for Serbia's fate and its growing desire to conciliate Vienna would help push Belgrade into Austria's waiting arms.

[96] AII, Ristić 22/?, Protić to Rustić, March 2/14. Protić claimed he had been primarily responsible, convincing Maikov of the righteousness of the Serbian position on the frontier question.

[97] *Istok*, March 8/20, no. 27, p. 1, reprinted Maikov's articles under the title, "Srpska-bugarska granica." Commented the editors, "We are grateful to Maikov for showing his countrymen that of all the Slavs, Russia should reveal the greatest sympathy for the Serbs."

[98] Ristić, *2*, 140–41. The Serbian foreign minister apparently took most seriously the report of the *Times* correspondent and Protić's pessimistic evaluation of Russian attitudes toward Serbia.

CHAPTER VIII

FROM SAN STEFANO

TO BERLIN

DURING the spring months, St. Petersburg concentrated on relations with the Powers rather than with the Balkan Christians. Russia promptly ratified the Treaty of San Stefano, although the court believed renewal of hostilities with the Porte was imminent. The Foreign Ministry, despite nationalist outcries that Russia's honor would be sacrificed, sought desperately and ultimately successfully to avert a disastrous coalition war. Until mid-May the issue of war or peace hung in the balance and a European congress appeared unlikely.

Russia and the Powers

English hostility and intense Anglophobia in Russia discouraged initially any approach to London. The Ministry, anxious to square Vienna and forestall an Anglo-Austrian alliance against Russia, sought Andrassy's consent to all or most of San Stefano.[1] To the Russian

[1] For detailed treatments of Russia's relations with the Powers in the spring of 1878 see Sumner, *Russia*, pp. 425–500; Stojanović, *The Great Powers*, pp. 234–66; Rupp, *A Wavering Friendship*, pp. 469–535; and Medlicott, *The Congress of Berlin and After* (London, 1938), pp. 12–35. Whereas Ignat'ev doubted that the Powers would accept the treaty, Gorchakov was confident that with Andrassy's and Bismarck's support he could obtain England's assent to it; thus he insisted on its immediate ratification (March 4/16). Ignat'ev, IV, *142* (Nov. 1915), 414–16. Neither Gorchakov nor Ignat'ev, asserts Miliutin, was anxious for a congress at this time. But if there were none, he predicted, there would be war with England and half of Europe. Russia, wrote the war minister on March 16, could not prepare in time for this seemingly inevitable conflict. Two days later, Gorchakov and the tsar had abandoned hope of a peaceful outcome. Miliutin, *Dnevnik*, 3, 27–30.

leadership, sacrifice of Serbian aspirations in the western Balkans seemed a modest price for mollification of the Dual Monarchy. At the end of March, when pessimism had been partially dispelled by reassuring news from Austria, the Ministry sent Ignat'ev to Vienna to explain and justify his treaty.[2] "C'est une tentative suprême," the chancellor explained to Shuvalov, "pour ranimer et resserer l'entente des trois cours Impériales." [3]

From Vienna, Ignat'ev reported that the kaiser desired agreement but that Andrassy was hostile and was seeking an alliance with England. To clarify the situation, the count sought to learn the details of the Austrian demands.[4] Ignat'ev's report of his discussions with Austrian leaders, submitted after his return, noted that Andrassy objected to San Stefano's provision for Bosnia and Hercegovina because it barred their annexation to the Monarchy.[5] When the Austrians protested strongly against the major territorial gains promised to Montenegro, Ignat'ev retorted that Andrassy had agreed in the Budapest Convention to advance it to the Lim and Drina. If the Black Mountain were to be virtually excluded from Hercegovina, simple justice demanded significant gains in Novi Pazar sandjak (the "Enclave"). But Andrassy firmly opposed such an exchange. In 1877, he admitted, Vienna had not contemplated annexing the "Enclave," but Bulgaria's extension south of the Balkan Mountains now required it. Montenegro would be permitted the territorial increase suggested by the Constantinople Conference, but the Monarchy, regarding the west Balkans as its exclusive sphere of interest, could not allow other powers to exert influence in the principality. "Andrassy's objective," wrote Ignat'ev, "clearly is to prevent any development of Montenegro and to surround

[2] Alexander II told Ignat'ev on March 11/23, "Go to Vienna tomorrow and try to clarify precisely what Austria-Hungary is demanding of us. Explain to them that we, by the conclusion of your treaty, have not departed at all from what was agreed to at Reichstadt." Ignat'ev, IV, *142* (Dec. 1915), 777–78; Miliutin, *Dnevnik*, *3*, 29–30. Ignat'ev took with him the tsar's letter announcing his desire "aplanir les divergences de vues" separating Russia and Austria but warning he was preparing for any eventuality. HHSA, Geheimakten I, Alexander II to Franz Josef, March 11/23.

[3] SR, *6* (1927–28), no. 429, Gorchakov to Shuvalov, March 29. Earlier, Shuvalov recommended concessions to Austria, rather than to England which did not appear to know what it wanted. No. 413a, Shuvalov to Gorchakov, March 23.

[4] Ignat'ev, IV, *143* (Jan. 1916), 36–40.

[5] *Ibid.*, pp. 53–58; (Feb. 1916), 357–67. Ignat'ev noted that in framing the treaty he had sought to spare these provinces from an Austrian occupation.

her with Austrian holdings, keep her in dependency by seizing all the harbors Montenegro might use and support the Catholics on her frontiers against the Orthodox."

At first, resumed Ignat'ev's report, Andrassy raised no objections to Serbia's San Stefano frontiers. Emperor Franz Josef declared he was satisfied with them although he supposed the Serbs would not be. But in their third discussion, Andrassy stated that Austria wished to annex the "Enclave" and compensate Serbia with territory (Vranje, Pirot, and Trn districts) taken from Bulgaria. "It is clear," warned Ignat'ev, "that Andrassy, exploiting the fact that in Belgrade they are dissatisfied at the Serbo-Bulgarian frontier, . . . wishes to give the appearance he is defending Serbian interests against us." Hearing reports that Vienna was supporting Karadjordjist activity in Serbia, the special envoy predicted that Austria would seek to re-establish there the influence she enjoyed during the reign of Alexander Karadjordjević.[6]

On Bulgaria, Andrassy was concerned with its dimensions, not its administration; he demanded that it be restricted to areas north of the Balkans. Ignat'ev replied that he had been guided at San Stefano by a War Ministry map, transmitted to Vienna early in 1877, outlining the boundaries of Bulgaria, Serbia, and Montenegro. Discovering this map in his desk, Andrassy, deeply embarrassed, admitted he had not paid proper attention to it.[7]

Ignat'ev found the Austrian demands of March 27 unacceptable. Andrassy's program, involving Austrian occupation of the insurgent provinces and the "Enclave," would also reduce the extent of Bulgaria and Montenegro. Vienna would be the major beneficiary of Russia's war, deprive her of future influence among the Balkan Slavs, and prevent their independent development. The Serbian people, subordinated to the Hungarian crown, would be relegated to vassal status similar to Croatia's. "My whole soul rebelled against destroying with my own hands my . . . work of fifteen years, killing all the hopes of

[6] *Ibid.*, pp. 357–58. Čukić, Belgrade's envoy in Vienna, requested Ignat'ev's support for Serbian claims to the disputed regions on the Bulgarian frontier. Such an increase could be arranged, urged Ćukić, if territorial exchanges resulted from Austro-Russian negotiations. On March 30, he informed Ignat'ev of Belgrade's alarm at rumors that the tsar would give Austria decisive influence over Serbia in the future. Ignat'ev sought to calm him with assurances that Russia would continually keep Serbian interests in view. He advised the Serbs to be content with their San Stefano frontiers.

[7] *Ibid.*, pp. 357–67.

the Slavs and strengthening Vienna's predominance in the east. I considered granting Bosnia and Hercegovina to Austria to be a crime against its Slav population and shameful for Russia." Instead, urged Ignat'ev, San Stefano's provisions must be executed fully before a European congress can convene.[8]

St. Petersburg pondered Andrassy's terms. Initially (March 28), Gorchakov defended San Stefano, arguing that it had created neither a new Bulgaria nor a strong Slav state under Russian control.[9] Andrassy's demands, affirmed Miliutin, exceeded St. Petersburg's fearful expectations and revealed that Austria was no longer content with the Reichstadt agreement. Ignat'ev's mission failed. The tsar and Miliutin nonetheless agreed that negotiations should continue—even a congress would be preferable to war—though the War Minister opposed the major concessions to the Austrians in Old Serbia suggested by Gorchakov.[10]

Ignat'ev, appalled at Austrophile sentiment at a meeting of top Russian leaders (about April 8), drew up a memorandum to the chancellor which stated, "The proposals of the Austro-Hungarian government in general cannot be accepted. They have the purpose of placing Montenegro and Serbia in complete dependence upon it and virtually [*fakticheski*] annexing to Austria-Hungary the entire western part of the Balkan peninsula." Russia, reminding Andrassy of his earlier pledges, should seek to reduce his demands. The Lim River could be accepted as Montenegro's eastern boundary, but

we cannot allow the Vienna cabinet to insist on removing from Montenegro the coastal strip and her ports on the Adriatic. Having deprived Montenegro fifty years ago of Cattaro in order to give it to Austria, we have no right now to deprive Montenegro of the seacoast conquered by her from the Turks and again give it to Austria-Hungary.

As to Serbia, the island of Ada Kale could be ceded to Austria and a railroad agreement with Vienna permitted. If an occupation of Bosnia and Hercegovina were inevitable, let it occur quickly and on a temporary basis. That might embroil Austria with Turkey, splitting a potential anti-Russian coalition. Should Vienna demand annexation of the "Enclave," contrary to earlier agreements, the Serbian states should be

[8] *Ibid.*, pp. 371–72, 376–77.
[9] HHSA, Varia Russie 1878, Gorchakov to Novikov, March 28 (handed to Andrassy April 12).
[10] Miliutin, *Dnevnik*, 3, 31–32, 39, 48.

compensated in Old Serbia. On Bulgaria's western frontiers, only changes should be permitted compatible with San Stefano (Article VI, Section 2).[11]

On April 27, reiterating his opposition to major concessions to Andrassy, Ignat'ev urged Gorchakov to insist unconditionally upon Montenegro's retention of its shore line, unless Prince Nikola consented to yield part of it. The "Enclave," though small, was vital in a moral sense. While it remained in Turkish hands. Montenegro could await a favorable moment to acquire the western portion and join Serbia on the Lim. Once the region became Austrian, warned Ignat'ev, the Serbian states would be encircled, Austria would obtain direct access to the Aegean by rail, and Macedonia would be brought under its influence. The division of Bulgaria and creation of a separate Macedonia would ignite Serbo-Bulgarian rivalry over its possession.[12] The count exerted his remaining influence to induce St. Petersburg to hold firm. Ignat'ev, as Shuvalov's conciliatory approach began to prevail, was losing his power to formulate policy.

Baron Langenau remained hopeful that the Russians would make concessions needed to avoid conflict. The tsar, he reported, had a noble heart but was "unendlich schwach"; he often failed to realize the significance of his acts. Gorchakov, regarding Andrassy's terms as too severe, especially on the Montenegrin seacoast, anxiously awaited reduced demands. However, Langenau informed him that Vienna expected Russian counterproposals.[13] And Andrassy adhered adamantly to his original demands in a conversation with Novikov (April 10), despite the evident desire of the kaiser and his generals to avoid war with Russia.[14]

The Russian counterproposals, handed to Andrassy on April 17, reflected Ignat'ev's views. Austria might construct a railway to Salonika through the "Enclave" but could not annex it, "being contrary to

---

[11] Ignat'ev, IV, *143* (March 1916), 656–60.

[12] *Ibid.*, *144* (April 1916), 49–54. This memorandum, explains Ignat'ev, was his final labor for the Foreign Ministry; after that he was not consulted nor shown diplomatic correspondence. Ignat'ev then fell ill (May 8) and could not combat the pacific influence of Count Shuvalov.

[13] HHSA, Langenau to Andrassy, no. 15 A-E, March 3/15; Privatschreiben and telegram 78 of April 7; no. 17 A-D, April 9, Geheim; telegram 81, April 10.

[14] Rupp, *A Wavering Friendship*, pp. 498–500. On April 16, they had a "heated quarrel" over the Montenegrin seacoast during which Andrassy declared he would leave it to the Porte rather than allow it to go to Montenegro.

the arrangements reached between us." These "Concessions éventuelles," reaffirming Montenegrin rights to the entire seacoast to the Bojana, would permit only minor modifications of the San Stefano frontiers of the South Slav states. Russia, though, would reduce the length of its Bulgarian occupation and the size of the occupying army.[15] Novikov telegraphed word that Andrassy found these concessions inadequate, especially on Montenegro.[16] Austro-Russian negotiations were deadlocked.

Various unsuccessful attempts were made to produce agreement. From Vienna, Novikov advised his government to yield on the Novi Pazar "Enclave" and Bulgarian frontiers; otherwise Russia might confront an Austro-British-Turkish coalition including Serbia, Rumania, and Greece.[17] Serbia, disillusioned with Russia after San Stefano, was already considering seeking Austrian protection. Gorchakov, asserted Ignat'ev, was prepared for major concessions, including partition of Bulgaria, and attempted without success to induce the count to sponsor them.[18] Bismarck sought to mediate the dispute, urging St. Petersburg to yield on Bulgarian frontiers and the Vardar valley in exchange for an Austrian agreement to concede a seacoast to Montenegro. Andrassy's demands, advised Bismarck, were not worth a war.[19]

The Russian Foreign Ministry, pressed by Vienna and Berlin to formulate more precisely the changes it would permit in San Stefano, composed a "Promemoria" for Andrassy.[20] Russia would accept division of Bulgaria into eastern and western portions but not any substantial reduction of its frontiers. The Russian military occupation there would be limited to the shortest possible time. Austria could occupy and annex Bosnia and Hercegovina, but the "Enclave" would be partitioned between the Serbian states. Montenegro would retain her San Stefano frontiers including the entire seacoast she had occupied. Andrassy promptly rejected these terms on the grounds that Austria would be

---

[15] HHSA, Geheimakten I, "Pro-mémoria verbale remis par M. de Novikov," April 17. Russia would permit Austro-Serbian commercial agreements and the cession of Ada Kale island to Austria.

[16] Ignat'ev, IV, *144* (April 1916), 32–33.

[17] *Ibid., 143* (March 1916), 668; Rupp, *A Wavering Friendship*, p. 499.

[18] *Ibid., 144* (April 1916), 32–33.

[19] *Ibid.,* p. 500. For Germany's relations with Austria and Russia in the spring of 1878 see GP, *2*; Sumner, *Russia*, pp. 461–62.

[20] HHSA, Geheimakten I, "Promémoria," transmitted by Novikov to Andrassy, May 8; Rupp, *A Wavering Friendship*, pp. 516–17; GP, *2*, no. 404.

excluded from the East. Chances of rapprochement with Vienna, wrote Miliutin, were receding.[21]

But prospects brightened for an Anglo-Russian accord. Replacing Derby as foreign secretary, Lord Salisbury on April 1 outlined London's objections to San Stefano, centering around a united big Bulgaria.[22] The Salisbury note provided moderates in St. Petersburg with an exit from their dilemma, and Shuvalov worked diligently in London to work out bases of an agreement. On May 12, Shuvalov arrived in St. Petersburg bearing Salisbury's proposals. The most distasteful of these to Russian leaders was division of Bulgaria at the Balkan Mountains, but they unanimously decided to accept a north-south partition if London supported Montenegrin access to the sea and other parts of San Stefano.[23] Shuvalov, after triumphing over Ignat'ev's nationalist group, returned to London and signed an agreement with England (May 30).[24]

The logjam had been broken and Andrassy outplayed. After England accepted Bismarck's invitation to the Congress of Berlin, Russia followed suit (June 4). Rather than face a possible Anglo-Austrian coalition, the tsar decided to make concessions to England. The tsar consented to discuss the entire Treaty of San Stefano, renounced a partition of the "Enclave" between the Serbian states, and agreed to allow the congress to determine the question of Montenegrin access to the sea. Andrassy reluctantly bowed to Bismarck's pressure to attend the Congress on this basis.[25]

Russia's concessions to the Powers provoked vehement reactions from the press and public. Even semiofficial organs, such as *Golos* and *Journal de St. Pétersbourg*, objected to European revision of San

[21] Miliutin, *Dnevnik*, *3*, 50. According to Novikov, reported Langenau, the latest Russian concessions had been given a poorer reception than St. Petersburg had anticipated; the peaceful mood of a few days before was evaporating. HHSA, Langenau to Andrassy, May 16, telegram 116.

[22] The complete text of the Salisbury Note is in A. Loftus, *Diplomatic Reminiscences, 1862–1879* (London, 1894), pp. 310–17.

[23] Miliutin, *Dnevnik*, *3*, 50–52, 57. Upon arrival in St. Petersburg, states Tatishchev, Shuvalov found government leaders tired of war and disposed toward peace. Russian resources were exhausted as were war supplies. Civil and military leaders agreed that it would be almost impossible for Russia to fight. Tatishchev, *Aleksandr II*, *2*, 486.

[24] For a detailed picture of Anglo-Russian relations at this time see B. H. Sumner, "Russo-British Relations . . . ," *Slavonic and East European Review*, *27, 28*; Sumner, *Russia*, pp. 436–38, 471–92, 637–51; Rupp, *A Wavering Friendship*, pp. 508–16; Medlicott, *Congress of Berlin*, pp. 15–21.

[25] Čubrilović, *Bosanski ustanak*, pp. 290–91; GP, *2*, no. 410.

Stefano.[26] For the nationalists, Katkov predicted that Russian attendance at a congress would produce war or humiliation. Conflict with Austria and England would be preferable to yielding, especially on the Bulgarian question. To satisfy the Powers' demands would mean tearing up San Stefano and granting the benefits of war to Russia's enemies.[27] If Russia were firm, predicted *Grazhdanin*, Austria and England would not fight to achieve minor frontier rectifications in the Balkans.[28] *Otechestvennye Zapiski*, organ of the legal left, was more realistic. No Balkan settlement is possible, it declared, which fails to conciliate the Powers' interests. War against an Anglo-Austrian coalition, even if victorious, would merely bring an uneasy truce; force, without the consent of Europe, could not create a solid political structure for the Balkan states.[29] "Colossal chauvinism" prevailed among the public, intoxicated by military successes over Turkey. The tsar, embodying the Russian spirit, must not yield to foreign pressure, chanted Aksakov and Ilovaiskii. Nationalist opinion was greatly disappointed that Germany had joined Russia's enemies to demand treaty revision; it emphasized Russia's preparedness and strength.[30] Visiting both the capitals and the provinces during the spring, Koshelev heard indignation expressed that Russia had consented to attend a European congress.[31] The vocal nationalist element, unlike responsible governmental and military leaders, disregarded Russia's financial and military weakness and believed she could defy Europe.

The Serbian States Face Russia and Austria

In the spring of 1878, the Serbian states had to reassess their relations with Russia and Austria-Hungary, the Powers with which they were

[26] When Langenau protested the hostile attitude of semiofficial papers toward Austria-Hungary, Gorchakov denied responsibility for them. Following Kraevskii's vehement editorial of March 9/21 (*Golos*, no. 68), however, his paper was prohibited from selling single copies. The government, noted Langenau April 24, does not wish to admit publicly that it has made concessions to the Powers for fear public opinion might boil over and compel it to adopt a less conciliatory attitude. HHSA, Langenau to Andrassy, March 3/15, 15 A-E; April 7, Privatschreiben; and April 24, no. 20D.

[27] Peredovykh, April 8/20, no. 92.

[28] *Grazhdanin*, March 19, no. 10. Wrote V. A. Panaev (April 10, no. 13): "We should concentrate 200,000 men on the Austrian frontier if Vienna rejects our terms; we can ignore England and the Salisbury Note."

[29] "Vnutrennee obozrenie," *Otechestvennye Zapiski*, 237 (April 1878).

[30] *Russland*, pp. 373-76. A. A. Kireev asserted that Russia would soon have 800,000 men ready to fight. Dnevnik Kireeva, 7, March 3/15, April 4/16.

[31] Koshelev, *Zapiski*, p. 234.

primarily concerned. Their vital interests were affected by Russian concessions which made possible the Congress of Berlin. As the Austrian shadow lengthened over the western Balkans, they were increasingly attracted into Vienna's orbit. And prospects for Serbian unity had been clouded by San Stefano. Treating Montenegro far more generously than Serbia, it had enhanced their mutual suspicion and weakened Serbdom's ability to resist Austria. Among the Serbs, Belgrade was the chief loser and had the greatest inducement to seek revision of San Stefano. On past occasions, Serbia, when repelled by Russia, had turned to Austria. Milan and Ristić, though not without agony, would now do so once more. On the other hand, Montenegro concentrated its efforts on obtaining areas promised to her—Cetinje had a vested interest in preserving the treaty. The insurgents, fearing Austria and detesting the Porte, saw no alternative to reliance upon Russia; they implored St. Petersburg to support their annexation to the Serbian states.

Serbia's relations with Russia during these months were troubled and uncertain. St. Petersburg still looked askance at political instability in Belgrade. The unresolved Serbo-Bulgarian border controversy created tension and the threat of violence—this was San Stefano's sad legacy. Serbian leaders feared that Russia, to reach agreement with Vienna, would sacrifice their vital interests. On the other hand, the danger of war against a powerful coalition made Russian leaders anxious to arrange future military co-operation with Belgrade and praise Serbia's contribution in the recent war.[32]

Austro-Russian negotiations—notably the Ignat'ev mission—aroused Serbian fears. Protić reported that Ignat'ev had gone to Vienna to propose a division of European Turkey granting the insurgent provinces to the Dual Monarchy.[33] Ristić, fishing for information, feared Russia would make major concessions at Serbia's expense.[34] To reassure the Serbs, Ignat'ev suggested to Ćukić that Vranje might be obtained as well as their San Stefano frontiers; he had no intention of sacrificing their interests to please Vienna.[35] A week later Protić telegraphed word that the Ignat'ev mission had failed, Austrian demands had been re-

---

[32] PRO, FO 78/2837, White to Derby, April 12, telegram.

[33] AII, Ristić 22/265, Protić to Ristić, March 12/24.

[34] *Ibid.*, 22/332, Ristić to Ćukić, March 17/29, telegram. Ćukić replied that the status quo could only be altered to Serbia's detriment since under pressure Russia would withdraw its support for Serbia's new western frontiers. *Ibid.*, 22/333, March 18/30.

[35] *Ibid.*, 22/334.

jected and the *status quo* for Serbia upheld.[36] When Foreign Ministry officials explained Russia's difficult international position, Protić warned that Serbia would not be the victim of an Austro-Russian partition of Turkey. Until it received natural frontiers, his country would be dissatisfied, and if Bulgaria obtained an Aegean port, Serbia must also get one. As he conversed with Giers, in burst Ignat'ev, exclaiming, "The devil knows what Austria wants; she has gone crazy, but nonetheless I arranged something for you Serbs and for Montenegro. Austria wants some agreement with Serbia and Montenegro, some railroad lines and God knows what else." He refused to elaborate.[37]

At the beginning of April, General Lješanin arrived in St. Petersburg ostensibly to confer on top Russian leaders the Serbian Takovo military decoration, but mainly to clarify Serbian-Russian relations. Gorchakov expressed surprise at the grandiose Serbian decorations, but his subordinates assured Lješanin of Russian support to retain Trn and Vranje, but not Pirot, for Serbia. At an audience with the tsar, the Serbian general expressed Prince Milan's gratitude and filial devotion. Emphasizing his appreciation of Serbian military co-operation, Alexander replied, "It is said that Russia is better disposed toward Bulgaria than toward Serbia, but this is untrue and you must not believe it. It is possible that Austria will win it [Serbia] over, but I hope that Serbia will not allow itself to be led astray and will in the future too remain with Russia." [38]

Both official Russia and the public, reported Protić, were now better disposed toward Serbia. Indeed, Russian leaders praised highly the Serbs' military role. To erase his unfortunate Kremlin pronouncement of 1876, the tsar told Protić, "You Serbs are fine fellows, you fought bravely." Commented Grand Duke Konstantin Nikolaevich, the liberal chairman of the State Council, "Last year you were considered revolutionaries here, and those who received [Takovo orders] were not allowed to wear them, but now that we have fought together, the tsar has permitted them to be worn." [39] Receiving his order of Takovo, Alexander replied, "I have done all that was possible to assure to Serbia

[36] *Ibid.*, 22/282, April 5, Protić to Ristić.

[37] *Ibid.*, 22/282, April 5/17.

[38] *Ibid.*, 22/325, Lješanin to Milan, March 26/April 7; 22/327, "Lješanin o svojoj misiji u Petrogradu," draft in pencil. Foreign diplomats provided a variety of interpretations of Lješanin's purpose. PRO, FO 260/8, Loftus to Derby, no. 454, April 23; HHSA, Wrede to Andrassy, May 3, no. 45.

[39] AII, Ristić 22/282 and 286, Protić to Ristić, April 5/17 and May 10/22; 22/468, Milan to Ristić, n.d.

in the present crisis advantages compatible with the military and political situation. . . . She [Serbia] can count upon my support to have them approved in Europe. It is up to Serbia to develop these advantages while preserving order, the only guarantee of prosperity." Other Russian leaders responded even more warmly.[40] But while protesting friendship for Serbia, they promised her nothing more than the treaty which the Serbs found unsatisfactory.

The Serbo-Bulgarian frontier remained the most troublesome issue in Belgrade's relations with Russia. Bulgarian officials, supported by the governor of Sofia, attempted to enter the Pirot-Vranje-Trn region occupied by Serbian troops; they demanded an immediate Serbian evacuation, although the Turks had not withdrawn from territory Serbia was to receive under San Stefano.[41] Reports that Russian troops were infiltrating the zone occupied by Serbian troops increased Belgrade's concern.[42] The Serbs responded by resolving to hold fast and appeal to St. Petersburg. Ristić instructed Serbian authorities to remain in the occupied zone until the frontier had been formally delimited, but to avoid quarreling with the Russians and to communicate their demands to Belgrade.[43]

The Serbs did not hesitate to proselytize in the occupied region. Seizing upon a statement in the Treaty of San Stefano (Article VI, Section 2) that frontiers should be determined on the basis of the majority of population, Prince Milan in late March declared, "I am in full agreement to put pressure upon the population [under Serbian administration] so that it expresses itself in favor of unification with Serbia." He left the details of this operation to Ristić. Meanwhile, Serbian officials in Pirot recommended expulsion of the Bulgarian *vladika* (bishop) and propagandists, and an end to requisitioning in order to win popular favor.[44] On April 2, Ristić ordered General Kosta Protić to

[40] *Ibid.*, 22/338, Alexander II to Milan, March 27/April 8, copy; 22/411, Gorchakov to Milan, n.d. Grand Duke Nikolai Nikolaevich declared that the decoration would always remind him of "notre confraternité d'armes." *Ibid.*, 22/412.

[41] *Ibid.*, 22/299, Ristić to Protić, April 3/15; HHSA, Wrede to Andrassy, May 3, no. 46.

[42] *Ibid.*, 19/378, General K. Protić to Ristić, March 27/April 8, telegram. If Russian troops enter Kula, asked Protić, how should we react?

[43] Grujić, *3*, 321–22; AII, Ristić 19/377, Ristić to K. Protić, March 27/April 8, telegram.

[44] *Ibid.*, 22/461, Milan to Ristić, n.d. Complaints of the governor of Rakovo were transmitted to Belgrade by Russian headquarters: the Serbs reportedly had been collecting taxes forcibly in the Vidin, Kula, and Belgradjik districts. The grand duke asked Belgrade to halt such activity. In reply Ristić argued that the Serbs

name delegations of "trustworthy people" from the disputed zone who would be sent to St. Petersburg and San Stefano to argue Serbian claims. "Naturally," added Ristić, "they should be partisans of unification with Serbia." [45] One result of Serbian agitation was a petition to the tsar from "the inhabitants" of Pirot, Trn, and Vranje, complaining of Bulgarian oppression and calling Serbia their fatherland.[46]

In late April, matters appeared to be moving toward a crisis. Russian soldiers in the Adlie area, reported Lieutenant Colonel Kalić (April 20), seized horses from the Serbs by force, and the commander of Belgradjik sent Russians into villages under Serbian administration to incite disobedience of the authorities. "The situation is such," concluded his report, "that a conflict appears certain." Ristić, bolstered by Catargi's admonitions from Russian headquarters to retain all occupied territories, appealed to Consul Persiani to secure recall of the Russian troops.[47]

Official Russia's conciliatory response and the Serbs' firmness averted further violence. Unlike Ignat'ev, who had pressed Belgrade to execute his treaty unilaterally, Giers generally shared Ristić's viewpoint. He promised to telegraph the Sofia governor to abstain from further encroachments on Serbian occupied territory.[48] The *status quo militaire*, agreed St. Petersburg, would be maintained until final delimitation of the frontier could be made.

General Bobrikov's memorandum of May 2,[49] rejecting as extravagant the Serbian claims to a frontier from Lom-Palanka to Radomir, thence along the Struma River to the Seres, presented the following objective summation of the boundary problem:

In view of the undoubted importance of establishing friendly relations between Serbia and Bulgaria, special significance attaches to an exact and fair drawing of their international frontier. It is extremely difficult to tell

---

had merely been meeting their temporary administrative expenses and would withdraw as soon as the Turks evacuated territory promised to Serbia. *Ibid.*, 22/430, n.d.

[45] *Ibid.*, 22/406, [Ristić?] to Milan, March 19/31 and Ristić to Srečković, April 15/27. "Give the delegation 100 ducats," instructed Ristić, "and tell it to hurry along to Russian headquarters." *Ibid.*, 22/375, March 21/April 2.

[46] *Ibid.*, 22/409, n.d.

[47] *Ibid.*, 22/436 and 439, Catargi to Milan, April 10/22 and (Milan?) to (Catargi); 19/110, Ristić to Persiani, April 13/25, draft.

[48] *Ibid.*, 22/300, Ristić to Protić, April 17, telegram; 19/398, Ristić to K. Protić, April 6/18, telegram.

[49] Os. Pr., no. 5, pp. 152–55. A copy went to the Russian ambassador in Constantinople; the original presumably was sent to War Minister Miliutin.

where one people ends and the other begins. Over the centuries the Turks have sought to obliterate the differences between them and turn all inhabitants into one herd of rayahs. At present both sides boldly claim rights to broad territories including not only doubtful territories but the primordial lands of the other. Scientific investigation by scholarly travelers is still too scanty here to be able to establish firm bases for a categorical delimitation. Much time and money would be required for such a study, yet the frontier question is urgent.

Serbian assertions that Russian authorities were openly partial to the Bulgarians, Bobrikov rejected as unjust. Belgrade's efforts to win the disputed regions by popular petitions and newspaper agitation he considered as specious as the statistical evidence it presented.[50] Such Serbian importunities, he felt, must cease so that uncontrollable passions would not drown the voice of reason and justice in Serbia. Evidence from the works of Serbian scholars, Bobrikov pointed out, refuted Belgrade's exaggerated claims.[51] The genuine patriotism of both peoples should be satisfied and land-hungry extremists frustrated. The ethnic boundary passes through Niš, concluded the general, but strategic necessity must move it somewhat further east. The Vranje region and the valley of the Bulgarian Morava should be joined with Serbia since its main inhabited points were predominantly Serbian.[52]

Serbia's internal political instability continued to cause concern. Belgrade's reputation in St. Petersburg, reported Protić, had been severely damaged by the army mutiny at Topola (December 1877) and the "communist ideas" accompanying it. It was particularly regrettable that Jevrem Marković, principal defendant in the ensuing court case,

[50] The statistical table which accompanied the map outlining Serbian claims, noted Bobrikov, listed 3,000 Serbian and 400 Turkish-Arnauti households in Pirot, omitting any reference to Bulgarians whose numerical predominance in the city "is beyond doubt."

[51] Bobrikov cited an article by Stojan Novaković, former minister of education, which noted that Vuk Karadžić himself had described the ethnic frontier as running along the Timok River. The Serbian government, added Bobrikov, which lists only Serbs for Pirot and Trn, had angrily accused the Bulgarians in the same region of lack of patriotism in 1876. Suddenly this same "treacherous, cowardly" Bulgarian populace now expresses in enthusiastic petitions its firm will to belong to Serbia or die! Belgrade, declared Bobrikov convincingly, had contradicted itself.

[52] Bobrikov recommended the following frontier: east of Niš, through Ak Palanka, from the Nišava River to the watershed of the basins of the Bulgarian Morava and Vardar, along the peaks of Suva Planina, Širena Planina, and Sveti Ilija, bisecting the Pirot-Leskovac highway.

had been decorated by Russia for bravery and had consorted with
Russian officials. The Topola affair, the envoy told A. A. Mel'nikov,
assistant director of the Asiatic Department, was directed not merely
against the Obrenović dynasty but at Serbo-Russian military co-operation during the recent campaign. Giers, though denying rumors that
Russia would dispatch a commissar to Serbia to investigate the mutiny,
admitted that Prince Milan would soon receive a letter counseling
prudence and magnanimity to avert further domestic disorder. Russian
intercession on behalf of convicted mutineers, warned Protić, had
produced an unfavorable effect in Serbia.[53] St. Petersburg abstained
from further action in this delicate affair.

Despite these disputes, the Russian military desired Serbian co-operation in case hostilities resumed. Bobrikov urged Prince Milan to order
reorganization and re-equipment of the Serbian army and accept a
commitment to aid Russia if war came. To ascertain the prince's
attitude, he drafted a letter for Milan to the tsar which stated:

Henceforth the basis of my rule will be dedicated moral service, to which
Serbs and Bulgars in their new life will be summoned by Your Majesty. But
it will remain difficult for the South Slavs, in the dangers surrounding them,
to adhere firmly to the road of development without brotherly alliance
among themselves and the protection of Russia. Take therefore, Sire, under
Your fatherly protection their resurrected forces and the Serbs will defend
their brother Bulgars with their breasts just as the Bulgars will become a
reliable support to their brother Serbs.

To send this would mean accepting Russian tutelage and ceasing anti-
Bulgarian agitation. Without rejecting Bobrikov's overture, Milan refused to commit himself. Though Ristić knew Serbia required military
strength to support his diplomacy, and War Minister Grujić drew up a
reorganization plan, Milan stalled and would not approve it. Explained
Bobrikov:

Not trusting the policy of our diplomacy and having a factual basis for this
unfortunately, Prince Milan sought by precautionary obsequiousness to
dispose the Vienna cabinet in his favor in order to have its assistance at an
international settlement. . . . Contrary to the logic of events and the les-
sons of Serbian history, the princely government embarked on the slippery

---

[53] AII, Ristić 22/282 and 285, Protić to Ristić, April 5/17 and May 2/14, 1878. A
Russian plan to send a commissar to Serbia to investigate the affair, claimed Protić,
had been scotched by his protests.

path of compromise, sacrificing to a brilliant mirage the traditional goal of unity of the Serbian people.[54]

In late May, incidents on Serbia's eastern frontier caused renewed friction with Russia. General Totleben protested to Milan against the entry of Serbian troops into villages under Russian administration (Lopuzno, Dragoman, and others). Such incursions could have "fatal consequences for the work we have achieved together." Extending the Serbian occupied zone, warned Totleben, could not affect future frontiers and could only benefit our enemies. He urged the prince to order his army to retire to the Trn-Zarlova-Dragoman line and await a final delimitation of boundaries.[55] Belgrade heeded this sharp, though friendly, warning.

Because of Russian military weakness in the Balkans and Turkish recovery, Totleben desired Serbian military aid. Consul Persiani had reported, "Serbia is greatly exhausted. Despite the undoubted sympathy toward us, one should not count on her as a military base. However, in case of a favorable turn in a new war and with very significant resources, she could raise up to 80,000 men and enter into co-operation with us." Totleben's appraisal was more optimistic. If war broke out between Russia and an Anglo-Turkish coalition, he wrote the tsar, Serbia would make maximum efforts to defend its conquests and could succeed with slight Russian aid. If Austria also joined the conflict, the Serbs, unable to fight in the field, could resist from fortresses and perform a valuable service to Russia. Threatened from the rear by its own Slavs, Austria could not operate freely on the right bank of the Danube, or in Rumania, until breaking Serbian resistance. "Serbia should now finally decide the question and tell us whether she would, in case of a breach with Austria, defend her interests by force of arms." If so, the Serbian army could be deployed at a fortified camp at Kragujevac and delay Turkish and Austrian advances while Russian forces hindered a Turkish invasion of the Niš region. If St. Petersburg approved this plan for military co-operation, Serbia must be supplied promptly with sufficient money to rebuild her army. The tsar responded (July 1), "I find your ideas on co-operation with Serbia

[54] Bobrikov, *Zapiski*, pp. 86–90. After the failure of his efforts to arrange further Serbo-Russian military co-operation, Bobrikov returned in disgust to St. Petersburg (May 8/20). He suggests that it was Milan who chose Austria from cowardice rather than Ristić out of general policy considerations.

[55] Os. Pr., no. 3, pp. 106–07, Totleben to Milan, May 17/29, copy. Conveying this letter to the prince, Captain Chichagov was instructed to size up Serbian military capabilities.

wholly correct." [56] Up to and during the Congress of Berlin, the Russians included Serbia in their military plans.

The Russian nationalist press was generally friendly toward Serbia in these months. The efforts of M. Protić and the articles of A. A. Maikov helped produce more impartial assessments of Serbian and Bulgarian claims in Russian newspapers. Declared *St. Peterburgskie Vedomosti*:

The Serbian people has been left in conditions which only weaken it. Serbian frontiers are rounded [by San Stefano], but when one realizes that the Bulgarian population is six million, it is evident this will be unbearable to the Serbs as the stronger people. . . . The task of Russian diplomacy should be to assist the union of the Serbian people which is related to us, not to divide it. If the Serbian people were united into a whole, it would comprise a force sufficient to restrain all Austrian pretensions beyond the Danube and there would be no cause for worry about the Straits.

On the other hand, noted *Zastava's* Belgrade correspondent, papers such as *Golos* and *Novoe Vremia* remained unfriendly toward Serbia as they "do not find in Serbia a people willing to follow blindly Russian policy and aspirations beyond the Balkans." [57] To *Russkii Mir*, Georgievič continued to send reports from Belgrade emphasizing Serbo-Russian friendship and prospects for military co-operation. Some of his comments coincided curiously with Totleben's military plans. He claimed that Andrassy feared little Serbia and was seeking its support. The Serbs could not resist the Austrian army in the field, but a small Serbian military demonstration would cause revolt among the Slavs of Hungary. Few Serbs dreaded an Austro-Serbian war. Vienna wished to bind Serbia with conventions and promises of territory, but its government and people trusted Russia unconditionally. The Serbian army stood ready, "realizing it may soon perform the greatest service to Russia and all Slavdom." Since Lješanin had cleared up all Serbo-Russian misunderstandings, concluded Georgievič, in a new war Serbia would follow Russia. [58]

As for the Serbian press, *Istok* remained Russophile and emphasized

[56] *Ibid.*, pp. 117–19, 125, 131. Totleben to Alexander II, June 1/13 and 8/20; Alexander II to Totleben, June 19/July 1.

[57] *Zastava*, March 24/April 5, no. 47, "Dopisi, Beograd," March 18/30. Many recent pro-Serbian articles in the Russian press, asserted the correspondent, had been inspired by danger of an Anglo-Russian conflict. Only *Russkii Mir* had invariably shown sympathy toward Serbdom and defended it before the Russian public.

[58] *Russkii Mir*, March 16/28, March 22/April 3, April 8/20, nos. 72, 78, 95, reports from Belgrade.

the probability of renewed conflict, whereas *Zastava* featured criticism of San Stefano and Russian policy. Convinced that Russia would not yield to the Powers, *Istok* declared it would greet any Russian move "to carry the holy cause of Slav liberation through to completion." Ignat'ev's mission to Vienna marked another step toward a war in which Russia would square accounts with all its enemies while Serbia defended her gains and occupied territory "belonging to her by every human and divine law." Why rejoice at "a rotten peace" giving the Serbs insignificant territories, preparing a foreign occupation for Bosnia, and leaving brethren in chains? If the tsar strives to complete Slav emancipation, Serbia will "understand its true interests." "Only after a new conflict can the victors dictate more glorious peace terms. Then the Slav element will celebrate its complete triumph and liberation, and all of Serbdom will be freed and united." *Istok* noted that Russia's opponents had promised much but delivered little; "*with them Serbia cannot enter into negotiations.*" Serbs could agree to a European congress, declared *Istok*, only if Slavdom lost nothing it had won. A congress should join Old Serbia with Serbia; that, rather than Bosnia, was the chief issue.[59]

Zastava, expressing deep Serbian discontent, which *Istok* was barred from voicing, repeatedly castigated San Stefano. The treaty, claimed its Belgrade correspondent, gave the Serbs less than other victor states; a congress would likely grant Serbia more. The cession of Pirot and Vranje to Bulgaria had aroused the indignation of the entire Serbian people. Serbia's sacrifices required annexation to it of all of Old Serbia. Much more bitter were his comments of April 23:

The Russian official, ruling, all-powerful and privileged German caste, which was the author of San Stefano [Germans like Ignat'ev and Nelidov? —DM], has shown clearly it cared nothing for Serbia and the Serbian lands except insofar as this was permitted by Austria-Hungary's interests which are opposed by the entire Russian press.[60]

[59] *Istok*, March 17/29, March 24/April 5, March 31/April 12, April 7/19, April 21/May 3, nos. 31, 34, 37, 40, 45. Plainly, the editors were optimistic that much additional territory could be acquired in a new war. Their repudiation of any deal with Austria is interesting since it coincided with Belgrade's efforts to achieve rapprochement with Vienna. See also April 26/May 8, May 21/June 2, nos. 47, 58.

[60] *Zastava*, "Dopisi iz Belgrad," in nos. 47, 51, 59, March 24/April 5, March 31/April 12, and April 14/26. In the "Dopisi" in no. 50, March 29/April 10, the correspondent asked, "Is it not clear that this entire war has been conducted in Russian and Austrian interests?" Commented the editor, "We shall discuss this question later, but it reveals sentiment in Serbia."

With Bosnia and Hercegovina lost to foreign domination, the recent war had been fought for Austrian and Russian selfish interests camouflaged with slogans of Christian liberation. The correspondent distinguished between the Russian government and the people:

As to our national [*narodnih*] relations with Russia and our Russian brethren, they can never cool, nor can the Serbs ever be wrenched away from our brother Russians. But as to official Russia, there cannot persist such a close relationship between our and Russian policy as heretofore, since it is evident that Russian diplomacy, in concluding the peace treaty, considered only the erection of a greater Bulgarian state at the expense of the Serbian nationality.

Let Russian diplomacy treat all Balkan peoples alike and alter the treaty to satisfy Serbdom's aspirations, then Serbian dissatisfaction would cease. *Zastava's* editor, rejecting this conclusion, found Serbian dismay over San Stefano understandable, but blamed Austria for the failure to achieve unification.[61] The Belgrade correspondent, accepting creation of a greater Bulgaria which provided Serbdom with a natural ally, protested that Russian partiality for the Bulgarians was undeniable. He ascribed it to their subservience to Russia: "The Serbs are a people which has developed independently without being subservient to anyone. The Pan-Slav ideas or Pan-Russianism of Aksakov find more favorable ground in Bulgaria than in Serbia: the Bulgarian intelligentsia is more Russian than Bulgarian."[62]

Zastava's editor, though critical of San Stefano, believed Russia might redeem its pledges to the Serbs at the congress. In a series of three articles, he stated that Russian diplomacy, attempting to satisfy everyone to some degree with the Treaty, had satisfied no one completely and had isolated Russia. San Stefano had robbed Serbia, Rumania, and Greece of legitimate gains and antagonized Austria and England; Russia had failed to impose a radical solution of the Eastern Question satisfactory to the Balkan peoples; she could still propose this at the congress.[63] As the congress convened in Berlin, the editor remained hopeful that Serbdom's interests would be respected. St. Petersburg, he wrote, had isolated the Austrians with timely concessions to England on Bulgaria and the Straits. No other power need support Vienna's

---

[61] *Ibid.*, March 29/April 10, no. 50, and April 4/16, no. 53, "Dopisi" (Belgrade).
[62] *Ibid.*, April 11/23, no. 57, "Dopisi" (Belgrade), April 5/17.
[63] *Ibid.*, May 12, 15, 17, nos. 67, 69, 70, "Posle sveti stefanskog mira."

claims to Bosnia and Hercegovina, so Russia could urge their annexation to the Serbian states. Bosnia was the key to Serbdom's future. Whoever ruled it would control the northwest part of the Ottoman Empire. Exhorting Belgrade to agitate the Bosnian question, he warned that abandoning it in order to expand eastward would be disastrous: "This would serve Andrassy's interests well, but for Serbia it would be truly a Danaan gift since Serbia could extend eastward only at the expense of the Bulgarians, and this would be fatal for both Serbia and Bulgaria and only favor those who wish to divide and rule." Nothing since the defeat at Kosovo would so upset Serbian development as loss of Bosnia. Russia's main Balkan bulwark against Vienna would crumble. If the Russians neglected Serbian interests at the congress, warned the editor, Serbdom would be alienated permanently and fatally: "And Russia has a hundred reasons to aid Serbia with its powerful voice and influence when it seeks Bosnia for itself. *Orthodox and Slav Russia cannot and should not permit anyone besides Orthodox and Slav Serbia to obtain Bosnia. The Serbs would forever part company with Russia if she allowed the Serbian future to be ruined by the sacrifice of Bosnia.*" [64]

Meanwhile, the bases of Serbo-Austrian rapprochement were being laid as Prince Milan completely reversed his foreign policy. Until San Stefano he remained firmly Russophile abroad and conservative at home. But the treaty revealed to him a great contradiction between Serbian and Russian interests. With his repeated pleas to St. Petersburg to assist in achievement of Serbian aspirations largely unheeded, he turned, somewhat fearfully, to Vienna. The prince recalled that the Austrian ruler had received him "as a young friend," while Alexander II treated him "like a corporal." Rapprochement with the Monarchy, upon whose success he staked his prestige, was Milan's first important independent step in foreign affairs. [65] Ristić, not opposing such a shift, expected less from Austria. True to his policy of balance, the Foreign Minister sought to preserve genuine Serbian independence by playing off Russia against Austria. Thus he approached Vienna with diplomatic reserve, not with Milan's decisive, sincere, and naïve spirit of submission. Preferring specific and temporary agreements with Vienna, Ristić

---

[64] *Ibid.*, May 31/June 12, no. 85, "U oči Kongresa"; June 4/16, no. 87, "Bosna je glavna." Both lead articles are signed "P." *Zastava*'s emphasis on the Bosnian question contrasts sharply with Belgrade's view that Serbian gains in the east were the most important.

[65] *Die Memoiren des Königs Milan* (Zürich, 1902), pp. 173–76. This Austrophile account incorrectly considers Ristić to be a convinced Russophile.

worked simultaneously to keep the bridges to St. Petersburg in good repair.[66]

Since initial steps were taken before San Stefano became public, it is evident that the change in policy was the result of calculation, not popular pressure. By March 4, Ristić had talked twice with the Austrian consul about Serbia's treatment under the preliminary peace; "contrary to . . . expectations," he found Wrede receptive to his overtures. Since Austria's attitude toward Serbian claims, he wrote Ćukić, would "be of great if not decisive significance" at a future European conference, he had considered it essential to initiate such discussions.[67] A few days later, Ćukić telegraphed him, "If you think it would not cause strong alarm and displeasure to Russia, we should, in my view, create here in advance on the part of the prince the best possible attitude. And you could come here [Vienna] personally, inquiring first, of course, whether this would be approved. *The situation is very critical for the future of Serbia.*" On March 18, Ristić responded affirmatively to this suggestion.[68]

Soon afterward a letter to Andrassy was drafted in Belgrade. It stated that since Austria-Hungary would exercise preponderant influence over the destiny of Serbia and the eastern Christians, Prince Milan wished to restore harmony to Austro-Serbian relations. During the recent campaign, the Belgrade government had avoided steps, such as entry into Bosnia, which might incur Austria's displeasure. Although his own Austrophile views, shared by "les individus éclairés" in Serbia, were not yet generally accepted there, they doubtless would be, provided Austria supported legitimate Serbian aspirations at a congress. Continued the prince's letter:

Your Excellency is certainly aware that the territorial advantages acquired by Serbia under the Treaty of San Stefano corresponded neither to the military successes nor the expectations of the nation. The latter viewed with true desolation the largest part of its ancient patrimony either annexed to a new principality [Bulgaria] or returned to the Porte.

Serbia was requesting Austrian support for its independence and aggrandizement justified by indisputable historic and ethnic rights. Even with these gains Serbia would remain "tout-à-fait inoffensive" for

---

[66] Vlada Milana, *1*, 419–20.

[67] Arhiv ministarstva inostranih dela (Belgrade), (Ristić) to Ćukić, March 4, no. 5.

[68] Ćukić to Ristić, Feb. 27/March 11 and Feb. 28/March 12, cited by Ristić, *2*, 161; Vlada Milana, *1*, 452.

Austria and would require continued Austrian support to protect its acquisitions.[69]

The crucial decision to place Serbia under Vienna's protection had been made; it needed only to be implemented. Preceding Ristić to the Austrian capital, Consul Wrede assured Andrassy that the Serbian government had reluctantly but definitely abandoned its immediate aspirations to Bosnia, turning its attention instead to the south and east. Action west of the Drina, the Serbs had concluded, would merely hasten an Austrian occupation of the insurgent provinces, which Belgrade wished to delay as long as possible. Similar considerations apparently had prevented Prince Nikola's advance beyond Nikšić during the recent campaign. Wrede then recommended emphatically, "I can say that if Bosnia and Hercegovina are not occupied and brought into Austria-Hungary at the definite conclusion of peace, the Serbs' aspirations for their unification with Serbia will be resumed." Unrest, threatening disastrous new complications, would continue until Austrian troops moved in.[70] Prince Milan, pleasantly surprised at intimations of Austrian backing for his claims in the east, proclaimed his indifference about Novi Pazar, accepting Vienna's contention that its annexation to Serbia would disrupt Austrian communications. Milan, noted Wrede, would conclude railroad and commercial agreements with the Monarchy but would reject a permanent military convention with any power. "They believe and generally say," declared the prince, "I am entirely devoted to Russian interests, but I can assure you that this is not at all the case and that I am anxious above all to preserve my full liberty of action."[71] The outlines of an Austro-Serbian bargain were becoming clear.

Arriving in Vienna June 6, Ristić next day read Andrassy the prince's letter.[72] Andrassy repeatedly nodded agreement, expressed general satisfaction, and pledged to aid Serbia at the congress despite anti-Serbian feeling in the Monarchy. He would advocate Serbian independence but not a European guarantee of Serbia. Provided Austrian terms were accepted, he would favor a territorial increase for

[69] AII, Ristić 13/2, draft headed "Excellence," and dated March 30. The text is also in Ristić, 2, 163–65.

[70] HHSA, Wrede to Andrassy (Vienna), May 14. Emperor Franz Josef commented at the top of this report, "Sehr gut."

[71] Ibid., May 27, no. 54.

[72] Ibid., Varia Belgrade, May 22/June 3, signed by Milan. This is a revised version of the draft letter of March 30.

Serbia in the east, including Vranje and Pirot, but he noted that the Serbs could not have Novi Pazar. "Although we regard Novi Pazar as an important historic point for Serbia," declared Ristić, "we are prepared not to insist on it because of your desires and in view of compensation on the other side." Retorted Andrassy, "Compensation or not, you cannot have that area. Our support for a territorial increase for Serbia has no connection with Novi Pazar—that is a question in itself." From this conversation Ristić gained a clear picture of the Serbian frontiers Vienna would permit.[73]

Andrassy's conditions included a commercial treaty and a railroad agreement. Ristić discussed (June 10) details of frontier and economic arrangements with Baron J. von Schwegel, director of the commercial section of the Austrian foreign ministry. The Austrians, reported Ristić, were anxious to remove the Serbian frontier as far as possible from the proposed Mitrovica-Salonika railroad. The most onerous Austrian demand, he felt, was that economic agreements be concluded formally before the congress ended. The Austrians made it plain "that Russian influence in the areas they regard as lying in the Austro-Hungarian sphere should be finally and completely smashed and excluded." Faced with an Austria assured of majority support at the congress for her principal desires, Serbia had little choice. Wrote Ristić,

If we agree to the Austro-Hungarian proposals, we shall obtain support of the neighboring Monarchy with prospects of territorial increase *even beyond the frontiers of the San Stefano preliminary;* should we not agree, then everything comes in question, even the boundaries of San Stefano and Niš. *This was made abundantly clear to me.*

When Vienna presents written proposals, he added, Belgrade can decide whether to accept them.[74]

[73] Ristić, *2*, 162–71; Ristić to Grujić, no. 1, May 27/June 8, in Grujić, *3*, 322–26. To Ristic's question whence Serbia's frontiers should start in the west, Andrassy indicated Kopaonik. Promising to support the annexation of the Pirot region to Serbia, the count would not commit himself on Vidin. In the east, Andrassy sketched in a line running from Gilan to Sveti Ilija, including Trn and Dragoman within Serbia, then ascending to the defile of Sveti Nikola. Reported Ristić, "It seemed to me in general that Count Andrassy would not object if in the east we extended [our territory] right to Sofia."

[74] Grujić, *3*, 327–30; Ristić, *2*, 171–81. Describing his meeting with Ristić, Schwegel noted he seemed to accept most Austrian demands, "but he is a thoroughly false man and naturally I cannot trust him." HHSA, Freiherr v. Schwegel, "Notizen über die Berliner Kongress," no. 10.

Initial responses of Serbian leaders to the Austrian conditions revealed doubt and divergence of view. Displaying its residual Rus-
sophilism, the cabinet expressed fear that such agreements would serve
Austrian interests, alienate Russia, and damage Serbia's future prospects. Russia, it suggested, should be consulted first. If an Austro-
Serbian accord were reached before the congress ended, Andrassy
might utilize it against the Russians. "For our government and people it
is easier to submit to a decision of a European congress than to an
unequal treaty concluded outside the congress and without consulting
Russia." Though agreeing that Serbia's main need was a territorial
increase, the ministers hesitated to accept increased economic burdens
to attain it.[75] Milan's reaction, however, was favorable and immediate:
"You know my view that in order to obtain Pirot and probably the
other frontiers of Serbia and to insure in general good relations with
Austria-Hungary, it is worth while to obligate ourselves to give the
exploitation of our future railroads to a Turkish company, but of
course Austria must agree to support us heartily at the Congress."
While Milan and Ristić realized that the Austrian terms had to be
accepted, the ministers remained to be convinced. As the congress
opened, Austro-Serbian negotiations were incomplete.

And Ristić had carefully avoided cutting Serbia loose from Russia.
Following his conversation with Andrassy, he had visited Ambassador
Novikov to seek Russian support at the congress. The Serbian government hoped, Ristić stated, that Russia would prove as helpful to its
cause as Austria, that it would not provide the unpleasant spectacle of
opposing Andrassy at the expense of Serbdom. Novikov replied that he
hoped and believed this would not occur.[76]

Prior to the congress, Montenegro's prospects of obtaining the fron-
tiers promised her at San Stefano waned steadily. Immediately after the
Treaty was concluded, realizing that Austria opposed its terms, Prince
Nikola sent Božo Petrović to Vienna to preserve his country's gains.
Although the prince had demonstrated subservience to Austrian de-
mands and had promised to co-operate in a subsequent Austrian occu-
pation of the insurgent provinces,[77] the Ballplatz proved adamant.
Leaving Petrović in no doubt of his basic hostility toward Montenegrin

[75] J. Grujić to Ristić, June 2/14, in Grujić, _3_, 330–33.   [76] Ristić, _2_, 173–74.
[77] See Nikola I to Franz Josef, Feb. 3/15, cited in Djordjević, _Crna Gora_, pp.
426–27.

aspirations, Andrassy stated openly that Austria would never permit her access to the sea. Therefore, Cetinje should withdraw its troops from Bar and the coastline it had occupied without awaiting the congress.[78] And the Austrian minister told Ignat'ev that Montenegro's frontier in the west could not extend beyond the Tara, while its San Stefano coastline would be eliminated or greatly curtailed.[79] Lieutenant Colonel Thömmel informed Božo Petrović that the Ballplatz was receiving numerous reports of Montenegrin military preparations and agitation among refugees and repatriates for Hercegovina's annexation to the Black Mountain. Such accusations, replied Božo, were untrue. Prince Nikola's pledges represented sufficient guarantee that Cetinje would undertake no hostile action against the Monarchy.[80]

Meanwhile, in dispatches to Constantinople, Andrassy sought to persuade the Porte to abandon Novi Pazar and the insurgent provinces to Austria. Andrassy argued that if Russia gave ground on the Bulgarian question, she would argue more stubbornly for a Montenegrin seacoast extending to the Bojana River. Were this permitted, the entire Turkish position in Europe would be endangered at the first Christian insurrection. Neither Turkey nor the congress could necessarily prevent such Montenegrin expansion; only the Dual Monarchy could do so by occupying Novi Pazar sandjak with the Porte's consent.[81]

Prince Nikola had ordered Stanko Radonić, his other envoy in San Stefano, to proceed to St. Petersburg to win Russia's support at the congress. Traveling with Grand Duke Nikolai Nikolaevich, Radonić arrived there at the height of Anglo-Russian tension. The tsar, anxious to obtain Montenegrin wartime assistance, told the envoy, "God grant we can hold what we acquired with such great sacrifices, but if it is necessary to fight again that the Montenegrins will respond as they always have." The prince, replied Radonić, would fight to the end rather than give up his new frontiers, especially the seacoast. In a May

[78] Nikola I, "Berlinski Kongres," Zapisi, 2 (1928), 95.

[79] HHSA, Geheimakten I, Mémoire, March 1878, cited in Čubrilović, p. 288.

[80] Djordjević, Crna Gora, p. 428. These reports apparently were part of a Turkish intrigue to alienate Montenegro from Vienna and stir up Arnauti and Turkish Moslems against the cession of their territories to Montenegro. Prince Nikola finally requested the Powers' consuls in Skadar to intercede with the Turkish authorities to prevent conflict in the Gusinje frontier region.

[81] HHSA, Andrassy to Zichy and Zichy to Andrassy, April 9, May 18, cited in A. Novotny, Quellen und Studien zur Geschichte des Berliner Kongresses 1878, 1 (Graz-Köln, 1957), 153.

25 dispatch communicated to the Russian and Austrian governments, Nikola was more cautious. Should the congress reject Cetinje's claims, Montenegro would battle for Bar to the death. There was fear in Cetinje, reported Thömmel, that at the congress Russia would yield many or all of Montenegro's gains. According to his information, Montenegro was so exhausted it would have to accept whatever terms were accorded it. To Radonić's reports that St. Petersburg doubted that even Bar could be retained, Prince Nikola telegraphed (June 5):

The attitude of the Russian government gives me deep concern and although I cannot imagine that Russia would place at stake Montenegro's winnings, and her peace and prosperity . . . since I have shown in the greatest measure how loyal I have always been to her and how useful in this war. But Russia will see what she has lost with Montenegro on this side if Montenegro perishes, since I shall adhere to my decision to die for the seacoast. This I declare again freely and openly.

Next day more encouraging tidings arrived from Radonić. "Here they have begun to believe that Austria, despite all her unwillingness, will consent to leave Montenegro the port of Bar, but will combine this with certain conditions." [82] On the eve of the congress the Black Mountain's chances had brightened somewhat because of Russian support.

In Bosnia the insurgents made desperate efforts to avoid an Austrian occupation. During the spring they continued to resist the Turks, and the provisional government called on the populace to fight. An assembly convened at Tiškovac (March 25–26), attended by some 450 delegates from all parts of Bosnia. Approved there were a memorandum to a future European congress and messages to the tsar and Slav societies of Russia. The memorandum, emphasizing Bosnian sufferings under Turkish rule and the struggle for freedom, avoided open rejection of an Austrian occupation. [83] But the petition to the tsar stated, "The ancient desire of the Bosnian people is to become an integral part of the Serbian principalities, but if for any reason this is prevented, then of necessity we are inclined to agree to become a separate, autonomous vassal state, such as our brother Bulgars have achieved." If Bosnia must be occupied, let Serbia do it. "All the sacrifices we have

[82] Nikola I, Zapisi, 2 (1928), p. 96; Thömmel to Andrassy, June 6, no. 127, cited by Djordjević, Crna Gora, p. 428.

[83] HHSA, "Eingaben an den Berliner Kongress 1878," 2, March 2; Čubrilović, Bosanski ustanak, p. 315; Ekmečić, Ustanak, pp. 343–45.

made would not bring us great and desired benefits or good fortune if the wishes of our people are not fulfilled," concluded the petition.[84] A similar appeal to "Slav brother, Aksakov" voiced open dissatisfaction with San Stefano: "After the victory of Russian arms, raised for the deliverance of all the Slavs in Turkey, we Bosnians are indignant . . . since we have been abandoned like the sweepings of humanity . . . to the mercy and injustice" of foreigners. The Russian public should demand annexation of Bosnia to Serbia. "Our peace and happiness are only in unity and freedom with our Serbian people." [85]

Vaso Vidović, a prominent insurgent leader, was selected as chief delegate to the European congress. He stopped off in Vienna to gain Ristić's support. Anxious not to antagonize Austria, he urged Vidović to delete references to Bosnia's unification with Serbia. But the Bosnian demurred, arguing that it must be made plain "to whom Bosnia wished to go." In Berlin, although he borrowed clothes from Ristić to give himself a civilized appearance, Vidović could obtain interviews only with Russian and Serbian delegates.[86]

The insurgent provinces were the subject of intensive Austro-Turkish negotiations. Asserting that the Turks could no longer preserve order there, Andrassy (March 28) urged the Porte to sanction an Austro-Hungarian occupation. This would secure remaining Turkish possessions from the expansionist Serbian states. In return for a free hand in Bosnia and Hercegovina, Austria at the congress would support the Turks elsewhere, especially in reducing Bulgaria's size. If the Turks sought to retain control of the insurgent provinces, Austria would have to "secure its interests." Andrassy declared that the Monarchy would occupy the two provinces to obstruct rising Pan-Slav agitation, with or without congress approval. On April 18, the Turkish cabinet unanimously rejected Andrassy's proposal. While Vienna and Budapest wrangled over how to justify occupation to the Austro-Hungarian public of more Slav territory, the Porte suggested (May 24) a joint operation: Austrian troops could occupy strategic points in Bosnia and Hercegovina, but they would have to withdraw when Turkey considered the crisis passed. Rejecting this Turkish offer as a piece of trick-

---

[84] Čubrilović, *Bosanski ustanak*, pp. 315–16.

[85] Ekmečić, *Ustanak*, p. 343.

[86] Čubrilović, *Bosanski ustanak*, pp. 314–16. Colonel Despotović eventually went to the Congress as second delegate after Golub Babić and Vid Milanović had declined to go. As assistants were named Vaso Pelagić and the merchant, J. Jovanović.

ery, Andrassy was now resigned to a full-dress Austrian occupation and was confident that the other Powers would approve.[87]

As the congress convened, continued fragmentation of the Serbian people was inevitable. The Treaty of San Stefano and Russian favoritism for Bulgaria and Montenegro promoted disunity. The Serbian states were unwilling to risk the gains they had been promised by supporting insurgent aspirations. Seeking maximum aggrandizement for themselves, Belgrade and Cetinje lost sight of the goal of Serbian unity. Once again Vienna profited from their jealousy and provincialism.

[87] Jakšić, *Evropa*, pp. 23–36.

CHAPTER IX

THE SERBIAN QUESTION AT THE CONGRESS OF BERLIN

NEGOTIATIONS had resolved the most dangerous issues before the delegates gathered for the Congress of Berlin on June 11–12. Voting delegates were present from the European great powers and Turkey as well as envoys from all of the Balkan countries concerned in the outcome. Russia had yielded substantially to Austria's demands for control over the insurgent provinces and to England's insistence on reduction and partition of Ignat'ev's Bulgaria. However, working out a Bulgarian settlement, determining Russia's gains in the Balkans and Asia Minor, and delimiting the frontiers of the Serbian states provided ample tasks for the assembled diplomatic talent, while the plenary sessions of the congress remained largely empty formalities. Austria's occupation of Bosnia and Hercegovina was assured, as was Serbia's reliance upon her to secure gains beyond those of San Stefano. But the Serbian states' long-term allegiance and the precise configuration of their frontiers remained uncertain.

Great power diplomacy at the Congress of Berlin has been treated in detail elsewhere.[1] Positions and attitudes of the major powers will therefore be described only as they pertain to the Serbian question.

---

[1] The best general work devoted to the Congress remains Medlicott's, *The Congress of Berlin*. The section in Sumner (*Russia*, pp. 501–53) is also excellent, especially for Russian aspects. Most useful for the Austrian position, although excessively laudatory of Andrassy's role, is Wertheimer, *Graf Julius Andrassy, 3*, 108–42. Summaries of the Austrian diplomatic correspondence are in Novotny's *Quellen und Studien*. For the British role see Wirthwein, *Britain and the Balkan Crisis*, pp. 390–415. See also E. L. Woodward, *The Congress of Berlin* (London, 1920), and Stojanović's account, *The Great Powers*, pp. 267–83.

Attitudes of the Powers

The Russian delegation [2] was headed by Chancellor Gorchakov, who had long desired to direct his country's case at a European congress and was not now to be denied this honor despite age and infirmity. Knowledgeable contemporaries mostly agreed, however they assessed his previous conduct of Russian foreign policy, that his faults now outweighed his abilities. The chancellor's impatience, tactlessness, carelessness about detail, ignorance of geography, and incredible vanity rendered him unfit to lead the defense of Russian interests in Berlin.[3] Gorchakov, wrote Lord Salisbury with devastating frankness, had become "a little insignificant old man, full of compliments, but otherwise having evidently lost his head." His presence "materially complicates matters, and . . . if some kindly fit of gout would take him off we should move much faster." [4]

The chancellor's incapacity placed heavy burdens upon Count P. A. Shuvalov, ambassador to England and Russia's second delegate, though

[2] The best assessment of the Russian delegates is found in Sumner, *Russia*, pp. 501–05.

[3] The tsar, claims Radowitz, had not wished Gorchakov to head the delegation, but he yielded when Gorchakov made his nomination a personal question. At the opening session, Gorchakov was too vain to admit he had not understood Disraeli's speech in English, and too slow to respond in Russian; his reply in consequence was irrelevant. J. von Radowitz, *Aufzeichnungen und Erinnerungen* (Berlin, 1925), *2*, 24, 36–37; HHSA, Langenau to Andrassy, June 21, telegram 145. Bartholomei, a Russian diplomat, stresses the chancellor's irresponsibility: he revealed to Beaconsfield a secret map, marked "only in case of absolute necessity," containing the maximum Russian territorial concessions on Bulgaria; henceforth, he was given only ordinary maps. In St. Petersburg, Gorchakov had mistaken Langenau for Schweinitz with embarrassing results. He had to be set straight by Giers, but he refused to acknowledge his blatant error. M. de Bartholomei, "Notes extraites des mémoires d'un diplomate russe," *Revue d'histoire diplomatique, 48* (Jan.–March 1934), pp. 104–06. Confirming the truth of the map story, General Anuchin wrote that he considered requesting the tsar to replace the chancellor with Miliutin as head of the delegation. Anuchin, "Berlinskii," pp. 9, 226. One of the few favorable assessments of Gorchakov at the congress is given by C. de Mouy, *Souvenirs et causeries, d'un diplomate* (Paris, 1909), p. 93, but the evidence of the chancellor's deficiencies appears irrefutable.

[4] G. Cecil, *Life of Salisbury, 2*, 279–81. Writing his wife June 20, Salisbury described Gorchakov's pathetic efforts to renounce the Anglo-Russian agreement on Bulgaria reached in London. After Gorchakov had "petulantly reasserted his purpose, and . . . flung himself angrily out of the room," Shuvalov whispered to Salisbury, "Faites pas attention—ce sont là un tas de bêtises." *Ibid.*, pp. 283–85.

he handled his manifold tasks with rare ability and good humor.[5] Shuvalov possessed the real authority among the Russian delegates; it was he, rather than Gorchakov, who made the vital decisions which averted conflict.[6] The count, frankly admitting his relative ignorance of Balkan affairs, worked assiduously before the congress to overcome this deficiency.[7] Count P. P. Ubri, ambassador in Berlin, was Russia's uninfluential and unhelpful third delegate.[8] The Russian military men at the congress (G. I. Bobrikov, D. G. Anuchin, and A. A. Bogoliubov) were conscientious and expert in Balkan affairs. One must nonetheless agree with Sumner that the Russian delegation, taken as a whole, did not constitute a powerful or united team.[9] Unconcealed hostility between Gorchakov and Shuvalov would prove damaging to Serbian as well as to Russian interests.[10]

Alexander II, after approving the Salisbury-Shuvalov agreement, convened his delegates to the Congress to confirm and clarify their instructions (June 8). Shuvalov complained later that many important issues were not even raised at this brief meeting. But War Minister Miliutin declared:

Why give you instructions, dear Count, and how would you want them? You know the situation. We cannot fight any more . . . either for financial

[5] Sumner, *Russia*, pp. 502–03. However, Sumner's statement that "all at the Congress agree that Shuvalov played his most thankless part with the utmost skill" is somewhat misleading. Russian nationalist diplomats criticized him for what they considered excessive concessions to the Austrians and English. See Mémoire of N. N. Giers in Jelavich, p. 74; Bartholomei, "Notes," pp. 99–100; Ignat'ev, IV, *144* (April 1916), pp. 331–32.

[6] Should Shuvalov break under the pressure of work, "fällt die ganze Pakete zusammen." Radowitz, *Aufzeichnungen*, 2, 24–25, 40. Shuvalov confers with Gorchakov only for show, wrote Anuchin later, since it is he who makes the basic decisions after conferring with the Russian experts. Anuchin, "Berlinskii," p. 12, June 9/21.

[7] Bobrikov, *Zapiski*, pp. 100–01.

[8] Ubri, writes Radowitz, had long been known to be unreliable and petty; he would make a good *maître d'hotel*. Jomini, however, was Gorchakov's indispensable assistant as usual. Nelidov, sad at the destruction of San Stefano, was nonetheless useful on Balkan questions. Radowitz, *Aufzeichnungen*, 2, 24–26.

[9] Sumner, *Russia*, p. 505.

[10] From the first day in Berlin, Shuvalov was convinced of the hostility toward him of Gorchakov and his subordinates. Thus Shuvalov established the condition that neither he nor Gorchakov would send any secret dispatches to St. Petersburg. Later, Shuvalov learned that the chancellor had sent a whole series of secret private letters to the tsar in an attempt to ruin his reputation. Khvostov, "Shuvalov," KA, *59*(1933), p. 101.

or military considerations. You have taken on yourself execution of a patriotic task, so defend us as best you can. Hold to the points you feel can be defended, and yield, better yield everything so as not to break up the congress.[11]

Chancellor Gorchakov hastened to adopt the pacific view of his government. Before departing for Berlin, he stated, "We are making great concessions, and I am prepared to take the unpopularity connected with it upon myself [*sic!*]. I desire peace and I know only one person who wants it even more urgently than I and that is the war minister." [12] Consequently, the Russian delegation arrived at Berlin in a conciliatory mood, resolved to avoid war if this were compatible with national honor.

And during the congress both the delegates and the leadership in St. Petersburg apparently realized how vulnerable was Russia's international position. Gorchakov, emphasizing his country's pacific intentions, announced, "Russia brings her laurels here, and she hopes the congress will convert them into olive branches." [13] Count Shuvalov warned his government that only Russia's minimum objectives could be achieved; "whoever wishes to go beyond this, wants war." [14] Russia was caught in an Anglo-Austrian vice, wrote Baron Jomini; she must make major concessions. He expressed the anguish of Russians in Berlin at their country's plight:

We are playing precisely the same role as at the Congress of 1856, judged and accused by Europe. . . . But then we were beaten! Today, after a victorious war, is this tolerable? But our envoys would bear a terrible responsibility if they exposed Russia to a new and triple war! They seek conciliation, propose deals, seek to save by desperate resistance at least some

[11] *Ibid.*, pp. 100–01.

[12] H. L. von Schweinitz, *Denkwürdigkeiten des Botschafters* (Berlin, 1928), *2*, 32. Actually, Gorchakov proved wholly unwilling to take responsibility for any concessions which might damage his popularity!

[13] In his speech, Gorchakov had used the phrase, "palmes de paix." But then he asked De Mouy to replace this with "branches d'oliviers" in the protocol, and was triumphant when this had been accomplished. The final version read: "La Russie apporte ici les lauriers, et il espère que le Congrès les convertira en branches d'oliviers." *Staatsarchiv*, *34*, nos. 6753, 6759. Protocols of sessions of June 13 and June 26; Busch, *Deutsche Rundschau*, p. 375.

[14] B. Bareilles, ed., *Le rapport secret . . . par Caratheodory Pacha* (Paris, 1919), pp. 119–21.

of our legitimate demands. But where to stop when one descends the staircase of concessions?[15]

Whereas Shuvalov attributed Russia's difficulties to Anglo-Austrian hostility, Gorchakov blamed Bismarck's failure to support its legitimate claims.[16] In St. Petersburg, Miliutin, while complaining bitterly about Russia's isolation and Bismarck's "betrayal," knew that Russia must yield to prevent war.[17] General Bobrikov's interpretation was different. He asserted that Russian representatives had been unable to repair grievous mistakes of previous years. Bismarck was as friendly toward Russia as one could expect; as mediator he supported its aspirations more strongly than those of its opponents.[18] But, in any case, Russian leaders did not believe they could support Serbian aspirations at the congress unconditionally.

Austria-Hungary, whose vital interests were at stake in Berlin, sent an unusually capable delegation, led by Foreign Minister Andrassy.[19] Regarding the western Balkans as the Monarchy's legitimate sphere of

[15] Jelavich, *Russia in the East*, p. 77, Jomini to Giers, June 14/26. He consoled himself with the thought: "La page future doit être le compte définitif à régler entre nous et l'Autriche."

[16] Goriainov, *Le Bosphore*, pp. 378, 380.

[17] Miliutin, *Dnevnik*, *3*, 72–73, June 17/29. He was surprised at the tsar's calm acceptance of "the impudent demands of Austria" to the "Enclave."

[18] "The Berlin Congress was not held in an atmosphere of general hostility toward Russia—such a view led us to overlook our own errors. The congress reduced our international significance not because of a hostile coalition, but because we worked too little." Bobrikov, *Zapiski*, p. 104. Stojanović (*The Great Powers*, p. 267), basing his account on Wertheimer (*3*, 102), incorrectly stresses "this unity of Europe against Russia" at the congress.

[19] Radowitz lists Andrassy's geniality and quick grasp of important issues as his chief assets. H. von Haymerle performed much of the routine work with great skill. Count L. Karolyi, the third delegate, lacked great gifts. Haymerle was assisted by an expert, hard-working staff including Kosjek, Mayr, Schwegel, Thömmel, and Teschenberg—all of them were intimately acquainted with Balkan problems. Radowitz, *Aufzeichnungen*, *2*, 27–28.

Freiherr von Schwegel asserted that "all the practical work which Andrassy does not do, falls on me. I shall have authored most of the ideas of the Berlin Congress." With similar exaggeration of his own importance, Schwegel wrote, "It is only due to my initiative that today the Russians renounced two thirds of their original claims in Bulgaria, though history will give the credit to Andrassy." HHSA, Schwegel, "Notizen," no. 32, n.d. and June 8. Sumner concludes justifiably (*Russia*, p. 508) that, taken as a whole, the Austrian delegation was the strongest at the congress.

interest, he aimed to extend its influence to Mitrovica, thus acquiring the insurgent provinces, securing maritime hegemony over the eastern Adriatic, and uniting most Serbs under the aegis of the Austrian kaiser.[20] Prior to the congress, Andrassy had been assured of the support of most other Powers in achieving these objectives. He would insist upon reducing Montenegrin gains and removing the Serbian states from the "Enclave." [21] From the outset, the Monarchy predominated in the affairs of the Serbs at Berlin.

The English aimed to restrict Russia's influence in Bulgaria and reduce its gains in Asia Minor. As to the frontiers of the Serbian states, Salisbury emphasized that the English delegation should support the Austrians and give European Turkey defensible frontiers. Otherwise, he instructed Lord Russell, "your aim should be to assure the welfare and good government of the populations concerned." [22] In Berlin the English, anxious to protect Turkey and accommodate Austria, generally opposed Serbian interests.

The remaining Powers, except the impotent Turks, were less vitally concerned with the fate of Serbdom. Bismarck, who dominated the congress and sought to hasten it along, remarked impatiently, "One does not come to a congress for purposes of discussion." Sympathizing neither with the Porte nor the Balkan peoples, he strove to prevent a collapse of the congress by mediating disputes between Russia, Austria, and England.[23] France and Italy, though often friendly toward the Serbs, occupied secondary positions. The Turkish delegation, declared Bismarck, consisted of "a Greek, a renegade, and an imbecile." It consistently opposed aggrandizement of the Serbian states but was kept

---

[20] HHSA, Schwegel on Austrian objectives at the congress. Wrote Schwegel, ". . . through the annexation of Bosnia and Hercegovina as a hinterland for Dalmatia, on the one hand can be secured the possession and development of that country and with it the proper maritime position of Austria-Hungary in the Adriatic, and on the other hand, through the unification of the overwhelming majority of the Serbian people under His Majesty, that decisive influence in a political and economic sense can be won and retained which is proper for that people and is essential to the Monarchy to preserve its position as a great power."

[21] Wertheimer, *Graf Julius Andrassy*, 3, 125.

[22] *Staatsarchiv, 35*, no. 6876, pp. 218–20, Salisbury to (Russell), June 8. The frontiers of Serbia and Montenegro, added Salisbury, and the arrangements for Bosnia and Hercegovina do not interest England especially. Should Russia insist on the provisions of San Stefano in regard to those issues, the congress should not be broken up. Bulgaria, however, "requires very material reduction."

[23] Bareilles, *Rapport secret*, pp. 65–67.

ill informed by Constantinople. The Turks' main task was to protest valiantly, then sign away provinces.

Serbia at Berlin

Bismarck, as presiding officer of the congress, insisted that questions be discussed in order of importance. Bulgaria's future was clearly the most controversial and dangerous issue; it absorbed the delegate's attention for the first two weeks.[24] Any settlement of Bulgaria's frontiers would significantly affect Serbia's boundaries. The Austro-British agreement (June 6) had stipulated that an autonomous Bulgarian principality could extend only to the Balkan Mountains on the south and the Morava Valley on the west. Encountering a solid hostile front on this issue, the Russians, though still strongly pro-Bulgarian, had to make major concessions. Anglo-Russian tension over Bulgaria was exacerbated by the London *Globe*'s disclosure (June 14) of the secret Salisbury-Shuvalov agreements. Salisbury's tactless remark (June 17) that the congress had convened "to destroy entirely the results of the war," provoked Shuvalov to retort that Russia had come to Berlin to co-ordinate the Treaty of San Stefano with the general interest of Europe.[25] Bismarck hastily intervened to arrange private Anglo-Russian negotiations to resolve differences over Bulgaria; Andrassy insisted upon participating. Consistent Austrian support for the British position in these *pourparlers* dismayed the Russians and compelled them to yield. On June 21, after receiving new instructions, Shuvalov agreed to Bulgaria's partition: an autonomous principality would be established north of the Balkan range, and a semiautonomous Eastern Rumelia to the south of it. Shuvalov secured Sofia sandjak for the Bulgarian principality by agreeing to restore the Mesta and Struma valleys to the Porte.[26] Disputes continued over delimitation of Bulgarian frontiers

[24] For the Bulgarian question at the congress see Medlicott, *Congress of Berlin*, pp. 45–71; Sumner, *Russia*, pp. 517–28; and Stojanović, *The Great Powers*, pp. 268–70.

[25] *Staatsarchiv, 35*, no. 6754, Protocol no. 2, June 17.

[26] Wertheimer, *Graf Julius Andrassy, 3*, 113–17; Sumner, *Russia*, pp. 517–25; Bareilles, *Rapport secret*, pp. 84–85, 94. Salisbury wrote triumphantly to his wife (June 22): "The Russians have very nearly given way on all material points. . . . Austria is still pulling with us heavily." And again on June 24: "We have very nearly finished Bulgaria—and entirely in our own sense." Cecil, *Salisbury, 2*, 286, 288. Shuvalov claimed, however, that he had obtained everything for Russia which had been agreed upon with Salisbury (May 30), as well as Sofia sandjak which St. Petersburg had not believed could be gained for Bulgaria. Khvostov, "Shuvalov," p. 100.

until late in the congress, which had an important bearing on Serbia's eastern boundaries.[27]

For Serbia the principal questions at Berlin were: (1) independence and a possible European guarantee; (2) frontiers; and (3) its economic relationship with the Dual Monarchy. The greatest difficulties were encountered in delineating Serbia's southern and eastern frontiers and concluding agreements with Austria-Hungary.[28] Foreign Minister Ristić, assisted by Kosta Ćukić, his envoy in Vienna, ably represented Serbia in Berlin. They were excluded from plenary session, but Ristić rightly regarded these as formalities.[29] The Serbs were free to confer with the Powers' delegates and present their case informally. Serbia's prospects were bright, Ristić confided to the German diplomat C. A. Busch, since the Austrians would probably support its claims in the southeast. Ristić personally was not so set upon territorial aggrandizement, but Serbian opinion, he explained, would accept only such compensation for its heavy wartime sacrifices.[30]

The Russians' attitude distressed Ristić. Their growing coolness since San Stefano he attributed to Serbia's approaches to Vienna, its independent attitude, and to their predilection for a Montenegro still regarded as "a poetical little country." Indeed, Russian efforts to salvage the Treaty of San Stefano could not possibly benefit Serbia.[31] General Bobrikov deplored his colleagues' behavior: "It was strange to see our own diplomats turn their backs on the Serbs and act disdainfully. They turned their backs on our stake in the strengthening of the Serbian nationality, on the balance of power in the Balkans upon which our importance in the Slav world depends." [32]

The Serbian question did not come formally before the congress until June 28, but in the interim Ristić was not idle. He discovered the

[27] Sumner, *Russia*, pp. 655-57.

[28] The chief source for Serbia at the congress is the confidential correspondence among Ristić, Prince Milan, and Acting Premier Jevrem Grujić contained in J. Grujić, *3*, 323-76. This material has been utilized in part by V. Georgewitch, "La Serbie au Congrès de Berlin," *Revue d'histoire diplomatique*, *5* (1891), 485-552, although few documents are presented there in their entirety. Even Grujić, *3*, does not contain the full correspondence; this can be found in AII, Ristić 22/1-89.

[29] The question of access to the formal sittings, wrote Ristić, was unimportant since important decisions were reached in private consultations. Ristić to Grujić, June 8/20, in Grujić, *3*, 334-36. Montenegro and Greece were treated similarly. Rumanian delegates were allowed to present their case to the session of July 1 (see *Staatsarchiv*, *35*, no. 6762).

[30] Busch, *Deutsche Rundschau*, p. 368; Vlada Milana, *1*, 418.

[31] Busch, *Deutsche Rundschau*, p. 368.

[32] Bobrikov, *Zapiski*, p. 95.

nature of Russian and Austrian frontier proposals and labored to secure a maximum gain for Serbia.[33] Everyone, reported Ristić, sought to avoid irritating Austria because of her powerful position at the congress. To succeed in Berlin, advised the French delegate, agree with Andrassy and avoid displeasing Austria. Ristić wrote that everything depended upon such an agreement, since only with Austrian support could Bobrikov's frontier proposal be defeated. Nonetheless, he preserved harmonious relations with the Russian delegates. "In no case," he warned, "can we utilize Austria-Hungary as a weapon against the influence of Russia in our areas." [34] On June 24, Ristić submitted to the congress a memorandum containing Serbia's maximum demands: independence under guarantee of the Powers and the territorial increases requested of Russia prior to San Stefano.[35] Thus he rejected Andrassy's advice to limit Serbian claims to what was obtainable. Serbian historic rights must be expressed, he asserted. But the memorandum's allusion to Bosnia was innocuous enough to be inoffensive to Andrassy.[36]

Ristić's position was difficult and delicate. Pressed by Austria to relinquish territory in the west, and by Russia to abandon the Pirot-Trn area to Bulgaria in the east, he strove to insure adequate territorial compensation for his country while maintaining friendly relations with both Powers. Ristić protested vigorously against the Russians' efforts to obtain the Pirot-Trn region for Bulgaria:

When the Austrians, say, drive us from Novi Pazar, you are not in a position to defend us, and when they offer us some compensation, you oppose it. Compensation, *especially that* [Pirot-Trn], is of such concern to us that we must have it at any price, and that it will come *dearer* to us will be your fault, since Austria-Hungary, realizing that because of your opposition it holds the key to our southeastern frontier, will not reduce its onerous demands. It is a sorry spectacle for us to see Russia quarreling with Austria *against us*. There have been enough mistakes. The San Stefano peace would have given almost all of Old Serbia to the Bulgarians. There is an opportunity now to correct these errors and not to leave an apple of discord

---

[33] Bobrikov had proposed the line: Giljan-Sveti Ilija-Snegpolje-Ak Palanka, leaving the Pirot-Trn region to Bulgaria. The Austrians suggested the frontier Kopaonik-Golak-Trnovac-Sveti Ilija-Trn-Dragoman-Stara Planina-Sveti Nikola, which would extend Serbia greatly in the east but reduce it in the west compared with the Treaty of San Stefano. AII, Ristić 22/36, Ristić to (Grujić), June 1/13.

[34] Ristić to Grujić, June 8/20, in Grujić, *3*, 334-36.

[35] See *supra*, p. 254.

[36] Ristić to Grujić, June 12/24, no. 4, in Grujić, *3*, 337-38.

between two brother peoples on the one hand, nor on the other to leave them with memories which will alienate the Serbian people from Russia.

Ristić objected particularly to Russo-Bulgarian claims to Pirot. "But according to our people," Shuvalov argued, "everything there is Bulgarian." "Perhaps so," retorted Ristić, "but we shall accept the result of a plebiscite from there, whatever it may be." When Russia settled accounts with the Austrians, he warned, Serbia would be a much more valuable ally than Bulgaria. Ristić believed his frank words had found their mark, since Jomini and Bobrikov now advocated consulting the people of Trn and Pirot if Serbian administrators and troops were withdrawn.[37] But this did not signify any basic change in Russian policy in regard to Serbia's eastern frontiers.

On the western side, Shuvalov, in preliminary discussions about the "Enclave," encountered heavy sailing. Andrassy demanded its annexation as far as Mitrovica to the Monarchy. Shuvalov, on instruction from St. Petersburg, remained obdurate. Finally, Andrassy, renouncing annexation, declared that the Porte could administer the "Enclave," but Austria would station troops there whenever Bosnia's security was threatened; however, Russia must pledge to support an eventual Austrian occupation of the insurgent provinces. In return Austria would back Russian claims to southern Bessarabia, the Asiatic frontiers it desired, and a seaport for Montenegro. Shuvalov reported home that only by accepting Andrassy's reduced demands on the "Enclave," could Austrian hostility toward Russia at the congress be overcome. However, he told Andrassy, "At the moment when the Russian tsar has retreated so far from the Treaty of San Stefano, Austria-Hungary should not ask that Russia herself subject its allies, Serbia and Montenegro, to encirclement." Andrassy retorted that Austria would occupy the "Enclave" by force eventually whether Russia approved or not.[38]

[37] *Ibid.*, June 14/26 and 15/27, pp. 339–41. Milan telegraphed Ristić (June 27) confidently that the population of Pirot and Trn would support Serbia, especially in the villages. "Positively, under present circumstances, the vast majority would vote for us and without any agitation on our part, but if it were necessary to withdraw our administration and give full scope to Russo-Bulgarian agitation, the situation would become more difficult. . . . Even then I feel we would succeed." *Ibid.*, pp. 339–40. This statement appears convincing since Milan had no reason to deceive Ristić on such a question.

[38] For Shuvalov's account see Khvostov, "Shuvalov," pp. 101–02, and Shuvalov to Giers, June 7/19, cited in Goriainov, *Le Bosphore*, p. 378. See also Anuchin, "Berlinskii," p. 9; Ignat'ev, IV, *144* (April 1916), 331–32; Novotny, *Quellen*, p. 107. Shuvalov attributed Andrassy's concession on the "Enclave" to his stubborn

In St. Petersburg the tsar at first was resolved to order Shuvalov to stand firm on the "Enclave"; Miliutin expressed indignation at the Austrian demands.[39] No final agreement was reached at that time on Serbia's eastern or western boundaries.

Serbian leaders were perplexed and embarrassed by the sudden appearance in Belgrade of General Fadeev, the noted Russian Pan-Slav. He informed Acting Premier J. Grujić that the War Ministry had sent him to Serbia on a secret mission to gather information about Austrian military strength and organize opposition to a possible Austrian occupation of the insurgent provinces. When Fadeev sought an audience with Prince Milan, the latter demanded proof of his official status and asked Ristić what should be done with him. And Grujić telegraphed Ristić, "I feel that the Russians on the one hand through Shuvalov seek peace, and on the other through Miliutin prepare for conflict with Austria in case the congress fails." Ristić responded (June 26): "Provide Fadeev with the information he seeks, but do not let him operate independently; that would compromise us with Austria-Hungary." [40] The Russian general soon departed for Bosnia, where he gathered additional data and encouraged Christian-Moslem co-operation against an Austrian occupation.[41]

On June 28, the Serbian question was first discussed formally by the congress. Only Caratheodory Pasha of Turkey raised objections to Serbia's independence. Bismarck declared firmly that since the Turks had granted this at San Stefano, they could not oppose it now. But Ristić's request for a European guarantee was ignored. The congress then approved a French proposal to assure religious freedom to all inhabitants of the principality. Accepting H. von Haymerle's vague formula —"la Serbie recevra un agrandissement territorial"—the delegates en-

---

resistance, but he blamed Gorchakov for undermining his bargaining position. According to Bismarck, the chancellor had told Andrassy, "You will get it [the "Enclave"]. . . . I would rather see it in your hands than in the hands of the Turks." This statement, noted Shuvalov, was diametrically opposed to the will of the tsar, who desired to leave it to the Turks, but in no case to Austria-Hungary. Khvostov, "Shuvalov," pp. 101–02.

[39] "Andrassy's insistence on the Enclave suggests," wrote Miliutin on June 27, "that he does not yet have the support of other Powers. But can Austria expect from Russia support in such scandalous pretensions which would strike a blow against the future of the Slav question in the Balkan peninsula?" Miliutin, *Dnevnik, 3,* 71.

[40] AII, Ristić 22/44, Milan to Ristić, June 10/22; Grujić, *3,* 338–39.

[41] Ekmečić, *Ustanak,* p. 355.

trusted delimitation of her frontiers to boundary and military commissions, composed of one representative from each Power. Turkey insisted Serbia's tribute payments be capitalized so that Serbia would bear a portion of the Ottoman state debt proportional to the territory it acquired. Since Russia was strongly opposed, this proposal was referred to the Editing Commission.[42] Serbia's fate would be resolved in the corridors and committees of the congress.

The future of the "Enclave" was the first controversial question to be settled. Andrassy's announcement in plenary session (June 28) that the sandjak would remain Turkish with Austria retaining the right to keep garrisons there led Shuvalov to request time to consult his government. Bismarck interjected, "But you have been discussing that question with the Austrians for almost ten months, and you still have not reached agreement! Will you be more fortunate in the course of twenty-four hours?" Next day Shuvalov informed Andrassy that the tsar would accept the Austrian terms.[43] Later (July 13), an Austro-Russian convention was concluded by which Russia pledged not to oppose Austrian occupation of the sandjak and the insurgent provinces.[44] A question of great significance for Serbdom had been decided without its representatives' participation.

The final determination of Serbia's frontiers should be viewed against a background of its deteriorating relations with Russia and conclusion of economic agreements with Austria. The Russian delegates persistently refused to support Serbian claims to the Pirot and Trn regions. Ristić, confident now that most of the population was Serbian, wrote Shuvalov (July 2) agreeing to a plebiscite. He rejected Shuvalov's suggestion that a special commission be established to investigate the problem:

Only the Slavs' adversaries could profit from the irritation which would result. . . . The entire Serbian nation would be distressed by such a delay. All Serbs would be surprised to learn that it depended only upon Russia to assure them certain advantages but that the Russian representatives refused it, whereas the representatives of all other powers were disposed to accord

---

[42] *Staatsarchiv, 35,* no. 6760, Protocol no. 8, pp. 171–74.

[43] Declared Miliutin, "The impudent demands of Austria anger me to the depths. To my amazement, the tsar accepted these demands quietly and indulgently," Miliutin, *Dnevnik, 3,* 72–73, June 17/29. Bareilles, *Rapport secret,* p. 145; Jakšić, *Evropa,* p. 55; Wertheimer, *Graf Julius Andrassy, 3,* 131.

[44] Novotny, *Quellen,* p. 132.

it to them. . . . Such an attitude would constitute a mistake which would remain historic. Serbia claims only her rights based on the Serbian nationality of the vast majority of the population in question and on the blood it has spilled in those regions [Pirot and Trn]. We have had to insist the more upon a good frontier in the east since the western one seems to have been established in a sense entirely unfavorable to us.

Ristić concluded that realization of Serbian desires rested with Russia.[45] With only the Russian vote needed to obtain Pirot and Trn for Serbia, Ristić requested Milan to telegraph the tsar to support Serbian claims. But Milan replied that an open telegram to the tsar would be a mistake since the work of the congress was secret. He regretted Russia's apparent separation from Serbia at the congress.[46]

Ristić realized that without Russian support prompt conclusion of an economic agreement with Austria-Hungary was essential. He asserted that his strong objections to the original Austrian drafts had induced Baron Schwegel to modify them by incorporating most of the Serbian suggestions.[47] Ristić summarized the final Austrian terms: (1) Austria-Hungary would link its railway system with the Serbian one at Belgrade in three years; Serbia would construct railway lines to Mitrovica and Niš in the same period; (2) the two governments would arrange connections with Bulgarian and Turkish lines; (3) construction and maintenance of these lines would be uniform; (4) a commercial treaty between Serbia and Austria would be signed immediately following the congress; (5) Austria would take responsibility for regulation of Djerdjap. Ristić favored immediate acceptance of these terms in order to assure a favorable decision on Serbian frontiers.[48] He considered onerous only the obligation to construct railways within three years, but he had been unable to extend the time limit. Everything else, he assured Grujić, left much latitude for subsequent negotiations. Convinced that the agreements were less harsh than Belgrade had antici-

---

[45] Ristić to Shuvalov, June 20/July 2, cited in Grujić, 3, 373–74.

[46] AII, Ristić 22/55, Ristić to Milan, June 20/July 2; 22/76, Milan to Ristić.

[47] Schwegel's original draft, Ristić believed, would impose such economic obligations on Serbia as to threaten its independence. To insist upon conclusion of agreements giving Baron Hirsch full rights to exploit Serbian railways before a territorial settlement, objected Ristić, "is to place a knife before our throats." Andrassy, denying any such intentions, advised him not to take Schwegel's draft so seriously. On June 30, Schwegel sent Ristić a revised proposal, and on July 3, Andrassy presented the Serbs with final draft agreements. Grujić, 3, 349–52. For the Austrian and Serbian proposals see *ibid.*, pp. 352–59.

[48] *Ibid.*, pp. 343–44.

pated and that further Austrian concessions were unobtainable, Ristić urged that they be approved.[49]

But the Serbian ministers were unconvinced. Grujić responded that until the cabinet learned what Serbia would obtain with Austria's support, it could not reach a decision. If most Serbian territorial increases depended on Austria, its terms must be accepted. "We shall rely upon your patriotism [to resolve that question]." That same day (July 5), Ristić warned, "The congress will come to an end and we will be passed over if there is further delay." Unless the cabinet approved immediately the convention with Austria, he would renounce responsibility for Serbia's fate. Andrassy had pledged to advocate inclusion of the Pirot-Trn area in Serbia and the western boundary proposed by the military commission[50] only if the Serbs accepted the convention. Its rejection would expose Serbia to unknown losses. Although Prince Milan reiterated unconditional support for the convention, Premier Grujić (July 7) continued to raise doubts:

When there are not only no guarantees of success and we are threatened with Austrian hostility . . . then there remains nothing else than to seek as a last resort the serious protection and support of the tsarist Russian delegates; if they cannot help us, then, depending upon the Russian view of the convention, conclude it with Austria on terms most favorable to Serbian interests.

Grujić apparently still believed Serbia could choose between Russia and Austria. To dispel such illusions, Ristić responded that to adopt the policy Grujić advocated would be ridiculous:

From my letters you know that the Russian delegate told me not only to reach agreement with Austria-Hungary, but to undertake nothing at the congress without its approval, and that we would succeed to the extent we agreed with it. Now, with the convention, we are on the verge of success on the eastern frontier, and precisely there Russia demands Pirot for Bulgaria despite all my oral and written appeals. Thus to seek her support in such circumstances would be equivalent to asking for Austria-Hungary's backing to acquire Novi Pazar.

[49] *Ibid.*, pp. 349–52, Ristić to Grujić, June 23/July 5, no. 10.
[50] In the east, Ristić noted that the line would run from Crni Vrh, along the frontier of Niš pashalik to Dragoman, Stara Planina, and Sveti Nikola. On the west the boundary proposed was Kopaonik, along the Kaniluč boundary of Niš pashalik (leaving the Lab Valley to Turkey), to Djak, Velika Glava, Poljanica, Koncul, Sveti Ilija, and ending at Crni Vrh.

The cabinet finally bowed to this dual pressure.[51] Ristić was authorized to sign.

On July 8, the Austro-Serbian agreement was formally concluded. Before signing, Ristić warned he would not recommend ratification by the Assembly unless Serbia received the frontiers Austria had pledged to support. "I am no bazaar trader," retorted Andrassy angrily. If Serbia failed to sign, he would oppose any extension of its frontiers. The convention, Ristić explained to Grujić, would insure Andrassy's support at the congress and prevent him from opposing Serbia's aggrandizement. What Serbia obtained beyond the frontiers of San Stefano, asserted Ristić later, was due primarily to the convention and Andrassy's efforts.[52]

Meanwhile, the military and boundary commissions wrangled over Serbian frontiers. The western boundary was settled easily after formal Russian acceptance (July 1) of Andrassy's proposals on the "Enclave." Ristić anticipated that Serbia would be excluded from the Novi Pazar sandjak, but he fought for the fertile Lab Valley.[53] Andrassy opposed this on strategic grounds, however, and Ristić's pleas to other delegates were ignored. In the west, Serbian claims encountered solid resistance from Austria, England, and Turkey. Ristić had to accept the commission's verdict.[54]

In the east, complications for Serbia arose from England's insistence that the Ihtiman-Djuma region in the eastern part of Sofia sandjak be

[51] Grujić, 3, 359–64; AII, Ristić 22/65. On July 6, noting the cabinet's hesitation, Milan wrote that of the ministers only R. Milojković understood the true situation of Serbia. The prince, obtaining the cabinet's consent to the agreement with great difficulty, urged Ristić to sign even without its full backing "and thus assure to Serbia an important territorial increase rather than leave us, because of your colleagues' ignorance of foreign affairs, . . . without any result or with reduced gains." On July 7, Milan telegraphed that he did not consider it essential, as did the ministers, to consult Russia because she was not supporting Serbia and "nous dispute élément serbe au profit de la Bulgarie." The prince added, "Vous avez carte blanche d'agir comme bon vous semble." AII, Ristić 22/85 and 89.

[52] Grujić, 3, 365–67.

[53] Ristić, learning June 30 that the Austrian delegate in the military commission had voted to assign the Lab Valley to Turkey, remonstrated with Andrassy. He declared, "I would be downcast and feel my mission had failed if I do not succeed in obtaining the Lab Valley, Vranje, Trn, and Pirot for Serbia." Grujić, 3, 354.

[54] Austrian interests, explained Ristić, include keeping the Serbs as far as possible from the left bank of the Vardar and the Mitrovica-Salonika route. Ibid., pp. 345–47. Anuchin claimed that he sought to draw a natural, impartial boundary. Anuchin, "Berlinskii," pp. 226–28.

left to Turkey, rather than Bulgaria, for strategic reasons. Andrassy and Shuvalov had agreed previously that the kazas of Trn and Pirot further west should go to Serbia. This decision was confirmed by the military and boundary commissions. On July 8, the report of the boundary commission was presented to the congress. C. von Hohenlohe Schillingsfürst announced that disagreement over Bulgaria's western boundaries persisted because of its decision to accept Anglo-Turkish demands for a strategic frontier. Shuvalov demanded the kaza of Trn to compensate Bulgaria for loss of the Ihtiman-Djuma region. But Andrassy, asserting that both Trn and Pirot contained Serbian majorities, claimed them for Serbia. As a compromise Shuvalov proposed that Trn remain in Bulgaria and Pirot go to Serbia. The congress adopted this view and empowered the boundary commission to draw up the actual frontier by majority vote.[55]

On the south, the commissions had approved the Koncul-Lužani line, awarding Vranje to Serbia. When Bismarck submitted this decision to the congress, it confirmed Serbia's right to Vranje, despite Anglo-Turkish contentions that the Porte's security would be endangered. The crucial vote went in Serbia's favor by a four-to-three margin, confirming the vital importance of Austrian support.[56]

The question of capitalization of tribute was debated July 11. Ristić had warned Shuvalov that capitalization could be imposed on Serbia only by force. The Russian had promised to do Serbia a favor by opposing any such measure in the congress. The Editing Commission's report, supported by England and Turkey, stated that the newly independent Balkan states should pay compensation to the Porte for its loss of annual tribute.[57] The Russian delegates promptly objected. Gorchakov argued that when Serbian and Rumanian independence were proclaimed at San Stefano, nothing was mentioned about capitalization of their tribute. Only newly annexed territories should bear a

[55] Over the issue of the eastern frontier of Serbia, Bismarck shouted angrily, "Does the peace of the world depend on the Serbian frontiers?" Nonetheless, Andrassy persisted in demanding Trn for Serbia. Only strong Austrian pressure, asserted Ristić, induced Shuvalov to abandon his earlier demand for the inclusion of Pirot in Bulgaria. Ristić to Grujić, June 29/July 11, no. 13, cited in Grujić, *3*, 367-70.

[56] *Staatsarchiv*, *35*, nos. 6767, 6768, Protocols nos. 15, 16. In the voting on Vranje, Serbian claims were backed by Austria, Russia, Germany, and France. Favoring its restoration to Turkey were England, Italy, and Turkey.

[57] *Staatsarchiv*, *35*, no. 6770, Protocol no. 18, July 11.

share of the Ottoman debt. Shuvalov declared that it would be unfair to capitalize their tribute since independence had been won in war, not by agreement. But these two states, objected Salisbury, owed their independence to Russian victories. Shuvalov replied: their own armies had gained important successes; Turkey must bear the consequences of defeat. The congress majority supported Russia's stand, and the capitalization proposal was defeated.[58] In a sense, Russia could still claim to be the protector of the eastern Christians against the Porte.

At Berlin, in addition to independence, Serbia acquired considerably more territory than she had been promised at San Stefano, despite Ristić's failure to secure gains on the west.[59] These increases, especially in the east, were due primarily to Austrian support. Russia, however, opposing Serbian aggrandizement only when it conflicted with Bulgarian claims based on nationality, had assisted Serbian expansion to the south. On the other hand, England and Turkey had revealed consistent hostility to Serbia's aspirations.

Treatment of Other Serbian Areas

Other Serbian lands fared worse at the congress. Montenegro's delegates, Božo Petrović and Stanko Radonić, faced dark prospects. From the outset it was evident that Montenegro would not gain all that the Treaty of San Stefano promised—how much it would lose depended primarily upon Austro-Russian agreements.[60] The Andrassy-Shuvalov conversation of June 13 established the main lines for a settlement of Montenegrin claims. San Stefano, admitted Shuvalov, had been a colossal piece of Russian stupidity. But they must reach agreement on the port of Bar, "the black point between us." Andrassy insisted upon Austrian control of the insurgent provinces and the "Enclave." "Wholly understandable," responded Shuvalov amiably. Russia, not opposing Austria's occupation of Bosnia and Hercegovina, would demand Bar for Montenegro; to leave Montenegro wholly

---

[58] *Ibid.*, pp. 265–67; Grujić, *3*, 372–73. Ristić later noted his appreciation of Russian efforts in this question. Ristić, *2*, 226–27.

[59] Serbia's area was increased from 783 to 993 kv. mil and its population from 1,360,000 to 1,640,000 by the Berlin Treaty. This amounted to 56 kv. mil and 54,000 people more than was stipulated at San Stefano. *Istok*, July 30/Aug. 11, no. 87.

[60] For Montenegro at the Congress the best source is Nikola I's memoirs, published in *Zapisi*. See also Jakšić, *Evropa*, pp. 54–55, and Protocols no. 10, 12. J. Vukić's article, "Crna Gora na Berlinskom Kongresu," *Zapisi*, 2, sv. 5 (1928), 281–87 is superficial.

dissatisfied would be unjust and unwise. Andrassy objected that Bar's inhabitants had petitioned Vienna against annexation to Montenegro. Because of Bar's commercial importance, Austria-Hungary must, in any case, attach conditions to secure her "general coastal interests." Shuvalov indicated he would accept this. And Emperor Franz Josef, approving the results of the Andrassy-Shuvalov parley, wrote that Montenegro could have Bar if it accepted Austrian terms. "In such a case," added the kaiser, "the necessity for occupation of Bosnia and Hercegovina, including the Enclave . . . becomes even more self-evident." [61]

Russia, renouncing support for Montenegro's acquisition of the entire coastal strip conquered by its armies, now merely sought Bar and environs. To achieve even this modest goal, Shuvalov would accept restriction on use of that port and sacrifice the "Enclave." Montenegro's prospects of retaining its Albanian coastline vanished, and Austrian troop concentrations in southern Dalmatia distressed Cetinje.[62] To buttress his country's case and win European support, Božo Petrović wrote an article for Le Temps of Paris (June 19). We Montenegrins, he pleaded, are a poor but proud people who have always had to fight to supply ourselves with food. We are tired of fighting and war poetry. If Europe grants us the coastal plain, we shall descend from our mountains and become peaceful farmers and merchants. Otherwise, we must remain warlike. Bar's possession will help make us a happy and peaceful nation. Let the Austrians take security measures; we shall submit to the verdict of Europe.[63] In a memorandum to the congress (June 27), Petrović explained that Montenegro's aspirations naturally exceeded its claims at the Constantinople Conference and that San Stefano's frontiers were just. Such boundaries would include 270,000 Orthodox and only 37,000 Catholics in Montenegro.[64]

The Montenegrins, excluded from formal sessions in the Palace Radziwill, worked privately to convince the delegates that their claims

---

[61] Novotny, Quellen, pp. 83–86, 112; Jakšić, Evropa, pp. 39–40. Austrian conditions for cession of Bar sought to insure Turkish control of both shores of the Bojana River, although Montenegro would be assured navigation rights along the river. Bar was to be closed to all foreign warships in order to prevent Russia from establishing a concealed Adriatic naval base. Austria was to obtain the right to patrol the Montenegrin coast line and construct a road and railway through Montenegrin territory into Albania. Novotny, Quellen, p. 112.

[62] Djordjević, Crna Gora, p. 430.   [63] Jakšić, Evropa, p. 44.

[64] HHSA, Promemoria, cited in Jakšić, pp. 54–55.

were valid. Most of the Powers' envoys realized that Montenegro could not live without access to the sea; but, anxious to satisfy the Austrians, they would not support its plea for the frontiers of San Stefano.[65] An Austro-Russian bargain, assuring Montenegro of Bar in exchange for Russian consent to eventual Austrian occupation of the "Enclave" and the insurgent provinces, was discussed at a Shuvalov-Andrassy conference (June 26–27).[66] At the insistence of Baron Schwegel, who drafted the proposed Montenegrin frontiers, Andrassy remained firm until the Russians accepted his terms on June 30.[67]

The Dual Monarchy asserted predominant influence over Montenegro before the congress decided its future. To obtain Bar, Prince Nikola instructed his envoys to agree to Vienna's conditions. These included neutralization of the port, limiting the ships Montenegro could keep there, and allowing Austria to patrol the coastline. Prince Nikola attributed Bar's retention to his personal appeal to the tsar, but actually it was assured by Russo-Montenegrin acceptance of Austrian terms.[68] Nikola lamented the loss of Hercegovina, the Bojana, and the Ulcinj littoral, but he had to acknowledge his subservience to Austria.[69]

Austro-Russian agreements on Montenegrin boundaries were upheld by the congress. Shuvalov declared (July 1) that since they had settled the principles of delimitation, details could be left to the boundary commission. Caratheodory Pasha, on ethnic and strategic grounds, opposed any major extension of Montenegro on the Albanian side. The Porte expressed willingness to cede the port of Spić, but claimed that Bar, Plava, and Gusinje were inhabited primarily by Catholics and Albanian Moslems. The Turks' protests were unavailing. Bismarck declared that they must adhere to San Stefano's provisions except for modifications accepted by the congress. By July 4, Montenegro's frontiers had been determined, mainly to Austrian satisfaction. Montenegro's independence was debated *pro forma*, but the congress decided

[65] De Mouy (*Souvenirs*, p. 130) attributed the hesitation of the delegates to support Montenegro to their conviction that it was "inféodé" to Russia.

Russian sympathy for Montenegro was reflected in Bobrikov's comments: "Could we throw this eagle's nest of Serbdom into the embrace of Vienna?" Prince Nikola "is the talented leader of Serbdom, fully equal to events." "To make a kingdom out of a cluster of rocks is a great achievement." *Zapiski*, pp. 110–11.

[66] Jelavich, *Russia in the East*, p. 78, Jomini to Giers, June 26; HHSA, Schwegel, *Notizen*, June 27, no. 29.

[67] *Ibid.*, nos. 29, 31, 33, 34.   [68] Nikola I, *Zapisi*, 2, sv. 3, pp. 159–61.

[69] Djordjević, *Crna Gora*, pp. 432–33.

to confirm San Stefano's provision guaranteeing its full sovereignty.[70]

The Montenegrin government could scarcely be expected to rejoice as the results of the congress. Austria-Hungary took Spič and the entire coastline from the Dalmatian frontier to Bar. The remainder of the littoral, except for Bar, was restored to Turkey. Montenegro was to receive Plava and Gusinje in compensation. Its prewar boundaries were considerably extended, but it was deprived of many of its gains at San Stefano.[71] Did Andrassy wish to prove to Montenegro and other Balkan peoples, wondered Nikola, that their master was Vienna, not St. Petersburg? In his final dispatch to his envoys in Berlin, he declared:

Once our affairs are completed and you are ready to leave, tell each of the great power representatives that Montenegro has not been properly rewarded and that her new frontiers in many places are completely unnatural. Also, that the Montenegrin people feels sorrow and fear, that because of these unnatural frontiers they will be agitated and hindered in their pursuit of peaceful development.[72]

The fate of Bosnia and Hercegovina was easily settled at Berlin without consulting their inhabitants. The Bosnian delegates, not permitted to speak, could merely submit a memorandum to the congress, but its demands for annexation to the Serbian states were heeded neither by the delegates nor by European opinion.[73] Before the congress, Andrassy had managed to obtain consent to an Austrian occupation from all the Powers except Turkey. He encountered more difficulty from his fellow Magyars, who were opposed to incorporating

[70] *Staatsarchiv*, 35, no. 6762, Protocol no. 10, pp. 195–97. Russia had always regarded Montenegro as independent since the sultan had never confirmed its princes in office nor had Montenegro paid tribute. England, on the other hand, had never recognized Montenegrin independence. The remaining Powers either recognized its independence formally or implicitly. Can one, however, regard as truly independent a country prohibited by treaty from fortifying its most exposed frontier and whose naval police would be under foreign (Austrian) control?

[71] Before the war, Montenegro's area was 78 kv. mil (4,405 sq. km.) and her population was 170,000. Under the Treaty of San Stefano it would gain 210 kv. mil (15,355 sq. km) and 137,000 inhabitants. The Berlin Treaty increased it by only 80 kv. mil (8,655 sq. km.) and 50,000 inhabitants. *Istok*, July 30/Aug. 11, lead; Jakšić, *Evropa*, pp. 54–55; J. Jovanović, *Stvaranje*, pp. 321–23.

[72] Nikola I, *Zapisi*, 2, pp. 161–62.

[73] The Bosnian memorandum, dated March 2/14 from Tiškovac, had been approved by the Bosnian Assembly; it was published in *Zastava*, June 21/July 3, no. 96.

more Slavs, than from Europe. To forestall Turkish opposition, Andrassy pledged to support the Porte on the Bulgarian question.[74] Constantinople proposed to Andrassy a joint, partial occupation of Bosnia and Hercegovina favorable to Turkish interests. But Andrassy, rejecting this plan, declared that if the Turks persisted in opposing his scheme, he would insist upon annexation.[75] If the Monarchy had to occupy the provinces without the Porte's consent, warned Andrassy, the Balkan peoples might seize territories restored to Turkey by the congress.[76] Vienna sought to silence embarrassing opposition by a combination of bribery and threats.

Andrassy had arranged presentation of the Bosnian question to the congress down to the last detail. He rejected Bismarck's offer to propose an Austrian occupation, explaining that this should come from "the least Turcophobe, the least Russophile power." When Salisbury agreed to sponsor an Austrian occupation of the two provinces, Bismarck declared in disgust, "I have heard of people refusing to eat their pigeon unless it was shot and roasted for them; but I have never heard of anyone refusing to eat unless their jaws were forced open and it was pushed down their throats." [77]

In plenary session (June 28), Andrassy opened the discussion affirming that all Powers had recognized the Monarchy's special interests in Bosnia and Hercegovina. San Stefano's grant of autonomy to them (Article XIV) was an impractical solution because of Turkish impotence and their national and religious diversity; autonomy would produce anarchy. Only "a strong and impartial power" could resolve their problems. The Austrian government, after spending large sums to maintain almost 200,000 refugees from Bosnia and Hercegovina, must now insist upon a solution insuring peace and stability. Rising to his

[74] Already on June 12, Andrassy assured Emperor Franz Josef that Russia would vote for an Austrian occupation of the provinces. As to Bulgaria, Andrassy intimated that he would advocate restoration of Turkish control over Eastern Rumelia if the Porte backed him on Bosnia and Hercegovina. Novotny, *Quellen*, pp. 83, 91, 97–98.

[75] Bareilles, *Rapport secret*, pp. 132–40; Novotny, *Quellen*, p. 157, nos. 544, 547A.

[76] Jakšić, *Evropa*, pp. 47–48. Throughout the congress, Andrassy hoped the Turks would approve an Austrian occupation, or at least not oppose one militarily. Haymerle felt Austria-Hungary should have taken Bismarck's advice and occupied the provinces months earlier. HHSA, Schwegel, *Notizen*, July 2; Busch, *Deutsche Rundschau*, p. 371.

[77] Novotny, *Quellen*, pp. 97–98, no. 128; Jakšić, *Evropa*, pp. 45–47; Cecil, *Salisbury*, 2, 281.

cue, Salisbury reinforced Andrassy's contention that San Stefano's proposed extension of Serbo-Montenegrin frontiers would threaten European Turkey's existence:

If a considerable part of them [Bosnia and Hercegovina] fell into the hands of one of the neighboring principalities, a chain of Slav states would be formed, extending across the Balkan peninsula, and whose military force would threaten the populations of another race [the Greeks?] occupying the territories to the south. Such a state of affairs would doubtless be more dangerous to the independence of the Porte than any other combination.

The two provinces, continued Salisbury, could contribute nothing to Turkey's wealth or strength; their defense should be entrusted to a capable power. "For these reasons the Queen's government proposes . . . that the congress state that the provinces of Bosnia and Hercegovina be occupied and administered by Austria-Hungary." Bismarck promptly seconded these arguments.[78]

Caratheodory Pasha rose to defend Turkish administration of the insurgent provinces. Having failed in desperate efforts to postpone public discussion until an Austro-Turkish agreement had been concluded, he had received instructions just prior to the session to oppose Austrian intervention.[79] He argued that Turkey was successfully restoring order and repatriating the refugees, making an Austrian occupation superfluous. Despite immense difficulties produced by three years of insurrection and war, Ottoman administration was intact, demonstrating Turkey's strength. But his words carried no weight. When Bismarck called for a vote, all other Powers supported Salisbury's resolution.[80]

The quick adoption of Andrassy's plan on Bosnia and Hercegovina caused joy among the Austrians, dismay in Serbia and Turkey. Ristić, who had hoped for an occupation which would cease when Russia evacuated Bulgaria, had to console himself with dreams of a subsequent "settling of accounts" between Russia and Austria-Hungary.[81] The

---

[78] *Staatsarchiv, 35*, no. 6760, Protocol no. 8, pp. 162–65.

[79] Bareilles, *Rapport secret*, pp. 141–42. Constantinople, noted Caratheodory, still believed its veto would prevent an Austrian occupation despite clear evidence of Vienna's military preparations and strong Anglo-German support. *Ibid.*, pp. 150–52.

[80] *Staatsarchiv, 35*, 165–71.

[81] Ristić to Grujić, June 28, no. 7, in Grujić, *3*, 342–43. Ristić's reaction to the efforts of Shuvalov and Jomini to soften the blow was his comment to Grujić: "Empty consolation." Čubrilović, *Bosanski ustanak*, p. 311.

Turkish delegates advised Constantinople to reconcile itself to an Austrian occupation and empower them to arrange favorable terms. They were instructed belatedly (July 9) to urge Andrassy to delay the occupation until an Austro-Turkish agreement had been concluded. But the draft article (July 10) on Bosnia and Hercegovina failed to stipulate any preliminary accord. Andrassy opposed any change; Bismarck was rude to the Turks. Waddington told the Turks they must submit to the law of the stronger as the French had done in 1871. "Bosnia and Hercegovina are lost to Turkey. . . . But try to obtain some profit from the Austrians." As usual, Constantinople lagged behind events, instructing its envoys (on the morning of July 13) to demand replacement of Article XXV by the formula: "The provinces of Bosnia and Hercegovina will be occupied provisionally by Austria-Hungary, and this occupation will be dependent upon a direct agreement between the Holy Porte and Austria-Hungary." By this time the Berlin Treaty had already been printed. The Turks' only recourse, noted Caratheodory, was to obtain an immediate agreement with Austria. At noon they went to Andrassy to obtain written confirmation of the occupation's provisional character and the need for a preliminary Austro-Turkish accord. Andrassy, yielding somewhat, signed a draft agreement containing those provisions. By his last-minute maneuver, Caratheodory helped preserve Turkish sovereignty in Bosnia and Hercegovina.[82]

The Bosnian insurgents, following the congress as best they could, soon realized that their aspirations would be denied. They provided General Fadeev with information, but although a Christian-Moslem alliance was suggested to resist an Austrian occupation, no important action was undertaken.[83] Some insurgent chiefs, like Petar Uzelac, defected to Vienna. Golub Babić led the rest across the frontier to surrender to the Austrian authorities (August 30). He declared, "I

[82] Bareilles, *Rapport secret*, pp. 153–95.

[83] A group of insurgent leaders, headed by Mico Ljubibratić, issued a proclamation to the Moslems urging their co-operation with the Christians in establishing a provisional government in Sarajevo to resist an Austrian occupation, but instructions and encouragement from Belgrade were lacking. Ristić 17/275, Skulić and Popović to Metropolitan Mihailo, July 6. On July 10, another appeal was made for Moslem-Christian reconciliation, armed resistance of all insurgents in Bosnia, Hercegovina, and Novi Pazar to a foreign invasion, and a declaration to the Powers that Austrian intervention was unnecessary. *Ibid.*, 17/277, Archimandrit Sava, *et al.*, "Dragoj braci muhamedancima i hrišćanima." See Ekmečić, *Ustanak*, pp. 357–58.

submit to His Majesty, the Austrian emperor, and lay down my arms." [84] Three years after it had begun, the Bosnian insurrection ended in complete defeat.

Russian and Serbian Public Opinion

Nationalist opinion in Russia and the Serbian lands, apprehensive as the congress convened, was dismayed at its outcome. In both areas, despite comforting official statements, nationalists interpreted the congress as a betrayal of the interests of Slavdom.

On the eve of the Berlin meeting, Russian nationalist newspapers deplored the important concessions already made to England and Austria-Hungary. The diplomats, predicted *Grazhdanin*, would produce confusion and might even revive moribund Turkey. Why had the congress not met soon after Russia's victory? The Salisbury-Shuvalov agreement, declared the paper with typical exaggeration (June 20), outlined a partition of Turkey leaving the "lion's share" to England and the insurgent provinces to Austria. Could a Russian representative actually sign such an accord? *Grazhdanin* continued, "No matter how pleasant and desirable for Russia a peaceful outcome of the congress would be, we will console ourselves with the hope that Prince Gorchakov does not wish to end his brilliant diplomatic career with the partition at the congress of the much suffering Slav lands, freed with rivers of Russian blood." [85] Russia had won the war, Katkov declared, but Austria was gaining predominance in the Balkans. Including the Serbian states in Vienna's sphere of interest would constitute a concealed form of annexation. Subordination of their armed forces to Austrian command and conclusion of commercial treaties would pave the way for their political absorption by the Monarchy. [86] The purpose of the congress, asserted Katkov, was to tear up the Treaty of San Stefano. The Powers' condescending attitude toward Russia insulted its national honor. [87]

At the start of the congress, though many Russians deplored the tsar's surrender to foreign pressure, it was widely believed that Russian diplomats would not make major concessions; there was confidence in Gorchakov's wisdom. But as reports of Russian setbacks in Berlin

---

[84] *Ibid.*, pp. 359–60.

[85] *Grazhdanin*, May 27/June 9, nos. 20–21, "Kongress," p. 396; June 8/20, June 8/20, "Kongress i soglashenie."

[86] Peredovykh, June 7/19, no. 144.

[87] *Ibid.*, June 24/July 6 and June 27/July 9, nos. 162, 164.

filtered back to Russia, public indignation increased.[88] Warned *Russkii Mir*:

We have the right to dispose of our own gains, but *in no case do we have the right to sacrifice others—those who trusted us with the defense of their interests.* We cannot be generous at the expense of the heroic Montenegrins even if a hundred Austrias demand it. Also we cannot cut off any part of liberated Bulgarian territory. *Russia will not sacrifice the interests of the eastern Christians.*[89]

Reports from Berlin provoked Ivan Aksakov to deliver a famous speech to the Moscow Slav Society (July 4), expressing the anger and sorrow of Russian nationalists: "We meet now . . . to attend a funeral . . . of whole countries—to attend the burial as it were of all the hopes of liberating the Bulgarians and of securing the independence of the Serbs. Are we not now burying the cause which all Russians have at heart?" Concessions already made by Russian diplomats, continued Aksakov, have sacrificed national honor and Russia's position in the Balkans. To accept such a verdict is "to formally abdicate one's post as the chief representative of all the Slav races and of all the Orthodox East; it means to lose not merely our influence and sacrifice our interests, but to forfeit the esteem of these peoples, our natural allies, the only allies we really have in Europe." War would be preferable to such a dishonorable peace, though England and Austria probably would not have dared fight Russia: "Invincible, invulnerable is the Russian tsar from the moment when he will lift up the standard of Russia which is also the standard of the Slavs and of all eastern Christians. The nation is agitated, irritated, troubled each day by the proceedings of the congress at Berlin."[90] Aksakov's fiery speech caused the government to close the Moscow Society and exile him to the provinces. "I could not, as president of the Slav Society," he explained, "remain silent before the Slavs; nor could I as a Russian." If hundreds of Russians had done likewise, continued Aksakov, Russia's cause might have fared better. "Such shame Russia has never suffered before in all her long-suffering history."[91]

[88] *Russland*, pp. 377–78, 381. The great majority of Russians, asserted *Russland*, viewed the congress as a betrayal of the cause of Russia and Slavdom.

[89] *Istok*, June 16/28, June 21/July 3, nos. 68, 70, "Pregled ruske štampe." The passages were italicized by the editors of *Istok*.

[90] Aksakov, *Sochineniia, 1*, 297–308; O. K. (Novikova), *Russia and England from 1876 to 1880* (London, 1880), pp. 98–106.

[91] Aksakov to Pobedonostsev, June 24/July 6 and June 16/28, RA, *3* (1907), 171–75.

As the nationalists learned of the treaty's provisions, their fury was unrestrained by censorship.[92] Their anger was directed at England, Austria-Hungary, and Russian diplomacy. The Powers, asserted *Grazhdanin*, had torn up San Stefano whenever it protected Christian interests; the new treaty was flagrantly unjust. "The Berlin Treaty can be recognized by Russia only upon condition of its quick destruction."[93] When the Austrians occupy Bosnia and construct a railway to Salonika, Vienna "literally becomes the master of the western half of the Balkan peninsula."[94] Serbia had been unjustly deprived of Bosnia and parts of Old Serbia, complained *Novoe Vremia*. "Toward Serbia the congress acted severely and unjustly throughout. . . . There is no doubt that Austrian jealousy and Hungarian arrogance have triumphed."[95] Even *Vestnik Evropy* deplored the division of Bulgaria, although generally it, and the semiofficial newspapers, defended the treaty.[96]

Among Serbian newspapers during the congress, *Istok* remained hopeful of Russian support, whereas *Zastava* turned strongly Russophobe. *Istok* predicted (June 14) that the congress would deprive Turkey of all European possessions except Constantinople and the Straits. Russia, it declared bravely (June 19), would not yield. On June 30, *Istok* greeted establishment of an autonomous Bulgaria as a great Russian moral victory over Europe. It admitted (July 3) that "no Serb and no Slav can be wholly satisfied with the work of the congress," but at least Serbia would retain its conquered territories. Though sharply critical of the impending Austrian occupation of Bosnia and Hercegovina, the paper predicted a *modus vivendi* with Vienna. The two provinces had not been lost permanently. "The future of Serbdom will not be crushed by the dictation of the congress; or if it is, then Serbdom never had a chance."[97]

[92] On public indignation see Grüning, *Öffentliche Meinung*, pp. 56ff.; *Russland*, p. 381. Declared Katkov, "Public opinion everywhere [in Russia] is stunned and confused." Peredovykh, July 4/16, no. 169.

[93] *Grazhdanin*, Oct. 10/22, nos. 23–25, "Mysli i nadezhdy posle molchaniia."

[94] Peredovykh, June 17/29, no. 154B.

[95] *Zastava*, June 28/July 10, no. 100, "Ruski listovi o srpskom pitanju."

[96] *Vestnik Evropy*, Aug. 8, p. 740. "Because we demanded more than we could really obtain [at San Stefano] we later received less than we considered essential." For defense of the treaty see *Golos*, July 18/30. On July 21, *Agence générale russe* declared that Russian diplomacy had registered great achievements in Berlin. Peredovykh, no. 177.

[97] *Istok*, June 2/14, 7/19, 16/28, 18/30, June 21/July 3, June 23/July 5, nos. 62, 64, 68, 69, 70, 71.

Zastava, at first avoiding direct commentary on the congress, urged Belgrade to abandon its narrow Serbian viewpoint on the disputed eastern frontier and work for reconciliation with Bulgaria. The Russians had erred in establishing the boundaries of San Stefano, stated the editor, but their mistakes could now be corrected:

We feel that the people in the disputed part of Old Serbia are neither purely Bulgarian nor Serbian. We feel that certain areas, such as Niš, should go to Serbia for strategic reasons, but otherwise disputes should be settled by plebiscite which must be completely free and perhaps under a European or Russian commission.[98]

Zastava believed that the new Bulgaria, despite its reduction by the congress, would develop properly and soon merge with Eastern Rumelia. The Serbs should rejoice at such a prospect—Bulgaria would be a natural ally. But have not the Serbs the same right to unite, queried the newspaper? Meanwhile, *Zastava* reserved judgment on its attitude toward Russia: "Should Russia agree to transfer Bosnia and Hercegovina to any power other than Serbia and Montenegro, then we are finished with her forever, and then between her and the Serbian people will be opened a bitterer gulf than between her and the Poles." This was not a threat, concluded the editor, but merely reflected the view of the Serbian people.[99]

Approval by the congress, with Russia's support, of an Austrian occupation of the insurgent provinces, completed *Zastava*'s disillusionment. Russia had opened her doors wide for Austrian entry into these Serbian lands. By instructing the Serbian delegates to reach agreement with Andrassy, claimed the newspaper, Russia yielded the entire western Balkans to the Monarchy. The result of a policy so unworthy of a Slav power must be the decline of Russian prestige among the Serbs: "We are anxious to bring to the knowledge of the Russian people that official Russia's policy rends the heart of every Serb, that it is unworthy of those vast sacrifices which the Russian people made for the liberation of their brethren." [100]

Serbian press reaction to the Berlin Treaty was mixed. *Istok* declared on July 14 that Russia, by unselfishly seeking freedom for the South Slavs, had created a much better situation for them than had existed before 1875. Five days later the same newspaper noted that the peace

---

[98] *Zastava*, June 9/21 and 14/26, nos. 89, 92, "Srpski-bugarski spor," leads.
[99] *Ibid.*, June 16/28, no. 93, "Nova Bugarska," lead.
[100] *Ibid.*, June 18/30, no. 94, "Srpsko pitanje i Austro-Ugarska intervencija," lead.

terms "do not satisfy the wishes of the peoples concerned"; only an insignificant part of Serbdom had been liberated.[101] *Zastava*'s reaction was negative and Russophobe. It denounced Russian diplomacy for permitting expulsion of Montenegro from territory it had conquered and for opposing Serbia's aspirations. "Serbia has been given enough to make her death difficult, but too little for a free and healthy life." Instead of satisfying Russian public opinion and assisting its natural allies, Russia at Berlin helped partition European Turkey into spheres of influence:

This division is death for the Serbian people since the Serbian lands have been left disunited and divided and Russia agreed to let Austria shove a wedge between Serbia and Montenegro and divide them from one another for good. What remains for Serbia and Montenegro? To be tools of Russia for her subsequent operations or to be devoured by Austria-Hungary—one of the two.[102]

Istok reflected the views of the satisfied Belgrade regime; *Zastava* spoke for frustrated Serbian nationalism.

---

[101] *Istok*, July 2/14, 7/19, Aug. 4/16, nos. 75, 77, 89, leads.
[102] *Zastava*, July 2/14, no. 102, "Zvanična Rusija i srpski narod"; July 5/17, no. 104, "Kongres i njegov domaćin," leads.

CHAPTER X

EPILOGUE AND CONCLUSION

THE Berlin Treaty shocked Russian leaders and the literate public. Gorchakov wrote, "I do not envy Shuvalov as bearer of this 'triste primeur,' and I only regret having had to add my signature to such a transaction. . . . I did not expect such a page at the close of my physical and political life." He told the emperor, "I consider the Berlin Treaty the darkest page in my life." Commented Alexander, "And in mine too." [1] Shuvalov was received coldly by the emperor, who felt humiliated though he had sanctioned Russian concessions in Berlin. Shuvalov defended his work before the top leadership and explained the problems involved in executing the treaty. [2] The soberer elements in the Foreign Ministry supported Shuvalov, but his sponsorship of the Berlin settlement finished his career. Even the government's official organ reacted critically, though with dignified restraint, toward the treaty. "Assuredly these results are far from realizing what Russia had a right to expect after the sacrifices of a victorious war." Balkan boundaries, asserted the paper, had been drawn for political reasons disregarding nationality. But its conclusion was hopeful:

Despite all our successes in Russo-Turkish wars, we have not been able to complete our task. We have always had to stop before the inextricable

---

[1] Jelavich, *Russia in the East,* p. 79, Gorchakov to Giers, July 12 (misdated as June 30); RS, *40* (Oct. 1883), p. 179; Ignat'ev, IV, *144* (April 1916), 341–42. When the dissatisfied emperor asked him to define the difference between San Stefano and Berlin, Ignat'ev replied, "The former was cooked with Russian sauce, the second with Austrian." Alexander II wept.

[2] Shuvalov delivered his report on the Berlin Congress on July 5/17 in the presence of the emperor, two of the grand dukes, Gorchakov, Miliutin, Giers, and Ubri. Miliutin, *Dnevnik, 3,* 78–80.

difficulties of this problem. But each of our wars has been an additional step toward the final goal and thus has been traced the sanguinary but glorious furrow which our traditions have left in history and which must lead up to the accomplishment of our national mission—the deliverance of the Christian east. However incomplete it may be, the work of the Berlin Congress marks a fresh step in that path—an important but painfully measured step.[3]

English and Austrian jubilation confirmed that Russian prestige had suffered in Berlin. The treaty, declared Salisbury, had removed most British objections to San Stefano. "The political outposts of Russian power have been pushed back to the regions beyond the Balkans."[4] Exaggerating Vienna's triumph, Baron Schwegel asserted that Russia had been deprived of most of its wartime gains and had bowed to Europe's will. More Serbs would now be ruled by the Dual Monarchy than by the Serbian states. "In my view," wrote the baron, "the Serbian people belongs in our sphere of power and thus it is important that we establish ourselves firmly in Bosnia and Hercegovina. Serbia under us, Greece with us, and Rumania not opposed to us—with these elements if used correctly we have little to fear from Russian encroachment in the Balkans or from Pan-Slavism with Bulgaria as its center."[5]

Belgrade's reactions to the Berlin Treaty were generally favorable. The Serbs of the principality, though mourning the imminent loss of Bosnia, rejoiced that the treaty had brought unanticipated aggrandizement in the east. Ristić's account of his work at the congress (July 25) was well received by the Serbian Assembly. Two leading nationalists protested bitterly against the coming Austrian occupation of the insurgent provinces and made impassioned appeals for the unification of Serbdom, but the delegates, though sympathetic, took no action.[6] Praising Ristić's achievement, General Lešjanin blamed Serbia's failure to acquire all the territory it desired upon the Powers' selfishness.[7] Prince Milan's proclamation of Serbian independence (August 22) expressed satisfaction with Serbian gains and for a change lauded Ristić publicly. The Berlin Treaty

---

[3] Novikova, *Russia and England*, pp. 107–09, citing *Pravitel'stvennyi Vestnik*.

[4] *Staatsarchiv, 35*, no. 6881, Salisbury to (Cross), July 13, p. 232.

[5] HHSA, Schwegel, *Notizen*, no. 47. Some of his comments were strikingly similar to those of Russian nationalists: "Russland hat auf dem Congresse so ziemlich alles verloren, was es auf den Schlachtfeldern früher erobert hat."

[6] *Istok*, July 9/21, no. 78, "Sa narodne Skupštine," July 12; July 12/24, no. 79, speech of Glica Geršić.

[7] AII, Ristić 22/192, Lješanin to Ristić, July 30/Aug. 11, 1878.

did not realize all the wishes of the Serbs, but under the circumstances . . . Serbia owes a debt of gratitude to the Powers. . . . Europe agreed to leave us most of the population of Old Serbia which we liberated. . . . We possess now a solid basis for development. . . . All in all we must be satisfied and proud. . . . With wise relations externally and solid relations within, that is the only path which can lead to the prosperity of independent Serbia.[8]

Execution of the Berlin Treaty, relatively simple in the case of a mollified Serbia, proved difficult for Montenegro. Delimitation of the Turko-Montenegrin frontier took years. Prince Nikola pressed the Porte to evacuate areas (especially the Gusinje-Plava region) assigned to Montenegro, but Constantinople was in no hurry to yield towns it considered strategic. Turkey and Austria urged Nikola to accept other territory in compensation; Cetinje insisted that the disputed area was Slav. Backed secretly by Vienna, one Turkish official noted, "At Berlin we had to sign the cession of Gusinje, but now in relation to Montenegro we are stronger and we will not yield." With Russian support Montenegro eventually obtained the port of Ulcinj instead of Plava and Gusinje.[9]

The occupation of Bosnia and Hercegovina was still more difficult. After abortive attempts to win the Porte's acquiescence and the support of the Christian populace, Austrian troops crossed the Bosnian frontier (July 29). They encountered desperate resistance from Moslem guerrillas stiffened at times by Turkish regulars. The principal cities were taken only after bitter battles. Dispelled was the legend so carefully fostered by Vienna that an Austrian occupation would encounter general popular support.[10]

The Serbian states looked on in helpless embarrassment. Belgrade had

[8] Milan's proclamation said of Ristić that he "a défendu [Serbian interests] avec une sagesse et un patriotisme qui m'imposent le devoir de lui donner publiquement en cette occasion le témoignage de ma reconnaissance." *Staatsarchiv, 35,* no. 6905, pp. 276–78, Aug. 10/22.

[9] G. Stanojević, "Prilozi za diplomatsku istoriju Crne Gore od Berlinskog Kongresa do kraja XIX vijeka," *Istorijski časopis, 2* (1960), 149–58; *Staatsarchiv, 35,* nos. 6898, 6900, Aug. 13, 20, pp. 271–73; *Grazhdanin,* Oct. 10/22, nos. 23–25, D. Bakić, "Chernogoriia noveishago vremeni—VII."

[10] North and northeast Bosnia and parts of Hercegovina around Livno and on the Montenegrin frontier were held by troops organized in regular battalions and aided by difficult terrain. In bitter fighting (Aug. 7–Oct. 7) the Austro-Hungarian army suffered over 5,000 casualties; the occupation force had to be doubled to a total of 135 battalions before resistance was broken. Mollinary, *46 Jahre, 2,* 307–08.

long anticipated such an Austrian occupation. Now it was so committed to Vienna that it observed scrupulously a policy of nonintervention. Austro-Hungarian newspapers spread rumors of Serbian intrigue and aid to the insurgents, but Wrede could discover no evidence to substantiate them. The consul concluded that Belgrade was wholly sincere in its expressed desire to remain on an intimate footing with the Monarchy.[11] Indeed, the official *Srpske Novine* went to unusual lengths to deny allegations of Serbian involvement. Unofficial Serbian elements led by Metropolitan Mihailo encouraged resistance to the occupation but lacked significant financial backing.[12]

Prince Nikola remained deaf to Hercegovinian entreaties to aid their resistance to Austria. Adhering instead to his promise to facilitate an Austrian occupation, Nikola pledged his loyal co-operation (July 26) just before the Monarchy's troops moved in.[13] Despite private sympathy for the Hercegovinians by his officials, the prince even offered to incorporate his Hercegovinian battalions in the occupation forces. At Vienna's request he kept them in Montenegro until the occupation was completed. Then Petar Vukotić led the 4,600 Hercegovinian troops back to their homeland, where they laid down their arms before Austrian General Jovanović. Declared Vukotić, "You Hercegovinians fought heroically. We Montenegrins stood at your side in brotherly fashion. Who can give you a country except Austria? Where is there more freedom. . . ? It is the oldest, most powerful and glorious empire on earth. . . . If I were not a Montenegrin, I would be an Austrian subject. Be true and obedient to her."[14] Thus the Serbian states, impotent before Austrian power, groveled before the kaiser, seeking his diplomatic and economic support.

[11] HHSA, Wrede to Andrassy, Aug. 4, no. 80; Aug. 12, no. 87. In the latter report, Wrede noted that Belgrade had detained Bosnian insurgent leaders in Serbia and had showed him orders it had sent to its commanders. These reports apparently calmed Andrassy's fears roused by Ambassador F. Zichy's communications from Constantinople.

[12] *Ibid.*, Sept. 4, no. 101; Actenstücke, 3, no. 207, Wrede to Andrassy, Aug. 23. *Srpske Novine* (Aug. 9/21, no. 176) declared, "No one in Serbia would take it on his conscience to continue a struggle which had already produced enough destruction and exhaustion. We are certain that the Austrian army will achieve its object and that no Serbian subjects will be found among the rebels."

[13] Djordjević, *Crna Gora*, p. 433. On August 8, Thömmel telegraphed Andrassy of Nikola's agreement to follow Austrian advice. When Moslem leaders in Hercegovina sought aid from insurgents there, Nikola persuaded the latter to return home and accept Austrian rule. Actenstücke, 3, no. 193.

[14] *Ibid.*, no. 260, Thömmel to Andrassy, Oct. 19.

But public indignation in Serbian lands over the Austrian occupation could not be wholly suppressed. In the Serbian Assembly, G. Glišić and M. Kujundjić made nationalistic, denunciatory speeches.[15] *Istok*, though unable to flout Belgrade's alignment with Vienna, printed without commentary A. A. Maikov's attack upon the occupation.[16] *Zastava*'s Sarajevo correspondent declared that the Austrian advance "sounded Serbdom's death knell," but that Vienna would be sitting upon an active volcano. "Serbia and Montenegro can destroy the decisions of the Berlin Congress as Italy . . . nullified the treaties of Villafranca and Zürich." [17] European diplomacy, stated *Zastava* several weeks later, had compelled Serbia to keep its agonizing watch on the Drina. The editors predicted that either Serbdom would be fully independent and united or completely dominated by Austria. Separate flags could not long wave in Belgrade and Sarajevo.[18]

For the moment such brave words could not alter the realities of power. The Berlin Treaty had confirmed the transfer of real authority over the destiny of the western Balkans from Constantinople to Vienna. And the Russian emperor, to whom the Serbian states had appealed so often, seemed powerless to resist the shift. In February 1879, when Montenegro requested Russia to represent it abroad temporarily, Andrassy protested strongly to Cetinje. Nikola hastily retracted his request, adding that he would soon name a permanent Montenegrin representative in Vienna. And Austria continued to exploit Serbo-Montenegrin rivalry to keep the Serbian states apart. Belgrade's efforts to establish permanent representation in Cetinje failed because of Montenegrin fears that it would promote its Piedmontese pretensions. Thömmel reported:

Eventual Serbian combinations as to Bulgaria, Bosnia-Hercegovina, and the sandjak could nowhere find a worse reception than in Montenegro. The unification of Bulgaria with Serbia under an Obrenović, even if in the form of a personal union, would throw Montenegro and her dynasty too much into shadow. Growth of Serbian influence in Bosnia and Hercegovina, or

---

[15] Čubrilović, *Bosanski ustanak*, pp. 373–74; Vlada Milana, *1*, 430–31.

[16] *Istok*, July 2/14, 5/17, nos. 75, 76, "Majkov o ulasku Austro-Ugarske u Bosnu i Hercegovinu" (reprinted from *Sankt Peterburgskie Vedomosti*). Maikov asserted that Russia's cession of the insurgent provinces to Austria had undermined its traditional policy and would alienate Serbian sympathies.

[17] *Zastava*, July 19/31, no. 112, Sarajevo July 6/18. The editors declared apropos of the death-knell prediction, "This is not so."

[18] *Ibid.*, Aug. 11/23, no. 125, "Beograd i Sarajevo."

even Serbia's penetration into the sandjak would be a fatal blow to the prestige and existence of Montenegro, which lives solely on the reputation of its heroism.[19]

Austria-Hungary—not Russia or the Serbs—appeared to be the heir of dying Turkish authority in the west Balkans.

Serbian-Russian political relations in the period immediately following the congress were cooler than before, though the Russian military, strangely enough, still counted upon Serbian assistance should persistent tension with Austria lead to war.[20] Metropolitan Mihailo's failure to make special mention of the tsar during celebration of Serbia's independence displeased the Russian envoy, who spoke sharply to Ristić.[21] Belgrade was still attempting to obtain the balance of the Russian subsidy for its participation in the Russo-Turkish War. Incidents on the Serbo-Bulgarian frontier involving Russian soldiers threatened complications, but Ristić carefully avoided trouble with Russia.[22] In February 1879, his old confidant, Milosav Protić, was appointed first Serbian ambassador to St. Petersburg and was promptly approved by the Russians.[23]

In the months following the Congress of Berlin, Pan-Slav influence declined greatly in Russia and in the Serbian lands.[24] *Grazhdanin*

---

[19] Djordjević, *Crna Gora*, pp. 440–41, 444–45, citing Thömmel to Andrassy, April 18, 1879.

[20] Of particular interest is the "Notice" of Russian Staff Captain Pleve of Nov. 11, 1878. "The political situation of Europe created by the Berlin Treaty is so complicated that we must continually be prepared for war with Turkey and even with Austria. . . . In case of war we count on the participation of the Serbian army." Pleve sought to discover: (1) how many Serbian troops were on the Austrian and Turkish frontiers; (2) how many Serbian troops Russia could count on in case of war against Turkey or an Austro-Turkish coalition; and (3) what operations the Serbian command had planned in case of war with Turkey. AII, Ristić 22/519.

[21] HHSA, Wrede to Andrassy, Aug. 23, 1878, no. 92.

[22] AII, Ristić 22/187, Ristić to Khitrovo, Aug. 17/29; 23/8, A. Marjanović to Minister of Interior, May 25/June 6, 1879. When a Russian officer claimed the Serbian part of Trn county to be Bulgarian territory, Ristić sent instructions: "Our vital interests demand avoidance of any quarrel with Russia. Protest but do not resist." *Ibid.*, 23/12, (Ristić) to D. Ćuprić.

[23] HHSA, Herbert to Andrassy, Feb. 26, 1879; March 12, no. 60; Langenau to Andrassy, Feb. 8/20, no. 7E.

[24] Pushkarevich, "Balkanskie slaviane," p. 226; HHSA, Langenau to Andrassy, Jan. 12, no. 2A; PRO, FO 181/573, Loftus to Salisbury, June 19, 1878, no. 614. Loftus wrote, "The Slavist party, although still influential at Moscow . . . *is considerably on the wane at St. Petersburg,* and from what I can learn, has

reaffirmed the traditional Pan-Slav viewpoint toward the Balkan Slavs in these terms:

Russia the liberator, strong politically, strong in its "reliable forces," strong in its generosity and unselfishness, naturally is in the eyes of all Slavs the sole support, the sole guarantee of their existence as national entities. To her all their glances are directed, their hopes and sympathies, and no hostile force can destroy that immaterial fortress being created in the Slav east which can serve Russia as a firm defense against enemies coming against her from every side.

It dismissed western reports of Slav dissatisfaction with Russia as baseless calumnies. Russia, therefore, could calmly await a better future for herself and the eastern Christians. When Russia finally liberated them, concluded *Grazhdanin*, its *faits accomplis* would not be disturbed by a European coalition.[25] However, the Russian government, instead of promoting a Pan-Slav policy, closed down the Moscow Slav Society and curtailed the activities of the one in St. Petersburg.

The attempt of Pan-Slavs in Russia and Serbia to develop closer cultural ties between their countries failed dismally. Late in 1878, A. Vasiljević, Serbian Minister of Education, traveled to Russia to confer with Pan-Slav leaders. The latter urged establishment in Belgrade of a philanthropic society to foster unity between Serbian and Russian intellectuals and reportedly supplied Vasiljević with 60,000 rubles to introduce Russian as a compulsory subject in Serbian schools. But Vasiljević overplayed his hand and was dropped from the Ristić cabinet for compromising it in Vienna's eyes.[26] Ristić maintained correct relations with St. Petersburg but refused to become involved with Pan-Slav schemes.

Baron Jomini of the Russian Foreign Ministry, assessing his country's future prospects in the Balkans, predicted that Austria-Hungary would exert increasing power of attraction upon the Slav states there. He

---

completely lost the influence it once exercised in the regions of the court." Metropolitan Mihailo noted regretfully, "I must halt all my efforts to influence the course and development of Slav affairs and limit myself to official functions." ROBibLen, f. Popova 13/48, Mihailo to Popov, Aug. 30/Sept. 12, 1878. See also A. Kireev, *Sochineniia* (St. Petersburg, 1912), 2, 14.

[25] *Grazhdanin*, Oct. 26/Nov. 7, no. 26, "Ogliadki vokrug da okolo"; Nov. 24/Dec. 5, nos. 29–31, "Russkii iazyk v slavianskikh zemliakh."

[26] HHSA, Wrede to Andrassy, Nov. 21, 1878, no. 146; Herbert to Andrassy, Dec. 24, 1878, no. 175; Jan. 31, Feb. 2, and March 2, 1879, nos. 24, 27, 64; AII, Ristić 26/776, Vasiljević to (Ristić?), Feb. 1, 1879, and "Primetbe."

pointed out that the Austrians possessed great advantages in the economic realm:

Their industrial and commercial superiority [over Russia] is evident. The material interests of the Slavs are all directed to that side. They have nothing to sell to us or buy from us, nor we to them. With the aid of railroads, their ties with Austria and the West will soon become indissoluble and from this time forward ties of race, language, and faith will be only weak arguments. The only thing which attaches the Slavs to us is the oppression from which they suffer and the hope which they place in our assistance.

As soon as that factor ceased to operate, the Slavs would turn their backs on Russia. European constitutional forms would provide an additional attraction. And Jomini emphatically rejected a Pan-Slav solution of the Balkan question: "The annexation of these populations to Russia is out of the question. It is impossible, and even if it were possible, it would be a great misfortune. There is only one means of realizing it: that would be a republican Slav United States. [But] that would be complete anarchy and the end of Russia as a great empire." [27] Instead, Jomini and his colleagues concentrated upon Russia's relations with the Powers and the preservation of European peace.

Jomini's pessimistic prediction was fulfilled for Serbia by 1881. After Ristić's fall in October 1880, Prince Milan concluded a political alliance with Austria-Hungary on June 28, 1881. The prince explained that in Serbia there had been deep aversion to Russia since San Stefano and that Bulgarian and Montenegrin hostility had convinced him that Balkan co-operation in defense of national independence was a dream. On September 13, Milan defended his Austrophile policy:

I have pursued this road out of conviction and will take no other path. Serbia must decide between Austria-Hungary and Russia. Russian policy has brought us no good but only humiliation. Especially since the creation of Bulgaria, we have been without worth or importance for Russia. We performed great services for Russia in the Turkish war. . . . But at San Stefano it was deaf to our wishes and aspirations. . . . Since then Russia has treated us as a minor and a subordinate, but I will not become a Russian prefect. Austria supported us at the Congress and even supported our claims against Russia. . . . I am convinced that I promote the well-being of Serbia when I adhere to Austria-Hungary.[28]

[27] Jelavich, *Russia in the East*, pp. 86–87, Jomini to Giers, Oct. 9/21, 1878. See also Giers to Jomini, Sept. 19/Oct. 1.

[28] Pribram, "Milan IV von Serbien," *Historische Blätter, 3* (1921–22), 473.

Such was destined to be Serbia's policy until the demise of the house of Obrenović in 1903.

During the eastern crisis, official Russia's co-operation with the European Powers generally took precedence over its ties with the Balkan Slavs. Except for two bellicose periods (November 1876 and June 1877–March 1878), the Foreign Ministry and the emperor were cautious and pacific. Men of the Diplomatic Chancellery—Gorchakov, Shuvalov, Novikov, and Jomini—sought to avoid war, especially a conflict with a European coalition. The emperor and Foreign Ministry aimed to preserve monarchical institutions in the Balkans and exaggerated danger from liberal and radical elements. Official Russian policy did not seek to destroy the Ottoman Empire but rather to ameliorate the Christians' status. Until October 1876, it pressed for a peaceful solution of the crisis on the basis of self-government for Bulgaria and the insurgent provinces and modest territorial compensation for the Serbian states.

The Turkish victory at Djunis and increasing Pan-Slav influence in Russia induced St. Petersburg to abandon temporarily its collaboration with Europe and to dispatch a unilateral ultimatum to the Porte. But this bellicose period, culminating in the emperor's Kremlin speech and partial mobilization, was brief; Russia at the Constantinople Conference resumed collective efforts to achieve a peaceful solution. To the very eve of the Russo-Turkish War, Russian leaders sought ways to avoid conflict. And in the war's initial phase St. Petersburg excluded Serbia and Rumania and favored a limited war and a "petite paix."

At Ploesti (June 1877), Pan-Slav diplomats (Ignat'ev and Nelidov) and military men converted the emperor to their drastic, unilateral approach to the Eastern Question. Ignat'ev, scoffing at the Foreign Ministry's fears of another Crimean coalition, advocated a Russian advance to Constantinople, fundamental reorganization of the Balkans, and participation of the Balkan states in the war. Russian national feeling, fanned by the Pan-Slav press, played a significant role in the emperor's shift to this position. Until after San Stefano, Ignat'ev determined the main lines of Russia's Balkan policy without much concern for the interests of other Powers. But under intense Anglo-Austrian pressure (spring of 1878), Alexander II reverted grudgingly to his earlier approach of accommodation and peace enabling the Diplomatic Chancellery to reassert ascendancy.

The duality of Russian official policy during the crisis contributed to its ultimate failure. The rift between a European orientation and unilateral nationalist one persisted until the Congress of Berlin. To the dismay of prominent spokesmen for the regime (Pobedonostsev, Miliutin), Alexander II and Gorchakov refused to make a final choice between these two contradictory approaches. Their vacillation placed them eventually at the mercy of nationalist opinion, involving Russia against their better judgment in the Russo-Turkish War and the disastrous Treaty of San Stefano.

In its relations with the Serbian states, official Russia attempted to avoid direct collision with Austrian interests and refused to take major risks to assist Serbian nationalism. Nonetheless, St. Petersburg considered it essential for reasons of prestige to prevent their conquest by Turkey. During the first year of the crisis, Russia co-operated with Austria to restrain them from war, although their own indecision and increasing Russian public support for the South Slavs deprived the emperor and his disorganized government of control over the situation. In the Serbo-Turkish War—which Russia had opposed—St. Petersburg adopted a nonintervention policy but permitted Russian volunteers to join the Serbian army and unofficially provided Belgrade with the funds it required to prosecute the war. Russia's November ultimatum rescued Serbia from certain disaster, but St. Petersburg soon ceased to regard it as an important factor in the Balkan crisis. Diplomatic reports and military missions convinced the emperor that Belgrade could provide little military assistance. His interest in Serbia's co-operation was aroused, however, by the Plevna reverses, though the Budapest Conventions with Austria-Hungary restricted its scope and direction. Belgrade's wartime achievements exceeded Russian expectations, but St. Petersburg, under Austrian pressure, refused to abandon the formula "correction of frontiers," which precluded major Serbian territorial gains. Russia's willingness to yield Bosnia to the Dual Monarchy and support Ignat'ev's big Bulgaria revealed its lack of concern for Serbia's vital interests.

During the 1870's, the policies of Russian Pan-Slavs (Ignat'ev, Fadeev, Cherniaev), by heightening intra-Slav frictions proved self-defeating. Favoring Montenegro and Bulgaria while neglecting the aspirations of the Serbian Piedmont, they helped split the South Slavs irreconcilably, increasing their susceptibility to west European influences. The Pan-Slavs' overweening ambition and attempts to exploit Serbia's difficulties antagonized the Belgrade leadership. Would the

Serbs be excluded from a future Slavic confederation as the Poles had been? The Bulgarian Exarchate promoted Serbo-Bulgarian antagonism; San Stefano intensified Serbo-Montenegrin rivalry. Whether intentionally or not, Ignat'ev—the architect of them both—had contributed mightily to fragmenting the South Slavs. Distrusting and disliking Jovan Ristić, his main objective was Russian domination of Turkey and the Straits and solidification of his own pre-eminence in Constantinople rather than unification of the Balkan Slavs. Other Pan-Slavs were torn between advocacy of a united Serbdom to block Austrian expansion and the desire to strike a bargain with the Monarchy to guarantee Russian hegemony over the eastern Balkans by sacrificing its western portion— and the Serbs—to Vienna.

Until Djunis, Serbia was the focus of attention for St. Petersburg and Pan-Slav elements; afterward they both favored Montenegrin and Bulgarian aspirations. Cherniaev's abortive campaign in 1876 disillusioned the Russians and revealed the deep cultural gulf between them and the Serbs. And to the Serbs it suggested that Pan-Slavism in practice was equivalent to Russian domination. Throughout the 1870's, conservative Russians idealized Montenegro because it was patriarchal and a tiny replica of autocratic Russia. Montenegro obeyed Russian advice, was stable and reliable and gained military victories. Bulgaria found favor because of its strategic location and subservience to Russian wishes. Serbia, on the other hand, had disregarded Russia's advice, pursued independent policies, was extremely unstable politically, and had adopted western constitutional practices. Thus it was not regarded after 1876 as a reliable instrument of Russian policy.

Vienna's success in gaining Serbia's allegiance in 1878 should be attributed to a variety of factors. Official Russia neither knew what it wished to achieve in Serbia nor how to accomplish its objectives. Its policy toward Belgrade was unclear and vacillating, and its envoys to Serbia were often inept. Like his predecessor, N. P. Shishkin, Consul Kartsov proved incapable of exploiting his opportunities and was sucked into the morass of Serbian politics; his tactlessness helped antagonize the Belgrade government. Special envoys Nikitin and Tseretelev bequeathed a legacy of suspicion and distrust which their abler successor, General Bobrikov, could not overcome. Reports of these poorly chosen representatives reinforced St. Petersburg's formidable ideological prejudices against Belgrade. Inflexible conservatism hampered Russia in its competition with Austria in Serbia. Perhaps the crucial factor in Russia's loss of influence was its failure to support adequate Serbian gains in compensation for its sacrifices in two wars with Turkey.

The Monarchy possessed important advantages in the struggle. Physically closer, it could exert its power in the Serbian area more effectively than Russia. Austria could offer much more to Serbia economically, and at any time it could paralyze Serbian trade. Prince Milan and many other Serbian leaders, but not the Serbian peasantry, were attracted by western culture or political ideas which reached them through the Monarchy. Austrian envoys in Belgrade (Kallay and Wrede) were better informed about Serbian conditions and aspirations than their Russian colleagues; generally they avoided tactless collaboration with the opposition and executed their instructions with precision. Wrede quickly informed Andrassy of the opportunity to exploit Serbian dismay over San Stefano. Andrassy's subsequent promises of eastern territory won with Serbian blood were crucial in gaining Belgrade's support. Vienna enjoyed the inestimable advantage of being in a position to profit from the numerous rivalries among the South Slavs; its leaders exploited this to maximum advantage in 1878. Inept Russian policies and Austrian promises and power enticed Serbia into the Monarchy's fold.

Russian society, as recent Soviet accounts emphasize, made a valuable contribution to the emancipation of most South Slavs from Turkish rule by 1878. Contrary to assertions of B. H. Sumner and the American historian, M. Florinsky, the Russian public's efforts in behalf of the Slavs in 1875–1876 were truly national in scope and not controlled by the tsarist court. Most contributions in money and kind came from the lower classes. But Soviet writers (Nikitin, Miroshnichenko) exaggerate the influence of the Russian Left in this movement. Conservatives and liberals directed the Slav committees, the leaders of this campaign of assistance. The effectiveness of unofficial aid was reduced by limited resources, poor organization, and disagreement over its objectives. Nonetheless, Russian society encouraged the insurgents to continue their valiant struggle and the Serbian states to come to their aid. Exploiting their government's hesitation, the Russian public involved it deeply in the fight for Slav liberation. But its success could not have been achieved without strong sympathy for this cause in high places.

Disunity and bitter rivalry prevented unification or complete liberation of Serbdom during the crisis. Jealousy between the Obrenović and Petrović dynasties precluded genuine and permanent co-operation between Serbia and Montenegro. Nowhere was this demonstrated more clearly than in their bickering over influence in Bosnia and Hercegovina and within the insurgent movement. In vain did *Zastava*, organ of the Vojvodina Serbs, warn of the destructiveness of fratricidal strife. Its appeals to Belgrade to achieve reconciliation with Bulgaria and Montenegro were unavailing. Only *Zastava*, indifferent to dynastic politics, remained true to the goal of Yugoslav unity. Prince Nikola's willingness to defer to Prince Michael's leadership of Serbdom in 1867 was not repeated when Milan became Serbia's prince. In their greed for territory and dynastic glory the Serbian princes turned their backs on national unity.

Serbia's chief leader in the crisis—Jovan Ristić—like the two princes, lacked the breadth of view of a Cavour. Concentrating upon territorial gain, he acquired for Serbia at Berlin all that it could reasonably expect. During his tenure in office, Ristić avoided the complete subservience to Vienna which Milan was willing to accept. Ristić remained true to his —and Ilija Garašanin's—policy of balance. He was a realistic and determined politician and diplomat, but his focus was narrowly Serbian. His successful gamble to involve Russia in war with Turkey destroyed remaining Turkish shackles and brought the Serbian Piedmont independence and expansion. But both he and Nikola, despite their cleverness, became Andrassy's victims. Exploiting Serbo-Montenegrin differences, Austria insured their physical separation and achieved temporary hegemony over the Serbs. The Monarchy's success revealed the underdevelopment of Serbian nationalism.

SELECTED BIBLIOGRAPHY

Unpublished Documents

AUSTRIA-HUNGARY

Haus-, Hof-, und Staatsarchiv, Vienna. The principal documents utilized were: (1) St. Petersburg. Gesandtschaft (1874–1878) and Depeschen nach St. Petersburg, P.A. X/66–73; (2) Belgrad. Konsulate (1873–1878), XXXVIII; (3) Varia Turquie (1875–1876), P.A. XII/230–243; (4) Geheimakten I, Beziehungen zwischen Russland und Österreich-Ungarn, 1873–1879, P.A. rot 453.

GREAT BRITAIN

Public Record Office, London. Foreign Office papers for Austria, Russia, Serbia and Turkey (1875–1878).

U.S.S.R.

Gosudarstvennyi Istoricheskii Muzei, Moscow. Fond M. G. Cherniaeva.
Otdel rukopisei biblioteki imeni V. I. Lenina, Moscow. The chief materials utilized were: (1) Fond N. A. Popova; (2) Dnevnik A. A. Kireeva; (3) Fond D. A. Miliutina; (4) Fond F. V. Chizhova.
Otdel rukopisei publichnoi biblioteki imeni M. E. Saltykova-Shchedrina, Leningrad. Fond I. S. Aksakova.

YUGOSLAVIA

Arhiv Istoriskog Instituta, Belgrade. Utilized were: (1) Hartije Matija Bana; (2) Hartije Jovana Ristića.
Arhiv ministarstva inostranih dela, Belgrade.
Arhiv narodne biblioteki u Beogradu, Belgrade. d. 174, Knjiga zvanične prepiske Kneza (Milana).
Arhiv Srpske Akademije Nauke, Belgrade.

Državni Arhiv Narodne Republike Srbije, Belgrade. Fond Poklon i Otkupa 13, 25–27, 29, 35, 39, 40, 70, 151.

Ph.D. Dissertations

Cerick, S. "The Foreign Relations of Serbia, 1868–1903" (Georgetown University, 1956).

Hehn, P. "The Constitutional and Party Struggle in Serbia, 1804–1878" (New York University, 1962).

Iakovkina, N. I. "Russko-serbskie otnosheniia, 1804–1812" (Leningrad State University, 1950).

Koz'menko, I. V. "Bolgarskii vopros i russkoe obshchestvo v period vostochnogo krizisa" (Moscow State University, 1945).

Lively, J. "Life and Career of Prince A. M. Gorchakov. A Political Biography" (Georgetown University, 1956).

MacKenzie, D. "Serbian-Russian Relations, 1875–1878" (Columbia University, 1961).

Miroshnichenko, P. Ia. "Otnoshenie russkogo obshchestva k balkanskim sobytiiam, 1875–1878 gg." (Stalino, 1946, 3 vols.).

Nikitin, S. A. "Russkoe obshchestvo i voprosy balkanskoi politiki Rossii, 1853–1876 gg." (Moscow State University, 1946).

Starnes, W. "The Diplomacy and European Foreign Policies of Prince Alexander Gorchakov" (University of Pennsylvania, 1951).

Tiutin, A. A. "Politika velikikh evropeiskikh derzhav v blizhnevostochnom krizise, 1875–77 gg." (Moscow State University, 1954).

Newspapers

Golos (St. Petersburg), 1875–1878.
Grazhdanin (St. Petersburg), 1878.
Istok (Belgrade), 1874–1878.
Moskovskie Vedomosti (Moscow), 1875–1876.
Pravitel'stvennyi Vestnik (St. Petersburg), 1875–1876.
Russkii Mir (St. Petersburg), 1875–1878.
Staro Oslobodjenje and *Oslobodjenje* (Kragujevac), 1875–1876.
Zastava (Novi Sad), 1875–1878.

Published Documents

Akademiia Nauk SSSR. Institut Slavianovedeniia. *Osvobozhdenie Bolgarii ot turetskogo iga.* 2 vols. Moscow, 1961, 1964.

Austria-Hungary. *Actenstücke aus den Correspondenzen des k. u. k. gemeinsamen Ministeriums des Äussern über orientalischen Angelegenheiten.* 2 vols. Vienna, 1878.

France, Ministère des affaires étrangères. *Documents diplomatiques: affaires d'Orient, 1875–1877.* Paris, 1877.

Germany, Auswärtiges Amt. *Die Grosse Politik der europäischen Kabinette, 1871–1914.* Vol. 2. Berlin, 1922.

Great Britain, Foreign Office. *Blue Book, Accounts and Papers. 84,* Turkey, 1876; *90–92,* 1876–77; *81–83,* 1878.

Iorga, N. *Correspondance diplomatique roumaine sous le roi Charles I.* Bucharest, 1938.

Jelavich, C. and B. *Russia in the East 1876–1880.* Leiden: Mouton, 1959.

Noradounghian, G. *Recueil d'actes internationaux de l'empire ottoman.* Vols. 3, 4. Paris, 1897–1903.

Novotny, A. *Quellen und Studien zur Geschichte des Berliner Kongresses 1878.* Vol. 1. Graz-Köln, 1957.

Onou, A. "Correspondance inédite du baron Jomini (1817–1889)," *Revue d'histoire moderne* (Sept.–Oct. 1935).

Pribram, A. F. *The Secret Treaties of Austria-Hungary, 1879–1914.* 2 vols. Trans. by A. Coolidge. Cambridge: Harvard University Press, 1920–21.

Russia, Voennoe Ministerstvo. Izdanie Voenno-Istoricheskoi Kommissii Glavnogo Shtaba. *Osobye pribavleniia k opisaniiu russko-turestskoi voiny 1877–78 gg. na Balkanskom poluostrove.* Nos. 1–5. St. Petersburg, 1899–1903.

——. *Sbornik materialov po russkoi-turetskoi voine 1877–78 gg. na Balkanskom poluostrove.* Nos. 8, 10A, 14. St. Petersburg, 1898.

Sbornik dogovorov Rossii s drugimi gosudarstvami 1856–1917. Ed. E. A. Adamov. Moscow, 1952.

Seton-Watson, R. W. "Russo-British Relations during the Eastern Crisis," *Slavonic Review, 3–6* (1924–28).

Das Staatsarchiv. Sammlung der officiellen Actenstücke der Geschichte der Gegenwart. Ed. H. von Kremer-Auenrode and Hirsch. Leipzig: Duncker und Humbolt, 1878.

Other Published Materials

Akademiia Nauk SSSR. Institut Slavianovedeniia. *Obshchestvenno-politicheskie i kul'turnye sviazi narodov SSSR i Iugoslavii.* Ed. S. A. Nikitin and L. B. Valev. Moscow, 1957.

Aksakov, I. S. *Ivan Sergeevich Aksakov v ego pis'makh, 4.* Moscow, 1896.

——. *Polnoe sobranie sochinenii I. S. Aksakova, 1.* ("Slavianskii vopros.") Moscow, 1886.

Aleksić, Lj. "Srpska štampa o engleskom javnom mnenju, 1875–1878 godine," *Istoriski Glasnik* (Belgrade), *3–4* (1953), 67–81.

Aleksinski, G. I. *Russia and Europe.* New York: Scribner's, 1917.

Alimpić, M. *Život i rad generala Ranka Alimpića u svezi sa dogadjajima iz najnovije srpske istorije.* Belgrade, 1892.

Almedingen, E. M. *The Emperor Alexander II.* London: Bodley Head, 1962.

Anuchin, D. G. "Berlinskii Kongress," *Russkaia Starina, 149, 150, 152* (1912).

——. "Kniaz' Vladimir A. Cherkasskii kak ustroitel' Bolgarii," *Russkaia Starina, 59* (July–Sept. 1888).

Aus dem Leben König Karls von Rumänien: Aufzeichnungen eines Augenzeugen, 3–4. Stuttgart, 1897–1900.

Aus der Petersburger Gesellschaft. Leipzig: Duncker und Humblot, 1873.

Austin, A. *Russia before Europe.* London, 1876.

d'Avril, A. *Négociations relatives au traité de Berlin.* Paris, E. Leroux, 1886.

Bareilles, B., ed. *Le rapport secret sur le Congrès de Berlin . . . par Carathéodory Pacha.* Paris, 1919.

Bartholomei, M. de. "Notes extraites des mémoires d'un diplomate russe," *Revue d'histoire diplomatique, 48* (Jan.–March 1934).

Besarović, R. "O prvom periodu djelovanja Vase Pelagića u Bosni," *Godišnjak istoriskog društva Bosne i Hercegovine, 2* (1950).

Billington, J. H. *Mikhailovsky and Russian Populism,* Oxford: Clarendon Press, 1958.

Bliokh, I. S. *Finansy Rossii XIX stoletii.* 4 vols. St. Petersburg, 1882.

Bobrikov, G. I. *V Serbii.* St. Petersburg, 1891.

——. *Zapiski G. I. Bobrikova.* St. Petersburg, 1913.

Bogičević, V. "Gradja za proučavanje ekonomskih odnosa u Bosni i Hercegovini pred ustanak," *Godišnjòg istoriskòg društva Bosne i Hercegovine, 1* (1949).

——. "Stanje raje u Bosni i Hercegovini pred ustanak," *Godišnjak istoriskòg društva Bosne i Hercegovine, 2* (1950).

Bolsover, G. H. "Aspects of Russian Foreign Policy, 1815–1914." In R. Pares, *Essays presented to Sir Lewis Namier.* London, 1956. Pp. 320–56.

Bratskaia pomoshch postradavshim semeistvam Bosnii i Gertsegoviny. St. Petersburg, 1876.

Brunswik, B. *Recueil de documents diplomatiques relatifs à la Serbie, de 1812 à 1876.* Constantinople: Weiss, 1876.

——. *Recueil de documents diplomatiques relatifs au Montenegro.* Constantinople: Weiss, 1876.

Busch, C. A. "Die Botschafterkonferenz in Konstantinopel und der russisch-türkische Krieg," *Deutsche Rundschau, 141* (1909).

Bushuev, S. K. *A. M. Gorchakov: iz istorii russkoi diplomatii, 1,* Moscow, 1944.

Cecil, G. *Life of Robert, Marquis of Salisbury.* 2 vols. London, 1921.

Ćetković, J. *Ujedinitelji Crne Gore i Srbije.* Dubrovnik, 1940.

Charles-Roux, F. *Alexandre II, Gortchakoff et Napoléon III*. Paris: Librairie Plon, 1913.

Charykov, N. V. *Glimpses of High Politics through War and Peace, 1855–1929*. New York: Macmillan, 1931.

Cherniaeva, A. "K perepiske M. G. Cherniaeva," *Russkii Arkhiv* (1914) no. 1, pp. 25–33.

Chichagov, L. M. *Dnevnik prebyvaniia Tsaria-Osvoboditelia v dunaiskoi armii v 1877 g.* St. Petersburg, 1887.

Clarke, J. F. "Serbia and the Bulgarian Revival, 1762–1872," *American Slavic and East European Review, 4* (Dec. 1945), 141–62.

Ćorović, V. *Borba za nezavisnost Balkana*. Belgrade: Balkanski institut, 1937.

———. "Iz istorii iuzhnikh slavian," *Iugoslaviia, 1* (1930), 85–106.

———. *Odnosi izmedju Srbije i Austro-Ugarske u XX veku*. Belgrade, 1936.

Čubrilović, V. *Bosanski ustanak, 1875–1878*. Belgrade, 1930.

———. *Istorija političke misli u Srbiji u XIX veku*. Belgrade: Prosveta, 1958.

———. and V. Ćorović. "Srbija od 1858 do 1903," *Srpski narod u XIX veku, knj. 3*. Belgrade, n.d.

Dabizh, V. D. "San Stefano i Konstantinopel' v fevrale 1878 g.," *Russkaia Starina, 57* (1888).

Danilevskii, N. Ia. *Rossiia i Evropa*. St. Petersburg: Obshchestvennaia Pol'za, 1871.

Devollan, G. A. "Nedavniaia starina. Poezdka v Serbiiu v 1876 godu," *Russkii Arkhiv* (1879), no. 7, pp. 339–76.

———. *Serbskii vopros pered sudom russkogo obshchestva*. St. Petersburg, 1877.

Djordjević, D. "Trgovinski pregovori Srbije i Austro-Ugarske, 1869–1875," *Istoriski Glasnik Narodne Republike Srbije, 3–4* (1958), 51–73.

Djordjević, M. *Politička istorija Srbije XIX i XX veka*. Belgrade: Prosveta, 1956.

Djordjević, V. *Crna Gora i Austrija, 1814–1894*. Srpska Kraljevska Akademiji Nauka i Umetnosti, Posebna Izdanja, knj. 159, Društveni i istorijski spisi, knj. 19. Belgrade, 1924.

———. *Srpsko-turski rat, uspomene i beleške na 1876, 1877 i 1878 godine*. 2 vols. Belgrade, 1907.

Dostian, I. S. *Bor'ba serbskogo naroda protiv turetskogo iga XV—nachalo XIX v*. Moscow: Akademiia Nauk SSSR, 1958.

Dragičević, R. "Prilozi ekonomskoj istoriji Crne Gore (1861–1870)," *Istorijski Zapisi, 7, knj. 10* (1954).

Dragović, M. "Vospominaniia Chernogortsa iz vremen gertsegovinskogo vozstaniia i chernogorsko-turetskoi voiny 1876–1878," *Russkaia Starina, 38* (April–June 1883), 363–86.

Dučić, N. "Borba dobrovoljačkog kora Ibarske vojske i ustaških ceta Javorskog kora 1876, 77 i 78 god," *Glasnik srpskog učenog drustva*, II od, knj. 13. Belgrade, 1881.

Dukmasov, P. *Vospominaniia o russko-turetskoi voine, 1877–8 gg. i M. D. Skobeleve*. St. Petersburg, 1889.

Durnovo, N. N. "K istorii serbskoi-turetskoi voiny 1876 g.," *Istoricheskii Vestnik*, 75 (Jan.–March 1899).

Edwards, H. S. *Sir William White: His Life and Correspondence*. London: Murray, 1902.

Ekmečić, M. "Uloga Don Ivana Musića u Hercegovinskom ustanku 1875–1878 godine," *Godišnjak istoriskog društva Bosne i Hercegovine*, 7 (1955), 141–69.

———. *Ustanak u Bosni 1875–1878*. Sarajevo: Veselin Masleša, 1960.

Erdmann, A. von. *N. K. Giers, russischer Aussenminister 1882–1895*. Tilsit, 1935.

Evans, A. J. *Illyrian Letters*. London, 1878.

———. *Through Bosnia and Hercegovina on Foot during the Insurrection, August and September 1875*. London, 1876.

Fadeev, R. *Opinion on the Eastern Question*. London, 1876.

———. *Sobranie sochinenii R. A. Fadeeva*. 3 vols. St. Petersburg, 1889.

Feis, H. *Europe the World's Banker, 1870–1914*. New Haven, 1930.

Fel'kner, A. *Slavianskaia bor'ba, 1875–1876*. St. Petersburg, 1877.

Fischel, A. *Der Panslawismus bis zum Weltkrieg*. Stuttgart and Berlin, 1919.

Florinsky, M. *Russia: A History and an Interpretation*. 2 vols. New York: Macmillan, 1953.

Forbes, A. *Czar and Sultan*. New York: Scribner's, 1894.

Geisman, P. *Slavianskii krestovoi pokhod*. St. Petersburg, 1902.

———. *Slaviano-turetskaia bor'ba, 1876–78 gg. i eia znachenie*. St. Petersburg, 1887–89.

Georgewitsch, W. (also Georgevitch, V.). *Die serbische Frage*. Stuttgart, 1909.

———. "La Serbie au Congrès de Berlin," *Revue d'histoire diplomatique*, 5 (1891), 483–552.

Ghikas, G. *Botschafter von Novikow über den Panslawismus und die orientalische Frage*. Vienna, 1907.

Giacometti, G. *Russia's Work in Turkey: A Revelation*. London, Wilson, 1877.

Gil'ferding, A. *Bosniia, Gertsegovina i Staraia Serbiia*. St. Petersburg, 1859.

Glaise-Horstenau, E. von. *Franz Josephs Weggefährte*. Vienna: Amalthea, 1930.

Golovin, K. *Moi vospominaniia, 1*. St. Petersburg, 1908.

Golubev, A. *Kniaz' A. I. Vasil'chikov.* St. Petersburg, 1882.

Gorchakov, A. M. *Sbornik izdannyi v pamiat' 25 let upravleniia MID Kniazia Gorchakovim.* St. Petersburg, 1881.

Goriainov, S. *Le Bosphore et les Dardanelles.* Paris, 1910.

——. *La Question d'Orient à la veille du Traité de Berlin (1870-1876).* Paris, 1948.

Grimm, E. "K istorii russkikh-bolgarskikh otnoshenii," *Novyi Vostok* (1924), no. 5. Moscow.

Grüning, I. *Die russische öffentliche Meinung und ihre Stellung zu den Grossmächten, 1878-1894.* Berlin, 1929.

Grünwald, C. de. *Trois siècles de diplomatie russe.* Paris, 1945.

Grujić, K. *Dnevnik iz Hercegovačkog ustanka.* Belgrade, 1956.

Grujić, S. *Bugarski dobrovoljci u srpsko-turskom ratu 1876 godine.* Belgrade, 1892.

——. *Operacije Timočko-Moravske vojske—beleške i uspomene.* 4 vols. Belgrade, 1901–02.

Harris, D. *A Diplomatic History of the Balkan Crisis of 1875-1878: The First Year.* Stanford, 1936.

Hasenkampf, M. *Moi dnevnik, 1877-1878 gg.* St. Petersburg, 1908.

Iasherov, V. "V Serbii, 1876-1877," *Russkii Vestnik, 133* (Jan. 1878).

Ignat'ev, N. P. "Zapiski Grafa N. P. Ignat'eva, 1864-1874," *Izvestiia Ministerstva Inostrannykh Del.* 1914-1915, no. 1, pp. 93ff.

——. "Zapiski," *Istoricheskii Vestnik, 85-87* (1914), *139-142* (1916), *143-144* (1917); *Russkaia Starina, 157-159* (1914), *161* (1915).

Istomin, F. M. *Kratkii ocherk deiatel'nosti Peterburgskogo Slavianskogo Blagotvoritel'nogo Obshchestva.* St. Petersburg, 1893.

Istoricheskie ocherki Rossii so vremeni Krymskoi voiny do zakliucheniia Berlinskogo dogovora, 1855-1878. 3 vols. in 2. Leipzig, 1878-79.

Ivanov, I. S. "Bolgarskoe opolchenie i ego sformirovania v 1875-1879 gg.," *Russkaia Starina, 62* (1889); *66* (1890).

Jakšić, G., *Evropa i vaskrs Srbije (1804-1834).* Belgrade: Narodna Misao, 1927.

Janković, D. *O političkim strankama u Srbiji XIX veka.* Belgrade: Prosveta, 1951.

——. "Prve radničke demonstracije u Srbiji (u Kragujevcu 1876 godine)," *Isotoriski časopis, 3* (1951-52), 157ff.

Jelavich, C. *Tsarist Russia and Balkan Nationalism: Russian Influence in the Internal Affairs of Bulgaria and Serbia, 1879-1886.* Berkeley: U. of California, 1958.

Jovanović, J. *Stvaranje crnogorske države i razvoj crnogorske nacionalnosti.* Cetinje: Obod, 1947.

Jovanović, J. "Veze Crne Gore sa Rusijom od druge polovine XVI vijeka do danas," *Istoriski Zapisi, 1* (1949), knj. 2–4.

Jovanović, S. *Druga vlada Miloša i Mihaila, 1858–1868.* Belgrade, 1923.

——. "Serbia in the Early Seventies," *Slavonic Review, 4* (1925).

——. *Ustavobranitelji i njihova vlada, 1838–1858.* Belgrade, 1925.

——. *Vlada Milana Obrenovića.* 2 vols. Belgrade, 1926–27.

Kaljević, L. *Moje uspomene.* Belgrade, 1908.

Kallay, B. *Die Orientpolitik Russlands.* Budapest, 1878.

Karasev, V. G. *Istoricheskie sviazi narodov Sovetskogo Soiuza i Iugoslavii.* Moscow, 1958.

——. "Osnovnye cherty sotsial'no-ekonomicheskogo razvitiia Serbii v kontse 60-kh-nachale 70-kh godov XIX v.," *Uchenye zapiski instituta slavianovedenii, 5* (1952), pp. 206–42.

——. "Serbskii revoliutsionnyi demokrat, Svetozar Markovich," *Uchenye zapiski instituta slavianovedenii, 7* (1953), pp. 348–77.

Karić, V. *Srbija: opis zemlje, naroda i države.* Belgrade, 1888.

Kartsov, Iu. "Za kulisami diplomatii," *Russkaia Starina, 133–135* (1908).

Katkov, M. N. *Sobranie peredovykh statei Moskovskikh Vedomostei 1863–1887 gg.* 25 vols. Moscow: Chicherin, 1897–98.

Khomiakov, A. *Polnoe sobranie sochinenii A. S. Khomiakova, 1.* Moscow, 1900.

Khvostov, A. *Russkie i Serby v voinu 1876 g.* St. Petersburg, 1877.

Khvostov, V. "P. A. Shuvalov o Berlinskom Kongresse 1878 g.," *Krasnyi Arkhiv, 59* (1933).

Kireev, A. A. *Sochineniia.* St. Petersburg: Suvorin, 1912.

Klaczko, J. *The Two Chancellors: Prince Gortchakof and Prince Bismarck.* New York: Hurd and Houghton, 1876.

Koetschet, J. *Aus Bosniens letzter Türkenzeit.* Vienna, 1905.

Kohn, H. *Pan-Slavism: Its History and Ideology.* Notre Dame, Ind., 1953.

Koliupanov, N. P. *Biografiia Aleksandra Ivanovich Kosheleva.* 2 vols. Moscow: Kushever, 1889–92.

Kolosov, A. *Aleksandr II, ego lichnost', intimnaia zhizn' i pravlenie.* London, 1902.

Koshelev, A. I. *Zapiski.* Berlin: Behr, 1884.

Kostyrko, M. "Ocherk grazhdanskoi deiatel'nosti nashi v Bolgarii v 1877–8 gg.," *Russkaia Starina, 135* (1908).

Kovačević, B. "O kulturnim vezama Srba s Rusima," *Letopis Matice Srpske, 359* (1947), pp. 99–112.

Koz'menko, I. "Iz istorii bolgarskogo opolcheniia, 1876–1877," *Slavianskii sbornik* (Moscow, 1948).

Lalić, R. "O tradicionalnim vezama izmedju Crne Gore i Rusije," *Istoriski Zapisi, 4,* knj. 7 (July–Sept. 1951), 273–93.

Langer, W. *European Alliances and Alignments, 1871–1890.* New York: Knopf, 1956.

Lazarević, L. "Pred rat: sećanje na 1875–76," *Zapisi, 2* (1928), 209–16.

Ljubibratić, S., and T. Kruševac. "Prilozi za proučavanje hercegovačkih ustanaka, 1857–1878 godine," *Godišnjak istoriskog društva Bosne i Hercegovine,* 7 (1955), 185–204; *8* (1956), 301–40; *9* (1957), 267ff.

Loftus, Lord A. *Diplomatic Reminiscences, 1862–1879.* 2 vols. London, 1894.

M-skii, "Kniaz' A. M. Gorchakov," *Russkaia Starina, 40* (1883).

McClellan, W. *Svetozar Marković and the Origins of Balkan Socialism.* Princeton, 1964.

MacKenzie, D. "Panslavism in Practice: Cherniaev in Serbia (1876)," *The Journal of Modern History, 36* (Sept. 1964).

Maksimov, N. V. *Dve voiny, 1876–1878.* St. Petersburg, 1879.

Maksimovich, V. "Voennye sviazi i otnosheniia Serbii i Rossii (1806–1917)," *Iugoslaviia, 1* (1930), 259–316.

Marković, S. *Srbija na istoku.* Novi Sad, 1872.

Matanović, A. "Stogodišnjica Praviteljstvujušeg Senata Crnogorskog i Brdskog Velikog Suda (1831–1931)," *Zapisi,* 7, sv. 6 (Dec. 1930), 355–63.

Medlicott, W. N. *The Congress of Berlin and After: A Diplomatic History of the Near Eastern Settlement 1878–1880.* London: Methuen, 1938.

Die Memoiren des Königs Milan, zehn kapitel aus dem Leben des ersten Serbenkönigs. Zürich, C. Schmidt, 1902.

Meshcherskii, Prince V. P. *Odin iz nashikh Mol'tke.* St. Petersburg, 1890.

——. *Moi vospominaniia, 2.* St. Petersburg, 1898.

——. *Pravda o Serbii.* St. Petersburg, 1877.

Mijatović, E. "Panslavism: Its Rise and Decline," *The Fortnightly Review, 20* (1873), pp. 94–112.

Milenković, V. *Ekonomska istorija Beograda.* Belgrade, 1932.

Miliutin, D. A. *Dnevnik D. A. Miliutina.* 4 vols. Moscow, 1947–50.

Miller, O. *Slavianstvo i Evropa.* St. Petersburg, 1877.

Milutinović, K. "Crna Gora i Primorje u Omladinskom pokretu," *Istoriski Zapisi, 6,* knj. 9 (Jan.–Feb. 1953), 1–46.

——. "Mihajlo Polit-Desančić i Crna Gora," *IZ,* 7, knj. 10, (1954).

——. "Protjerivanje Vase Pelagića iz Novog Sada," *Godišnjak istoriskog društve Bosne i Hercegovine, 4* (1952), 225–52.

Mollinary, A. von. *46 Jahre im österreich-ungarischen Heere, 1833–1879.* 2 vols. Vienna, 1905.

Mousset, A. *La Serbie et son église, 1830–1904.* Paris, 1938.

Mouy, C. de. *Souvenirs et causeries d'un diplomate.* Paris, 1909.

Muir-MacKenzie, G., and P. Irby. *Travels in the Slavonic Provinces of Turkey in Europe.* 4th ed., 2 vols. London, 1877.

Naglovskii, D. "Kishinevskoe sidenie," *Russkaia Starina, 112* (1902).

Nathalie, Queen of Serbia. *Mémoires de Nathalie, Reine de Serbie.* Paris, 1891.

Nelidov, A. I. "K dvadtsatipiatiletiiu osvobozhdeniia Bolgarii," *Istoricheskii Vestnik, 91* (1903).

———. "Souvenirs d'avant et d'après la guerre de 1877–78," *Revue des deux mondes* (May 15, July 15, Nov. 15, 1915).

Nemirovich-Danchenko, V. I. *God voiny (dnevnik russkogo korrespondenta), 1877–8 gg.* St. Petersburg, 1879.

Nevedenskii, S. *Katkov i ego vremia.* St. Petersburg, 1888.

Nikitin, S. A. "Podlozhnye dokumenty o russkoi politike na Balkanakh v 70-e gg. XIX v.," *Izvestiia Akademii Nauk SSSR,* Seriia istorii filosofii, *3* (1946).

———. "Russkaia politika na Balkanakh i nachalo Vostochnoi Voiny," *Voprosi Istorii* (1946), no. 4.

———. *Slavianskie komitety v Rossii v 1858–1876 godakh.* Moscow, 1960.

Nikola I of Montenegro. "Berlinski Kongres," *Zapisi, 2* (1928), 91–96, 159–62.

———. "Crna Gora i Hercegovina," *Zapisi, 7,* sv. 1 (July 1930), 99–106.

———. "Crna Gora i kretanje u narodu srpskom za oslobodjenje i jedinstvo," *Zapisi, 8,* sv. 6 (June 1931), 348–63.

———. "Hercegovački ustanak," *Zapisi, 11,* sv. 5 (Nov. 1932), 246–56, 304–19; *8,* knj. 13 (Jan. 1935), 8–14, 75–84, 137–40.

———. "Stanje Crne Gore po ratu 1862," *Zapisi, 8,* sv. 1 (Jan. 1931), 22–33.

Novikova, O. A. *Krizis v Serbii.* Moscow, 1882.

———[O. K.] *Russia and England from 1876 to 1880.* London, 1880.

Ocherk bor'by slavian s turkami na Balkanskom poluostrove v 1875–6 god. Odessa, 1877.

Onou, A. "The Memoirs of Count N. Ignatiev," *Slavonic Review, 10, 11* (1932).

Ovsyany, N. R. *Blizhnii vostok i slavianstvo.* St. Petersburg, 1913.

———. *Russkoe upravlenie v Bolgarii v 1877–78–79 gg.* St. Petersburg, 1906.

———. *Serbiia i Serby.* St. Petersburg, 1898.

Paléologue, M. *Aleksandr II i Ekaterina Iurevskaia.* Petrograd, 1924.

Parensov, P. *Iz proshlago.* St. Petersburg, 1901–08.

———. "Perepiska P. D. Parensova s K. B. Levitskim pered nachalom voennykh deistvii v Turtsii," *Russkaia Starina, 124* (1905).

Pelagić, V. *Istorija bosansko-ercegovačke bune u svezi sa srpsko- i rusko-turskim ratom.* Budapest, 1879.

Pervye 15 let sushchestvovaniia S.-Peterburgskago Slavianskago Blagotvoritel'nago Obshchestva, po protokolam obshchikh sobranii. St. Petersburg, 1893.

Petrovich, M. *The Emergence of Russian Panslavism, 1856–1870.* New York: Columbia, 1956.

Piročanac, M. *Beleške povodom jedne diplomatske istorije.* Belgrade, 1896.

——. *Knez Mihajlo i zajednička radnji balkanskih naroda.* Belgrade, 1895.

Pobedonostsev, K. P. *Pis'ma Pobedonostseva k Aleksandru, III.* Moscow, 1925.

——. *Pobedonostsev i ego korrespondenty.* Moscow, 1923.

Pokrovskii, M. *Diplomatiia i voiny tsarskoi Rossii v XIX stoletii.* Moscow, 1923.

——. *Russkaia istoriia s drevneishikh vremen.* 5 vols. Moscow, 1913.

Popov, N. A. *Gertsegovina i nyneshnee vosstanie v nei.* Moscow, 1876.

——. *Rossiia i Serbiia. Istoricheskii ocherk russkago pokrovitel'stva Serbii s 1806 po 1856 god.* 2 vols. Moscow, 1869.

Popov, R. S. *O Serbakh.* St. Petersburg, 1877.

Porokhovshchikov, A. A. "Zapiski starozhila," *Istoricheskii Vestnik,* 67 (1897), 9ff.

——. *Tsar' 'osvoboditel' i Rus' pravoslavnaia vo dni serbsko-turetskoi voiny.* St. Petersburg, 1898.

Pribram, A. "Milan IV von Serbien und die Geheimverträge Österreich-Ungarns mit Serbien, 1881–1889," *Historische Blätter,* 3 (1921–22), 464 94.

——. *The Secret Treaties of Austria-Hungary, 1879–1914.* 2 vols. Cambridge: Harvard, 1920.

Prodanović, J. *Istorija političkih stranaka i struja u Srbiji,* Belgrade: Prosveta, 1947.

Propper, V. *Bor'ba serbov s turkami (1389–1878).* Moscow, 1901.

Pržić, I. *Spolašnja politika Srbije (1804–1914).* Belgrade, 1939.

Pushkarev, S. *The Emergence of Modern Russia, 1801–1917.* New York: Holt, 1963.

Pushkarevich, K. A. "Balkanskie slaviane i russkie 'osvoboditeli,'" *Trudy instituta slavianovedeniia Akademii Nauk SSSR,* 2 (1934).

Pypin, A. *Panslavizm v proshlom i nastoiashchem.* St. Petersburg, 1913.

Radenić, A. "Vojvodjanska štampa prema namesničestvu, 1868–1872," *Istoriski časopis,* 6 (1956), 65–108.

Radojčić, N. "Svetozar Miletić o jugoslovenskom jedinstvu—1870 god." *Glasnik istoriskog društva u Novom Sadu, 1,* sv. 1 (1928), 92ff.

Radowitz, J. M. von. *Aufzeichnungen und Erinnerungen aus dem Leben des Botschafters Joseph Maria von Radowitz,* ed. H. Holborn. 2 vols. Berlin, 1925.

Radulović, J. "Političke veze izmedju Hercegovine i Vojvodine u drugoj polovini prošlog vijeka," *Istoriski Zapisi, 3,* knj. 6 (Oct.–Dec. 1950), 414–32.

Radulović, J. "Ruski uticaj u Hercegovini u XIX veku," *Istoriski Zapisi, 2,* sv. 5–6 (Nov.–Dec. 1948), 269–79.

Radziwill, E. *Behind the Veil at the Russian Court.* New York: John Lane, 1914.

Rakočević, N. *Ratni planovi Srbije protiv Turske.* Belgrade, 1934?.

Ražnatovic, N. "Položaj i uloga crkve u Crnoj Gori, 1852–1878," *Istoriski Zapisi, 14,* knj. 18, sv. 4 (1961).

Reiswitz, J. A. von. *Belgrad-Berlin, Berlin-Belgrad, 1866–1871.* Munich and Berlin, 1936.

Reitern, M. "Dnevnik," *Russkaia Starina, 143* (1910).

——. *Die finanzielle Sanierung Russlands nach der Katastrophe des Krimkrieges 1862 bis 1878 durch den Finanzminister Michael von Reutern.* Berlin: Reimer, 1914.

Ristić, J. *Diplomatska istorija Srbije za vreme srpskih ratova za oslobodjenje i nezavisnost, 1875–1878.* 2 vols. Belgrade, 1896–98.

——. *Još malo svetlosti.* Belgrade, 1898.

——. *Spolašnji odnošaji Srbije novijega vremena, 3.* Belgrade, 1901.

Riustov, V. *Voina s Turtsii.* St. Petersburg, 1876.

Rovinskii, P. A. "Belgrad, ego ustroistvo i obshchestvennaia zhizn'," *Vestnik Evropy* (April 1870), pp. 530–79; (May 1870), pp. 132–88.

——. *Chernogoriia v eia proshlom i nastoiashchem.* 2 vols. in 4. St. Petersburg, 1888–1905.

Rupp, G. H. *A Wavering Friendship: Russia and Austria, 1876–1878.* Cambridge, Mass., 1941.

——. "The Reichstadt Agreement," *American Historical Review, 30* (1925), 503–10.

Russian Intrigues. Secret dispatches of General Ignatieff and consular agents of the great Panslavic societies. London, 1877.

Russkie dobrovol'tsy 1876 goda. St. Petersburg, 1876.

Russkii Arkhiv (1897) no. 2, "Nakanune nashei poslednei voiny."

——(1914), no. 1. "K. M. G. Cherniaevu."

Russland vor und nach dem Kriege. 2d ed. Leipzig, 1879.

Schmid, F. *Bosnien und die Herzegowina unter der Verwaltung Österreich-Ungarns.* Leipzig: von Veit, 1914.

Schweinitz, H. L. von. *Briefwechsel des Botschafters General von Schweinitz.* Berlin: Hobbing, 1928.

——. *Denkwürdigkeiten des Botschafters General von Schweinitz.* 2 vols. Berlin: Hobbing, 1927.

Semanov, S. *A. M. Gorchakov, russkii diplomat XIX veka.* Moscow, 1962.

Seton-Watson, R. W. *Disraeli, Gladstone and the Eastern Question.* 2d ed. London, 1962.

——. "Les relations de l'Autriche Hongrie et de la Serbie entre 1868 et 1874:

la mission de Benjamin Kallay à Belgrade," *Le monde slave, 3* (Feb.–March 1926).

——. "The Role of Bosnia in International Politics," 1875–1914," *Proceedings of the British Academy, 17* (1931).

——. "Russian Commitments in the Bosnian Question and an Early Project of Annexation," *Slavonic and East European Review, 8* (March 1930), 578–88.

Šišić, F. *Jugoslovenska misao.* Belgrade, 1937.

——. *Okupacija i aneksija Bosne i Hercegovine.* Zagreb, 1938.

Skalon, D. A. *Moi vospominaniia, 1877–1878 gg.* 2 vols. St. Petersburg, 1913.

——. *Ocherk deiatel'nosti glavnokomanduiushchogo v rusko-turetskuiu voinu 1877–1878 na Balkanskom poluostrove.* St. Petersburg, 1907.

Skarić, V. "Iz prošlosti Bosne i Hercegovine XIX vijeka," *Godišnjak istoriskog društva Bosne i Hercegovine, 1* (1949), 19ff.

Skazkin, S. *Konets avstro-russko-germanskogo soiuza.* Moscow, 1928.

Skerlić, J. *Istorijski pregled srpske štampe (1791–1911).* Belgrade, 1911.

——. *Omladina i njena književnost* (1848–1871). Belgrade, 1906.

Škerović, N. "Iz odnosa izmedju Srbije i Crne Gore," *Istoriski Zapisi, 4,* knj. 7 (Jan.–March 1951), 16–40.

Sklifosovskii, N. V. *Iz nabliudenii vo vremia slavianskoi voiny 1876 goda.* St. Petersburg, 1876.

Slavianskii Sbornik (1875–1877). 3 vols. St. Petersburg, 1875–77.

Slavianskii Sbornik: Slavianskii vopros i russkoe obshchestvo v 1867–1878 godakh. Ed. I. Koz'menko. Moscow, 1948.

Sosnosky, T. von. *Die Balkanpolitik Österreich-Ungarns seit 1866.* 2 vols. Stuttgart and Berlin, 1913–14.

Srpska Akademija Nauka. *Pisma Filipa Hristića Jovanu Ristiću (1868–1880).* Ed. G. Jakšić, knj. 206, Odelenje Društvenih Nauka, knj. 8. Belgrade, 1953.

——. G. Jakšić. *Bosna i Hercegovina na Berlinskom Kongresu,* Posebna izdanja, knj. 228, Odelenje Društvenih Nauka, nova serija, knj. 11. Belgrade, 1955.

——. "Pisma Ilije Garašanina Jovanu Ristiću," 2, *Zbornik za istoriju, jezik i književnost srpskog naroda,* prvo odeljenje, knj. 22. Belgrade, 1931.

——. "Pisma Jovana Ristića Filipu Hristiću od 1870 do 1873 i do 1877 do 1880," *Zbornik za istoriju, jezik i književnost srpskog naroda,* prvo odeljenje, knj. 20. Belgrade, 1931.

——. "Zapisi Jevrema Grujića," knj. 3. Belgrade, 1923.

Stanojević, G. "Prilozi za diplomatsku istoriju Crne Gore od Berlinskog Kongresa to kraja XIX vijeka," *Istorijski časopis, 11* (1960).

Stavrianos, L. S. *The Balkans since 1453.* New York: Rinehart, 1958.

Stavrianos, L. S. "Balkan Federation," *Smith College Studies in History*, 27 (Oct. 1941–July 1942), pp. 1ff.

Stefanović, J. ("Jedan stari vojnik"), "Černjajev u Srbiji kao vojskovodja i političar," *Otadžbina*, 8 (1931), 513–42.

Stillman, W. J. *Herzegovina and the Late Uprising.* London, 1877.

Stojanović, M. *The Great Powers and the Balkans, 1875–1878.* Cambridge, England, 1939.

Stranjaković, D. "Politička propaganda Srbije u jugoslovenskim pokrajinima, 1844–1858," *Godišnjak istoriskog društva u Novom Sadu*, 9 (1956), 151–79, 300–15.

——. *Srbija Pijemont južnih Slovena, 1842–1853.* Belgrade, 1932.

Sumner, B. H. "Ignatyev at Constantinople, 1864–1874," *Slavonic Review*, 11 (1933).

——. *Russia and the Balkans, 1870–1880.* Oxford: Clarendon Press, 1937.

Tatishchev, S. S. *Imperator Aleksandr II: ego zhizn' i tsarstvovanie.* 2 vols. St. Petersburg, 1903.

——. *Iz proshlago russkoi diplomatii.* St. Petersburg, 1890.

Taylor, A. J. *The Struggle for the Mastery of Europe, 1848–1918.* Oxford, 1954.

Temperley, H. V. *A History of Serbia.* London, 1919.

Terekhov, A. *Istoricheskii ocherk dvizheniia Rossii na Balkanskii poluostrov.* St. Petersburg, 1888.

Tiutcheva, A. F. *Pri dvore dvukh imperatorov.* 2 vols. Moscow: Sabashnikovykh, 1928–29.

Todorović, P. *Odlomci iz dnevnika jednog dobrovoljca.* Belgrade: Srpska Književna Zadruga, knj. 280, 1938.

Tomasevich, J. *Peasants, Politics and Economic Change in Yugoslavia.* Stanford U., 1954.

Trivanovitch, V. "Serbia, Russia and Austria-Hungary during the Reign of Milan Obrenovich, 1868–78," *The Journal of Modern History*, 3 (1931).

Trubetskoi, Prince G. N. "La politique russe en Orient: le schisme bulgare," *Revue d'histoire diplomatique*, 21 (1907), 185ff.

——. *Russland als Grossmacht.* Stuttgart and Berlin, 1913.

Tunguz-Perović, D. "Uloga Knjaza Nikole od početka Nevesinjske puške do stupanje službene Crne Gore u rat," *Zapisi*, 3 (1928), 257–64.

Uebersberger, H. *Russlands Orientpolitik in den letzten zwei Jahrhunderten.* Stuttgart, 1913.

Valuev, S. *Dnevnik, 1877–1884.* Moscow, 1961.

Vasil'ev, A. F. *Sredi narodnikh stradanii—Chernogoria, Gertsegovina i Bosniia v 1875–1878 gg.* St. Petersburg, 1905.

Vöguė, E. M. de *Journal du Vicomte E. M. de Vöguė, Paris-St. Pétersbourg, 1877–1883.* Paris: Grasset, 1932.

Voina serbov, gertsegovintsev i chernogortsev ili bitva slavian s turkami. Moscow, 1877.

Voronich, K. I. *Iznanka serbskoi voiny.* St. Petersburg, 1877.

Vostochnyi vopros i slaviane na Balkanskom poluostrove. St. Petersburg, 1876.

Vučo, N. *Privredna istorija Srbije do prvog svetskog rata.* Belgrade: Naučna Knjiga, 1955.

Vukčević, M. "O politici grafa Andrašija prema našem narodu u oči istočne krize," *Glasnik istoriskog društva u Novom Sadu, 5,* sv. 13 (1953), pp. 403–17.

———. *Crna Gora i Hercegovina u oči rata, 1874–1876.* Cetinje, 1950.

Vukić, J. "Crna Gora na Berlinskom Kongresu 1878 god," *Zapisi, 2,* sv. 5 (1928), 281–87.

Vuković, G. *Hercegovački i Vasojevički ustanak.* Sarajevo, 1925.

Vuksan, D. "Jedan memorandum Družine za oslobodjenje i ujedinjenje srpskoga naroda," *Zapisi, 2,* sv. 1–6 (1928), 49–52.

———. *Pregled štampe u Crnoj Gori, 1834–1934.* Cetinje, 1934.

Wendel, H. *Der Kampf der Südslawen um Freiheit und Einheit.* Frankfurt-am-Main, 1925.

Wertheimer, E. von. *Graf Julius Andrassy, sein Leben und seine Zeiten.* 3 vols. Stuttgart, 1910–13.

———. "Neues zur Orientpolitik des Grafen Andrassy," *Historische Blätter, 2* (1921), 252–76; *3,* 448–63.

Wesselitsky-Bojidarovitch, G. de. *Dix mois de ma vie, 1875–1876.* Paris, 1929.

Wirthwein, W. G. *Britain and the Balkan Crisis, 1875–1878.* New York: Columbia University Press, 1935.

Wittrock, G. "Gorčakow, Ignatiew und Šuvalov—verschiedene Richtungen in der äusseren Politik Russlands 1876–78," *Historische Blätter, 5* (1932).

Zhigarev, S. *Russkaia politika v vostochnom voprose.* Moscow, 1896.

Živanović Ž. *Jovan Ristić: knježevski i kraljevski namesnik i mnegogodišnji ministar inostranih poslova.* Belgrade: Sveti Sava, 1929.

———. *Politička istorija Srbije.* 3 vols. Belgrade: Gece Kon, 1923–24.

Zotov, P. D. "Voina za nezavisimost' slavian," *Russkaia Starina, 49* (Jan.–March 1886).

INDEX